A PRACTICAL TREATISE

ON THE

TECHNICS AND PRINCIPLES

OF

DENTAL ORTHOPEDIA

AND

*Prosthetic Correction of
Cleft Palate*

BY

CALVIN S. CASE, M.D., D.D.S.

FORMERLY, PROFESSOR OF ORTHODONTIA, CHICAGO COLLEGE OF DENTAL SURGERY. DEMONSTRATOR OF PROSTHETIC
DENTISTRY, UNIV. OF MICH.; PROFESSOR OF ORTHODONTIA, W. R. U.; AND PROFESSOR OF PROSTHETIC DEN-
TISTRY AND ORTHODONTIA, C. C. OF D. S. AUTHOR OF "FACIAL AND ORAL DEFORMITIES";
"THE DEVELOPMENT OF ESTHETIC FACIAL CONTOURS," IN THE AMERICAN TEXTBOOK
OF OPERATIVE DENTISTRY, ETC. MEMBER OF THE INTERNATIONAL DENTAL AND
INTERNATIONAL MEDICAL ASSOCIATIONS, NATIONAL DENTAL ASSOCIA-
TION, ILLINOIS STATE DENTAL SOCIETY; HONORARY MEMBER
FIRST DISTRICT DENTAL SOCIETY, NEW YORK CITY;
HONORARY MEMBER OF THE ODONTOLOGICAL
SOCIETY OF NEW YORK CITY; AND
MEMBER OF ALL CHICAGO
DENTAL SOCIETIES

CHICAGO
PUBLISHED BY THE C. S. CASE COMPANY
1921

Copyright, 1921
In Great Britain and All Countries
Subscribing to the
International Copyright Convention at Berlin

Copyright, 1921
In the United States of America
By
CALVIN S. CASE

All Rights Reserved

The Lakeside Press
R. R. DONNELLEY & SONS COMPANY, PRINTERS
CHICAGO

In the interest of creating a more extensive selection of rare historical book reprints, we have chosen to reproduce this title even though it may possibly have occasional imperfections such as missing and blurred pages, missing text, poor pictures, markings, dark backgrounds and other reproduction issues beyond our control. Because this work is culturally important, we have made it available as a part of our commitment to protecting, preserving and promoting the world's literature. Thank you for your understanding.

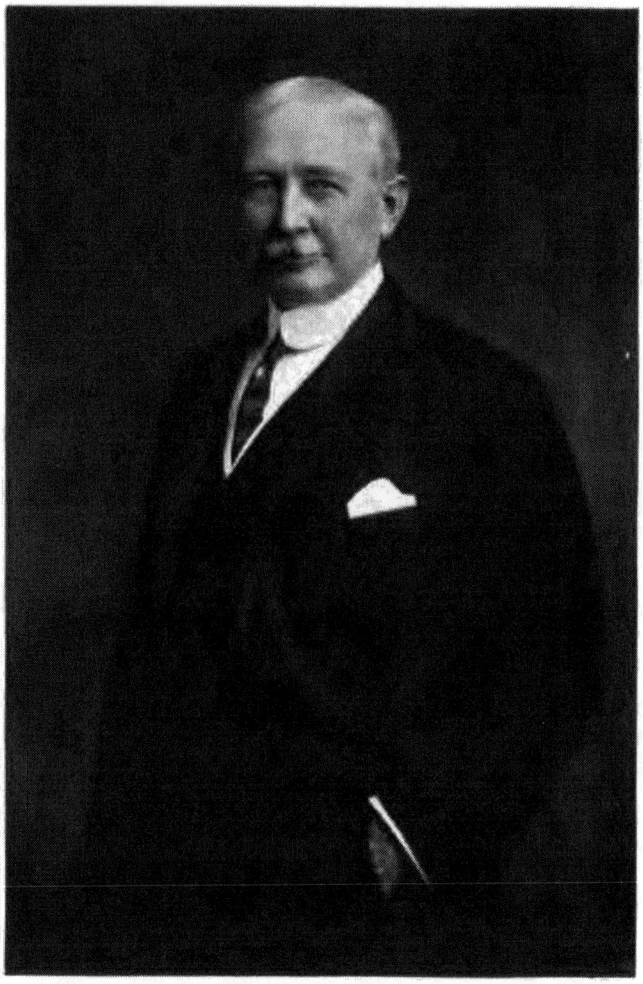

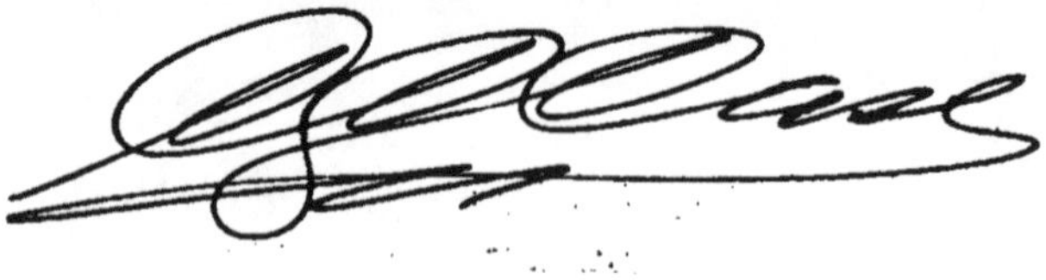

*To my friends and all
who are interested in the highest
possibilities of Dental Orthopedia, and the most
scientific correction of Cleft Palate,
this book is respectfully
dedicated*

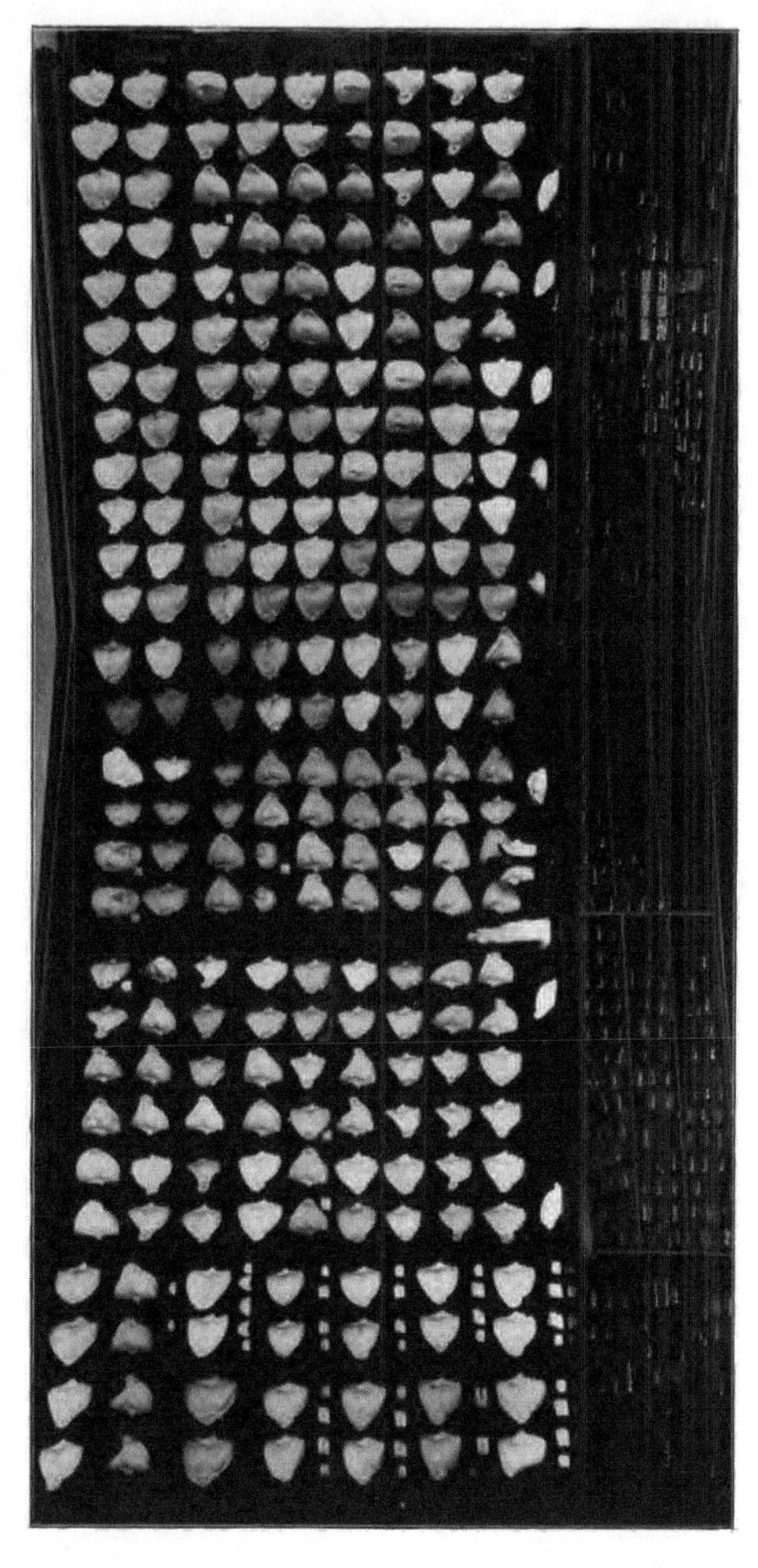

The above illustration represents a corner in the model room of the author's office in 1903. One can get something of an idea of the number of cases upon which the deductions of the present work are founded by remembering that only about one-sixth of orthodontia cases are afflicted with marked dento-facial deformities that call for facial casts.

PREFACE TO SECOND EDITION

The present and second edition of this work, which now bases malocclusion upon the dento-occlusal classification, has required a complete rewriting and readjustment of nearly every department.

The part which taught the "technic preparation of stock material and instruments," has been eliminated, and in its place the technic construction of appliances in Part V has been greatly enlarged.

The work proper now starts with Etiology of Malocclusion, with particular reference to Heredity. As the principles of heredity are founded upon and pertain to the principal laws of biology, an intelligent understanding of the foundation principles of biology seems imperative.

The work is not intended as an unabridged treatise upon the various systems employed for the correction of malocclusion, but it is one that is especially designed for teaching the technics and practical principles of correcting dental and dento-facial irregularities in colleges where thorough training is desired. It will also be found convenient and instructive as a reference book in practice.

In the presentation of the work, an endeavor has been made to arrange systematically the different branches in the sequence that would develop in the natural demands of training and practice. It commences with the foundation principles of the science, and carries the work through the several progressive stages to the final construction and adjustment of regulating apparatus and retaining appliances. It deals concisely with general and special principles relative to the application of force, diagnosis, classification, causes, treatment, and retention. The description of specific methods of treatment commences with Practical Treatment of Classified Dento-facial Malocclusions in Part VI, with a view to a co-ordinate systematic arrangement especially useful in teaching, and also useful to those who contemplate operations in orthodontia.

An important feature of the work is the employment of the half-tone illustrations of cases selected from the author's practice to illustrate from a practical standpoint the three Classes of Dento-facial Deformities and the results of correction.

Lengthy and verbose histories of cases, with a detailed account of the successive methods and steps that were pursued, which would in all probability never be the same, even in two apparently similar cases by the same operator, will not be found in this work. The time will be far more profitably spent in a study of the underlying principles of the science — in the acquirement of the peculiar knowledge that is essential to diagnosis and treatment, and in gaining an intimate knowledge of the principles of mechanical forces and technic methods of applying them to a single tooth, so as to move it in every possible direction.

Realizing how difficult it is for students to gain a clear conception of some of the underlying principles of this branch of dentistry, the author has not refrained from repeating many times throughout the work the same ideas, whenever the particular subject in hand has seemed to demand it. This will be found especially true in regard to the principles of occlusion in its various phases and relations to the art of correction and retention.

On account of the large number of irregularities treated in this work, with nearly every malposition that is common to the teeth, and the variety of forms of the appliances applicable for their correction, the system will doubtless appear to the casual observer as more or less complicated. But if one carefully considers the proposition here presented, i. e., that a systematic arrangement and classification of every distinctive character of irregularity will enable him to readily and surely find in the illustrations a malposition that is similar to the one which he wishes to treat, with every technic instruction for the construction or purchase of the whole or any part of an apparatus that is scientifically applicable for its correction, he will never again resort to other methods whose greatest recommendation is their apparent simplicity.

While it is always desirable to simplify the apparatus and methods of applying force to the teeth, the attempt to use certain methods or appliances solely because of their apparent simplicity, which may be inadequate to meet the special requirements of the case, greatly increases the difficulties of the operation, and often is the sole cause of failure. In fact, simplicity of treatment, ease and satisfaction in the adjustment and management of regulating appliances, and comfort to the patient, are always in proportion to the special adaptability and adequacy of the apparatus to accomplish the work successfully. Even this would fail without the skill of an operator capable of making slight but important variations in its construction or adjustments, of determining when, where, and how to apply the force, and especially when to reduce or stop it, and change the whole or parts of the appliances for methods or variations that more fully meet the demands of the changed and changing conditions.

A grateful appreciation is most heartily acknowledged for the aid derived from the teachings of others to whom honor is due for the upbuilding of this branch of dentistry; and while the work will be found free from any attempt to copy the various published methods, it is not that their importance is undervalued, or that the system here presented is not largely permeated by and dependent, in many of its important principles, on the work of others, but principally because the aim has been to teach only that which has been practically applied in the author's own practice. Wherever principles and methods from the works of others have been employed that could be located in the field of common property literature, due credit is given. Dr. Angle has truly observed: "To fair minds, recorded dates are usually sufficient evidence of priority." Unfortunately, this rule has not always been strictly observed.

Among the men of this country to whom the author is particularly indebted for many ideas pertaining to the practice of dental orthopedia, may be mentioned Drs. Kingsley, Farrar, Angle, Black, Guilford, Matteson, Cryer, Jackson, and others. The author is especially indebted to his son, Dr. Carl B. Case, for many important suggestions, and the invention and improvement of numberless ingenious and effective appliances, instruments, etc., and also for valuable aid in the preparation of drawings which illustrate this work.

An important addition to this work is the treatise upon the Prosthetic Correction of Cleft Palate. It is a branch of dentistry which most perfectly co-ordinates with the practice of orthodontia, for while it pertains principally to the correction of speech, the correction of malposed teeth and deformed facial outlines frequently forms the most important and indispensable part of a successful cleft palate operation. There is no branch of dentistry which can bring more pleasure, satisfaction, and grateful appreciation, than the correction of speech for cleft palate patients. or one which is founded so wholly upon scientific principles of practice.

C. S. C.

CHICAGO, 1921.

CONTENTS

INTRODUCTORY PREFACE

PART I

PRELIMINARY PRINCIPLES OF PRACTICE

CHAPTER I
SCOPE OF DENTAL ORTHOPEDIA

PAGE

An Appeal for a Higher Education and Thorough Training in those Branches of Science, Art, and Mechanics which Pertain to this Department 3

CHAPTER II
NOMENCLATURE

A Résumé of the Terms Employed in this Work and Applicable in Dental Orthopedia, with the Author's Objections to the Misapplication of Terms of Definite Meanings, and the Dropping of Terms of Established Usage and Scientific Applicability for New and Odd Terms, However Applicable 8

CHAPTER III
DENTO-OCCLUSAL CLASSIFICATION OF MALOCCLUSION

Explains Objects of a Classification — Basis of Present Classification — The Disto-Mesial Occlusion of Buccal Teeth — The Three Classes, Normal, Distal, and Mesial — Why Certain Malocclusions Arising from a Local Cause Cannot be Classified — Classified Chart of Malocclusions 15

PART II

ETIOLOGY OF MALOCCLUSION

CHAPTER IV
ETIOLOGIC PRINCIPLES OF MALOCCLUSION WITH REFERENCE TO TREATMENT

Unknowable Causes — Compound Causes — Relation of Causes to Treatment — Importance of Correct Diagnosis — Influences of Heredity 23

CHAPTER V
ETIOLOGIC INFLUENCES OF DECIDUOUS AND ERUPTING PERMANENT TEETH WITH PRINCIPLES OF TREATMENT

Why this Stage Is the Most Prolific of the Local Causes — Maleruption of Labial Teeth — Importance of Preserving the Deciduous Second Molars and Cuspids — Thumb-Sucking — Influences of Heredity — A Local Cause of Protrusion — Comparison of Childhood and Adult Physiognomies 30

CHAPTER VI
LAWS OF BIOLOGY REGARDED AS ETIOLOGIC FACTORS IN MALOCCLUSION

General Principles of Biology — Heredity — Natural Variation — Natural Selection — Environment 37

CHAPTER VII
HEREDITY AND VARIATION ETHNOLOGICALLY CONSIDERED

General Consideration — Mendel's Law — The Possibility of Mendel's Law as One of the Etiologic Factors in Malocclusion — Men of the Old Stone Age — Atavistic Heredity and Its Possible Influence upon Races and Present Types of Physiognomies 43

CHAPTER VIII
PRACTICAL APPLICATION OF BIOLOGIC LAWS

General Influences of Heredity — Direct — Atavistic — Union of Disharmonious Types — Influences of Heredity in Relation to Treatment 51

PART III
BASIC PRINCIPLES OF PRACTICE

CHAPTER IX
ARRANGEMENT OF THE TEETH AND ALVEOLAR PROCESS ANATOMICALLY CONSIDERED
By Dr. G. V. Black

Arrangement of the Teeth — The Alveolar Process and Alveoli 61

CHAPTER X
TYPICAL AND ATYPICAL OCCLUSION OF THE TEETH IN RELATION TO THE CORRECTION OF IRREGULARITIES
By Dr. Matthew H. Cryer

Shows Absurdity of Regulating Teeth by Rule — Typical vs. Actual Anatomy and Occlusion — Extraction for the Correction of Irregularities — Characteristic Features of Caucasian and Negro Skulls — Prognathous Appearance Caused by Hypertrophied Gums and Alveolar Processes 68

CHAPTER XI

DENTO-FACIAL PRINCIPLES OF OCCLUSION WITH REFERENCE TO PRACTICE

Occlusal Relations — Importance of Striving for a Normal Occlusion, but not at the Expense of Producing or Leaving a Facial Deformity — Importance of Angle's Teaching in Comparison with that of the Author — Why a Normal Occlusion should not be Regarded as a Basis of Correction 78

CHAPTER XII

THE QUESTION OF EXTRACTION IN ITS RELATION TO CAUSES, DIAGNOSIS AND TREATMENT

Rules of Extraction — Injudicious Extraction of Permanent Teeth — Judicious or Rational Extraction of Permanent Teeth 83

PART IV

TECHNIC PRINCIPLES OF PRACTICE

CHAPTER XIII

PRINCIPLES OF MECHANICS IN THE MOVEMENT OF TEETH

Inclination Movement — Levers — Post Levers — Tooth Levers — Relations of Power, Stress and Movement — Relating to Bodily Movement — Rotating Movement — Intrusive and Extrusive Movements 95

CHAPTER XIV

BODILY MOVEMENTS

Principles of Bodily Movements — Always through the Lever Action of the Third Kind — Torsional Force Applied to Bodily Movements 109

CHAPTER XV

PRINCIPLES OF DENTAL ANCHORAGES

Character of Force Regulating Immovability — Principles of Anchorage Stability — Stationary Anchorages — Root-wise Anchorages — Sustained Anchorages — Reciprocating Anchorages 118

CHAPTER XVI

PRINCIPLES OF INTERMAXILLARY AND OCCIPITAL FORCE

Intermaxillary Force — Occipital Force 126

CONTENTS

PART V
PRIMARY PRINCIPLES OF PRACTICE

CHAPTER XVII
IMPRESSIONS AND CASTS

Modeling-Compound — Dental Casts — Facial Impressions and Casts 139

CHAPTER XVIII
PRIMARY PRINCIPLES AND TECHNICS IN THE CONSTRUCTION OF BANDS

Separating Teeth — Orthodontia Bands — Soldering Bands — Silver Solder 147

CHAPTER XIX
ADVANCED PRINCIPLES AND TECHNICS OF REGULATING BANDS

Preliminary Fitting — Relation of Coronal Zones — Placing Bands — Removal of Bands — Soldering Attachments — Management of Solder and Blowpipe — Bands for Midget Appliances — Finishing and Plating — Advantages of Nickel Silver 155

CHAPTER XX
MODERN PRINCIPLES AND METHODS IN ORTHODONTIA

Three Characters of Malocclusion in One Case — Midget Apparatus — Bodily Movement Apparatus — The Technics of Attachments — Assembling Apparatus, and Adjustment Treatments — Bodily Working-Retainer 166

PART VI
PRACTICAL TREATMENT OF DENTO-FACIAL MALOCCLUSIONS

CHAPTER XXI
ORTHODONTIC PRINCIPLES OF DIAGNOSIS AND GENERAL RULES OF TREATMENT

Introduction — Scope of the Dento-Facial Field — Dento-Facial Area — Zones of Movement — Remarkable Changes in Facial Expression with Slight Movements — Dento-Facial Outlines in Diagnosis — Observation Training — Practical Diagnosis — Principles of Diagnosis According to Classes 181

CLASS I. NORMAL DISTO-MESIAL OCCLUSION

Table of Divisions and Types 199

CONTENTS

CHAPTER XXII
PRINCIPLES OF DIAGNOSIS IN MALERUPTION OF THE CUSPIDS
Diagnosis — Practical Application of Rules 200

CHAPTER XXIII
TYPE A, DIVISION 1, CLASS I. UNILATERAL MALERUPTION OF THE CUSPIDS
Full Description with Apparatus for the Treatment of Simple and Complicated Cases . . 205

CHAPTER XXIV
TYPE B, DIVISION 1, CLASS I. BILATERAL MALERUPTION OF CUSPIDS CORRECTED WITHOUT EXTRACTION
Full Description with Apparatus for the Treatment of Simple and Complicated Cases . . . 209

CHAPTER XXV
TYPE C, DIVISION 1, CLASS I. BILATERAL MALERUPTION OF UPPER CUSPIDS, REQUIRING EXTRACTION
Differential Diagnosis and Treatment 215

CHAPTER XXVI
TYPE D, DIVISION 1, CLASS I. THUMB-SUCKING PROTRUSION OF THE UPPER FRONT TEETH 218

CHAPTER XXVII
TYPE F, DIVISION 1, CLASS I. LATERAL MALOCCLUSION
First Form — Second Form 220

CHAPTER XXVIII
TYPE G, DIVISION 1, CLASS I. OPEN-BITE MALOCCLUSION
Diagnosis — Causes — Treatment 227

CHAPTER XXIX
DIVISION 2, CLASS I. BIMAXILLARY PROTRUSION AND RETRUSION
Diagnosis — Causes — Treatment 232

CLASS II. DISTAL MALOCCLUSION OF LOWER BUCCAL TEETH
Table of Divisions and Types 245

CHAPTER XXX
INTRODUCTION TO CLASS II 246

CHAPTER XXXI
TYPE A, DIVISION 1, CLASS II. PRONOUNCED RETRUSION OF THE LOWER DENTURE WITH UPPER NORMAL

Principles of Diagnosis, Treatment, and Retention 249

CHAPTER XXXII
TYPE B, DIVISION 1, CLASS II. MODERATE RETRUSION OF THE LOWER DENTURE, AND PARTIAL PROTRUSION OF THE UPPER

Diagnosis and Treatment — Intermaxillary Force 255

CHAPTER XXXIII
DIVISION 2, CLASS II. INTRODUCTION 259

CHAPTER XXXIV
TYPE A, DIVISION 2, CLASS II. UPPER CORONAL PROTRUSION 262

CHAPTER XXXV
TYPE B, DIVISION 2, CLASS II. UPPER BODILY PROTRUSION 266

CHAPTER XXXVI
TYPE C, DIVISION 2, CLASS II. UPPER CORONAL PROTRUSION WITH APICAL RETRUSION 270

CHAPTER XXXVII
TYPE D, DIVISION 2, CLASS II. UPPER APICAL PROTRUSION 274

CONCOMITANT CHARACTERS OF CLASS II

CHAPTER XXXVIII
RETRUSION OF THE MANDIBLE AND LOWER DENTURE 279

CHAPTER XXXIX
CLOSE-BITE MALOCCLUSION 283

CLASS III. MESIAL MALOCCLUSION OF LOWER BUCCAL TEETH

TABLE OF DIVISIONS 290

CHAPTER XL
PRINCIPLES OF DIAGNOSIS, CAUSES, AND TREATMENT 291

CHAPTER XLI
DIVISION 1, CLASS III. BODILY RETRUSION OF THE UPPER DENTURE AND MAXILLA 295

CHAPTER XLII
THE PROTRUDING CONTOUR APPARATUS 298

CHAPTER XLIII
DIVISION 2, CLASS III. CONTRACTED RETRUSION OF THE UPPER DENTURE 301

CHAPTER XLIV
DIVISION 3, CLASS III. UPPER RETRUSION WITH PROTRUSION OF LOWER DENTURE 312

CHAPTER XLV
DIVISION 4, CLASS III. RETRUSION OF THE UPPER DENTURE WITH PROGNATHIC MANDIBLE COMMONLY ACCOMPANIED WITH OPEN-BITE MALOCCLUSION 317

PART VII
PRACTICAL TREATMENT OF UNCLASSIFIED MALOCCLUSIONS
TABLE OF CHARACTERS. 328

UNCLASSIFIED MALPOSITIONS
FOREWORD 329

CHAPTER XLVI
INFRA AND SUPRA-OCCLUSION
Infra-Occlusion of Cuspids — Infra-Occlusion of Upper Incisors 331

CHAPTER XLVII
CROWDED MALALIGNMENTS 333

CHAPTER XLVIII
MALTURNED TEETH 339

CHAPTER XLIX
NARROW AND WIDE ARCHES. 346

CHAPTER L
ABNORMAL INTERPROXIMATE SPACES 354

CHAPTER LI
IMPACTED TEETH AND THEIR TREATMENT 362

PART VIII
PRINCIPLES AND TECHNICS OF RETENTION

CHAPTER LII
PRINCIPLES OF RETENTION

Influences of Heredity — Local Influences — Occlusal Influences — Importance of Interdigitation of Cusps — Importance of Extraction — Importance of Bodily Movement — Summary of Principles — Imperative Demands of Retaining Fixtures 377

CHAPTER LIII
LABIAL RETAINING FIXTURES

Quality and Technics of Bands — Technics of Construction — Six-Band Labial Retainer — Details of Construction — Placing the Appliance — Removal of the Appliance — Restoring Broken Extensions. 384

CHAPTER LIV
SUPPLEMENTARY RETAINING ATTACHMENTS AND APPLIANCES

Retention of Lateral Expansions — Retention of Retruded Movements — Intermaxillary Retention — Reciprocal Retaining Action — Direct Intermaxillary Retention — Occipital Retention — Retention of Bodily Movements — Permanent Retaining Fixtures . . . 393

PART IX
THE PROSTHETIC CORRECTION OF CLEFT PALATE

CHAPTER I
GENERAL PRINCIPLES IN THE MECHANISM OF SPEECH, AND THE TRAINING OF CLEFT PALATE PATIENTS AFTER OPERATIONS

Importance of Proper Instruction — Practical Teaching — Sound-Images — Practical Application of Methods of Instruction 409

CHAPTER II
PHYSIOLOGIC AND PHONETIC PRINCIPLES IN THE ART OF SPEAKING

Mechanism of Speech — The Velum-Palati — Resonance — The Oral Elements of Vowels and Consonants — The Vowels — The Consonants — The Intrinsic Value of Illustrations — Classification of Consonant Oral Elements — The Nasals — The Explosives — The Aspirates — The Open Aspirates — The Explosive Aspirates — Relative to the Chart . 420

CHAPTER III
THE TECHNIC CONSTRUCTION OF THE VELUM-OBTURATOR

The Impression and Model of the Cleft — Small Clefts — Two-Section Impression — Three-Section Impression — Plaster Working-Model of the Cleft 437

CHAPTER IV
THE TRIAL MODEL OF THE OBTURATOR

The Body of the Obturator-Model — The Veil of the Obturator-Model — The Most Scientific Part of the Operation 450

CHAPTER V
THE LABORATORY TECHNIC CONSTRUCTION OF THE OBTURATOR-MODEL

Preparation of the Plaster Model — The Flask — Preliminary Principles — The First Set of Plaster Models — Plaster and Investment Models — Investment Models 456

CHAPTER VI
TECHNICS OF THE METAL CASTS AND OBTURATOR

Metal Casts of the Models A, B, and C — Preparatory to Packing and Finishing the Obturator 466

CHAPTER VII
COMPLICATIONS WITH IRREGULARITIES AND SURGICAL FAILURES . . 471

PART I

Preliminary Principles of Practice

BOSTON UNIVERSITY
School of Medicine
Department of Stomatology
Graduate Orthodontics

DENTAL ORTHOPEDIA

CHAPTER I

SCOPE OF DENTAL ORTHOPEDIA

Dental Orthopedia, more commonly designated Orthodontia, or Orthodontics, is the science which has for its object the correction of dental and dento-facial malocclusion. The term Malocclusion in its present broad acceptance, not only applies to every form of dental irregularity, but to all imperfections in facial outlines that are caused from malpositions of the teeth and jaws, or that may be corrected through the medium of mechanically constructed appliances attached to the teeth.

In commencing the study of orthodontia, a preliminary knowledge of the elementary and general basic principles is imperative. The student should first become conversant with the nomenclature of orthodontia (Chapter II), and the classification of malocclusion (Chapter III), in order that he may have a clear and immediate understanding of the exact meaning of the technical terms employed, and the general characters of Classes and Divisions of Malocclusion. This will enable him to start with an intelligent understanding of the work from the very beginning, and thus he will be able to fully grasp and think out for himself each one of the steps as he progresses.

As the science relates to the correction of malocclusion for the promotion of normal functions, esthetic relations, and the beautifying of facial outlines, it will be seen that it pertains to physical changes in the structure and position of important parts of the human body which we have no right to touch except with proficient knowledge of subjects which pertain to causes, diagnosis, and treatment. As the treatment consists principally in the application of force appliances to the teeth, and is dependent largely upon a knowledge of mechanics and art, it is important that the student should lay a broad and firm foundation through the acquirement of all branches which pertain to this subject, and then with a knowledge of the various causes of malocclusion, and an understanding of the true principles of diagnosis, he will more fully appreciate what it is that established the standard of correction, and why it is necessary, desirable, and possible.

Let us briefly consider the present status of dental and dento-facial orthopedia, and the character and scope of the requirements which are necessary to the highest standard of its attainment. To sense all that is implied by dental and dento-facial malocclusion, one must know what is implied by the normal, the ideal, and the esthetic, relative to this branch of dentistry, and to realize that the growth and development of dental orthopedia has carried it beyond the mere mechanical correction of irregularities of the teeth, their malrelations to each other and to occlusion, and has placed it in a position where facial art is one of the indispensable bases of treatment. In nature's laboratory, things rarely occur mathematically, mechanically, or ideally perfect in all their parts. This is attested by every organ and part of the human body. If opticians should copy exactly the lines and refractibility of a normal natural lens, they would fall far short of the mathematical requirements of an artificial lens.

Some orthodontic authors wishing to visually illustrate by an anatomic specimen what they have most beautifully and ideally described as a "normal occlusion" are confronted with the almost impossible object of their search, because they seek for a specimen of *ideal* rather than normal or anatomic occlusion; whereas, any quantity of normal occlusion of the teeth could be found everywhere.

The apparently frantic efforts of authors along this line have led them to accept certain specimens for their illustrations, quite regardless of the race, or incongruity of the facial outlines of the living individual to whom the specimen belonged. See Cryer, Chapter X. As one becomes more fully informed in regard to the science of orthodontia, he will more deeply appreciate the fact that its highest attainment is harmony in dental and dento-facial relations, for use, health, development, and beauty. As by far the largest proportion of dentures require to be placed in normal occlusion in order to fulfill the desired perfection of facial outlines, a study of normal occlusion lies at the very foundation of orthodontic requirements.

The student is urgently referred to Dr. Angle's perfect description of an "ideal normal occlusion" under the heading "Occlusion" in his work entitled "Malocclusion of the Teeth." In connection with this, the chapters in this work entitled "Arrangement of the Teeth and Alveolar Process Anatomically Considered," by Black; "Typical and Atypical Occlusion of the Teeth in Relation to the Correction of Irregularities," by Cryer; and "Principles of Occlusion and Dento-Facial Relations," by the author, will be found replete in everything of practical value which relates to occlusion of the dentures, and its importance and rightful place in dental orthopedia.

The advancement of dental orthopedia to a gradually increasing position of permanency and reliability has undoubtedly been accomplished through the natural evolution toward a higher order of attainments and skill, stimulated no doubt by certain teachers who possessed special qualifications. There is probably no department of dentistry in which the relative branches of applied science and art are so indispensable to its highest success, or one, moreover, in which training in advanced principles of mechanics is so important. It, therefore, becomes necessary in the teaching of this department to dwell more or less upon these basic principles, to aid the student in laying the proper foundation for practice, with the hope also that it will stimulate him to a thorough equipment in the future that will fully prepare him for high professional attainments, whether or not he decides to practice this branch as a specialty.

In the present broad scope of advancement in orthodontia, or dental and dentofacial orthopedia, the science demands for its highest attainment an intimate knowledge of all relative branches of applied science, art, and mechanics.

Science.—One should know the anatomy, histology, physiology, and pathology of the teeth and all associate parts which enter into the formation of the oral, nasal, and naso-pharyngeal cavities, the bones, their embryologic and post-natal development, structure, and functions; the muscles, their physiologic activities in mastication, in speech, and in controlling or marring the normal development and form of the dental arches. He should be capable of immediately recognizing local pathologic conditions which interfere or inhibit normal development, and which frequently demand the services of other specialists.

In the biologic field will be found much of interest and practical instruction to orthodontists, especially in principles of heredity and natural variation which pertain to causes, and in ethnology which relates to the origin and development of races of peoples, with their characteristic types of physiognomies. This is especially important inasmuch as it is thoroughly proven that through the admixture of dissimilar racial types, and types of the same race that are quite dissimilar in sizes and physical characters, that many of the individual disharmonies and dento-facial irregularities of our own race have arisen. There is probably no branch of science, from an educational and practical standpoint, that is so important to orthodontists, and in fact all men of the medical and dental profession, as the principles of biology, because biology is a science which is founded upon thoroughly proven investigations that are accepted as true by all learned minds, and because it relates to the origin, development, evolution, and continued co-ordination of all living things, it has much to do with the interests, the pleasures, and the practical benefits of our everyday lives. It lies at the very foundation of nearly all the scientific branches which we regard as imperative to teach in our dental colleges, and it is especially important to orthodontists, because it shows them the true etiologic origin of many of the dento-facial malocclusions they are called upon to treat; and in so doing, it guides them toward their true correction.

It would seem, however, from the many unreliable statements that have been made within the past few years by some of the men who stand high in our specialty, that our education as a class in the principles and truths of biology had been sadly neglected. And because these statements strike at the very root of important principles in our advancement, it has seemed necessary, in order to effectually combat them, to give far more space in the etiologic branch of this work, to the laws and principles which govern these important questions, than would otherwise be necessary.

Art.—From the first activities of the senses, the mind intuitively commences to be educated and early acquires a rudimentary conception of relations in qualities, forms, sizes, distances, colors, etc. As the mind becomes more educated solely through these repeated contacts of the senses with physical things and natural phenomena, there arises involuntarily, and without our seeking or realizing why, a pleasurable appreciation of the regular, the beautiful, and the harmonious, in the blending of colors, the rhythmic union of musical tones, the combination of graceful lines, etc., until subconsciously we know without being told when a perceptible disharmony arises which we are almost sure to intuitively feel in proportion to its degree.

In no branch of dentistry does there arise the need of so much artistic ability as in the department of dento-facial orthopedia. One who possesses the true artistic temperament will more quickly discern, as if by intuition, esthetic imperfections in dento-facial outlines, and will be able to determine in advance the direction and amount of the various possible movements of the teeth and bony framework required for correction.

Those who fail to appreciate, or are so constituted they cannot comprehend the importance of this particular branch of applied art in the diagnosis and treatment of dento-facial imperfections and deformities, will never know the satisfaction of true success which comes to him who reaches the higher planes of this specialty.

But let no earnest seeker after these high attainments in dento-facial art become discouraged by the many mystifications which will arise in the minds of students and in practice, providing he rises to a realization of his failures, and persists in an earnest faithful endeavor to master the principles which are so thoroughly taught in this and other works on dental orthopedia. In other words, the faculty of intuitive artistic discernment in diagnosis, while doubly valuable to the possessor may be duplicated to a very large extent by observation, training, good judgment, and experience, with careful and intelligent study of the conditions which arise in practice.

Mechanics.—It is not so very many years ago that dentists who aspired to high professional standing considered it somewhat beneath their dignity to acknowledge that the highest achievements of their practice depended upon their mechanical ability. Today, it is freely accepted that nearly every department of dentistry is dependent for true success upon the art of mechanical manipulation and principles of mechanics. Throughout the entire universe from the greatest to the smallest, we see how everything is developed and guided by mechanical forces. In the biologic field we find in every living thing, for its protection and development, a wonderful display of mechanical ingenuity for the propagation and stimulation to action, in all histologic and anatomic forms and structures, from the simple cell to the most heterogeneous organism.

Consider the jaws, their structure, physical forms and relation to each other and to other parts and auxiliary organs, how exactly and mechanically in accord with their use and functions in the arrangement, strength, and attachments of the muscles to produce the required movements and forces; in the form and structure of the component parts of the teeth and alveolar processes to resist the stresses of mastication without injury or discomfort; in the form and structure of the enamel, the cusps, their interdigitation and interdependence in occlusion to sustain the forces and produce the most perfect trituration of foods; in everything everywhere we see that same wonderfully mechanical ingenuity employed for the protection, preservation, and action of the several parts according to their needs and the physical activities of their normal functions. One has but to become thoroughly acquainted with the activities of primary and secondary dentition to be filled with wonder and admiration at nature's mechanical expedients for the development, eruption, and arrangement of the teeth.

In no department of dentistry is there so great an opportunity and need for mechanical ingenuity and skill based upon the laws of mechanics, as in orthodontia. The reasons for this are, first, no two cases of malocclusion are exactly alike, they having variations which frequently demand individual inventive capacity for which no guiding rules can be found. Two cases which seem to be similar and are alike in occlusion and relations of dentures to each other, are frequently found, by an intelligent diagnosis of facial relations to be widely different in their demands of treatment, and in the application of forces. Second, the correction of malocclusions does not consist as formerly in merely pulling and pushing the crowns into alignment and occlusion, but one of its most common demands is a bodily movement in order to place the teeth in positions of greatest usefulness and beauty, and, moreover, to apply the forces in such a manner that the dental and alveolar arches, and the yielding developing jaws will take their proper relations to each other and to the facial outlines. Third, the limited opportunity for applying the various forces through the medium of attachments soldered to thin bands cemented to the crowns of teeth, requires a thorough knowledge of the laws of applied forces which relate to this department, with ingenuity to determine the most effective methods and skill to carry forward the movements according to the required mechanical and physiologic demands.

This branch is of such very great importance to a successful practice of dental orthopedia, the author has devoted much space to the scientific principles of applied mechanics, which relate to the movement of teeth, and also to practical details in the construction and application of appliances and apparatus for the correction of all the common forms of malocclusion, fully explaining various forces which are exerted, and the probable movements of the teeth that are produced. This will give to the student a mental training which, supplemented with the manual training of the technic department, should thoroughly prepare him for an intelligent understanding of the more advanced didactic teaching and duties of infirmary and final office practice.

CHAPTER II

NOMENCLATURE

A correct use of terms that may be universally adopted is greatly to be desired in this department of dentistry. At present we are hampered by the use of wrong or ill-chosen terms which we are unable to discard, because of general established usage. Unfortunately, there has been an effort to force into our nomenclature an enlarged and changed definition of words which are not compatible with their dictionary meaning or common use. Again, the effort to force us to accept terms whose root meanings are not at all like the words they are intended to represent, is very bad form, and should be stopped in our textbooks and teachings before these misnomers become too thoroughly established. We are unhappily mystified also by the use of terms which prominent writers have from time to time adopted in their efforts to find words that would more clearly and concisely express their meaning, and perhaps also to simplify that which should be more specifically and scientifically defined.

But when these new terms are odd and unfamiliar, whatever their scientific applicability, they should not be forced into our nomenclature to take the place of other terms of anglicized established usage which have an equal claim to derivative applicability. An established nomenclature in orthodontia, or any branch of science, is not a thing that can be molded like putty and changed in form by any one man, or by chosen "committees on nomenclature," and especially not, if they attempt to enlarge or restrict the definition of words of exact meaning, purely by *fiat*, or to discard scientifically correct terms for others whose roots render them inapplicable. In fact it is next to an impossibility to discard the employment of established terms which in the first place were wrongly chosen as regards the real meaning of their roots, even though other terms are offered in their place that are absolutely correct and far more applicable.

This is well illustrated in the selection of the word "Orthodontia" as the title of that branch of dentistry which has for its object the correction of malocclusion, or irregular teeth. Its choice was unfortunate, because the word means in the Greek "straight tooth." We do not straighten or correct the *shape* of an individual tooth as the orthopedic surgeon corrects the form and shape of a child, but we correct its position in relation to surrounding parts. The choice, however, was excusable as long as the art was confined to the correction of dental arch alignment and occlusion; but now that one of the principal accomplishments of the art is to correct facial deformities through the medium of force applied to the teeth, the term Dental and Dento-Facial Orthopedia is far preferable, and is quite universally employed in other languages, but the long established use of the term "orthodontia" in this country has doubtless made it a permanent fixture. It is, therefore, freely used in this work in its restricted sense.

The word "Orthopedia" is derived from two Greek words which literally translated mean "straight child." Originally, the word was chosen to indicate that branch of general surgery which has for its object the straightening or correcting deformities of children by the moderate application of force to the yielding and developing bones. Orthopedic surgery in its present and broader sense includes the correction of all deformities accomplished in a similar manner. "Orthopedic Dentistry," or "Dental Orthopedia," therefore, would plainly specialize the art to the correction of all dental and facial deformities accomplished by orthopedic movements of the teeth and connecting bones.

The following terms as defined will be used in this work as the standard expressions in this department of dentistry.

Dento-Facial Area is the facial area which is supported and characterized by the teeth and the alveolar process.

Dento-Facial Relation refers to the relation which the teeth in masticating occlusion bear to the physiognomy. In normal **dento-facial relations, or dento-facial harmony** the teeth and overlying features are in the most perfect harmony to the general facial outlines, according to the type of the individual.

Naso-Labial Folds, Depressions, or Lines, extend from the lateral borders of the wings of the nose diagonally downward to a point slightly below the corners of the mouth, marked by the action of the orbicularis oris and risorius muscles.

Labio-Mental Curve or **Depression** is the concave depression beneath the lower lip and above the chin.

Occlusion.—The term "occlusion" will be employed in this work to mean the same as defined in every dictionary. It is a word of long established and unwavering usage, and refers anatomically only to the action of parts or organs of the body whose function is to open and close. When the lips, the eyelids, or the teeth are brought temporarily together in the full performance of their immediate functions, they are in "occlusion." We, therefore, have no right to take a word of such definite and established anatomic meaning, and assert purely by *fiat* that it must henceforth be used to mean "normal occlusion," or that "normal occlusion" means "dento-facial harmony." In orthodontia, the term **occlusion** refers to the closure of the teeth or dentures one upon the other. When the jaws are closed, the teeth that fully touch each other are in **"occlusion."** If the teeth are irregular, but with buccal cusps striking well into closely fitted sulci, they are in **"masticating occlusion,"** though they may not be in normal interdigitation. If no teeth are missing, and the dentures are not irregular and close according to the anatomic standard, they are in **"normal, or anatomic occlusion."**

The terms **Normal,** and **Anatomic,** mean "according to rule," or "in conformity to natural law." In orthodontia they are useful words, because slight variations from the typical are the rule rather than the exception.

Malocclusion.—The terms "dental irregularity," and "irregularity of the teeth," while perfectly proper in a restricted sense, have been gradually succeeded by the more comprehensive and popular term "malocclusion," which in the present wide scope of its meaning refers to all dental and dento-facial malpositions which may be corrected by mechanical forces applied to the teeth.

Posed and **Malposed.**—Teeth are **normally posed** when regular or in normal positions. The terms **"malposed"** and **"malposition"** are used with varying shades of distinction as synonymous with **irregular** and **irregularity.**

Alignment and **Malalignment.**—Teeth are in alignment when they are in proper relation to the line of their dental arch. A tooth or teeth in malalignment constitutes an irregularity, yet all the teeth of the dental arch may be in perfect alignment with the dentures in malocclusion, as instanced by abnormal protrusions of the upper teeth and other conditions.

Interdigitate and **Interdigitation** have reference to any closure of the buccal teeth in which the cusps of one denture strike fairly into the occluding sulci of the other. When the teeth are in normal occlusion, the buccal cusps are in **normal interdigitation.** When the buccal cusps interdigitate, with the teeth in abnormal occlusion—as in upper protrusions, for instance, where the upper buccal cusps are fully the width of a premolar in front of a normal occlusion with the lower—the cusps are in abnormal interdigitation or **"malinterdigitation."**

Open-Bite Malocclusion.—When the labial, or "biting" teeth cannot be brought together, through an occlusal interference of the back teeth, leaving a space of more or less width, the condition may be properly termed an **"open-bite malocclusion."** See Fig. 152, Class I, Division 1.

Close-Bite Malocclusion.—The opposite condition of the above would therefore apply to those cases in which a closure of the back teeth causes the front teeth to pass their normal occlusal planes, frequently forcing the lower incisors deeply into the gum back of the upper front teeth. See Class II, Division 1. This may be an infra-occlusal position of buccal teeth, or a supra-occlusal position of the labial teeth.

The Occlusal Plane.—When the lips of esthetic facial outlines are in perfect repose, the standard line of a typical occlusal plane should be even with or but slightly below the lower edge of the upper lip, which should indicate the normal line of the occlusal edges of the upper labial teeth. The front part of the lower plane curves upward to a point slightly above this to allow the occlusal ends of the lower labial teeth to pass back of the uppers. From this point, posteriorly, the plane curves slightly downward, and then as it passes the first molars, it again curves slightly upward.

Infra and **Supra-Occlusion** are terms which refer to teeth whose occluding surfaces are below or above the normal occlusal plane. See "Intrusive" and "Extrusive."

General Bimaxillary Supra and **Infra-Occlusion.**—We frequently meet people whose dentures are in normal occlusion, and not protruded, and yet they cannot possibly bring their lips together without an effort, and when they are laughing or talking, the crowns of the front teeth, and often the gums far above, are in unpleasant evidence. This is because the teeth are too long in relation to the normal occlusal plane, and the condition may be properly termed **"General Bimaxillary Supra-Occlusion."**

Occasionally, the teeth are in the opposite, or infra-occlusal malposition. This does not refer to that frequent "close-bite malocclusion" found in Class II in which the lower front teeth strike into the gums back of the upper, and is due to an **infra-occlusal position of the back teeth,** but it refers to cases in which both the front and the back teeth are too short in relation to the normal occlusal plane. Patients with this character of malocclusion, can open their jaws from ¼ to ⅜ of an inch without disturbing a reposeful closure of the lips, and when the jaws are closed, the lips in contact are forced forward with a marked and unpleasant redundancy of lip tissue. This condition may be properly termed **"General Bimaxillary Infra-Occlusion."** See description and illustration of this character which is placed in this work in Class I, Division 2.

Mesial and **Distal,** when used to define malpositions, locations, occlusion, movements, etc., will be used only in the sense in which these terms were originally intended to be used in dentistry, i. e., toward or from the median line in a direction along the curve of the dental arch. Therefore, they should not be used as they frequently are in the sense of anterior and posterior, front or back, or protruded and retruded, except in referring to the buccal teeth. Again, if the lower first molars occlude mesially to normal, or distally to normal in relation to the upper molars, this malocclusion should not be defined as one "in mesial malocclusion," or one in "distal malocclusion," *without other qualifications* as it frequently is, because this term has reference to the upper teeth as well as to the lower in occlusal contact. This would indicate that only the lower denture assumed these distal and mesial malpositions. Moreover, the mesio-distal relation of the molar occlusion in no sense defines the real irregularity, because this relation does not necessarily indicate that the lower or the upper teeth are protruded or retruded. The fault may be entirely with either denture alone, or it may be partly with the lower and partly with the upper denture.

Arch.—The dental arch is that inscribed by the teeth. The **alveolar arch,** that inscribed by the alveolar process and overlying gum. It is an unfortunate confusing misnomer to call arch-bows, "arches." They are not "arches" in any sense of the word, and they *are* bows for correcting dental arches.

Dome.—The **dome** of the oral arch refers to the upper curve or area of the roof of the mouth.

Zone is a favorable word for locating sections of the dental and alveolar arches that we frequently wish to refer to in describing different characters of general malpositions and movements. **Dental Zones** may be considered as narrow band-like areas extending along the dental arch parallel to the occlusal plane, as **"Occlusal, Gingival,** and **Apical Zones."** (For "Dento-Facial Zones," see Chapter XXI.)

Malturned is used in reference to a tooth that is abnormally turned on its central axis. The term "malturned," though somewhat of a mongrel, is much preferred to "torsion" and "torso-occlusion," which is very bad and improper. The dictionary states: "Torsion (torsio, torquere), the act of twisting a body—such as a thread, wire, rope, etc., by the exertion of lateral force tending to turn *one end* or part of it about a longitudinal axis, while the other is *held fast* or turned in the opposite direction." A tooth is never twisted or in a twisted posture, nor do we twist teeth as we do a string, or any yielding body. We *rotate* them bodily on their central axes. Moreover, the term **"torso occlusion"** is suggestive of "torso," the trunk of the human body.

Rotate is used in reference to the **process** of turning a tooth. Many authors have heretofore used "rotate" and its suffixes to define both position and action. The same is true of "torsion." The author finds that it avoids much confusion in teaching and writing—besides being more proper—to use distinct words for position and action. Thus a "malturned" tooth demands "rotating" force for its correction.

Compound Terms.—The adjectives **mesial, distal, labial, buccal, lingual,** and **occlusal,** and their combinations can be happily used to exactly define certain malpositions, movements, points of attachment, direction, etc. The direction in which a tooth is malturned or requires rotating on its central axis may thus be fully defined with a compound word, if it is understood as in other departments that the first member of the compound word indicates the location upon the surface of the tooth, and the last member the direction of the movement. For instance, we may say that a central incisor is malturned labio-mesially, or that it requires the application of labio-distal rotating force. Again, it may be in mesial, distal, labial, buccal, or lingual inclination, or in labial or lingual malalignment, etc.

Anterior and **Posterior** are words that are so well established by common usage it would be difficult if not impossible to drop them from our nomenclature, even if we wished. When used to define relative position or movement in a direction parallel to the median line, they are frequently of great advantage.

Trudo.—A number of quite commonly employed and useful English terms are derived from the Latin root "trudo," "to thrust." The syllable "trude" with its prefixes "pro" (forward), "re" (backward), "ex" (out from), "in" (into), "con" (in upon), with their suffixes, "ed," "ing," "sion," and "sive," gives us a class of words of distinct and scientific applicability. Moreover, they are of such common usage in our language, and especially in the sciences in expressing relative positions and movements, and their applicability is so quickly comprehended by students, it seems strange that so many orthodontic teachers and authors of textbooks in their nomenclatures should employ in their place terms that are odd, and of very uncommon usage, whatever their scientific applicability.

Protrude, Retrude, etc.—Teeth are in a **protruded** or **retruded** position only in respect to the esthetic standard of dento-facial relation, and in no instance can this be determined or defined by the occlusal relation. The esthetic facial lines, accord-

CHAPTER II. NOMENCLATURE

ing to the type of the physiognomy, are taken as a **standard** of position, and therefore should not be confounded with the relative position of the teeth or the dentures in relation to each other. If the teeth are in front of a line which forces the lip or lips forward of the true dento-facial line, they are **protruded** to the extent of their malposition, and are denominated **Upper Protrusion, Lower Protrusion,** or **Bimaxillary Protrusion.** The same is true in regard to retruded malpositions.

The front teeth alone may be protruded or retruded, or these adjectives may be applied to the entire dentures or even the jaws in these characters of malrelations to dento-facial harmony.

If the crowns alone are protruded with labial inclinations forcing the orbicular portion of the lip or lips forward, it is **coronal protrusion.** If the crowns and roots are protruded forcing the entire labial area forward, it is **bodily protrusion.** If the jaws are protruded, it is **maxillary,** or **mandibular protrusion, or prognathism.**

Intrusive and **Extrusive** are relative adjective terms which refer to movement or position in relation to the socket or the normal occlusal plane, and always in the line of the central axis. For instance, a tooth in a supra-occlusal malposition demands an **intrusive movement,** and vice versa. The expression "compressing teeth into their sockets," is quite as bad form as "torso." Nothing is "compressed," except compressible substances, like cotton, wood, etc., which can be forced into a more compact form.

Contrude is a useful word, not supplied by any other, to indicate an abnormal inward curve of any portion of the line of the dental arch. Thus, in a "club-shaped arch," the sides are *contruded*. It may also be used to refer to a single tooth which is crowded lingually into malalignment. The term in geology refers to a downward or inward curve of the line of strata.

Labial, Lingual, and **Buccal** are terms employed to define position, direction, or movement. For instance, the front teeth are moved labially when they are moved forward or toward the lips, etc.

Gingival, Occlusal, Approximal, etc., are well known.

Rootwise is employed to define position or direction of force. Rootwise attachments "are those which extend above the gingival line for the force attachment." If force or movement is in a rootwise direction, it is toward the ends of the roots in a line with their central axes, or intrusively.

Labial Teeth and **Buccal Teeth.**—It is frequently desirable to speak of the six front upper or lower teeth as having moved or requiring movement in phalanx. The same is true of the right and left upper and lower side teeth. Therefore, the term **"Labial Teeth"** will be used to refer to the incisors and cuspids in single phalanx; and the **"Buccal Teeth"** to the premolars and molars in single phalanx.

Front, Back, Upper, and **Lower.**—In referring to the general location of the teeth, the terms **"Front"** and **"Back"** will be used in preference to the terms **"Anterior"** and **"Posterior,"** and the terms **"Upper"** and **"Lower"** instead of **"Superior"** and **"Inferior"** teeth.

In this work, the terms **Cuspid** and **Canine** will be used synonymously, though preference is given to the former. **Premolar** instead of Bicuspid; **Deciduous Molar** instead of "Premolar"; **First Permanent Molar** instead of "Six Year Molar"; **Third Molar** instead of "Wisdom Tooth."

In the present unfixed state of our dental nomenclature, the author believes it inadvisable to wholly discard the use of any term which by long usage and strict scientific application may be properly applied, and especially those which are correctly employed by our best writers.

The term "Cuspid" instead of "Canine" is the choice of Dr. G. V. Black in our leading Dental Anatomy. In a letter in reference to these terms he says:

"I wish to say this: that Dental Nomenclature in dentistry is not necessarily dental nomenclature in comparative dental anatomy. The comparative dental anatomist's nomenclature never will answer the purpose of the dentist, and neither will the nomenclature of the dentist answer the purpose of the comparative dental anatomist, and the quicker this is recognized the better it will be for all parties. We do not write of dog's teeth and we have no use for the term 'canine tooth'."

The author does not object or refrain from using any advisedly established term which is applicable and calculated to convey the desired meaning. The term "Canine" has come into quite general use of late, and the fact that it is wholly adopted by the "Cosmos," and a number of leading journals and textbooks, are good reasons for adopting it in this work, but it seemed unreasonable to drop "Cuspid" as long as we retained "Bicuspid." The two words as a pair were plainly indicative: the one referring to a tooth having one cusp, and the other to one having two cusps. But cuspid is so fixed by usage it is almost impossible to drop it.

The term "Premolar" when referring to the bicuspids has certain objections, because if there are any teeth in the mouth which are premolars according to the strictest meaning of the term, **they are the deciduous molars,** as these are the only teeth which, in form and function, are like the permanent molars, and they are also "pre" to the permanent molars both as to position and time. Dr. Cryer rightfully calls them premolars, though he also uses this term in referring to the bicuspids; while others confine the term to the bicuspids alone. The fact, however, that "premolar" instead of "bicuspid" has come into quite general use by orthodontists, and also because it has been adopted by many of the latest scientific works, practically necessitates adopting it in this work.

Unilateral, indicating location, refers to one side of the mouth.

Bilateral, indicating location, refers to both sides of the mouth.

Unimaxillary, indicating location, refers to one jaw.

Bimaxillary, indicating location, refers to both jaws.

The term **Oro-Nasal** is introduced to take the place of naso-pharyngeal, when applied to the passage leading from the mouth to the nose.

Oral Element is an indivisible element of speech.

CHAPTER III

DENTO-OCCLUSAL CLASSIFICATION OF MALOCCLUSION

Like nomenclature, it is important that the student should acquire a perfect knowledge of the accepted classification of malocclusion employed in the textbook, at the very beginning of his study of orthodontia in order that he may be able to intelligently locate by name the various malocclusions that are mentioned in the text, as he progresses. By the aid of the "Table of Classes" herewith, to which the student can immediately turn, he will soon familiarize himself with the special characters of the Classes and their Divisions.

The principal object of a classification in any of the sciences is to enable one to quickly obtain a general mental grasp of the thing referred to, and to recognize it, or define it as distinguished from other things of a similar nature, thus producing a clear mental flash-light word picture of the thing itself. This is accomplished through a systematic arrangement of the objects or material into distinct groups, classes, divisions, types, etc., each one of which is characterized by some stable peculiarity in form, structure, or property of *recurring constancy, not found elsewhere in the classification*. Therefore, in naming a class in any classification with the division of that class, and the type of the division of the class, we have presented a mental picture of the thing and its peculiar distinguishing characteristics.

In an attempt to follow this commonly accepted system of nomenclature in classification of malocclusion of the teeth, we are confronted with somewhat the same difficulties that confront the science of medicine in classifying diseases.

In orthodontia, the present most popularly accepted basis for the classification of malocclusion is the disto-mesial occlusal relations of the buccal teeth. This naturally divides malocclusions into three classes as follows: In Class I, the disto-mesial occlusal relations of the buccal teeth are normal or nearly so. In Class II, the disto-mesial occlusal relations of the lower buccal teeth are about the width of a cusp distal to normal; and in Class III, the disto-mesial occlusal relations of the lower buccal teeth are about the width of a cusp mesial to normal.

The consistent reason for this natural division into the three classes is as follows: In a normal occlusion of the teeth, the cusps of the buccal teeth of one denture fit evenly and anatomically into the sulci of the other. During the eruptive stage, if from some cause they do not quite take this exact anatomic relation, the forces of mastication soon drive them fully into it along the inclined planes of the sliding facets; except in those cases where certain causes, local or inherent, have forced the teeth to erupt so that the crests of the cusps of one denture are more or less outside the grasp of the normal spheres of influence. In this instance they at once commence to drift along the inclined planes toward the wrong, or abnormal sulci, until they have fitted themselves as closely as possible into their interlocking grasps, with the result that the buccal teeth of one denture in relation to the other, on the right or the left, or both sides, are commonly found to occlude in normal, or about the width of a cusp mesial or distal to normal occlusion.

As the teeth erupt and come into contact with their masticating fellows, they are often forced to move disto-mesially and bucco-lingually, from their erupted positions through the fitting processes of their cusps, in exactly the same way that they are moved by orthodontic forces. There is no doubt that whole dentures are frequently caused to move antero-posteriorly to a considerable extent by the mesial or distal movement of their masticating teeth in nature's process of fitting the cusps into their normal or abnormal interdigitating sulci, which constitutes the basis of our present three classes of malocclusion.

While this **dento-occlusal classification** here presented is quite different from the Angle classification, it will be found, by teachers and students, of the greatest practical value, enabling a systematic presentation of the most advanced principles of dento-facial orthopedia, at present unequaled by any other classification. For the very great advantage of perfect harmony and unanimity in our literature and teaching, the author would have gladly adopted the Angle classification were it not for the fact that as it now stands it cannot be made to express a large number of very important characters of malocclusion which should be fully recognized and systematically scheduled as independent Divisions or Types of Divisions of one or the other of the three Classes. Furthermore, the Angle classification does not recognize those *wide differences* in the character of certain malocclusions which have the *same disto-mesial occlusion* of the buccal teeth. It will be found by a careful study of malocclusions that these differences in dento-facial characters and demands of treatment *within each class* are fully as great and quite as important in orthodontia as the differences which arise between one class and another. Note the distinctively different characters within each one of the three classes shown by the chart. When we take the disto-mesial occlusal relations of the buccal teeth as the distinguishing bases of the three classes, we should necessarily place in each one of the classes—either in divisions or types—*all the distinctive recurring characters which correspond to the chosen basis of the class.*

When we name a class to which a certain malocclusion belongs, we convey a mental picture of *only* the disto-mesial occlusal relations of its buccal teeth, and nothing more, except the fancied conception of its real character and dento-facial relations. And when we go further and name the Division of its class, we still have placed it only as one of a family of malocclusions whose individual members may differ quite decidedly from each other when dento-facially considered, though all are alike in one distinguishing characteristic of buccal occlusion. Neither can we place in the mind's eye the individually completed characters of the case in hand until we have named its Type, its Division, and its Class. There are, however, certain divisions whose different types are so similar they require no mention in a classified chart, though in practical treatment they may differ considerably; all of which with a variety of variations should be fully outlined in the textbook teaching.

In this classification, while the class to which a malocclusion belongs is determined solely by its occlusal disto-mesial relations, its family or Divisional characteristic is based upon its general dento-facial relations, and when there are found to be distinctive variations within the Division, they constitute its Types. But when these distinctive type variations are common to all the Divisions of the Class, they are placed under "Concomitant Types" as in Class II.

As a large majority of orthodontists have already become accustomed to divide malocclusions according to the three distinct occlusions of the buccal teeth —normal, mesial, and distal—the placing of all the commonly recurring dento-facial types which have a similar occlusion, in one class, will doubtless give a greater opportunity to define their wide differences in character and demands of treatment, and thus prevent as far as possible the too common error of treating cases alike on the basis of their occlusal similarity. It is hoped also that it will tend toward preventing the insistence of placing certain dentures in a normal occlusion whose deforming facial protrusions demand extraction. And on the other hand, it is most earnestly hoped that it will prevent the extraction of teeth by those who unfortunately have made a wrong interpretation of the author's teaching. It certainly should appeal to those orthodontists who favor the occlusal classification, and whose highest aim in practice is a truthful and scientific diagnosis of their cases.

To those who believe that teeth should never be extracted for the dento-facial correction of the decided unimaxillary and bimaxillary protrusions, Dr. Angle's classification will be found quite consistent with that system of practice.

It was because of the marked differences in the character, facial outlines, and required treatment of malocclusion in Class II—in which the upper denture is about the width of a cusp in front of a normal occlusion—that led the author to divide this class in a former classification, into Classes II and III, as he believed this would more strongly emphasize the importance of a differential diagnosis of dento-facial characters having the same occlusion of the teeth, certain types of which demand the extraction of teeth in their proper correction, while with others, such a procedure would be decided malpractice. In other words, it was his desire to free it from the mechanical and mathematical trend toward which the science seemed to be drifting, and to induce a deeper consideration and study of facial art and beauty as important factors of diagnosis and treatment. With the present advancement in the practical principles of orthodontia, it is hoped that a systematized arrangement of all the distinctive types of malocclusion under three heads, upon the basis of their occlusal peculiarity, will enable a full appreciation of the wide differences in dento-facial outlines with patients having, practically, the same occlusal relations of the teeth.

By carefully scanning the author's present classification, it will be seen that while the distinct characters of malocclusion are now divided among the three classes upon the basis of their disto-mesial occlusion, their true basis of diagnosis and treatment is dependent very largely upon the facial outlines in relation to the standard of esthetic perfection for the individual, because it is not otherwise possible as a guide to treatment to determine whether the dentures—one or both—are really protruded or retruded.

While the dento-occlusal classification possesses the advantage of enabling us to divide and segregate a great variety of malocclusions into a small number of classes, it will be found as one becomes more and more advanced in the science of orthodontia, that there will arise a fuller appreciation of the fact that the disto-mesial occlusion of the buccal teeth is a very uncertain and often misleading guide as a basis of diagnosis in determining real conditions, and the kind of treatment demanded, because in every one of the three classes, if all the distinct characters inside of each class are tabulated, there will be found a remarkably diverse variety of dento-facial deformities.

One of the most dangerous features of the Angle classification, as formerly set forth, and one which, strange to say, has tended to popularize it in the minds of orthodontists, is the universally applied teaching that when dentures are placed in normal occlusion, the facial outlines will take care of themselves; and, therefore, the highest possible orthodontic attainment for that individual is accomplished. If this were as true as it is believed by many, it would simplify the whole practice of orthodontia, because in theory it eradicates the necessity of a deep comprehension of dento-facial art, and many other important principles which are so difficult for orthodontists to understand.

A careful study of the great question of extraction which is so largely dependent upon Causes, and which lies at the very foundation of advanced dento-facial orthopedia, must convince every receptive truth-seeking mind of the delusiveness of a teaching which asserts the *universal applicability* of the "normal occlusion theory,"—which is: that "every tooth or its artificial substitute is necessary for the perfect correction of dental or dento-facial malocclusions."

In adopting the occlusal classification, therefore, it should be remembered that the disto-mesial character of a buccal malocclusion is no more or less than one of the incidents of the case in hand, requiring correction if demanded along with other malpositions which may be present, and which are equally important to correct. It is one moreover that demands to the fullest extent that the masticating cusps shall be in perfect interdigitating occlusion; and furthermore—it goes without saying—they should always be placed in normal occlusion, except in those comparatively few instances where this rule is inconsistent with imperative facial demands.

There are, however, certain special and quite common malpositions which are found in every one of the three classes, because they arise from local causes which

CHAPTER III. DENTO-OCCLUSAL CLASSIFICATION

Classified Table of Dento-Facial Malocclusions

CLASS I. NORMAL DISTO-MESIAL OCCLUSION OF THE BUCCAL TEETH.

DIVISION 1: LOCALLY CAUSED DENTO-FACIAL MALOCCLUSIONS.

TYPE A: UNILATERAL MALERUPTION OF CUSPIDS.
TYPE B: BILATERAL MALERUPTION OF CUSPIDS.
TYPE C: BILATERAL MALERUPTION OF CUSPIDS REQUIRING EXTRACTION. (From Class II)
TYPE D: PROTRUSION OF UPPER FRONT TEETH. (From Thumb Sucking)
TYPE E: RETRUSION OF UPPER FRONT TEETH. (Treated in Division 2, Class III)
TYPE F: LATERAL MALOCCLUSION.
TYPE G: OPEN-BITE MALOCCLUSION.

DIVISION 2: BIMAXILLARY PROTRUSION AND RETRUSION.

CLASS II. DISTAL MALOCCLUSION OF LOWER BUCCAL TEETH.

DIVISION 1: RETRUSION OF LOWER DENTURE.

TYPE A: PRONOUNCED RETRUSION OF LOWER DENTURE, WITH UPPER NORMAL.
TYPE B: MODERATE RETRUSION OF THE LOWER DENTURE, WITH PROTRUSION OF THE UPPER DENTURE.

DIVISION 2: PROTRUSION OF THE UPPER, WITH LOWER NORMAL.

TYPE A: UPPER CORONAL PROTRUSION.
TYPE B: UPPER BODILY PROTRUSION.
TYPE C: UPPER CORONAL PROTRUSION WITH APICAL RETRUSION.
TYPE D: UPPER APICAL PROTRUSION.

CONCOMITANT CHARACTERS OF CLASS II.

RETRUSION OF THE MANDIBLE AND LOWER DENTURE.
CLOSE-BITE MALOCCLUSION.
MALERUPTION OF CUSPIDS. (Treated in Class I)

CLASS III. MESIAL MALOCCLUSION OF LOWER BUCCAL TEETH.

DIVISION 1: BODILY RETRUSION OF THE UPPER DENTURE AND MAXILLA.
(With lower normal though apparently protruded)

DIVISION 2: CONTRACTED RETRUSION OF THE UPPER DENTURE.
(Due to inhibited development of Maxilla)

DIVISION 3: RETRUSION OF THE UPPER WITH PROTRUSION OF LOWER DENTURE.
(With no protrusive position of the Mandible)

DIVISION 4: RETRUSION OF THE UPPER WITH PROGNATHIC MANDIBLE.
(Commonly accompanied with Open-Bite Malocclusion)

may attack any inherited disto-mesial occlusion of the teeth, and therefore they cannot be classified as special divisions or types of any one particular class, notwithstanding the fact that they frequently dominate and characterize the whole malocclusion of the case in hand. This refers to **Maleruption of Cuspids, Thumbsucking Protrusions, Lateral Malocclusion, Open-Bite Malocclusion, Infra** and **Supra-Occlusions, Malalignments, Malturned Teeth, Contracted** and **Expanded Arches, Abnormal Interproximate Spaces,** and **Impacted Teeth.** It is quite as important that the principles and treatment of these malocclusions be taught, as those of the distinctly classifiable characters.

Inasmuch as the first four of this group produce at times quite marked facial imperfections, and as all locally caused malocclusions arise most frequently in connection with normal occlusions, these special characters of malocclusion are placed in the **Practical Treatment** of **Class I, Division 1.** The **Practical Treatment** of the rest of this group is fully described in Part VII.

In regard to the **Classified Table** of **Dento-Facial Malocclusions** here presented, it should be understood that only the distinguishing types of the different Divisions of the Classes are stated in the Table. Many of these Divisions possess a variety of Types which demand variations in treatment. These will be found fully described and illustrated from cases in practice, with their diagnosis and treatment in the "Practical Treatment of Dento-Facial Malocclusion," in Part VI of this work.

PART II

The Etiology of Malocclusion
with Reference to
Principles of Diagnosis and Treatment

ETIOLOGY OF MALOCCLUSION

CHAPTER IV

ETIOLOGIC PRINCIPLES OF MALOCCLUSION WITH REFERENCE TO TREATMENT

The common causes of the different types of malocclusion will usually be found in this work in connection with their practical treatment. There are, however, certain underlying principles which must govern an intelligent determination of so many of the most prolific causes of dental and dento-facial malpositions, it seems important to consider this subject extensively in its general relations to the science of orthodontia. While there are certain conditions of which it is impossible to determine definitely the cause, though it may lie within the field of conjectural possibility, there are other conditions which when examined in the light of intelligent investigation can be seen to have arisen undoubtedly from heredity or certain well known postnatal causes. There are also a number of malocclusions which are the final result of a series of causes, one following as a sequence of the other.

So many of the more pronounced dento-facial malocclusions arise through one or more of the many channels of heredity, or from the law of natural variation, a brief review of some of the well established principles of biology which relate to this subject, seems indispensable to an intelligent understanding of all the etiologic factors under consideration.

Unknowable Causes

In orthodontia, we are mainly engaged with treating results from causes that are inactive at the time; and this is true of all cases, except the malocclusions or threatened malocclusions of childhood in which the cause is active. Therefore, in many cases, to know the cause which may be far in the past, has been considered heretofore of no practical advantage so far as the treatment of the particular case in hand is concerned. But this does not lessen the importance of a knowledge of all causes from an educational orthodontic standpoint, or the necessity at times of positively determining whether a certain condition has arisen from heredity or from some local cause. Moreover, it is especially important to fully understand the causes which arise from improper or inadequate care and treatment of children's teeth, and to be able to recognize all conditions prevalent with children, which tend to produce malocclusions. A special chapter is devoted to this branch of the subject.

Through advanced training and modern equipment, the unknown causes of malocclusion are gradually being reduced to a minimum. Formerly, it was impossible to determine why certain teeth did not erupt. Now, the radiograph tells us why and much more that is of the greatest advantage in dentistry. (See Chapter LI.) It may show that the germs of the said tooth or teeth are extinct, and we may find upon investigation that this is a family peculiarity found in one parent or the other, and perhaps known to have come down through several generations, proving atavism. Or the radiograph may show that the failure of the teeth to erupt is due to one or more supernumerary teeth or odontomata buried in the alveolar process in such a position as to prevent the desired eruption; and if it is a cuspid, we may find it lying at a decided abnormal angle with its occlusal end near the central incisor, deeply imbedded under the process. Though we may never know the prime causes of these conditions, we can now more intelligently proceed to the correction of their results. This is but one of the many examples illustrative of the progress and evolution of ideas relative to causes and many other things pertaining to orthodontia.

Compound Causes

There are many malocclusions which arise from certain evident local causes, of which the primary cause, or the cause of the cause, is quite obscure. With other cases, the primary cause of the local or immediate cause is plainly heredity, or some other local cause. One of the simple instances of this is the low attachment of the frenum of the upper lip, whose muscular fibers extend through the proximal space between the central incisors with attachments to the lingual aspects of the ridge, and whose local action tends to separate the centrals with every movement of the lip. No intelligent person can claim that this character of frenum could possibly arise from a local cause; besides it has been frequently found following the same condition in one of the parents, proving direct heredity; though one can understand how this abnormality of the frenum, and many other anatomic anomalies might arise originally in a moderate degree from the law of **natural variation,** which is neither heredity nor local causes, as will be explained in Chapter VI.

Crowded malalignments of the upper teeth amounting to many of the most decided malocclusions, are often caused by a lack of growth development of the superior maxilla during the early years of childhood. This, in turn, is mainly due to continued early mouth-breathing, thus depriving the nasal passages and sinuses of the natural nutrient forces of air upon which the lining membranes are dependent for their health and functional activities, and in turn all the connecting bones dependent upon the health of these tissues for their normal growth development. This deprivation when long continued will at times force the sensitive mucous membranes into a chronic inflammatory state, resulting at times in hypertrophied walls dripping with diseased exudations which the stagnated action of its cilia are unable to eliminate as they would in health, resulting finally in a partial or complete inhibition of the normal growth development of the maxilla, and a variety of dental and dento-facial malocclusions, and even general physical and mental inhibitions, through some mysterious disturbances of those glands or ganglia which preside over normal developing activities.

The early mouth-breathing habit may, in turn, be due to any one or more of three local causes, i. e., chronic rhinitis, adenoid vegetations, and enlarged tonsils, which result in a partial or complete stenosis of one or both nasal fossæ; and while it is conceded that the abnormal activities of these diseases are mainly due to some local infection, no one can assert that the peculiar glandular structures in the nose and naso-pharynx were not constitutionally the predisposing cause, while other children with more normally inherited structures would be immune to the same infection. Moreover, it is a well known fact that abnormally enlarged tonsils are due to heredity. Jackson says: "Chronic enlargement of tonsillar tissue is one of the causes of mouth-breathing. It is a disease of child life. Some authors claim that enlargement of these glands has been observed in children born prematurely, indicating direct heredity."

While the evidence instanced does not necessarily prove that the condition did not arise from intra-uterine infection, there are any number of instances which do prove that enlarged tonsils frequently arise from heredity. Moreover, there is such an intimate relation between the tonsillar glands and those from which adenoids develop, they may reasonably be included. In one family of three boys who came under the intimate observation of the author, the tonsils were all abnormally large in their most quiescent state, but from the slightest exposure and even from unknown causes they would pass quickly into active inflammatory conditions of the most painful and obstructive character. The mother and grandmother of these boys had both been afflicted with these same conditions, during childhood, and the mother still retained, in a lessened degree, the same predisposing tendency.

It will be seen by this that there may be at times four definite stages of causes—one dependent upon and following the other—before the final result of malocclusion: First, heredity; second, enlarged tonsils or adenoids; third, mouth-breathing; fourth, inhibited growth of maxilla with its concomitant contraction, followed by crowded malalignments; open-bite malocclusions; upper retrusions, etc. During the sleeping hours, these causes are most active when the mouth is commonly stretched widely open with the masseter and buccinator muscles pressing in on immature arches narrowing them and raising the domes, and aided by the strong pressure of air striking the vaults. Again, the mechanical action of the various forces of the muscles upon immature mandibles held long in that position is the main cause of open-bite malocclusions, as is fully explained in Class I, "Open-Bite Malocclusion."

While it is true that a very large proportion of pronounced malocclusions of Classes II and III arise in the main from some form of heredity, it is nevertheless true that certain dominating local causes arising in connection with these cases, will impress themselves upon them in such a manner as to quite decidedly change the main inherited type, and give the impression that the malocclusion is due wholly to local causes.

It is true also, that many pronounced malocclusions of these two Classes are caused wholly by local causes, even to the full disto-mesial malrelations of the buccal occlusion.

One of the most pronounced and interesting incidents which arises wholly from a combination of local causes, is the mesio-distal malocclusion of Class II with its resultant dento-facial disharmonies. Again, instances arise in children of inherited normal occlusions in which the early habit of thumb-sucking produces all the characteristic malrelations of the labial teeth and deforming facial outlines of pronounced upper protrusions. In other cases of inherited normal occlusions, the early loss of the deciduous upper molars is frequently followed with a mesial malocclusion of the upper buccal teeth, and this in many instances results in a full malinterdigitation of buccal cusps. This is one of the frequent causes of maleruption of upper cuspids. When these two causes arise in the same case, as they undoubtedly do at times, the resultant malocclusion may have all the dental and dento-facial characteristics of a pronounced upper protrusion, and wholly from a combination of local causes.

Relation of Causes to Treatment

While the practice of orthodontia is quite different from the practice of medicine in which the removal of the cause is the prime factor of treatment, and while it is true that we mainly correct conditions by mechanical procedures from the standpoint of their existent malpositions, it is nevertheless frequently of the greatest importance to know whether the malocclusion arises from heredity, or from causes operative after birth, because this may be the only guide to correct treatment.

For example, one of the most common forms of malocclusion is that which is characterized by a maleruption of the upper cuspids, which is immediately due to a partial or complete closure of the spaces between the lateral incisors and first premolars. Let us suppose that a case of this character at the age of ten or twelve presents for treatment, and we find upon an examination that the upper buccal teeth are in mesial malocclusion with the lowers to the extent that the crests of the mesio-buccal cusps of the upper first molars are slightly in front of the mesio-buccal cusps of the lowers, instead of closing into the sulci between the mesial and distal buccal cusps of the lowers as they should. And when we compare the relations of the lower denture to the mandible—the lower lip with the chin—and the chin to the general facial outlines, we find that the malocclusion is not due in the slightest degree to a retrusion of the lower denture, it being in perfect dento-facial relation; consequently the upper buccal teeth being in mesial malposition more than one-half the width of a cusp, they are protruded to that extent in relation to dento-facial harmony.

CHAPTER IV. ETIOLOGIC PRINCIPLES

If it is true that this is caused by a premature loss of upper deciduous teeth permitting the buccal teeth to drift forward of their normal positions, or if it has arisen from any of the local causes, fully explained in other chapters, it should be our greatest endeavor to force the buccal teeth back to the normal relations and occlusion which nature intended they should occupy. But if, on the other hand, we find that the mesial malrelations of the upper buccal teeth have arisen from heredity—this diagnosis being frequently confirmed by protruding types of upper teeth in the same family, or relatives, and the absence of any indication of a local cause—it would show that the front teeth of our patient would also have been protruded had not the cuspids been forced out of alignment—not by a mesial movement of the buccal teeth, as in the other instance—but by the incisors which were held back, or forced back, by pressure of the lips. We would under these conditions hesitate before attempting to move the upper buccal teeth distally to the extent that would be necessary to place them in normal occlusion with the esthetically posed lower denture, for many reasons, all of which are fully outlined in the practical consideration and treatment of this malocclusion.

The older members of the dental profession will remember many cases like the above which have been very satisfactorily corrected—occlusally and dentofacially—by no other treatment than the simple extraction of the first upper premolars. This allowed the cuspids to take their proper places in relation to the unprotruded lower teeth, and the cusps of the upper buccal teeth to become adjusted to a mesial interdigitation through use, with quite an adequate masticating occlusion. It was through successes of this kind by dentists in the early years of orthodontia, as stated elsewhere, that led to the criminal extraction of thousands of teeth in cases of crowded malalignments; and especially where the cuspids were forced to erupt through the gums above their proper positions. Whereas, we now know that among the frequent malocclusions of this character there is probably not more than one case in ten for which extraction is indicated. This is only one of the many examples which may be cited showing the importance of correct differentiation in diagnosis between conditions which arise through the channels of heredity and those from local causes.

Until the acceptance of modern principles of biology, the theory of special creations led to the gravest errors relative to causes. It is unfortunate in this day of advancement that prominent teachers so frequently interlard their teachings with statements which are wholly dependent upon the unscientific phases of belief that have been long discarded by all well informed minds.

If it were true that "all malocclusions arise from local causes," as has been repeatedly claimed, and that the "placing of dentures in normal occlusion will invariably be followed by harmony and perfection of facial outlines according to the type of the individual," many of the difficult problems of orthodontia would not arise. It would completely exclude the difficult question of extraction which has led so many into quagmires of malpractice; and, furthermore, it would eradicate to a considerable extent the complex question of diagnosis and treatment, by reducing the science to mathematical and mechanical procedures, while the practice of dento-facial orthopedia would require no artistic ability or brain-racking study and anxiety. We would then unhesitatingly place the teeth of every case in normal occlusion, and if teeth were missing, we would open the spaces and insert artificial teeth to maintain normal relations and arch widths of the dentures. Especially in the treatment of children's teeth, without a single thought of heredity or facial outlines we would invariably see that the first permanent molars were placed and retained in normal disto-mesial relations so that the dentures would be guided to a normal occlusion, all with the view, as this false teaching asserts, that the jaws and even all the bones of the skull—since there would be no such things as inherited disharmonies—would in every case grow to harmonious proportions as was intended by nature. Fortunately for humanity, nearly all competent orthodontists of today are following, or will soon follow, in their practice, the more rational scientific teachings abundantly proven by experience and ethnologic investigation. While it is a fact that a very large proportion of malocclusions arise from causes of post-natal origin, it is equally true that many irregularities—from simple malpositions to decided antero-posterior malrelations of the dentures and jaws, including every variety of dento-facial deformity—arise through the same channels of reproduction that produces the normal, resulting if not prevented, in exactly that which is stamped upon them by the laws of heredity in the union and admixture of harmonious and inharmonious types.

One often hears and sees from the lips and pens of men of high standing in orthodontia relative to causes that malocclusions of the teeth never arise from heredity, but always from post-natal or intra-uterine local causes, which follows the erroneous teaching that "all persons are destined by nature (or through inheritance) to have normal occlusions of the dentures." They might as well assert their disbelief and consequent ignorance of the laws and principles of evolution, of biology, of ethnology, of hybridism, and of irregularities in all parts of the body which everywhere confront us in offspring and that are plainly seen to have arisen through direct heredity, and from unions of different types. Furthermore, they must also assert their disbelief in the commonly known results in artificial cross-breeding in both plants and animals.

The laws of biology teach throughout the entire evolution and development of all living things, that nature does not "start out in each individual to build a physically or esthetically perfect being," but she builds that which is forced upon her by the inexorable laws of biologic development, with the result that disharmonies in the sizes, forms, and positions of the teeth, jaws, and all bones which characterize physiognomies are quite as possible and even much more liable than esthetically perfect types. It must be remembered that within the domain of normality, the physically ideal and the esthetic is a rarity and not the rule. Outside of the domain of what is erroneously called the "normal," but by which is more often meant the typically perfect, nature under the biologic activities of heredity reproduces in the offspring in some form that which is impressed upon the germ cells by progenitors.

These deeper questions of heredity cannot be appreciated without at least a superficial understanding of the laws and principles of biology outlined in Chapter VI.

It is not strange that many should believe and teach that all malocclusions of the teeth arise from local causes when it is seen that so many malpositions of the teeth and jaws do undoubtedly arise in this way, and these moreover are frequently in close duplication of those which arise from heredity.

Nor is it strange that many who have observed the remarkably beneficial effects following the removal of adenoids for patients of inhibited physical and mental development, should conceive an exalted opinion of local causes and the power of mechanical stimulation toward bone growth.

The rapid beneficial development in these instances is no doubt due: first, to the removal of the cause, without which little could be accomplished, and second, the consequent renewal of natural physiologic activities of growth, stimulated secondarily by the operation itself, and its improved resultant occlusion.

There can be no doubt from a scientific standpoint that the jaw bones proper —and especially the mandible which is not subjected to the same influences that retard the development of maxilla—assume the forms and sizes determined by the unchangeable laws of heredity under healthy growth conditions in the same way as other bones of the body. While the rapidity of their early growth may be hastened, and while inhibited developments may be stimulated to normal growth, and while the forms of the bones may be varied slightly by bending, it is contrary to the laws of biology that environing forces, or any kind of artificial stimulation has the power to cause them to grow interstitially larger than their inherent normal size.

It would be far more advisable in early childhood cases of marked disto-mesial malocclusion of the buccal teeth which are not distinctly due to local causes, or to retrusions of one denture or the other, to wait for a more mature development of the facial outlines, which would enable a sure and correct diagnosis of the conditions, and then treat the case along the lines of art and within the realms of physiologic demands.

CHAPTER V

ETIOLOGIC INFLUENCES OF DECIDUOUS AND ERUPTING PERMANENT TEETH WITH PRINCIPLES OF TREATMENT

One of the most prolific of the **local causes** of malocclusion arises through improper care and treatment of the deciduous teeth. A large proportion of the malocclusions which arise from this cause are due to the fact that parents and dentists do not appreciate the imperative importance of preserving the teeth of the temporary dentures up to the very moment when each succeeding permanent tooth is ready to erupt; and they also fail to understand the character of influences which are exerted by the premature loss of one or more of these teeth toward marring the positions and occlusion of the permanent teeth.

The errors of dentists in this field of their profession are so frequent and so serious it would seem that there is a thoughtless disregard of principles which are plainly shown in the natural physiologic processes of secondary dentition, and which no thinking mind can contemplate without amazement and admiration.

In view of the large amount of literature upon this subject, and the competent teaching in the various colleges, showing the importance of preserving the deciduous teeth, it would seem that we should be free from those conditions which frequently confront us, and which must be regarded as caused by a ruthless interference with one of nature's most important provisions.

The deciduous teeth are most evidently for the purpose of affording means of mastication during the early years when the full-sized permanent teeth would be all out of proportion in size and appearance for the undeveloped jaws and features. They are there also for the purpose of giving nature an opportunity to develop and erupt the permanent teeth, and in bringing them forward in successive and systematic stages, timed according to the needs of general growth and use. They are, moreover, for the purpose of establishing occlusal relations of the permanent teeth and harmonious relations of the facial outlines.

At about five years of age the first permanent molars commence to crowd their way into the arches between the bases of the deciduous arches on one side, and the rami and tuberosities on the other. Nature, apparently conscious of the forceful influences of this eruptive process toward an interstitial forward movement of the entire deciduous dentures, has provided the deciduous molars with broad spreading roots so as to take a sufficiently firm and immovable hold of their surroundings to successfully combat this force, in the same way that will be found with the roots of trees which are subjected to the force of strong winds. Note also how perfectly nature under normal conditions has timed this eruptive stage to prevent that possibility which she so evidently fortifies herself against, and at the same time to take advantage of the general developing forces of eruption. Under the needs of increasing age for greater masticating facilities, she starts the eruption of the first permanent molars at a time when the strong phalanx of the deciduous denture is there, or should be there, to resist the forward pressure of these erupting teeth; nor does she commence it before there is nearly enough room by growth for those large teeth back of the temporary set; nor before the alveolar surroundings of the deciduous roots are developed to comparative stability; nor does she wait until the temporary molar roots have become weakened by resorption from the eruptive forces of the premolars.

What could be more prophetic than these provisional acts on the part of nature in emphasizing the importance of preserving the natural relative position of the bases of the deciduous arches in order that the permanent molars which are destined to establish the occlusal relations of the adjoining permanent buccal teeth will not be allowed to drift forward of their natural positions, since it is upon the established position of the first permanent molars that the relative positions of adjoining buccal teeth are dependent, and also the final occlusion and dento-facial relation of all the teeth. From this we may draw a lesson of the importance of preserving these temporary piers to the future arches until the time of the eruption of their successors, because at whatever stage the arch is long deprived of their support, the permanent molars will surely tend to drift forward to fill the gaps, notwithstanding the restraining influences of perfect interdigitating occluding cusps.

Another of nature's acts along this line is worthy of the deepest consideration, because it seems to be prophetic of the apparently recognized tendency of the permanent molars to drift forward, and of the importance of preventing it up to the last moment. In the typically normal processes of secondary dentition, when the second deciduous molars are thrown off, the second premolars are ready to prick through the overlying gum tissue, and soon take their places in preserving the integrity of the arch. This is another reason for the spreading of the deciduous roots in order that the resorptive forces of eruption may have an opportunity, without the necessity of extraction, to make a place beneath for the premolar crowns, and thus permit them to erupt as much as possible up to the last moment of their power to hold the required space open. Otherwise, as is frequently seen—especially on the lower—the second premolars are impacted in the dovetailing inclination of adjoining teeth, because of the premature extraction or loss by decay of the second deciduous molars. It may be that this is one reason why the second premolars are the only ones of the permanent dentures which occupy less space than the deciduous teeth that precede them in order, perhaps, that they may have a little better chance to get into place before the drifting tendencies of the adjoining teeth can shut them out.

Maleruption of Labial Teeth

From five to six years of age under normal processes, the arches commence to expand in the incisal area in co-ordination with the erupting forces, and from six to seven years of age, the roots of the temporary central incisors are so completely resorbed that the crowns fall out or are forced out by the erupting permanent centrals. As these teeth prick through the gums, the cutting edges are commonly in front of the deciduous line, and are not uncommonly malturned. Their disto-mesial widths are so much greater than the deciduous centrals, that notwithstanding the expansion of the arches there is usually not sufficient room between the deciduous laterals for their perfect alignment at this time. This has frequently led to the premature extraction of the deciduous laterals under the false impression that they were causing a permanent irregularity of the centrals. Whereas, in this very act one of the important physiologic forces of nature—the eruptive force—for the expansion of the arches is stopped. The forces of growth are far greater than we are accustomed to imagine; nor can it be appreciated fully unless one has observed the power which the growth of the roots of trees exert which extend under strongly imbedded cement sidewalks, and which will often break the cement blocks and raise them several inches. With the extraction of the deciduous laterals, and the growth of the arch inhibited, there is soon found to be far less than sufficient room for the permanent laterals, and this leads to the premature extraction also of the deciduous cuspids, followed by an alignment of the laterals which partially fill the cuspid spaces. Soon after this, or at about eight or nine years of age, the first upper premolars erupt, taking the places of the first deciduous molars. If the deciduous cuspids are not there they naturally drift forward to partially fill the distal portion of the cuspid spaces, with the tendency also for the teeth back of these to drift forward, so that when it is time for the cuspids to erupt, there being no room, or not sufficient room for them, they are obliged to force their way through the gums above their proper places, where they have often been regarded by many ignorant people as unnatural "tusks," and have frequently been wrongfully extracted by dentists as the shortest if not the best means of correcting a deforming irregularity, which has seemed to them impossible to correct properly in any other way. See "Question of Extraction," Chapter XII, and "Maleruption of Cuspids," Class I.

Next in importance to the preservation of the deciduous second molars is the retention of the deciduous cuspids up to the last moment of their usefulness, whatever the apparent irregularity of the incisors; and while the permanent cuspids are very much wider than the space occupied by the deciduous cuspids their wedge-like form impelled by the forces of eruption and natural provisional enlargement of the jaws, will usually enable them to take their places in normal alignment.

Another cause of the maleruption of cuspids is the premature loss of the first or second deciduous molars, which not only inhibits the growth development of the arch in that area, but permits a mesial movement of the first permanent molars which are forced forward by the oncoming erupting second molars. The premolars

CHAPTER V. DECIDUOUS AND ERUPTING PERMANENT TEETH

having also been forced to a mesial malposition, the cuspids are forced to erupt out of alignment; especially if the deciduous cuspids have been prematurely extracted as frequently occurs in this condition, to give room for the eruption of the premolars.

The maleruption of lower cuspids is not so frequent as the upper cuspids. One of the reasons for this is: the lower permanent cuspids erupt before the first premolars, and consequently are not so liable to be interfered with. However, if the first molars are forced forward of their normal positions by the erupting and fixed mesial malposition of the second permanent molars, the cuspids are the ones which are forced out of alignment whatever their position or stage of eruption. One can see by the many causes direct and indirect, which so frequently arise, why it is that the irregularity that is characterized by maleruption of cuspids, is one of the most common of all the malocclusions.

By far the larger proportion of temporary dentures are in normal occlusion and in correct dento-facial relations according to age and type, because that is the dominant type toward which the natural biologic forces tend. And were it not for maltreatments and certain local and constitutional causes, there would be a far greater number of cases than at present that would attain to a normal occlusion of the teeth.

THUMB-SUCKING

The one cause which most often affects the normal relations of the deciduous dentures is the habit of thumb-sucking, which if allowed to continue into the early years of secondary dentition will frequently produce all the dento-facial characteristics of an upper protrusion, but with no effect upon the disto-mesial relations of the buccal teeth, except to narrow the arches.

The *modus operandi* of the cause, its correction, and final treatment of the resultant malocclusion, will be found in the Practical Treatment of Division 1, Class I.

INFLUENCES OF HEREDITY UPON DECIDUOUS DENTURES

In regard to the malocclusions which arise from heredity, from the simplest to the most pronounced dento-facial deformities, it is somewhat rare that the deciduous dentures and jaws indicate in an appreciable degree the condition which is destined to affect the permanent teeth and more mature jaws. This is because inherited physical dental malformations rarely commence to develop before the beginning of secondary dentition, nor are they often sufficiently pronounced to become apparent before the period of adolescence.

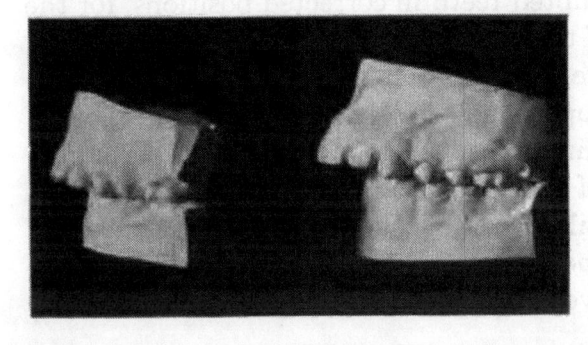

FIG. 1.

While there are exceptions to this rule which is illustrated by Fig. 1, showing the plaster models of the deciduous and the permanent dentures of a Class

II case at five and eleven years of age, *it is nevertheless true that early interference with the temporary dentures, such as expanding the arches, or the disto-mesial shifting of occlusal relations, is rarely advisable,* unless one is sure that the threatened condition has arisen from some definite local cause which the natural physiologic processes of nature will not correct. If teeth are prematurely lost, threatening maleruption or crowded malalignments, the areas should be properly expanded and retained for the free eruption of the succeeding teeth. But under other circumstances where the erupting permanent teeth do not seem to have sufficient room and are forced into overlapping malalignments—a condition quite common with the lower incisors—it should be remembered that this is the only way in which nature is enabled to get those large teeth into the small and as yet undeveloped jaws which she is rapidly enlarging by interstitial growth for that purpose. If left to herself as she has been during all past ages when the same character of activities has repeatedly presented itself with results that were nearly if not quite invariably normal, there is no reason to believe that the same results would not now obtain without artificial interference. Besides, anyone of long experience has seen any number of these decided cases of overlapping malalignments of the erupting permanent teeth fully right themselves through natural forces alone.

It is therefore not always necessary or advisable to attempt any artificial preparation for the eruption of the permanent teeth; nor is it always advisable to begin at a very early age the regulation of children's permanent teeth, except in those cases in which the effects of a local cause still remain that cannot be corrected by natural forces.

It may be that the habit of thumb-sucking has narrowed the arches and protruded the upper incisal area and retruded the lower, or that the injudicious extraction or premature loss of the deciduous teeth has inhibited the growth development, and contracted the spaces required for the aligned eruption of the permanent teeth, or it may be that it is one of the many threatening malocclusions which arise from adenoids or nasal stenosis. Under such conditions, the early regulation of children's teeth is always admissible and advisable, and should be accomplished with the most delicately constructed appliances for both movement and retention. Furthermore, there should be a definite understanding with the parents that the operation is intended to place only the erupted teeth in corrected positions, for the purpose of permitting the free eruption of the remaining permanent teeth.

One of the greatest objections to the early regulation of children's teeth, is that we usually have them on our hands up to and through the eruption of the second molars, while the little ones up to nine or ten years of age could be running free and building up stable conditions of future health; moreover, the operation in many instances could be far more easily accomplished for everyone concerned by commencing after the eruption of the premolars—except of course in those cases where simple demands are imperative.

CHAPTER V. DECIDUOUS AND ERUPTING PERMANENT TEETH

Another phase of this branch should not be forgotten: It has reference to the early disto-mesial malrelation of the first permanent molars whose correction must be determined, as before explained, by the character of the cause. If seen to be purely local, correct by all means, but do not be in haste to correct if there is any doubt that the cause may be an inherited protrusion, upper or lower. The student is referred to fuller explanation of this phase in Chapter XXI.

A Local Cause of Protrusions

Before leaving the subject of secondary dentition, one of its greatest lessons cannot be too often repeated. This relates to that large majority whose permanent teeth are, or would have been, normal in occlusion and dento-facial relations in all instances had the deciduous teeth been preserved, or retained according to nature's requirements. With these naturally normal conditions, if the loss of deciduous teeth has permitted the permanent buccal teeth to drift forward, ever so slightly, from an otherwise normal dental and facial relation in the arch, and the front teeth then erupt in alignment, *an abnormal protrusion of the facial outlines will be exactly in proportion to this movement.* If the extent of this mesial movement is sufficient to carry the crests of the cusps in front of those of the occluding teeth, a full mesial malinterdigitation of the upper cusps is inevitable. This shows how from premature extraction, or unnecessary loss of deciduous teeth alone, protrusion of the permanent teeth may arise, and though in amount it but slightly changes the facial contour, it may be sufficient to mar the expression of an entire physiognomy. When this occurs with both upper and lower dentures, as at times it no doubt does—all of the teeth having been forced forward of their normal position, and with a possible preservation of normal occlusion and alignment—it is a most unfortunate affair, because people in general, and among them dentists of renowned ability in orthodontia, seeing these perfect conditions of normal occlusion, interpret the facial imperfections which have resulted from this local cause, as inherent, or one intended by nature, and as perfect as it is possible for that individual.

We hardly imagine that in the many faces we meet, there has occurred during their childhood days a thoughtless or ignorant disregard of important principles in the treatment of the deciduous teeth, which has resulted in an unnatural and unnecessary protrusion of the permanent teeth, slight or great, over the upper or entire dento-facial area, characterizing the features, producing unesthetic expressions, and marring those perfect facial outlines which nature would have produced had she been permitted, or aided in having her way.

Comparison of Childhood and Adult Physiognomies

The common normal peculiarity of childhood physiognomies, between the ages from six to twelve, is that of a slight protrusion of the upper and lower lips in relation to the other undeveloped features. By association, we intuitively and unconsciously accept this appearance in late childhood and early youthhood without a thought of facial imperfection. And yet were we to analyze the facial outlines of these young people from the artistic viewpoint of the adult perfect outlines, we would find that a large proportion are similar to those which if seen in adult life would be truthfully denominated bimaxillary protrusion.

This is due to the fact that the teeth are the only bones in the body which do not grow larger than their first formations; and therefore during the development and eruption of the adult-sized permanent teeth in the small jaws of childhood, where they are crowded in one upon the other, in their different stages of development, they necessarily expand the dental and alveolar arches prematurely, during the stage of secondary dentition; and as the entire maxillary and other facial bones do not keep pace with this rapid development, the lips are unesthetically, though naturally, forced forward in their outlines—all of which the ultimate growth of other parts finally harmonizes.

By continued observation of the development of childhood and adolescent features, one will frequently see, even as late as twelve years of age, prominent mouths and apparent receding chins, that at seventeen or eighteen years of age will entirely disappear. This goes to prove that which the author has endeavored to emphasize in other chapters, that the bones which characterize physiognomies do not always begin to show at twelve years of age that which is destined by the dominant strains of heredity to characterize the features during later adolescence.

The author remembers a mate of his school days who at twelve years of age was smaller than the other boys, with effeminate features and small nose like his mother's, but who at twenty years of age was six feet tall with large angular strong features and prominent Roman nose like his father's more dominant type.

CHAPTER VI

LAWS OF BIOLOGY REGARDED AS ETIOLOGIC FACTORS IN MALOCCLUSION

General Principles of Biology.—Before proceeding to a study of those malocclusions which arise partly, and to a large extent from some form of heredity, it is important for the student to be informed in regard to the general laws of biology upon which is dependent the entire scientific basis of that which pertains to this branch of our subject, so that he may have a more intelligent appreciation of the various propositions presented along this line.

The science of biology lies at the very foundation of all knowledge pertaining to living things—their origin, development, propagation, and all co-ordinating and environing influences. Unfortunately, the principles of biology and general evolution are quite commonly regarded, even by people who pride themselves upon their education, as of no more practical value than the sciences of astronomy and geology; whereas, there is no branch of learning which enters so intimately and extensively into other branches that are regarded as the essentials of life and education.

While this is particularly true in the general practice of medicine and dentistry, there is no branch in which the laws and principles of biology are of such importance as in the study of the causes and treatment of malocclusion and dentofacial disharmonies, because they present an authentic foundation for a broader understanding and application of the possibilities of ethnologic influences in the admixture of different types of races, and in the union of physical disharmonies everywhere. Therefore, a brief epitome of biologic laws seems essential to an intelligent comprehension of certain principles which enter so largely into the etiology of malocclusions. It is hoped, moreover, that this will stimulate students to a more extensive study of this important branch of literature.

Biology and biologists deal only with the natural laws of organic evolution. By long, patient, and scientific investigation, biologists verify every proposition over and over again before it is stated as a scientific truth. These pertain principally to the problems of life, heredity, variation, natural selection, and influences of environment.

Every anatomic form or structure—barring inhibited development—which arises from the **Law of Heredity** is laid down in the metabolic activities of the germ cells at the time of fertilization and forced upon the offspring by the laws of reproduction.

Fortunately, there is another law which is quite as important in biologic development as the law of heredity. This is the law of **Natural Variation** which also lays down in the germ cells the elemental beginnings of variations which arise in the offspring that differ from the parental stock and like those of heredity are capable of being propagated to future generations.

The other two laws, **Natural Selection** and **Environment** may be said to act extrinsically—the one being nature's selection of those whose qualities are best adapted to the environment and propagation of their kind; and the other deals purely with adaptive variations in structure, etc., which fits them a little better to live and thrive in the environment into which they are thrown.

This presents two important truths: First, no physical form or variation in anatomic structure can arise except through the channel of the germ cells, though the environing influences upon already endowed properties of the individual after birth may result in a more adaptive degree of development. Second, it shows the impossibility of appreciably increasing the inherited sizes or forms of any of the bones by local or environing stimulation.

Heredity

The **Law of Heredity** is that which determines the propagation of physical forms, structures, peculiarities, and even traits of character. Its importance along these lines is clearly related by J. Arthur Thomson, of Aberdeen, in his recent book, "Heredity." "There are no scientific problems of greater human interest than those of Heredity; that is to say the genetic relation between successive generations. Since the issues of individual life are in great part determined by what the living creature is, or has to start with, in virtue of its hereditary relation to parents and ancestors, we cannot disregard the facts of heredity in our interpretation of the past, our conduct in the present, or our forecasting of the future."

Those who have not given much thought to the subject of heredity are accustomed to think only of *direct* heredity, or the inheritance of some physical peculiarity or characteristic which had its existence in one of the parents; whereas, this is only one of the many forms of heredity. It may be a blending or composite union of quite distinctively different features or family types belonging to both parents harmoniously or disharmoniously united in the offspring; or it may be that the undiluted forms or features of one parent will be found closely associated in the offspring with the characteristic features of the other parent, as the large nose, ears, jaws, or teeth of one parent in connection with the smaller and more delicate features of the other parent.

How often do we see beautiful children from homely parents, because of the transmission to the child of those special features of the two physiognomies that harmonize in union? On the other hand, how often do we see plain and homely children from parents whose physiognomies individually are symmetrical and attractive, because of the transmission to the child of a combination of the features of both, which being dissimilar in size are inharmonious in union? And as the osseous framework is the principal medium that characterizes the various forms, even the large teeth of one parent and the small jaws of the other—though never claimed as more than a rare occurrence—will probably continue to be placed among the causes of irregularities by intelligent dentists, especially as it can be so easily verified.

The condition in question may be some physical or mental peculiarity which had no existence in either parent, but which obtained in some more distant forebear. This **atavistic heredity** may have passed without recurrence through many generations, to suddenly crop out in the offspring without any apparent known cause; or it may have arisen from an exceedingly complicated propagation under the forces of natural sexual selections, similar to that which is produced by artificial selection or hybridizing, demonstrated by what has been achieved in the past in regard to horses, cattle, poultry, pigeons, fruits, flowers, etc.

Among the vast number of trial and experimental efforts along this line, there has been discovered a number of almost unbelievable laws of heredity which are as dependable, when the exact requirements are fulfilled, as **direct heredity.** One of these is known as "Mendel's Law." A further consideration of the subject of heredity in its various phases and practical application to diagnosis and treatment of malocclusion, will be found in other chapters.

Natural Variation

Next in importance to the laws of **Heredity** is the law of **Natural Variation,** without which everything would have repeated itself from the start, and consequently there would have been no science of biology or organic evolution. One of the stable peculiarities of all living structures is the production of variations in otherwise original hereditary forms and characteristics. These **natural variations** which innumerably arise in all living things are commonly very slight, varying in degree from the almost indiscernible to marked or anomalous modifications from the typical or inherited type. All **natural variations** invariably arise during the metabolic activities of the germ cells in both plants and animals, and when once started are under the same transmissible laws of heredity as those of the established lines of heredity; the difference being the latter are not so likely to become extinct because of their established adaptability to environment; whereas, **natural variations** are quite likely to be unnecessary, or opposed to their environment, and, therefore, not being stimulated toward continued development soon die out in future generations. On the other hand, the variation may be one which more perfectly fits the individual for the struggle of life and a higher adaptation to the requirements of environment. In this event, the variation becomes one of the stable forms of heredity, along with other variations which have arisen in the same way, thus fulfilling the highest function of this particular law in the great work of evolution, and in the development of species.

Natural variations which begin with or are inherited by the individual are quite as likely to be in disharmony as in harmony with progressive development. The difference being that those which are contrary to the needs of life are not as capable or as prolific, and consequently die out.

It may be well to state that the law of **natural variation** has no reference in biology to perceptible physical changes in structure that arise or that may be produced in individuals from the adaptive forces of environment, or from local causes, or any form of artificial stimuli. All forces which arise from extrinsic causes have little or nothing to do with biology proper, because that kind of variation is not transmissible, except when the cause and its results obtain through many generations so as to finally become a natural variation.

Moreover, physical growth enlargements or "bone growths," which are caused from extrinsic forces, other than those which arise after inhibited developments through a revivification of functional activities, are never of a normal structural character, and certainly never result in healthy interstitial growth of the bones to the extent of carrying their development to a larger than their inherent size or form. This assertion is made advisedly, basing it on the opinions which have recently been obtained from some of the most advanced authors and teachers of biology, and which hardly accord with the somewhat recent propaganda promulgated by certain orthodontic teachers relative to the fantastic possibilities of "bone growth."

Natural Selection

Darwin's law of **Natural Selection** is not, as is popularly supposed, the selection of mates through instincts and qualities of the individual, or sexual selection, but it is that which was intelligently stated by Huxley when he invented the term **"survival of the fittest,"**—in other words, nature's selection of those who are best fitted for thriving and procreating their kind amid the environment into which they are thrown.

When individuals in plant or animal life are forced to exist amid environment in which they are not physically adapted, or are under destructive influences, against which they are not fully protected, they gradually diminish and die out; though adaptive natural variations may arise in certain of the offspring, similar to adaptive artificial variations which are forced to arise in crossbreeding and which tend to restore the species to the possibilities of progression.

Environment

In the struggle of life, the influences of **Environment** are exerted very strongly upon each individual toward the production of adaptive qualities and variations in form, to render them more fitted for sustaining their lives amid the surroundings into which they are forced. Whole libraries have been written upon this phase of biology alone, but in all these volumes adaptive variations induced to arise in the individual after birth are rarely considered as factors in biologic development, because, as stated before, they are not transmissible, and certainly one finds nothing in regard to the possibility of producing adaptive or harmonizing physical growths in the framework of animals after birth by mechanical or any other stimuli, because biologists are engaged with problems of *natural* reproduction and development.

Such variations in the individual are seen at times in plants whose roots and limbs reach out after moisture and sunlight, but rarely if ever in animal life; except perhaps in superficial tissues, with no effect upon the framework or skeleton, except in instances of inhibition, resulting in diminished growth. What does occur and through the forces of which all the various forms of life and species have sprung, is: an offspring appears, among the many, with a *natural* or an inherited variation, perhaps induced in fertility by the stimulation of needs which surround the parents, resulting perhaps in only a slight change in form or structure, and yet sufficient to make life easier and more vigorous, and capable of greater protection, and possibly more attractive to mates, with increased chances of reproduction. Thus from generation to generation other adaptive variations are added—and inherited by the offspring — the higher adaptive qualities crowding out the weaker.

The neck of the giraffe and the necks of its million progenitors, back to the first variation which marked the beginning of this type, did not grow to its present length by increasing the inherited lengths of its seven cervical vertebrae during the lives of each of the successive individuals, even though strongly stimulated by the demands of hunger and repeated efforts to reach higher for its tropical foods. Every marked change in the slow development of these adaptive qualities arose first with some **natural variation** in the offspring, which added a little to the length of the vertebrae of the neck, giving them a better chance; and in the next, or some succeeding generation, another slight adaptive variation arose rendering them still more fitted for the environment, and so on, through myriads of variations to the present form. During these long periods, those who were less fitted were dropped from this progressively developing species by dying out, or by becoming a factor in the development of some other kind of animal, through being forced into a different environment for food, protection, etc.

The science of organic evolution which is now accepted by all competent biologists asserts that variations in plant and animal types, through all the past and present forms of life, have not originated because of the stimulation of use or influences of environment, but they have arisen solely because, first, of the *law* of "natural variation," and second, the law of heredity, through the admixture of dissimilar types. Not the smallest portion of an extra cusp of a human tooth ever started to develop because of use or needs that was not first laid down in the germ cells of that individual through the laws of heredity or "natural variation." The influences of use and environment are *subsequent* forces upon already endowed forms and qualities, adapting the fitter types of life to the needs of surroundings, and stimulating them to more vigorous growth and reproductive activities.

What these unseen guiding forces are—or any of the objective qualities of all natural forces—we probably will never know in this life, or anything beyond the subjective cognition of the phenomena produced. No one can intelligently contemplate the probable forces which have been at work during the millions of past years in the origin and development of organic life from its simplest form up to man, without a profound feeling of awe for the unknowable guiding forces which set in motion and control this orderly sequence of events.

The men who have been devoting their lives to the possibilities of these laws in the biologic field, in patient and painstaking investigation, tell us that these are the only ways in which structural variations in organic life are brought about. This is not to underrate the important part which environment plays in the great work of evolution. Nature selects only those whose endowments permit them to live, and those who possess the more adaptive qualities are to that extent more capable of co-ordination, development, and propagation. They are, moreover, better fitted through their vigor to aid in the transmission of those adaptive natural variations which they may have been the very first to possess.

It can be seen by this that there are three great laws which have produced and governed organic evolution, i. e., Heredity, Natural Variation, and Natural Selection. Influences of Environment upon individuals through immediate adaptability to surrounding conditions are of far less importance, as has been explained; and yet a co-ordination of Environment with Natural Selection has led to the preservation and continuation of those which are naturally best adapted to thrive, and the weeding out of those which are incapable of adaptation to the environment.

Thus it has been with everything, everywhere throughout the past ages in the developmental processes toward surrounding us with untold variety of living things. When one begins to comprehend the wonderful co-ordination and interdependence of the forces of heredity, variation, natural selection, and environment, a far far deeper veneration and love arises for the great Prime Mover of all things.

Man steps in and discovers these laws and their action, and then with his artificial selective breeding facilities, he hastens the operation—that is all. He does not alter or add to it one single biologic law that nature has not employed through æons of time. While this is wholly true in the science of biologic evolution, the wonderful work which man has accomplished in the last fifty years, and particularly in the past few years, in creative chemical transformation of the organic compounds, which were supposed not long since to arise only from vital living forces, is something which now far outstrips the works of nature—freely demonstrated in the chemical transformation of the coal tar products and their creative combination with other compounds, as in the making of the aniline dyes, etc.

CHAPTER VII

HEREDITY AND VARIATION ETHNOLOGICALLY CONSIDERED

If the parents come through long lines of normal symmetrical forms of proportionate size in relation to each other, the offspring will follow the normal type—barring natural variation and atavistic heredity from distant inharmonious progenitors. If one of the parents is characterized by some definite disharmony of features, as a marked disproportion in the size of the nose, the ears, the jaws, the teeth, etc., there may arise in the offspring any one of a number of definite forms of products, or their blending gradations; the dominant and recessive types being largely dependent upon the strength or persistence of parental strains.

It is not a rare occurrence, as stated in the previous chapter, to find in one such family a child having features which show a blending diminution of disharmonizing characteristics; another will show a predominance of the type of one parent or the other; and in another will be seen the disharmonizing features of one parent in immediate association with features which are distinctly that of the other, etc. Thus, every variety of change and interchange of *inheritable* features and characteristics—or those which have not arisen in the individual from extrinsic causes or environment—possessed by parents, may arise in the offspring from direct inheritance.

Again, a child of fairly symmetrically formed parents will have some one part of the face quite out of proportion in size, form, or relative position to the otherwise harmonious features, but one which has been a characteristic feature of a grand or great-grand-parent, or known to have had existence in some more distant progenitor. Moreover, the laws of heredity present a variety of possibilities which can neither be regarded as direct, nor as atavistic heredity *per se*.

Mothers who have brought their children to orthodontists have frequently said: "I don't see where the child got those prominent protruding teeth, neither his father nor I have teeth like that, and so far as we can learn no member of either of our families for generations back ever had such teeth." This does not refer to the many similar expressions from the lips of loving mothers upon the eruption of the first permanent incisors, which are always far out of proportionate size with the "baby" teeth and childhood features, and thus erroneously regarded as abnormal; but as the case in question may be one of the dento-facial protrusions, let us suppose by way of examining biologic possibilities from a scientific standpoint, that it is one of those extreme cases of **bimaxillary protrusion** in which the entire dentures of both jaws are protruded in relation to the mandible and other bones of the skull; this deformity being always enhanced by a "receding chin effect." See Figs. 157

and 158, Chapter XXIX. We will take it for granted it is true, that no one in either of the two immediate families referred to above, ever had a similar condition of the teeth, and that the said patient is a child of legitimate birth. If this condition of pronounced bimaxillary protrusion were one of very great rarity, seen perhaps only once in a lifetime, it would be called a "freak" by many. Others who are firm in their belief of atavism, even through many generations of progenitors, would see in it a recurrence of some former type. But as this particular form of malocclusion, in different degrees of its prominence, happens to be one of somewhat common occurrence, seen plentifully in large cities of nations composed of mixed races, there is every reason to believe that this and other irregularities of the teeth and jaws have at times arisen through the activities of **"Mendel's Law"** in biologic generation, *which precludes the usual hereditary necessity that some one of the forebears must have been characterized by a similar general disharmony of the features.* Modern biologic investigations in crossbreeding have abundantly proven that combinations of the most complex nature may be brought about through the activities of this law, with results which are at times highly beneficial in the offspring, and again with results which are exceedingly abnormal in appearance, and so deficient in adaptive variations, that—under the law of natural selection—they soon become extinct.

Mendel's Law

In the short space of this chapter it will be impossible to give more than a glance at recent investigations along this line. The student is referred to any one of the modern works upon biology for a fuller description. The following excerpt from a somewhat recently published textbook entitled "Biology," by Stackpole, teacher of biology in Columbia University, will give a brief summary of this phase of heredity: "Much attention has in recent years been given to the experimental study of variation and heredity. These experiments are of interest in connection with Mendel's Law, a law so important in the science of biology that Professor Bateson has written of it, 'The experiments which led to this advance in knowledge are worthy to rank with those that laid the foundation of the atomic laws of chemistry.' The discoverer of this law was Gregor Johann Mendel (1822–1884), an Augustinian monk. . . . To gain an idea of the scope of these principles, one cannot do better than turn to Mendel's own account of his experiments. Punnett's 'Mendelism' and Thomson's 'Heredity' give such an account:

" 'The new science of heredity has much to teach the practical man' says Punnett. 'Let us suppose that he has two varieties, each possessing a desirable character, and that he wishes to combine these characters in a third form. He must not be disappointed if he makes his cross and finds that none of the hybrids approach the ideal which he has set before himself, for if he raises a further generation he will obtain the thing which he desires. He may, for example, possess tall green-seeded and dwarf yellow-seeded peas, and may wish to raise a strain of green dwarfs. He makes his cross—and nothing but tall yellows result. At first sight, he would

CHAPTER VII. HEREDITY AND VARIATION ETHNOLOGICALLY CONSIDERED

appear to be further than ever from his end, for the hybrids differ more from the plant at which he is aiming than did either of the original parents. Nevertheless, if he sow the seeds of these hybrids, he may look forward with confidence to the appearance of the dwarf green [in proportion of 1 to 3 of the dominant tall yellows]. And owing to the recessive nature of both greenness and dwarfness, he can be certain that for further generations the dwarf greens thus produced will come true to type.'"

Experiments with mice and many of the lower animals have so repeatedly confirmed these results in all instances where the conditions and requirements are fulfilled, that the principle is now recognized as one of the established laws of heredity. One who is skilled in crossbreeding can produce in the offspring any combination of characters or strains which are well established by heredity in the parent stock. Not only that, but he can cause to be completely dropped from the combination in the offspring and subsequent generations of the type, strongly marked characters of the parent stock. For examples, look at the work that Burbank is doing today.

Now let us apply this law to our patient whose protruding teeth seem to have arisen from no cause. Both parents may have passed down from long lines of typically formed progenitors, both families of which were fairly symmetrical in physical forms, according to racial type, and yet when the two lines are compared to each other, they are genetically quite disproportionate in size, physique, and character of features; the one characterized by large strong bones, muscles, and sinews, as occurs with dominant types in certain tribal races, while the other family is built on a more delicate effeminate plan, and yet with this strain of its characteristic type none the less persistent.

When one considers the endless variety of unions which arise in mixed races, it must be realized that it is no far-fetched proposition that marriages have and do take place between dissimilar types who possess all the exacting requirements which place them under the rule of Mendel's Law, and with the strong probability that the first offspring of these unions are characterized by the dominant type—as in the production of the "tall yellow" peas. Let us suppose that this pertains to the large heavy bones and teeth of the stronger parent. If this character of offspring should meet and marry other similar offspring that have arisen in the same way (which is more than possible), in the second generation there will be a strong hereditary tendency for a recessive type to arise, or parts of the recessive in combination with the dominant. This means that undiluted physical characters, parts or properties of the delicately constructed grand-parents upon one side, will arise in combination with the strongly marked physical characteristics of the other grand-parents, both of whom composed the original characters of these distinctively dissimilar types. It is not more than possible that this typal mixture may express itself through the laws of heredity by a disproportionately large mandible or maxilla or both as compared to the other bones of the skull of the individual, or may it not be the large strong teeth of the dominant type in combination with the smaller and more delicate jaws of the other as in cases which Dr. Cryer has mentioned? The large teeth striving to force themselves into the small jaws are with their alveolar processes naturally carried forward rather than backward, because of the obstructing rami and tuberosities, with the production of any one of the decided dento-facial protrusions; and through the same biologic processes that have produced other imperfections in facial outlines by an association of immediate parts of physiognomies that are inharmonious in size or relation.

Through careful artificial selection in the processes of hybridizing, excessive protruding mandibles and teeth of bulldogs have been produced, together with equally marked physical variations in domesticated animals, fruits, flowers, etc., and, too, through methods of crossbreeding not unlike those which possibly may, and very probably do obtain in the multitudinous variety of natural unions of dissimilar types in the human race, which so often result in disharmonious combinations in the facial outlines of individuals.

The short upper jaws and prognathic mandibles of pug and bull dogs arose originally either from a natural variation or from cross fertilization. This has been increased to the present types largely by selective breeding or hybridization. For bench show purposes this biologically developed abnormality is still further enhanced artificially in the individual by mechanical devices which inhibit the growth development of the maxilla, and through the same channels of forces that obstructive diseases produce pathologic inhibitions. Physical changes in the individual, wrought in this way from intra-uterine, post-natal, or any of the extrinsic local causes, however, are never transmitted to offspring, it being one of the accepted laws of biology that all inheritable characteristics invariably receive their propagating qualities during the metabolism of the germ cells.

It has been erroneously asserted that "nature does not place in one organ two or more parts that are disharmonious in their sizes," also that "it is impossible for two component parts of any section derived from the same embryonic bud of development to be in disharmony with the whole." This is abundantly disproven by the many disharmonies in closely related parts repeatedly exemplified everywhere by heredity alone. Moreover, it is one of the most constant and expected products of hybridizing. Were it not for this, we would not today be enjoying the great variety of fruits and flowers of our times.

In regard to this phase of the subject, it may be pardonable to quote the words of a prominent biologist to whom this principle of teaching was submitted for criticism: "A statement like—'nature never puts teeth into a mouth that do not belong to that physiognomy,' always arouses my ire. Variation is so thoroughly the rule in nature, not only in individuals, but in parts of individuals, that there is *just as apt to be disharmony as harmony.*"

In this connection it may be interesting to note certain evidences for the theory of far reaching atavistic heredity, by comparing the physiognomies and jaws of the present quite common bimaxillary protrusion of the dentures, shown in

CHAPTER VII. HEREDITY AND VARIATION ETHNOLOGICALLY CONSIDERED 47

Figs. 157 and 158, Chapter XXIX, with the physiognomies and jaws of early prehistoric peoples, shown in Figs. 2 and 3, which are from a recently published work entitled "Men of the Old Stone Age : Their Environment, Life, and Art," by Henry Fairfield Osborn, of the American Museum of Natural History, and Professor of Anthropology in Columbia University, published by Charles Scribner's Sons. By permission of the Publishers.

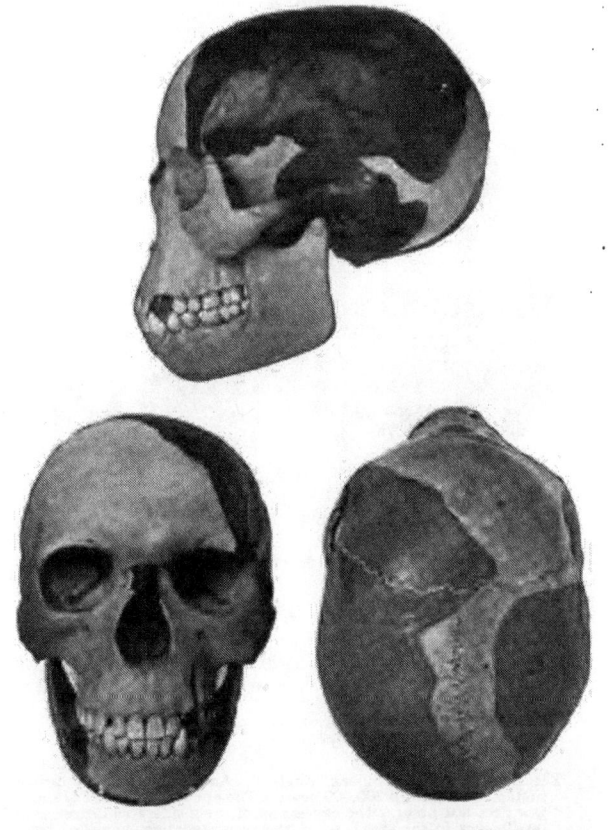

FIG. 2.

Three views of the Piltdown skull as reconstructed by J. H. McGregor, 1915. This restoration includes the nasal bones and canine tooth, which were not known at the time of Smith Woodward's reconstruction of 1913. One-quarter life size. Copyright, 1915, 1918, by Charles Scribner's Sons.

The receding chin was such a predominating characteristic of the early races of the old stone age that they are frequently spoken of as the "chinless men." In other words, their stage of evolution still had left stamped upon them certain characteristics of the teeth and jaws which doubtless had arisen in their anthropoid progenitors from prehensile needs. This consisted in protruding dentures in relation to the maxillæ in which they were placed, a condition of all ape tribes and common to Negroid races. And though this type prevailed ages before the chin development of the mandible, which later characterized the men of the upper palæolithic age and the present *"homo sapiens,"* it will nevertheless be seen that

48 PART II. ETIOLOGY OF MALOCCLUSION

the facial outlines of these early races were not far unlike those of many physiognomies of today, which are, from some form of heredity, characterized by the same bimaxillary protrusion of the dentures, or with the same receding chin effect as the chinless men.

In the illustration of a paper read before the 1913 meeting of the National Dental Society, the author presented fifteen cases of bimaxillary protrusion. In nearly all the cases shown, the buccal teeth were as perfect in alignment and occlu-

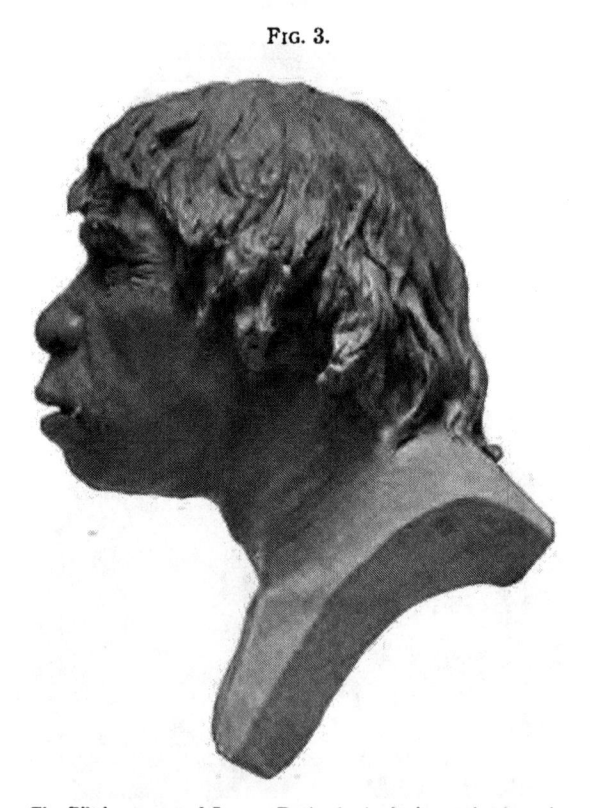

FIG. 3.

The Piltdown man of Sussex, England. Antiquity variously estimated at 100,000 to 300,000 years. The ape-like structure of the jaw does not prevent the expression of a considerable degree of intelligence in the face. After the reconstruction modelled by J. H. McGregor. Copyright, 1915, 1918, by Charles Scribner's Sons.

sion as we commonly find in normal dentures. With the exception of one of these cases, so far as can be learned, no condition which resembled this character existed with the parents or any of the known forebears; and this was true also of Dr. Cryer's case. See Fig. 24, Chapter X.

One thing which very strongly illustrates the persistent forces of heredity in physical structures and their relations, which have arrived at a condition of equilibration or state of high perfection in relation to environment, is obtained by a careful study of the photographic pictures of the jaws and dentures of prehistoric man, and the scientific restorations found in many of the illustrations of Professor Osborn's book, one of which is shown in Fig. 2. It proves that the inherited

CHAPTER VII. HEREDITY AND VARIATION ETHNOLOGICALLY CONSIDERED

standard type of normal occlusion of the human dentures—contrary to the opinion of many teachers of modern orthodontia—has come down to us essentially unchanged through the ages from the prehistoric men of the "old stone age," and kept in line through "the law of natural selection" ("survival of the fittest"), and its perfect adaptation to needs.

Even as far back as the second "interglacial period"—200,000 to 350,000 years ago—the forms, number, and relative position of the teeth and their buccal occlusion was essentially the same as the standard normal occlusion of today. And though in earlier stages of that vast period, the jaws were of a heavier type and the bimaxillary protrusive mouths, enhanced by chinless mandibles, showed their distant descent from their anthropoid progenitors, the occlusion of the teeth, their alignment and arch form—even the canines which had thrown off nearly all their carniverous characteristics—*were all practically the same as today.* In this connection compare the protruded malposition of the dentures in relation to the maxillæ and mandibles, shown in Fig. 2, illustrative of the men who lived hundreds of thousands of years ago, with illustrations of more recent skulls; first, the Fan Tribe West African Negro, Figs. 21 and 22, and second, Dr. Cryer's patient, Fig. 24, all in Chapter X. He assures the author that in the latter case the buccal teeth were in normal occlusion.

There is no doubt in the minds of advanced anthropologists that the form, structure, and relation of the bones of the human skull like those of other bones of the body were evolved from beings very much lower in the animal scale, through the unwavering laws of heredity, variation, natural selection, and influences of environment. And that peoples from the very earliest age of man up to the present time, through segregations in distantly located parts of the globe, presenting marked differences of environment, have become through slight ethnologic variations during many ages, the different races, characterized by distinct types in color and character of skin and hair, and of physical framework of physiognomies.

While there are at present only three markedly distinct races—the white or Caucasian, the yellow or Mongoloid, and the black or Negroid—through admixtures by intertribal relations and more distant migrations, many quite distinct races have been formed, with the production of intervening types, of which it is said, if they could be collected and compared, would blend into each other with imperceptible gradations.

This is a subject which pertains to the established sciences of stomatology and ethnology—branches of anthropology—which are today taught in our colleges, and which are founded upon many years of patient careful investigations by the most learned scientific minds.

It is shown that the present white race, more than any of the others, is decidedly a mixed race, there being few if any left of the original representatives of the Caucasian type, to which we are accustomed to refer as the standard of beauty and physical perfection. Yet because of the fact that our taste and appreciation of these qualities are being varied under the same adaptive guiding forces of evolution which have characterized the physical, we not uncommonly meet with types which fully accord with our own understanding of manly and womanly beauty and perfection. This doubtless has been true also of all isolated races of peoples, the more primitive of which we would now regard as exceedingly unattractive and perhaps repulsive.

In this brief mention of a few of the well established principles and possibilities of the laws of heredity and their co-operating forces with reference to the influences they exert in producing dental and dento-facial malformations, the author has endeavored to place before the mind of the reader a broader appreciation of the subject than that which is popularly understood as heredity, with the hope that it will lead to a more comprehensive study of these great principles which have such an intimate bearing upon many conditions which come within the scope of dental orthopedic practice.

CHAPTER VIII

PRACTICAL APPLICATION OF BIOLOGIC LAWS

What interests us most as orthodontists, especially as we essay the correction or improvement of facial beauty that is marred or deformed by malpositions and malrelations of the teeth and jaws, is the fact that in our country—the United States above all other countries—the union of dissimilar types occurs most frequently. The laws of heredity do not necessarily produce in the offspring a blended composite type. In fact, such an occurrence from parents of dissimilar types of both plants and animals often exhibits an association of separate distinct physical characters that have come from both parents or their progenitors. A slight observation of family physiognomies must fully demonstrate the inheritance of distinct features of both parents, and when this occurs in the associated parts of a physiognomy, it may result in decided disharmony of the features. "For nature knows no laws of esthetics, as beautiful and harmonious as her products are."

Under the forces of atavistic heredity, also, there have frequently arisen peculiar and inharmonious characteristics which could not be remembered as having previous existence in immediate forebears, but which have been definitely traced through records of history to some very distant progenitor.

These laws were fully recognized by both Darwin and Wallace in the earlier researches of evolution. Huxley, more than forty years ago, in writing upon the laws of heredity and variation, said: "It is a matter of perfectly common experience that the tendency on the part of the offspring always is to reproduce the form of the parents; that is a matter of ordinary and familiar observation. In all cases of propagation and perpetuation, there seems to be a tendency in the offspring to take the characters of the parental organisms. You do not find that the male follows the precise type of the male parent, nor does the female always inherit the precise characteristics of the mother—there is always a proportion of the female characters in the male offspring, and of the male characters in the female offspring. There are all sorts of intermixtures, and intermediate conditions between the two of dissimilar types, when complexion, beauty, or fifty other different peculiarities belonging to either side of the house are reproduced in other members of the same family. You will also see a child in a family who is not like either its father or mother; but some old person who knew its grandparents, or it may be an uncle, or perhaps a more distant relative, will see a great similarity between the child and one of these."

The disharmonies in esthetic facial outlines which are caused from malposed teeth are quite as diversified as disharmonies in size, form, and relation of the features of different physiognomies compared to the symmetrical. How often do we see some one feature of a face too large or too small for the rest of the features of which it forms a part, and this is true in varying degrees of every feature and organ of the human body as compared to that which may be considered as the truly normal or symmetrically formed type.

The surface-contour, form, size, and varying positions of the features which compose the human physiognomy are largely dependent upon the osseous framework, which in turn is, normally, either an inherent type or the union in the offspring of types which vary from harmony to the distinctively disharmonious. In all conditions of health and normality, these same influences and laws of development constitute the causes which govern and determine the relative sizes and forms of every organ and natural contour. From these sources have mainly arisen all the distinctively different types of races.

In America, where the union of disharmonious types has had full sway, we find a great variety of disharmonies in the physical forms of its inhabitants. On the other hand, among peoples such as the Japanese and the Chinese, whose native countries are not so extensively encroached upon with the intermingling of foreign types, individual disharmonies and variations from the racial type are comparatively uncommon. And while their characteristic type, from our viewpoint, may be far from that which we recognize as the highest physical development in beauty and perfection of form, it nevertheless is that which has normally arisen under the influence of heredity, natural selection, and environment, and consequently **to them it is a normal type.**

One of the characteristic dento-facial types that is common with a Japanese physiognomy is a depression or unesthetic retrusion along the upper part of the upper lip, and at the base of the rarely prominent nose. This depression heightens the usual pronounced malar prominences and shortens the somewhat thin upper lip in its relation to the incisal ends of the teeth—the lip itself approaching a prehensile inclination of 45 degrees. In a number of cases which the author has examined, the disto-mesial relations of the buccal teeth were normal in occlusion, while the labial teeth, particularly the incisors, were more labially inclined than we would consider esthetically normal. The cutting edges, especially of the upper incisors, were more or less protruding, which seemed to be due to a retrusion of the apical zone, or that which we would denominate from an esthetic standpoint, a repression of the normal development of the middle features of the physiognomy. If this condition, which is a normal Japanese type, occurred with an Anglo-Saxon, **as it occasionally does,** it would be diagnosed as **decidedly abnormal,** notwithstanding the perfect occlusion of the buccal teeth. And in all probability, if not an inherited type, it would be caused by some abnormal condition of the maxillary sinuses, and result in a lack of development of the intermaxillary processes, and would demand a bodily protrusive movement of the apical zone of the incisors, and a retrusive movement of the incisal zone to correct the facial outlines. See Type C, Division 2, Class II.

CHAPTER VIII. PRACTICAL APPLICATION OF BIOLOGIC LAWS

Much could be written and quoted along this line, but space will not permit. With a moderate understanding of the ethnologic principles of biologic development, it will be seen that all forms of animal life about us are the offspring of progenitors whose physical and mental characteristics they repeat to a very large extent, either by direct inheritance with the blending of types or with the association of the distinct characters of one or both parents, or through atavism from more distant progenitors, etc.

The immediate association in the physiognomies of individuals of distinct characteristics of the different racial types from which they sprung, through some form of heredity in which Mendel's Law may have played a part, is one of the most important ethnologic considerations. In connection with these sources of reproduction, one should not forget that the law of natural variation is always and everywhere in action through the metabolic activities of the germ cells, with the same transmissible properties as those of long lines of heredity.

Principles of Heredity in Relation to Treatment

The following phase of this subject pertains to that which we find exemplified everywhere about us. First, to the relationship as regards size, form, and relative position of the mandibular and maxillary bones proper, to the rest of the bones which form the framework of physiognomies; second, to the relations of the dental and alveolar arches to the mandibles and maxillæ—both with a view of comparing the disharmonies we commonly find, to that harmony of dento-facial relation which accords with our present standard of perfection and beauty.

It will be seen that the types of people present the most marked differences in the form and size of the bones which constitute the framework of human bodies. Thus we have tall and short men, either of whom may possess strong heavily built bones or slender delicate ones. Nor does esthetic harmony or the typically anatomic prevail, except rarely. Moreover, it is common to find disharmonies in the sizes and relations of bones which are closely associated as the bones of the face, and which can frequently be traced to direct inheritance or the admixture through some channel of heredity of disharmonious types.

In this investigation, which anyone with an observing mind may pursue, there will be found to exist every possible variation between the so-called "freaks" and those of Apollo-like harmony and perfection. We find noses of every possible shape in relation to harmony with the features upon which they are placed, and jaws prognathous and retruded in relation to the rest of the features. This must be equally true of the sizes of teeth whose width measurements have been erroneously employed to determine the sizes of the newly regulated dental arches. If the sizes of dental arches are made in exact mathematical proportion to the width of the upper central incisors, will not these arches be found at times too large or too small for facial harmony, and to an extent that is noticeably deforming? We frequently find the sizes of the front teeth quite out of proportion with the features. Moreover, the circumference measurements of the right and left centrals and other teeth are rarely exactly the same, and commonly vary in their circumferences under normal conditions, $1/64$ to $1/32$ of an inch, and at times even more.

Many of the facial disharmonies pertain to the dental and maxillary framework, and characterize the physiognomies as plain, homely, or deformed, according to the character and amount of the protrusion or retrusion over the dento-facial and mandibular area.

In many protrusions, both unimaxillary and bimaxillary, the entire bodies of the maxillary bones are protruded in their dento-facial relations, and this is easily determined by the prominence of the chin and the prominence at the base of the nose and along the upper portion of the upper lip. In many of these cases the teeth are in perfect harmony of size and position with the protruded jaws—in arch width, alignment, and inclination—and yet distinctly out of balance with the esthetic relations of the rest of the features. In bimaxillary malpositions the dentures are often found in typical occlusion in the white as well as in colored races, because both dentures are equally protruded. Again, in a large proportion of protrusions, the protrusion pertains mostly or wholly to the dental and alveolar arches alone. As an illustration of this, see the beginning of Dr. Cryer's case, Chapter X, and the physiognomies of bimaxillary protrusions illustrated in this work. Moreover, in nearly all typical protrusions of the dentures not due to local causes, the teeth are crowded closely together, showing that the buccal teeth partake of the protruded malposition quite as much as the labial teeth.

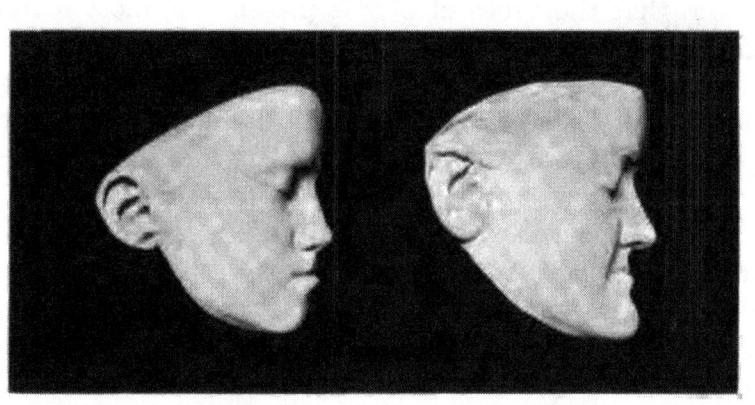

Fig. 4.

Attention is called also to the variety of antero-posterior malpositions of the lower denture in relation to the mandible. Fig. 4 is made from the facial casts of two cases before treatment. The mandible of the one on the right, judging from the facial outlines, is seen to be decidedly prognathous, but from the relative position of the lower lip, the lower denture must be in about normal dento-facial relations. With the case on the left, judging from the relative positions of the chin, the lower

CHAPTER VIII. PRACTICAL APPLICATION OF BIOLOGIC LAWS

lip, and labio-mental curve, these conditions are reversed, that is: the mandible is in esthetic dento-facial relations, but with the lower denture protruded.

These two cases like many others which could be pointed out in this work, illustrate the decided dissimilarity in types which may arise *with the same character of occlusion of the dentures.* These belong in Class III in which the upper denture is more or less retruded, and with the lower denture closing far in front of a normal occlusion with the upper denture. Illustrations of this kind, moreover, definitely show that through that most prolific form of heredity—i. e., the sexual union of dissimilar characters—even entire upper or lower dentures take decidedly different positions at times in relation to the bones in which they grow.

Thus many of the most pronounced, as well as minor malocclusions, having every possible malrelation of the teeth, jaws, and facial outlines, have arisen through one of the many avenues of heredity. The proof of this statement is so plainly shown on every hand, and, moreover, it accords so thoroughly with the laws of biology in both flora and fauna, that the fantastic claims that "all malocclusions arise from local causes," and "God does not make such mistakes in forming the human anatomies, etc.," must be regarded as crass ignorance of the well established principles of heredity.

This brings us to a point which should be emphasized, because it pertains to the question of early correction, and particularly to the teaching of shifting the deciduous buccal teeth and recently erupted first molars to normal, in all cases of disto-mesial malocclusion, even though the buccal cusps are in full malinterdigitation.

It should be understood that the author is heartily in accord with this movement for young patients, where it is distinctly seen to be demanded. The cases that demand it are: first, those which arise from local causes and which otherwise would have been in normal relations; and second, from whatever cause, if one denture or the other is retruded in its dento-facial relations, and the other is not so protruded but that the slight distal movement that is necessary for its correction can be safely and advisedly performed.

If it is other than this, as it is quite liable to be, where the lower denture is destined to be normal or not protruded, and the opposing denture, *through heredity*, is destined to be decidedly protruded, the operator can rest assured that the shifting of the first molars to a normal occlusion, *at whatever age, will ultimately result in a bimaxillary protrusion*, permanently marring the beauty of the face. Nor can one be sure what the adult conditions are destined to be at this very early age, when the bones are just beginning to take on the inherent stamp of their progenitors.

In the hundreds of cases which have come under the author's observation during the ages of childhood and youth, there is no room to spare in the jaws back of the deciduous molars, except at the time preparatory to the eruption of the first permanent molars, and finally the second, and then the third molars; the latter being often obliged to occupy quite as crowded positions in protruding cases as are seen when teeth are not protruded. In other words, in all cases of typical protrusion in the white race due to heredity, the natural position of the back teeth in relation to the tuberosities and rami allows no more than a very moderate distal movement without encroaching upon space demanded for the succeeding molars, a demand which nature will at one time or another insist upon, or else make trouble.

Therefore, in all marked inherent protrusions of the upper, for example, if the first molars are extensively moved distally for the purpose of placing them in a normal occlusion in early childhood or later, one may count quite surely upon ultimate disappointment of intention. If the teeth do not go back to their former inherited malinterdigitation, as they are quite liable to do through the eruptive forces of the second or third molars, a bimaxillary protrusion, which is quite as bad, will be stamped upon the features through life.

In the discussion of a paper read before a prominent society upon the advantages of radiographs in orthodontia, a prominent teacher in a dental college—who evidently had caught the "bone growing" fever—criticised Dr. Cryer's warning in regard to the excessive distal movement of molars, and he did this upon the bare evidence of a single case that he illustrated with the lantern, showing a third molar which evidently had been impacted by a distal artificial movement of a second molar, and which had finally erupted to normal position. This speaker expressed in unmistakable terms his belief that the crowding of the teeth and the artificially applied forces will stimulate an interstitial extra growth and elongation of the jawbone itself, and thus carry all the denture forward and give plenty of room for the third molars. This is abundantly proved to be untrue by the many instances of crowded dentures that are protruded in relation to the jaws in which they are placed.

If nature possessed this power in the individual to cause the jaws and associate bones to grow to meet the requirements of room and facial harmony, or if it were possible for us to stimulate nature to an extra interstitial growth, there would be far more harmonious relations between the sizes of dentures and jaws than are seen to exist. We would not so frequently see retruded chins in connection with crowded and prominent lower teeth, or those marked cases of bimaxillary protrusion which are not usually noticeable until ten or twelve years of age, and which seem to increase in prominence during adolescence.

There is every reason to believe from the most advanced authorities upon biology that the bones of individuals cannot be forced to *grow* larger than their inherited sizes, nor would they have ever grown larger than any primitive fixed state, had it not been for the laws of *natural variation* and "survival of the fittest."

The following quotation from Stackpole's "Biology," should forever set at rest the fantastic theory of "bone growth." "*It is well known that all animals and plants have a definite limit of growth.* From the cytological point of view, the limit of body-size appears to be correlated with the total number of cells formed rather than

CHAPTER VIII. PRACTICAL APPLICATION OF BIOLOGIC LAWS

with their individual size. This relation has been carefully studied by Conkline ('96) in the case of the gasteropod Crepidula, an animal which varies greatly in size in the mature condition, the dwarfs having in some cases not more than one-twenty-fifth the volume of the giants. The eggs are, however, of the same size in all, and their number is proportional to the size of the adult. The same is true of the tissue-cells. Measurements of cells from the epidermis, the kidney, the liver, the alimentary epithelium, and other tissues, show that they are on the whole as large in the dwarfs as in the giants. The body-size therefore depends on the total number of cells rather than on their size, individually considered, and the same appears to be the case in plants."

PART III

Basic Principles of Practice

BASIC PRINCIPLES OF PRACTICE

CHAPTER IX

ARRANGEMENT OF THE TEETH AND ALVEOLAR PROCESS ANATOMICALLY CONSIDERED

The foundation of all training calculated to fit one to enter the practical field of Orthopedic Dentistry must lie in a perfect knowledge of nature's **anatomical arrangement** and **occlusion of the teeth,** and the form and structure of the **alveolar process.**

This is most perfectly described in the incomparable work "Dental Anatomy," by Dr. G. V. Black, who has kindly permitted the re-publication of it in this chapter.

ARRANGEMENT OF THE TEETH

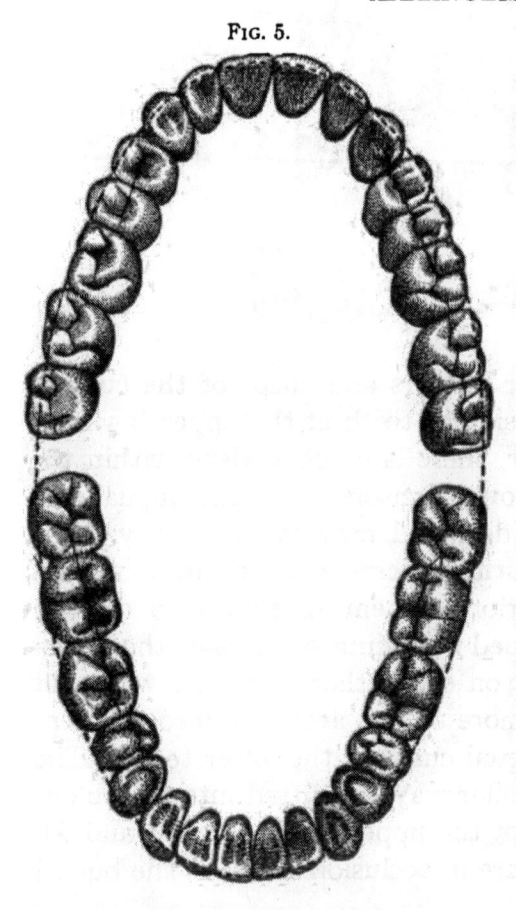

FIG. 5.

"The **upper teeth** are arranged in the form of a **semi-ellipse,** the long axis passing between the central incisors. In this curve, the cuspids stand a little prominent, giving a fullness to the corners of the mouth. In different persons there is much variation in the form of the arch within the limits of the normal. Occasionally the bicuspids and molars form a straight line, instead of a curve, and frequently the third molars are a little outside the line of the ellipse. In the examination of casts of the most perfect dentures, it is found that the two sides do not perfectly correspond, and that certain teeth deviate slightly from the perfect line. The incisors are arranged with their cutting edges forming a continuous curved line from cuspid to cuspid, and this line is continued over the cusps of the cuspids and the buccal cusps of the bicuspids and molars to the distal surface of the third molars. From the first bicuspid to the third molar the lingual cusps of these teeth form a second line of elevations. Be-

PART III. BASIC PRINCIPLES OF PRACTICE

tween these two, the lingual and buccal cusps, there is a continuous but irregular valley, or sulcus.

"The **lower teeth** are arranged similarly but on a slightly smaller curve, so that the line of the ellipse, which falls on the buccal cusps of the upper bicuspids and molars, will fall upon the buccal surfaces near the gum on the lower teeth (Fig. 5). Therefore in occlusion the upper teeth project a little to the labial and buccal of the lower at all points of the arch (Fig. 6). The incisors and cuspids

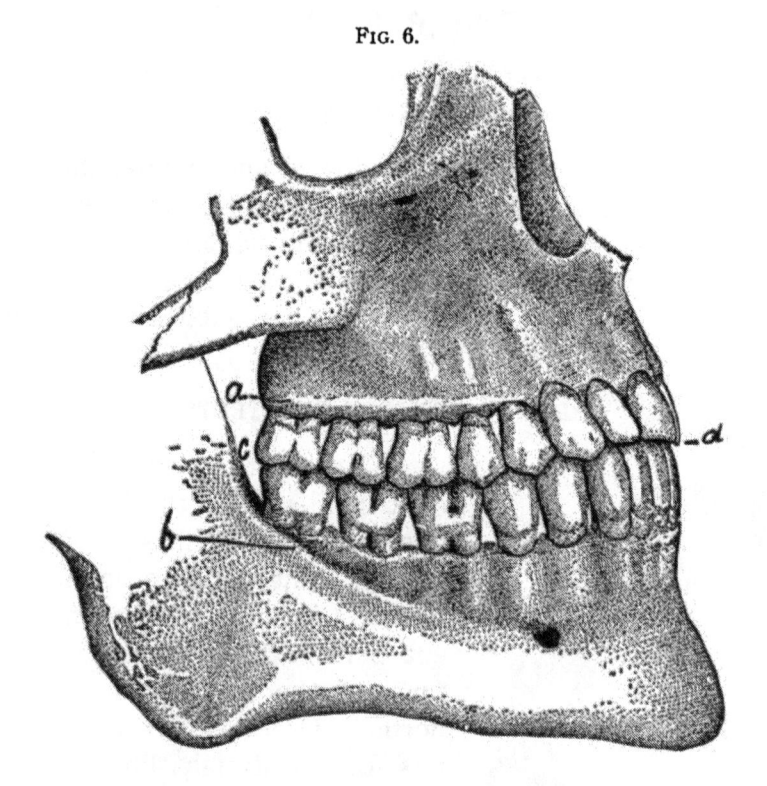

FIG. 6.

occlude so that the cutting edges of the lower incisors and cusps of the cuspids make contact with the lingual surfaces of the similar teeth of the upper jaw near their cutting edges (Fig. 7). In this, however, there is much variety within the limits of a **normal occlusion.** Sometimes the lower incisors strike the lingual surfaces of the upper near the linguo-gingival ridge, and may strike at any point between that and the cutting edges. In **abnormal occlusions** the lower incisors may miss the upper, striking the gums posterior to them, or they may occlude anterior to the upper incisors. The broad cusped occluding surfaces of the bicuspids and molars of the opposing dentures rest on each other in such a way that the lingual cusps of the upper teeth fit with more or less accuracy into the general sulcus formed between the buccal and lingual cusps of the lower teeth. The buccal row of cusps of the lower teeth, in a similar way, are fitted into the sulcus formed between the buccal and lingual cusps of the upper teeth (Figs. 8 and 9). This arrangement is such that when the teeth are in occlusion it leaves the buccal

CHAPTER IX. ARRANGEMENT OF THE TEETH

inclines of the buccal cusps of the upper teeth outside the buccal surfaces of the upper teeth (a). And, also, leaves a ledge formed by the abrupt lingual inclines of the lingual cusps of the lower teeth along the lingual line of the occlusion (b). This brings the occluding surfaces of the teeth in the best form of apposition for the purposes of mastication. The forms presented to the cheek and to the tongue hold these soft tissues a little apart from the actual contact points of the occlusion, and thus prevent them from being caught and pinched, or crushed, between the teeth in the act of mastication. In youth, while the permanent teeth are taking their places, and before the cusps are properly fitted to the sulci, we often find the cheeks or tongue wounded by being caught between false occluding points. With the after movements of the teeth, by which they are more perfectly arranged, this difficulty disappears.

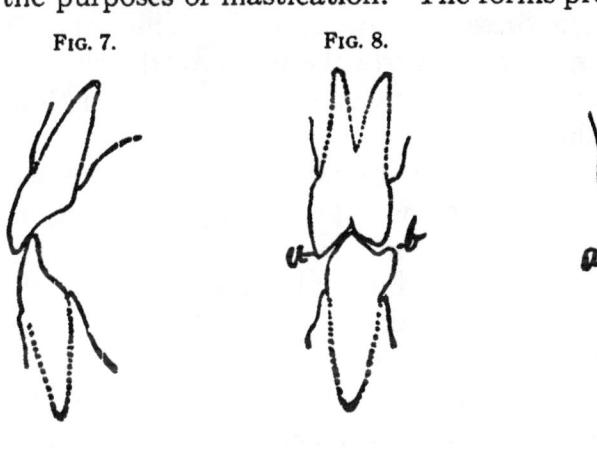

FIG. 7.   FIG. 8.   FIG. 9.

"The **line** from before backward on which the occlusion occurs is not quite a plane; in the lower jaw it presents a slight curve, or concavity, and in the upper jaw a convexity (Fig. 6, c to d). The concavity of the line of the occluding surfaces of the lower teeth is a little greater than the convexity of the upper, so that the cutting edges of the lower incisors pass a little beyond, and to the lingual of the cutting edges of the upper incisors.

"In the **occlusion**, the relative mesio-distal position of the particular teeth of the upper jaw to the lower is important (Fig. 6). At their cutting edges the upper central incisors are about one-third wider from mesial to distal than the lower centrals. The upper central, therefore, occludes with the lower central, and also with from one-third to one-half of the lower lateral incisor. The upper lateral occludes with the remaining portion of the lower lateral, and the mesial portion of the lower cuspid. The upper cuspid is usually rather broader from mesial to distal than the lower, and in occlusion covers its distal two-thirds and about half of the lower first bicuspid so that its lingual, or triangular ridge, is between the cusp of the lower cuspid and the buccal cusp of the lower first bicuspid, the point of its cusp overlapping the lower teeth. The buccal cusp of the lower first bicuspid occludes in the space between the upper cuspid and the upper first bicuspid. This order is now maintained between the bicuspids. The buccal cusp of the upper first bicuspid overlaps (to the buccal) the space between the two lower bicuspids, and its lingual cusp occludes in the sulcus between them, while the buccal cusp of the lower second bicuspid occludes in the sulcus between the two upper bicuspids. The cusps of the upper second bicuspid occlude between the lower second bicuspid and lower first molar. The broad surfaces of the molars come together, so that the mesial two-thirds of the upper first molar covers the distal two-thirds of the lower first molar; and the distal third of the upper first molar covers the mesial third of the lower second molar. This brings the transverse ridge of the upper molar between these two lower teeth. This order is continued between the remaining molars, but less perfectly as the teeth are more irregularly formed. The upper third molar is usually smaller than the lower third molar, yet it generally extends over its distal surface.

"The **inclination of the teeth** is the deviation of their long axes from the perpendicular line. The direction of the inclination is expressed by some accompanying word. The upper incisors and cuspids are so arranged that their crowns are inclined more or less forward, or towards the lip, and slightly towards the median line. The mesial inclination is continued in the bicuspids and molars, diminishing from before backward, and is usually lost at the second or third molar. As a rule, the bicuspids and molars of the upper jaw are also slightly inclined towards the cheek, but in many dentures this inclination is slight, or wanting in the bicuspids and first molars, to re-appear in the second and third molars, though it may be absent even in these without necessary malformation.

"The **lower incisors** and **cuspids** are also inclined with their crowns towards the lip, but in less degree than the upper. And even the perpendicular position of these is not inconsistent with a normal arrangement. They have, however, a mesial inclination, but usually much less than the corresponding upper teeth. The **lower bicuspids,** within the limits of the normal arrangement, vary considerably in their inclinations. Sometimes they have a strong mesial inclination, and at other times they are nearly or quite perpendicular. In many dentures, they also have a lingual inclination, but may be perpendicular or even have a slight buccal inclination. The **lower molars** usually have a slight mesial and lingual inclination. In many examples, however, the mesial inclination is wanting, especially in the second and third molars.

"All the teeth are a little broader from mesial to distal at or near the occluding surfaces than at their necks. Therefore, when arranged in the arch with their proximate surfaces in contact, there is a considerable space between their necks (Fig. 6). These are known as the **interproximate,** or **V**-shaped, **spaces.** The sharp angle or apex of the **V**-form is toward the occluding surface or at the contact point of the proximation, and the open end or base is at the crest of the alveolar process. In normal conditions, this space is filled by the soft tissues, or gums (Fig. 10). The average arch measures about **127** millimeters (5 inches) from the distal surface of the right third molar to the distal surface of the left third molar, following the curve of the arch. This

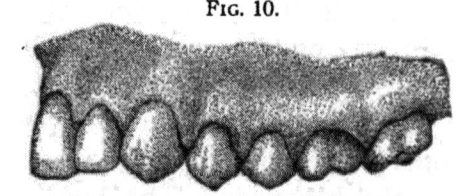

Fig. 10.

represents the average mesio-distal measurement of the crowns of the teeth of the upper jaw taken collectively. The average measurement of the teeth at their necks is about 89 millimeters (3.5 inches). The remaining 38 millimeters (1.5 inches) represent the average sum of the **interproximate spaces** taken collectively.

"On account of the difference in the **conformation of the crowns** and the **inclination of the teeth,** the interproximate spaces vary much in width in different dentures. They are much wider between bell-crowned teeth than between thick-necked teeth; but some interproximate space exists in every normal denture. When the crowns of the incisors and cuspids are much inclined towards the lip, the necks of the teeth form a smaller circle than the line of the contact points of the proximation, and in this way the interproximate spaces may be considerably narrowed. Generally, the interproximate space is wide between the necks of the central incisors. The suture joining the maxillary bones passes between the roots of these teeth, and they are somewhat farther apart than the roots of the central and lateral incisors, or those of the lateral incisor and the cuspid. Therefore, in these latter, the interproximate spaces are of less width. Between the bicuspids the interproximate spaces are wider at the necks of the teeth than between the anterior teeth, on account of the greater breadth of the crowns as compared with the roots. The widest interproximate spaces are usually between the necks of the molars.

"The **points of proximate contact** in the best formed arches are near the occluding surfaces of the teeth. In imperfectly developed teeth, in which the crowns are much rounded towards the occluding surfaces, the contact points are more toward the gingival. In the incisors and cuspids they are in direct line with the cutting edges. In the bicuspids the contact is near the buccal angles and nearly in line with the buccal cusps.

"The mesial and distal flattened surfaces of these teeth converge to the lingual to such an extent that, though they are arranged in arch form, the contact points remain close to the buccal angles. In many excellent dentures there is a decided interproximate space opening to the **lingual,** but in thick-necked teeth and those of a more rounded contour the contact points are often more toward the lingual, and there is no appreciable lingual interproximate space. In the molars the contact points, as a rule, are removed rather more to the lingual, but still in the best formed dentures they will be found nearly in line with the buccal cusps. Between the upper first and second molars the contact point is often extended toward the lingual by the prominent disto-lingual cusp of the first molar; and, even when otherwise the general rounding of the distal surfaces of the upper molars often brings the contact points near the middle line of the teeth. In lower first molars the large distal cusp brings the contact point with the second molar close to the buccal side, with a considerable lingual interproximate space. If the distal cusp is small the contact point is usually extended toward the lingual, often as far as half the bucco-lingual breadth of the teeth. Between the second and third molars the contact point is most frequently near the central line of the teeth. In the best formed dentures the **form** of the **proximate** contact is such as to prevent food from being crowded between the teeth in mastication; and, therefore, such as to keep these spaces clean and the interproximate gingivus in health. But many **faulty forms** are met with, which allow food to leak through into the interproximate space and crowd the gum away, forming a pocket for the lodgment of debris, giving opportunity for decomposition, and resulting in caries of the proximate surfaces, or disease of the gum and peridental membrane. **Exceptionally, cases are met with** in which the teeth stand so widely apart that the spaces are self-cleaning. The form of the interproximate spaces is very variable. It is best studied in skulls in which the teeth are all present, and by careful consideration of the forms of the proximate surfaces of the teeth, together with their relative positions.

THE ALVEOLAR PROCESS AND ALVEOLI

FIG. 11.

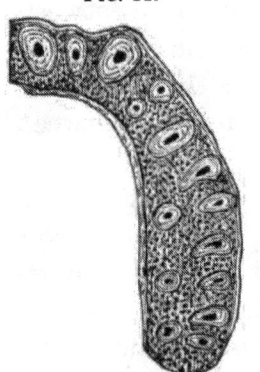

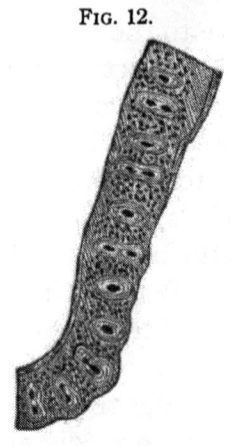

FIG. 12.

"The **alveolar process** is the projecting portion of the maxillary bones within which the roots of the teeth are lodged in alveoli, or sockets, accurately fitted to their surfaces (Figs. 11 and 12). The form of the alveolar process seems to depend on the teeth, the conformation of their roots, and their arrangement in the arch. If any teeth are misplaced, or from any cause stand out of the regular and normal line, the alveolar process is formed about their roots in this irregular position. Also, when teeth are lost, the alveolar process mostly disappears by absorption, and the remaining portions of the alveoli are filled with bone.

"**Normally,** the alveolar process envelops the roots of the teeth to within a short distance of the gingival line (Figs. 6 and 13), varying from one to three millimeters in the young adult. This distance increases somewhat with increasing age. The borders of the alveolar process are reduced to a thin edge about the necks of the teeth on both the labial and lingual sides of the incisors and cuspids of the upper jaw. About the lingual sides of the necks of the bicuspids and molars the borders are also reduced to a thin edge, becoming slightly thickened about the second and third molars, especially of the latter. On the buccal sides of these, a thickening of the immediate borders of the alveolar process, in the form of a marked ridge, begins about the first or second bicuspid, more commonly between these two, and extends to the distal of the third molar (Fig. 6, a). This ridge varies in different examples, from a very slight thickening of the immediate border, to a thickness of two or three millimeters. It forms a border standing squarely out from the necks of the teeth. The alveolar process then thins away so that, in many instances, the buccal roots of the teeth, especially the mesial root of the first molar, have but a thin covering of bone.

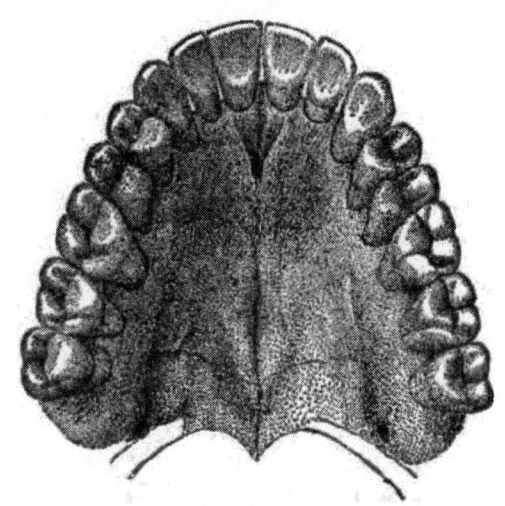

FIG. 13.

"**Anteriorly,** the bony covering of the roots of the upper incisors presents much variety. In some examples, the middle portion of the roots has but a slight covering of bone, but more generally it is progressively thickened from the neck to the apex. The roots of the cuspids are prominent towards the lip, and, for most of their length, have only a thin bony covering, and this forms a ridge along the line of the root, which may easily be traced with the finger through the soft tissues of both the gum and lip. In many instances the bony covering is entirely wanting for a little space near the middle of the length of the root of the cuspid, the buccal root of the first bicuspid, the mesial root of the first molar, and, occasionally, of other teeth.

"On the **lingual side** of the upper teeth (Fig. 13), the progressive thickening of the alveolar process, from the border towards the apex of the root, is much greater; so that the roots of the teeth seem to lie towards the labial and buccal side of the alveolar process (Fig. 11). Even the large lingual root of the upper first molar, diverging strongly to the lingual, seldom forms a ridge or prominence of the process covering its lingual surface."

CHAPTER X

"TYPICAL AND ATYPICAL OCCLUSION OF THE TEETH IN RELATION TO THE CORRECTION OF IRREGULARITIES"

The following chapter is an extract from a paper entitled as above, by Dr. Matthew H. Cryer, Professor of Oral Surgery in the University of Pennsylvania, read before the New York State Dental Society, May, 1904, and published in the Dental Cosmos, September, 1904.

It should be carefully studied in its general and scientific teaching of the anatomical, physiological, and surgical aspects of the teeth in relation to Orthodontia. The teachings of men of Dr. Cryer's long experience and eminence in the dental profession, relative to the principles of tooth movement and regulation, should receive the profoundest consideration. Attention is particularly called to his opinions in regard to some phases of the much exploited theory of regulating all cases without extraction, upon the basis that "the most esthetic facial outlines are dependent upon the production of a typically normal occlusion."

EXTRACT FROM DR. CRYER'S PAPER

"During the past three years many papers have been published on the subject of irregularities of the teeth and their treatment, and while some of them are of unquestionable value, covering points of capital importance in the field of Orthodontia, the author feels, however, that due consideration has not always been given to the outlines of the face which are molded upon the topographical anatomy of the facial bones, the alveolar processes, and the teeth.

"Some writers have given fixed rules for changing the position of the teeth, without bearing in mind the fact that each case demands the adoption of a special mode of procedure in its treatment. This wholesale correction by rule is causing many of the young members of the profession to perform operations which are damaging to the patient and which cannot be rectified in later years. It is for this reason that the writer desired to present a paper which would bring out a general discussion upon 'Typical and Atypical Occlusion of the Teeth.'

"In the correction of irregularities of the teeth and their processes, three fundamental principles should always be considered. First, the operator should carefully regard the outlines of the face, especially as they should appear in early adult life; the difference in treatment demanded by the male and female type should be observed; the variations in each individual should be considered, and each case treated according to its own requirements. Second, due consideration

CHAPTER X. TYPICAL AND ATYPICAL OCCLUSION OF THE TEETH

should be given to the appearance of the teeth when the lips are open, as in talking and laughing. Third, the importance of occlusion in regard to vocalization, appearance, and mastication. As malocclusion often brings serious pathological conditions, such as impacted teeth, neuralgia, etc., this condition should receive most careful attention. It is the writer's opinion that the surgeon should have a full knowledge of the superficial and internal anatomy of the maxillary bones, with that of the alveolar process, which is only the connecting structure between the teeth and the bones proper. He should also be thoroughly conversant with the physiology of this region and with the pathological changes of which it may become the seat.

TYPICAL VS. ACTUAL ANATOMY AND OCCLUSION

"After close study of the forms of various bones of the human skeleton, both disarticulated and articulated, and the open spaces of the face, such as the oral cavity, the orbits, the nasal chamber with its associated pneumatic sinuses and cells, etc., the writer came to the conclusion that typical anatomy as taught in textbooks is more ideal than true, and is something different from that with which the surgeon comes into daily contact, and it is his opinion that this divergence applies to a notable extent in reference to the jaws and teeth at rest and in occlusion.

"In order to bear out this statement a few illustrations will be given showing the typical anatomy of the external and internal structures of the jaws and the occlusion of the teeth.

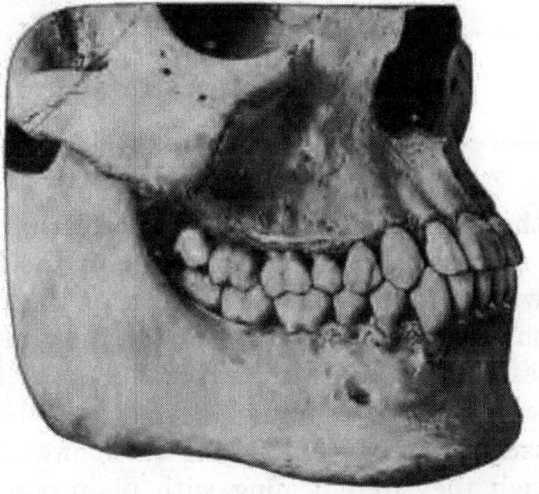

FIG. 14.

Upper and lower jaws of a negro skull, showing considerable prognathism.

"The illustration Fig. 14 is from a slide kindly loaned by Dr. I. N. Broomell, from a photograph of a negro skull which is in his possession. The reason for showing this picture is the fact that various authors give it as an illustration of **normal occlusion** of the teeth, omitting to state that it is from the **negro race**—in

70   PART III. BASIC PRINCIPLES OF PRACTICE

other words, that it belongs to a race more or less prognathic. The occlusion of the anterior teeth shows that it belongs to this type of skull; it is a fine specimen, except that the upper second and third molars do not occlude typically with the lower third molars, even according to the negro type.

"Fig. 15 is a side view made from an almost perfect skull of a white woman. The teeth are so nearly typical in occlusion that but a few persons have found any fault with the specimen. The incisor teeth may possibly protrude too much

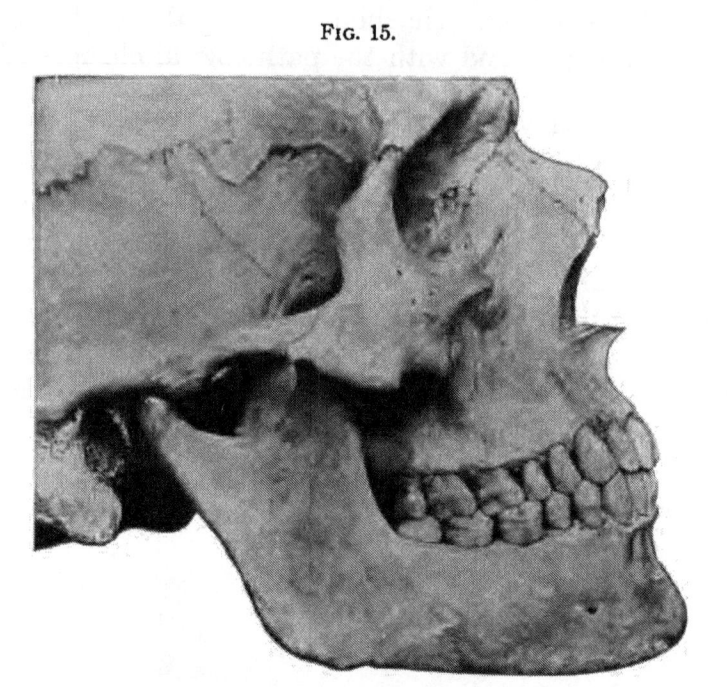

FIG. 15.

Side view of upper and lower jaws of a Caucasian skull, showing typical occlusion of the teeth.

to be in harmony with some Caucasian faces. The teeth, especially the anterior ones, must be in harmony with the general outline of the face and lips. In the general occlusion it will be found that each tooth of the upper jaw comes into contact with two teeth of the lower jaw, except the third molar, while each tooth of the lower jaw comes into contact with two of the upper teeth, except the central incisors. The interlocking of the premolars and the molar teeth is ideal.

"Some orthodontists speak of moving the teeth inward, outward, forward, or backward, as though they were dealing with plain porcelain teeth set up in wax on a mechanical articulator, without taking into consideration the anatomy, physiology, or pathological conditions presented in the jaws or the general system.

"The writer can readily understand how teeth can be moved forward, as a rule, by orthodontists, as that is the direction of their general or usual movement during development or eruption into their proper positions. But he doubts the ability of any man to successfully move a lower first molar backward half its width

CHAPTER X. TYPICAL AND ATYPICAL OCCLUSION OF THE TEETH

when the other molars are in position. It may be possible—though it is somewhat doubtful—for the lower first molar to be moved half its width backward in the mouth of a child about seven or eight years of age, but your essayist fears serious results even in such a case.

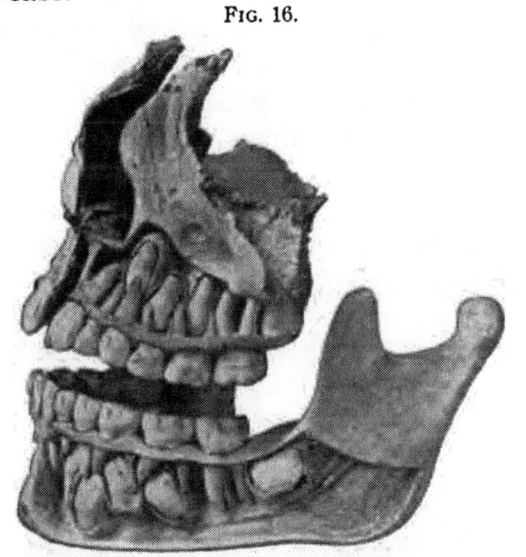

FIG. 16.

Side view of the upper and lower jaws of a child about seven or eight years of age, showing the deciduous teeth, the first molars, and the germs of other permanent teeth.

"Fig. 16 is from a specimen of jaws belonging to a child seven or eight years old. We find all the deciduous teeth in position, also the first molar. The developing crown of the second molar is just posterior to it. The germ of the third molar is not shown. Suppose it were possible to move the first molar backward

FIG. 17.

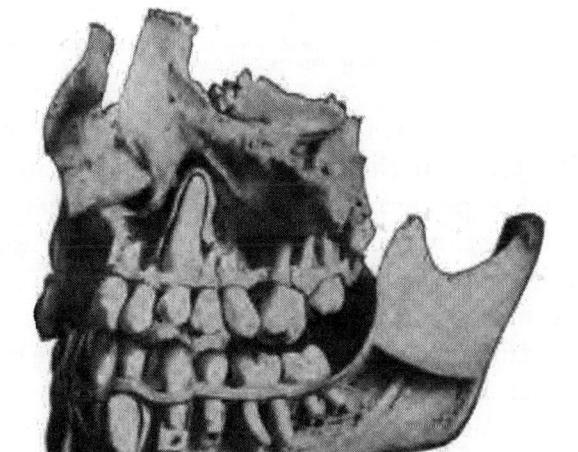

Side view of upper and lower jaws of a child about twelve or thirteen years of age.

half its width, would it not interfere very materially with the second molar by disturbing its true position—by carrying it backward and turning it over to a greater or less extent?

"Fig. 17 is from a similar preparation, of a child about twelve or thirteen years of age. If the first molar had been moved backward half its width, at the age of seven or eight years, the second molar would have been carried back with it. This would not have allowed proper space for the third molar, which would more than likely have become impacted.

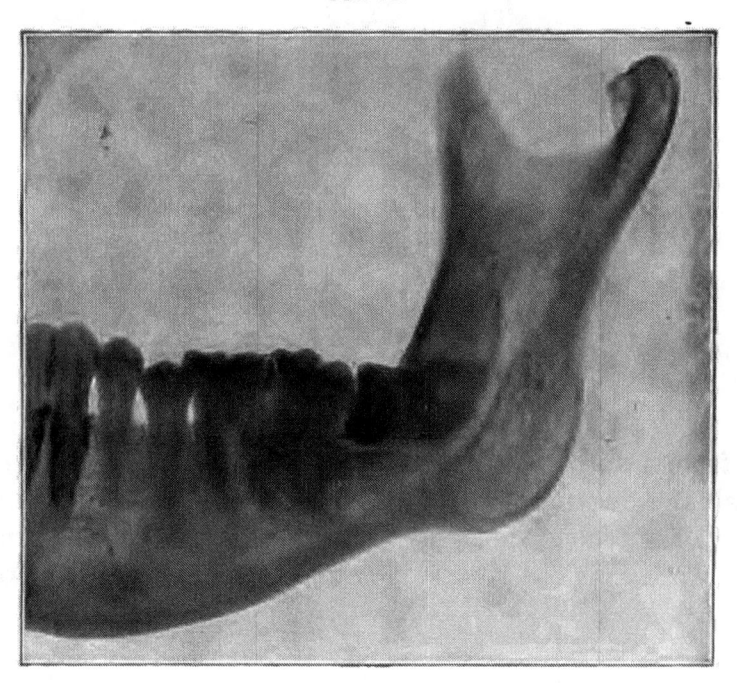

FIG. 18.

From a radiograph taken from a cleaned specimen of the left side of the lower jaw, showing an impacted third molar.

"Fig. 18 is a radiograph taken from a cleaned specimen of the left side of the lower jaw showing the teeth in their position with the cancellated tissue. One might well imagine that a modern orthodontist had moved the first molar half its width backward or held it in such a manner that it could not advance. Whether this was done by a mechanical appliance or was the result of pathological causes, the tooth was held and impaction resulted. If the cancellated tissue be examined, as seen in the X-ray picture, it will be noticed that it is more dense around the first and second molars than anteriorly to these teeth. As the result of an inflammatory condition the cancellated tissue has become united with the cortical bone, thus making another factor in preventing its sliding forward. It will be noticed that the roots of the molar teeth are also thickened by the overaction of the cementoblasts caused by this inflammatory condition.

CHAPTER X. TYPICAL AND ATYPICAL OCCLUSION OF THE TEETH

Extraction for the Correction of Irregularities

"Many writers, especially of late, claim that irregularities of the teeth should always be corrected without the extraction of one or more teeth, as 'Nature never puts teeth into a mouth that do not belong to that physiognomy.' Your writer thinks this is doing Nature a great injustice; many teeth are found within the mouth which should be removed, not only for the correction of irregularities but for the general comfort and health of the patient. Modern civilization demands that we live contrary to rather than in accordance with Nature, and so long as this is so, we cannot blame Nature for existing irregularities or depend entirely upon her for beneficent results. Our numerous dental and medical colleges testify to the necessity of assisting Nature to become reconciled with modern methods of living.

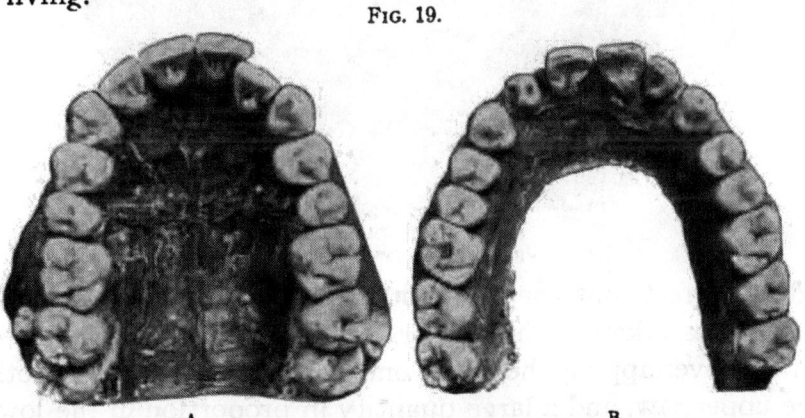

FIG. 19.

A B

Made from two upper jaws, showing a large amount of tooth tissue in the smaller jaw, A, and much less in the larger jaw, B.

"Fig. 19 is made from two photographs of upper jaws taken on the same plate. These pictures are to demonstrate that a small jaw can be crowded with large teeth, while a large jaw may have small teeth with space between them. It has been given as a reason for this condition that a child may inherit the jaw of one parent and the teeth of another, and for lack of a better explanation it may be well to accept this one for the present.

"From a practical standpoint it matters not why such irregularities exist; they are there, and must be corrected. Notice the size of the teeth in the left picture. Beginning with the incisors and passing backward, the first bicuspid is extraordinarily large, as are also the molar teeth; there seems to be too much tooth tissue, as in addition two rudimentary fourth molars can also be seen. What would the non-extractor do with these two teeth? Would he endeavor to place them in their regular position, as shown in the illustration Fig. 23, or would he not rather acknowledge that these teeth should be extracted because they interfere with the general hygiene of the mouth?

"Fig. 20 is a lateral view of the left picture of Fig. 19. The teeth are in occlusion with its mate, the lower jaw. It has been claimed by many that if the first

74 PART III. BASIC PRINCIPLES OF PRACTICE

molars or bicuspids be properly locked, the other teeth would be in good occlusion. The writer cannot agree with these two assertions. The illustration before us shows that the first and second molars of each jaw are typical in occlusion as well as the bicuspids. (The molars and bicuspids on the opposite side are in equally good occlusion.) If the above rules are to be followed, then the canine and incisor

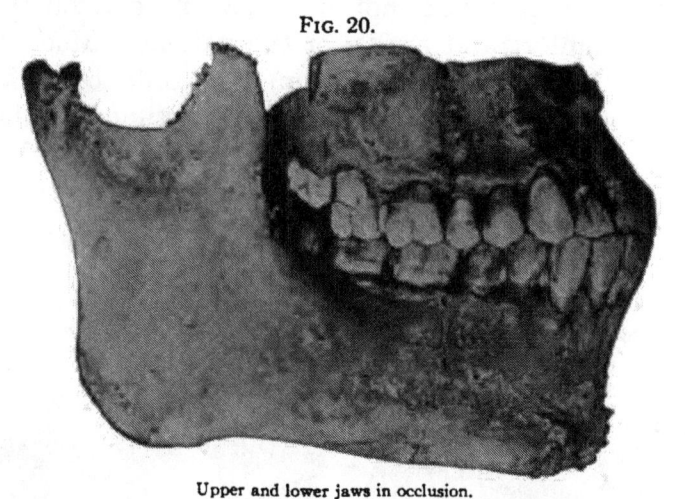

FIG. 20.

Upper and lower jaws in occlusion.

teeth should be correct, but they are not to be found so in the skull from which this illustration was taken. The incisors are in occlusion, edge to edge, instead of the upper one overlapping the lower one. A large amount of tooth tissue was shown in the upper jaw, and a large quantity in proportion in the lower jaw. In order to have had proper occlusion it would have been necessary to have lost tooth tissue laterally, in the lower jaw. If this be granted, then the question arises, when should it have been lost, and what tooth or teeth should have been extracted?

CHARACTERISTIC FEATURES OF CAUCASIAN AND NEGRO SKULLS

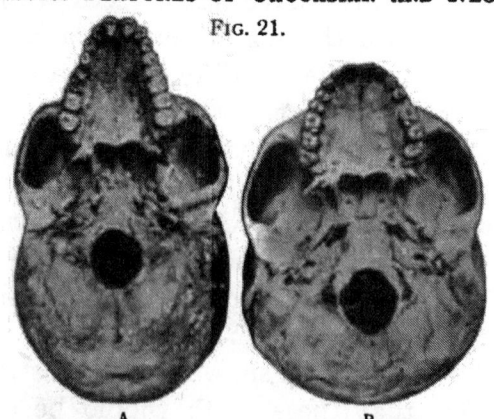

FIG. 21.

A   B
View of the under surfaces of skulls, showing difference between Fan Tribe West African skull and the Caucasian.

"Fig. 21 is made from the under surface of two skulls. The one on the left is that of a Fan Tribe West African, the other is from a Caucasian. They differ

CHAPTER X. TYPICAL AND ATYPICAL OCCLUSION OF THE TEETH

greatly in the shape of the roof of the mouth and the line of the occluding surfaces of the teeth. For these types of skulls they are normal in the arrangement of the teeth, with the exception of those lost by decay. The line of the occluding surfaces of the white skull is too nearly circular, however, to be termed typical. The special difference in these skulls is this: In the negro, if the outer line of the zygomatic arch be carried around until it intersects the teeth, that line will be near the anterior surface of the second molars; while in the other skull the line would be in front of the first molar, showing that the teeth are carried forward in the negro skull the width of a molar tooth.

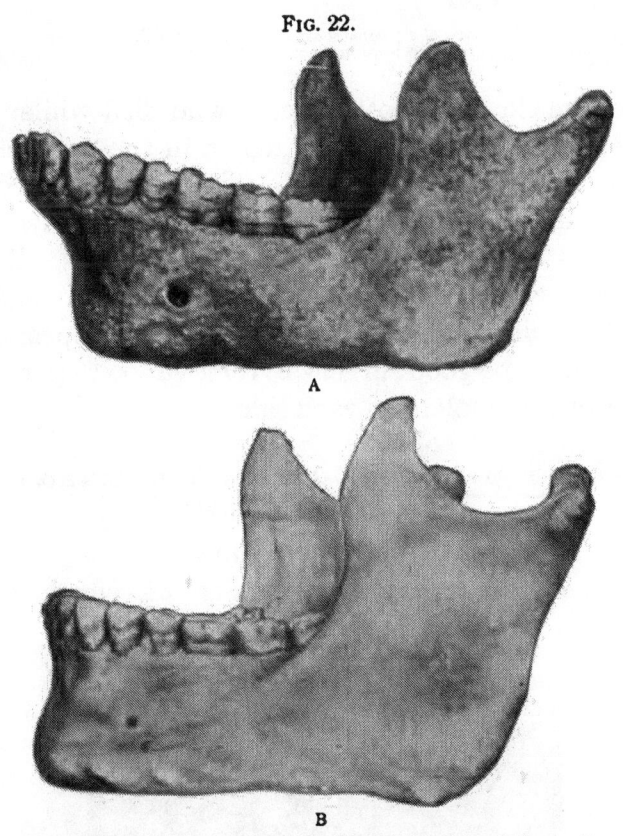

FIG. 22.

Two mandibles — A, from a Fan Tribe West African negro; B, from a Caucasian, showing difference in position of teeth relative to the ramus, mental foramen, and symphysis menti.

"Fig. 22 is made from two mandibles. The upper one is from the same Fan Tribe negro as shown in Fig. 21; the lower one is from another Caucasian skull. If the position of the third molar of the negro jaw be examined, it will be seen that there is room for another molar back of the third, while in the mandible of the white skull the third molar is far back, leaving no room for another tooth. In the negro jaw the mental foramen will be found below the first molar, while in the white jaw it is on a line drawn downward from between the bicuspids, showing again that in the negro skull the teeth are carried forward about the width of a molar tooth.

76   PART III. BASIC PRINCIPLES OF PRACTICE

FIG. 23.

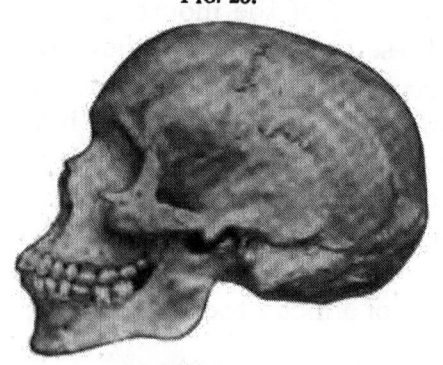

Side view of a prognathous negro skull with eighteen
teeth in the upper jaw.

"Fig. 23 is from the skull of another negro who died while in the Philadelphia Hospital. The prognathism is not so marked as in the one belonging to the Fan Tribe West African. The mental foramen in this case is situated on a line between the second bicuspid and the first molar. In the upper jaw there are eighteen teeth, the two most distal being rudimentary fourth molars. Barring these fourth molars, all the other teeth are in good occlusion. If this condition of the teeth were exhibited in the white race, which would give the appearance of that shown in the next figure, it would be good surgery to remove the upper and lower bicuspids or the upper and lower first molars on each side.

PROGNATHOUS APPEARANCE CAUSED BY HYPERTROPHIED GUMS AND ALVEOLAR PROCESSES

"Not having an anatomical specimen showing this kind of prognathism, your essayist has taken the liberty to show Fig. 24, which was made from the

FIG. 24.

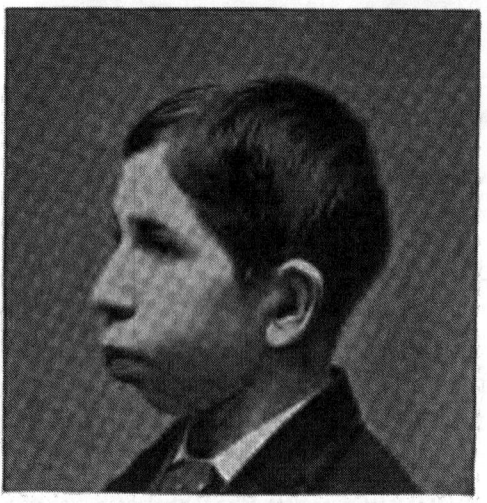

From photograph of a lad suffering from hypertrophy of the
gums and alveolar process.

CHAPTER X. TYPICAL AND ATYPICAL OCCLUSION OF THE TEETH 77

photograph of a boy about fifteen years old. When this picture was shown to one of our leading orthodontists, he declared it was that of a degenerate. The boy had a most marked hypertrophied condition of the gums and alveolar process of both jaws, which protruded forward. It was thought advisable to remove the alveolar process along with the teeth and gums, which gave him the appearance shown in the next picture.

FIG. 25.

FIG. 26.

From photograph taken three weeks after removal of the pathological tissue.

From photograph taken five years after operation upon the person represented in Fig. 24.

"Fig. 25 was taken three weeks after the operation. The prognathism is lost, leaving somewhat sunken cheeks.

"Five years afterward he had a picture taken shown in Fig. 26. No one would claim that this picture was that of a degenerate.

"These last three illustrations have been exhibited in order to justify the removal of gum, tooth, and alveolar tissue, or even bone, to correct such deformities, even if artificial teeth have to be worn afterward."

CHAPTER XI

DENTO-FACIAL PRINCIPLES OF OCCLUSION WITH REFERENCE TO PRACTICE

As a number of prominent orthodontists are still following the teaching that a normal occlusion should be regarded as the indispensable standard of attainment in the correction of all cases of malocclusion, it is important that students, while being taught to appreciate its full value should also be prevented from overestimating its limitations as a basic principle in diagnosis and treatment.

Occlusal Relations.—In the correction of all malocclusions of the teeth with a view to their future permanency of retention, occlusion and dento-facial relations are the most important factors for consideration in diagnosis and treatment.

In every case where the masticating teeth have established a fixed occluding position with cusps that interlock or interdigitate, whether or not it be typically normal in its relations, any change of that position necessary for the accomplishment of correction *should place them in a new occlusal adjustment of self-fixation;* otherwise, nature either in her forceful efforts to perfect the function of mastication, or in response to the law of heredity, will mar or wholly destroy the perfect results of treatment, even though they be artificially retained for years.

In cases where one or more teeth of either jaw are crowded out of arch alignment, or are malturned and overlapping, if held in that malposition by the fixed occlusion of other teeth, any movement to accommodate them that is destined to affect the relative positions of the premolars or molars will usually require a concomitant movement of the occluding teeth of the opposing jaw.

In a large proportion of malocclusions among youths whose inherited disto-mesial relations of the buccal teeth were normal, there will be found no marked abnormal dento-facial disharmony; and even those facial imperfections that are caused by a malrelation of the teeth in occlusion, will frequently disappear upon proper corrective treatment after being followed by the harmonizing influences of growth. Therefore, in all of these cases, however jumbled the irregularity, the rule should be **imperative** that we strive to produce a **typically normal occlusion.**

This does not mean that the principal and only object in practice in *all* cases is to attain to the production of a **normal occlusion** at the expense of producing or retaining a **facial deformity;** and especially if by the extraction of the first or second premolars we can place the operation within sure and easy possibilities of correcting the facial deformity and leave the patient with a good masticating occlusion—often so perfect that only an expert is able to discover that teeth are missing. Nor does it mean that the correction of the facial deformity or imperfection should be accomplished, if possible, at the expense of a **masticating occlusion** whose cusps interdigitate. One is quite as important as the other. The facial outlines should always be considered, because they frequently **mark the course** that should be pursued in a correction of the dental irregularity, with the concomitant correction of the facial outlines, as they indicate whether we should move the upper or the lower teeth, or both, and also the relative amount of movement demanded. They indicate also, whether it will be inadvisable to attempt correction without extraction. The failure to extract teeth when demanded, is quite as much malpractice as the extraction of teeth when not demanded.

In the contemplation of obtaining room for the correction of malposed teeth, or for the freer eruption of the permanent teeth of youths by the expansion of immature arches, or by the extraction of temporary or permanent teeth, the harmonizing influences of growth with the natural enlargement of the alveolar arches should never be lost sight of. If dentists would give more thought to this subject, and to the possibilities of judiciously enlarging the arches in keeping with the present and future development of other parts, there would not be that ruthless and uncalled-for interference and that wholesale malpractice of extraction which has so often disgraced the science of dentistry in former years.

With modern methods and principles of applying force to the teeth, the dental arches can always be sufficiently enlarged to place all the teeth in alignment and in normal occlusion if demanded, however extensively malposed. Therefore, the question of extraction should never arise as a means toward making an operation easier or possible in the correction of any *dental* irregularity. Nor should it ever arise, except in cases of decided dento-facial protrusion which cannot be corrected by the most skillful methods toward placing the dentures in normal occlusion. It is not always possible to decide this question at the beginning of an operation, especially for young patients whose mature growth development of other features will frequently harmonize the facial relations. Therefore, if the facial outlines show no very marked protrusion of one denture, or both, the safer way, at times of uncertainty like this, would be to place the teeth in normal occlusion subject to a future operation involving extraction, if found to be demanded for the correction of a resultant facial deformity. Read the history and study the illustrations of Fig. 164, Chapter XXIX.

Every dentist, and especially those who essay the regulation of teeth, whether he limits his practice to this specialty, or not, should consider it imperative to his professional education to fully understand the mechanical, anatomical, and physiological principles of normal occlusion of the teeth. In fact a full appreciation of normal occlusion and all that is implied by that term, as a standard of perfection to imitate or strive for, has always been one of the greatest influences toward the progress and development of the science of dentistry and its branch, orthodontia. One has but to carefully peruse the first works of note upon orthodontia —"Oral Deformities," by Dr. Norman Kingsley, published in 1880, and "Irregularities of The Teeth," by Dr. J. N. Farrar, published in 1888—to become convinced that the importance of restoring teeth to a normal occlusion in orthodontia was fully appreciated, and one of the principal factors of treatment, by some of the leading minds then, as now. And since that time in all the teaching and practice of prominent orthodontists it has been regarded as a **self-evident principle** in the regulation and retention of teeth.

Importance of Dr. Angle's Teaching.—While it is probably a fact that the true anatomic relations of normal dental occlusion have long been well understood by dentists, and the importance of striving for its attainment in the correction of irregularities of the teeth has been dwelt upon by numberless writers and published by dental journals and textbooks, it has nevertheless remained for Dr. Edward H. Angle in his very admirable work entitled "Malocclusion of the Teeth," to present this phase of the subject in so forcible a manner that the dental profession—or at least that part of it who essay the regulation of teeth—have awakened to a fuller appreciation of its importance as a guide to correction and as a means to permanency of retention.

He places the occlusal relations of the first permanent molars as the real guide-posts in diagnosis for determining the general relations of occlusion. This should meet with the hearty approbation of all experienced orthodontists. **First:** Because the occlusal relations of the first permanent molars are usually in distinct evidence when other teeth which might be used as guides have not erupted, or are in decided malalignment. **Second:** The first permanent molars are the true bases of their respective dental arches, because the relative antero-posterior positions of other teeth are largely influenced by the relative positions which these teeth assume in the jaws. **Third:** With a very large proportion of the human family—and especially those to whom abnormal disturbances in secondary dentition have not occurred—the natural occlusion of the teeth is normal, while their sizes and relative positions in the White Race are that which we have come to recognize as harmonious with the physiognomies in which they are placed, so that we have always before us a fairly perfect type of normal occlusion and esthetic dento-facial relations. **Fourth:** It being true that the relative mesio-distal positions of the buccal teeth are dependent upon those of the first permanent molars, in connection with the fact that the first permanent molars are often subjected to early influences—such as the premature loss of deciduous teeth, etc.—which causes them to shift their otherwise normal positions in the arch, we are led at once to the importance of preserving or establishing **early,** the normality of these natural piers to the future arches, in order that normal occlusion, natural esthetic facial relations, and permanency of retention, be attained in correction of malocclusions.

But it should be remembered that this is but **one** of the basic principles in orthodontia, and that it refers **only** to that important numerous class of irregularities in which the natural or inherited disto-mesial relation of the buccal teeth are—or were intended to be in the individual—in harmony with all dependent physical structures, and that correction with the proper maintenance or attainment of a normal occlusion without the loss of permanent teeth is indispensable to normal dento-facial relations.

This covers so large a class of irregularities that are met with in practice, and for which the proper correction of occlusion without extraction is the only true treatment, that many in following its teachings with happy results have unfortunately been led to believe in its unlimited applicability.

One of the greatest errors in this teaching is that whatever the irregularity or facial deformity, the main and indispensable object in the practice of orthodontia is to place the dentures in normal occlusion. Today a very large proportion of orthodontists who are striving for the highest attainments in their specialty, have learned by experience the dangers of this arbitrary and autocratic teaching and are endeavoring to treat their patients according to facial as well as occlusal demands. The only danger in this return swing of the pendulum of progress is that it will too often be permitted to swing beyond the true equilibrium of rational practice by those who will not take the time to acquire the scientific principles of diagnosis, and thus again lead to the inexcusable extraction of teeth whose presence in the arches are indispensable to the attainment of perfect results.

The perfect type of **normal occlusion** is beautifully illustrated in Dr. Cryer's collection of skulls, shown in Chapter X. Attention is especially called to that shown in Fig. 20, because it is one which has been frequently selected to represent **a normal occlusion.** It is probably from a *negro skull;* and while looking at it, one can readily see—in the mind's eye—the characteristic protruding lips and receding chin effect. Should the same character of occlusion, with protruding relations of the teeth to the jaws, occur in an Anglo-Saxon type—*as it certainly does* at times, even to a greater extent—it would produce a facial effect that could not be diagnosed otherwise than a bimaxillary protrusion, demanding extraction.

In the Dental Cosmos for February, 1905, Dr. Cryer, in speaking of this same specimen, says: "It is certainly normal for that particular negro, but it would be just as reasonable to give the occlusion of a horse or a dog and state they are normal. The point is this, modern orthodontists show upon the screen a profile portrait of an Apollo Belvedere, as an illustration of manly beauty, and then follow it with Fig. 20—the skull of a prognathous negro—as an illustration of normal occlusion."

In regard to this phase of the subject, glance again at the two faces before and after treatment reported in Dr. Cryer's chapter, and shown here under Fig. 27. The beginning face on the left had all the characteristics of an excessive bimaxillary protrusion. The dentures, as Dr. Cryer has since stated to the author, were in normal occlusion. This case was corrected, as shown in the face on the right, by the surgical removal of the front teeth and alveolar processes, and the insertion of artificial dentures to restore the facial outlines. The face on the left presents the expression of a degenerate, despite *a normal occlusion of the teeth*, while that on the right is now characterized by the highest type of intellectuality. We can well imagine that the lower jaw of this patient, if dissected at the beginning of the operation, would look like Fig. 22, Chapter X, and that the upper denture would be similarly protruded.

In pursuance of this phase of the subject, turn again to the text matter and illustrations of Bimaxillary Protrusions, Division 2, Class I, Chapter XXIX, and then ask yourself: if the hackneyed and oft-repeated teaching is of any scientific value, which avers in various forms that "a full complement of teeth is necessary

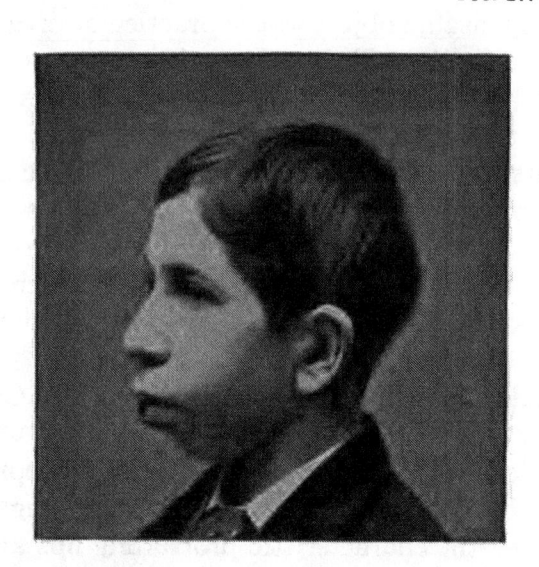

FIG. 27.

to establish the most pleasing harmony of the facial outline;" or that "normal occlusion is incompatible with any degree of irregularity;" or that "normal occlusion and normal facial outlines are inseparable." *

Throughout this work the author has endeavored to teach that decided disharmony of facial outlines frequently exists with the general disto-mesial relations of the dentures in normal occlusion. This can be verified to the satisfaction of any inquiring mind by an observation of the people to be found everywhere about us. The teeth may not be irregular in their relations to **each other;** but what is malocclusion broadly and truly speaking, if it is not malposition of the teeth in relation to the facially esthetic, as well as the anatomic, and expressed by a dental marring or deforming of that perfect type which, from the birth of classic art, has appealed to the esthetic senses?

In the author's opinion, the statement is irrefragable that all of that large class of cases whose teeth are in **normal occlusion,** but with overlying facial contours, protruded or retruded, to a deforming extent, should be regarded as **malocclusions, demanding correction,** according to our present nomenclature, if the science of Dental Orthopedia means anything beyond the mere correction of irregularities of the teeth for mastication alone.

*Angle and Pullen, International Dental Journal, October, 1903, and Items of Interest, July, 1904.

CHAPTER XII

THE QUESTION OF EXTRACTION IN ITS RELATION TO CAUSES, DIAGNOSIS, AND TREATMENT

Injudicious, and judicious or rational extraction of teeth, as a preliminary step to orthodontic operations depends entirely upon causes and dento-facial diagnosis. Therefore, the discussion of this branch of dental orthopedia naturally follows that of principles of etiology, and being interwoven with that most important of all branches, diagnosis, it will serve to lay a foundation for the practical treatment of all orthodontic cases in which the question of extraction of permanent teeth should arise. Moreover, this chapter and a principal part of the teaching throughout this work, is intended to prevent uncalled-for and needless extraction of teeth quite as much as it is to teach and fully define those characters which at times demand extraction.

In a paper read before the National Dental Association of the United States, in 1911, the author showed from the statistics of his own practice that in all the cases which presented for treatment, there was only about one case in twelve to fifteen in which the question of extraction should ever arise. Inasmuch as there are so comparatively few cases which do demand extraction, and for which it is quite as much malpractice to avoid extraction as it would be to extract teeth when not demanded, it is doubly important for us to know exactly the character of those cases, and the kind of diagnosis by which they are determined.

RULES OF EXTRACTION

If the author were to lay down rules relative to the extraction of teeth, he would say: (1) Never extract teeth for the purpose of making the operation of correction easier, for whatever the malocclusion, the teeth can always—or with very few exceptions—be placed in arch alignment and in normal occlusion, and in a very large majority of all cases, they are needed in the arches, not only to perfect occlusion, but to aid in beautifying the facial outlines. Therefore, so far as the relations of the teeth to each other are concerned, no *dental* malposition should be regarded as a basis for extraction.

(2) Teeth should never be extracted in orthodontia, except in cases of excessive protrusion, producing decided facial deformities, or at least marked dento-facial imperfections—and not even then, especially in young children, unless there is every indication of an *inherent* protrusion that will ultimately mar the beauty of the face for life. In nearly all locally caused malocclusions in immature arches, the final development of the jaws and general growth enlargement of the features

demand all of the teeth and their sustaining alveolar arches to harmonize the facial relations. Therefore, in every case in which dento-facial protrusions can be corrected without extraction, we should strive to produce a normal occlusion, not only for the sake of its more perfect masticating character, but because of its normal developing influences upon associate bones.

In former days when the science of orthodontia was in its infancy, and the wonderful yielding and responsive property of the alveolar processes and surrounding tissues was not generally known, dentists indulged quite freely in the extraction of teeth in all cases of pronounced malalignments, and in disto-mesial malocclusions, with little thought of the true possibilities of treatment, or the demands which are now determined by dento-facial diagnosis. Unfortunately, this practice prevailed to a considerable extent until Dr. Edward H. Angle proclaimed to the world that no teeth should *ever* be extracted in the correction of malocclusion.

In this remarkable paper read before the New York State Dental Society in 1903, he said: " Extraction is wrong. The full complement of teeth is necessary to the best results, and each tooth should be made to assume its correct relations with its fellows. I shall try to impress you" he said "from the orthodontist's standpoint with the full value of each individual tooth and with the **absolute necessity** of preserving the full complement of teeth or its equivalent in **every case.** I shall try to bring conclusive evidence that the sacrifice of teeth for either the intended prevention or correction of malocclusion is not only wrong practice and fallacious teaching, but most baneful in its results. I shall further try to show that the full complement of teeth is necessary to establish the most pleasing harmony of the facial lines."

No one can say that a radical statement of this kind from a man of such eminence, did not do more good in stopping the general ruthless extraction of teeth than any half-way measures, even though untrue and not according to the rational teaching which is practiced by advanced orthodontists of today.

Injudicious Extraction of Permanent Teeth

One of the most frequent errors in the extraction of teeth for the correction of malocclusion has arisen in that most common of all irregularities, maleruption of the upper cuspids. Without regard to the demands of facial diagnosis, dentists seeing those large cuspids protruding through the gums above their proper places and often with no room for their eruption between the laterals and first premolars, have imagined that their correction is impossible without extraction. Fig. 28 is a fair sample of many cases. It will be seen upon the left side of the beginning dental models, that the space for the cuspid was completely closed; and notwithstanding the very crowded condition of the dental arch, it was evident at the start, from the undeveloped facial area, that the adult physiognomy would require all of the teeth in the arches for the development of perfect dento-facial outlines and beauty.

CHAPTER XII. THE QUESTION OF EXTRACTION

This is well shown in the photo-print of the face, which was made from a photograph of this patient taken several years after treatment. One who would mar the beauty of such a face by extracting teeth to aid in the operation for correction, would not deserve the title of orthodontist.

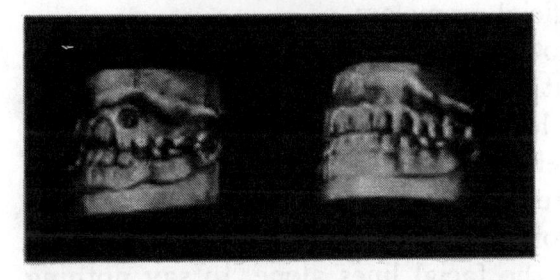

FIG. 28.

The author once listened to a paper by a dentist who claimed to be an authority upon the subject of regulating teeth, and who after throwing upon the screen pictures made from dental models of this character of malocclusion, said in effect:

"These cases are usually corrected by extracting the first premolars, but sometimes we are obliged to extract the cuspids;" this really tells the whole story. There certainly are many cases of maleruption of the cuspids in which the extraction of the premolars is demanded, as explained under the head of judicious extraction, but *never* the extraction of cuspids, for the reason that the upper cuspids, more than any other teeth, serve to give character and esthetic contour to the features, because their large long roots form and sustain the canine eminence of the maxillae, and this in turn prevents an unesthetic retrusion of the facial lines over the area which supports the wings of the nose, and naso-labial lines. This is well illustrated under Practical Treatment of Class I. Youths whose permanent upper cuspids have been extracted, or are lingually impacted, have a mature expression far in advance of their years, because as people grow older, the naso-labial lines deepen. This is one of the common facial characteristics of advancing years, and one which is greatly increased with edentulous mouths. One of the greatest difficulties in attempts to restore the original facial expression with artificial dentures, is the impossibility of extending the rim of the plate high enough to restore the normal contour of the canine eminences, which in consequence leaves a more or less deepened depression at the wings of the nose.

Some years ago a prominent Chicago dentist called at the office of the author and said: "Doctor, when you have cuspids that are erupting through the gums above, and with no spaces between the laterals and first premolars, you have to extract teeth to get them into the arch, do you not?" In reply, he was shown

PART III. BASIC PRINCIPLES OF PRACTICE

FIG. 29.

the plaster models of a number of cases which proved that however irregular the teeth, however bunched, malaligned, or malposed, they could always be placed in their respective places in the arches and in normal occlusion, and therefore, so far as the relations of the teeth to each other are concerned, **no dental malposition should be regarded as a basis for extraction.**

When these truths dawned upon his mind he said: "I believe I have made a very great error, doubly so, because it is in the family of some very dear friends of mine. Wishing to do the very best for their little daughter whose upper cuspids were erupting in that way, I extracted the first premolars, and now at about fifteen years of age, I find that all the upper front teeth are biting back of the lowers, with quite a depression of the upper lip, which gives her the appearance of a protruding lower jaw."

Fig. 29 shows on the left the position of her teeth when she was brought to the author; and, on the right, is shown the position of her teeth after correction, by a bodily labial movement of the upper front teeth, opening spaces for the insertion of artificial premolars.

FIG. 30.

Another case similar to the above, sent to the author from Ohio, is shown in Fig. 30. In the letter of introduction from the dentist who referred the case, he said: "I have extracted the first premolars knowing that you would find it necessary." Anyone can see by the facial lines alone, to say nothing of the fact that the upper front teeth close back of the lowers, that it was the very height of orthodontic malpractice to extract teeth from the upper arch. The only excuse for extracting sound permanent teeth—an axiom which cannot be too often repeated—is the impossibility of otherwise correcting the malocclusion without leaving a facial protrusion. To remove one or more teeth from immature arches for the purpose of more easily correcting an irregularity that has arisen wholly from local causes, will inevitably produce its effect. And the effect upon arches that would otherwise be ultimately correct in size and occlusion is to abnormally contract them and to force the occluding teeth of the opposing jaw into malalignments, besides producing more or less imperfections in esthetic facial contours. And under certain circumstances as instanced by the two cases illustrated, it may result in an actual facial deformity, and, too, when the operation is performed by men who are supposed to know better.

Besides the thousands of occlusal malrelations that have been caused by the needless and even criminal extraction of permanent teeth, there are numberless dento-facial imperfections and deformities that have gone through life from this cause alone. It has frequently been a matter of great surprise to see the results of poor judgment shown by dentists, even of advanced standing, in extracting deciduous and permanent teeth; and when one considers the thousands of young dentists of less experience who are let loose upon trusting communities, it is not strange that there arise so many examples of criminal malpractice along this line, especially in the extraction of permanent teeth from crowded arches in which all the teeth are necessary to perfect occlusion and dento-facial relations. Many seem to be wholly ignorant of the quality, possibilities of movement, and function of the alveolar process, which is always susceptible of any required degree of arch enlargement to accommodate the teeth, however crowded or malaligned.

Judicious or Rational Extraction of Permanent Teeth

While it is true that too much cannot be said in regard to the needless extraction of teeth, the principle of non-extraction of teeth, nevertheless, has its limitations from a true orthodontic standpoint. The question may well be asked: Do the untold evidences of this character of malpractice prove that extraction should never be resorted to under any condition? In other words, does this prove "that extraction is wrong and that the full complement of teeth or their equivalent is necessary to the best results *in every case?*" Most certainly not. It simply proves that the injudicious and needless extraction of teeth when not demanded for the correction of dento-facial protrusion should be condemned in the strongest possible terms. The collection and portrayal of disasters in railroad travel and in the use of anesthetics would be quite as legitimate to prove that humanity should desist from the employment of these benefits as that such evidences should be presented as frequently have been to prove that extraction is *never* demanded in the correction of dento-facial deformities.

It has been frequently asserted or implied that a **normal occlusion**—which means: "without the loss of a single tooth"—is the only occlusion which presents sufficient opportunity for healthful mastication of food and perfect retention of teeth in corrected positions. This is not true, because the ultimate masticating closure of many quite irregular dentures, and especially those cases of full malinterdigitation of buccal cusps supply every need for perfect mastication. And because the teeth have assumed that position through intrinsic local forces, their retention is assured, unless artificially changed. Therefore, this theory cannot be used as an argument for non-extraction any more truthfully than the statement that a normal occlusion is the only occlusion that is compatible with esthetic facial outlines. In fact, it will be found that an extensive disto-mesial shifting of the dentures with the intermaxillary force to produce the relations of a normal occlusion *is far more liable to result in non-retention* than are those cases where premolars have been extracted and the six front teeth retruded, with the original disto-mesial occlusion of masticating teeth undisturbed, or slightly shifted to correct lateral relations and the more perfect interdigitation of the cusps. Furthermore, when the first or second premolars are extracted, the spaces are perfectly closed, the interdigitation of the cusps of the back teeth is adjusted, mastication of food and permanency of retention are assured, while the relations of the dentures should be such that they give no appearance of missing teeth.

In Class I, the buccal teeth are disto-mesially normal in occlusion, and though presenting a great variety of irregularities from the simplest to the most complex, when they are corrected for youthful patients, and the dentures are placed in normal occlusion with proper arch width, usually the most perfect results possible are accomplished. But, if after such an operation it is found that they produce a facial protrusion, it must be a protrusion of both dentures, protruding the upper and lower lips. This, when characterized by a receding chin effect, may have all the appearances of a **typical bimaxillary protrusion.** If any teeth are extracted to correct this condition it must be from both upper and lower dentures, and if the protrusion is bilateral, as it is very liable to be, it would mean the extraction of right and left upper and right and left lower teeth.

Then the very grave question arises: Does the facial imperfection warrant the extraction of four sound teeth from youthful dentures which are now in perfect normal occlusion? If the protrusion is not very pronounced and cannot be traced to one or the other parent as a family type, and the patient is under 12 years of age, one should never think of extraction until he has seen what the developing forces of nature will accomplish. If at 14 or 15 years of age it has partially disappeared, there is very good reason to believe it will wholly disappear at 18.

It was shown in Chapter V, how through premature loss of the deciduous teeth, protrusions both unimaxillary and bimaxillary may arise. Again, it was shown under the last heading of that chapter that during the years of rapid secondary dentition there is nearly always a general protrusion of the lips and all that facial area supported by the large erupting teeth and alveolar processes, which is accepted by us with no anxiety because it is the common childhood facial characteristic. Moreover, the forces of heredity which characterize the framework of physiognomies, as in other parts of the body, are not often sufficiently pronounced before the beginning of adolescence, or of puberty, for us to determine definitely what the final facial characteristics will be. Therefore, it will be seen by these foundation principles of diagnosis that great caution and judgment should be exercised before attempting early capital orthodontic operations which later development may prove to be decidedly wrong.

On the other hand, if after correcting the alignment and occlusion of a **Class I case,** it is found at fourteen years of age, or older that the physiognomy bears all the characteristics of a developing pronounced bimaxillary protrusion, or if a new case presents with that facial characteristic determined by protruding lips and receding chin effect, it is then up to the patient or the parents to say whether they are willing to undergo the required operation for the purpose of beautifying the face—an operation that is not guesswork if properly performed, but one which is just as sure in its results as any other operation of dento-facial orthopedia.

In Chapter XXIX, under practical treatment of **Bimaxillary Malocclusion, Division 2, Class I,** there is described and illustrated under Fig. 164 a very interesting case which is quite apropos to the question of extraction. It shows how an endeavor was made to correct an apparently simple irregularity in a Class I case of a miss fourteen years of age, by placing the dentures in normal occlusion, which resulted in a prominence of the mouth, but one which it was hoped that adolescent growth would harmonize in the general development of the surrounding bones of the physiognomy. Instead of this, however, at nearly seventeen years of age, the unpleasant protrusion seemed more pronounced, if anything, than when the case was first corrected. This was doubtless due to the fact that the maturing development of the features had assumed the delicate type of the mother, and this brought out in stronger relief the labial disharmony, which is well shown by the facial cast which was made at that time. The four first premolars were then extracted, and this enabled a comparatively easy retruding movement of the twelve labial teeth, and resulted in a beautiful harmonizing effect of the entire dento-facial outlines, as shown by the final facial cast, and a photograph taken two years later.

Like all other cases that are properly treated in this way, the remaining teeth were in normal occlusal relations, affording an opportunity for the mastication of food fully equal to any normal occlusion.

In a **Class II case,** if after correcting it by shifting the dentures to a normal occlusion, it is found at fourteen or fifteen years of age that the lips are unpleasantly protruded, marring the facial outlines that would otherwise be perfect, it will be because the case originally *was not a lower retrusion*, but *an upper protrusion* which demanded the extraction of the first upper premolars. Dr. Cryer has said that he has seen a number of cases with protruding mouths right from the hands of orthodontists who doubtless believed it was wrong to extract in the correction of any case.

Should such a contingency arise in practice, with a desire or willingness on the part of the patient to have the protruded facial outlines corrected by a second operation, the following would be the proper treatment: If the protrusion is not excessive, extract the first upper premolars and then, with stationary anchorage on the upper buccal teeth, retrude the lower denture with the intermaxillary force to its original normal position. In connection with the movement—from rootwise extensions on the anchorages—retrude the six upper front teeth to close the spaces of the extracted premolars. If, however, the protrusion is quite decidedly pronounced, with a receding chin effect, extract the four first premolars. Proceed in these operations as fully described under "Practical Treatment of Bimaxillary Protrusions."

The large majority of the most advanced orthodontists today are practicing the judicious extraction of teeth according to the teaching which is outlined in this work. But unfortunately there are a number of prominent orthodontists who are still practicing the extreme autocratic teaching of Dr. Angle, with results no doubt, in many cases that should not satisfy anyone whose aim is the attainment of the highest plane in modern orthodontia.

As an illustration of this: A family of very moderate means consulted an Angle orthodontist of high reputation in regard to the correction of their son's teeth, who at that time was twelve years of age. The prominent feature of the case was a deforming labial maleruption of the upper cuspids, which was locally due to the premature extraction of the deciduous cuspids in a mouth which distinctly indicated an inherited upper protrusion, shown by the mesial malocclusion of the upper buccal teeth in connection with a normally posed chin and lower lip, and proven by a similar occlusion in one of the parents. The straining force of the upper lip had caused the incisors to drift back and shut the spaces for the normal eruption of the unusually large permanent cuspids. One of the complications of the case was the decayed and broken down condition of the right lower first molar in which the pulp had long since died, and had given trouble from abscessed condition.

The treatment outlined by the said orthodontist was to place the dentures in normal occlusion and restore the molar with a crown; this is the same principle of treatment that has been strictly followed in the past by the Angle school of orthodontia, and is unfortunately still followed by many who earnestly believe it to be the true principle in the correction of all malocclusions.

The case fell into the author's hands because of the—to them—prohibitive fee, which led the father to inquire if it could be corrected at the college. It is needless to say that the extraction of the two upper first premolars was ordered; this gave very little more room than necessary for the eruption and alignment of the cuspids. The diseased lower molar was also extracted, as no capable dentist in these days would attempt to restore it.

With the exception of appliances for the bodily mesial movement of the second molar to close the space of the extracted first molar, the case would have corrected itself if given time under ordinary circumstances. It was hastened with an upper apparatus having a resilient bow for the cuspid movements, and the intermaxillary force for adjusting the occlusion and as an aid in the mesial movement of the molar.

Fig. 31 shows the facial and dental models of the case at the beginning and when the operation was completed. Fig. 32 shows occlusal aspect of the dentures.

CHAPTER XII. THE QUESTION OF EXTRACTION

The whole subject of extraction of permanent teeth in the practice of dentofacial orthopedia resolves itself into the question of its importance to the patient. Is it important to correct facial imperfections and deformities caused by protruding

FIG. 31.

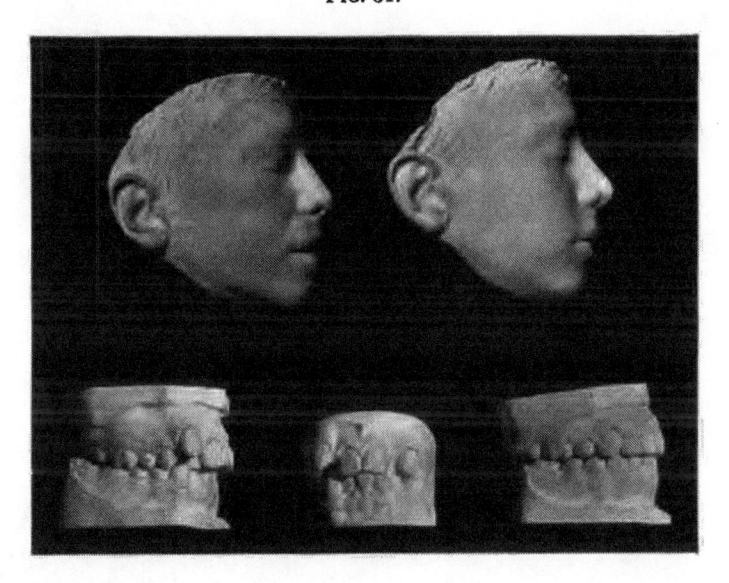

FIG. 32.

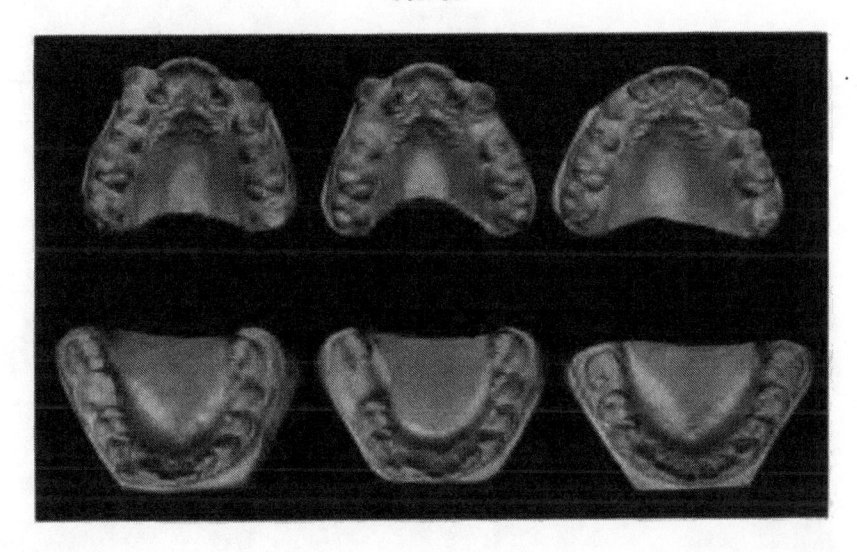

teeth which cannot be accomplished without extraction, and when by the sacrifice of certain teeth a most satisfactory result of the operation in this regard and also in permanency of retention is assured?

The subject is of so much importance in dento-facial orthopedia, it will be continued in other chapters in connection with allied principles and practice, so that the student will have an opportunity to study it from many viewpoints.

PART IV

Technic Principles of Practice

TECHNIC PRINCIPLES OF PRACTICE

CHAPTER XIII

PRINCIPLES OF MECHANICS IN THE MOVEMENT OF TEETH

In the contemplation of applying force to a tooth for its movement, every condition should be considered: (1) its situation in relation to the arch and adjoining teeth; (2) the number, probable length, shape, and inclination of its roots; (3) the probable yielding quality of its alveolar imbedment in relation to the required movement; (4) the possibility of attaching appliances to the crown which will permit the proper application of force; (5) and finally, the influences of occlusion, dento-facial relations, and the possibilities of retention.

A dental regulating apparatus—however simple or complex—is a *machine* for the application and transmission of power which is given to it by the operator in the form of potential energy for the movement and correction, primarily, of malposed teeth; and secondarily for the correction of all forms of malocclusion and dento-facial imperfections.

A machine is a contrivance, or device, or a combination of mechanical elements by means of which a force or forces may be **advantageously** applied. Every machine, however complicated, is reducible to five elementary forces, which have been named **"the mechanical powers,"** i. e., the **lever;** the **wheel** and **pulley;** the **screw;** the **inclined plane;** and the **wedge.** A little thought will show that the mechanical principle of the wheel and axle (see Fig. 47) is exactly that of a lever; and that the advantage derived from the inclined plane and wedge is the same as that of a screw. Therefore, the real elemental mechanical powers are the lever and the screw.

One of the most important factors of a regulating machine or apparatus is that obtained from the backward spring or elasticity of metal, rubber, silk, etc., by virtue of the quality of these substances to regain their former positions when their molecules are forced out of equilibrium. This resilient property enables the storing up of potential energy to be slowly liberated in the form of continuous force—a form of force which seems especially calculated to arouse bone-cell activities, where the real metamorphic work in the movement of teeth is carried on.

There is, however, a very erroneous impression prevailing in regard to the action of the so-called "positive forces of a screw," when applied for the movements of teeth, which grew out of Dr. Farrar's statement that it was in accord with the common physiologic functional requirement of "work and rest." With properly constructed appliances and properly conducted treatments, a nut is never turned more than to give a slight snug feeling, which passes away in a few moments. This is accomplished by giving two or three-quarter turns about every third day. *The real work in the regulation of teeth by this movement is not accomplished when the nuts are turned, but it occurs only during the long intervals of so-called "rest."*

The immediate action in screw force, is to move the roots slightly—bodily or otherwise—in the direction of the applied force, but the surrounding alveolar process is not moved at this time, because the root never comes into actual contact with its bony socket. The highly elastic and more or less thickened peridental membrane upon which the root impinges is forced out of equilibrium, and is thereby stored with the same kind of potential energy as occurs from the resilient powers of extraneous forces. When the force is transmitted through the medium of a bow, even though the bow is apparently quite rigid, it also stores potential force, and from both of these sources the force is slowly transmitted to the alveolar process where the real work of movement is carried on.

The intrinsic action of the spring cushion is exactly the same as the extrinsic action of any kind of the resilient forces; the only difference being that in one the intensity of the force gradually diminishes until it comes to rest, but if the treatment adjustments are timed and modified exactly in accord with the possibilities of work, it is as continuous as any of the continuous forces. In fact, whenever teeth are moved physiologically, by whatever means, it is always through a continuous pressure of the crowded peridental membrane upon the alveolar process, which causes it to slowly move out of the way, either through the property of resorption, or by a more or less bodily movement *en masse*, so that the immediate tissues which are necessary for the vitality of the teeth may return to equilibrium.

Kinds of Movement

The mechanical processes of correcting malposed teeth may be divided into five **Primary Movements** which, placed according to their degree of demands, are: **Inclination, Rotating, Bodily, Extrusive,** and **Intrusive.** The movements which are most commonly demanded are **Compound Movements** which are made up of two or more of the Primary Movements.

Inclination Movement.—Inclination Movement in Orthodontia is the most important, because it is by far the most common. It also presents a far greater variety of possibilities and demands in the application of force.

In nearly all orthopedic movements of teeth the apical ends of the roots do not move, at least not in the direction of the applied power, unless the apparatus is especially constructed for that purpose, as will be explained later under the head of Bodily Movement. Therefore, while nearly all movements are produced by forcing the occlusal end of the tooth along the arc of a circle whose pivotal point is near the apex of the root, it usually is eminently desirable that the movement be kept at a minimum of its inclination tendency, in order that the teeth when properly aligned will stand in normal pose.

CHAPTER XIII. PRINCIPLES OF MECHANICS

When a pull or push force is applied to the crown of a tooth at any point whose line of direction is at right angles to its central axis, the movement that takes place will be purely that of **Inclination,** providing that perfect freedom of movement is permitted at the point of applied power.

FIG. 33.

When force is applied in this way to the incisal zone "a," Fig. 33, of a tooth, far less power is required for its movement, with a greater tendency toward inclination, than if applied at the gingival zone "b" or at any point further root-wise. There will also be a greater tendency toward a movement of the apical zone in the opposite direction. By this example it will be seen that a tooth imbedded in a yielding medium which forms its socket, and subjected to force appliances attached to its crown for its movement, is practically a lever, responding approximately to the same laws which govern levers everywhere under like conditions of stress.

LEVERS

The ordinary mechanical lever is a **rigid bar, or inflexible rod, straight or bent, resting upon a prop called a fulcrum, and with power and weight disposed at some two other points.**

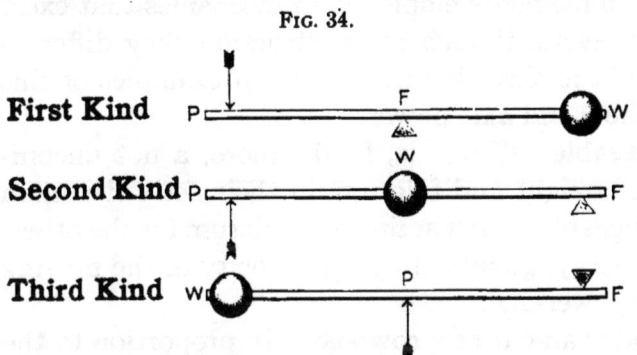

FIG. 34.

First Kind

Second Kind

Third Kind

The different ways in which the three factors, **power, weight,** and **fulcrum,** may be disposed give rise to three kinds of levers. See Fig. 34.

In mechanics the important factors of levers are **power** and **weight** and the **length** of the **power** and the **weight-arms.**

Given three of these factors, the other can always be determined by the following rule which applies to all true levers:

Law of Levers.—Power and weight are in the inverse ratio to their distance from the fulcrum.

The distance from the fulcrum at which power and weight are placed indicates the length of the power and weight-arms respectively. If we wish to know, for example, how much power will be required with a 6-foot lever of the **"first kind"** to sustain a weight of 25 pounds, with the **fulcrum** placed one foot from the **weight,** we have but to state the inverse ratio as follows: Power-arm (5) is to Weight-arm (1) as Weight (25) is to Power (X), or

$$5 : 1 :: 25 : X. \text{ Ans. 5 pounds.}$$

Again, how much weight will 5 pounds of **power** lift with a 6-foot lever of the **"second kind,"** with the **weight** placed one foot from the **fulcrum?**

98 PART IV. TECHNIC PRINCIPLES OF PRACTICE

Weight-arm (1) is to Power-arm (6) as Power (5) is to Weight (X), or
1 : 6 :: 5 : X.   Ans. 30 pounds.   Etc.

Levers in Relation to Laterally Moved Teeth.—Applied Mechanics in computing quantities deals only with **power** and **weight** or work, exemplified in the above general law of levers. Little is said of the force of reaction, or the force sustained at the **fulcrum**; whereas, with a **tooth** considered as a lever, the action at **fulcrum,** as will be shown, is quite as important for us to consider as the force which is exerted at the points known as **power** and **weight**; and, moreover, it is important to keep in mind approximately the relation which this force bears to the other factors. While it is never possible or necessary to calculate these quantities accurately, still, in order to arrive at the rough estimate desirable, a clear conception of the mathematical methods employed according to the laws of physics, especially those relating to levers, is very important. This can easily be approximated with levers when we remember another law of levers, i. e.: **Force exerted or sustained by the middle factor of a lever at equilibrium, be it fulcrum, weight, or power, is equal to the sum of the other two factors.** This law shows why a lever of the second kind is always chosen where great force is required at the expense of motion.

Again, in the typical lever the **fulcrum** is always considered a fixed point, but we are aware there are a number of implements employed in mechanics that exert force according to the principles of levers, though in construction they differ in certain particulars from every one of the three kinds. Common examples of this are all forms of the **pulley** and the **wheel and axle** power.

Fulcrum and Weight Interchangeable.—There is, furthermore, a not uncommon kind of lever in which points of weight and fulcrum, in their activities upon each other, are more or less interchangeable—each acting as a fulcrum for the other, with varying stability and relative energy, governed by the velocity of the moving power and the relative length of the power-arm.

An example of a lever of this kind is an oar of a rowboat. In proportion to the velocity of the moving power exerted by the rower, above the possibilities of the water to get out of the way of the blade, the oar becomes a lever of the **second kind** and the boat or work moves forward. But if the velocity of the moving power is not sufficient to overcome the inertia of the boat, the only work that the oar or lever can be said to accomplish is the movement of the yielding water in front of the blade, with fulcrum at the oarlock—or the action of a lever of the **first kind.** It can be seen in this common example of a lever of the second kind that the fulcrum, or so-called point of resistance, is a broad moving area of water. And it would be none the less a lever if its so-called point of work was also spread over a broadened area upon the lever, both areas of fulcrum and weight moving and reacting upon each other.

This combination of activities is exactly that which is exemplified in the alveolus of a tooth when force is applied in a lateral direction upon the crown. It is perfectly illustrated also in the following example of the post lever.

CHAPTER XIII. PRINCIPLES OF MECHANICS

Fig. 35.

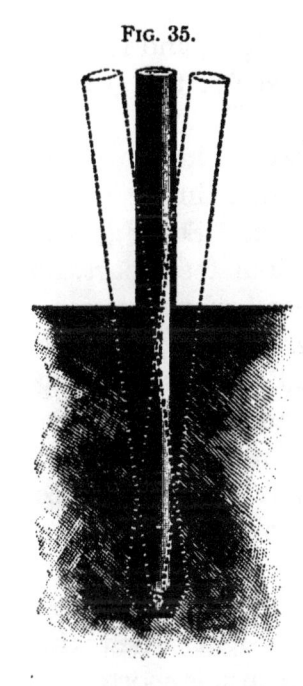

Post Lever.—If you should drive a four-foot post one-half its length into clayey soil of uniform quality, and then take hold of the top of the post and move it back and forth with a view of subsequently pulling it out of the ground, you would be working a lever which combines the qualities of the first and second kinds, or one like the oar in which the so-called areas of fulcrum and weight act as fulcrums to the other. See Fig. 35. After pulling the post out of the ground, if it were possible for you to make a transverse section of the soil for the purpose of examining the shape of the hole you had made, you would find it somewhat the shape of an hour-glass; the upper portion of the opening being about twice as large as the lower.*

As the post is forced in one direction the soil in front of it, along its upper sphere of action, will become impacted, or thrust to one side, the post thus acting as a lever of the second kind, with fulcrum at the lower end. At some point along its imbedded length, however, it will cease to move in the direction of the applied power, because the resistance of the soil in the upper area causes it, in turn, to act as a fulcrum, and the whole as a lever of the first kind, with work or movement at the lower end in the opposite direction.

The reason that the upper area of work is about twice that of the lower in the above example, and also the changed relations with **power** applied at different points, may be found in an examination of other examples which refer to the relation of the three factors of levers.

Levers of the First Kind.—The beam of balance scales is a lever of the first kind. The support or central standard is the fulcrum, with points of power and weight at the end attachments for the pans. See Fig. 36. It can now be seen at once that when the beam or lever is at equilibrium the fulcrum sustains the sum of power and weight, and this would hold true of any lever of the first kind at whatever intermediate point between power and weight the fulcrum is placed. Therefore, when the fulcrum is exactly in the middle of the lever of the first kind, at equilibrium,

Fig. 36.

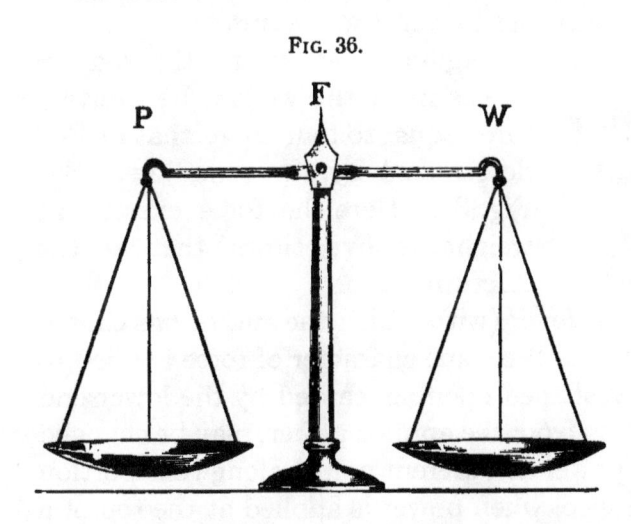

---
*In mathematical exactness, a post moved in this way, with its imbedded portion completely surrounded with a homogeneous resisting medium, the depth of the upper V-shaped opening would be somewhat less than two-thirds the entire depth of the hole.

it receives twice as much stress as that exerted at the point of weight; and for this same reason the post lever moves through the soil at the surface of the ground about twice as far as at the lower end in the opposite direction.

Levers of the Second Kind.—An example of a lever of the second kind may be a rod or a pole supporting a weight carried by two men. See Fig. 37. If the points are four feet apart, at which the two men—whom we may call P and F—grasp the pole, and the weight is a pail of water weighing thirty pounds swung in the center of the pole, each man would exert a force equal to fifteen pounds. In other words, the force exerted at W, exactly in the middle of a lever at equilibrium, would be twice that at the fulcrum. Here, again, we have the same result as shown by the action of a lever of the first kind.

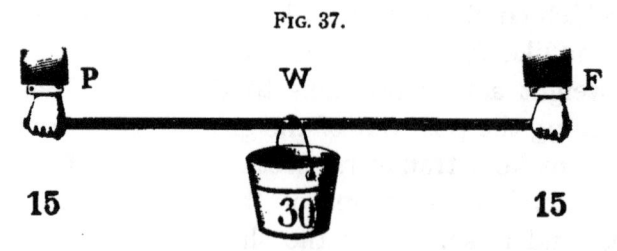

Now, if you please, note the change in the relative magnitude of force exerted at fulcrum and weight when the length of the power-arm is shortened. See Fig. 38. If P grasps the rod one foot from the pail, we have a three-foot lever with P exerting twice as much force as F, which may be proven by the law of levers, i. e., "power and weight are in the inverse ratio to their distance from the fulcrum."

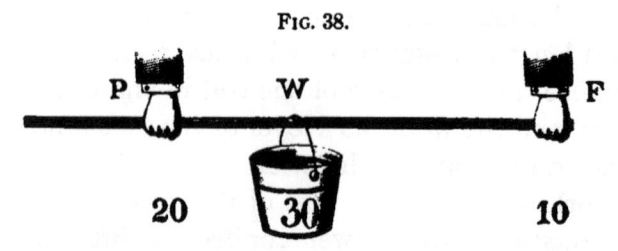

Power-arm of the above lever (3 feet) is to W-arm (2 feet) as weight (30 pounds) is to P, or 20 pounds; which leaves 10 pounds to be sustained by F. Therefore, the force exerted at weight in this lever is three times that at the fulcrum.

Again, if P grasps the rod six inches from the weight, he exerts a force equal to four times that of F—determined by the same law. See Fig. 39. Here the force exerted at weight is five times that at the fulcrum.

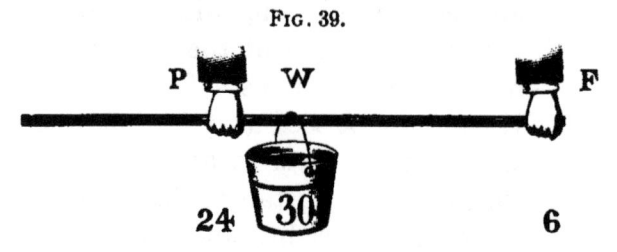

When we apply these rules to our post lever (with which the author has chosen to illustrate, on a general scale, the action of the same character of force applied to a tooth), we can see that the inverted V-shaped opening, caused by the lower end of the post moving in the opposite direction from the applied power, may be changed quite decidedly in area by applying the power at different points along that portion of the post above the surface. For instance, when power is applied at the top of a four-foot post imbedded one-half its length in the ground, the movement at the lower end in the opposite direction will be about one-half that at the surface of the ground in the direction of the power. When power is applied one foot from the ground, or at a point one-half the length of the exposed end, the movement at the lower end will be about one-third that at the surface, and when applied six inches from the ground (or in a tooth lever, as near to the alveolar margin as the gum will permit) the movement at the lower end will be about one-fifth that at the surface.

Teeth as Levers.—While teeth differ in shape from each other and from the post lever which has been described, and while their alveolar surroundings do not present a uniformity of resistance to their movement, and therefore while we cannot calculate force and motion with mathematical accuracy, the fact that they are imbedded one-half their length in a yielding substance and subject to the frequent application of force for the correction of irregularities, the only way we can approach an exact science in the application of power for their movement is to consider them as levers propelled by a machine doing work on the tissues in which they are imbedded.

In the process of moving a tooth by inclination—in a lingual direction, for instance—there are two principal spheres of resistance in the socket, i. e., one over that portion of the wall that is pressed upon by the tendency of the root to move in the direction of the applied force "c," Fig. 40, and the other upon the opposite wall at the apical area, that is pressed upon by the tendency of that portion of the root to move in the opposite direction "d." Within the boundaries of these two spheres of action, the force exerted upon the resisting surfaces gradually diminishes as they approach each other until a certain zone, or pivotal point "e," is reached, upon which it may be said no force is exerted in either direction, and consequently no movement occurs toward or from the direction of the applied power. By far the greater portion of the force is expended at the gingival and apical boundaries of these two spheres, which therefore may be considered as the true points of Fulcrum and Weight, when the tooth is a lever of the first and second kinds.

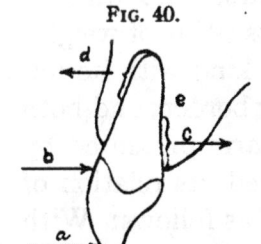

Fig. 40.

Tooth Levers of the Second Kind.—With the application of inclination force at any point upon the crown, the apical area of the alveolus is the natural fulcrum or immovable point, and the gingival area that of weight or movement. A tooth is, therefore, naturally a lever of the **second kind.** One of the reasons for this is due to the greater relative stability of the apical walls of the sockets, especially of long roots which penetrate the real bone. But the principal reason which applies to all conditions, and is determined by the law of levers is: with force applied laterally at a single point upon the crown, only one-half to one-fifth the amount of power can be exerted in this way at the apical area as compared to that of the cervical.

First Kind.—When retruding force is applied at the incisal zone—"a," Fig. 40—of a central incisor, about one-half as much power is exerted in the opposite direction upon the alveolus at the apical sphere of its influence "d" as at the cervical, "c," and if applied at the gingival zone of the crown, the force in the opposite direction at "d" is greatly decreased. Consequently, the apical end is naturally the fulcrum or immovable point, and the tooth a lever of the **first kind.**

On the other hand, in proportion to the resistance at the alveolar border "c," this point also becomes a fulcrum with tendency to move the apical end of the root in the opposite direction. The said spheres of action, therefore—apical and cervical—of a tooth lever under the influence of inclination force applied to the crown are both fulcrums, reacting upon each other for the production of weight, work, or movement, proportionate to the conditions.

Relations of Power, Stress, and Movement

The relative degree of force exerted at these spheres of action is largely governed by the position upon the crown or root at which power is applied; while the actual movement that takes place is further governed by the relative stability of the resisting spheres, form and number of the roots, etc.

If a tooth (say a central incisor) were a true lever of the first kind with its point of immovable fulcrum at the border of the alveolus, and its point of weight, work, or movement at the apex, or again, a lever of the second kind with its immovable fulcrum at the apex, and point of weight at the alveolar border; and both with the same possibilities of changing the length of the power-arm presented by the different points upon the crown at which force can be applied, its relation of applied forces could be determined with mathematical precision, as follows: With power applied at the incisal zone, the amount of force exerted at the apex in the opposite direction, in either case, would be exactly one-half that at the alveolar border, providing that the latter was equally distant from the other two factors, or exactly in the center of the lever; and with power applied at the gingival border of the crown, or upon the so-called power-arm at one-fourth the same distance from the central factor of the lever, the force exerted at the apex would be exactly one-fifth that at the alveolar border; as proven by the examples of the pail and lever of the second kind.

When applied to inclination movement, this law of levers teaches us why we obtain a more ready response to force that is applied at or near the occlusal borders; but with a far greater tendency toward tipping or abnormal inclination of the crown than if applied at or above the gingival margins. To illustrate this, note the different movements that would probably take place in a central incisor by applying force at different points and directions upon the crown, as follows:

With retruding power applied at "a," Fig. 40, the relative amount of force exerted at "c" compared to that at "d" would be as two to one. But if the usual stability of the cortical surface of the process obtains at "c," quite as much movement might occur at "d" in the opposite direction; and in either event a minimum amount of power would produce inclination movement. This example fairly represents the activities of a lever of the first kind.

CHAPTER XIII. PRINCIPLES OF MECHANICS

With protruding power applied in the opposite direction, at "f," Fig. 41, the relative stability of the resisting spheres would be reversed, and, according to the law, as the force exerted at "g" (or "c") would be about twice that at "h" (or "d") with the present example the apical sphere of resistance "h" would be the real fulcrum, with almost if not quite the entire movement at "g," and the lever that of the **second kind.** In both these examples a minimum amount of power would produce inclination movement.

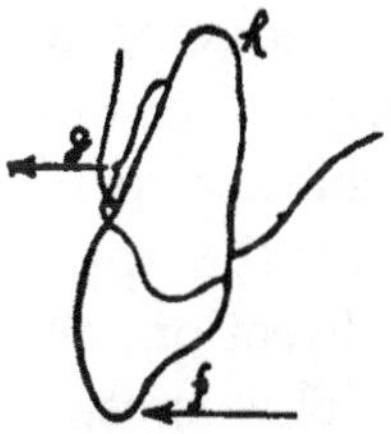

With retruding power applied at "b," Fig. 42, the relative amount of force exerted at "c" compared to that at "a" would be as five to one, and even greater in some instances, in proportion as the line of force approached the center of resistance. With this example there would be far less tendency toward inclination movement, because the main portion of the power would be distributed to the posterior wall of the alveolus. The fact also that it requires far more power at this point, and above, to move the tooth is of the greatest importance in the construction of stationary anchorages.

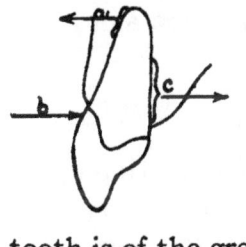

Approaching a Bodily Movement.—With power applied above the point, "b," at "i," Fig. 43, as could be accomplished by attaching to the crown a rigid root-wise extension or bar, the line of force might be sufficiently above the point of greatest resistance at "c," to exert no force in the opposite direction at the apical sphere. In fact a more or less bodily movement of the entire root in the direction of the force would probably occur in some instances, though not with the absolute certainty that would follow the more scientific control of the force for this character of movement, described later. For instance, in the construction of an appliance for the retrusion or retraction of the incisors with a traction bow extending from molar anchorages, if we wish the least movement possible of the roots in the opposite direction, the bow should rest upon the incisors as near to the gingival margins as the gums will permit. Usually upright bars are soldered to the bands, and these extend to the highest points of the exposed faces of the crowns. Grooves or rests are cut at the upper ends of these for the bow, enabling it to span the interproximate gingivae. See Figs. 44 and 45. Frequently the bars are extended above the gum margins, in order to apply power that is equivalent to direct force upon the roots at points above the margins of the alveoli, and it is found in these procedures of the greatest importance in arriving at results for which they are designed.

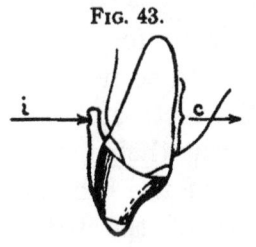

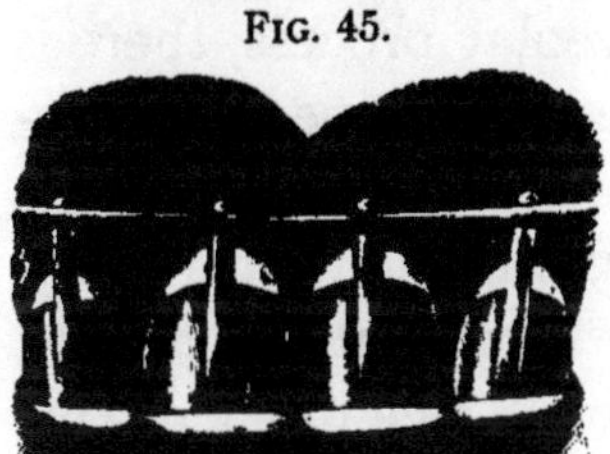

It is not necessary to multiply descriptions of methods relative to other teeth and conditions where the important principles of inclination movements may be employed, further than to say that whenever it is desired to avoid producing an abnormal inclination of the crowns of teeth in the direction of the applied power, it is nearly always possible to take advantage of some effective mechanical principle. On the other hand, whenever in the movement of a crown under the application of a single force, it is desired to move the root in the opposite direction, the force should be applied as near as possible to the occluding border. This is especially true in cases of protruding crowns of the superior incisors, with a retrusion of the roots; of which the common cause is thumb-sucking—the teeth often assuming a decided labial inclination, with the production of a depression along the upper portion of the upper lip.

Power in Relation to the Possibilities of Movement

It has been shown that the tendency to **inclination movement** or tipping of teeth is somewhat in proportion to the nearness to the occlusal zone at which power is applied. There is another cause of the tipping movement that is too frequently overlooked, i. e., **power applied in excess of the possibilities of orthopedic movement.**

In correcting the positions of malposed teeth, it should never be forgotten: first, that the important and indispensable part of the operation is to so regulate the force that the normal functions and healthful conditions of the teeth and surrounding tissues are preserved; and secondly, that nature will permit their movement, physiologically, only so rapidly as she is able to take care of the broken-down tissue of retrogressive metamorphosis caused by pressure of the tooth upon the walls of the alveolar socket. The rapidity of the movement will be influenced largely by the age of the patient, and will differ as other things differ with people.

The point which interests us may be stated as follows: As soon as the applied force overreaches the possibilities of natural physiologic changes, the surplus is liable to spend itself in producing some undesired and unlooked-for condition. In other words, nature can be made to work only so rapidly. Any attempt to force her beyond her natural powers will certainly result—if not in disaster—in a misdirection, and transference of the surplus force to other parts which should not, and otherwise would not be disturbed.

On account of the relatively hard surface layer of the alveolar process, there is always a tendency for it to act as a fulcrum over which the tooth is tipped; but fortunately the apical region of bone in which the roots are imbedded usually presents sufficient resistance to the lessened degree of force at this point for it to remain as the true and immovable fulcrum of the lever so long as the force is not increased beyond the powers of resorption in other portions of the socket. The moment this does occur, however, the border area of the alveolus becomes the fulcrum, while

CHAPTER XIII. PRINCIPLES OF MECHANICS

the extra force is delivered at the end of the root in the opposite direction and in exact proportion to the surplus force.

As before mentioned, notice the action of the force of an oar in propelling a boat in still water. If only sufficient pressure is used against the oar to permit the water to pass from in front of the slow-moving blade, there will not be sufficient pressure at the fulcrum, or oarlock, to overcome the inertia of the boat; but immediately upon the force being increased above the possibilities of the water to get out of the way, the fulcrum of the lever is transferred to the water and the over-load of surplus force is delivered at the oarlock with a movement of the boat. There is another and perhaps more forcible example: Drop the point of a crowbar into the ground at the side of a large cake of ice, fixed immovably in place. See Fig. 46. Now if we heat the bar and press it against the cake with only sufficient force to permit the ice to melt in front of it, little or no change of position will take place at the point or fulcrum of the bar, but the moment we increase the pressure above the melting possibilities of the ice, the fulcrum of the lever is transferred to the cake and the surplus force is delivered at the point of the bar, with a tendency in proportion to the surplus pressure to force it laterally in an opposite direction in the ground. This illustration is only one of many conditions which may be and often are produced by excessive or misapplied force in operations for correcting irregularities of the teeth.*

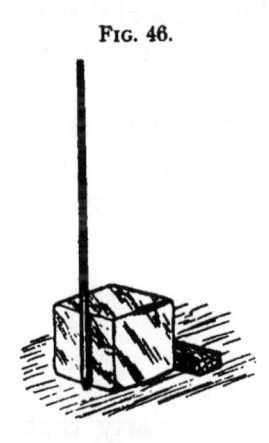

FIG. 46.

In a desire to hasten an operation, dentists will commonly push the amount of force to the limit, not fully realizing the fact that the orthopedic movement of the teeth, within the bounds of physiologic safety, cannot be made to move faster than the processes of nature will permit, however much force is exerted. With force properly applied near the gingival borders of the teeth, they will usually move by inclination, but with no appreciable movement of the ends of the roots in the opposite direction. When, however, the magnitude of power is in excess of the requirements of the most rapid possible movement at the cervical sphere of action, it reacts upon the apical sphere with perhaps the production of a movement in the opposite direction with far greater inclination; and one which would not have occurred had the power been kept within the bounds of the possibilities of the movement desired. In other words, the cervical sphere of action being unable to respond by proportionate movement to more than a certain degree of power, becomes in turn a stationary fulcrum to the excess force, which causes movement at the apical end. This principle of force is important when applied to teeth which are moved by virtue of the limited possibilities of the alveolar process "to get out of the way," and it is also applicable between all alveolar spheres of action and fulcrum; as for instance, the general movement of teeth from dental anchorages. See Stationary Anchorages, Chapter XV.

*Case—Dental Review, August, 1892.

The above examples are presented to illustrate that the force exerted at different areas of the alveoli with power applied at different points upon the crown is quite similar to that of true levers; but that the actual movement that is produced is often far from that which would obtain under the exact conditions and requirements of mechanics. The difference being caused: *first*, by the fact that the power cannot be exerted in the socket at two exact points of weight and fulcrum, but instead, upon the broadened spheres of the alveolar process which is pressed upon by the roots of the teeth under the influence of force appliances attached to the crowns; *second*, by the variability of the resisting spheres; and *third*, by the peculiar quality of the alveolar process to move only in accord with its physiologic possibilities, which frequently results in the transference of the force of action to points of reaction.

Furthermore, these principles and activities of force are quite as applicable in the movement of any of the teeth, and especially important, as it is always possible with a little careful thought and management to approximate and control the relative variability of probable movement at the resisting spheres.

ROTATING MOVEMENT

One of the most common forms of dental malposition is that of malturned teeth. It enters more or less into every class of irregularity, particularly that of the simple and complex characters. There are a number of effective methods of correction, applicable to different conditions, which are treated at some length in Chapter XLVIII, where the several appliances are shown with full description of their respective force activities. There are certain important principles in the application of force for the rotation of teeth which it would be well to remember.

Wherever force is applied for the rotation of a tooth, the mechanical power of the appliance is dependent largely upon the distance from the central axis at which the force is exerted. This is quite important when applied to the labial teeth, the peripheral surfaces of whose crowns present points of attachments that greatly differ from each other in this regard.

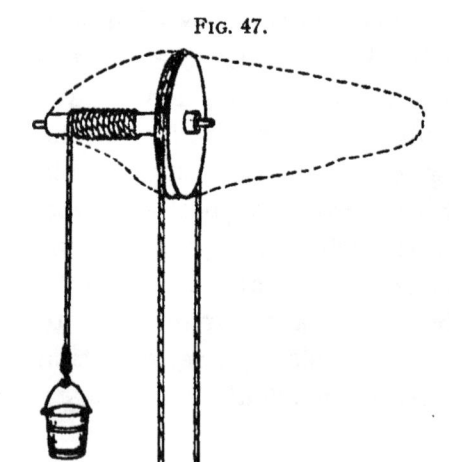

FIG. 47.

The action of the "wheel and axle" as one of the secondary mechanical powers will serve to illustrate this principle. Fig. 47 demonstrates at a glance the mechanical advantage of applying a rotating force at the gingival margins of incisors and cuspids. This principle is especially true of the spring lever rotator, which is one of the most convenient and effective appliances in the author's practice for nearly all cases where a moderate force is sufficient. See Fig. 241.

CHAPTER XIII. PRINCIPLES OF MECHANICS

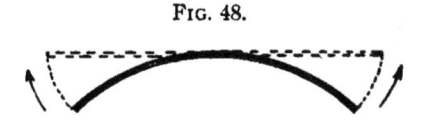

Spring Lever Rotator.—When a straight resilient bar is bent in the form of a bow and its ends are immovably attached, the only force which it potentially exerts is in the direction of the arcs which its ends would inscribe if released and allowed to return to equilibrium. See Fig. 48.

Fig. 48.

Fig. 49.

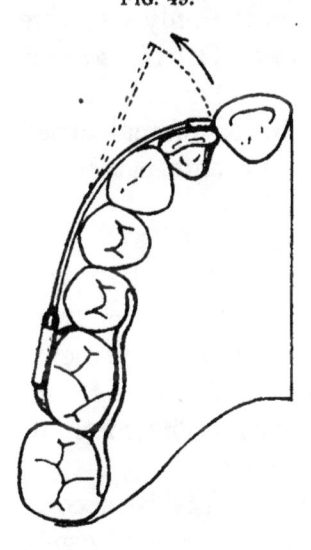

If one end is fastened to a stationary point or anchorage, and the other to a movable body, such as an incisor tooth, the only force which it would exert upon the incisor would be in the direction of the arc which that end would inscribe in returning to the originally straight form of the bar, as shown in Fig. 49.

If instead, the distal end is hooked to an alignment bow along which it can freely glide, as in Fig. 50, the bar will then exert the additional force of tooth rotation. See Fig. 241. If the incisor is prevented by the alignment bow from responding to the outward spring of the end of the bar to which it is attached, the only movement of the tooth will be that of rotation on its central axis, in response to the force of the bar to return to equilibrium; and this force will always be in proportion to the freedom given to the bar to straighten itself by the distal end gliding along its attachment. Therefore, to obtain the greatest rotating power of a spring lever rotator, the free end should not be clasped by a tube attachment, as shown in Fig. 49, or by any long-bearing attachment, as the friction caused by the spring of the bar would retard its rotating movement.

Fig. 50.

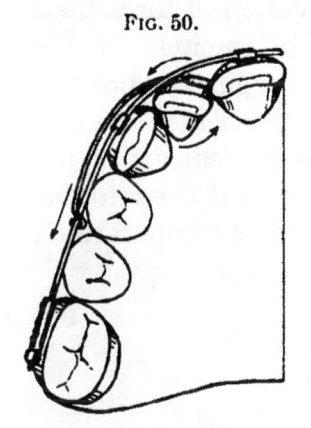

In all cases where this appliance is employed, an alignment arch-bow is indispensable to prevent the rotating tooth from being forced out of alignment. The bow is also well adapted for the gliding movement of the free end of the rotating lever, with a proper distribution of its tangential force. Frequently the reciprocally reacting force exerted by a spring lever can be utilized in bringing the tooth or teeth to which it is attached at one end, or both, into alignment. But no patient should be allowed to leave the chair with appliances of this kind attached to the teeth, without the controlling power of an alignment bow or other effective attachments for preventing the teeth from being forced out of alignment.

Whenever a single rotating force is applied upon one side of a tooth, as with levers, ligatures, pull and push screw-bars, etc., there is also the tendency toward inclination movement unless prevented by an arch alignment bow or other means. Frequently both movements are demanded, i. e., the rotation of a tooth while forcing it to alignment. Numerous instances will be shown in the illustrations of **Specific Methods** where this principle is taken advantage of.

True rotating force which exerts no tendency other than to rotate the tooth upon its central axis, can only be produced by reciprocally acting pull and push forces applied upon opposite sides of the tooth. This principle is applicable in all cases where considerable force is demanded and frequently it is the only effective method. The appliances, with the text descriptions, in Chapter XLVIII so perfectly illustrate this principle that it need not be explained here.

One of the most modern and effective forces for the correction of malturned teeth, and for nearly all the malalignments common with young patients, is through the resilient action of very light spring arch-bows, Nos. 24 and 25.

INTRUSIVE AND EXTRUSIVE MOVEMENTS

When force is applied in the line with the long axis of a tooth, toward or from the apical end of the root, it tends to produce intrusive and extrusive movements respectively. Movements of this character are necessary in the correction of Supra and Infra-occlusions, and in Open and Close-bite Malocclusions. The methods employed are fully outlined under practical treatment of these cases.

Intrusive Movements are far more difficult, because they can only be accomplished by a resorption of the bone forming the sockets and are governed largely by the age of the patient.

Extrusive Movements are commonly the easiest of all movements of the teeth, and when performed within the bounds of a reasonable application of force there is no danger of rupturing the vessels and nerves at the apical foramina. In this movement the gum rarely if ever changes its relative position at the gingival borders, the movement seeming to take place solely by stretching the pericemental and gum tissues. Judging from the difficulty in permanently retaining movements of this character after correction, however, we are led to the conclusion that the reformative process in building new alveoli, under these circumstances, is comparatively slow. See Chapter XLVI.

CHAPTER XIV

BODILY MOVEMENTS

As has been explained, when force is applied to a tooth for its movement in a right-angled direction to its central axis, it practically becomes a lever. When a push or pull force is applied at one point upon the crown for its inclination or tipping movement, there are two areas of resistance in the socket—gingival and apical—upon which the strain comes from opposite directions. These are the areas or points of fulcrum and work. The mechanical advantages in all levers are in proportion to the increased distance between the point at which power is applied, and the fulcrum, and the decreased distance between points of fulcrum and work. But in bodily movements, the entire alveolar socket is the area of work, its mathematical "point" being located at the center of its alveolar resistance, while the fulcrum of the lever is now placed outside of the socket at some point upon the crown through the medium of the mechanical device, and the power is applied at another point between the fulcrum and point of work.

Many fail to understand or appreciate the mechanical principles and requirements of bodily movements of the teeth. For instance, we often see the published statement that a single small arch-bow or bar .036″ in diameter, that is rigidly attached to the buccal or labial surfaces of teeth, can be made to move them bodily through the alveolar process. While this might be possible with very young children when time is a matter of no importance, it is not practical from a general orthodontic sense.

This principle of bodily movement may be fairly illustrated by soldering, or firmly attaching an iridio-platinum bar to a firmly attached cuspid band—the threaded end of the bar resting in a molar anchorage; the object being to move the cuspid bodily in a mesial direction.

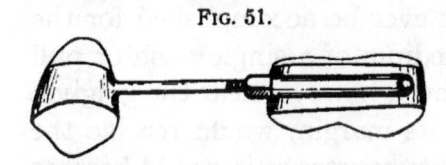

FIG. 51.

It does not take a mathematical calculation for an ordinary mind to see that when force is applied in this manner instead of being evenly distributed over the entire mesial or distal surface of the socket, as it must be in order to move the root bodily, a weak and short-bearing attachment of that kind would not be of sufficient rigidity to stand the strain, in any case requiring more than a very moderate degree of bodily movement for young patients. The upper surface of the bar at its point of attachment may be regarded as the point of applied power, and the lower edge, the fulcrum, the whole device being a lever of exceedingly low mechanical advantage, because of the nearness of points of power and fulcrum compared to that of weight, or alveolar resistance.

110   PART IV. TECHNIC PRINCIPLES OF PRACTICE

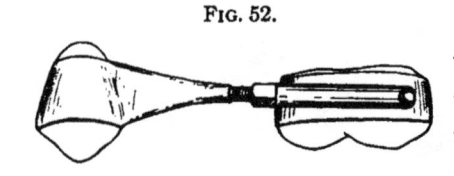

Fig. 52.

If the bar is widened at its point of attachment to the cuspid by soldering to it a rigid plate, the mechanical advantages toward a bodily movement would be increased in proportion to the width of its attachment. Fig. 52. But even this device with its absolutely rigid bar and attachment to a cuspid would be found in practice to be very defective, because the tendency toward inclination movement of the cuspid would exert a strong extrusive force upon the anchorage, and as an extrusive movement requires far less force than any other movement, especially that of a bodily movement, it would not take long to produce a supra-occlusion of the molars that would result in an open-bite malocclusion.

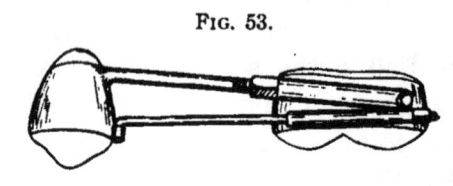

Fig. 53.

Observe how this illustrative device may be put into practical form by causing the power and fulcrum forces to act independently of each other with reciprocal action upon the anchorage and movable points of attachment to the cuspid. See Fig. 53.

It will be seen by this method that when force is applied on the power bar, any inclination movement of the cuspid which is not overcome with the fulcrum bar can have no extrusive tendency on the anchorage, because of the movable attachments of the bars. Again, the reciprocal action of the push and pull forces upon the molar, nullifies the reactive force upon the anchorage, and consequently stabilizes it. The main advantage is the perfect control of the bodily movement of the cuspid.

With very rare exceptions, lateral force applied at a **single point** upon the crowns of any of the teeth, and especially the molars, would require for the bodily movement of the roots in the direction of the applied power, a far more rigid propelling arm and grasp of the crown than is possible with all ordinary regulating appliances. The limited area upon which force can be applied to a tooth, compared with that portion imbedded in the socket and covered by the gum, has made it next to impossible to move the apical end of the root in the direction of the applied power in that way. Nor could a bodily movement ever be accomplished for the customary cases with power applied through the medium of a single push or pull bar, or arch-bow, attached at any point upon the crown, however near the gingival margin, as the opposing wall of the alveolus, near its margin, would receive the magnitude of this direct force, and in proportion to its resistance it would become a fulcrum exerting a tendency to move the apical end or ends of the roots in the opposite direction.

If force is applied at "A" in the direction of the arrow in Fig. 54, it will be principally received by the opposing walls of the alveolus near the margin, or at "B," where the greatest, if not the only, movement of the alveolar process would occur, but in proportion to the resistance of the labial wall it will become a

CHAPTER XIV. BODILY MOVEMENTS

fulcrum, creating a tendency to move the apical end in the opposite direction. This would also be true if a single force is applied in the direction of the arrow at

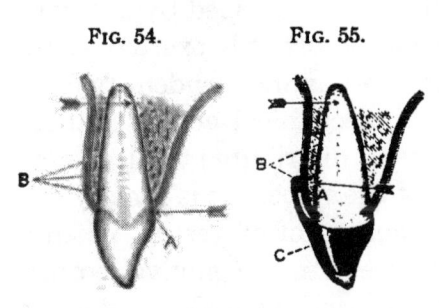

FIG. 54.   FIG. 55.

"A," in Fig. 55, except that it would be distributed over a greater area of the alveolus with lessened tendency to move the root in the opposite direction. But if in the construction of the apparatus, the incisal end is prevented from moving forward, or its movement is placed under positive control, it becomes the real fulcrum with possibilities of directing the power toward a bodily movement of the entire root.

But if in the construction of the apparatus a **static fulcrum** is created outside of the alveolus and made to act independent of the osseous imbedment at a point near the occluding or incisal end, while the power is applied as far root-wise as permitted, the tooth will then become a lever of the third kind of considerable mechanical advantage having power, directed to a movement of the entire root in the direction of the line of force.

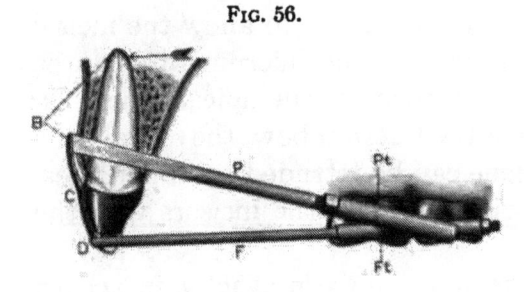

FIG. 56.

In the diagrammatic drawing, Fig. 56 shows the principles of the combination for a bodily labial movement of the incisors. The power bar "P" exerting a push force of considerable magnitude for extensive movements for the older class of patients, should be as large as No. 13, or 14, to prevent its springing laterally, while the fulcrum "F" exerting a traction force, need be no larger than No. 23. The reaction of these two forces from opposite directions, centered in the same anchorage, neutralize each other at this point to the extent of the lesser force. When they are equal, or exactly reciprocal, no distal or mesial force is exerted at the anchorage.

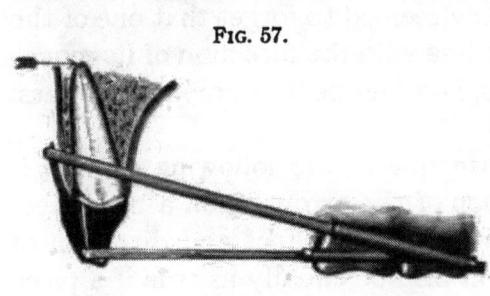

FIG. 57.

Fig. 57 shows the combination for bodily lingual movement of the incisors. It will be seen that the direction of the two forces is reversed. The power bow now exerting a pull force need not be larger than No. 16, while the fulcrum bow now exerting a push force should be as large as No. 16, or 17. For practical apparatus, see Chapter XXXVII.

If an attempt were made by grasping the top of a post imbedded one-half its length in some yielding substance with the view of moving it bodily in a lateral direction, it might be found that the upper portion could be easily moved back and forth, but with every movement, the lower end of the post would move in its imbedment in the opposite direction. See Fig. 35, Chapter XIII. Again, if the post is grasped near the surface of the ground, it will require far more force to move it, because of the lessened mechanical advantage, but even then the lower end would move in the opposite direction. If now the top of the post is grasped by one hand and prevented from tipping, while the whole force of the other is exerted at the base, the difficulty will at once be solved. In the last effort an independent fulcrum is established at the top of the post, and the whole mechanical action changed to that of a lever of the third kind, with the entire power distributed to all the imbedded portion toward a movement in the direction of the force. It is exactly this principle that should be employed for the bodily movement of all teeth. When it is possible to apply the power at a point further root-wise than the gingival border, through the medium of a root-wise bar soldered to the band, or a rigid extension of the band attachment, the mechanical advantage of the lever will be increased, and the force upon the artificially arranged fulcrum proportionately lessened.

A study of these principles will show that the operator has perfect control over the peculiar character of movement imparted to the incisors. For instance, in Fig. 55, if it is desired to bodily move the incisors forward and retain the same inclination which the teeth possessed at the start, the distal nut of the fulcrum bow should be judiciously unscrewed as the movement progresses, to allow the incisal zone to move forward with the roots. The loosening of the fulcrum wire can be carried to such an extent that there will be no movement at the apical zone. On the other hand, by exerting a traction force upon the fulcrum bow, the apical zone can be protruded, and if desired, the occlusal zone can be retruded. Similar rules, with movements reversed are applicable in bodily retruding the incisors with the combination shown in Fig. 57.

In the early introduction of the above principle which is exactly in accord with the laws of mechanics, the author was severely criticised, and the principal contention was that power applied upon a rigid root-wise bar soldered to an incisor band, as shown in Fig. 56, was equivalent to applying it at the gingival margin of the tooth, in as much as the extension bar was attached at that point, and because the force was applied through this medium. They seemed to forget that one of the basic laws of physics is: **"Force always acts in a line with the direction of its movement,"** and that this applies equally to all levers, however bent or crooked the bars, providing they be rigid.

Students will recognize the truth of this principle in the following drawing:

Force applied at "A," Fig. 58, in the direction of the arrow, upon a rigid steel ring, will be transmitted to "a," and will have the same effect and direction of influence as it would if applied at "x." This will also be equally as true if a piece is cut out of the ring on one side—providing it is rigid—as at "B–b." This being true, the same principle will apply at "C–c" and "D–d." The latter is similar to the appliance which we rigidly attach to a tooth for the purpose of applying the force in a line further root-wise than would be possible at any point upon the crown proper.

CHAPTER XIV. BODILY MOVEMENTS

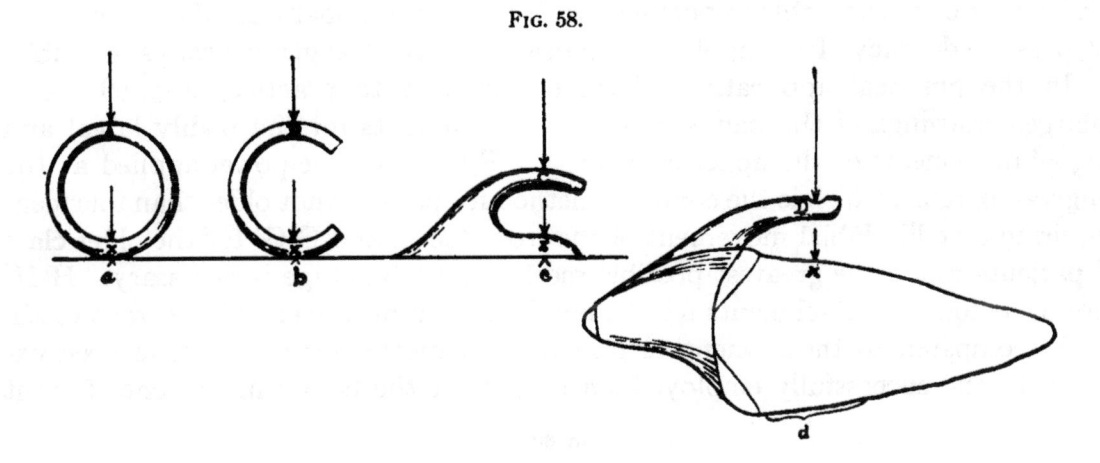

Fig. 58.

In the combination for bodily moving the teeth, through the possibilities of establishing an independent fulcrum at the occlusal or incisal zone, the only object

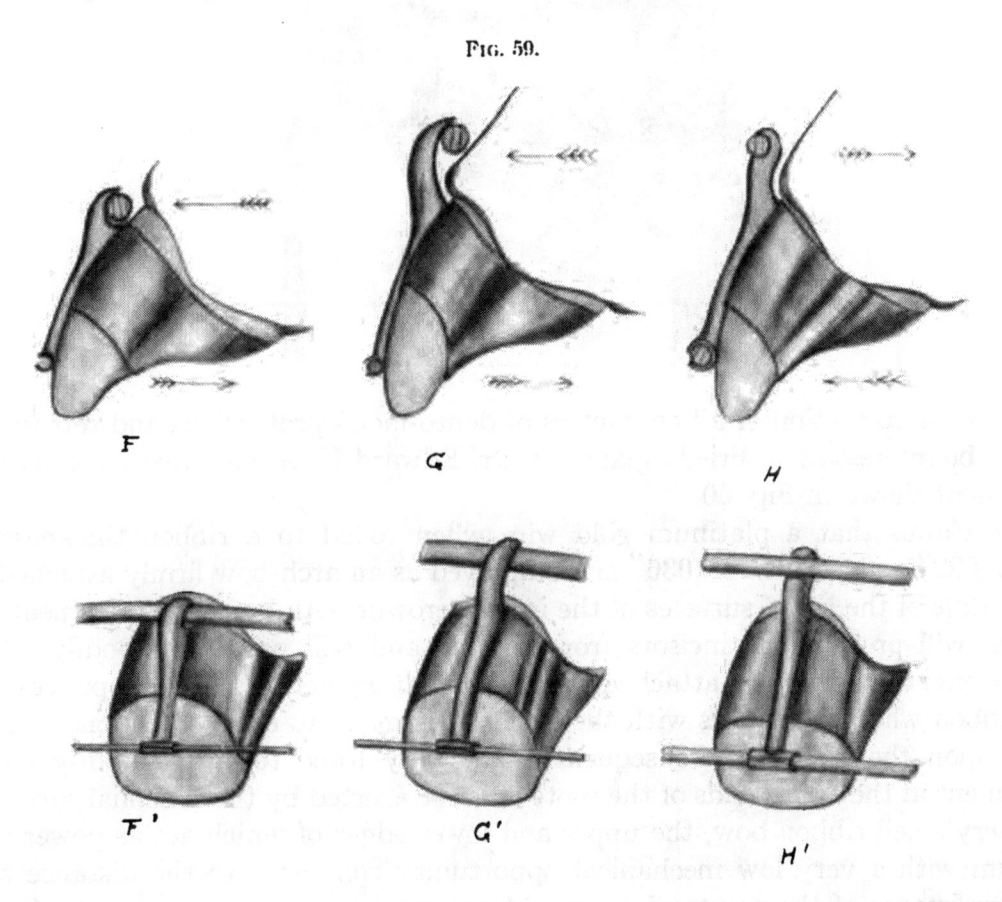

Fig. 59.

of applying the power at a point upon the root is to increase the mechanical advantage of the lever, by increasing the distance from points of power and fulcrum, which proportionately relieves the strain upon the power and fulcrum bows. This is a feature of considerable importance with regulating apparatus where the greatest possible delicacy of the appliances consistent with strength is always desirable.

In the practical application of these principles to practice, Fig. 59 shows enlarged drawings of the bands and their attachments for the bodily labial and lingual movements of the upper front teeth. F F' shows the power applied at the gingival margins, which is the common method for patients not older than fourteen, requiring a bodily labial movement of the front teeth, and G G' for the older class of patients where the greatest possible mechanical advantage is necessary. H H' shows the form of attachments for the bodily lingual movement of the front teeth.

As compared to these scientific principles of mechanics which have been extensively and successfully employed since 1891 for the bodily movement of front

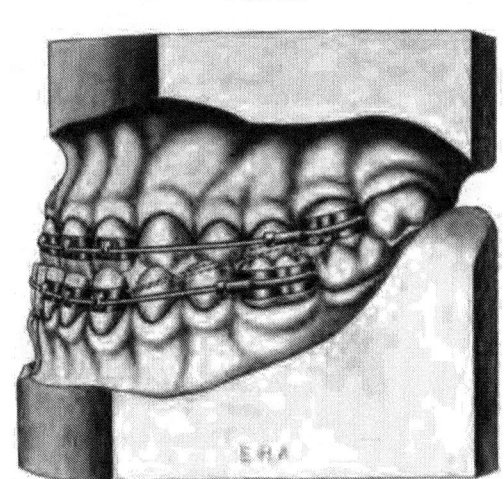

FIG. 60.

teeth in the correction of all characters of dento-facial protrusions and retrusions, it may be interesting to briefly glance at Dr. Edward H. Angle's method of bodily movement shown in Fig. 60.

He claims that a platinum gold wire when rolled to a ribbon thickness of about .022" and a width of .036" and employed as an arch-bow firmly attached to the middle of the labial surfaces of the incisor crowns with bracket attachments as shown, will prevent the incisors from tipping and will produce a bodily labial movement; the bow being attached to single molar anchorages. The upper edge of the ribbon where it engages with the brackets is made to exert a tortional spring force upon the incisors. Consequently, the only force toward a bodily labial movement at the apical ends of the roots must be exerted by the torsional spring of this very small ribbon bow, the upper and lower edges of which act as power and fulcrum with a very low mechanical opportunity compared to the distance and great resistance of the points of work. Moreover, no more than a very moderate degree of labial force applied at the anchorages can be obtained from a ribbon bow of that size.

CHAPTER XIV. BODILY MOVEMENTS

Fig. 61 "A" is a mesio-distal view of Dr. Angle's method. It shows by the two lower arrows the approximate distance between power and fulcrum, and by the upper arrow, the distance to the center of the area of work. "B" shows the prin-

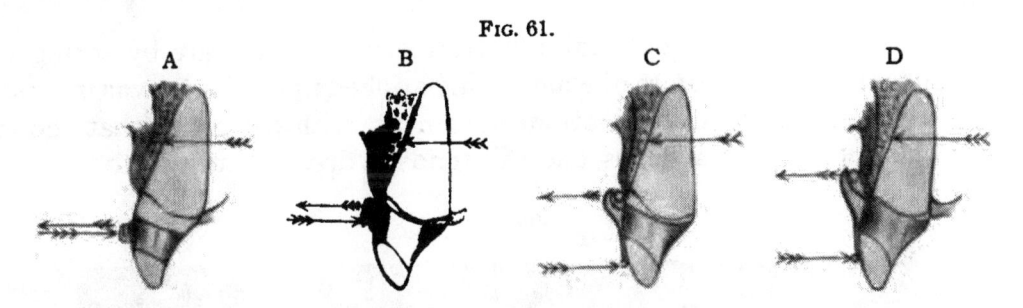

FIG. 61.

ciples of a modification by the author, to increase the mechanical advantage of the method by employing a No. 18 bow rolled to a thickness of .020" and a width of .050". This greatly increases the comparative distance between the points of power and fulcrum, and being placed at the gingival margins, it decreases the distance to the area of work or alveolar resistance, both of which greatly increase the mechanical advantage. Again, the arch-bow being rolled only over its incisal dimensions, as shown in Fig. 62, the protruding power of the bow is greatly increased.

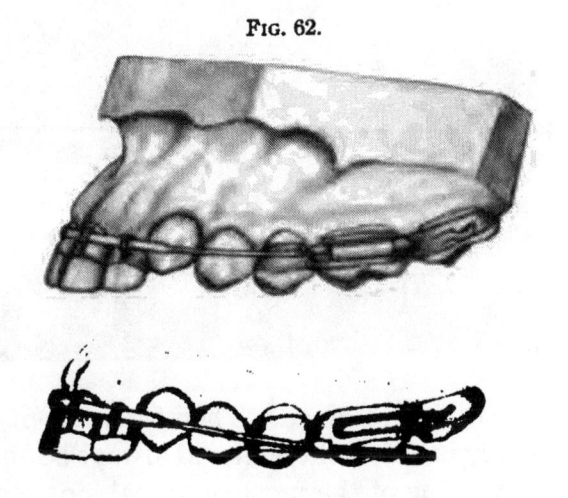

FIG. 62.

This torsional method of bodily movement is hardly to be compared with the long tried effectiveness, mechanical advantages, and physiologic control of the regular bodily movement apparatus, the principles of which are shown in Fig. 61, "C" and "D." Note the relatively increased distances between power and fulcrum, and decreased distances to the center of resistance or weight, shown by the arrows.

The bodily disto-mesial movement of buccal teeth to close spaces after extraction so as to leave no inverted V-shaped interproximate space to pocket food is of the greatest importance. This is accomplished by ingenious devices for applying the power upon lingual and buccal root-wise extensions aided by an occlusal screw

116   PART IV. TECHNIC PRINCIPLES OF PRACTICE

bar fulcrum resistance, or by long-bearing telescoping tubes at the occlusal area. See "Stationary Anchorages," Chapter XV, and the closing of "Abnormal Interproximate Spaces," Chapter L. Also see Figs. 266 and 268, Chapter L; and Fig. 166, Chapter XXIX.

The ordinary methods of expanding narrow dental arches, are by spring arch-bows, or lingual jacks, the forces of which being applied upon the crowns in a buccal direction, produce purely an inclination movement, with the result that the teeth soon close only on the lingual cusps, and this tends to drive them back to their form-

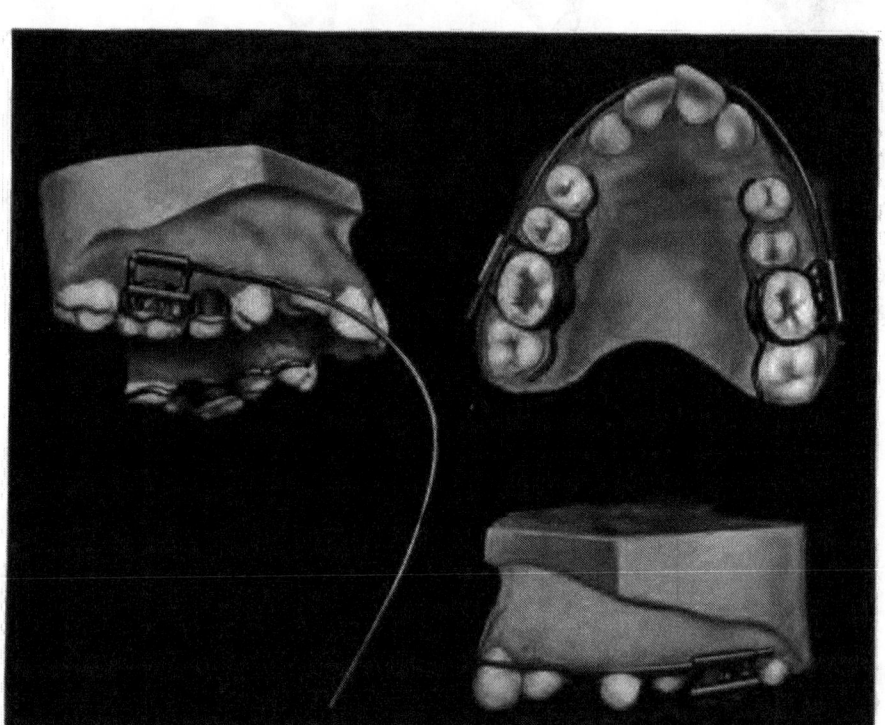

FIG. 63.

er malpositions, unless positively retained. Therefore, except in those cases where the buccal teeth are lingually inclined, there should always be an endeavor to produce a *bodily* buccal movement. One of the most practical aids toward this movement is the root-wise extensions soldered to the buccal surfaces of the bands. To these, the open-tube attachments are soldered to the extreme root-wise positions permitted by the muscles. When high-grade spring arch-bows No. 18 or 17 are sprung into these tubes, the line of force is far nearer to the center of alveolar resistance in the sockets, and consequently with a greatly increased tendency toward bodily expanding movement.

It very commonly arises that this expansion arch-bow is threaded at the ends for nuts, to exert distal or mesial force; the ends resting in open-tubes, which may be partially closed after placing the bow. The bow can then be utilized for a

CHAPTER XIV. BODILY MOVEMENTS

labial or lingual movement of the front teeth, and at times also, as a power bow for bodily movements.

Fig. 63 illustrates an appliance that has been constructed to show how a combination of torsional and root-wise forces may be employed in the bodily expansion of arches. The arch-bow in this appliance is No. 19 special spring nickel silver, rolled distal to the cuspids, to a ribbon form of about $2/3$ its diameter, and at an angle—in equilibrium—that will twist the ends of the bow one-quarter to one-third the way around when sprung into the U anchorage tubes, and in a direction so that the force of the upper, or root-wise edge of the ribbon will be exerted in a buccal direction. The lingually directed force of the lower edge is supposed to be more than neutralized by the direct expanding force of the bow. The model on the left, shows the position of the arch-bow at rest with one end in its anchorage tube, in a position to be grasped firmly at the other end with a pair of pliers, with which it is twisted while carrying it to its seating in the opposite U tube. It will be seen that this apparatus may be constructed to produce a bodily buccal movement on one side alone if so desired, by leaving one end round to be carried to place in a round open anchorage tube. This torsional arch-bow may be employed as a pull or push bow by threading its ends for nuts to operate in connection with the anchorage tubes.

CHAPTER XV

PRINCIPLES OF DENTAL ANCHORAGES

The most important of the laws of force in the mechanical movement of malposed teeth is Newton's third law: **To every action there is an equal and contrary reaction.**

Nowhere is this law so important as in the application of force in **dental** anchorages, and in all movements of teeth from points of dental resistance, because whatever the magnitude of force that is exerted toward the correction of one or more malposed teeth, an equal force must always be exerted in the opposite direction upon the tooth or teeth that are chosen for the bases of action. While the forces exerted at points of action and reaction are always equal, the relative amount of *movement* that is induced is proportional to the respective resistances.

As the amount of movement in proportion to the resistance is largely dependent upon the mechanism employed for the application of force, and consequently, upon the peculiar construction of the appliances and their attachments, a perfect knowledge of the principles involved, with the technics of construction and application of dental anchorages, is of the utmost importance.

Bands for anchorage teeth that are intended to sustain considerable force should be made of material no thinner than .005"; and for stationary anchorages two and sometimes three adjoining bands should be soldered firmly together.

The ordinary clamp-band attached to a single molar tooth, and also the long band clamping two or more teeth together, are not stationary anchorages. In fact, some of them should be termed "movable anchorages," because they offer so little resistance to inclination movement, especially when the bands are thin, or are uncemented, as is sometimes advised; for even when well supported by the adjoining teeth there is nothing to prevent the sliding of contact surfaces, which is the main principle of anchorage stability.

It may be laid down as a rule that all single band anchorages of the above type will surely result in an inclination movement of the teeth to which they are attached if much force is applied. A band that is clamped around a tooth with a screw has no superiority in sustaining capacity over one that is accurately fitted, even though the bands be of the same thickness and both cemented; and the claim that "it will move a first molar bodily through the process, after the eruption of the second molars, if it moves it at all," is simply absurd. With the most scientifically constructed anchorage, with thick molar bands reinforced and properly supported so as to thoroughly distribute the applied force to all its resisting areas, if the power is applied in the usual way on the crown, the molar tooth to which the anchorage is attached is rarely if ever moved **bodily** in a mesial or distal direction, and if **too much force** is applied, there is always danger of inclining the teeth by a slight bending or yielding in the rigidity of the appliance or its cement attachments.

If one will study from a mechanical standpoint the anatomic shapes of the first and second molar teeth—their position, inclination, and length of roots in relation to their natural imbedment in the alveoli—and intelligently note the direction of movement which each root will take in its socket during the process of inclining the tooth mesially or distally, and again if he will note the resistance which the three upper roots and the two broad lower roots offer to a bodily mesial or distal movement, and if he will then turn his attention to the crowns, their smooth rounded contours, the narrowness of the coronal zones as compared to the length of the teeth to which we are permitted to attach bands—then and not until then can he appreciate the difficulties of preventing inclination or of producing bodily movements of molars with the force applied to the crowns with any form of attachment.

By "too much force" is meant, more force than the limit of physiologic tooth movement requires. This surplus force, be it little or great, added to the already adequate force reacting upon the anchorage, may be sufficient to overcome its stationary inertia, which otherwise would not have occurred with an exhibition of greater moderation and patience. In other words, the active end of the machine becomes the inactive anchorage for every ounce of the surplus force, because its resisting tissues are already strained to their fullest extent, and are now reacting upon the original anchorage tissues that are ready to move as soon as the force of reaction becomes sufficient to overcome their inertia.

The dissolving and bending processes that are induced in the alveolar process by direct pressure of the roots of teeth upon the surrounding pericemental tissues are limited in their possibilities of rapidity of movement. And when we go beyond the possibility of this movement with greater than a sufficient force, we are opposed by the same sort of resistance that occurs when we attempt to thrust a heated poker into ice faster than it is possible for the ice to melt and get out of the way of its movement; with the result, that this surplus force reacts and often does something that was not intended. It may break the appliance, strip a thread, cause the anchorage attachment to give way and the teeth to incline, and perhaps more frequently than anything else, produce extrusive movements and greater inclination than desired of the teeth we are trying to correct.

The same simple law of physics which applies to front teeth under the active stress of movement applies equally to anchorages. When lateral force is applied to the crown of a tooth at some point, with a hinge movement attachment, that tooth becomes a lever of the second kind, with its natural fulcrum at the apical end, and with its greatest stress upon the alveolar border. If, therefore, we do not exceed the possibilities of movement at the gingival area in proportion to the apical inertia, we may get no movement at the apical end of the tooth in the opposite direction.

FIG. 64.

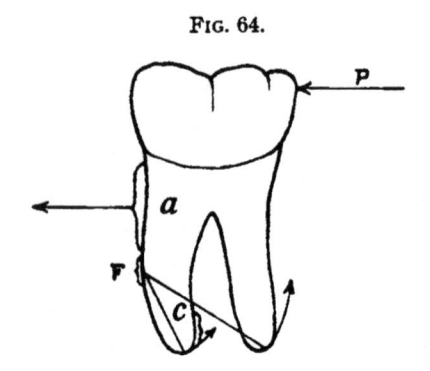

If power is applied at "P," Fig. 64, or at one point on the crown of a lower molar tooth in a mesial direction, the principal area of the alveolus which is pressed upon will be that of the mesial root; the greatest force being exerted at the mesio-gingival wall "a," and a lessened force in the opposite direction at the disto-apical wall "c." The immovable center of the circle of inclination movement in this instance would, therefore, be at "F," with a combination movement of the entire tooth which would tend to lift the distal root from its socket with a moderate degree of resistance other than that of its membranous attachments. The same principle will also apply to a distal movement of these teeth; and because of it, molar teeth, which are unsustained by adjoining teeth, offer little or no more resistance to inclination movement than do teeth with one root.

It would seem that the three roots of the upper molars would enable them to present the greater resistance to inclination movement, but it has been found that they tip quite as easily as the lower molars.

Principles of Anchorage Stability

In contemplating the construction of a molar anchorage appliance that will prevent, as far as possible a movement of the included teeth, the principal object should be to construct the device so that the great tendency of the crowns to tip will be prevented. If this is fully accomplished and the tooth or teeth are held in an upright position, the applied force will be equally distributed over the entire mesial or distal surfaces of the alveoli for all the roots, increasing the stability of the anchorage to an incalculable degree. If the appliance is loosely attached to the teeth or permits the slightest hinge movement, as would arise from a removable crib or a single uncemented band that encircles two or more teeth, there would be nothing to prevent this tipping tendency; though such an anchorage might be sufficient for many purposes, if attached to a sufficient number of teeth and the applied power always less than their combined natural inertia. But instances frequently arise in the regulation of teeth where it is eminently desirable to obtain an anchorage of the greatest possible stability. When it is necessary to employ the back teeth as a stationary base for a considerable movement of front teeth, two or three teeth should be included in the grasp of the anchorage appliance.

The addition of a second tooth to the anchorage, united scientifically, will far more than double its stability by the support which the two teeth can be made to give to each other through a proper construction of the appliance; on the same principle that the strength of a T or a double T girder is increased far out of proportion to the difference in the added material, over that of a plain girder.

CHAPTER XV. PRINCIPLES OF DENTAL ANCHORAGES

Fig. 65.

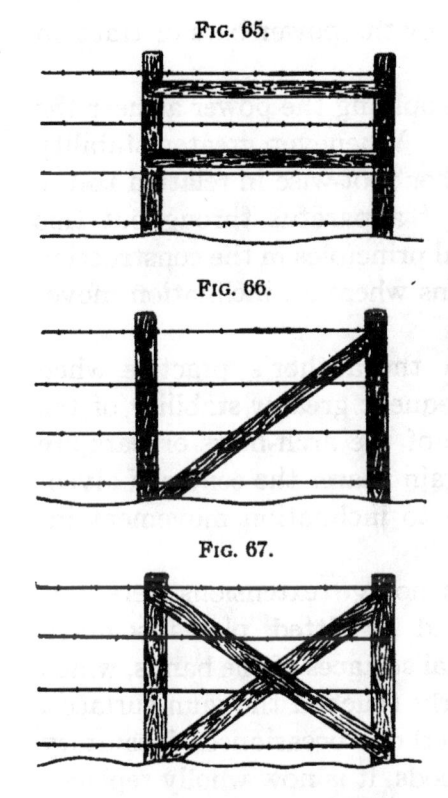

Fig. 66.

Fig. 67.

This principle is well illustrated by the simple mechanical methods adopted in constructing the terminals of wire fences. If the two terminal posts were united by parallel bars which permitted a hinge movement at their attachments as shown in Fig. 65, their movement would depend solely upon the united stability of their imbedment in the ground, but with a single bar placed as shown in Fig. 66, the stability of the terminal is seen to be greatly increased, because inclination movement of the terminal post is obstructed, nearly all the stress of the wires now being exerted at the base of the second post. This device is sufficient for all ordinary purposes of wire fence building. If necessary the terminal stability of the fence could be greatly increased by attaching a second bar as shown in Fig. 67, which would absolutely prevent the slightest inclination movement of either post, and establish an immovability to the extent of a power sufficient to pull their imbedded ends bodily through the ground.

The application of this principle is exactly what we endeavor to apply in the construction of stationary anchorages.

STATIONARY ANCHORAGES

In the construction of stationary dental anchorages, banding material should be selected that is .005″ or .0056″ in thickness (No. 36 or 35 gauge), and as wide as the teeth will permit. When these are soldered, festooned, contoured, and fitted to the teeth chosen for anchorages, take a plaster impression of each anchorage separately, using the anchorage trays shown in Fig. 68, or similar trays which can be easily made of sheet lead; and then use only sufficient plaster to cover the bands. Carefully remove the bands from the teeth with the band-removing plier, to avoid distorting their shape, and place them accurately in the impressions. See that the proximal surfaces are forced *closely* together, and the joints filled with hot wax, and after luting with liquid plumbago, fill with investing plaster, forming small casts of only sufficient size to hold the bands in place during the soldering process. Solder should be flowed between the bands, uniting their approximal surfaces and filling the V-shaped spaces on either side. To more perfectly reinforce the stability of the appliance, fit and solder to the lingual surfaces a piece of No. 16 hook wire in the form of a yoke, in

Fig. 68.

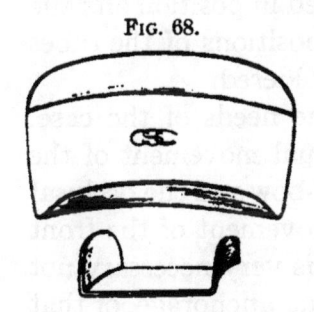

addition to the buccal tube or tubes to be attached for the power bars or traction bows for the movement of the anterior teeth.

In attaching the buccal tubes, the advantage of applying the power as near the gingival margin as possible should be remembered. Whenever greater stability is demanded, the power tubes should be placed further root-wise in relation to the gingival margins, as shown in many illustrations of apparatus throughout this work. This is one of the most advanced and practical principles in the construction of stationary anchorages, and in fact in all conditions where an inclination movement is to be avoided.

Root-wise Anchorages.—In nearly all cases in the author's practice when considerable anchorage force is demanded and consequent greater stability of the anchorages, the tubes for sustaining the main force of the arch-bows or bars are attached to root-wise extensions, which places the strain nearer the center of alveolar resistance, and thus by nullifying the tendency to inclination movement increases the stability of the anchorage.

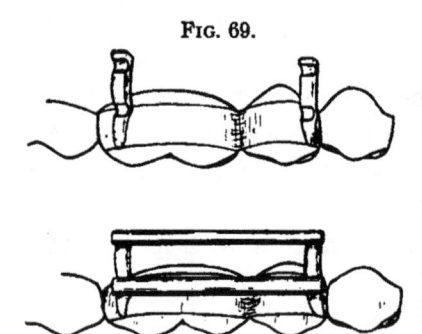

FIG. 69.

These root-wise anchorage extensions were formerly made of swaged or fitted plates soldered to the buccal and lingual surfaces of the bands, which conformed to and nearly touched the gum surfaces. But because this method occasioned insanitary pockets for decaying foods, it is now wholly replaced by the following improved method, which has the advantage of being far easier to construct and fit. In Fig. 69, the root-wise attachments are made of No. 16 wire rolled to about two-thirds its diameter. With the anchorage bands mounted on investment models of the teeth, the prepared wire is cut in pieces about one-half inch long, and bent to fit the buccal surfaces of the bands and gum as shown, and at proper distances apart to rigidly support the long-bearing power tubes. When these are soldered in position and the bands are soldered together with a reinforcement flow, the positions of the tubes are marked and deeply grooved to obtain firm seating when soldered.

The size and character of the tubes are regulated by the needs of the case. For instance, if the anchorage is for the bodily labial or lingual movement of the front teeth, the root-wise or gingival tube is for the power arch-bow and the occlusal tube is for the fulcrum arch-bow. In retrusive inclination movement of the front teeth after the extraction of the first premolars, and when it is very necessary not to disturb the buccal occlusion, as would arise with a single-band anchorage, or that might occur with an ordinary two-band stationary anchorage, the root-wise application of the greatest force will be found to be invaluable. If the object is to retrude the cuspids with a traction bar and with a traction arch-bow encircling the front teeth, the gingival tube should be chosen for the cuspids, and the occlusal tube for the traction arch-bow.

In the final finishing after the anchorage is removed from the model and boiled out, the projecting ends of the bars and all excess material is cut away. In fitting this anchorage to the teeth preparatory to cementing it, the positions of the tubes in relation to the gum surfaces should be finally adjusted by bending their root-wise supports.

When a stationary anchorage of this character is fitted and cemented to the teeth, it will tend to hold them rigidly in its grasp in an upright position. If the bands are thin and narrow, or the apparatus is not sufficiently reinforced, or if for any reason there is a lack of absolute stability in the work or its attachments, the slight yielding of its integrity under great strain permitting inclination movement, will cause the bands to break loose from their attachments.

Sustained Anchorages

Conditions not infrequently arise where it is necessary, in correcting a malposition, to employ an isolated molar for an anchorage. In protruding cases, where the first molar has been extracted, for instance, and the third molar has not erupted, though the main forces may be the occipital and intermaxillary, it nevertheless is necessary to employ the single molars for anchorages, if for no other reason than to support the bow and retain the movement as it progresses. One cannot expect much resistance from a single isolated molar whose inclination movement is not prevented, and even where it is wholly prevented, much anchorage force will always tend to partially extrude or lift it from its socket. If properly sustained, however, it will answer the purposes of a moderate degree of force, perhaps sufficient to move the premolars distally, one at a time, with elastics, and also to sustain and retain the movement of a retruding bow which is acting on the front teeth propelled by other forces.

In the construction of the appliance, the same rules should be fully observed that apply to sustaining the stability of all anchorage teeth, i. e.:—(1) The bands should be wide and thick so as to possess a firm grasp of the crown; (2) the engaging tubes should be firmly soldered at the gingival margins, or upon root-wise extensions; (3) the tubes should be of sufficient length, strength, and size to carry rigid inflexible traction bars or arch-bows for communicating the force, and thus prevent, as far as possible, the slightest inclination movement of the anchorages.

A principle which the author presented at the meeting of the American Dental Association in 1907, for sustaining a single molar anchorage is as follows:

"Instances frequently arise where only one tooth can be used for an anchorage on one or both sides of the mouth. These teeth not being supported by the adjoining teeth will readily tip if not properly sustained. In fact, a molar tooth that is allowed to tip will offer but little more resistance to force than a premolar, but if sustained in an upright position its bodily stability will greatly increase its resistance to movement. When a single isolated molar is used for an anchorage attachment, the band should be wide and thick, fitted and cemented as carefully as a crown, with rigid attachments for inflexible extensions. However perfect the band and its attachments, if a flexible traction wire is used to transfer the power, no obstruction is offered to the tipping tendency of the molar. The same is true with an inflexible power rod if the band is thin, narrow, and yielding, or in any way movable upon the tooth, or if the power tube is short and loosely fitted to the rod."

Fig. 70.

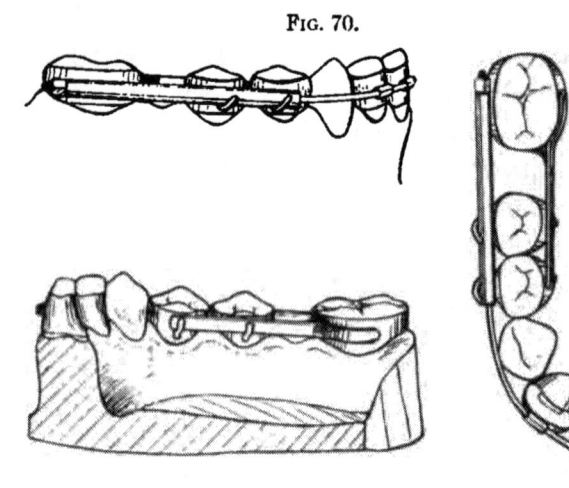

Where great immobility of a single anchorage tooth is required, use for banding material nickel silver or platinized gold, .0035" thick, and as wide as the tooth will permit. When this is contoured and fitted, solder to the buccal surface a long bearing power tube at the gingival margin. See Fig. 70.

The power tube should extend forward to the first premolar resting upon narrow projecting hooks soldered to the premolar bands, as shown. This will add greatly to the stability of the anchorage. It will be seen that any tendency of the molar to tip forward will carry the mesial end of the tube almost directly toward the roots of the premolars, the movement being prevented by the rests. Nor will such a device offer any special obstruction to the distal movement of the premolars—the rests sliding along the tube.

In addition to this, a flattened rigid bar may be soldered to the lingual aspect of the molar bands to rest upon hooks attached to the premolars as shown. This is especially applicable where it is desired to correct a protrusion with a small flexible traction bow encircling the teeth, or even in combination with more inflexible buccal devices. Again, it may be desired to move the premolars distally to relieve a crowded maleruption of the cuspids, but with no lingual movement of the incisors. See Fig. 71. In addition to the long-bearing lingual tube sustaining the single molar anchorage through the medium of the lingual push bow resting in the incisor hooks, the doubly reinforced and sustained anchorage may carry a buccal tube soldered to root-wise extensions for a traction bar to the malposed cuspids, and also hooks for the attachment of elastics to move the premolars distally.

Fig. 71.

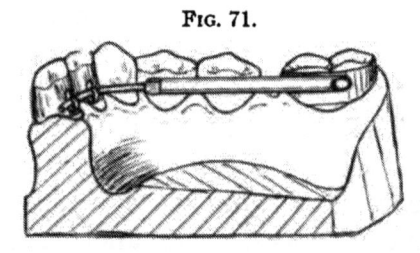

A similar device is especially applicable for children who have inherited a decided protrusion of the lower teeth. The lingual supporting tubes should be sufficiently large to allow the ends of the bow to easily glide into them as the incisors are forced back with the labial traction bow. A practical result in the application of this method of treatment with a full description of the apparatus, will be found in Chapter XLIV.

CHAPTER XV. PRINCIPLES OF DENTAL ANCHORAGES

RECIPROCATING OR MOVABLE ANCHORAGES

Dental anchorages may be considered as any point of resistance which is made to receive the reaction of the force required for the movement or correction of malposed teeth. Wherever it is possible to do so, these points of resistance should be chosen with a view to utilizing the reactive force for a reciprocal movement of other teeth that require correction. This is one of the most practically scientific laws of orthodontia, though sadly neglected, and one, moreover, that is applicable in some form in almost every case of irregularity.

In the choice or invention of a regulating apparatus, after the several required movements of the case have been determined, a careful study of the demands with the reciprocating possibilities in view, will present surprising opportunities for its application. This will be found well exemplified in the details of regulating apparatus presented in this work. Instances arise where it is eminently desirable to move the buccal anchorage teeth mesially or distally to correct occlusion by the same force that is used to protrude or retrude the front teeth. This is accomplished purely by the method in which force is applied through the peculiar construction of the appliances that permits or induces inclination or bodily movement of the anchor teeth. Nowhere is it more applicable than in that common irregularity which is characterized by maleruption of the cuspids, shown in illustrations of apparatus in Class I of this work.

It will be seen by a number of the appliances that the reaction of the force to protrude the front teeth in opening spaces for the cuspids, is received upon the premolar attachment whose peculiar construction is such that the force of reaction is applied at, or near, the occlusal zone, and as near as possible to the line which bisects the central axis, with a tendency to produce distal inclination without rotation; the whole apparatus being calculated to utilize to the fullest extent the reactive force from the front teeth, in moving the buccal teeth back to normal occlusion while opening the spaces for the alignment of the cuspids.

CHAPTER XVI

PRINCIPLES OF INTERMAXILLARY AND OCCIPITAL FORCE

INTERMAXILLARY FORCE

One of the most important methods of applying force in the regulation of teeth, and one which is now recognized as an indispensable factor in modern orthodontia, is the **Disto-mesial Intermaxillary Force.** This principle, together with the principle of **bodily movement of teeth,** was introduced by the author at the February 1893 meeting of the Chicago Dental Society, and at the International Dental Congress in August of the same year.* It essentially consists in the attachment of elastic rubber bands from the cuspid area of one jaw to distal buccal points upon the molar area of the other, for the purpose of producing a distal or mesial movement of the buccal teeth of one jaw, or a reciprocal distal and mesial movement of both in correcting a disto-mesial malocclusion of the buccal teeth, and as an aid in correcting protrusions and retrusions of the front teeth. Throughout practical treatment of malocclusion will be found many illustrations showing different methods for applying this force.

The peculiar application and action of disto-mesial intermaxillary force in orthodontia, is quite distinctive in its character, and, moreover, decidedly different from all forms of direct intermaxillary force that have been used in various ways for many years.

The rubber bands that are well adapted for **intermaxillary force** are known to the trade as "election rings," and can be purchased in two or three sizes at almost any rubber house. Where greater force is required, two may be employed or the single ring may be doubled or looped twice upon the hooks.

The action of these small elastic bands exerting a continuous force upon the teeth of youths, will at times accomplish results that are surprisingly remarkable. Moreover, the ease and facility with which the elastics are adjusted and worn by even the little patients uninterruptedly—even while eating—proves the practical applicability of this force in the regulation of teeth.

This method of applying force is particularly useful in all cases of general protrusion and retrusion, and especially in cases of protrusion of the teeth of one

---

*As the origination of the Intermaxillary Force has been claimed by others, and as it was erroneously named the "Baker Anchorage" by Dr. Angle nearly ten years after it had been quite extensively published by the author and employed by many prominent dentists, the reader who is interested in the historical part of the subject is referred to the articles entitled "Origin, Use and Misuse of the Intermaxillary Force," published in the Dental Cosmos, May 1904, and "Rise and Development of Intermaxillary Force," published in the Dental Cosmos, May 1907. The fact that the voluminous evidence presented in these papers, which pertained to published proceedings of prominent dental societies, and the historical acts and statements of prominent *living* dentists, has never been controverted, except by bald assertions and untruthful claims *unsustained by the slightest attempt to produce legitimate evidence*, is sufficient in itself to place the honor where it belongs.

CHAPTER XVI. INTERMAXILLARY AND OCCIPITAL FORCE 127

jaw, and retrusion of those of the other where the full reciprocating activities of the force can be utilized. When properly applied in this way to the teeth of youths, the correction of malocclusion and facial contours is found to be easily accomplished in numberless instances that would have been considered at one time impossible without extraction. Frequently the teeth are moved by this force alone one-half the width of a cusp, or reciprocally the full width of a premolar which is equivalent to the operation of "jumping the bite."

FIG. 72.

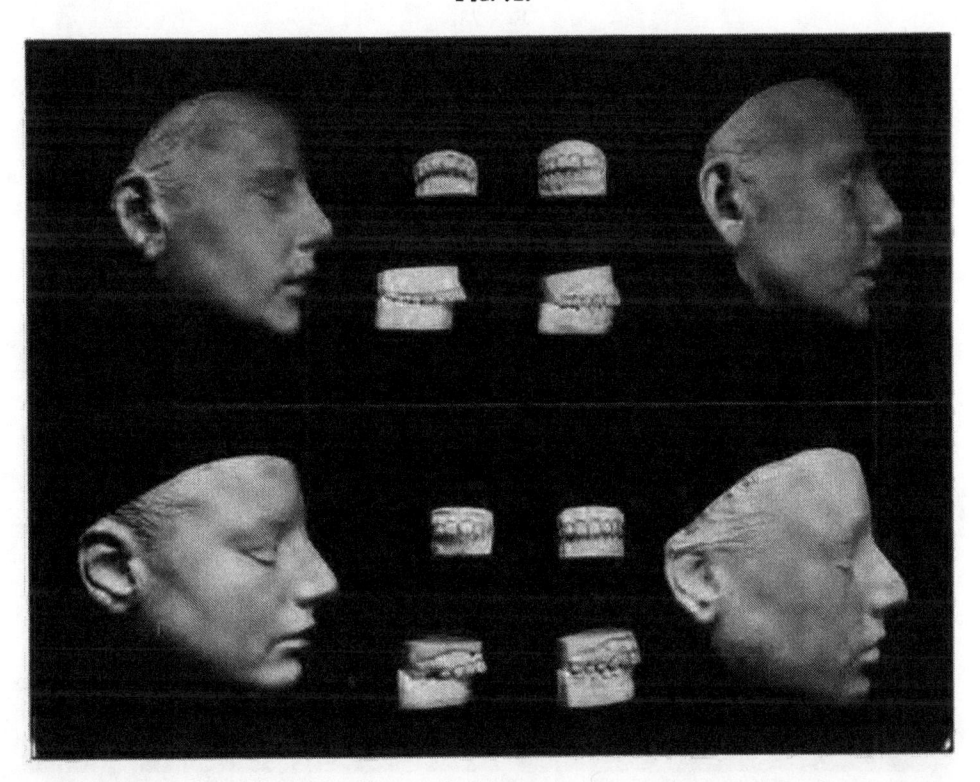

In Figs. 72 and 73, the facial and dental casts on the left show the beginning malocclusions of four cases in practice whose diagnosis places them in Division 1 of Class II—"retrusion of the lower denture with upper normal or nearly so." It will be seen in all of these cases that there is a full distal malocclusion of the lower buccal teeth in relation to the upper, with the usual malrelation of the front teeth. On the right are shown the finished cases with the dentures in normal occlusion, and the facial outlines corrected, the work being mainly accomplished with the intermaxillary force in shifting the dentures to a normal occlusion. See also Figs. 173 and 174, Chapter XXXI.

For the protrusive or retrusive movements of the teeth of one jaw with the intermaxillary force, as explained elsewhere, the force of **the reaction** should be distributed to the teeth of the opposing jaw so as to avoid their movement. If a

128   PART IV. TECHNIC PRINCIPLES OF PRACTICE

retrusive movement of the teeth of one jaw be required, with no mesial movement of the opposing buccal teeth, the hooks for the attachment of the elastics to the opposing jaw should be placed at the disto-buccal extremity of **stationary anchorages** and near the occlusal zone, in order that the line of force will be as nearly parallel as possible to the occlusal plane, to reduce the extruding tendency of the force when the jaws are opened. Its extruding action is one of the main objections to this principle of applying force, and certainly one that must be limited in its application. Especially is this true when the rubber bands are attached to single

FIG. 73.

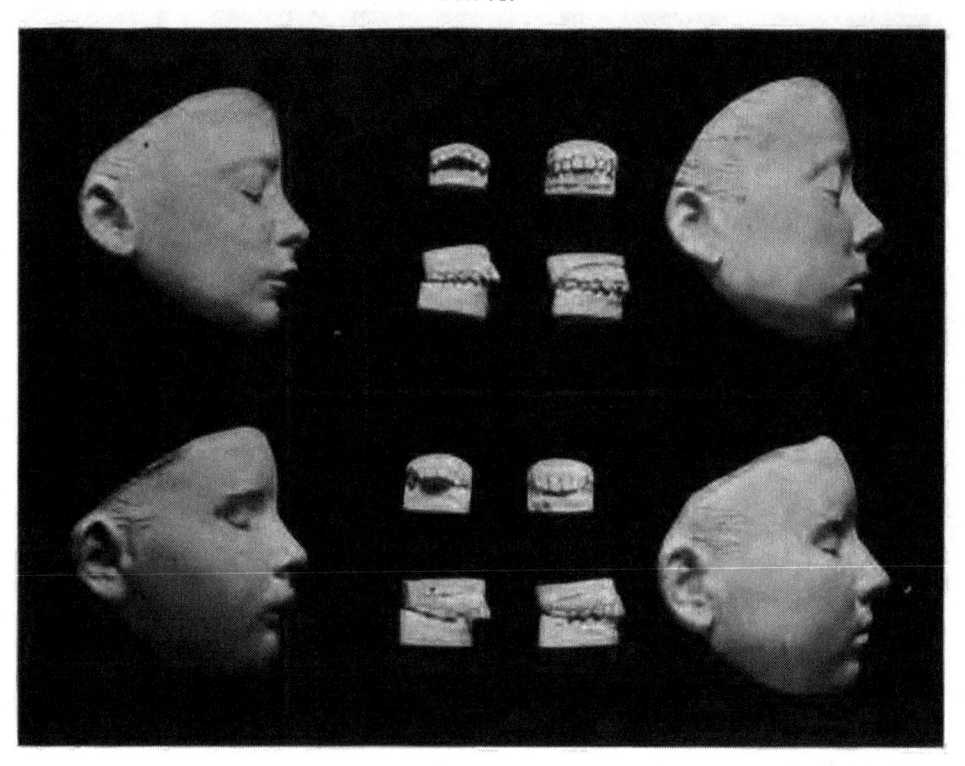

molar anchorages, particularly the first molars with no retaining arrangements, as has been wrongly advocated.

Moreover, the disto-mesial action of the intermaxillary force is an indispensable adjunct to the occipital force in a great variety of conditions, particularly where the buccal teeth—both upper and lower—have drifted forward from local causes. It is also one of the most important adjuncts for the reinforcement of weak molar anchorages, or whenever it is desirable to transfer the force from a weak point of reaction to the teeth of the opposing jaw. It is also indispensable in the treatment of many conditions which heretofore have baffled our possibilities of applying force.

The disto-mesial intermaxillary force is of the greatest value in opening spaces for the alignment of malerupted cuspids by a distal movement of the buccal teeth which have drifted forward and partially or wholly closed these spaces.

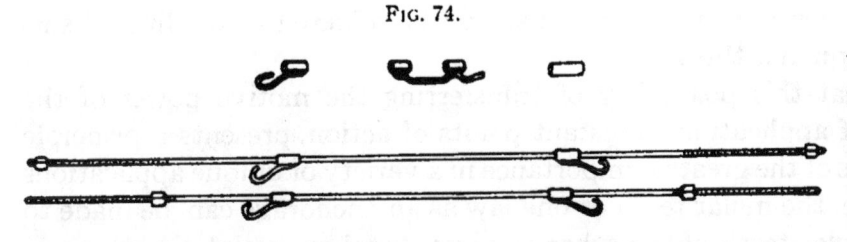

CHAPTER XVI. INTERMAXILLARY AND OCCIPITAL FORCE 129

Fig. 74.

As a distal movement of buccal teeth is always difficult, the entire force of the intermaxillary elastics may be directed upon any one or all of the buccal teeth through the medium of sliding tubes or span-hooks. See Fig. 74.

The **sliding intermaxillary hook** is a hook soldered to a short section of an open or seam tube for quickly attaching the intermaxillary force to any appliance having an arch-bow. This **sliding hook** communicates the force immediately to any band attachment on the cuspids or premolars or through the medium of sliding tubes to the molars, as shown in 3 and 5, Fig. 141, Chapter XXIV. They may also be immovably attached to the arch-bow with soft solder.

The **span-hooks** are made by soldering two short open tubes to a No. 19 or 18 bar. The bar is bent to conform to the line of the arch-bow and to span any intermediate attachment, thus communicating the force directly to the back teeth.

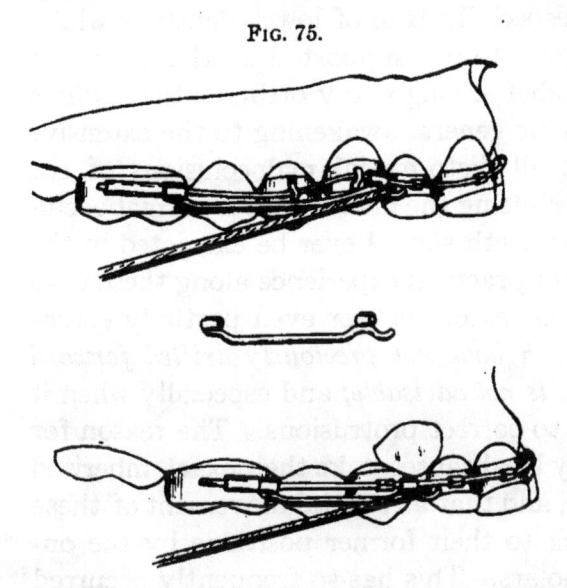

Fig. 75.

These span-hooks should be made of different lengths to supply every immediate demand.

Fig. 75 shows two conditions in which the intermaxillary long span-hooks are particularly applicable. In both these cases the malposition of the cuspids is due to premature loss of deciduous teeth permitting the buccal teeth to drift forward, demanding a distal movement of these teeth to their normal occlusal relations, with no labial movement of the incisors, thus properly opening the required spaces for the eruption and alignment of the cuspids. In the upper drawing, the required movement of the buccal teeth, though slight, is nevertheless necessary, because of the erupting second molars, which tend to increase and hold the malposition. The apparatus shows how the distal force of the intermaxillary elastics may be directed upon the molars, while their extruding tendency is utilized upon the nearly erupted cuspids.

In the lower drawing, the required distal movement of the buccal teeth is far greater; consequently the tube attachments on the molars are short and loosely fitted to the bow, so as to permit free distal inclination movement. In both of these cases, the distal movement of the premolars is accomplished with ligatures to the molars. Hook attachments for this purpose should be soldered to the lingual surfaces of the bands to equalize this force.

It will be seen that this possibility of transferring the motive power of the elastics from points of application to distant points of action, presents a principle in orthodontia which is of the greatest importance in a variety of unique applications of force. For instance, the molar teeth of one jaw as an anchorage can be made to move the opposing molar teeth of the other jaw in a distal or mesial direction. It also enables moving both the upper and lower teeth disto-mesially by a reciprocating action of the force, *and all with no movement of the front teeth.*

It will be seen, moreover, with a little thought, that the sliding span-hook permits a labio-lingual reciprocating action of the elastic force, to be applied to the upper and lower front teeth, the one to be moved labially, and the other lingually, or either one to be moved separately.

It should always be borne in mind, as elsewhere stated, that the distal movement of buccal teeth requires far more force than their mesial movement, because the distal bases of the respective arches, at whatever age the operation is undertaken, will be found to rest against a solid foundation of alveolar process and true bone, or against erupting teeth which are forcibly crowding their way into the arch between firmly resisting masses. This is especially true of lower dentures whose bases are composed of broad and solid ridges of bone supported by the ascending rami. It was through quite a prevailing belief among many orthodontists, which arose about fifteen years after the enthusiastic general awakening to the extensive employment of intermaxillary force, that all disto-mesial malocclusions of the dentures of Class II should be corrected by shifting the dentures to a normal occlusion with this force, which premised that no teeth should ever be extracted in the correction of malocclusions. Fifteen years of practical experience along these lines has shown to all advanced orthodontists that extensive—or even partially extensive—distal movement of buccal teeth *which have not previously drifted forward from the loss of deciduous or permanent teeth, is not advisable;* and especially when it involves the retrusion of an entire denture to correct protrusions. The reason for this is that the buccal teeth, uninfluenced by local causes, take their exact inherited disto-mesial positions in relation to the jaws, and that any distal movement of these teeth will almost invariably be forced back to their former positions by the oncoming eruption of the second and third molars. This has so frequently occurred even after operations for quite young children, notwithstanding the perfect interlocking of buccal cusps, in forced normal occlusions, that attempts to correct decided upper or lower protrusions in this way are rapidly being abandoned for more rational and scientific methods which present assurances for the perfect correction of the facial outlines, a good interdigitating masticating occlusion, and permanency of retention. A distal movement of molar teeth, however, is often demanded in nearly all cases in which they have been allowed to drift mesially from local causes, and for the correction of which the disto-mesial action of the elastics is of the greatest value. A favorable method for this purpose is to employ span-hooks, as described, which slide upon the arch-bow and communicate a distal intermaxillary force directly, or through the medium of sliding tubes, from the hooks in the vicinity of the cuspids to which the elastics are attached, to hooks at the distal end of lower stationary anchorages.

In whatever direction the disto-mesial movement, the apical ends of the roots are rarely if ever moved with the application of intermaxillary force—the movement being purely that of inclination. In Chapter X are pointed out by Dr. Cryer some of the objections and dangers in a considerable distal movement of the molars.

In the contemplation of employing the intermaxillary force for the correction of malocclusion and dento-facial relations, it should be remembered that the ungoverned action of the elastics will in all probability produce a far greater mesial movement of one denture than a distal movement of the other. While this may perfectly correct the occlusion, the dento-facial outlines may be left in quite a protruded state, because the case may have been one which required a greater distal movement of one denture than a mesial movement of the other. And this would also hold true, though to a less extent, in cases where an equally reciprocal movement of both dentures is demanded. On the other hand, in cases where the mesial movement should be greater, as in slight protrusions of the upper in connection with a considerable retrusion of the lower, as described in Division 2 of Class II, the unrestricted action of the intermaxillary elastics may perfectly perform the disto-mesial correction demanded, and without recourse to the extraction of teeth.

In addition to restricting or preventing the movement of one denture by anchoring the teeth together in phalanx, there is a variety of effective methods for accelerating the movement of the other denture, or rather of producing the greatest possible movement with the least exhibition of force. This is accomplished principally in two ways: First, by applying the force through the medium of movable attachments at the occlusal zone with its advantage toward inclination movement, and second, by applying the force, first to the most distantly located teeth in line with its action, and then to the next teeth in line, etc., until all have been moved. The various methods and technic principles will be found fully described and illustrated in detail in the respective classes of irregularities where the intermaxillary force is applicable.

Direct Intermaxillary Force.—Direct intermaxillary force of silk ligatures to aid the eruption of retarded teeth was employed in the latter part of the 60's by Dr. Jerry A. Robinson, of Jackson, Michigan.

The most practical form of *direct* intermaxillary force is that which was introduced by Dr. E. H. Angle, and published in the Dental Cosmos, September 1891, which described the employment of this method for correcting impacted upper cuspids and incisors. See Fig. 273. The principal use which the author makes of this form of force is in the correction of **Open and Close-bite Malocclu-**

sions, **Bucco-lingual Malocclusion of the Molars,** and **Lateral Malocclusion of the Dentures,** and in fact all forms of **Infra-occlusion** requiring extrusive force, a description of which will be found in Specific Methods of Regulating.

In Chapter XXVIII, is fully described a case showing, among other things, the common method now employed for correcting open-bite malocclusion with direct intermaxillary force. And, in Chapter XXVII is described and illustrated in Figs. 147, 148, and 149, one of the common intermaxillary aids in the correction of Lateral Malocclusion.

An important discovery in the application of direct intermaxillary force on molar teeth is: When elastics are attached to hooks on the buccal surfaces of upper and lower molars for an extrusive movement, the molars to which they are attached are also moved lingually, and when attached to the lingual surfaces, they are also moved bucally. This is important to remember, because if these lingual or buccal movements are not desired, two elastics should be employed attached to lingual and buccal hooks to equalize this force.

This bucco-lingual movement from a purely extrusive force is an important one, especially in those cases where one or both arches have been expanded, resulting in an inclination buccal movement, causing the molars to occlude upon the lingual cusps alone. While the expanding appliances are at work or in place, strong direct intermaxillary buccal elastics will tend to move the roots of the molar teeth buccally.

FIG. 76. In other words, the expanding process will be in the nature of a **bodily movement.** See Fig 76. If this or some other provision is not made for a bodily expanding movement, the malocclusion of the cusps will soon drive the arches back to their former malposition after the expanding force is removed, unless firmly retained. See Torsional Apparatus for bodily expanding movements, Fig. 63.

FIG. 77. Fig. 77 shows another important use of direct intermaxillary elastics in those cases where one arch has been expanded with the production of buccal inclination movement, or one molar has been abnormally expanded or moved buccally by an inadvertent expanding force of an alignment or expansion arch-bow. This is easily corrected with elastics from buccal hooks to lingual hooks on opposing molar anchorages.

OCCIPITAL FORCE

The principal force with which the Intermaxillary is an important auxiliary, is the **Occipital,** and as these two forces, in the author's practice, have become so largely dependent upon each other, working together and in conjunction with dental anchorage forces, he deems it advisable for all who essay the regulation of teeth to thoroughly acquaint themselves with the principles and latest methods of its application.

The **Occipital Force** was among the first to be used for the regulation of teeth —the early practitioners recognizing the advantage of locating the base of anchor-

CHAPTER XVI. INTERMAXILLARY AND OCCIPITAL FORCE

age completely outside of the immediate field of action. This same need or necessity was the "mother of the invention" of the **intermaxillary force.** As means develop for applying these forces in a scientific and skillful manner, they will be considered more and more among the indispensable powers for the regulation of teeth. This can only be accomplished by a full appreciation of dento-facial relations, and the adoption of applicable variations in methods and apparatus which will make the proper corrective movements possible.

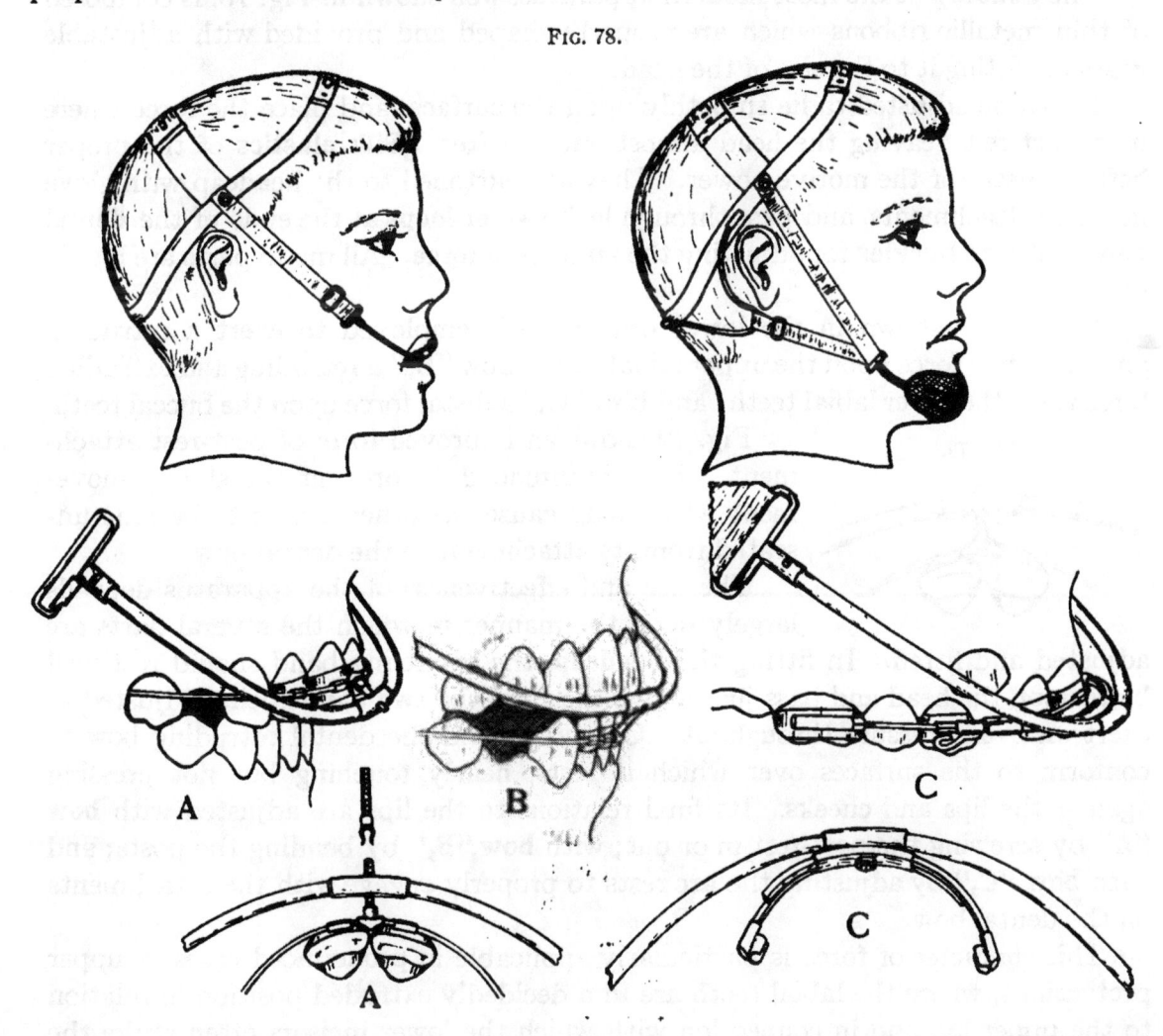

FIG. 78.

One of the greatest objections and drawbacks to the more general adoption of the **occipital force** has been the discomfort and irritation, if not actual pain, which the various forms of headgear apparatus that are sold on the market give to sensitive patients, and which so frequently causes them to omit wearing it a sufficient portion of the time to be of real service.

An **occipital apparatus** should be one that can be perfectly fitted by the operator to the form and requirements of the individual patient, with no prominent or projecting portions to interfere with the pillow while at rest, and one which can be easily adjusted by the patient and worn with the least possible discomfort during sleeping and waking hours. The principal direction of its movement is upward and backward, with a tendency toward the production of a movement when applied to the teeth that is frequently demanded, and **which can be accomplished in no other way.**

The **headcap** of the most modern apparatus, well shown in Fig. 78, is composed of thin metallic ribbons which are properly shaped and provided with adjustable gears for fitting it to the size of the head.

It can be adjusted to lie smoothly upon the surface, and place the force where it is least felt, leaving the head almost entirely free. **Silk elastics** of the proper heft are used for the motive power. They are buttoned to the headcap with glove fastener attachments, and pass through **lock swivel loops** at the ends of the **dental bow** to **sliding buckles** for adjusting the amount of force. All metal parts are highly nickel-plated.

Bow "A"—shown in the lower drawings—is employed to exert a retruding and intruding force upon the upper labial teeth; bow "B," a retruding and extruding force upon the lower labial teeth; and bow "C," a distal force upon the buccal teeth.

FIG. 79.

Fig. 79 shows an improved form of post-rest attachment, which is intended to prevent the sliding movement which may cause the other device to become unseated from its attachment to the dental bow.

The use and effectiveness of the apparatus depends largely upon the manner in which the several parts are adjusted and fitted. In fitting the **headcap,** the encircling band should rest well back upon the head and pass just above the ears; the two bands being adjusted to exert an even pressure throughout. Carefully bend the dental retruding bow to conform to the surfaces over which it rests, nearly touching but not pressing against the lips and cheeks. Its final relations to the lips are adjusted with **bow "A"** by screwing the post-rest in or out; with **bow "B,"** by bending the posts; and with **bow "C,"** by adjusting the arc rests to properly engage with the attachments on the dental bow.

This character of force is particularly applicable in pronounced cases of upper protrusions, where the labial teeth are in a decidedly extruded position in relation to the upper lip, and in connection with which the lower incisors often strike the gum back of the upper incisors. In Close-bite Malocclusions, with short upper lip and prominent teeth, the post-rest **bow "A"** is especially adapted for this movement.

Another irregularity for which the occipital force is especially applicable is in **protrusion of the lower teeth with an open-bite malocclusion,** for which the lower **bow "B"** will often be found exceedingly effective. The possibility which is now presented for applying the occipital force directly to the lower labial teeth in phalanx through the medium of a lower dental bow as an aid to the correction of open-bite malocclusions, where the lower jaw and teeth are protruded, renders the occipital force indispensable in the author's practice, even if it could not accomplish another object.

One of the most modern and valuable possibilities of the occipital apparatus is that which now enables the application of this force directly to the **buccal teeth** through the medium of the **bow "C."** See 2 and 4 under Fig. 141, Chapter XXIV. In this connection it is especially valuable as an auxiliary to the intermaxillary force. By this means, as is fully explained, the two retrusive forces can act upon the most distal upper molars, or all of the buccal teeth, without exerting any force, if not desired, upon the labial teeth. In fact, the incisor teeth can be moved labially from the molar anchorages while the premolars and molars are moved distally with the occipital and intermaxillary forces to open spaces for the eruption of crowded cuspids.

It will be seen that the entire apparatus is so constructed in its several parts that it may be easily adjusted by the operator to any size of head, and thus perfectly fitted to each individual case. If proper care is exercised in this regard, with the usual co-operation, no patient will object to wearing it. Many patients older than twenty years, in the author's practice, are wearing the apparatus without the slightest complaint. Younger patients of course will always adjust themselves to anything that is reasonable.

The **chin-cap** is made of fine wire gauze, soldered to a frame of proper form and provided with the swivel attachments for the elastics. When fitted to the chin, it presents a ventilated cap which exerts an even and comfortable pressure.

The application of occipital force to the chin for the bodily retrusive movement of the lower jaw, which has been in the past quite a popular practice, is now rarely considered of practical advantage after the years of childhood. If the apparatus can be made comfortable for the little ones so they will voluntarily wear it with sufficient persistence, no doubt much can be accomplished in this way.

PART V

Primary Principles of Practice

PRIMARY PRINCIPLES OF PRACTICE

CHAPTER XVII

IMPRESSIONS AND CASTS

In commencing the correction of an irregularity, good impressions should be taken of the dental arches separately, and a labial impression of the front teeth with the jaws in masticating closure. Perfect plaster casts of these impressions will show the exact malposition of the teeth; while the labial cast will enable an adjustment of the upper and lower casts to their occlusal relations.

Absolute duplication of the parts, as required for artificial dentures which may be obtained from plaster impressions, is rarely if ever demanded. In fact, the slight difference between dental casts made from skillfully taken Modeling Compound Impressions, and those taken with plaster, for all purposes of study and use, is not important; nor is it always advisable to attempt so trying an ordeal as a plaster impression at the first sitting with many nervous children and youths. If the occlusal relations of the teeth were a competent guide for their correction, as many seem to think, or if the plaster teeth instead of the natural teeth were used for taking the measurements and fitting the bands, it might then be different. Moreover, it is usually advisable to have a number of casts of each case, some of which may be used to hold the measurements and bands in place, and to set up the apparatus, where it can remain undisplaced until the final fitting and attachment at the chair. Again, it is frequently desirable to take impressions for casts during the progress of the case with appliances on the teeth, or at times when the apparatus is removed for radical changes of force, and during times when the sensitiveness of the teeth should preclude the use of plaster.

In the author's teaching, competent and successful diagnosis to determine the movements demanded, can be accomplished only at the chair where the natural occlusion of teeth, and the influences which the teeth and alveolar processes exert in characterizing the facial outlines, may be carefully and intelligently studied in all their phases of malrelation. The author wishes it to be understood, however, that he has no objection to the practice of taking preliminary plaster impressions for models of study—especially by those who cannot or do not obtain perfect impressions with plastic material—if for no other reason than it tends to cultivate habits of nicety and exactitude in other more important branches which pertain to the art of regulating teeth.

For the taking of Modeling Compound Impressions of the teeth, a **Tray** should be selected that can be easily introduced, and one which will carry the compound well over the labial and buccal surfaces of the teeth and gums. Trays shaped and constructed similar to certain forms of the Ash and Sons' trays, but differing in important particulars to facilitate introduction, are procurable, and in sizes adapted

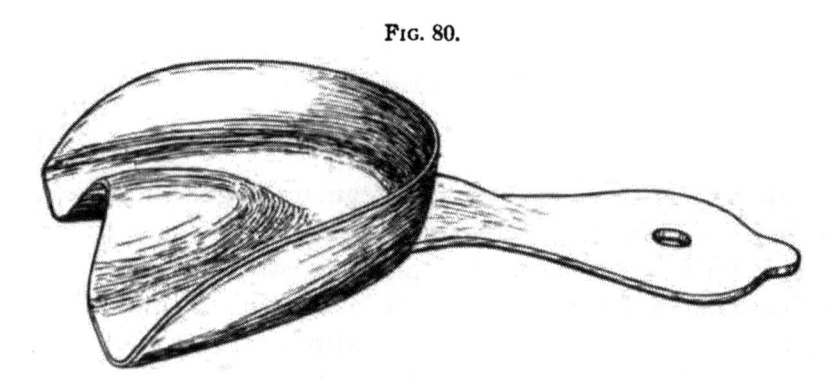

FIG. 80.

to the mouths of children as well as to adults. In Fig. 80, it will be noticed that the posterior buccal extensions are considerably lowered.

Use good modeling compound, softened in hot water to a consistency that will take a sharp imprint. (The author prefers the white compound manufactured by the Dental Mfg. Co. of New York City.) Warm the tray and place only a sufficient amount of the compound in it to take the complete impression. See that the impression surface is smooth and free from creases. Finally, warm the surface by passing it lightly over dry heat.

One of the greatest faults, and the one too that is the most common, is to allow the surface of the compound, before introduction, to become cooler and consequently harder than the body of the compound beneath, whereas, the opposite consistency should be the endeavor. The compound should never be heated to the extent of stickiness, or allowed to lie long in very hot water. The time required to place it in the warmed cup, shape and smooth it, will cause the surface to become stiffer than the body. If it is introduced in this condition, it cannot make a sharp impression, because the softer compound beneath is not stiff enough to press the harder surface into the deep sulci to sharply define the gingival borders.

Give the compound sufficient time for the entire mass to lose its very soft consistency before passing it lightly over a small Bunsen Burner. This will cause the softer overlying portion to be forced to place. In introducing the tray, place it so as to leave plenty of material for the labial portion and then speedily carry it bodily in a line with the long axes of the teeth. When the labial surface of the compound has passed the gum line, in the process of forcing it to place, raise the lip and press the compound firmly back into the cup and against the gum surfaces to sharply define the labio-gingival borders. Then, and not until then, carry the impression fully to place, and hold the tray perfectly still until the material is

CHAPTER XVII. IMPRESSIONS AND CASTS

sufficiently hard to remove without dragging. The time may be hastened by spraying with ice-water, or the air syringe.

In its removal, do not attempt to pull the impression away at the extreme end of the handle, but grasp the tray firmly so as to have complete control of its movement exerting a slight but firm tilting motion until you feel the first indication that the impression has started to leave its imbedment; then with gentle force partially allow it to take *its own direction of movement* from the teeth. If it does not start readily, see that it is not held by atmospheric pressure. Pull the tissues away from its borders and allow air or a little water to penetrate beneath.

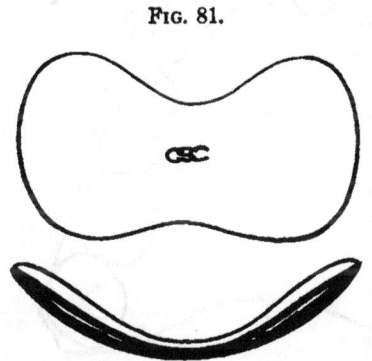

FIG. 81.

After obtaining good impressions of the upper and lower dentures, take an **occlusal impression** of the labial teeth as follows: See that the teeth are closed in masticating occlusion and admonish the patient not to open them during the operation. With a small amount of modeling compound placed in an **occlusal tray** (Fig. 81), press it against the front teeth including the cuspids and gums. In removal, ask the patient to open the mouth and then gently force it from its attachment to the upper teeth.

Duplicate impressions should be taken at another sitting to insure against imperfections in filling or breakage. The imperfect ones are used for working models during the entire process of constructing the apparatus.

The filling of impressions is so perfectly described in textbooks of other departments that it is not necessary to speak of it here. In the teaching of this branch, neatness and precision in shaping the casts should be insisted upon.

If the base lines of the upper and lower casts are trimmed as "a" and "b" in Fig. 82, and parallel to the occlusal plane, and the sides and front at right angles to the base from the extreme borders of the impression, it will have a symmetrical appearance. Overhanging "Dutchman's cap" extensions are silly. The occlusal casts, "c," may be trimmed as shown. Do not varnish the casts with shellac. If a preservative is desired, dip them in hot stearine. The name and age of the patient and date of taking the impression should be written plainly on each of the casts.

FACIAL IMPRESSIONS AND CASTS

In all cases of dento-facial deformities, or marked imperfections of the facial outlines, which are caused by malpositions of the teeth and jaws, **facial plaster casts,** from plaster impressions which exactly represent the natural contours, are far superior to facial photographs for all purposes of study and comparison of the features at different stages of the operation, because they permit an examination of every outline from different angles of observation.

If a **plaster cast** of the physiognomy is indicated, the operation should be deferred until you have gained the full confidence and friendliness of the patient.

142   PART V. PRIMARY PRINCIPLES OF PRACTICE

Without this, all operations which require for their success the full co-operation of the patient should not be undertaken.

Say nothing to young patients upon the subject of an impression of the face until you are all ready to take it. Then treat it as a matter of course and with no apparent thought that there will be any objection. Explain what you are going to do and just how they are going to help you; tell them it will not give the slightest

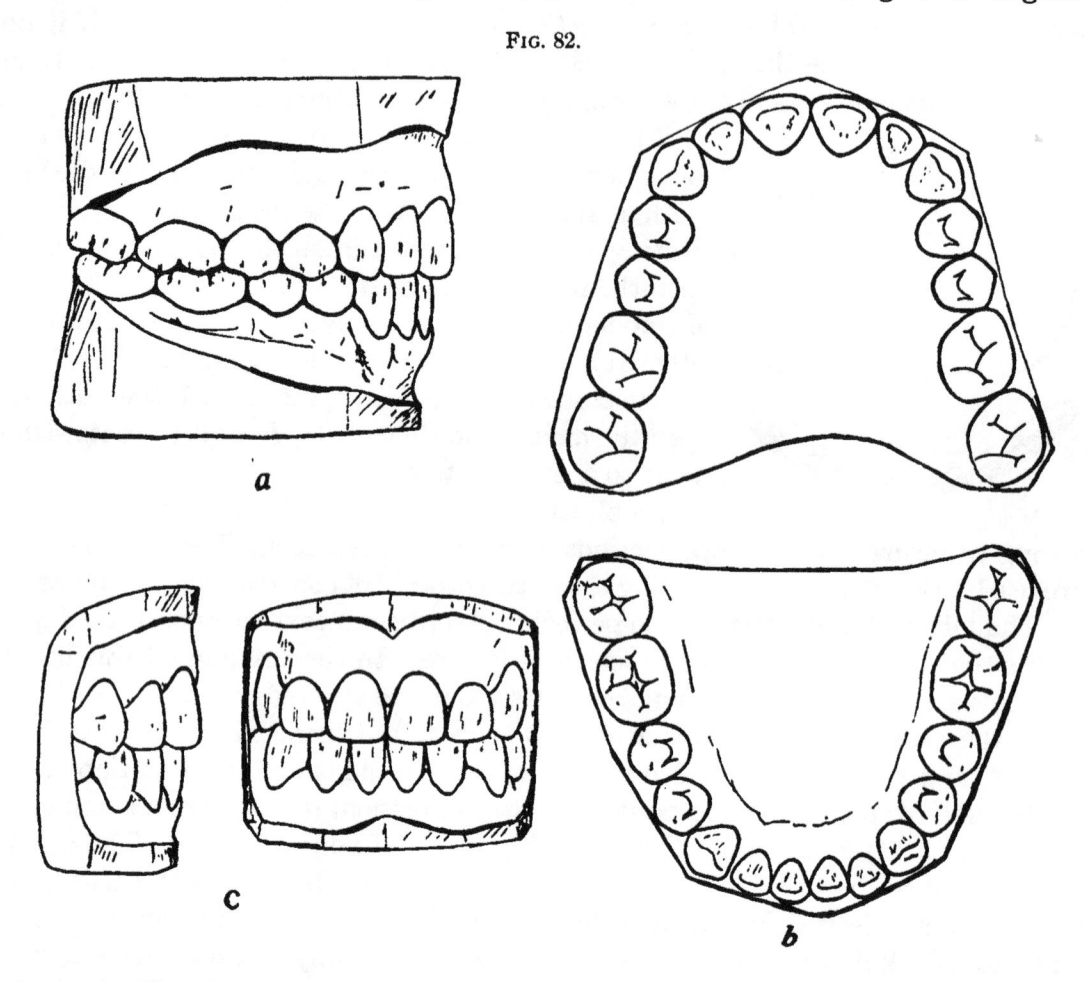

FIG. 82.

pain, and will only take about ten minutes. Exclude parents and friends from the room, or at least from standing by the chair, and have no one looking on within their sight after you commence with the plaster. If the patient is young, do not let him see that this is an intentional ostracism. You know the effect which the consciousness of some one gazing into your face would have upon your control of the facial muscles during a long sitting for a photograph, and how this would be increased if you were allowed to "catch the eye" from time to time of an acquaintance or relative.

Repose the patient well inclined in an easy position with the face turned from you, and make all preliminary arrangements with the least possible appearance of preparing for a difficult, or even a particular operation.

Have ready a small quantity of white perfumed vaseline in a small thin glass, placed in a clean white bowl of warm water, to partially liquidize the vaseline. Use an inch wide flat camel's hair brush, to apply the vaseline rapidly, and be sure that every part is gone over where you intend to lay the plaster. If the eyebrows are heavy, use the vaseline more or less congealed; nor should any of the vaseline be hot or in a fully liquid state. Do not feel obliged to brush the hair away from the forehead or ears to an unnatural position. It adds to the artistic effect of the model to show a portion of the hair naturally arranged and even partially covering the ear.

Commence with the vaseline upon the cheek, and then the mouth, lips, and teeth—if the latter are exposed. Assure your patient that the vaseline, and also the plaster which is to follow it, is perfectly clean, that none of it will drop into the mouth even though the lips are slightly open; and ask him to avoid if possible any movement of the lips while the plaster is being laid over the mouth, as it will spoil the natural pose which you are striving to catch. The involuntary tendency of the muscles to tightly close the lips to keep out offensive substances will mar the habitual pose of the lips and chin. This may be easily overcome, even with very nervous patients, with a little patience and kindly persistence in applying the vaseline, which they soon realize is in nowise disagreeable, and that the same will be true of the plaster.

In carrying the vaseline well up under the eye, ask the patient to look upward and tell him that when the plaster is being put on at that point to maintain that position for a few minutes, without winking, to prevent the lashes of the upper lid from becoming smeared with it while soft—that it will soon be hard and free from this danger.

Place a small pledget of cotton in the ear, and work the vaseline well into the surrounding depressions and out over the rim. You will now arrange the hair, if you have not previously done so, and vaseline it and the eyebrows as described. Ask the patient to close the eyes, and lubricate the surface of the upper lid down to the lashes; then the depression surrounding the canthus—down over the nose to the very borders of the nostrils; and join that portion of the vaseline which you first laid on. Let the operation be thorough, even to going back over surfaces that do not seem to be well lubricated, as upon this depends the ease of removing the impression. In fact, the titillating effect of the brush is good discipline to the muscles for acquiring immovability during the application of the plaster.

If it is to be a cast of the profile only, the vaseline should stop just beyond the border of the median line of the face. If a front view impression is intended to be taken in one piece, its distal borders should not extend beyond the malar prominences, as otherwise it will be difficult to remove without breaking. However, an impression can be taken in any number of sections by covering the borders of the plaster where you decide to stop with vaseline before proceeding with the next section. These sections can then be removed separately and fitted together before filling. In this way, the whole face, head, and neck can be taken; although such an extensive attempt is not advisable until you have had considerable experience in the work.

Above all things, do not admonish the patient about laughing or smiling, before or during the process of putting on the vaseline or plaster. If you see such a tendency, pay no attention to it, not even when in laying the plaster over the mouth you fear it may spoil the impression. If he is at once made to believe that you are seriously unconscious of his emotions, by some commonplace remark which you may make to your assistant about the weather, or of something you pretend to see out of the window, the danger will usually be averted by leading his mind into another channel, with an immediate subsidence of the smile before the plaster has become sufficiently hard to be affected by it.

On occasions, it has been observed by the slight quivering of the lips and moisture in the eyes of little ones, that the opposite tendency was uppermost. This should be treated in the same way, perhaps with some cheerful confident remark to your assistant complimenting the patient's fine behavior, and that it will be all over in a few minutes, etc., but by no means with a word or action of sympathy unless you wish them to break down. In almost every case, out of the hundreds of facial impressions the author has taken, even little ones who at first trembled at the sight of the dental chair, will become seriously and cheerfully interested, because of the fact that they have been made to feel they are in safe hands and that everything will transpire exactly as told to them.

In a serious operation of any kind, children should never be treated as babies requiring expressions of sympathy. Treat them rather as individuals of character who possess self-control, pluck, and bravery. They possess the canine instinct of knowing who are their friends, though they will rarely give you their whole confidence in the presence of a loving and sympathetic mother, who unfortunately will sometimes imagine it helps her children to stand by the chair and hold their hands, etc.

The plaster should be of a fine but slow setting quality. Mix with a slight excess of water that will not chill, and stir thoroughly to a smooth, clinging consistency, which may be handled easily with a spatula and will stay in place on inclined surfaces.

Use for the main work a spatula that is full width but about two-thirds the usual length. This can be made from an ordinary plaster spatula. A narrow spatula should be at hand when needed for certain deep places, or where small quantities of plaster with delicacy of manipulation is required.

Everything being ready, call for the first bowl of plaster. Hold it in the left hand just beneath the face with the arm over the head, and with the spatula lay the plaster first upon the cheek and approach the area of the mouth, extending it beyond the median line, and from the wings and septum of the nose to a point well beneath the chin. Then cover the cheek to the border of the lower lid while the patient is looking steadily toward the ceiling.

The thickness of the plaster should at first be only sufficient for the impression. You will reinforce it finally at the weaker points for strength, when it is not so important to avoid the dragging force of its heft.

In carrying the plaster along from the borders of each spatulaful, give a slight shaking or trembling motion to the spatula, to tease the plaster smoothly over the surface and down into deep depressions, as between lips, around exposed teeth, etc.

The plaster should be handled with skill and delicacy of manipulation, with no abrupt or awkward motion, as for instance, striking the skin with the spatula—that would cause pain or even surprise and a lack of perfect relinquishment.

The same is true in an ethical sense in regard to all your conversation, words of warning, direction, etc. Inspire your patient with a kind, cheerful, and confident atmosphere. Never speak loudly or peremptorily to your assistants, as calling to "hurry up with that plaster," etc., or in unkind criticism, even though you have the best of reasons, and things seem to be going all wrong; for the little ones, like the "gallery gods," are quick to note a discordant strain, and it may come at a time when they are all but ready to break down in one way or the other, and at the crucial moment when the plaster has commenced to set over the mouth. Here the slightest movement of the muscles indicative of the emotions will destroy the really important part of the impression.

The advice which was given in explaining the lubricating process, relative to the ethical management of the patient, will be especially important while you are striving to safely pass the critical point around the mouth; after this there is usually little occasion for anxiety.

Follow the same course with the plaster that was described in laying on the vaseline. The first mix of plaster will usually cover the mouth, cheek, ear, hair, and eyebrows, providing that you work rapidly; then you can finish with the second mix; although three and even four mixes are sometimes necessary when the plaster sets rapidly. The last and thicker portion of the first mix should be used over the hair and eyebrows, as it is not so liable to cling upon removal. To do this, it is often necessary to skip the ear, which should then be covered with the first of the second mix. As soon as the plaster commences to thicken, call for another bowl, continuing with the one in hand until it has become too thickened to spread well. If an extra mix is required for finishing the impression of the nose—which should be with plaster that flows readily with a slight shaking motion—have a small quantity of potassium sulphate mixed with the water, then the remaining portion of the plaster will serve to reinforce the impression, and you will not be obliged to wait so long for it to set.

It requires considerable delicacy of manipulation to work the plaster over the upper eyelid till it nearly touches the lashes, and around the borders of the canthus also at the end of the nose down over the septum and to the very borders of the nostril, without closing the opening so as to obstruct breathing. Do not attempt to put anything into the nose, such as quills, etc., for this purpose, it only serves to annoy the patient and is never necessary.

After waiting until the plaster is hard, place the fingers under the edge of the mesial border of the impression and lift with a gentle force, working it slightly with a lateral movement. Do not use force as you would in removing a plaster impression from the mouth. It will soon yield if the lubrication has been thoroughly performed. If it clings to the eyebrows or hair, as soon as you have raised it sufficiently to pass the fingers or a rubber spatula beneath, you will be able to feel the clinging hair or hairs, and by pressing downward toward the skin, they can be gently dislodged from the plaster. This part of the operation is usually performed by the assistant.

FIG. 83.

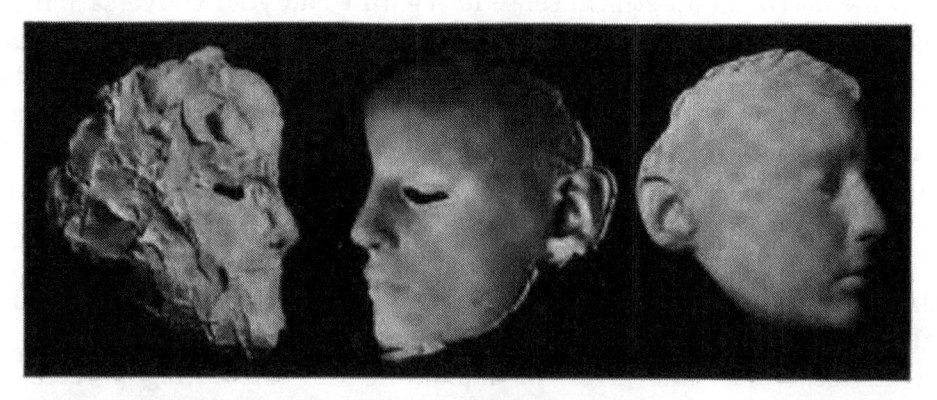

The above illustration shows from left to right, the outside and inside of the impression, and the final facial cast made from the impression.

Unhinge it slowly and carefully from the ear, working out the clinging portions of the rim or hair with the finger. The pledget of cotton generally comes away with the impression, where it is allowed to remain during the filling process, and if waxed and shaped to the proper form it serves to represent the external meatus.

In preparing the impression for filling, the eye and nostril holes are covered with wax (externally) in such a manner as to leave the borders well defined; this will allow for an excess of plaster at these points that can be finished by carving. Varnish with a thin coat of shellac, followed with sandarac, and then thoroughly soak the impression in water just before filling. In the process of filling, imbed two corks in the back of the cast so as to raise it to the proper angle, if desired to fasten it to a board with screws.

Before separating, soak it thoroughly in warm water and dip it occasionally while chipping off the impression. In other particulars follow the same rules as in separating plaster impressions of partial dentures. In carving the borders of the closed eyelid and open nostril, continue the curves of the natural surfaces. This will cause the greater prominence of the upper eyelid to rest upon the lower, and carry the lines of the nostril to the more abrupt curve which enters the orifice.

When the cast becomes soiled at any time later, a thin coat of light pink calcimine will give it an agreeable flesh color. This can be renewed at any time by washing off the previous coat.

CHAPTER XVIII

PRIMARY PRINCIPLES AND TECHNICS IN THE CONSTRUCTION OF BANDS

Separating the Teeth.—In practice, when the character of any irregularity and the appropriate apparatus for its correction is determined, the **measurements** of the natural teeth for the required bands should be taken. As a preliminary step, see that the teeth are sufficiently **separated**. For the purpose alone of taking the measurements, the operation of separating should never be performed, unless absolutely necessary, as the separators usually require to be left between the teeth twenty-four hours, and with some nervous and sensitive patients this is exceedingly annoying, if not painful.

Fig. 84.

Separating Tape.

Separating Tape.—In operations for youths, if it is necessary to first separate the teeth slightly in order to force the bands between them for the measurements, use the thinnest and narrowest **flax waxed tape** that will stay in place without dislodgment. Thus, by a gradual approach, the severer conditions that may be found necessary with a greater separation will be withstood later in the operation without a murmur.

Waxed tape is made in three widths, Nos. 1, 2, and 3, Fig. 84. Where space is demanded for taking the measurements, etc., at first use the No. 1, and if necessary, follow it with No. 2, or No. 3, folded with one edge slightly projecting to facilitate introductions. Where the No. 1 has remained between the teeth for several hours, the folded tapes can be easily introduced, and the teeth will speedily respond.

Between back teeth where the thicker interproximate portions of double-band anchorage or adjoining bands of completed appliances are to be attached, the folded tapes, finally, will always be necessary. With older patients it may at times be found advisable, especially when the contact point is near or at the occlusal surfaces, to tie floss silk, or twist, around the contact point with the knot in the interproximate space. A few fibers of cotton placed in the loop may in this way be drawn in and held firmly between the teeth.

Method of Introducing Tape.—In inserting the tape, hold the roll in one hand with a sufficient length unrolled to be grasped firmly and extended tautly with the other; then, with the forefingers on the occlusal edge of the tape near the teeth, press the gingival edge into the space with a sawing motion.

When the separating tape is inserted between the teeth, it is important that it be cut off closely within the interproximate spaces in order that no projecting ends or fraying threads are left to act as sources of irritation or inducements to the removal of the separators during the twenty-four or forty-eight hours they are required to remain between the teeth. For this purpose, scissors should be used with blades that are short, sufficiently narrow, and properly curved to enable the operator to place the pointed ends on either side of the tape as it emerges from its lodgment, and cut it cleanly to the shortest possible length. A fine grade of curved manicure scissors may be used whose blades have been ground to the narrowest limit consistent with strength. **Tape scissors** that are especially constructed for the pur-

FIG. 85.

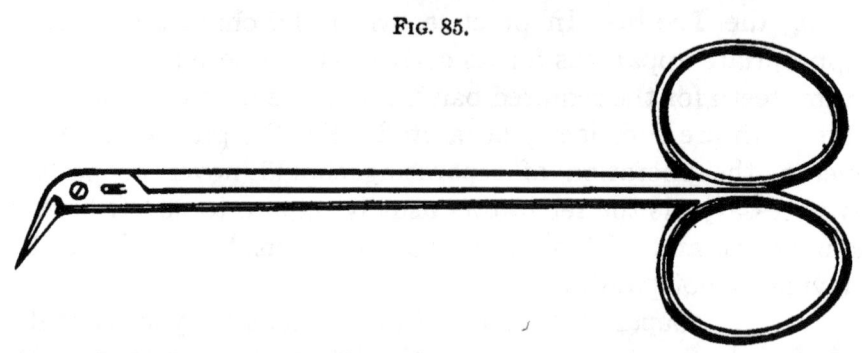

pose, as shown in Fig. 85, will be found convenient, especially in reaching the most distal requirements of the back teeth.

When the separating tapes have been cut off as closely as they should be in this manner, the difficulty of removing them is increased, and it is often impossible with ordinary tweezers and pliers. Fig. 86 shows specially constructed **Tape Pliers** whose beaks are strong and pointed with interdigitating serrations calculated to penetrate the interproximate space and firmly grasp the tape.

FIG. 86.

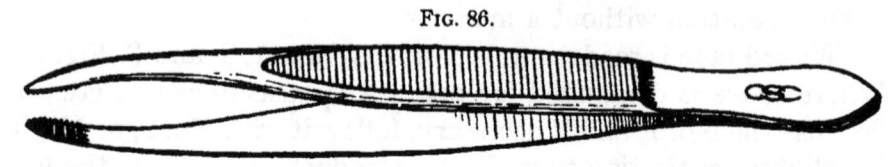

FIG. 87.

Band Material.

Orthodontia Bands.—Band Material, Fig. 87, is made in three widths,—narrow, medium, and wide,—and in thicknesses which range from .003″ to .006″.

The consistent place for the joints of front bands requiring attachments is on the **labial surfaces,** not only because of the greater ease and more assured accuracy in taking the band measurements, but mainly because the finished bands take a more natural and stable position in relation to the crowns. It will be noticed that when a piece of straight band material is passed around an upper central incisor, for instance, and drawn or pressed forward so that its middle portion lies flat against the lingual surface of the tooth, for the purpose of making the joint in front, its free ends incline upward toward the gum. Consequently, when the ends are properly pinched for the joints and soldered, the location of the labial portion is considerably more root-wise than the lingual, and therefore more

CHAPTER XVIII. CONSTRUCTION OF BANDS

in accord with the mean gingival border lines of gum and enamel. See "a," Fig. 88. This is true to a more or less extent of all the front teeth. On the other hand, when straight band strips are passed around these teeth in the opposite direction for lingual joints, and pressed evenly against the labial surfaces, the bands will take the opposite inclination in relation to the gingival zone, with the frequent necessity, when taking the measurements, of forcing the edges into the lingual and interproximate gingivae in order to secure sufficient gingival nearness in front. This is important in most instances, because in the application of all linguo-labial and linguo-buccal forces which are not intended for inclination or "tipping" movements, whether direct or torsional, the attachments to the bands should always be placed as near the gingival borders as admissible, if one wishes to obtain the greatest mechanical advantages toward moving the teeth bodily or semi-bodily. See "b," Fig. 88.

Fig. 88.

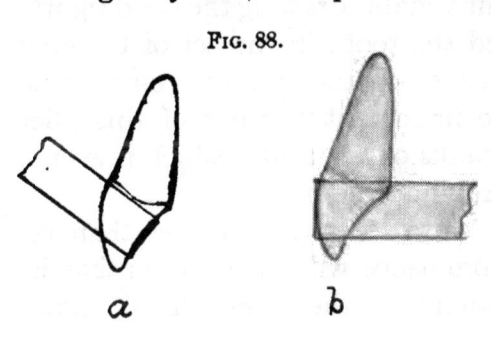

Among the minor advantages, when the rib of the band joint after soldering is trimmed to project about a 32nd of an inch, and is then mashed flat and the surface contoured with fitting pliers for the front teeth, and contour pliers for the buccal teeth, so that they exactly fit the labial and buccal contours of the crowns; and finally when the joint and adjoining surfaces are reinforced with No. 18 gold solder, or No. 2 silver solder—as will be explained—there is no other method that affords a greater degree of strength, perfection of fitting, and permanency of attachment to the tooth, or one that is superior in artistic effect; particularly because this method of reinforcing the joint and labial surfaces with solder nearly obscures the joint while its strength permits narrowing the front of the labial bands to the minimum width, especially for all operations in aligning the teeth with the resilient forces of light arch-bows.

Dr. Angle's *insistence* that the joints of the front bands should always be located on the lingual surfaces may be partly due to the fact that there is no other way of placing on the market his modern appliances with their difficult technic. And it may be also for the same reason that he insists upon those cumbersome, irritating and unsanitary lingual clamp-band joints for molar anchorages.

Fig. 89.

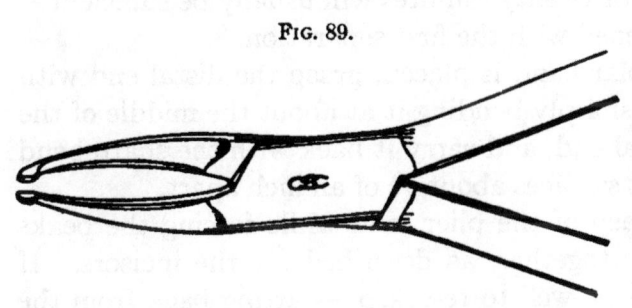

For taking the band measurements, the **Banding Plier** shown in Fig. 89 is recommended. The extreme ends of the beaks are shaped to obtain three grasping positions of the plier, "a," "b," and "c," Fig. 90, which will be found convenient for the different angles in which the plier must be held in crimping the joints of the bands for different teeth. By placing the sharpened edges back from the crimping points of the band, while pressing them firmly against the teeth, they will bite into the surfaces, and thus enable drawing the band tightly around the tooth in the act of bringing the beaks together for the joint. One of the important features of this plier is the open and rounded inner surfaces of the shanks of the beaks, which prevents pinching the lips when the crimping edges are brought together.

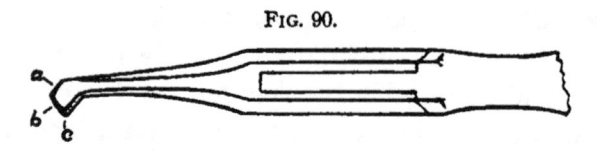

FIG. 90.

The **Band Material,** Fig. 87, should be cut into lengths no longer than required to facilitate adjustment. If students commence with the incisor bands, they will have acquired a certain degree of training for the more difficult molar measurements.

Grasp the ends of the looped piece of banding material between thumb and fingers of one hand, and force the loop between the proximal surfaces of the teeth with the other, and while drawing it firmly to place, bend it to fit the lingual inequalities of the tooth in order to give proper direction to the joint ends. Still holding the ends between finger and thumb, place the open jaws of the plier with ends resting back upon the band on either side of the joint. Pressing the band against the tooth, bring the jaws firmly together, and move the pliers slightly to and fro to sharply bend the joint marking.

Carefully remove each band as it is measured to avoid obliterating the mark, and place it in the proper position on a form, or on its proper tooth of the working model—the teeth of which have been sawed apart for this purpose. Proceed in a similar manner with the cuspids and premolars. Working forms are easily made with thin pieces of wood into which short brads are driven in the positions and alignment of the teeth in the dental arch.

Molar Measurements.—The molar bands being much thicker and more rigid are more difficult to adjust and perfectly fit; considerable force, often with the plier, is required to force the band between the teeth. If the spaces are insufficient, insert the wider folded tape. Fifteen or twenty minutes will usually be sufficient—the teeth having become slightly loosened with the first separation.

When the band material for a molar band is placed, grasp the distal end with the plier and bring it firmly forward, sharply bending it at about the middle of the buccal surface. Then grasp the mesial end, and carry it back with the sharp bend at a point that will leave the two joint surfaces about $\frac{1}{8}$ of an inch apart.

Now include both ends in the grasp of the plier, and while forcing the beaks against the tooth, bring them firmly together, as described for the incisors. If the bands are wide and thick, it may be well to re-grasp—starting back from the joint—and repeat the movement. In fact, after a band is soldered and found to be too large, a tuck can be taken up in it in this way, showing the utility of the movement for drawing the band to a perfect fitting. Quite frequently, in taking the measurements for second molar bands, it will be found more convenient to pinch the joint on the lingual surfaces.

Measurements for Partially Erupted Cuspids.—A perfect fitting band can be made for a cuspid not fully erupted without causing more than a slight pain, if the measuring process is managed properly. Loosen the surrounding gum covering the enamel, which will be found to have a slight attachment, then carefully work the loop of the band, held as described, beneath the lingual border of the gum. Sometimes it can be passed under the linguo-gingival border the full width of the band without even drawing blood. In this position the ends on the labial aspect may be pinched for the joint.

Soldering Bands

Preparatory to soldering the joints, the ends of the bands should be cut off to about ¼ of an inch, then placed in the grasp of the **Band Burnishing Plier**

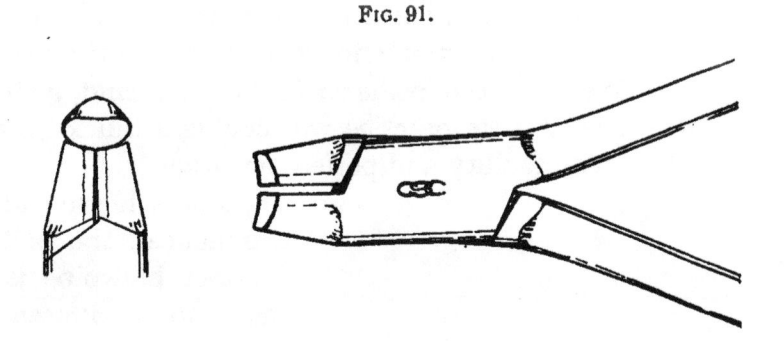

Fig. 91.

(Fig. 91), or a blunt square-nosed plier, and burnished toward the joint on the inside of the band so as to carry the ends deeply between the jaws to form a perfectly united joint when soldered.

Before placing the band in the grasp of the Solder Plier, Fig. 92, lute the ends of the plier with liquid plumbago to prevent them from adhering to the work. The joint edges of the band should come evenly and perfectly together. In soldering

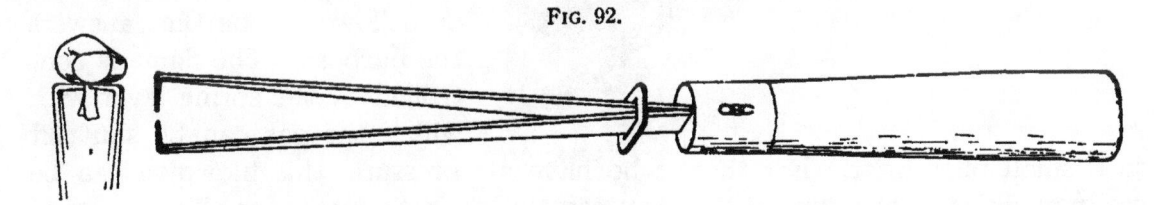

Fig. 92.

all parts of appliances, the pointed blue blaze is rarely employed. The blaze that is made with less air blast pressure whose greatest heat area is farther away from the point of the blowpipe, and of a more distributing character, is far preferable and safer. Its hottest central point can be quite as accurately directed; and it is

152 PART V. PRIMARY PRINCIPLES OF PRACTICE

safer, because its softer spreading quality distributes a more general heat to the surrounding area where its danger degree in relation to the fusing point of the solder can be seen and guarded against. Remember always, that the solder should be forced to flow through the medium of the heated joint or surface to be soldered. One should have a sufficient number of these inexpensive solder pliers to enable shaping the ends to properly grasp the different attachments to be soldered.

In soldering bands, direct the soft blaze of the blowpipe always upon the ends beneath the band until the joint starts to turn red, then quickly run along the joint the point of an instrument dipped in partially liquified borax with the view of drawing the subsequently fused borax down into the joint, and not on the inside surface of the band. Then place a very small piece of solder—only sufficient to fill the joint—exactly over the joint so that it touches both sides, and continue the heat as before, always beneath, never upon the band itself, or upon the solder, until it is fused and drawn down into the joint. In placing the small piece of solder, it may first be touched to the surface of the liquified borax. If the heat carries it to one side of the joint, stop and replace it exactly over the joint; otherwise it is likely to flow on to the inside surface of the band, instead of being drawn into the joint. A very little practice will enable a quick performance of this part of the operation with facility and perfect accuracy.

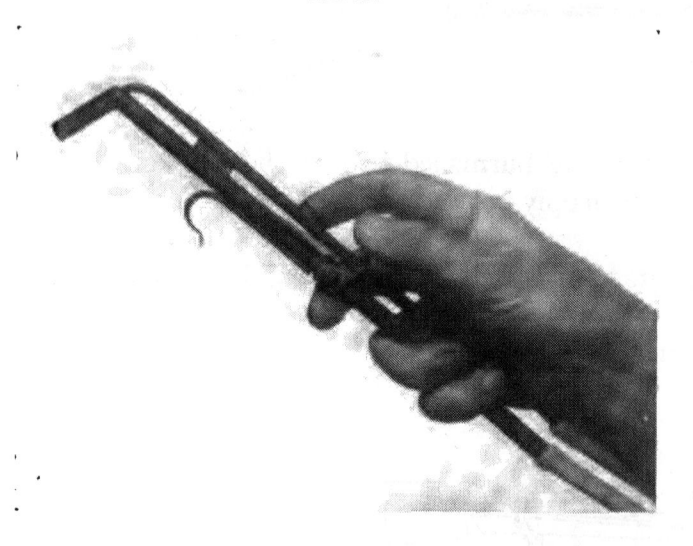

FIG. 93.

For soldering all regulating appliances, the skillful use of a perfect blowpipe is far preferable to a Bunsen Burner, or any stationary instrument. In selecting a blowpipe, it should be one that can be held lightly in the hand, so as to be manipulated easily and quickly in response to demands. The Lee blowpipe, shown in Fig. 93, which is operated by the mouth, or bellows, is one that answers the purpose. The flame is controlled by the spring lever with which the gas can be shut off to a small pilot light. For those who have air pressure, this blowpipe can be easily modified to form one of the most convenient instruments for all purposes of soldering. This is accomplished by cutting an oblong finger-hole in the air tube of the blowpipe, through which is passed a short half-section of a thin tube curved and contoured at one end, as shown below in Fig. 94, and soft-soldered to the inside of the air tube, as shown by the dotted lines, in such a position that the continuous

CHAPTER XVIII. CONSTRUCTION OF BANDS

stream of air under pressure is directed out through the hole. Around the hole is soldered an elevated rim beveled to exactly fit the end of the forefinger. This enables one to completely close the hole with a very light pressure. When the finger is in place covering the hole, the air is forced over the curved inner lip and on to its work forming the air blast.

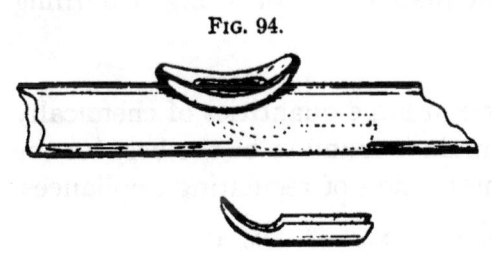

Fig. 94.

A small spur is soldered to the side of the pipe to which is attached a fine spiral spring which connects with the gas lever. The flame is controlled with the thumb on the spring lever which when released shuts the gas down to the pilot light. At any moment the operator drops or hangs up the blowpipe, the spring lever is released, and the gas shut down to the pilot light, but not blown out by the air pressure which now escapes through the hole.

The main advantage in this device is that it enables a quick and delicate regulation of the gas and air, which with little practice becomes an involuntary movement. With small work that is not invested, only sufficient gas and air should be allowed to pass the valves that will form a blaze of this kind about two inches long to its extreme end. Before commencing to solder, only a trifle more than the required amount of air should be turned on to the pipe, and this is further regulated by slightly raising the finger. Perfection and delicacy of adjusting and manipulating the blaze is of the greatest importance in skillful soldering.

In regard to the solder, it is quite as easy and safe to solder nickel silver appliances with different grades of gold solder as with silver solder. In all appliances where gold solder is to be used throughout, as in retaining appliances, the joints of the bands should be soldered with 22k. For the rest of the work, the author rarely employs less than 18k. It requires far more care to use a low grade of solder than a high one—providing of course that the fusing point of the solder is lower than the things to be soldered—for the reason that a slightly overheated thin band or base will quickly absorb and become alloyed with the zinc of the solder, and immediately fuse or "burn out" over that surface.

Whenever the solder of any kind does not flow freely, or "balls up," so to speak, it is due to one of two things: First, to the lack of borax, and second,—which is commonly the cause with beginners—the solder itself is fused before the joint or surfaces to be soldered are first heated to, or slightly above, the fusing point of the solder. If the case is invested, it should be first thoroughly dried out over a Bunsen Burner, and when it is placed on the solder block, the flaming blaze should be directed upon the investment and continued until the bands, at the point to be soldered, commence to turn slightly red—as in free-hand soldering—then add the borax and fuse that, and then the solder. Always commence the blaze back on the investment, and gradually draw the heat toward the band or joint until brought to the fusing point of the solder which will then flow freely into the joint; then stop at once, and add more solder if required to complete the work. If the heat is carried a very little beyond the free fusing point of the solder, it is liable to alloy the base and lower its fusibility, and this is one of the main causes of fusing or burning thin bands.

Silver Solder

The most perfect flowing silver solder is made in large quantities of chemically pure silver, copper, and zinc. The following formula is found to be the best for the three grades of silver solder required in the construction of regulating appliances.

		No. 1	No. 2	No. 3
Silver Solder	C. P. Silver	8	8	8
	C. P. Copper	4	4	4
	C. P. Zinc	1	2	3

An eight-ounce crucible is first completely coated on the inside with borax, using a gas oxyhydrogen furnace. The copper of one of the grades is first fused, and when at its lowest fusing point, the silver, in small pieces or pellets is added one at a time, increasing in amounts until all are in. Then when again reduced to its lowest fusing point, add the zinc—thrusting small pieces into the mass so as to bury them quickly beneath the surface to prevent oxidation or burning them up before they can be united with the alloy. The alloy is then brought to a high heat that will cause it to roll and thoroughly mix, before pouring into ingots to be rolled to 28 gauge, and cut into 1 pwt. pieces.

CHAPTER XIX

ADVANCED PRINCIPLES AND TECHNICS OF REGULATING BANDS

Preliminary Fitting of Bands.—After the joints of the bands have been soldered with No. 1 silver solder or 22k gold solder, the projecting ends of the joints should be trimmed off close, and firmly mashed between the beaks of fitting pliers, and then properly contoured to fit the labial and lingual surfaces of the teeth. It is usually an advantage to fit the bands to the natural teeth to correct any imperfection in size, and to mark the position and direction of attachments. In giving to the band the exact shape of its tooth form, it insures greater perfection to the fit of attachments, especially those of the long tubes upon molars.

At this time the proximal borders of the bands may be trimmed so they will not extend beneath the borders of the gums or lie upon occlusal surfaces. Whenever it is necessary that the edges must extend under the gingivæ, they should always be carefully burnished to fit the surfaces of the teeth at the time of cementing them. Where attachments are to be soldered to front bands merely for the purpose of bow rests, or where there is no great tendency of the force to dislodge the band, the labial surfaces may be considerably narrowed. An apparatus requiring a very small alignment arch-bow for the retrusion or alignment of the labial teeth can in this way be made quite inconspicuous. In most **drawings of apparatus** in this work, the bands are shown wide for the purpose of more distinctly illustrating the attachments and their respective positions. They should not, therefore, be viewed as the finished band in this particular.

FIG. 95.

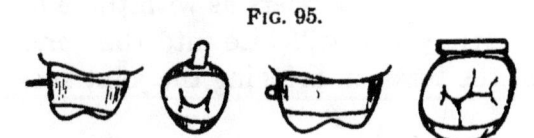

FIG. 96.

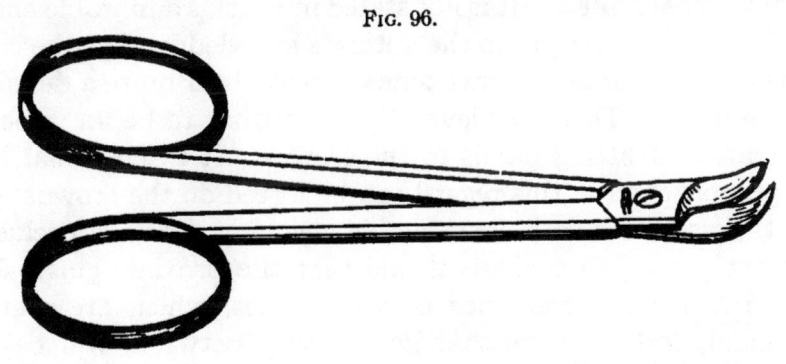

The lingual and buccal portions of molar and premolar bands should be contoured and the sharp edges filed preparatory to the final finishing, as shown in sample bands, Fig. 95.

The instruments necessary for the above work are: **Curved Scissors,** Fig. 96, a six-inch half-round **jeweler's** file No. 6, a six-inch **rat-tail** file No. 5, and the **Band Contouring Pliers,** Fig. 97. The latter are far more perfectly adapted for this work

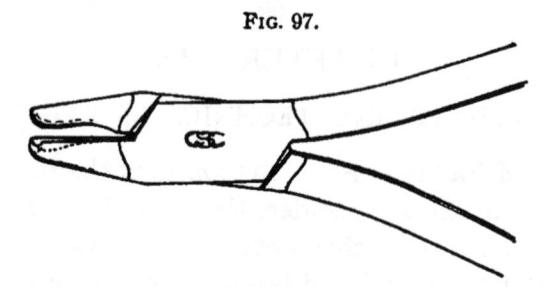

FIG. 97.

than the ordinary crown contourers, as they are constructed to avoid crimping the edges of the band.

The Technics of Band Fitting.—One of the essentials to the perfect retention of a band, is that it should fit the teeth as tightly as it can be driven on. Some writers have instructed that the bands should fit somewhat loosely, so as to leave space for the cement; this is about as reasonable as leaving a space for the cement or glue in mending broken earthen or glassware, or in making a wood joint.

In taking the **measurements** it requires considerable practice to draw a band —especially the thicker ones—around a tooth tightly, and sharply bend it for the joint; nor can it be done as easily with any of the ordinary pliers as with those of more delicate ends having somewhat sharp edges, which will bite into the band material itself while pressing the band against the tooth in bringing the joint surfaces closely together.

Again, in burnishing the joint preparatory to soldering: if the joint has not been sharply marked, it requires considerable judgment to avoid leaving the band too large, by failing to force the joint sufficiently into the grasp of the burnishing pliers. In fitting a band on a tooth after it is soldered, if it is found to be slightly too small it can be easily enlarged on the horn of an anvil.

Relation of Coronal Zones.—It is not stated in Black's admirable and exhaustive "Dental Anatomy," or elsewhere to the author's knowledge, that the circumference measurements of the different **coronal zones** of teeth bear quite a definite anatomic relation to each other. This is believed by the author to be an important factor in the consideration of fitting bands to the crowns. It teaches that bands which are properly proportioned in this regard can be forced on the crowns of any of the teeth and fit their surfaces with considerable accuracy, from an occlusal line even with the contact points, to a gingival line near the proximo-gingival borders of enamel. The relative circumference of these zones, which are marked by the edges of the band, and the zone that lies midway between, will be found quite definite in all teeth of the same character.

The relative circumferences of the crowns of **incisors** and **cuspids**—upper and lower—gradually taper in size from the gingival to the occlusal zones. The incisors taper in the proportion of 2 to 1 in 4 inches, and the cuspids 2 to 1 in 1 inch. That is to say, bands of the proper size that are made to fit mandrels which taper in this proportion will quite accurately fit these teeth from the mesio-distal angles to the linguo-gingival ridges.

With **upper premolars** and the upper and lower **first** and **second molars,** the gingival band zones are about the same size as the occlusal, but the largest zone lies between, somewhat nearer to the gingival. If these bands are made of the proper size upon a mandrel which tapers in the proportion of 2 to 1 in 12 inches, and of a width that covers well the buccal and lingual surfaces, and are festooned so as not to cover the occluso-mesial and occluso-distal ridges on the one hand, or extend far beneath the interproximate gingivæ on the other, and then are contoured on the buccal and lingual sides so as to draw in the occlusal edges, the bands will be found, when driven on, to fit these teeth quite accurately from the gingival to the occlusal margins.

With **lower premolars** the occlusal and gingival zones are about the same size, the two zones lying nearer together and with no marked difference between them in proportional taper. If bands are made for these teeth of the proper size, with very slight taper, and as above, in other particulars, they will be found to fit with sufficient accuracy for all practical purposes.

From this it will be seen that if **bands** are shaped and contoured properly and are of the right size and taper they may be **driven** on the crowns to a point where they will tightly fit all the surfaces. Again, there is usually so much difference between the general sizes of the right and left tooth, even though not perceptible to the eye, that if the bands are transposed they will commonly be surprisingly too large or too small. Therefore, in taking the measurements, a model or form should always be at hand upon which the bands can be placed in their respective places when removed from the teeth; a precaution that should be strictly observed throughout the entire construction of the apparatus.

Placing Bands.—In placing a band upon a tooth, one should be able, on account of the slight conical shape of the tooth and band, to force it nearly to place with the fingers or thumb, if the spaces between the teeth will permit; after this the use

FIG. 98.

of a hickory or hardwood **Band Plugger,** Fig. 98, used with a heavy mallet, is invaluable. The broad and somewhat yielding surface of the wood resting upon the edge of a band—especially when it is nearly in place—will not double or mar the edge as will any steel instrument. It will also catch the edge that has passed the occlusal angle and enable one to force it to a more perfect fitting than seems possible with anything else.

158   PART V. PRIMARY PRINCIPLES OF PRACTICE

A heavy **Lead Mallet,** one weighing 6 ounces, will be found far more effective and cause less pain to the patient than one of the ordinary lighter kinds used for filling. With the same amount of momentum, the velocity is decreased in proportion to the weight, producing a blow that approaches a push force, without rebound, and being one of a more distributing quality, will not produce the amount of shock to sensitive teeth which often obtains in the use of lighter mallets.

Removal of Bands.—The removal of bands that have been driven on the teeth for trial, or to mark position of attachments, is made easy with the **Band Removing**

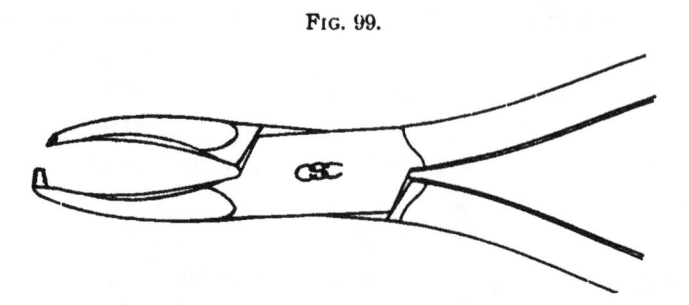

FIG. 99.

Pliers, Fig. 99. These are constructed with one jaw to engage with the gingival edge of the band, while the other, which is longer and turned at right angles, is shod with copper to rest upon the occlusal surface and act as a fulcrum, without danger of cracking the enamel. The shape of the extreme end of the fulcrum beak is such that while retaining its position upon the tooth, it enters the band as it is being lifted, thus permitting its free disengagement. These pliers are indispensable for the removal of cemented and uncemented bands, for the purpose of changing their position or to add attachments for the application of other forces. The reciprocal action of the two beaks causes little or no strain upon the teeth and consequently a minimum amount of pain to patients, as would certainly always arise in such an attempt with a free hand action of any instrument lifting or pulling upon the band.

Slitting the Bands.—When a preservation of the band is unnecessary and its removal is at all difficult, it should be cut with the **slitting pliers,** Fig. 100.

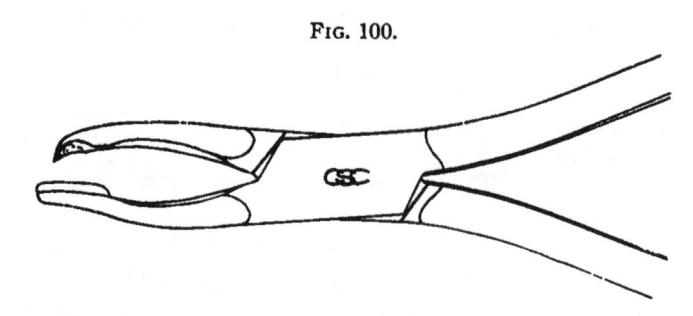

FIG. 100.

The longer fulcrum beak is shod with copper to rest upon the occlusal surface of the tooth without injury to the enamel, while the shape of the cutting beak is peculiarly adapted for slitting the band.

Soldering Attachments.—Preparatory to soldering attachments, the bands should be first festooned and the premolars and molars perfectly contoured, and then replaced upon the plaster model or natural teeth in the exact position they are intended to occupy, in order to determine and mark the correct positions and directions of the attachments. In removing the bands, the natural tooth shape of the bands should be preserved, especially for fitting and soldering long-bearing attachments. For long **rotating** and **molar tubes,** groove the band with a **fine round** or **joint file** to give the tube a long bearing close seating, while preserving the natural contour of the band. The ends of the **anchorage tubes** should not project more than is necessary to freely turn the nuts; and where no distal nuts are to be used, bevel and finish the ends of the tubes to prevent the laceration of tissues.

In some instances when a part of the apparatus is complicated, or requires special care as to the position of the attachments in relation to the teeth and gums, and in the construction of **stationary anchorages** and retaining appliances, a plaster impression of the teeth with the bands in position with a view of placing them on an **investment model** in the exact positions they occupied on the teeth, will be found necessary.

The only objection to this procedure in all cases, is the necessity of heating up a large model when the soldering of the attachments can usually be accomplished far more easily and safely while held in the solder pliers, and with sufficient perfection, if their positions have been properly marked upon the bands.

Management of Solder and Blowpipe.—When the attachment is in place on the band, and held in the grasp of the solder plier, lightly throw a spreading—not a pointed—blaze from the blowpipe over the point to be soldered, heating it to a near red; then quickly touch the point with liquified borax to cover only that portion where the solder is to flow. Follow this immediately with a soft blaze as before until the borax is thoroughly fused between the joints, then, and not until then, place over the joint or into it a piece of No. 2 solder nearly if not fully sufficient for the whole of that immediate work, and direct the same character of blaze, *not* upon the solder, but with the view of heating up the surfaces or joint to be soldered, and make this heated area fuse the solder and draw it into the joint. If the solder becomes oxidized over its surface in a half-fused condition, quickly touch it with more borax, and continue the heat, which will at once cause it to flow to place. When you see the solder suddenly jump to its place, *stop at once.* Too much heat at this point will cause the zinc of the solder to alloy the nickel silver band, lowering its quality and weakening it. For the same reason never use the No. 3 solder, except in places where there is danger of loosening a previously soldered attachment. In fact, in all soldering whether of silver or gold, the higher grades of solder when used with skill, will be found to flow far more evenly, safely, and perfectly than the lower grades.

Construction of Bands for the Midget Appliances.—In the construction of all front bands and their attachments, an endeavor should be made to make them as inconspicuous as possible. The front bands of the Midget Appliances, and also those for the bodily labial movement of children's teeth, afford an opportunity to exercise this desire to a greater degree than any of the other appliances as follows:

When the front bands are soldered with 22k gold solder, and their joints mashed, they are placed on the teeth and driven firmly to place. As some of the bands will go further on the teeth than others producing an unevenness in their line, this should be noted and an even gingival line marked on the front with a steel point. The bands are then removed, and their gingival edges are evened, and their occlusal edges are festooned with the curved scissors to the minimum of width along this line, which need not be wider in the middle than one-eighth of an inch, and even less if attachments are to span the joints. The bands are then slightly contoured on the front to fit the curves of the teeth, and again placed on the teeth to verify their alignment; finally shape the front surfaces. Moreover, a careful removal of the bands after the final fitting is important so that they will retain the form of the teeth, because over the entire front of each of these bands is flowed a thin layer of 18k gold solder which stiffens and strengthens them.

Nothing adds so much to the artistic effect of appliances as an evenness in the width and relation of the bands to the occlusal edges of the front teeth. The object in flowing the 18k solder over the front of the band is twofold: First, no other solder is required in placing the attachments; all that is necessary is to hold the attachments in place with the solder plier, and direct the pointed blue blaze of the blowpipe *upon the attachment* until the solder beneath starts to fuse. Second, because of its quality and light color, it gives to the bands a durable and pleasing finish.

In this process, the band is held freely in the solder plier, and the labial surface gently brought to a red heat with a soft blaze flared back and forth; then add borax and flush it over the entire front surface with the same kind of gentle heat. Then add the gold solder commencing at the joint, and fuse it in the same manner, causing the heat to carry it completely and evenly over the surface. This should entirely obliterate the appearance of the joint.

The labial attachments, of various forms to meet all requirements, are shown enlarged in Fig. 101. A shows a long open tube attachment with very thin wall to be employed for retention of position. When closed around the arch-bow, which these attachments should exactly fit, they present a smooth finish. B and C show variations in correcting malturned teeth through the resilient forces of very light arch-bows, the wire ligature being employed until the bow can be inclosed in both short open tube attachments. D, E and F show different views of the finger-spur attachment, which is the method most frequently employed with light resilient bows, Nos. 24 to 26, for the rotation and alignment of incisor teeth. Tiny abridged **U-tubes** are soldered on these bands in positions to meet the requirements of intrusive or extrusive movements and to steady the bow. The **finger-spurs**

CHAPTER XIX. TECHNICS OF REGULATING BANDS

are cut from No. 24 annealed wire and flattened at one end on the anvil. These are soldered to the extreme distal or mesial surfaces permitted by the crowded position. When the arch-bow is in position in the tubes, it is sprung lingually, and the finger-spurs are bent sharply over it with a pair of pliers so as to exert a rotating force; the surplus ends are then cut off. This may need to be repeated in subsequent treatments—each time making a new bend in the finger-spurs until the position of the teeth is corrected.

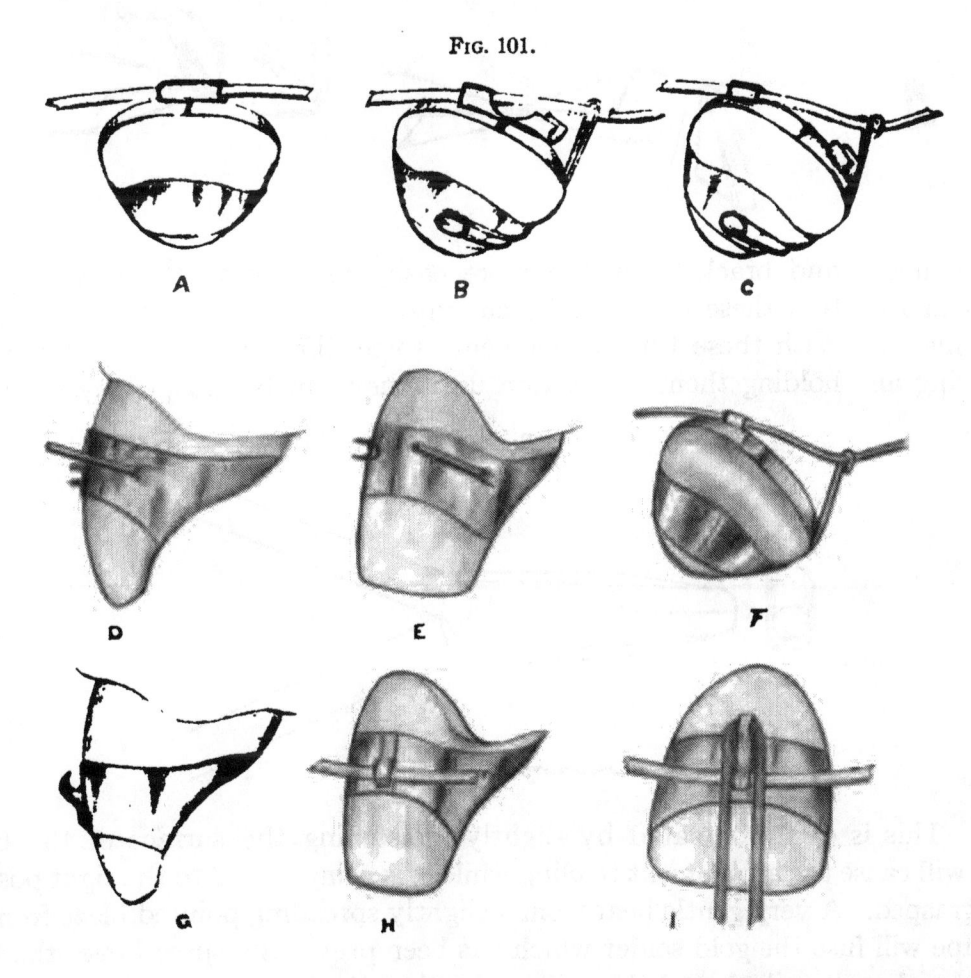

FIG. 101.

The finger-spurs are also of great value in the correction of marked malalignments when little or no rotation of the tooth is required. The spur is bent sharply in the form of an L at the flattened end, and soldered at any point upon the front of the band to exert the proper pulling force. The finger-spur is then lapped over the bow as before. G and H show the common hook attachment. When employed with the very light resilient bows, Nos. 24, 25, and 26, they are made by rolling No. 23 (.0225″) round wire to a thickness of about .018″. This is bent sharply with thin flat-nosed pliers to the desired form and finished neatly so that it will project no more than slightly beyond the bow when in place.

162   *PART V. PRIMARY PRINCIPLES OF PRACTICE*

Fig. 102 shows the double hook or bracket which is useful at times for the attachment of intermaxillary elastics in the correction of open-bite malocclusions.

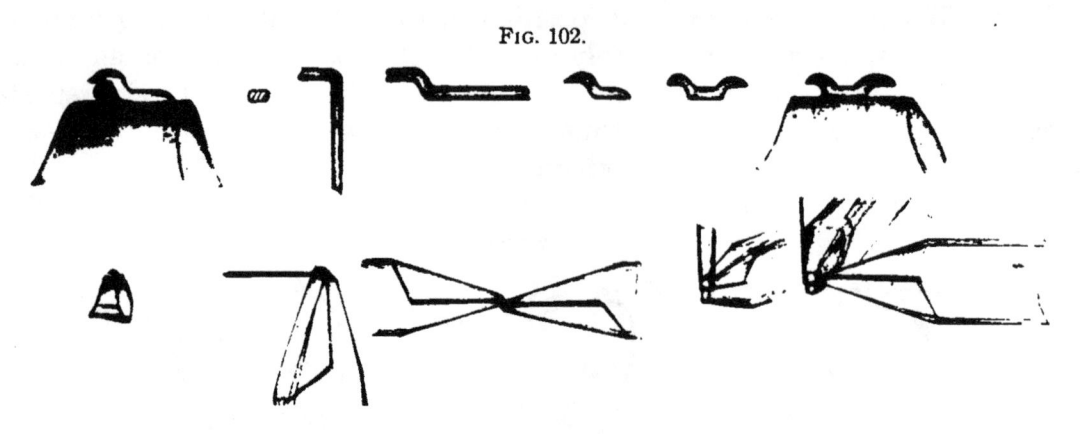

FIG. 102.

The hooks and brackets can be more easily made with the crimping plier shown in Fig. 103; these can then be cut into the proper sizes for the required attachments. With these tiny attachments some difficulty may be experienced in placing and holding them in position until they can be grasped by the solder

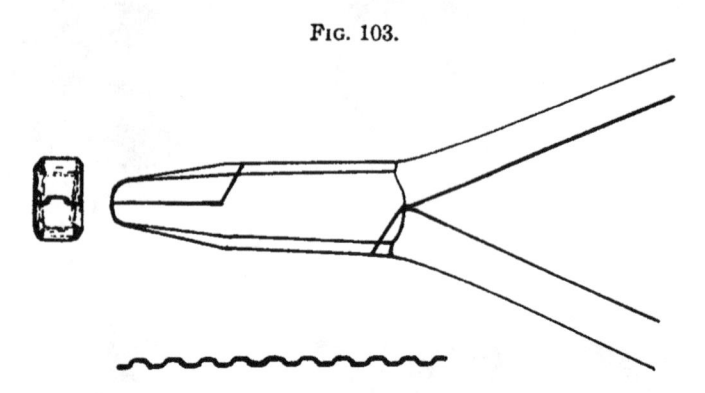

FIG. 103.

pliers. This is easily obviated by slightly moistening the surface of the band, which will cause the attachment to cling while it is being teased to the right position to be grasped. A very gentle heat from a slightly spreading pointed blaze from the blowpipe will fuse the gold solder which has been previously spread over the front of the band as described, and this will solder the attachment.

FINISHING AND PLATING

After the necessary attachments are soldered to the bands, they are boiled about fifteen minutes in a solution of sulphuric acid, and neutralized in a solution of sal soda, then thoroughly rinsed in hot water; this is to remove the borax and loosen the oxide preparatory to polishing and plating them. In finishing the bands, hold them on a wood mandrel somewhat the form and taper of the respective teeth. All sharp and projecting portions that are likely to irritate the mucous

CHAPTER XIX. TECHNICS OF REGULATING BANDS

membrane should be removed with a file, or with a fine emery wheel, and the surfaces rounded, smoothed, and polished with tripoli on a felt wheel and a coarse hair brush wheel; then a fine brass wire brush wheel is used for the final polishing and burnishing. If care has been observed to prevent oil or grease of any kind from coming in contact with the parts, from the hands, or otherwise, while polishing, they can be carried immediately into the plating solution.

When the appliances are of platinum and gold alloy, if highly polished and kept in that condition, they present a far more artistic and inconspicuous appearance without gold-plating.

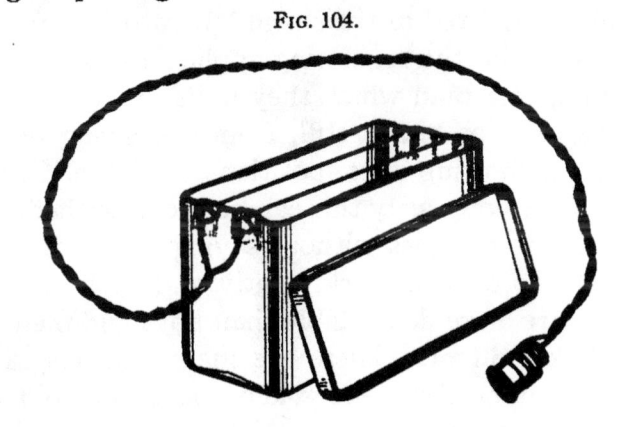

FIG. 104.

The **Plating Outfit** for regulating appliances employed by the author is shown in Fig. 104. It takes its current directly from the Edison 110-volt direct current through the medium of a series current tap supporting a 16-candle-power lamp. If this seems to produce a current of too high voltage, it may be reduced one-half by inserting an 8-candle-power lamp. Where the direct current is not at hand, a single one-gallon cell (Daniel, Smee, Bunsen, or preferably, an Edison Lelande) can be substituted.

The gold-plating solution advised by the author is made by dissolving 30 grains of Mallinckrodt's Gold Chloride in about one quart of hot distilled water; then add chemically pure cyanide of potassium until the solution is clear; it can be used cold or slightly warmed. This solution contains far less cyanide than the usual solution recommended, and will be found to preserve the anode much longer. Use for an anode a piece of pure gold plate about two inches square; this should be removed from the solution when not in use. After plating the parts, polish with whiting on a soft hair brush wheel.

The Personal Factor in Technics

When one is properly equipped with all the requisite tools, implements, and material, the construction, or personal direction and supervision of the construction of regulating appliances in the office laboratory will be found one of the greatest pleasures in the practice of orthodontia, and one, moreover, that will require less time and annoyance with far more assurance of perfect applicability than the selection and fitting of commercial appliances. Besides, nearly all commercial appliances demand considerable fitting and soldering; then why not go a little further and solder the attachments to the bands, and thus be sure that they are exactly in the right places and attitudes for performing the most effective work?

This does not mean that one shall prepare banding material, tubing, or threaded bows, bars, nuts, jackscrews, etc., or prepare the stock material for the small attachments, all of which may be purchased, but it is an appeal to orthodontists to construct or have constructed in their own laboratories, under their immediate supervision and personal aid, the regulating appliances used in their practice, and made exactly according to a plan which they have previously thought out as the most efficient for the case, or better still, from a drawing of the whole apparatus set up on the teeth, showing sizes, positions, etc., etc. A very little practice along these lines will show how easily this can be accomplished, while the efficiency and satisfaction to be derived goes without saying. It is remarkable, moreover, how quickly girls learn to do this work, neatly and with dispatch, because they enjoy it; besides, they are more dependable than boys and men.

Advantages of Nickel Silver.—There are many reasons in favor of the employment of nickel silver in preference to gold or platinized gold, etc., in the general construction of regulating apparatus. The nickel silver material is fully as harmless for the teeth and gums as any of the royal metals. One of the things in favor of nickel silver bands is: the material is softer and can be more easily and perfectly fitted to the depressions on the lingual surfaces of the incisors and along gingival borders than the platinized metals, and therefore, less likely to loosen from the teeth or to leave spaces for the washing out of the cement.

The fusing point of nickel silver is sufficiently adequate for every practical purpose. For instance, in constructing the retainers, the joints of the incisor bands which are not over .003" or No. 40 B. & S. gauge, are soldered easily with 22k gold solder, and for the rest of the work not less than 18k solder may be safely used by one who is skillful in its management, thus entirely covering the nickel silver bands with the gold solder and reinforcements.

The main argument in favor of nickel silver is not because of the difference in cost, which of course amounts to considerable in a large practice, but it is the perfect willingness and even desire on the part of the operator to at once remove and *throw away* any apparatus or part as soon as it is found to have done its work, or is not quite perfect, and replace it with another. He is not trying to make it do, when he knows it ought to be changed, nor is he saving the bows and bands for another case for which they are not perfectly adapted. As for the difference in appearance—for that is all that it really amounts to—the gold-plated nickel silver is certainly objectionable when compared to the fresh clear white-metal appliances, but when the nickel silver is highly polished, and not plated, there is comparatively no difference in appearance; and while the latter is perhaps more likely to become tarnished in the mouth, unless there is a perfect co-operation on the part of the patient or parents in keeping regulating appliances of *whatever metal* clean and polished—which is always possible—they all soon become tarnished and turn dark at points which are difficult to reach with the brush.

Boys are usually far more difficult to control in this regard than girls, because they have less pride. But parents should be made to understand at the outset, that it is incumbent upon them to attend to this necessity, and if they fail, they should be called sharply to account, for the difference in appearance of the appliances is small compared to the danger to the teeth if great care and attention is not given to cleanliness during the regulating process.

CHAPTER XX

MODERN PRINCIPLES AND METHODS IN ORTHODONTIA

In order to bring to the minds of students some of the most modern methods in orthodontia, it has been deemed advisable to devote this chapter to the history and treatment, from start to finish, of a somewhat complicated case in the author's practice, revised from a paper which was read before the American Society of Orthodontists in 1917.

Three Characters of Malocclusion in One Case.—The object in selecting this particular case for this purpose, is that it presents a combination of several distinctive malpositions, and a variety of distinctive characters of movements, with the requirement of a number of different kinds of appliances for its correction and retention. It will give an opportunity to describe from a practical standpoint the efficiency and value of the **new midget appliances** for correcting the alignment of the teeth for children and youths; the value of direct intermaxillary elastics in the correction of open-bite malocclusions; the value and modern technics of comparatively light appliances for the **bodily labial movement** of the upper front teeth; the principle and practical application of **torsional force** for the bodily expansion of arches; the value and practical action of the **working-retainer;** and finally, the finished result with the **regular retaining appliances** in place.

The case is one of peculiar interest and applicability, because in the first place it teaches the importance of a careful and thorough study of every case, however apparently simple and uncomplicated it may at first appear, and why an artistic observation of the facial outlines should be regarded as one of the foundation principles of intelligent diagnosis.

It shows how there may arise three distinctive characters of malocclusion from the local cause of adenoids followed with long continued early mouth-breathing and inhibited maxillary development, i. e., decided malalignments of the permanent teeth, open-bite or infra-occlusion of the front teeth, and finally, a bodily retruded position of the upper incisors and entire intermaxillary process.

It will conclusively demonstrate the remarkable effectiveness of the resilient forces of exceedingly light arch-bows and delicately constructed bands and unique attachments. It will show the most modern technique and application of the regular bodily movement apparatus whose principles of force have been successfully employed for twenty-five years for the correction of the most extensive retrusions and protrusions. This was originally named the "contouring apparatus." It was afterwards discovered that this same principle of applying force to the teeth, according to the law of levers of the third kind, was quite as applicable

CHAPTER XX. MODERN PRINCIPLES AND METHODS 167

for bodily *lingual* or retruding movements of the front teeth; and in recent years this same mechanical principle has been extensively employed for bodily movements of the teeth in every direction. In fact, no teeth were ever moved bodily, except through the application of this principle of force, which consists in the establishment of independent points of fulcrum and power in relation to the alveolus or area of work. Even that addition to our technic principles of torsional force for the bodily movement of teeth presented recently by Dr. Angle and exemplified in his new "pin and tube" and " bracket and ribbon" appliances, is reducible in its direct action to that of a lever of the third kind.

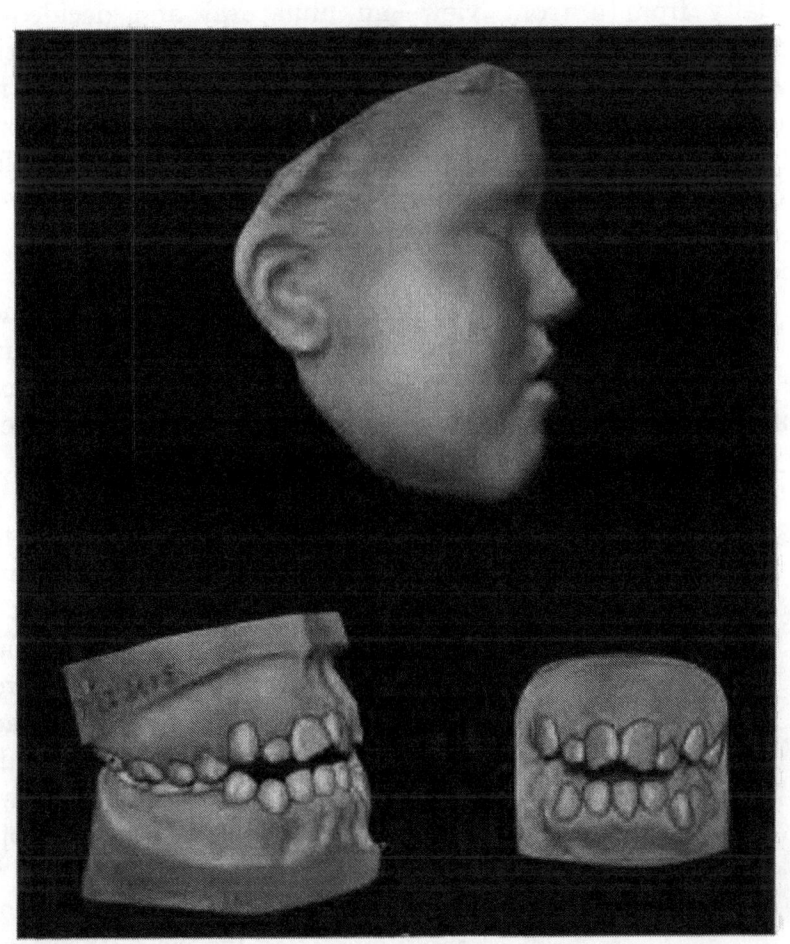

FIG. 105.

The first impressions of this case—the plaster casts of which are shown in Fig. 105, were taken September 27, 1916, and are those of a miss thirteen years of age. Both right and left sides of the denture were so alike in buccal occlusion, it is unnecessary to show but one side. As will be observed by an examination of the buccal occlusion, the upper denture is slightly distal to normal, and the upper incisor teeth, though appearing to be prominent at their occlusal edges, distinctly show by the retruded facial outlines that they are quite labially inclined from deepened incisive fossæ. The apparent prominence of the upper incisor crowns is enhanced by the retruded position of the lower incisors, which was caused by the criminal extraction of a lower lateral incisor which happened to erupt—as incisors often do—in lingual malalignment. From the facial cast, it can be seen that the chin and lower lip are quite perfectly posed, and in harmonious relation to the main or unchangeable features of the physiognomy, showing that the mandible and lower denture are in normal dento-facial relations. The moderately retruded outlines of the upper part of the upper lip with the abnormal deepened nasolabial lines, enhancing the prominence of the cheek bones, gave to the physiognomy—especially from a front view—an unnatural and decidedly unesthetic broad and flattened appearance. The facial diagnosis, in connection with the retruded relations of the upper incisors and marked open-bite malocclusion, definitely indicates that its cause was early adenoids and mouth-breathing; the former inhibiting the normal development of the maxilla, and the latter—which doubtless continued through several years of early development—resulted in the open-bite malocclusion.

From the above diagnosis it will at once be observed that the case belongs in Class III of the dento-occlusal classification, and that the main and imperative part of the operation demands a bodily labial movement of the upper incisors and incisive alveolar process, accompanied by a general maxillary expansion and alignment of the teeth through bone-growth development, to correct dental and facial relations.

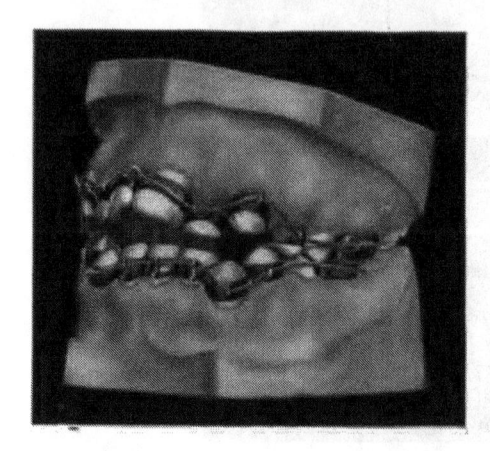

FIG. 106.

The Midget Apparatus.—In all cases in which a bodily movement of the front teeth is demanded, it is first quite imperative that the front teeth be placed in alignment so that they can be brought evenly within the firm grasp of the power arch-bow, and thus moved bodily in phalanx. For the purpose of accomplishing this first stage of the operation, and incidentally to correct the alignment of the lower teeth and open-bite malocclusion, the first apparatus worn is that shown in Fig. 106 which is similar in general character to that which has been commonly employed by the author for years in the correction of all simple irregularities and malpositions of the teeth of children and youths. It is that which derives its main motive force from the resiliency of very light arch-bows which range in diameter sizes from Nos. 22 to 26 (.025″ to .016″). To those who are not familiar with the gauge sizes, it may be well to state that No. 22 is about the size of a small pin, and No. 26 is but a trifle larger in diameter than the thickness of a 28-gauge plate with which all dentists are familiar.

CHAPTER XX. MODERN PRINCIPLES AND METHODS 169

There is no objection to employing any of the alloys of gold and platinum for the arch-bows, if specially drawn, but for all intents and purposes 18 per cent nickel silver spring wire if properly drawn, will answer every requirement. Orthodontists who have not tested the possibilities of high-grade nickel silver can hardly realize the higher degree of spring temper and resiliency that can be given to arch-bows of this material when drawn *cold* from very much larger sizes.

Fig. 107.

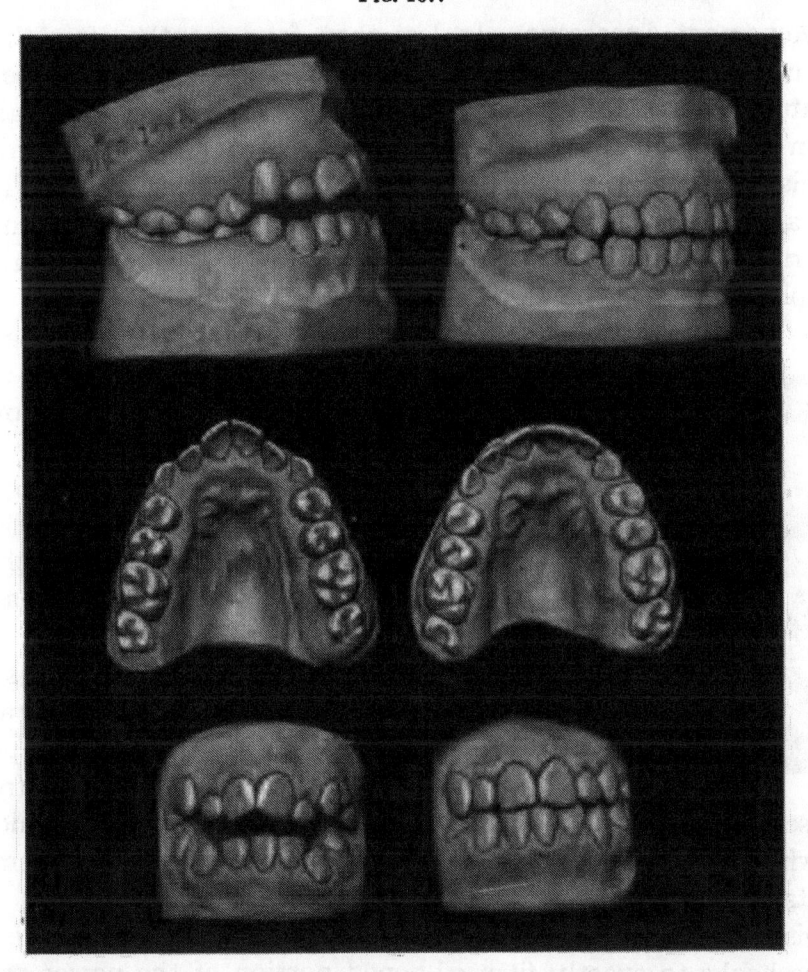

The arch-bows of the above small sizes, if intended for the purposes referred to, should be drawn from Nos. 14 to 16 high-grade spring nickel silver wire, without annealing, and kept cold in the process with a small bag of crushed ice placed over the draw plate.

The particular characters of malocclusion for which these very light resilient arch-bows are especially adapted, are those which are commonly composed of a variety of malpositions which arise during the early eruptive stages of the permanent teeth, and which are commonly due to local causes. In the apparatus shown in Fig. 106, the arch-bows are No. 26. In the bracket attachments on the lower incisors, the gingival hooks are for direct intermaxillary elastics to aid in closing the open-bite. See "Construction of Bands for the Midget Appliances," Chapter XVIII. After this apparatus was placed on the teeth and the patient instructed in the adjustment of the elastics, the case was not seen oftener than once in two weeks. Occasionally at these times, the arch-bows were removed and replaced with new ones, and minor treatments performed as the changing conditions demanded.

Bodily Movement Apparatus.—In less than four months after the case was started, the upper front teeth being sufficiently in alignment for the **bodily movement apparatus,** the appliances were removed and impressions were taken for the models shown on the right of Fig. 107. On the left is a view of the beginning models. It was at this time that the **bodily movement apparatus,** shown in Fig. 108, was made and placed. The power arch-bow in this case is No. 16 spring nickel silver rolled to a ribbon form of about $\frac{2}{3}$ of its diameter over the labial area, and placed to apply its force at the gingival line of the front teeth.

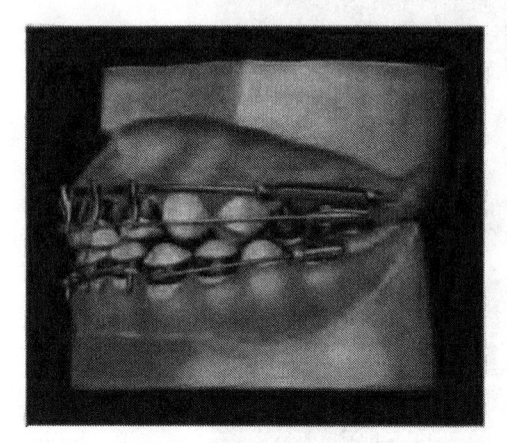

FIG. 108.

For the younger class of patients, the power is now rarely applied above the gingival margins, and often the fulcrum bow is placed near the middle of the crowns. It must be seen however, that the farther the line of power is placed from the area of alveolar work, and the nearer it is to the artificial fulcrum, it proportionately decreases its mechanical advantage for bodily movement, and consequently increases the strain upon the power arch-bow and its molar anchorages.

The object in applying the power upon root-wise attachments to the front teeth, is to increase the mechanical advantages of the whole apparatus, which is quite important when extensive bodily movements of front teeth are demanded for older patients.

If one wishes to combine with this the **torsional bodily force,** he can easily construct the hooks to exactly fit a ribboned portion of the power arch-bow, as shown by Fig. 62, Chapter XIV. The bow is rolled at such an angle that when placed in its front attachments, the distal ends of the bow, at equilibrium, will stand below the occlusal plane, from which they are sprung upward into their positions in the U or open tubes. It would be advisable, however, from some experience which the author has had with this method, that the fulcrum bow be not omitted, and the power bow be not less than No. 19.

The Technics of Attachments.—The incisor attachments for bodily labial movements for young patients are made in the following manner: No. 18 (.040″)

CHAPTER XX. MODERN PRINCIPLES AND METHODS

nickel-silver or platinum-gold wire is rolled to about ⅔ its diameter, as shown in the enlarged view of Fig. 109 ("a"). At one end, on the flat side of the rod, a groove is filed ("b"), using a jeweler's fine cut joint-file. This file is ⅛ of an inch thick, ½ inch wide, and cut only on its edges half-round. The end is then rounded off so as to form a quarter-round open tube at the end of the bar having a wall thickness of .005″ ("c"), designed to grasp the small-sized fulcrum arch-bow when closed around it. The line of the fulcrum arch-bow should be fully 3/32 of an inch above the incisal ends of the laterals. The distance from the fulcrum grooves to the gingival border of the lateral bands, having been determined by exact measurement of the tooth, the bar is then grasped in heavy pliers, or a small vise, and sharply bent at right angles at this point ("d"), using a small hammer to perfect the sharpness of the right angle. It is then bent back in the form of a hook or staple ("e"), being careful not to disturb the right-angled bend which represents the gingival border of the band. The finished hook of the root-wise attachment ("f") is formed to fit the labial faces of the incisors, and to support the power and fulcrum arch-bows, as shown in Fig. 110. Its position in relation to the band should be such as to allow the power bow to span the interproximal gingivæ. It should not extend above the power arch-bow, which, being always at tension, requires but a slight groove to prevent it from slipping off; otherwise, it would be difficult if not impossible to lift the bow from its attachments at any time when desired. The fulcrum bow is a No. 23 (.0225″) alignment bow threaded at one end. After placing it the ends of the upright attachments are closed around the wire to make a smooth finish.

FIG. 109.

FIG. 110.

It will be seen that the right-angled gingival bend of this attachment, starting as it does from the gingival margin of the band, and ending in a fitted hook for the power bow, presents a mechanical principle of great strength, and enables the application of more than sufficient power through the medium of a very delicate mechanism. In the construction of appliances for bodily labial movements which demand the application of a greater bodily mechanical advantage above the gingival margins for the older class of patients, the root-wise extensions of the attachments require to be made much heavier where they join the bands, because the line of force is far to one side of their line of attachment to the teeth, and from that point they may be tapered to a finished edge, thus securing required strength with the least amount of material.

In soldering the attachment to the band, place it to one side of the joint on the band, and grasp it with the solder plier, which for this purpose is grooved on one of its grasping points for a firm seating on the attachment.

The power arch-bow for this apparatus may be No. 18, or 17 (.040", .045"), spring nickel silver, or platinized gold. A round wire bow is much more rigid than one that is flattened, and less conspicuous. If flattened at all, it should be only over the incisors. It is important that it be shaped to lie evenly over the gingival surfaces in front, but distal to the cuspids it should take a straight line to its anchorage tubes to insure its rigidity. It goes without saying that a power arch-bow for bodily labial movement of the incisors, which necessarily bends nearly at a right angle from its front attachments to its molar anchorage, must possess considerable rigidity to prevent the push force from springing it buccally. The power anchorage tubes should lie evenly with the line of the bow so that the threaded ends will rest evenly in the open tubes.

In assembling this apparatus for its final fitting and adjustments, place the anchorages first and then the power arch-bow, adjusting its relations in front with the anchorage lock nuts. Finally, in placing the incisor bands, see that the gingival hooks for the power bow are properly adjusted so that they will not press the bow into the gums, and also that the bow can be lifted from its seating without injury to the gums, which might arise if the hooks lapped on to the bow too far. It is at this point in the preliminary fitting that the final bend of the hooks should be made. This is accomplished by grasping the band in the root-wise plier, one beak

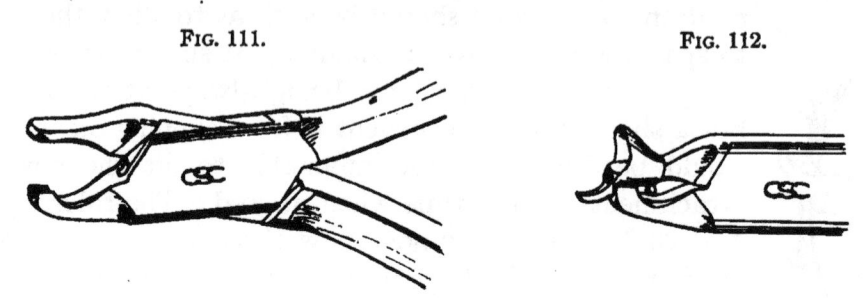

FIG. 111.

FIG. 112.

of which fits over the attachment (Figs. 111 and 112). The hook is then safely given its final bend to adjust the relations of the power bow to the gums. These rules apply also to the fitting and adjustment of the more root-wise power attachments. The same order of assembling the apparatus is pursued in the final placing and cementing. The fulcrum arch-bow is placed last. So far as strength is concerned, a midget arch-bow No. 26 (.016"), or even an Angle wire ligature would be sufficient, but these small wires, under the strain of considerable traction force, are likely to press on the cuspids and narrow the labial arch.

Fig. 113 was made from a photograph of one of the lighter forms of contouring apparatus where the power arch-bow may be no larger than No. 18, or 19 (.040" or .035") spring nickel silver or platinum gold, and the fulcrum bow,

No. 26 (.016″). The U-power anchorage tube is not shown in this illustration because it occurs only upon the right side.

FIG. 113.

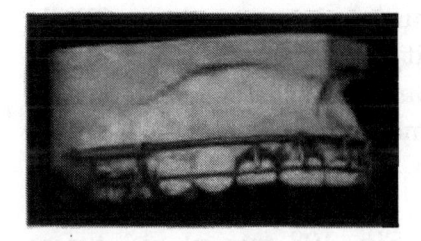

If the case is a pronounced retrusion of the entire upper denture with full mesial malinterdigitation of the lower buccal teeth, the author has learned from many unsatisfactory experiences that it is not advisable to shift the dentures to a normal occlusion, except for very young patients, because of the improbability of permanency of retention. Instead, spaces are opened between the premolars of the retruded dentures for the insertion of artificial premolars. This rule in the author's practice applies also to pronounced inherited retrusions of the lower dentures in those cases where the chin is in normal pose and the upper denture is not materially protruded. It is mentioned here, because, if the case is one of this character, the reaction of the fulcrum force may be utilized in the mesial movement of: first, the cuspids, as shown, and then, the first premolars to open spaces for the insertion of retaining artificial teeth. The insertion of artificial teeth absolutely prevents a retrusive movement of the crowns of the front teeth, but they must not be expected to take the place of the regular retainer whose main function is to prevent the roots from returning toward their former positions until nature has been given time to equilibrate and solidify the surrounding alveolar structure. See Chapter XLII.

There are no cases in orthodontia which so forcibly and invariably tend to return to their former positions after treatment as inherited retrusions of the dentures which have demanded for their correction a bodily labial movement, or none, moreover, in which there is greater need for the fulfillment of the highest principles of retention.

The amount of correction of the open-bite at this stage of the case under consideration is shown on the right of Fig. 107, as compared to that on the left. This was accomplished mainly by direct intermaxillary elastics attached to the midget hook and bracket attachments upon the front teeth.

At the anniversary clinic of the Chicago Dental Society, January 27, 1917, four months after the case was started, the patient attended by her older sister, kindly consented to appear and submitted to hours of examination and questioning by hundreds of dentists. She was wearing at that time the upper contouring apparatus shown in Fig. 113. The plaster dental and facial casts, and the mounted apparatus which had accomplished its work up to that time, were shown and explained. The author is particular to mention this circumstance—parenthetically—because it establishes the unquestionability of the above dates.

From the presentation of the true chronological history of this case, some might imagine that rapidity of orthodontic movements should be regarded as a test of the value of the appliances, whereas, it will be found throughout the entire teaching in this work that that particular phase of an operation is negligible compared to the selection and application of methods which are best suited to the needs of the case in hand, and the methods which will accomplish the most favorable results. In fact, the best accomplishments cannot be attained in the correction of many cases of malocclusion in an attempt to hurry the operation. While time, ease of adjustments, painlessness, non-irritability, and artistic effect are of great importance, they should never stand in the way of the true principles of practice. Occasionally, as in this instance, we will meet with cases which safely respond with phenomenal rapidity, if the forces are skillfully adjusted to their needs.

The second lower apparatus, which is shown in Fig. 108 was placed a few weeks after the patient had become accustomed to the upper. The lower front teeth were nearly in alignment, and consequently in a position to be more firmly grasped by a No. 23 expansion arch-bow which would sustain, with greater stability, the distances between the molars and front teeth, and exert a slight general expanding force, and at the same time permit the proper action of the disto-mesial elastics for the reinforcement of the upper anchorages, and the adjustment of the occlusion. Provision will be seen on the lower for the direct intermaxillary elastics to continue the extruding force—particularly the upper cuspids and first premolars.

It should not be inferred that the forces of any of these appliances alone were the only treatments employed, because in this, as in nearly every case, the skillful orthodontist will employ subsidiary forces as the case progresses, which are quite as important as the main forces for keeping the machinery in perfect co-ordinating action. With the author, these side forces are mainly obtained with light silk ligatures and elastics. Moreover, it is the office rule that when bands or their attachments have outgrown their usefulness, or are not properly constructed or adjusted to perform their best work, they are immediately removed and corrected—more often with new bands and attachments for varying the forces.

There is one thing to which attention is particularly called as a recent and most important improvement in the technics of anchorages. It is the employment of the U or open-tubes, instead of closed or seamless round tubes, for the anchorage ends of the arch-bows as shown in Fig. 108. For the very light resilient bows, a seamless tube on one side, and a U or open-tube on the other are usually sufficient. But for the larger bows, with locked attachments to the front teeth, which are designed to exert a bodily expanding force, U or open-tube anchorage tubes are invaluable, because they enable giving to the bow any desired spring force, and with assured ease of assembling. And then when desired, the ends can be readily lifted from the tubes and given an extra spring force and replaced without the necessity of unlocking the bow from its front attachments. This is especially important for the more rigid power arch-bows of the bodily movement apparatus. It occasionally becomes necessary to remove these bows to increase or decrease their expanding properties, or to correct some irritating action that arises at

CHAPTER XX. MODERN PRINCIPLES AND METHODS

the front. Formerly, this was impossible without a complete removal of all the front bands, or the stationary anchorages; and this is not always an easy operation, without slitting them. Now, the counter-sunk nuts, shown in Fig. 114, which lock

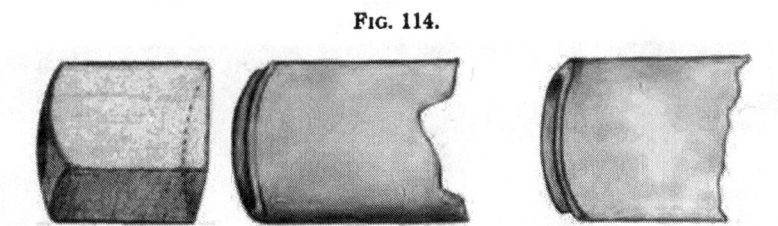

FIG. 114.

the ends of the bow in the tubes, are unscrewed and the bow is easily lifted out of its attachment at the back, and then at the front, and as easily replaced, without disturbing any of the bands. The drawing shows the way to cut the ends of open tubes to fit the counter-sunk depression in the nuts; but if U-tubes are used, the corners of the open lips should be cut back so that the counter-sunk nut will draw the bar or bow deeply into the tubes. See latest locking device for power U-anchorage tubes, Fig. 210, Chapter XLII.

The importance of applying the anchorage power above the gingival margins upon root-wise anchorage attachments shown in Fig. 108 cannot be overestimated. This places the direction of the power more nearly in a line with the center of alveolar resistance, and proportionately increases the stability by decreasing the tendency to inclination movement. The root-wise method of applying force is invaluable in all bodily movements. Besides the labio-lingual bodily movement of the front teeth, it is of great advantage in the bodily expansion of dental arches, and in the bodily disto-mesial movements of both the front and back teeth to close interproximate spaces from whatever cause, where it is important to avoid inclination movement.

Bodily Working-Retainer. To return to the case under consideration: After the bodily movement apparatus had been worn about four months, the patient was obliged to return to her home in Oklahoma on account of the sickness of her father, which would prevent the author from seeing her until near the close of the operation. As the bodily movement of the upper teeth and the general correction of the malocclusion had progressed quite favorably, and fearing to trust to others in this advanced stage the treatment adjustments, the author decided to place the **bodily working-retainer** on the upper incisors which would continue more slowly but safely their bodily movement.

Fig. 115 shows two views of the working-retainer on the model of the upper teeth at this time. The lingual push bars are No. 19 spring nickel silver, fitted but not soldered into the thick wall clasp-metal tubes which are attached to the clasp-metal reinforcement-backing of the retainer. The distal ends of the bars at equilibrium are about ⅜ of an inch below the occlusal plane, and when sprung

176   PART V. PRIMARY PRINCIPLES OF PRACTICE

into the U or open-tube attachments on the lingual surfaces of the stationary anchorages, they exert a labial force upon the roots of the incisors; this, in connection with the action of the nuts at the mesial ends of the anchorage tubes,

FIG. 115.

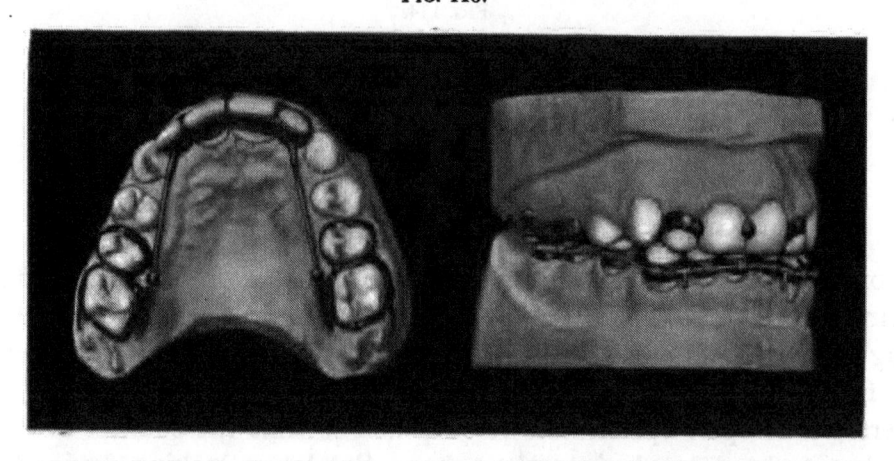

results in a bodily labial movement. The open sides of the tubes cannot be seen in the illustration because they are turned toward the roof of the mouth; this causes the spring bars to be locked in place without closing the tubes.

FIG. 116.

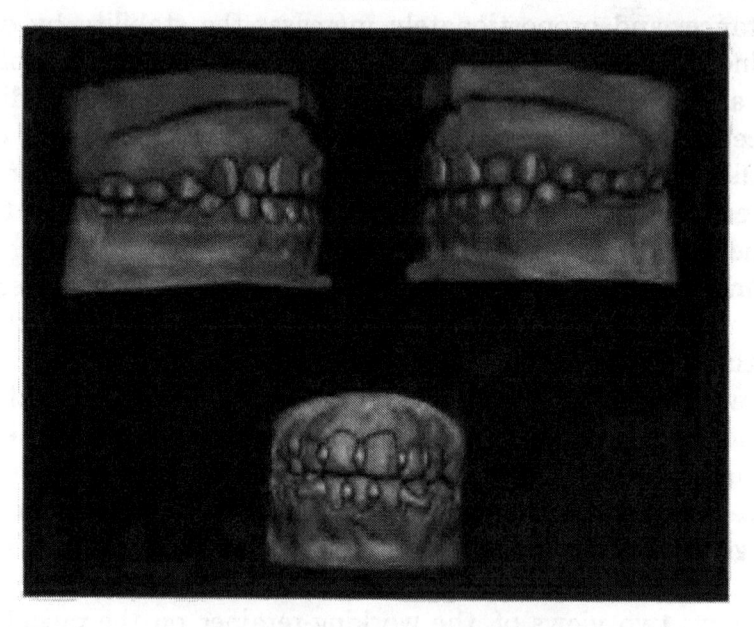

The object of the two-band stationary anchorages is to distribute the extrusive spring force of the bars and prevent a supra-occlusal movement, as would naturally occur if this force were sustained by single molar anchorages. The disto-mesial and direct intermaxillary and other forces were continued with this appara-

CHAPTER XX. MODERN PRINCIPLES AND METHODS 177

tus. The **working-retainer** is fully described under "Principles and Technics of Retention," in Chapter LIV.

During the absence of the patient, she very faithfully kept up the application of the various forces. On Wednesday, August 29, 1917, eleven months after the case was started, all the appliances were removed, and the impressions were taken for the plaster casts shown in Fig. 116. Notwithstanding the unfortunate fact that there are only three lower incisors, the dentures are in fair occlusion, which time will improve. Below, is a front occlusal view of the teeth with the final retainers in position. You may be able to see the supplemental spurs for the attachment of the direct intermaxillary retaining elastics for continuing the extrusive force, to prevent a return of the infra-occlusal position, and also the hooks on the lower for continuing the disto-mesial intermaxillary force.

FIG. 117.

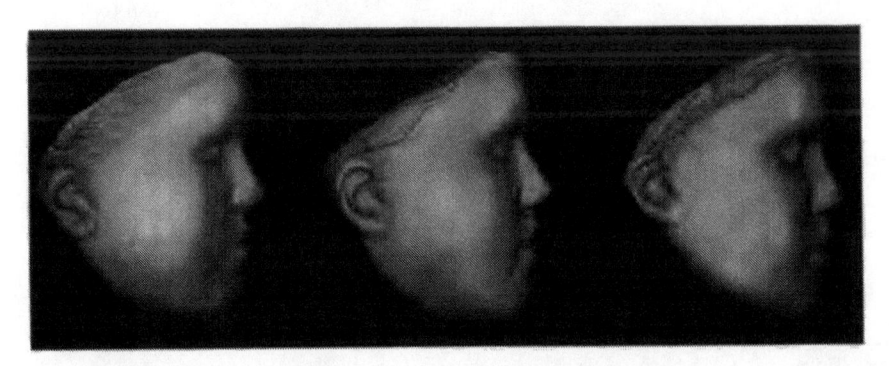

Fig. 117 will give a fair idea of the development in the facial outlines by immediate comparison with the beginning facial cast on the left. The plaster impression for the one in the middle was taken upon the removal of the regular bodily movement apparatus which was worn about four months. The impression for the one on the right was taken upon the removal of the entire regulating apparatus. The protruded prominence of the roots of the incisors are very faintly shown in the illustration. If the upper incisors are retained in their present bodily labial position, the facial outlines will no doubt continue to improve through stimulated growth development.

PART VI

Practical Treatment
of
Dento-Facial Malocclusions

CLASSES OF DENTO-FACIAL MALOCCLUSIONS

CLASS I. NORMAL DISTO-MESIAL OCCLUSION OF THE BUCCAL TEETH
CLASS II. DISTAL MALOCCLUSION OF LOWER BUCCAL TEETH
CLASS III. MESIAL MALOCCLUSION OF LOWER BUCCAL TEETH

For General Classified Table of Divisions and Classes, see page 19
For Table of Types and Divisions of Class I, see page 199
For Table of Types and Divisions of Class II, see page 245
For Table of Divisions of Class III, see page 290

DENTO-FACIAL MALOCCLUSIONS

CHAPTER XXI

ORTHODONTIC PRINCIPLES OF DIAGNOSIS AND GENERAL RULES OF TREATMENT OF ALL CLASSIFIED MALOCCLUSIONS

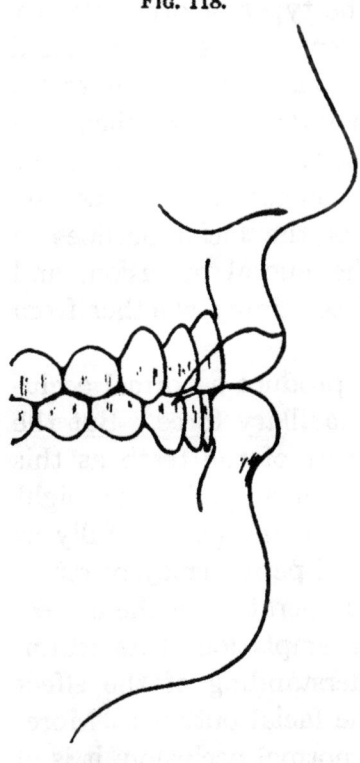

Fig. 118.

Introduction.—This chapter relates particularly to the foundation principles and diagnosis of dento-facial malocclusions, with general outlines of treatment. It also comprises a comparison of the different characters which have deceptive similarities, with the view of establishing their treatment upon an artistic and scientific basis.

In order to accomplish this most successfully, one should have in mind a standard of perfection of facial outlines. In other words, one should be able to see in the mind's eye the symmetrical outlines to be worked for or toward in the correction of the case in hand.

Fig. 118 represents the common relations which the lips sustain to the teeth in normal dento-facial position and occlusion. The facial outlines of this figure will be employed throughout Classified Malocclusions as a standard of comparison solely for the purpose of showing the probable degree of disharmonies in the facial outlines in different characters and types of protrusion and retrusion of the teeth and jaws.

While it is important to observe the occlusion, the malalignments and malrelations of the teeth and jaws to each other, the diagnosis should always be accomplished with an intelligent and artistic observation of dento-facial outlines. *There is no other way of determining the real character of a case or the direction and degree of movement demanded in its correction.* In a diagnosis and prognosis of malocclusion, a disregard of facial outlines and the marring effects which malrelations of the teeth and jaws produce, or a belief that "the attainment of a normal occlusion will always result in the most perfect correction of dento-facial imperfections and deformities," is rapidly taking its rightful place as one of the fantastic theories of the past.

Those who appreciate and desire the highest attainment in practice must in time become convinced that the only true basis of diagnosis and treatment is **dento-facial harmony**—harmony in the occlusal relations of the dentures to each other for purposes of mastication, and harmony in the dento-facial area and its relations to the other features. It includes a normal occlusion of the teeth as one of its highest attainments, except in those comparatively rare instances where extraction is demanded to correct or prevent a dento-facial deformity, and it always includes an adequate masticating occlusion with the most exact interdigitation of buccal cusps it is possible to attain.

In a consideration of the facial outlines of the three classes of malocclusion, there will be found in each class a variety of distinctive types which differ quite as much from each other as they differ from many of the types of other classes. In fact the facial effects in a number of instances in different classes will be found quite similar, being due to similar dento-facial malpositions of the front teeth; and yet because of the difference in buccal occlusion, they demand for their correction quite different treatment. Therefore, true diagnosis for determining the character and treatment of all marked cases of malocclusion can only be successfully accomplished by a careful and intelligent study of the facial outlines in connection with the dental irregularity, particularly the buccal occlusion, and finally, the probable causes, mainly with the view of determining whether from local or inherent origin.

It is always possible, and it is usually not difficult to produce a normal occlusion of the dentures by a judicious application of intermaxillary force. But the question should arise: "Will such an extensive movement of the teeth as this often portends, *leave the overlying features undeformed*, or not as perfect as might be produced with a lesser movement which would secure to the patient fully as perfect masticating forces and with a greater probability of permanency of retention?" While a normal occlusion should be regarded as imperative in the correction of a very large majority of all malocclusions, the contemplation of its attainment should always be based upon an intelligent understanding of the effect which this condition of the dentures will produce upon the facial outlines. Moreover, in the disto-mesial shifting of the buccal teeth to a normal occlusion, it is of the greatest importance at times to govern the extent of the movement of one denture or the other to obtain the best facial effect. This principle is especially outlined in the treatment of Class II.

Standards of Diagnosis.—In the diagnosis and treatment of all dental malocclusions which produce disharmonies in the facial outlines, a mental standard of comparison is imperative. In almost every act of our lives there is or should be a guiding mental standard of perfection. In the art of speaking perfectly, there should be a fixed mental standard of true articulation and phonation in the enunciation of all the oral elements of speech. This in phonology is named the "correct sound-image." In the practice of orthodontia, and especially in diagnosis, we

CHAPTER XXI. DIAGNOSIS AND TREATMENT

should have firmly fixed in our minds a perfect understanding and appreciation of normal occlusion and dento-facial harmony. The ability to establish a mental standard of beauty should not be confined to a fixed idea of the facial outlines of classic art as shown in that of the Apollo Belvedere, but it should be one which may be adjusted in the mind's eye to the different types of physiognomies which present for treatment, according to the rules laid down in the following principles of Diagnosis. Thus the most desirable harmony in the dento-facial area it is possible to produce in the correction of every dental irregularity, may be determined and attained.

In a normal occlusion of the teeth, the condyles of the mandible rest in their most posterior positions in the glenoid fossæ; while the incisal edges of the lower labial teeth pass slightly back of those of the upper.

The labial teeth and all of that portion of the adjoining osseous structure which it is possible to move with dental appliances, constitute the main framework of the **dento-facial area.** And while no artistic or mathematical rules can be laid down as a standard of facial beauty because of the variety of different types that are denominated as "beautiful," it is nevertheless true that certain standards of physical relation must always obtain with every physiognomy which lies within the field of what is termed beauty and esthetic perfection.

As the chin should always be sufficiently prominent in relation to the lower lip to produce no suggestion of a "receding chin," the antero-posterior relations of the lower teeth to the mandible—upon which this portion of the facial outlines depend—should be such as to bring into decided evidence the graceful concave

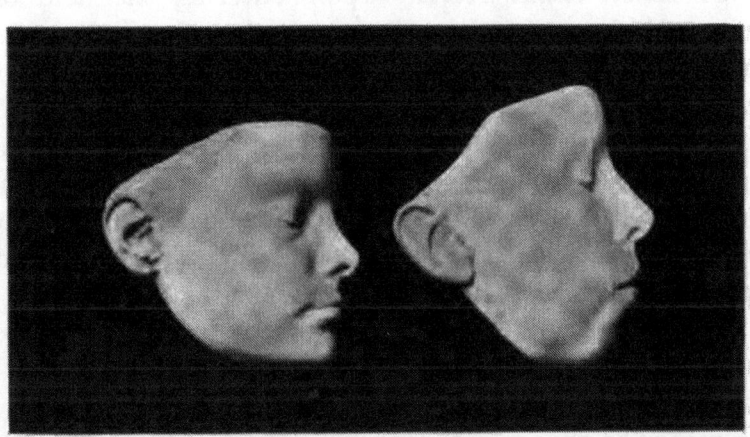

Fig. 119.

curve of the labio-mental depression. The normal closure of the lower labial teeth, slightly back of the upper labial teeth, permits the desired esthetic harmony in the relations of the upper and lower lips. If, therefore, the upper labial teeth in arch alignment are not protruded or retruded in relation to the bones which form the framework of the middle features of the physiognomy, the upper lip will also assume the desired form and pose in relation to the cheeks, malar prominences, and bridge of the nose, and this is necessary for the perfection of this portion of the facial outlines.

To complete the esthetic requirements of this *ensemble* of dento-facial harmony, the perfect ease and pose of the lips when closed and at rest are largely dependent upon the harmony in distance between the upper and lower jaws when closed with the muscles relaxed in relation to the labial and buccal tissues. If an infra-occlusal or intrusive malposition of the buccal teeth causes the jaws to come too closely together, as in short and close-bite malocclusion, the redundancy of labial and buccal tissue is evidenced by the pouting attitude of the lips and other concomitant disharmonies to the facial outlines, as shown on the left of Fig. 119. In this connection it would be well to remember that in all normal conditions, when the features are in unconscious repose with the lips closed, the teeth are rarely if ever in occlusion, as the relaxed muscles more restfully sustain the mandible with the teeth slightly apart.

On the other hand, as shown on the right of this figure, if a supra-occlusal or extrusive malposition of the teeth or an open-bite malocclusion prevents the jaws from coming together in harmonious relations, the effort to close the lips, even when the teeth are not protruded, will mar the ease and perfection of their pose, with a frequent obliteration of the labio-mental curve, and a retraction of the surface contour of the chin. Again, it is very important in dento-facial orthopedia that rules which are acknowledged as the standard of esthetic beauty with adults, should never be strictly applied to the facial outlines of childhood and early adolescence, without an intelligent recognition of the developing influences of growth.

Scope of the Dento-facial Field.—Upon entering the field of dento-facial malocclusion, it would be well for the student to first deeply consider the scope of this department. The possibilities of **Dento-facial Orthopedia** in the correction of facial outlines are confined in their action to a comparatively small area of that which constitutes the framework of the human physiognomy. The labial teeth and alveolar process in which their roots are imbedded, and the incisive or intermaxillary portion of the upper jaws, constitute the principal extent of the facial framework, which it is possible to move with dental regulating appliances.

While a lateral expansion of arches—especially the upper—will often produce a more rounded fullness to the cheeks, it is not due so much to the direct support of the buccal teeth as to the relief of tension upon the labial and buccal tissues that has followed the concomitant retrusion of the front teeth which the expansion permitted. In regard to changing the position of the chin, it is quite rare that one has an opportunity to apply force at a sufficiently early age to retrude the mandible with occipital pressure, while a permanent movement of the mandible in the opposite direction, in the operation of "jumping the bite," is very uncertain. Therefore, we must place the chin on the outside of the **dento-facial** area proper, and consider it as one of the most prominent landmarks of the physiognomy from which to draw comparisons in diagnosis.

CHAPTER XXI. DIAGNOSIS AND TREATMENT

The Dento-facial Area.—The principal portion of the human face, therefore, which it is possible to beautify by moving the teeth and alveolar process, is that formed by the upper and lower lips and the lower portion of the nose, bounded laterally by the naso-labial lines and below by the chin. This is the "**dento-facial area.**" (See Fig. 121.)

Within this ovoidal area, the slightest change of muscular movement expressive of the emotions will produce an apparently marked effect upon the physiognomy. The same is true of any physical imperfections of contour, particularly around the mouth, which will seem to change the entire features. It is here that an inherited or acquired lack of symmetry in the size, shape, or position of the teeth and jaws produces those marked changes of facial contour which characterize the several types of dento-facial malocclusions. In nearly all cases of decided protrusion or retrusion of the roots of the upper labial teeth, the incisive portion of the maxillæ, with its anterior nasal spine and cartilaginous nasal septum, will be protruded or retruded in its dento-facial relations. As this is the framework which supports the extreme upper portion of the upper lip and forms the base of the entire lower portion of the nose, with the naso-labial depressions on either side, including the end and wings of the nose, the form and relative position of this facial zone will be frequently affected to a marked degree in certain characters of protrusion and retrusion of the upper teeth. In most cases for youthful patients, this area is susceptible of being changed considerably in the outlines of its contour by a bodily protruding and retruding movement of the teeth, as it fortunately happens to be a fact that all of that portion of the superior maxilla in which the incisor teeth are developed with its alveolar ridge, will usually be carried bodily with the roots of the incisor teeth in a protruding or retruding phalanx movement. This may be largely due to its early separate development.

FIG. 120.

Inferior Surface.

From Gray's Anatomy.—Gray, in describing the superior maxilla, says: "In some bones a delicate linear suture may be seen extending from the anterior palatal fossae to the interval between the lateral incisor and the canine tooth. This marks out the **intermaxillary** or **incisive bone.** It includes the whole thickness of the alveolar process, the corresponding part of the floor of the nares, and the anterior nasal spine, and contains the sockets of the incisor teeth. . . . The incisive portion is indicated in young bones by a fissure which marks off a small segment of the palate, including the incisor teeth. (See Fig. 120.) In some animals this remains permanently as a separate piece, constituting the **intermaxillary bone;** and in the human subject, where the jaw is malformed, as in cleft palate, this segment may be separated from the maxillary bone by a deep fissure extending back between the two into the palate."

A bodily protruding or retruding movement of the roots of the lower labial teeth and alveolar ridge, which constitute the framework that supports the labio-

186   PART VI. DENTO-FACIAL MALOCCLUSIONS

mental area, will be found far more difficult to accomplish than a like movement of the upper.

Zones of Movement.—The **dento-facial area** shown in Fig. 121 is naturally divided into four transverse segments or zones of movement, according to the areas that can be moved **separately** by a movement of the crowns or the roots of the underlying teeth and alveolar process. The zones lying over the crowns of

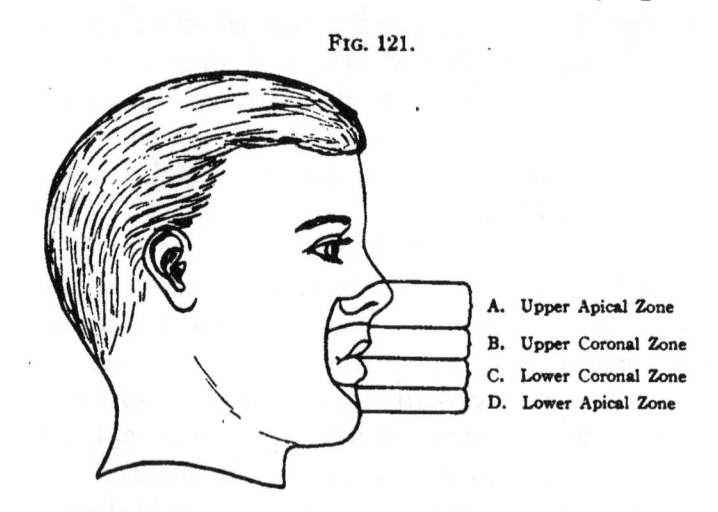

FIG. 121.

A. Upper Apical Zone
B. Upper Coronal Zone
C. Lower Coronal Zone
D. Lower Apical Zone

the upper and lower front teeth are properly named the **upper** and **lower coronal zones,** and those over the roots, the **upper** and **lower apical zones.** If the labial teeth are moved bodily backward or forward, the overlying dento-facial zones will respond in proportion to the movement. In cases of bodily upper protrusions or retrusions, the end of the nose will often partake of the malposition. In these cases, a bodily corrective movement of the upper labial teeth will usually straighten the lines of the nose, and thus place it in a more esthetic pose.

REMARKABLE CHANGES IN FACIAL EXPRESSION WITH SLIGHT MOVEMENTS

It is not often realized what a very small physical change in the outlines and contours of a face will produce in the appearance and expression of the entire physiognomy. This is especially true of physical changes within the dento-facial area that are possible to produce by the movement of the teeth and surrounding alveolar process. This is diagrammatically illustrated in Fig. 122, which shows the correction of the common upper protrusion. The outlines of the two faces on the left are drawn exactly alike, except that which pertains to the tip of the nose and upper lip, between the two parallel lines and in front of the vertical one. The exact amount of this difference in the two faces is seen on the right. This illustrates how a very slight and easily possible change in the facial outlines will at times seem to change the entire physiognomy and expression of the face, and how also in an artistic practice of dento-facial orthopedia, many apparently wonderful and even unbelievable corrections are so frequently accomplished. It is not so

CHAPTER XXI. DIAGNOSIS AND TREATMENT 187

much because the physical change in the actual measurement of the framework is great, as it is that slight movements of facial contours, if produced at the proper points, will bring about remarkable esthetic results. It shows, moreover, the possi-

FIG. 122.

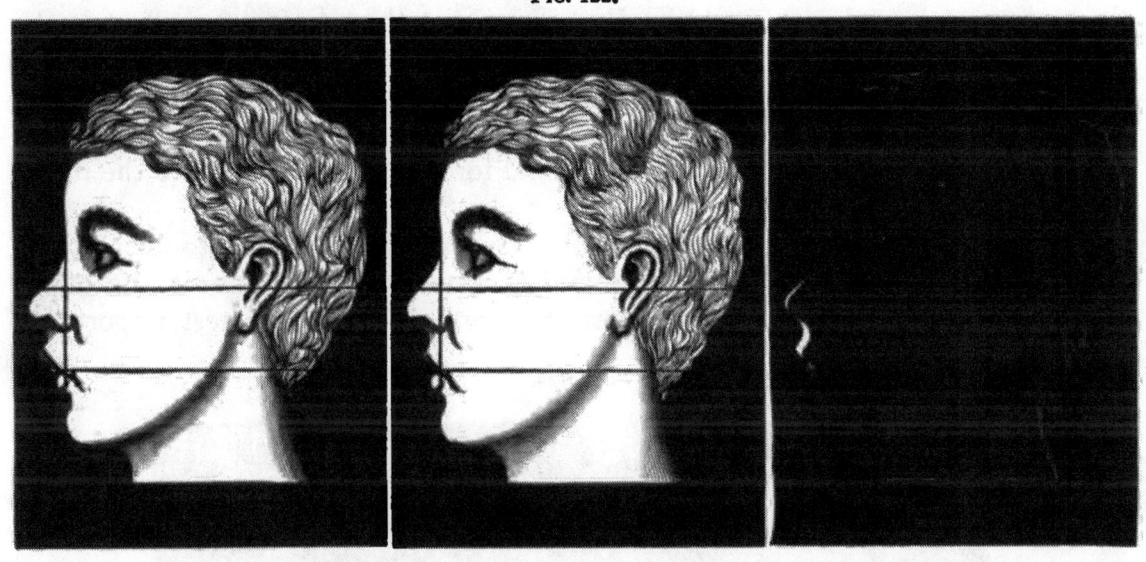

bilities of orthodontia when one has arrived at a true conception of artistic relations in determining the character and type of dento-facial malocclusions, and the movements demanded for their most perfect correction.

FIG. 123.

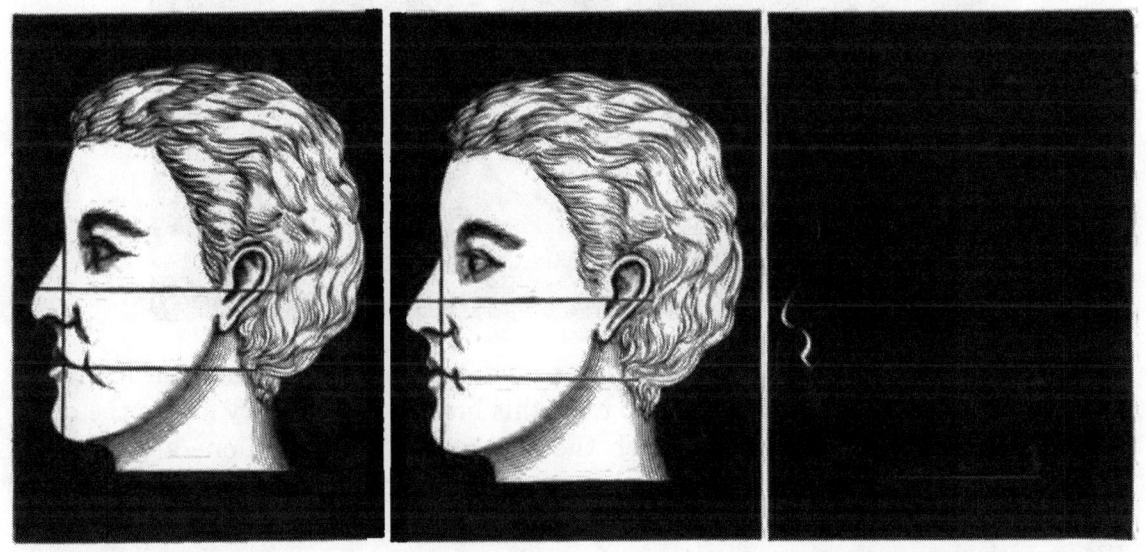

This principle is further illustrated in the diagrammatical drawings under Fig. 123. Like the former illustration, the two faces on the left are drawn exactly alike in every particular, except a slight change in the profile outline of the upper

PART VI. DENTO-FACIAL MALOCCLUSIONS

lip and the end of the nose. The amount of difference in the facial outlines of the two faces on the left is shown on the right, which illustrates how a very little depression of the central features of the physiognomy, shown in the first figure, will produce the effect of prognathism of the lower jaw. If the cross lines of these figures were removed, one would hardly believe that the harmonizing effect in the central face was not partly produced by retruding the outlines of the lower lip and chin, or that it had been accomplished with so little change as that shown on the right. This change is exactly that which may be accomplished in any case under eighteen years of age, with bodily labial force properly applied to the upper front teeth.

Again, force may be applied so as to move any one of the dento-facial zones mainly, or it may protrude one zone and at the same time retrude the other. These principles within the possibilities of force, are of the greatest importance

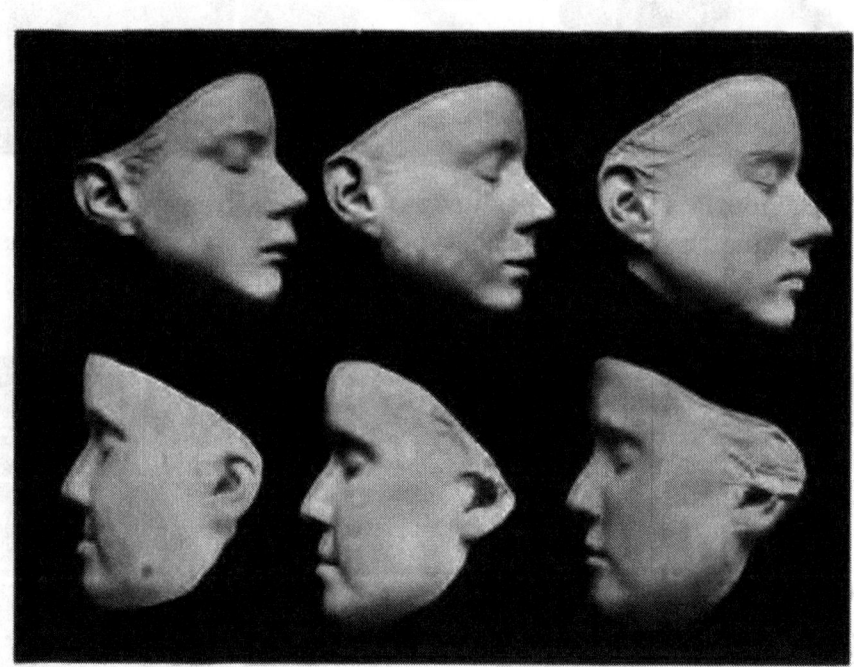

Fig. 124.

in the esthetic correction of facial outlines, and are among the main principles of the science which have tended most to raise this branch of dentistry above the ordinary methods of orthodontia in which the crowns of the teeth alone are moved.

As a part of the training in facial diagnosis, and also as an education in the possibilities of practice, examine carefully each one of the physiognomies in Fig. 124, which represent the correction of a full upper protrusion and a full upper retrusion. Give attention first to the original conditions as shown by the facial casts on the left. Please note that the chin and lower lip in both these cases are in normal pose, or nearly so, in relation to the unchangeable area. What appears

CHAPTER XXI. DIAGNOSIS AND TREATMENT

to be a deficient chin in the upper case, and a too prominent one in the lower, is due to a visual error caused by the immediate malrelations of the upper lip. If the chin and lower lip are in perfect dento-facial harmony, the whole fault must lie with the upper, which is true of these cases.

The upper figures show the progressive facial stages of treatment in a case of upper bodily protrusion, which is one of the characteristic types of Division 2, Class II. At its beginning stage, as shown on the left, the fact that the naso-labial depressions at the wings of the nose are obliterated, the end of the nose slightly protruded, and the upper part of the upper lip, or apical zone, is protruded in proportion to the coronal zone, shows that perfect correction can only be accomplished by a bodily lingual movement of the upper labial teeth and surrounding alveolar process. This type of malocclusion always demands the extraction of the first premolars.

The lower figures show the progressive facial stages of treatment in a case of upper bodily retrusion, which is one of the characteristic types of Division 1, Class III. At its beginning stage, as shown on the left, the fact that the naso-labial depressions at the wings of the nose are deepened, the end of the nose retruded, and the apical zone of the upper lip retruded in proportion to the coronal zone, shows that true correction can only be accomplished by a bodily labial movement of the upper labial teeth and entire intermaxillary process.

The central profiles in both these cases were made after the crowns alone had been moved lingually in the one case, and labially in the other. It will be seen by examining the intermediate stages of the operation, that the upper apical facial zones in both cases were practically unchanged; in fact the original protrusion and retrusion along the upper portion of the upper lips seem increased.

In the first stage of the protruded case, the lingually directed force was applied at the gingival margins of the upper labial teeth, with the hope that this would correct the facial outlines, but it was found that this affected only the coronal zone and brought into more pronounced evidence the protruded condition of the apical zone; a condition which is not always at first discerned in the diagnosis of pronounced upper protrusions. Nor is there any special loss of time, as the bodily lingual movement of the apical ends of the roots is only a continuation of the lingual movement of the coronal portion of the roots accomplished in the first stages.

In regard to the second case, it is frequently necessary to first move the retruded upper crowns from their inlocked malpositions with the lowers, and occasionally align them before it is possible to properly place the bodily movement apparatus. This inclination movement of the crowns corrected the coronal facial zone without affecting in the least the apical zone, as can be seen by the intermediate facial cast.

The profiles on the right were made after a bodily lingual movement of the roots had been performed in the upper case, and a bodily labial movement in the lower case, with a fairly perfect correction of the facial outlines. Note the changes which took place in the two entire upper dento-facial zones, even to the ends of the noses; this shows that the upper apical and coronal zones of any youthful case may be moved separately, together, or in the opposite directions, with an equal probability of success. Note also that the chin and lower lip in both these cases remained in their original positions in relation to the unchangeable area.

As one advances more deeply into this subject of facial diagnosis and treatment from a clinical standpoint of practice, he realizes the great possibilities of orthodontia in correcting and beautifying every face within a reasonable limit of age, whose facial outlines are marred and more or less deformed by malpositions of the teeth. Heretofore, when only the crowns of the teeth were moved, these possibilities were greatly limited in extent, but now, when every dento-facial zone can be moved labially or lingually, separately or together, it places dento-facial orthopedia on the highest possible artistic plane where its art workers are dealing with human flesh and bones instead of canvas and marble. In no treatment are these possibilities more strongly emphasized than in instances where the upper apical zone is moved in a labial or a lingual direction and at the same time the coronal zones are moved in the opposite direction. (See Types of Class II, Chapters XXXVI and XXXVII.)

In one of these cases the upper part of the upper lip, or apical zone, was in a retruded position with deepened naso-labial lines. In the other, these conditions were reversed with flaring nostrils and complete obliteration of the naso-labial lines. In both cases the buccal occlusion was that of Class II. As shown by the finished facial and dental casts, they were beautifully corrected as described.

The Dento-Facial Outlines in Diagnosis

In the correction of all malocclusions, the facial outlines should be regarded as the main guide in determining the proper treatment. They point the course to be pursued, and the special character of movements in the correction of the occlusion and alignment of the teeth to obtain the most perfect dental and facial results for the individual. Even a casual artistic examination and comparison of the occlusion and facial outlines of cases in practice will soon teach the futility of depending wholly upon the buccal occlusion, or the facial outlines alone, in determining their character and treatment. To illustrate this, examine the dental and facial casts of three diametrically different facial characters of malocclusion in Class I, shown in Fig. 125.

In characters similar to each of these cases, the buccal occlusions may be absolutely normal, and yet, as can be easily determined by diagnosis, the case on the left is an upper protrusion, caused by the malrelations of the labial teeth due to thumb-sucking; that in the middle is an upper retrusion due to inhibited incisive maxillary development; and that on the right is a bimaxillary protrusion due to heredity.

CHAPTER XXI. DIAGNOSIS AND TREATMENT 191

In Classes II and III, there will also be found quite different characters and demands of treatment, though they will have the same disto-mesial occlusal malrelations of the buccal teeth. This may be illustrated by a careful examination of the beginning facial and dental casts of five cases in practice from Class II, shown in Fig. 126. The lower buccal teeth in all these cases are in full distal mal-interdigitating occlusion in relation to the uppers, and yet their dento-facial diagnoses are briefly as follows: Case A is an upper coronal protrusion. Case B is an upper bodily protrusion. Case C is an upper coronal protrusion and lower

FIG. 125.

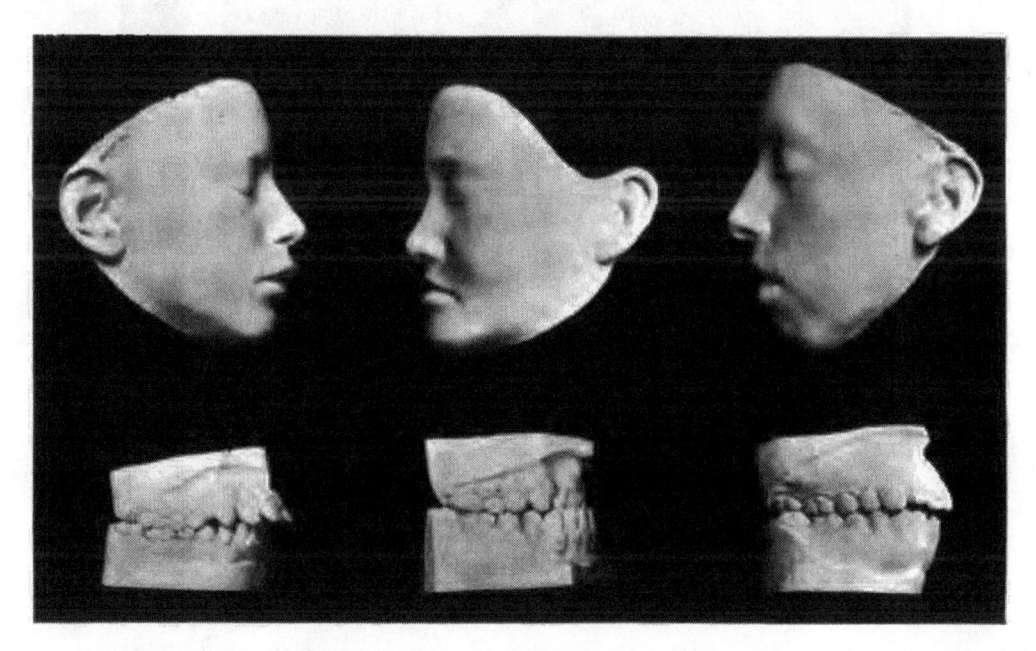

bodily retrusion. Case D is an upper coronal protrusion and upper apical retrusion. Case E is a lower bodily retrusion.

Before a formal consideration of the principles of dento-facial diagnosis of malocclusion, according to Classes, it would be well for the student to remember that every one of the so-called unclassified, or *locally caused characters*, when regarded individually in a clinical examination at the chair, must all fall into one or the other of the three Classes, in accord with the buccal occlusion that is found. Therefore, in a case which presents for treatment, if it seems to be mainly characterized by some special form of irregularity, it is important to first determine the Class to which the case belongs, by a careful examination of the buccal occlusion, particularly the first molars, and then by a comparison of the different zones of the dento-facial area with the unchangeable and main portions of the face. The Division of the Class to which the case belongs will at once be apparent. This is really necessary as a first guide to correct treatment.

192   PART VI. DENTO-FACIAL MALOCCLUSIONS

While there are doubtless many who will arrive at correct conclusions in diagnosis through natural artistic discernment (See "Art," Chapter I), their channels of subconscious thought, if intelligently interpreted, would amount to about the same thing. Nor does it relieve us of the fact that the great majority of students require well defined rules in a proceeding of which they have little or no knowledge.

FIG. 126.

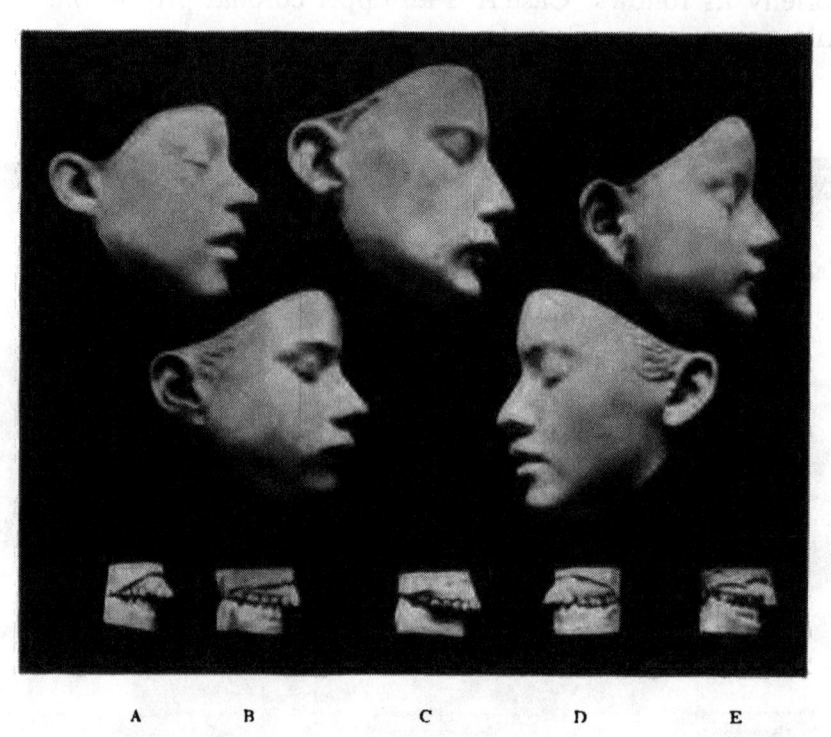

A   B   C   D   E

Observation Training.—In training the mind to a fuller appreciation of the needs of this department, one cannot do better than to study, unobtrusively, the faces one meets in suburban cars and local transits of a large city. In a face under observation, note the general character and relations of the various parts of the principal features, or unchangeable area, shutting out for the time the dento-facial area. Note the relative position and **pose of the chin,** with the malar prominences, forehead, bridge of the nose, etc. Then turn to the **dento-facial area,** or that portion of the physiognomy that it is possible to change in dental orthopedia—its general and localized relations from an esthetic standpoint. Compare the outlines of the **dento-facial zones** with each other, and with the adjoining areas of the physiognomy outside of this sphere of possible influence. Note first: the character and shape of the **chin** and its relation to the **lower lip.** Do the lines of the **labio-mental area** form a graceful and concave curve to the border of the lip, or are they abnormally deep with pointed chin, or straight, with character lacking? Second: note the antero-posterior relations of the **upper** and **lower lips** to each other, the lips in repose and in talking and laughing; do they close with ease, or with a muscular effort? Is the natural parting of the lips even with the occlusal plane of the teeth, or does the lower lip lap over the occlusal ends of the upper incisors? Is this due to a short upper lip, or to a supra-occlusal malposition of the upper labial teeth? Third: note the **shape** and **relations** of the **upper lip**. In its perpendicular lines, is it slightly concave, as it should be, or is it straight or convex? Over the incisive area, does it gracefully curve with a slight deepening of the **naso-labial lines** where it joins the cheeks? Or is the entire upper lip protruded, with a partial or complete obliteration of the naso-labial lines and with that peculiar prominence of the middle features which produces the effect of a **retruded lower** denture and mandible? Or is the entire upper lip retruded, with an abnormal deepening of the naso-labial lines at the wings of the nose, which produces the effect of lower prognathism?

Practical Diagnosis.—When these oft-repeated observations are put into practical use in contemplating the treatment of a dental irregularity, the first thought of the operator will naturally be directed to the physiognomy in an intelligent and critical observation of the temperament, age, development, the character of the facial outlines, then the character of the occlusion, especially that of the first molars, and finally the probable causes.

This may usually be accomplished without special display, or without occupying more time than would be necessary for examining the teeth. In fact, it may require but a glance to show that the case does not belong to any of the Classes of Protrusion or Retrusion, and that you may expect to find it characterized by one or more of the locally caused malpositions of Class I.

If there are no marked imperfections in the contours and outlines of the dento-facial area in relation to its different zones and the rest of the features, the disto-mesial relations of the buccal occlusion will usually be found normal, or nearly so, providing all the permanent teeth forward of the first molars have erupted. The teeth may be decidedly malposed, malturned, and in fact so irregular in their alignment, that their correction may *seem* to be impossible or inadvisable without extraction. *This is a consideration which should never seriously arise except in those rare cases when one is positively sure their alignment will produce an objectionable facial protrusion; and even then, if it is for children under twelve years of age, a normal occlusion with a somewhat protruded mouth will commonly correct itself in the subsequent growth and development of other parts.*

If permanent teeth are missing through injudicious extraction, impaction, or extinction of tooth germs, the teeth back of these spaces will usually drift forward, changing the occlusion from what otherwise would have been normal. The local cause of this malrelation is not difficult to determine, and in nearly all cases demands a restoration of the buccal teeth to normal occlusal positions.

If, however, the case is seen to belong to the dento-facial division, it may require a far more careful observation, extending through several sittings to determine the special division of type to which it belongs. This study may demand a full acquaintance with all the relations—the teeth to each other, their malpositions and occlusion, the relation which they bear to the facial contours, and the esthetic relation which different zones of the dento-facial area bear to each other and to other portions of the physiognomy.

In the study of a physiognomy with the view of determining its particular **facial disharmony,** and the **Class, Division,** and **Type** to which a case belongs, as a guide to the general movement demanded for its correction, the head of the patient should be in an upright position, somewhat in a line with that of the observer, and the face studied from different angles, in repose, and in action. In the absence of the patient, the facial cast will be of great value for this purpose, and also for comparison during the progress and finish of the work, as are the original dental casts. A cursory examination of the dentures, particularly the buccal occlusion on both sides, will give one a line on determining the character of the dento-facial relations.

While you are looking at a profile in repose, the first thing to determine is the relative position of the **chin** to the unchangeable area of the physiognomy, the landmarks of which are, the **forehead, malar prominences,** and **bridge of the nose.** If the position of the chin is in proper relation, and the lower lip is well posed, it indicates that any movement of the teeth of the lower denture to correct malpositions or malrelations, should be performed, if possible, without changing the general labio-lingual relations of the lower front teeth. It may be necessary to widen the lower arch to correct crowded malalignments of the lower front teeth, or it may be needful to move the lower buccal teeth distally to correct cuspid maleruptions caused by premature loss of deciduous teeth, etc.

If the chin and lower lip—with the graceful labio-mental curve—are in harmony with each other, it means that the lower labial teeth are in normal mandibular relations; and this is true also of the entire lower denture if the back teeth are not materially irregular. Now, if the said lower facial outlines are in esthetic relations to the principal features of the physiognomy, the facial outlines of the upper, and the occlusion of the buccal teeth must at once determine the Class to which the case belongs, and the general course of treatment. These rules and their relations are applicable in all characters of dento-facial malocclusion.

Whatever the complication, the position of the chin and lower lip in relation to esthetic facial outlines should always be regarded as one of the main guides to treatment. Thus, through this same system of diagnosis, each one of the Divisions and Types of the three Classes of Malocclusion may be intelligently determined, and its general treatment outlined.

It will also be observed that the disto-mesial relations of buccal occlusion signify only the Class in which the case belongs, and that the relation of the dento-facial zones to each other and to the rest of the features signifies the Division and Type which stands for the real character and indicates the treatment.

CHAPTER XXI. DIAGNOSIS AND TREATMENT

Principles of Diagnosis, According to Classes

Class I.—In the diagnosis of dento-facial malocclusions, if the disto-mesial relation of buccal occlusion is normal, or nearly so, the case evidently belongs to that great Division 1, of Class I, which is composed of malpositions that arise from local causes. When they occur in this Division, therefore, the usual treatment should consist in placing the dentures in normal occlusion. But on the other hand, it should be remembered that in Division 2 of this Class—which refers to Bimaxillary Protrusion and Retrusion which arise from some form of heredity—the buccal teeth are not only in normal disto-mesial relation, but the entire dentures are often in absolute normal occlusion. In these characters of dento-facial malocclusion, the facial outlines alone are the guides for determining the Division to which they belong, and the treatment demanded.

As has been previously stated: The original plan or inherited anatomic position of the dentures in a very large proportion of the human race is that of normal occlusion with dento-facial harmony; consequently, the many local causes of malocclusion have a very much larger field to attack in Class I occlusions than in the inherited disto-mesial malocclusions of Classes II and III. In Class I, therefore, we find almost every variety of malocclusion which arises from local causes. Often two or more local causes working at the same time or following each other in sequence, have contributed toward producing the various results.

Of course, these same local causes quite freely arise in connection with inherited disto-mesial malocclusions of Classes II and III, and will be found to produce their characteristic stamp, though varied more or less by the original condition. Thus we find in every disto-mesial malrelation of buccal occlusion, crowded malalignments, impacted teeth, maleruption of cuspids, and in fact every malposition which arises from local causes, though not so frequently as in Class I.

There is, however, one exception to this rule relative to open-bite malocclusion, which is found most frequently in connection with Class III, because its local cause is mainly that which produces many of the general malocclusions of that Class. But in the main, the foregoing rule holds good, which shows why so large a proportion of locally caused irregularities arise in Class I, and also why these often very pronounced characters cannot be assigned individually to any one of the three Dento-occlusal Classes, even though they frequently dominate the entire irregularity.

As it is a fact, however, that locally caused malpositions arise so extensively in this Class, it has been deemed advisable for the teaching purposes of this work to place under Division 1 those special malocclusions of a **dento-facial character** which are most frequently found in this Class. The rest of the locally caused characters will be found in "Unclassified Malocclusions" in Part VII. This arrangement presents an opportunity to place the diagnosis and technic treatment of four of the most dominant types of this group within the domain of Classified Malocclusions where they can be studied and compared in closer proximity to similar conditions found in other Classes, i. e., Maleruption of Cuspids, Thumb-sucking Protrusions, Lateral Malocclusions, and Open-bite Malocclusions.

For the same reason, retrusion of the upper incisors and intermaxillary process due to inhibited development, when occurring with normal occlusions, is strictly a type of Division 1 of this Class, but in its practical treatment, it is described in this work in Class III, because of its similarity in facial character to nearly all the types of that Class, and because it gives an opportunity in teaching, to draw sharp lines of comparison and treatment.

Class II.—There are probably no two malocclusions which so decidedly differ in their demands of treatment, as Divisions 1 and 2 of Class II, notwithstanding the fact that the occlusion of the teeth is the same. Division 1 is mainly characterized dento-facially by a retruded malposition of the lower denture, and Division 2 is mainly characterized by a protruded malposition of the upper. Between extreme cases of these two Divisions will be found every reciprocal gradation of dento-facial malocclusion, the composite of which is a partial retrusion of the lower denture and a partial protrusion of the upper. The common treatment, under the Angle teaching, was unfortunately based almost solely upon the malocclusion of the buccal teeth which characterizes this Class, and consisted principally in a disto-

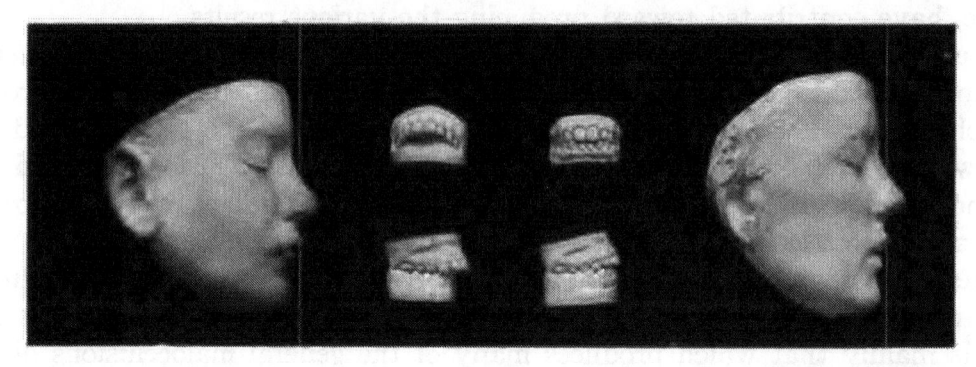

FIG. 127.

mesial shifting of the dentures to a normal occlusion *in every case*. During later years, there has been an effort on the part of those who persisted in following this system to place the greatest movement on the denture which needed it the most. This, with the abnormal expansion of the upper arch, in upper protrusion, resulting no doubt in an improvement of the facial outlines, has led many to imagine they were practicing the true principles of orthodontia. Let us hope that the futility of this effort will be seen by all orthodontists in the correction of pronounced upper protrusions.

In both of these divisions, the upper denture in a masticating closure is about the width of a cusp in front of a normal occlusion in relation to the lower, and

CHAPTER XXI. DIAGNOSIS AND TREATMENT

with the chin in normal dento-facial relation. Therefore, if the upper lip is not protruded, as in Type A, Division 1, the lower denture *must* be retruded in relation to a normally posed chin and the rest of the facial framework, to the full extent

FIG. 128.

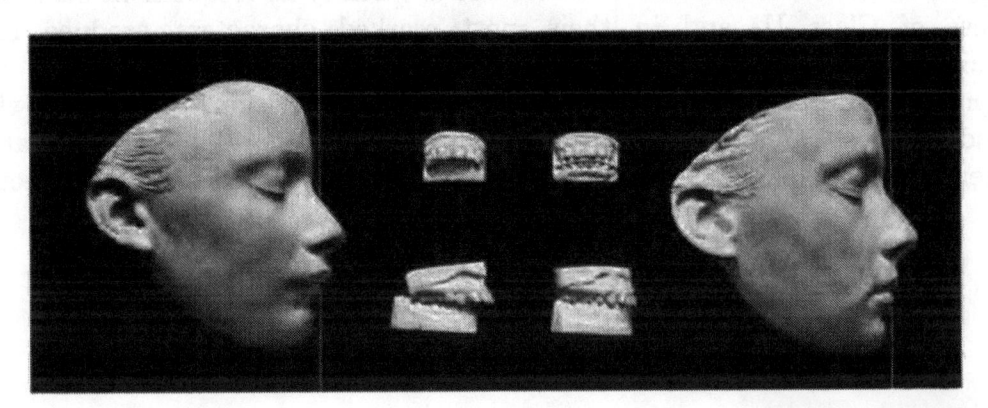

of the buccal malocclusion. This is proven by the retruded position of the lower lip and deep labio-mental depression in relation to the chin and all other parts. It is somewhat rare, however, to find a case with this character of buccal occlusion in which the upper lip is not even slightly protruded in relation to the main or unchangeable features of the physiognomy. Figs. 127 and 128 quite fully illustrate this type. In viewing the beginning facial outlines of these faces, the inclination to compare the position of the upper lip with the lower instead of the other features, will produce the effect of an upper protrusion, when perhaps it is purely a lower retrusion or what is most common of this Type, a very slight upper protrusion, as in Fig. 127.

In Division 2, the lower lip and chin are in normal dento-facial pose, which is characterized by a graceful labio-mental curve, and shows that the lower denture is in normal relation to a perfectly posed mandible. Therefore, if the upper denture is the width of a cusp in front of a normal occlusion with the perfectly posed lower, the upper denture *must* be protruded to the full extent of the buccal malocclusion. This is readily evidenced by the protruding lip in relation to the other features. See Fig. 128.

With the same mesial malocclusion of the lower buccal teeth, which characterizes this entire Class II, there will be found every reciprocal gradation of dento-facial malocclusion which lies between Divisions 1 and 2. In addition to this, there are certain complications which arise in both Divisions 1 and 2, and which are placed in the practical treatment under "Concomitant Characters," where a full description and diagnosis will be found.

Class III is characterized dentally by a mesial malocclusion of the lower buccal teeth—the lower labial teeth closing in front of the upper. Facially, it is characterized by an abnormal retrusion of the upper dento-facial zones with deepened naso-labial lines, and often with a slight abnormal retrusion of the end of the nose. Malocclusions of this Class are nearly as frequent in occurrence as those of Class II, and in their most marked characters produce facial deformities that are quite as unpleasant in appearance. Like Class II, also, they present a number of important and interesting Divisions and Types which demand the most careful and intelligent comparisons of dental and facial relations to determine their real character and the treatment demanded in their correction.

CLASS I
NORMAL DISTO-MESIAL OCCLUSION

Table of Divisions and Types

DIVISION 1: LOCALLY CAUSED DENTO-FACIAL MALOCCLUSIONS

    Type A: UNILATERAL MALERUPTION OF CUSPIDS
    Type B: BILATERAL MALERUPTION OF CUSPIDS
    Type C: BILATERAL MALERUPTION OF CUSPIDS IN CLASS II
    Type D: PROTRUSION OF UPPER FRONT TEETH
    Type E: RETRUSION OF UPPER FRONT TEETH (See Division 2, Class III)
    Type F: LATERAL MALOCCLUSION
    Type G: OPEN-BITE MALOCCLUSION

DIVISION 2: BIMAXILLARY PROTRUSION AND RETRUSION

CLASS I

CHAPTER XXII

PRINCIPLES OF DIAGNOSIS IN MALERUPTION OF THE CUSPIDS

Diagnosis.—The most frequent dento-facial irregularity of the teeth is that which is characterized by a Maleruption of the Cuspids; and since it arises from various local causes, it will be found in connection with every disto-mesial malrelation of the buccal teeth. In other words, it will be found at times characterizing every one of the three Classes of Malocclusion. It arises far more frequently in Class I—as in all locally caused malocclusions—because in inherited normal occlusions of the teeth, there is a far larger field for local causes to attack than in inherited malocclusions of the buccal teeth.

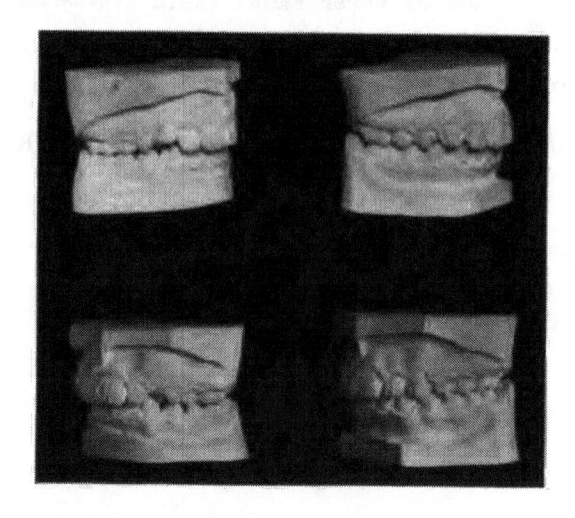

FIG. 129.

The most common characteristic is that of a labial maleruption of the upper cuspids, and occasionally upon one side alone, as shown in Fig. 129. While this condition will frequently be found with both the upper and lower dentures, it far more commonly occurs with the uppers alone. If in these cases it is accompanied with an irregularity of the lower, it will usually be a malalignment of the incisors with the cuspids more or less prominent, though fully erupted. The reason for the more frequent maleruption of the upper cuspids as compared to the lower, is partly due to the earlier eruption of the lower cuspids, which permits them to take their positions before the loss of the deciduous molars, and the eruption of the premolars. It is also due to the fact that the temptation to prematurely extract the lower deciduous cuspids to correct a seeming irregularity, does not arise as frequently as with the upper.

While the technic correction of this character of malocclusion, illustrated in the following pages, deals principally with the upper denture, it should be remembered that the methods and principles of movement which are here described, are in the main equally applicable to like conditions upon the lower. There are a number of complications which arise in connection with this character demanding quite radical variations in treatment, which can only be determined by a careful and intelligent consideration of dental and dento-facial relations.

Maleruption of the Cuspids arises so rarely from heredity, we may consider it as arising wholly from local causes, though of course heredity in malposing the disto-mesial occlusion of the buccal teeth, frequently plays an important part as an aid to the local cause, increasing the difficulties of correction.

In a large majority of cases, the position of the malposed cuspids is caused by the premature loss of the deciduous teeth, which permits an abnormal mesial movement of the buccal teeth with more or less retrusion of the incisors, partially or completely closing the cuspid spaces. If this cause arises with the upper teeth alone, or only upon one side, the approximating lower teeth will usually be driven into malalignment. When this has occurred with young patients whose inherited occlusion is normal, there should be no hesitation in placing the teeth in normal occlusion even though the crests of the cusps have passed the crests of the opposing buccal teeth, and the spaces for the cuspids are entirely closed. As an illustration of this, turn to Fig. 28, Chapter XII.

In some instances, the mesial drifting movement of the upper buccal teeth will amount to a complete jumping of the cusps, and a full malinterdigitation, which judged from the malposition of the teeth alone, might easily be mistaken for an inherited mesial occlusion of the upper buccal teeth, which would produce an upper protrusion if the cuspids were in alignment.

In cases of this character, if there is a general lack of fullness in the dento-facial area, particularly over the **lower coronal zone,** showing that the adult features will require all the teeth in the arches to properly develop the facial contours, they should be placed in normal occlusion.

One can understand by this case, how a person may have a full coronal upper protrusion due wholly to the combined forces of two local causes, i. e., first, the loss of deciduous teeth permitting the mesial drift of the first permanent molars, causing a mesial maleruption of the premolars to a sufficient extent that permits them to pass the crests of the lower premolars into a final full malinterdigitation; second, if this occurs with a thumb-sucking patient, the crowns of the labial teeth and alveolar process will be forced forward, giving room for the perfect eruption and alignment of the cuspids, with a result that may have all the dento-facial characteristics of the ordinary Type A, Division 2, Class II case.

Practical Application of Rules

The following common examples will serve to illustrate the clinical application of the main rules of diagnosis and treatment when applied to those malocclusions that are characterized by a maleruption of the cuspids.

Let us suppose, first, that the case in hand is mainly characterized by a pronounced **labial maleruption** of the **upper cuspids,** with the spaces between the laterals and first premolars nearly or quite closed, and that the buccal occlusion places it in Class I. Then by following the rules of dento-facial diagnosis, outlined in the previous chapter, if you find that the chin and lower lip are in esthetic pose, and the lower denture is in normal arch alignment, the case is at once located in Division 1, as Type B, in which correction demands placing the dentures in normal occlusion with no mesial movement of the lower. See Fig. 28, Chapter XII.

Second: With the same normal, or nearly normal buccal occlusion, accompanied with crowded maleruption of upper cuspids, if the lower lip is decidedly protruded in relation to a normally posed chin, the placing of the dentures in normal occlusion, without a decided and very inadvisable distal movement of the lower denture, would protrude the upper lip to the same degree as that of the lower with the production of a bimaxillary protrusion, as in Division 2 of Class I, in which perfect correction would demand the extraction of two upper and two lower teeth—preferably the first premolars—everything else being equal. See Fig. 160, Chapter XXIX.

Third: Let us suppose that with the same peculiar strongly marked maleruption of the upper cuspids, the lower buccal teeth are in distal malocclusion, and upon an examination of the facial outlines, we find that the chin and lower lip are in normal pose. The case in all probability is an inherited upper protrusion, notwithstanding the fact that the upper lip is not materially protruded except over the canine area, because the incisors are in a retruded position, closing the cuspid spaces. If the upper teeth are placed in alignment with no other movement, it would be a typical upper protrusion, as in Division 2 of Class II. Therefore, the extraction of the first upper premolars is indicated, to allow the cuspids to take their places, correct the facial outlines, and leave the patient with a perfect interdigitating occlusion. For practical treatment of this character, see Type C, Division 1, Class I.

Fig. 130 is a good illustration of this type. It belongs to Class II, as one can see by the mesial malinterdigitation of the upper buccal teeth. It is placed in Class I to draw a sharp comparison between cases in which locally caused maleruption of the upper cuspids arises with normal occlusion and with inherited upper protrusions. The retruded position of the incisors entrapping the cuspids has prevented the case from assuming a typical inherited protrusion, because it should

CHAPTER XXII. DIVISION 1. CLASS I.

be remembered that whenever the results of a local cause arise in connection with an inherited Class II malocclusion of the buccal teeth, the treatment should always be regulated by the dento-facial character of its original inherited state, or the state in which it would be if the front teeth were placed in alignment.

FIG. 130.

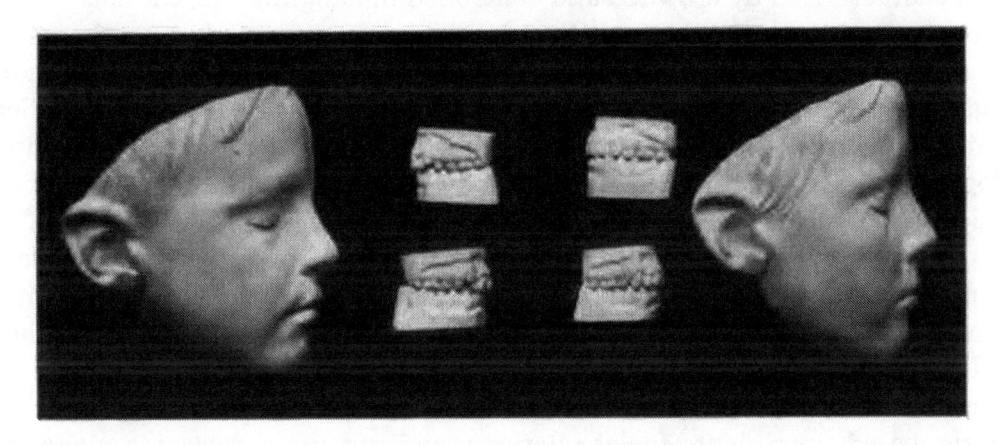

Fourth: With the same dental character of malocclusion as in the above case, if there is a pronounced retrusion of the lower lip in relation to a normally posed chin, the placing of the upper teeth in alignment will produce little or no upper protrusion, showing that the case belongs to Type A, Division 1 of Class II, where its treatment will be found fully defined.

On the other hand, if the lower lip is only moderately retruded in relation to the chin, the placing of the upper teeth in alignment will produce a moderate upper protrusion, as in Type B of that Division. Commonly, the dentures can be shifted to a normal occlusion in these cases without producing a disharmony to the dento-facial outlines. It should be borne in mind, however, that any extensive reducive movement of the entire upper denture, especially that of inherited Types, is very liable to be impossible to retain.

In all cases, it is important to determine whether the malocclusion of the buccal teeth is due to local or inherent causes. If from local causes, and the disto-mesial malocclusion is only half the width of a cusp, there should be no hesitation in placing the buccal teeth in normal occlusion for children, even after the eruption of the second molars, and in many cases, after the crests of the cusps have passed their normal boundaries, but always with a reciprocal disto-mesial movement that is regulated according to the demands of the facial outlines. On the other hand, if the cause is heredity, and the case arises in practice after the second molars have fully erupted, and with *no retrusion of the lower denture and lower lip* in relation to the chin, as in the case illustrated by Fig. 128, the propriety of extracting should be considered rather than attempt to retrude all the buccal teeth one-half the width of a cusp or more from an inherited position in the jaw.

It must not be forgotten that maleruption of the cuspids arises in connection with every Division and Type of Class II, and that the treatment of the case after the Type is determined by an intelligent dento-facial diagnosis, is exactly the same as it would be if cuspids were fully erupted and in alignment.

Fifth: One of the common forms of maleruption of the upper cuspids is that which is characterized by crowded and contruded malalignments, the entire maxilla being contracted, with the dome of the arch high and narrow, frequently resulting in one of the forms of upper retrusions in Class III. The cause of this condition may usually be traced to early diseases of the naso-maxillary sinuses, adenoid vegetations, enlarged tonsils, mouth-breathing, etc., resulting in a lack of normal development of the superior maxillary bones. In some instances, the effect of this condition upon the facial outlines is quite marked, the upper dento-facial area being more or less retruded with deepened naso-labial lines and narrowed seating of the nostrils. When associated with open-bite malocclusion, which arises from the same cause, the mandible will frequently be prognathic. See Figs. 212, Chapter XLIII, and 228, Chapter XLV.

Particular attention is called to these facts to show the need of an intelligent diagnosis, based upon dento-facial relations, and not upon occlusion alone in the correction of all irregularities.

Such a very large proportion of maleruption of the upper cuspids arises in connection with Class I occlusion, and from local causes, demanding a general enlargement of the upper and lower arches to make room for the cuspids and perfect the occlusion, the **extraction of teeth** should never be resorted to as an aid to the process of correction, but always as a **dernier resort,** when convinced that it is demanded for the greater perfection of occlusion, dento-facial harmony, and final retention. If over-zealous dentists would view these conditions from the broader standpoint of future relations, sure to be brought about in the developing and enlarging influences of growth, and consider the importance of a normal occlusion of the teeth and the retention and preservation of means to that end, they would be rendering the only true professional service that would redound to their credit and the future good of their little patients. Many instances can be shown where the injudicious extraction of the first or second premolars, or the first molars, for young patients, has caused a disharmony in the size of the arches, and a malocclusion impossible to correct without either the extraction of premolars from the lower arch, or the opening of space on the upper for the insertion of artificial teeth.

CHAPTER XXIII

Type A, Division 1, Class I

UNILATERAL MALERUPTION OF THE CUSPIDS

When an upper cuspid is prevented from properly erupting because of a partial or complete closure of its space, it will frequently be impossible for it to ever align itself unaided through the natural influences of growth, because of the general contraction of the arch from causes that continue to exert their influence, even to driving the lower teeth into malalignment.

A **unilateral irregularity** of this type is often more difficult to correct properly than one that is **bilateral,** because the forces on each side of the mouth are not

Fig. 131.

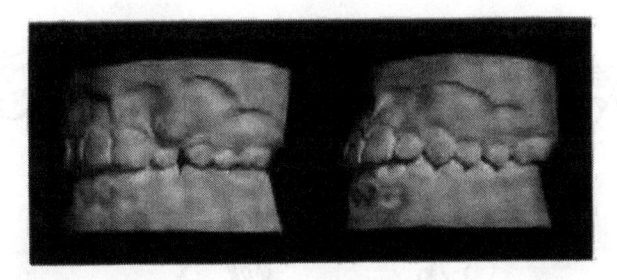

reciprocal; consequently they require greater skill and a peculiar application of force to keep the arch in symmetrical form.

The cuspid spaces at times are entirely closed, principally through a mesial drifting movement of the buccal teeth, and a partial retrusive and lateral movement of the incisors toward that side, permitted by the premature loss of deciduous cus-

Fig. 132.

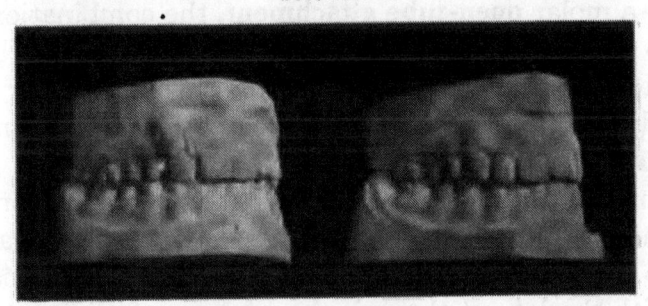

pids. The contraction of the upper arch usually contracts the lower, crowding the teeth into malalignment, demanding a concomitant enlargement of the lower arch with that of the upper.

At the beginning of the case illustrated in Fig. 131, the mesial movement of the left upper premolars and molars had caused the crests of the cusps to strike upon the crests of the lowers, while on the right side the teeth were nearly in normal occlusion. Again, in Fig. 132, is shown another case in which the right upper buccal teeth were nearly in complete mesial malinterdigitation, with the cuspid space fully closed, while on the left side, the occlusion was nearly normal.

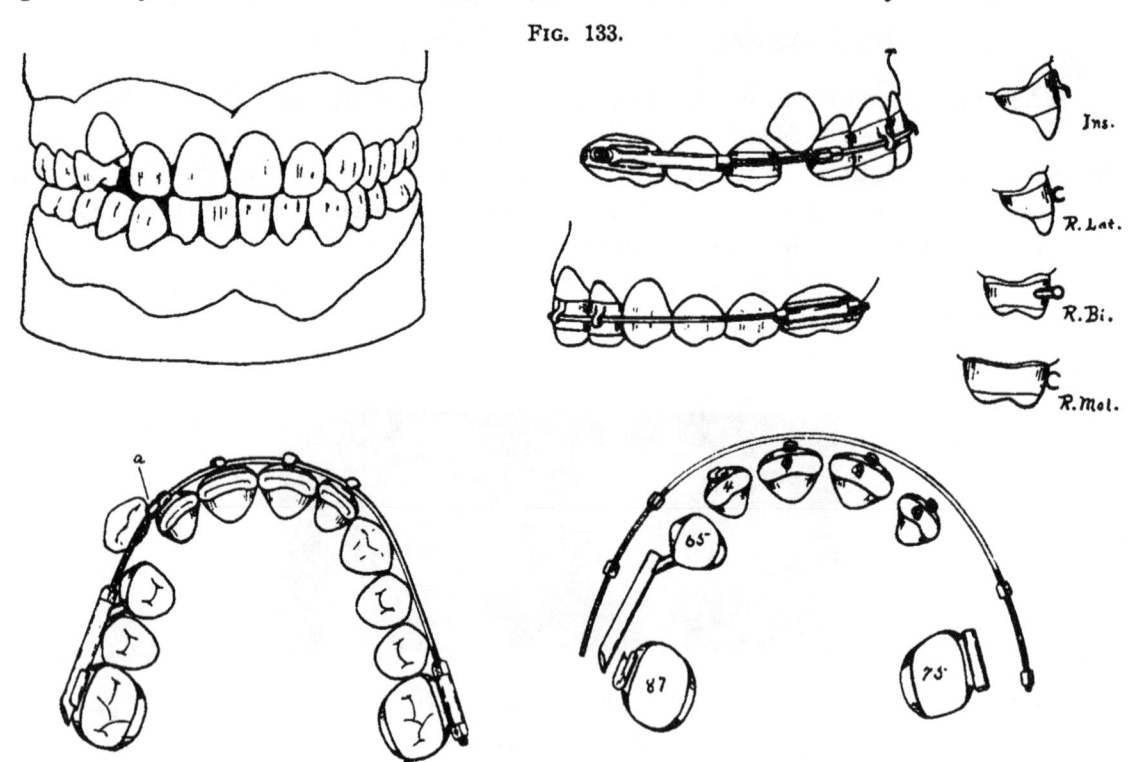

Fig. 133.

The apparatus shown in Fig. 133 is well calculated for regulating slight unilateral irregularities of this character. One end of the **arch-bow,** No. 19, rests in a **buccal T-tube attachment** on the premolar, the distal end of which is supported in a molar **open-tube attachment,** the combination being calculated to promote a distal inclination movement of the buccal teeth. See Movable Anchorages in Chapter XV. The other end of the bow is adjustably fastened with two nuts to the left molar **tube attachment.** The bow carries a fixed **lug-tube** "a" soft-soldered at a point to engage with an **open-tube attachment** on the lateral band. Instead of the lug "a" the thread of the bow may extend mesially to carry another nut—as in the disassembled apparatus—to engage with the lateral through the medium of **sliding tubes,** as shown in Fig. 134. This combination permits lessening the direct stress upon the lateral by unscrewing the **lug-nut** "b" with a distribution of the protruding force of the bow upon all the incisors.

Fig. 134.

CHAPTER XXIII. TYPE A. DIVISION 1. CLASS I.

The incisor bands, with hook or **open-tube attachments,** clasp the bow to force the teeth forward with its movement. Should one or more of the incisors be malturned, or in malalignment, the proper attachments for producing the desired force should be soldered to the bands.

The expanding force of the **nut** at the mesial end of the **premolar tube,** forces the incisor teeth forward and to the left, with the teeth attached to the bow. The lateral movement of the incisors can be aided or prevented by a pull or push movement of the bow at its left anchorage. The reaction of the protruding force will tend to retrude the right buccal teeth to normal occlusion by virtue of the free inclination action of its peculiar attachments. (See Movable Anchorages, Chapter XV.) If it does not fully accomplish this, the **intermaxillary force** will be indicated.

When the cuspid space is more completely closed, and the arch proportionately contracted, a greater degree of expanding force for the general enlargement and symmetrical expansion of the arch will be demanded.

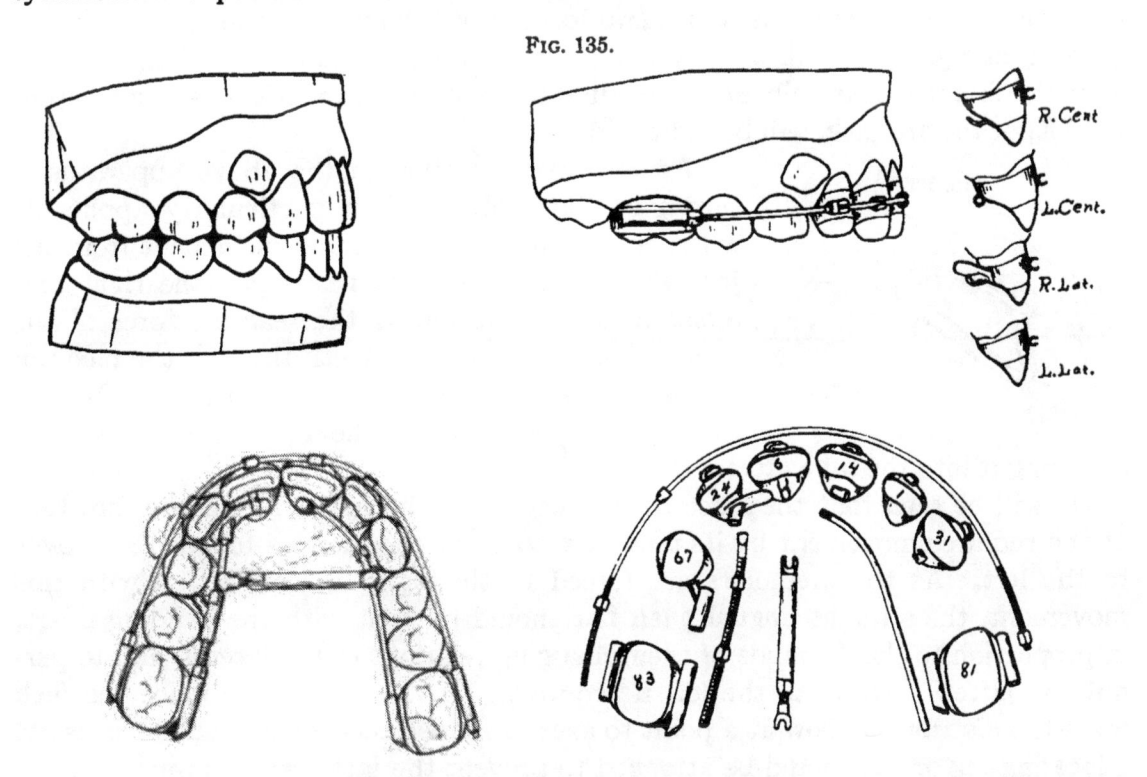

Fig. 135.

In the apparatus shown in Fig. 135, the **arch-bow,** No. 19, or 20, with fixed **lug** or **nut** to engage with the right lateral, is principally for the purpose of alignment, to keep the arch in symmetrical form, and aid in the correction of minor malalignments, etc. It, however, aids in the distal movement of the right buccal teeth by acting directly upon the molar. The lingual appliance is unique in its adaptability for retruding the buccal teeth, and is one of the most common methods employed in the author's practice.

The possibility of applying the reaction force upon the molar and at any moment transferring it to the premolar, with attachments that permit free inclination movement, is of the greatest advantage.

The mesial end of the right **lingual push bar,** No. 16, or 18, is received into a **flattened tube attachment** on the right **band 24,** which carries an extension to engage with the central to distribute the protruding force. The left lingual **distributing bar,** No. 18, rests in a seamless tube attachment on the left central **band 14.** This is done to preserve the rigidity of the bar which would be softened if soldered to the band. Should it be found desirable that this bar exerts a push or pull force upon any tooth or teeth to which it may be attached, it can be threaded at the distal ends for nuts working against the lingual tube on molar **band 81.** The lingual **open-tube attachment** on left cuspid **band 31,** is to prevent the bar from sliding on its inclined lingual face.

The **bar-rest jack,** No. 16, can be located at any point best adapted to exert the proper lateral force. As its general location will be near to the incisal alveolar ridge, a **straight jack** will usually not interfere with the functions of the tongue, after the first few days. Should it be found to do so, the **drop jack** shown in Chapter XLIX, or the **arc jack,** will be indicated.

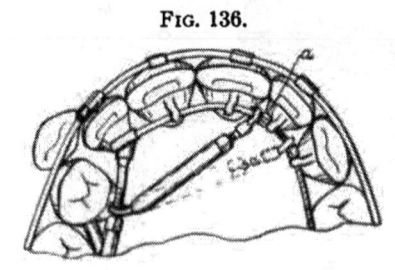

FIG. 136.

An effective variation in the above apparatus is shown in Fig. 136, which is particularly applicable when nearly all of the expanding movement from the **jack** should be brought to bear upon the right premolar area by distributing the reacting force of the **jack** to a larger number of teeth through the medium of the **lingual distributing bow.** This bow, No. 18 extra hard, is attached to the right lateral by soft-soldering it into the **tube attachment.**

It will be seen that the force of the **jack** upon the **bow** will aid the direction of the required movement by its tendency to carry the incisors forward and over to the left. As the premolars are forced to the right, in connection with this movement, the straight **lingual push bar** should be bent with the bending pliers, in proportion to the demands of their changing relations to the lateral, and to permit the latter to move to the left if required. If it is desired to place the **jack** upon the **distributing bow** at a point to exert a more direct force upon the incisors, a **locating lug** or **nut** should be attached to prevent the **jack** from slipping.

CHAPTER XXIV

Type B, Division 1, Class I

BILATERAL MALERUPTION OF CUSPIDS CORRECTED WITHOUT EXTRACTION

Bilateral maleruption of the cuspids is subject to the same rules in diagnosis and prognosis as those which govern the Unilateral characters. The correction of these cases usually requires less skill, because the applied forces being reciprocally bilateral, balance each other and thus aid in preserving the symmetry of the arch.

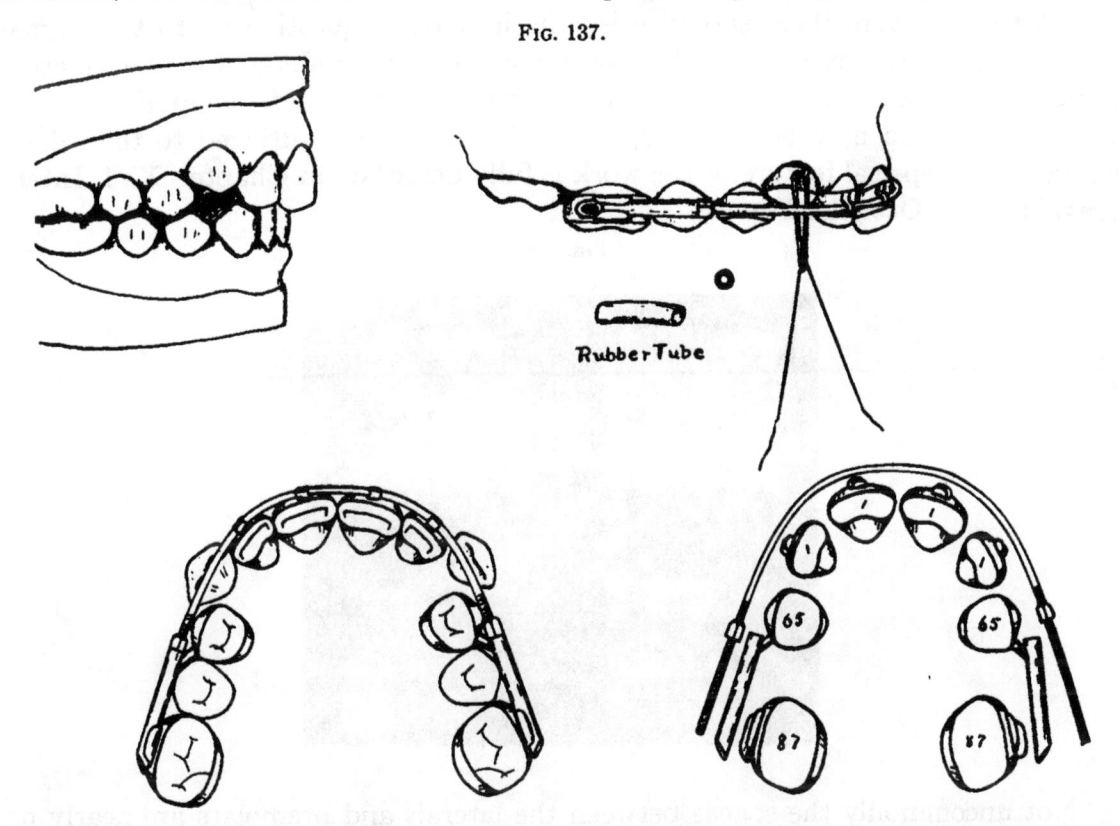

FIG. 137.

When the dental arch is not contracted laterally, and the cuspid spaces are only partially closed, the apparatus shown in Fig. 137 will usually be found sufficiently effective for the entire correction. An arch push bow, No. 18, or 19, attached to the incisors, as shown, reacts upon the buccal teeth through the medium of the same character of reciprocating anchorage attachments that were described in the apparatus shown in Fig. 133, which is constructed with a view of inducing a distal movement of the buccal teeth upon one side.

In the diagnosis of all characters of irregularities, and especially those of this class, the occlusion of the teeth in relation to the facial outlines is of the greatest importance.

In a large proportion of cases of this character, the buccal teeth have moved slightly forward of their normal occlusion, which may be corrected by the reaction of the bow alone, but it will be seen that this force is only that which reacts from moving the four incisors forward, and when distributed to all of the buccal teeth of both sides, one cannot expect more than a slight proportional distal movement of these teeth from that source. Therefore, the intermaxillary force, which may properly be termed **the great adjuster of occlusion,** will be indicated in a large proportion of cases. This is readily attached to the upper by clasping to the arch-bow the **intermaxillary hook-tubes** from which the elastics extend to the disto-buccal aspect of the lower anchorages.

At this juncture there should arise the important question as to the degree of movement—if any—which the lower teeth should undergo for the greatest perfection to the facial outlines, so that in the construction of the appliances, the forces of reaction may be nullified, or on the other hand, utilized to the fullest extent. This special feature of the work is fully described in Chapter XVI, **Intermaxillary** and **Occipital Force.**

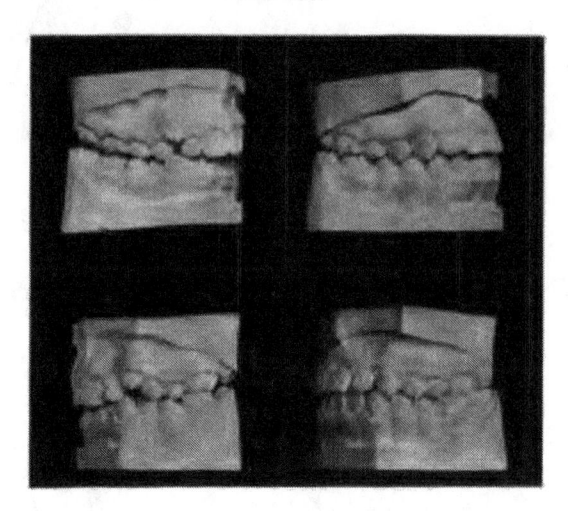

Fig. 138.

Not uncommonly the spaces between the laterals and premolars are nearly or quite closed, and the eruption of the cuspids has advanced so far they prevent placing a heavy arch-bow on the outside of the dental arch. This is well shown in Fig. 138. When this occurs, the apparatus shown in Fig. 139 will be indicated. The lingual yoke push bow here shown with premolar movable anchorage attachments, is one of the most practical and effective combinations in the author's practice. It is similar in its action to that shown in Fig. 137, but is far more applicable for extensive movements.

CHAPTER XXIV. TYPE B. DIVISION 1. CLASS I.

The **lingual yoke bow** is designed to exert an evenly distributed pressure upon the front teeth and prevent the lateral incisors from sliding along the bow. The yoke and bow are attached together by fitting the two into an elliptical tube which has been made by slightly flattening a round seamless thin tube, by passing it through the rollers. When in place, the V-spaces are closed by pinching the central portion of the tube with blunt cutting pliers. The joint is then firmly attached with soft-solder.

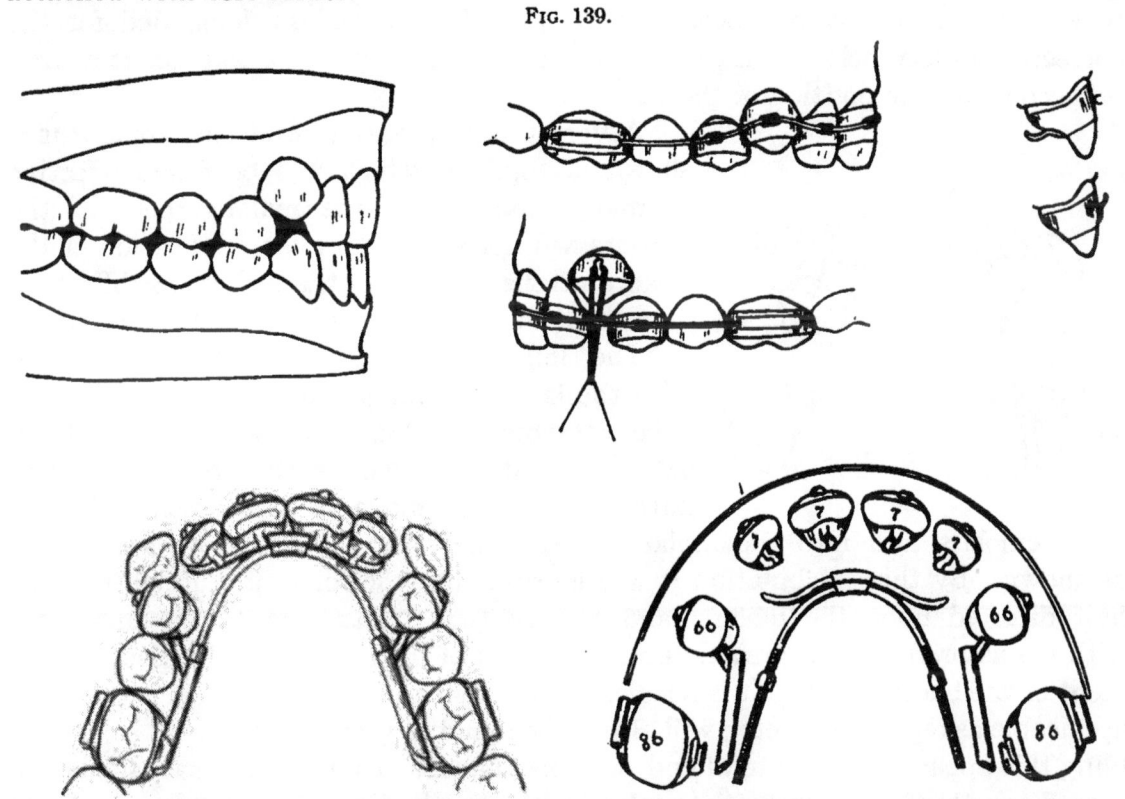

FIG. 139.

In connection with this, the author usually employs at the beginning of the operation a light alignment bow, No. 22 or 23, principally for its resilient action as shown in the buccal views of the apparatus.

There is no use in attempting to force a cuspid or other teeth into alignment until there is sufficient room for them to move in. In nearly all instances where the cuspids are in the position shown, they will usually move into place without artificial aid as rapidly as space is made for their eruption into normal position.

In assembling the apparatus, the yoke of the lingual bow is bent to rest properly against the front teeth, engaging with hook attachments on the incisor bands. If the arch is of normal width, the distal ends of the bow should lie evenly in the anchorage tubes without pressure; but if the molar area of the arch is laterally contracted or expanded, the bow should be bent to exert a corrective force. The molar bands may be placed first, then one of the premolar bands with the bow in its tube. In placing the other premolar band, lift the free end of the bow and slip the tube over the end, and then with a hinge movement carry the band on to the tooth. Another way is to place the premolar bands with the bow in the tube attachments together. This may be done before or after placing the molar bands, as the premolar tubes can be easily sprung into the molar tube attachments. The incisor bands should be placed last, the lingual hooks having been bent properly in the preliminary assembling so as to go easily to place and subsequently clasp the bow. The alignment arch-bow may be placed later, unless demanded for the correction of the incisors; and even then it may be impossible to place it at first on account of the position of the cuspids.

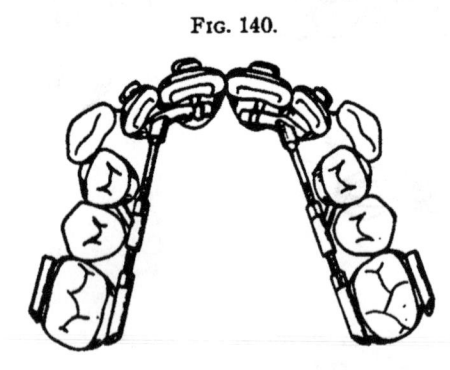

Fig. 140.

A very practical variation of this apparatus is shown in Fig. 140, which will be found effective in many cases where the malalignment of the incisors will not permit an even application of the yoke, and especially where there is quite a difference demanded in the amount of force on each side.

The lingual bars, No. 18, engage directly with the laterals through the medium of elliptical tube attachments, Fig. 135, which support an extension plate to engage with the central. The bars pass through movable attachment tubes on the premolars, and into the molar tubes. They are threaded for mesial nuts, as shown. By this combination it will be seen that the force of reaction may be first directed upon the molars, and at any time transferred to the premolars with the assurance of the greatest possible utility of the force toward a distal movement of the buccal teeth. It is needless to say that the arch-bow, that is the most applicable as regards size, etc., will always be found of great assistance. In assembling this apparatus, the lateral and premolar bands, with the push bar, should be placed together. In placing the molar band, slip the lingual tube over the distal end of the bar and then with a hinge movement, carry the band to place. Finally, place the central incisor bands.

In the case illustrated by Fig. 138, is shown the common occlusion of the buccal teeth in this type. This will usually demand the application of the disto-mesial intermaxillary force at the first moment that it can be properly applied. This, added to the reactive force of the lingual bow, will force the buccal teeth distally to their originally intended normal occlusion. When considerable distal movement of the buccal teeth is demanded, the force may be applied first to the most distal molars through the medium of sliding-tubes or span-hooks, then the force can be transferred to the next tooth in front, etc. This is fully described in connection with the appliance shown by "5," Fig. 141.

In those cases when the incisors demand a bodily labial movement, the front teeth are first placed in alignment so that the incisors are in position to be grasped

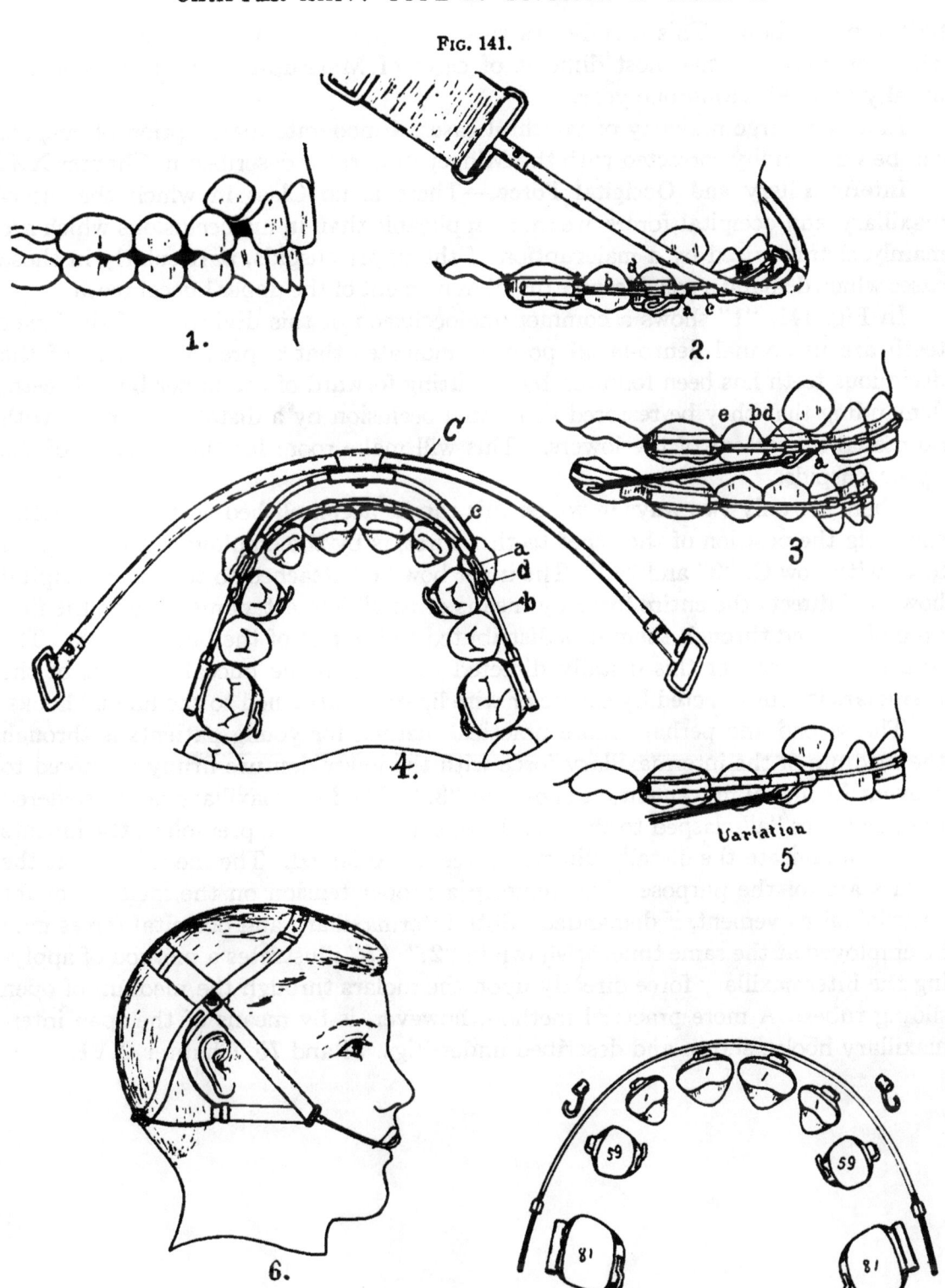

CHAPTER XXIV. TYPE B. DIVISION 1. CLASS I. 213

Fig. 141.

by the power bow. This is fully described and illustrated in Chapter XX. The whole operation in the most difficult of cases of Maleruption of the Cuspids, is usually finished within one year.

In a very large majority of youthful cases, a moderate maleruption of cuspids can be very readily corrected with the Midget Apparatus described in Chapter XX.

Intermaxillary and Occipital Force.—There is no Class in which the intermaxillary and occipital forces are more applicable than in malocclusions which are mainly characterized by a maleruption of the upper cuspids, particularly in those cases which demand a considerable distal movement of the upper buccal teeth.

In Fig. 141, "1" shows a common malocclusion of this division. If the lower teeth are in normal dento-facial pose, it indicates that a premature loss of the deciduous teeth has been followed by a drifting forward of the upper buccal teeth, demanding that they be restored to normal occlusion by a distal movement, with no mesial movement of the lowers. This will make room for the eruption of the upper cuspids.

There are only two ways in which this can be accomplished without materially changing the position of the other teeth. First, is by the employment of occipital force with bow C, "2" and "4." The inner bow "c" attached to the main occipital bow "C" directs the entire force by means of its sliding attachment upon the first premolars, and through them it is distributed to the rest of the buccal teeth. The rotating tendency of this distally directed force upon the buccal surfaces of the premolars is counteracted by elastic or wire ligatures attached to the lingual hooks.

The second and perhaps more practical method for young patients is through the medium of the intermaxillary force with the lower denture firmly anchored to prevent its mesial movement, as shown in "3." The intermaxillary hooks soldered to open tubes "a" clasped to the arch-bow, engage with the premolar attachments and communicate the distally directed force as explained. The mesial nuts at the molars are for the purpose of keeping up a proper tension on the incisors, or for their labial movement, if demanded. Both intermaxillary and occipital forces may be employed at the same time, as shown in "2;" "5" illustrates a method of applying the intermaxillary force directly upon the molars through the medium of open sliding tubes. A more practical method, however, is by means of the span intermaxillary hooks, shown and described under Figs. 74 and 75, Chapter XVI.

CHAPTER XXV

Type C, Division 1, Class I

BILATERAL MALERUPTION OF UPPER CUSPIDS, REQUIRING EXTRACTION

As has been repeatedly stated, the malocclusion which is characterized by a maleruption of the upper cuspids arises in all three Classes; and while it is found far more frequently in Class I—where its correction should be performed without extraction—it is not uncommon to find this same character of maleruption of the cuspids in every type of inherited disto-mesial malrelations of the buccal teeth of Classes II and III.

Differential Diagnosis and Treatment

Though the present Type C under consideration is distinctly a Class II Type, it has been deemed advisable for teaching purposes to place its practical treatment in connection with Maleruption of the Cuspids of Class I, where close comparisons in diagnosis and treatment can be drawn.

Specifically, it is a locally caused irregularity which has arisen and has been ingrafted upon an inherited Class II malocclusion of the buccal teeth, in the same way that this same character of irregularity of the cuspids is ingrafted upon inherited normal occlusions of Class I.

As fully explained in the previous chapter relative to Type B, a full mesial malocclusion of the upper buccal teeth may also arise purely from a local cause, with the production of the characteristic Maleruption of Cuspids through the premature loss of deciduous teeth, permitting the upper buccal teeth to drift forward until they jump the cusps, and thus entrap the cuspids and force them to erupt through the gums above. If one is sure that the condition has arisen in this way, and the case is presented before the eruption of the second molars, it would be proper to force the upper buccal teeth back to the normal occlusion which nature intended; and especially is this true if the lower denture is more or less retruded in relation to the mandible, as in Types of Division 1, Class II.

On the other hand, if there is every reason to believe from the occlusion of the buccal teeth and their relations to the facial outlines that the cuspid maleruption has arisen in connection with a true Class II malocclusion, the next thing to determine is the Division and Type of that Class in which it has occurred, and then treat the case according to its demands. All of this is fully outlined in the diagnosis and treatment of Class II, where it will be found.

Notwithstanding the fact that the malrelations of the dentures are the same, there is a very decided difference in the facial outlines which they produce, and consequently a very decided difference in the character of treatment they demand. For instance, if the maleruption of the cuspids has occurred in a case of Class II, in which the distal malrelation of the lower denture is due to its retruded position in relation to the mandible, causing a pronounced retrusion of the lower lip in relation to a normally posed chin, the extraction of premolars to correct the cuspid malposition would be decided malpractice. But on the other hand, if the lower lip and chin are normally posed, it indicates that the case is an inherited upper protrusion demanding the extraction of premolars to align the cuspids.

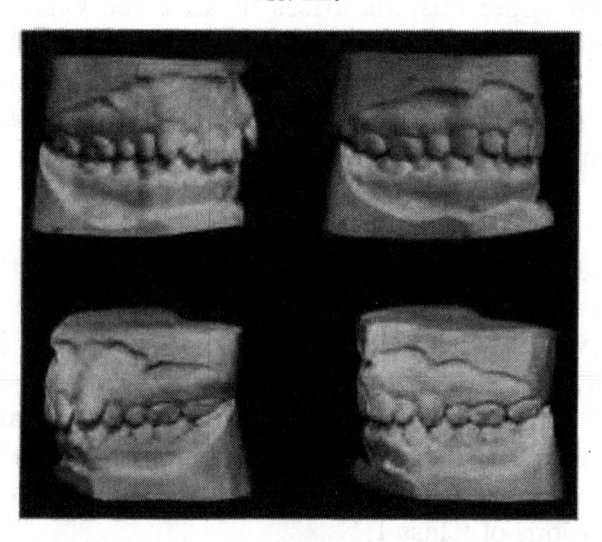

FIG. 142.

In Fig. 142 is shown a case which would have been a pronounced upper protrusion with lower normal had it not been that the maleruption of the cuspids permitted a retrusive movement of the incisors through the action of the upper lip. This patient being twenty years of age had established a perfect interdigitating occlusion of the buccal teeth, as shown on the left. The result of treatment by extracting the first premolars is shown on the right.

Originally, the lips of this patient were somewhat protrusive, which would have been decidedly enhanced had there been an attempt to shift the dentures to a normal occlusion without extraction.

Hundreds of cases of this particular character were perfectly corrected by dentists in the past with no other treatment than the extraction of the first premolars, and as mentioned before, this was one of the reasons which led to the frequent malpractice of extraction in all maleruptions of upper cuspids.

Fig. 130, Chapter XXII, will serve to illustrate the facial and dental character and results of treatment in a case of this Division of malocclusion. It will be seen by the facial cast on the left that the lower lip and chin are in normal dento-facial pose; and consequently with the upper buccal teeth in mesial malocclusion, this case—had it not been for the maleruption of the cuspids—would have resulted in a pronounced upper protrusion, demanding the extraction of the first premolars; consequently, that points the way to the proper treatment of this type. When the cuspids are moved to the places of the extracted premolars, the overlying prominences of the lips are reduced with a complete correction of the facial outlines.

In the treatment of these cases, this type is the easiest to correct and retain of all the maleruptions of the cuspids. In the case of the young man shown in Fig. 142, correction was accomplished in a little over six months. Afterwards, he wore the retainers only about the same length of time, and now after four years, his teeth have never changed their positions, except to more perfectly correct their occlusion.

In this case, as in others of its kind, three-band stationary anchorages were employed on the upper to prevent the slightest mesial movement of the buccal teeth. To these were soldered two buccal tubes. The upper tubes carried traction bars No. 19 to the cuspids, and the lower tubes carried a No. 22 alignment archbow to the incisors. If the arch requires lateral expansion, the arch-bow may be No. 18 extra spring, though if considerable expansion is demanded, a lingual spring or jack expander is preferable.

CHAPTER XXVI

Type D, Division 1, Class I

THUMB-SUCKING PROTRUSION OF THE UPPER FRONT TEETH

Fig. 143.

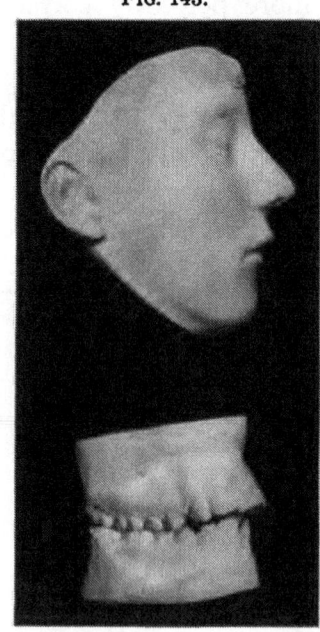

The childhood habit of thumb-sucking when occurring with patients whose dentures would otherwise have assumed a normal occlusion, frequently produces a dento-facial appearance that is quite similar to upper protrusions found in Class II. Therefore, in cases of dento-facial upper protrusion, if the buccal teeth are found in normal occlusion, and the chin and lower lip are in esthetic pose, and in harmonious relation to the facial outlines, outside of the dento-facial area, the malposition has undoubtedly been caused by thumb-sucking. Commonly, the upper arch is narrowed by the contracting action of the buccinator muscles, and the upper front alveolar ridge and front teeth are pulled forward by the ball of the thumb resting in the roof of the mouth, usually causing a decided labial inclination and wide interproximate spaces. The lower incisors, moreover, will often be found retruded, enhancing the protruding effect of the upper.

One has but to place the thumb in the roof of the mouth and suck on it to fully understand the mechanical action of the several forces, i. e., the pressure of the buccinator muscles, the forward pull of the ball of the thumb upon the upper, and the pressure of the knuckle upon the lower incisors, with the muscles of the arm relaxed and its weight pulling downward.

Fig. 144.

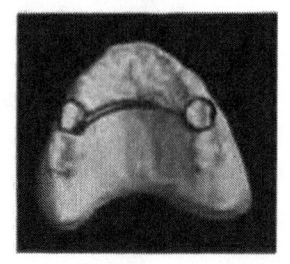

A very little thought will determine also the effect of this cause upon Classes II and III Malocclusions.

The habit which commences in infancy, and frequently continues into the early periods of secondary dentition, may be readily stopped with the appliance shown in Fig. 144, which consists of a loosely telescoping **bar** and **tube,** straight or curved, one end of each being soldered to deciduous molar bands, as shown. The easy gliding movement of the bar permits the natural growth expansion of the arch. This appliance produces no material disturbance, except that it prevents the thumb from taking its accustomed position, and at once stops the habit.

The most pronounced protrusion arising from this cause in Class I, is usually not difficult to correct with a light traction arch-bow from stationary anchorages on the upper. If the lower front teeth are in a retruded malposition, an expansion arch-bow No. 20, or 19, from lower stationary anchorages to attachments on the incisors, will usually be sufficient to align these teeth. The main action of this bow should be through its resiliency from the cuspids. The demands for variations to correct other complications will be apparent from an acquaintance with other cases.

The object of the stationary anchorages on the upper and lower buccal teeth is to prevent disturbing their normal disto-mesial occlusion and dento-facial relations. Any disto-mesial malrelations of occlusion are easily corrected with the intermaxillary force.

CHAPTER XXVII

Type F, Division 1, Class I

LATERAL MALOCCLUSION

There are two very distinct forms of lateral malocclusion of the dentures, both of which arise from local causes. One is due to an acquired malposition of the buccal teeth which forces the mandible far to one side during a masticating closure of the dentures, while the other form is due to a unilateral malformation of the mandible itself, through causes that will be fully explained.

First Form

The first form of lateral malocclusion is apparent only during the mastication of food. At other times when the muscles are at rest with the jaws slightly apart, and if the patient is laughing or talking, the condyles are evenly posed in their sockets with the chin in the median line, but immediately upon any attempt to masticate, the features are more or less disfigured by this necessary movement of the mandible.

This condition which probably arises during secondary dentition, becomes permanently fixed by the eruption and malocclusion of other oncoming teeth seeking the fulfillment of their masticating functions.

In the pronounced form of this malocclusion, the decided lateral movement of the jaws in the effort to masticate food is at times so noticeably awkward and deforming to the facial outlines, reminding one of a cow chewing her cud, it becomes exceedingly annoying and embarrassing to the patients and their friends.

Fig. 145 was made from the occlusal-bite models of three cases in practice. Those on the left represent the dentures in occlusion at the beginning of the operation. Note the pronounced lateral malrelation of the upper dentures to the lower front teeth. On the right are shown the corrected cases. The one at the top is from the models of a miss sixteen years of age, of high social standing, and beautiful when her features were in repose or when she was talking or laughing. That in the center is from the models of a miss twenty-seven years of age, a ceramic artist by profession, whose facial deficiencies were decidedly emphasized by the same deforming action of the jaws in eating that characterizes this malocclusion. The one below is from a child about seven years of age.

In the correction of this character of malocclusion, it is necessary to break up the entire occlusal relation of the dentures and place them in normal bucco-lingual dento-facial relations. This is not an easy operation with ordinary appliances, because of the deep and strongly fixed occluding lateral planes—some of the premolars often shearing by each other without touching their occluding surfaces.

The work in the more pronounced cases may be greatly facilitated by placing hollow crowns over the first lower molars with heavily built inclined planes to open the bite and force the dentures to a normal linguo-buccal position while eating.

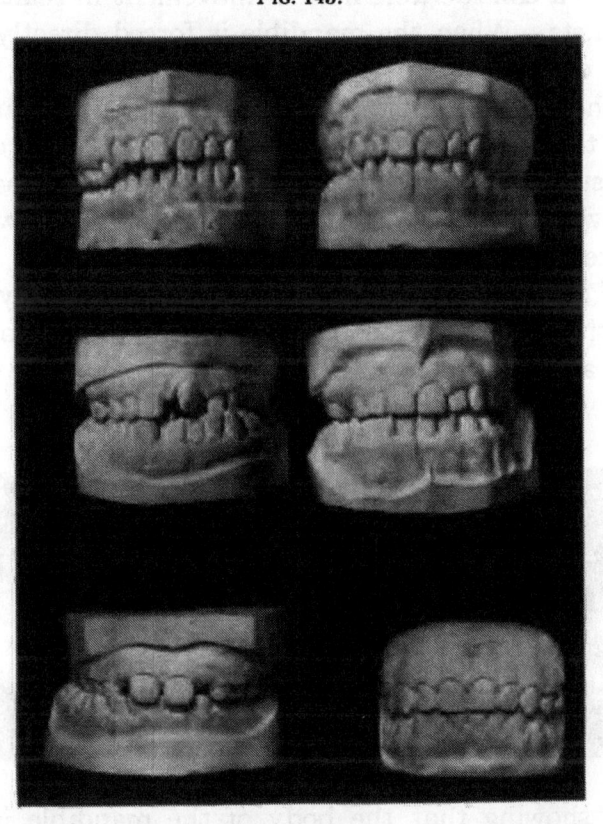

FIG. 145.

The teeth are then more easily shifted to their new positions and occlusal relations. Other than this, the various means which may be successfully employed are applicable variations of the usual methods, which need not be described in detail as no two cases are alike. For children who have not shed the temporary buccal teeth—as shown at the bottom of Fig. 145—strong guiding plates attached to stationary anchorages are usually sufficient for the entire correction of the buccal occlusion.

SECOND FORM

The second form of lateral malocclusion is due to a unilateral malformation of the mandible, and arises during the very early developmental processes of the bones, resulting in the production of a more obtuse or straightened angle of the ramus and its condyle *upon one side only*, in its relation to the body of the mandible.

While this condition is not so very rare in its minor degrees, its occasional pronounced state forms one of the most unpleasant dento-facial deformities and one of the most difficult to correct, because of the profound complications it produces. Moreover, it is so distinctive in its dento-facially deforming character and demands of treatment, it is important that every orthodontist should give to it a careful consideration and study.

The temporo-maxillary articulation in the normal state, is the only one in the body which permits a considerable normal movement in relation to its functional seating in the sockets. When the mandible is forced directly forward in normal movements, both condyles glide evenly forward upon their inter-articular fibro cartilages, until they rest against the posterior inclined planes of the articular eminences, where they are prevented from passing over the crests by the strong tension of the capsular and other ligaments. When the normal movement is only in a lateral or sidewise direction, one condyle alone moves forward, while the other remains in its socket.

In this second form of lateral malocclusion, both condyles remain in their most posterior positions in the glenoid cavities, while the front of the mandible—shown by the chin and the lower front teeth—is far to one side of its normal medio-

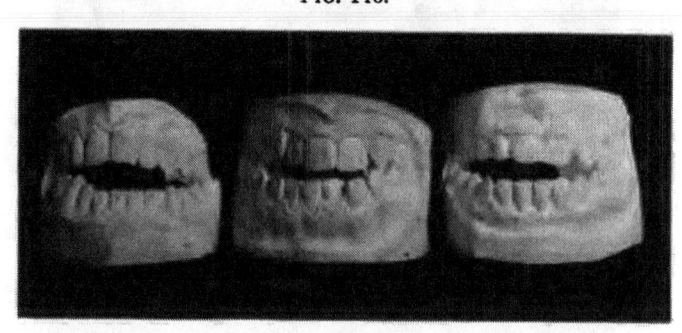

FIG. 146.

occlusal relations, showing that the body of the mandible is bent to one side. Fig. 146 shows a few characteristic positions of the front teeth made from occlusal impressions of three cases in practice having this peculiar malocclusion. The condition may be caused by intra-uterine or accouchement forces, or more probably from the thoughtless habit of some mothers in causing the young babe to nurse and lie far more often upon one side than the other. From the latter cause, the mandible is forced to remain in a strained lateral malposition for repeated periods of time during the very early years of its yielding immaturity when very slight continued pressure will result—if not corrected—in a permanent malformation of the bones.

It seems probable that this is the main if not the only cause, in that it so exactly corresponds to the condition which would inevitably arise under these circumstances through the forces of the ligaments and muscles exerted in that manner and at that age. The *modus operandi* of this action may be explained as follows: The condyle upon one side is forced firmly back against the posterior articular wall of the glenoid cavity, and the other condyle with the ramus being held forward by the forced position of the body of the mandible is under the strain of the ligaments and muscles, which tend to force it back into its socket; with the result that this slight continued force, during early growth development, prevents the ramus and condyle upon that side from assuming the normal form which is more nearly that of a right angle in relation to the body. This action is somewhat similar in its results to that which straightens the angles of both rami in the regular open-bite malocclusion from mouth-breathing.

By increasing the obtuseness of the angle of the ramus upon one side without debarring its growth development in other particulars, the distance from the symphysis of the chin to the condyle is necessarily increased upon that side, and the body of the mandible and its contained teeth is forced abnormally forward, while on the opposite side the disto-mesial relations of occlusion may be unchanged; though the lateral malposition of the jaw, however, forces the lower front teeth, the premolars, and sometimes the first molar upon this side, into bucco-labial malocclusion. This forward movement of the buccal teeth upon the one side frequently amounts to a full mesial malinterdigitation of the cusps; and in one case, fully described under Division 4, Class III, and illustrated with Fig. 230, which arose in connection with a retruded upper, the mesial line of the left lower first molar was even with the point of the upper cuspid. In connection with this condition also, the almost invariable result is an open-bite malocclusion, for the reason that any change toward straightening the normal angles of the rami must to that extent prevent the front teeth from coming together, thus permitting only the most distal molars to occlude, while all teeth mesial to this are evenly opened toward the front, resulting in the production of all the characteristics of an open-bite and general malocclusion of the entire dentures, while the protruded lateral malposition of the mandible and lower teeth usually gives to these cases all the peculiar facial characteristics of Class III.

If this lateral malposition of the lower jaw is discovered during babyhood, it doubtless can be easily corrected with a moderate degree of digital manipulation. At five years of age, and possibly at ten, some ingenious orthopedic appliances could be constructed that would probably bend the mandible back to the normal shape, and thus prevent this very unhappy dento-facial deformity. Later, the usual possible method of correction consists in shifting the crowns of both dentures toward the normal occlusal relations—the one to the right and the other to the left. In connection with this lateral movement, the open-bite can be corrected by an extrusive and retrusive movement of the lower front teeth. If the case is complicated with an abnormally retruded upper, this feature should be corrected by a bodily labial movement of the upper front teeth in the usual manner, but with forces applied, also to move them laterally toward their normal relations with the

224 PART VI. DENTO-FACIAL MALOCCLUSIONS

lower. In those cases where the lower denture and chin are carried far to one side by the lateral bending of the mandible, there is very little hope, after twelve years of age, of accomplishing anything toward a restoring movement of the mandible, or in other words, a permanent movement of the chin toward the median line. But a surprising dental and facial correction will always ensue by moving the front teeth of one denture to the right and the other to the left toward their normal

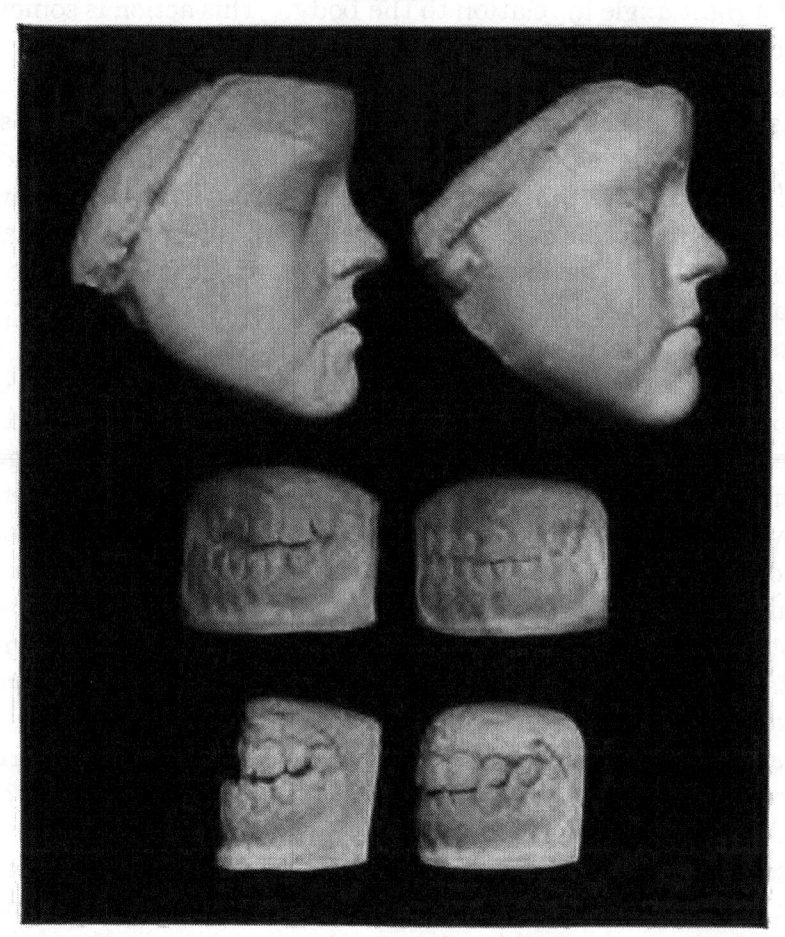

Fig. 147.

occluding relations, thus harmonizing the immediate relations of the dental and facial lines. This is well illustrated in the following case.

If the lower denture is protruded, as commonly obtains in these cases, a first lower premolar may be extracted on the protruded side, and the forces applied so as to carry all the front teeth and opposite premolars over to that side mesio-distally and lingually, to close the space.

Fig. 147 shows this character of lateral malocclusion with the usual open-bite and prognathic mandible and lower denture. On the left it illustrates the facial and dental casts of a miss, seventeen years of age when she presented for treat-

CHAPTER XXVII. TYPE F. DIVISION 1. CLASS I.

ment. From some cause, the lower jaw was bent decidedly to the right, as can be seen by the relations of the upper and lower incisors; while all the teeth assumed exactly the malrelations described in the foregoing text. In this case the malrelation of the dentures was enhanced by a retruded position of the upper front teeth. This was apparently due to the early extraction of the upper left lateral, and a lingual maleruption of the upper right cuspid. The profile plaster casts do not show, as a front view would have done, the extent, on the one hand, of the facial deformity caused by the protruded lower jaw carried far to the right in connection with a retruded upper and open-bite malocclusion, and on the other, the final improved facial effect. The latter is more perfectly illustrated in Fig. 148, which was made from a photograph of the patient taken several years after the case was finished.

FIG. 148.

The auxiliary appliance for shifting the occlusal relations of the lower front teeth to the left in this case, is shown in Fig. 149. It shows the plaster casts in an articulator in the original occlusal position of the case, with a duplicate of the lower apparatus which the patient wore to correct the open-bite malocclusion, and move all the lower front teeth to the left. The upper apparatus for the bodily labial movement of the incisors is not shown. After the lower left first premolar was extracted in this case, a No. 22 arch-bow was made to pass through open-tube attachments on all the front teeth to correct and hold them in alignment. The bow was fixedly attached to the right lower cuspid though its

FIG. 149.

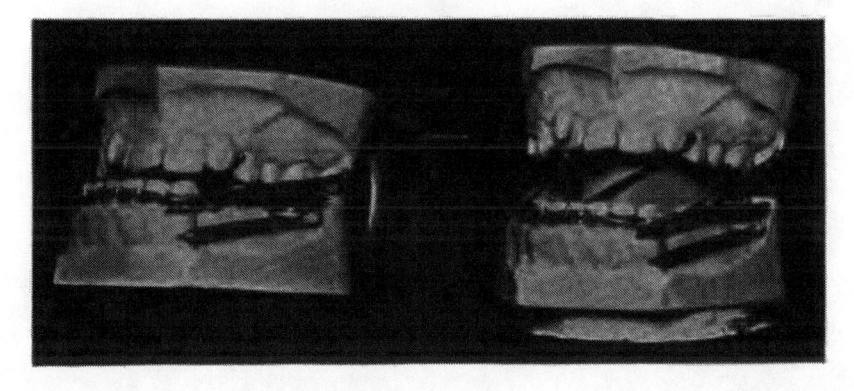

distal end, on that side, passed through a single molar anchorage tube for alignment security. Its motive force was from a three-band stationary anchorage on the left side. The directions of this force upon the lower front teeth were toward the left, lingually and extrusively. In addition to this, and the regular disto-mesial elastic on the left side, intermaxillary elastics were attached to hooks upon the lingual surface of the right lower cuspid, and extended to attachments on the left upper cuspid. This force which tends to pull the lower to the left and the upper to the right is distributed through the medium of the arch-bows to the entire front portion of both dentures. This may be further supplemented with short elastics, as shown, from hooks on the lingual surfaces of the upper right premolars and molars to attachments on the buccal surfaces of the teeth below. The latter resort is the common method in the author's practice for the lateral shifting of buccal occlusion. It would seem as if this apparent complicated arrangement of elastics would be a very difficult one for the frequent necessary readjustments at mealtimes, but patients—especially the young ones—soon learn to remove and readjust the elastics far more quickly and adroitly than a skilled operator.

To produce a bodily distal movement of the left lower cuspid, root-wise labial and lingual bars were soldered to the cuspid band with hook attachments for elastics to extend to root-wise attachments on the anchorage. To further insure and sustain a bodily movement of the cuspid, a small tube was firmly soldered to the cuspid band which telescoped into the anchorage tube with an easy sliding movement. This is not distinctly shown on account of the position of the elastics. The arch-bow passed through these tubes to engage with a distal nut. This is one of the common methods in the author's practice, either with elastic or screw force, for closing spaces after the extraction of buccal teeth, by a bodily disto-mesial movement of the adjoining teeth.

One of the most important and effective auxiliaries in the correction of this character and every form of open-bite malocclusion which demands an extrusive and lingual movement of the lower front teeth, is the occipital force. (See "Open-bite Malocclusion," Chapter XXVIII.)

CHAPTER XXVIII

TYPE G, DIVISION 1, CLASS I

OPEN-BITE MALOCCLUSION

DIAGNOSIS

In the malocclusion which is characterized by open-bite, the front teeth are apart or open when the jaws are closed in an effort to masticate food. The extent of the malocclusion varies in its scope from conditions in which only the most distal molars occlude, to conditions in which all of the buccal teeth may quite perfectly occlude while the labial teeth are apart. In pronounced cases of open-bite, when the jaws are in their nearest occlusal relations, with the lips in repose, the mouth is usually open, often with a drooping of the lower lip, which even with patients of more than common intellectuality, often produces the expression of imbecility. See Fig. 150. Again, the forced effort to close the lips in these cases, especially if complicated with bimaxillary protrusion, will retract and retrude the muscles of the chin and give to the features an awkward receding chin effect, which enhances the deformity, as shown in Fig. 151.

The occluso-labial casts of a few typical characters of open-bite malocclusion are shown in Fig. 152. The impressions for these cases were taken by pressing modeling-compound against the teeth while the jaws were as fully closed as possible. Fig. 153 shows on the right a common result after treatment.

Occasionally, the condition obtains far more upon one side than upon the other. Usually, however, the space between the upper and lower teeth quite uniformly increases from the point of occlusion toward the front, just as if the mandible had been bent downward or straightened at the angles of the rami. In fact, in pronounced cases

FIG. 150.

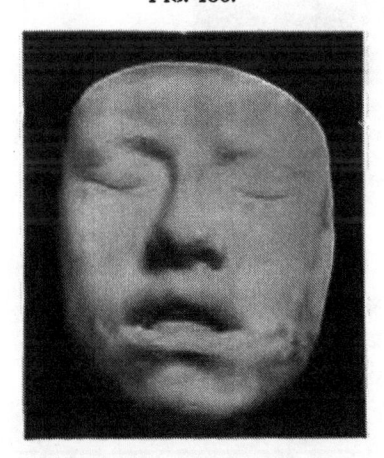

The above is a common facial expression in open-bite malocclusion.

FIG. 151.

where only two or more molars on each side occlude, the back ones will at times seem to have been driven into their sockets through the force of mastication, or prevented from growing to their full height, so that the tuberosities come into close proximity to the angles of the rami when the jaws are closed.

The author has met with a number of cases, however, older than twenty-five years of age, where the entire forces of mastication had been sustained from childhood by single molars on each side, with no apparent intrusive movement.

FIG 152.

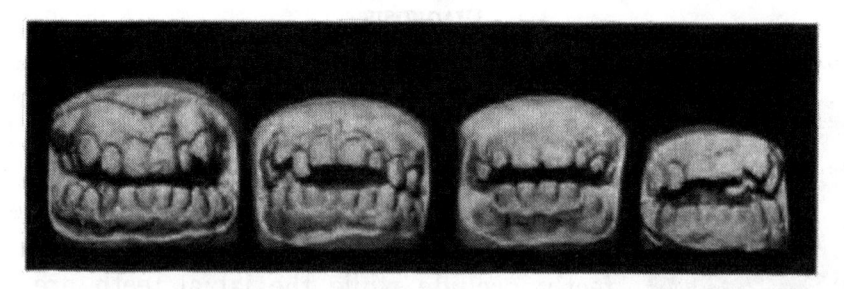

Notwithstanding the fact that this irregularity is the sole characteristic of many pronounced dento-facial deformities, it nevertheless cannot be classified as belonging to any particular one of the three dento-occlusal classes of malocclusion for the reason that it arises in every character of disto-mesial occlusion of the buccal teeth, and consequently in every class.

FIG. 153.

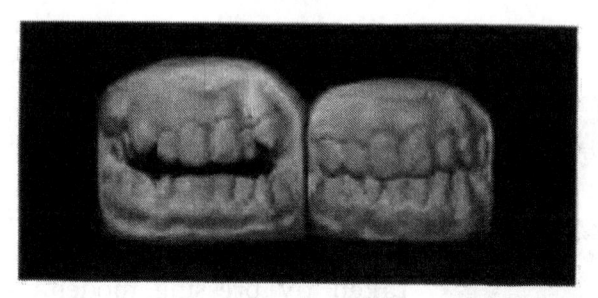

Unfortunately a few orthodontists in their writings have denominated this character of malocclusion as cases of infra-occlusion; while others quite as earnestly believe that they are cases of supra-occlusion; whereas, the fact is, while some of the cases are due to an infra-occlusal position of the front teeth, and others are due to a supra-occlusal position of the back teeth, the greater number are due to neither one nor the other, but to a maldevelopment of the mandible in which the rami and body of the mandible have assumed a more obtuse angle than is normal, and which consequently prevents the occlusion of the front teeth.

In order to arrive at an appreciation of the causes of open-bite malocclusion, it would be well to remember that the terms "supra and infra-occlusion," are

CHAPTER XXVIII. TYPE G. DIVISION 1. CLASS I.

merely relative terms, like distal and mesial, labial and lingual, etc., that are employed to define malpositions or movements in relation to the normal or typical standard line of occlusion. The typical line of the occlusal plane is that which may be said to arise when, with dentures in normal occlusion, and the lips of esthetic facial outlines in perfect repose, the incisal edges of the upper front teeth are even with, or very slightly below, the parting of the lips, though the curve of the lower occlusal plane carries its labial portion slightly above this.

There are people on every hand with normal occlusions, and with apparently no dental irregularity, who cannot close their lips without an awkward and deforming effort, and when they are laughing or talking, the entire crowns of the front teeth are not only exposed, but the gums far above are in decidedly unpleasant evidence, and solely because the dentures, both front and back, upper and lower, are in a supra-occlusal position in relation to a typical dento-facial occlusal plane. In many of these cases, the lips would reposefully close with perfect dento-facial outlines if all the teeth could be proportionately intruded. The fact that we at times see this condition running through whole families, proves the cause to be that of heredity.

On the other hand, the dentures are frequently in the opposite, or infra-occlusal malposition. Occasionally this is so pronounced that it amounts to a facial deformity. This does not refer to those frequent close-bite malocclusions commonly found in Class II, in which the lower front teeth strike into the gums back of the upper, but with the incisal edges even with the lips when the jaws are apart, and which can only be due to an infra-occlusal position of the back teeth, but it refers to cases in which both the front and back teeth are in an infra-occlusal position in relation to the typical dento-facial occlusal plane, shown by the fact that the occlusal edges of the front teeth are in a marked intrusive position in relation to a reposeful parting of the lips, and also by the fact that when the jaws are closed in mastication, the lips in contact are forced forward with a marked redundancy of lip tissue. This character is illustrated, and its treatment described in connection with Close-bite Malocclusions, in Concomitant Types of Class II.

Causes

Many cases of open-bite malocclusion undoubtedly arise from some form of heredity. This is proven in families in which some one or more of the children duplicate the exact peculiarities of the teeth, with an open-bite which obtained with one of the parents or grand-parents. One of its most common inherited forms is that which is occasioned by a supra-occlusion of the back teeth. This is well illustrated in Fig. 151.

The most prolific sources of open-bite malocclusion, however, are from local causes. There are three quite distinct kinds, all of which arise from different characters of local causes operating during the early years of childhood development. In the **first kind,** the front teeth are in an infra-occlusal malposition, caused by the early habits of tongue, lip, cheek, and thumb-sucking, and in fact any postnatal cause which tends to retard or inhibit the normal growth development of the erupting permanent teeth. These habits no doubt start during the irritating periods of dentition, because of the relief afforded in biting upon some resisting tissues, or resilient substances of which rubber rings and so called "pacifiers" have played a more or less active part.

The **second** and **third kinds** are produced by a malformed development of the mandible itself which forces the dentures into an open malocclusion. In the **second kind** the mandible is forced to one side with the production of a decided lateral malocclusion, and with an open-bite which often extends from the most distal molar upon one side to the premolars upon the other. This character is fully described in the previous chapter.

The **third kind** arises from that most prolific of all the local causes of malocclusion, i. e., adenoids and enlarged tonsils, causing partial or complete stenosis of the nasal air passages, resulting in mouth-breathing; open-bite malocclusion; inhibited development of the maxillæ; upper retrusions; and prognathic mandibles. All of these conditions at times occur in one case. The direct cause of the open-bite is through the mechanical forces of the muscles acting upon the early developing mandible in mouth-breathing, mostly during the long sleeping hours. This character of open-bite is so intimately associated with malocclusions of Class III, arising as it does from the same local cause which produces some of the principal characters of that class, the *modus operandi* of its cause and its complete practical treatment will be found under Division 4 of that Class.

Treatment

In those cases when the open-bite is due to an infra-occlusal position of the incisors, they can usually be easily corrected for young patients with a light resilient arch-bow, providing the cuspids are fully erupted and will stand the reaction

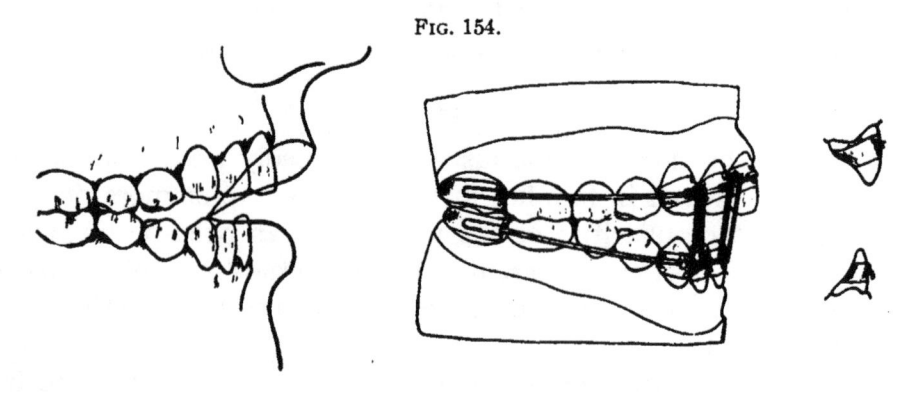

Fig. 154.

of this force. (See Fig. 233.) When the open-bite involves the cuspids and other more distal teeth, the most effective correcting medium is direct intermaxillary elastics. In Chapter XX, "Modern Principles and Methods in Orthodontia," is shown the effectiveness of the "Midget Apparatus" in correcting an open-bite malocclusion, largely through the medium of intermaxillary elastics which are attached to specially designed bracket attachments which also support a very light resilient arch-bow.

When the infra-occlusion commences with the premolars, and evenly opens the bite toward the front, a No. 22 arch-bow (.025″) may be effectively employed with spurs for the elastics attached to the bow, as shown in Fig. 154. With this arrangement, the force of the elastics is distributed evenly to the teeth through the medium of the bow.

For older patients, with longer standing pronounced cases of open-bite malocclusions, the correction and retention is attained with far greater difficulty. The causes, extent, and peculiarity of the malocclusion, together with the complications which are commonly present, must always govern the treatment, which will depend largely upon the skill and ingenuity of the operator, and his ability to cut loose from stereotyped commercial appliances for those which are individually constructed to meet the demands of the case in hand.

In pronounced cases caused by mouth-breathing, when only one or two molars on each side imperfectly occlude, it is generally advisable to freely grind the occluding surfaces (of the molars) in connection with the regulating, to increase as far as possible the area of occlusion and then correct the rest of the open-bite with extensive movements.

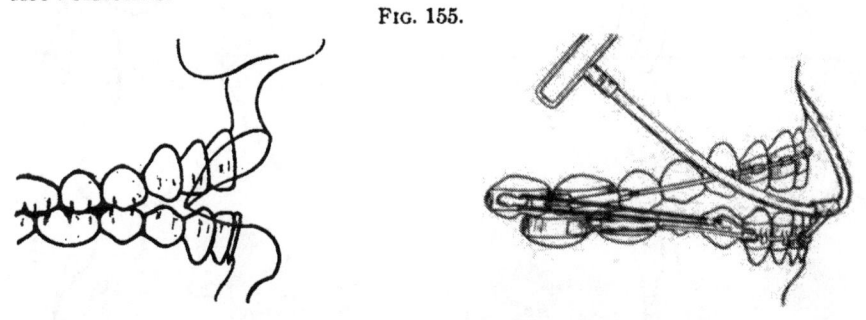

FIG. 155.

As many of these cases in practice will be found complicated with retruded upper dentures and maxillæ in Class III, demanding a bodily labial movement of the upper front teeth, in connection with a protruded mandible, demanding a lingual movement of the lower front teeth, it has been found that the intermaxillary and occipital auxiliary forces are of the greatest possible value in closing the open-bite as an aid to the general correction. Fig. 155 is designed to show the application and direction of the intermaxillary and occipital forces employed solely for a retruding and extruding movement of the lower front teeth. In those cases where the upper denture is in normal dento-facial relations, a bow (No. .036″) similar to the one shown is indicated to offer a static resistance to the forces. In nearly all cases of this character, however, the upper will demand the bodily labial movement apparatus, described in Class III.

CHAPTER XXIX

DIVISION 2, CLASS I

BIMAXILLARY PROTRUSION AND RETRUSION

Between the extreme boundaries of Bimaxillary Protrusion and Bimaxillary Retrusion, which are diagrammatically illustrated in Fig. 156, lies every gradation of these two pronounced characters, which merging toward each other should result in a composite of typically perfect occlusion and facial outlines. There is probably no dento-facial malocclusion which so frequently arises to mar or deform

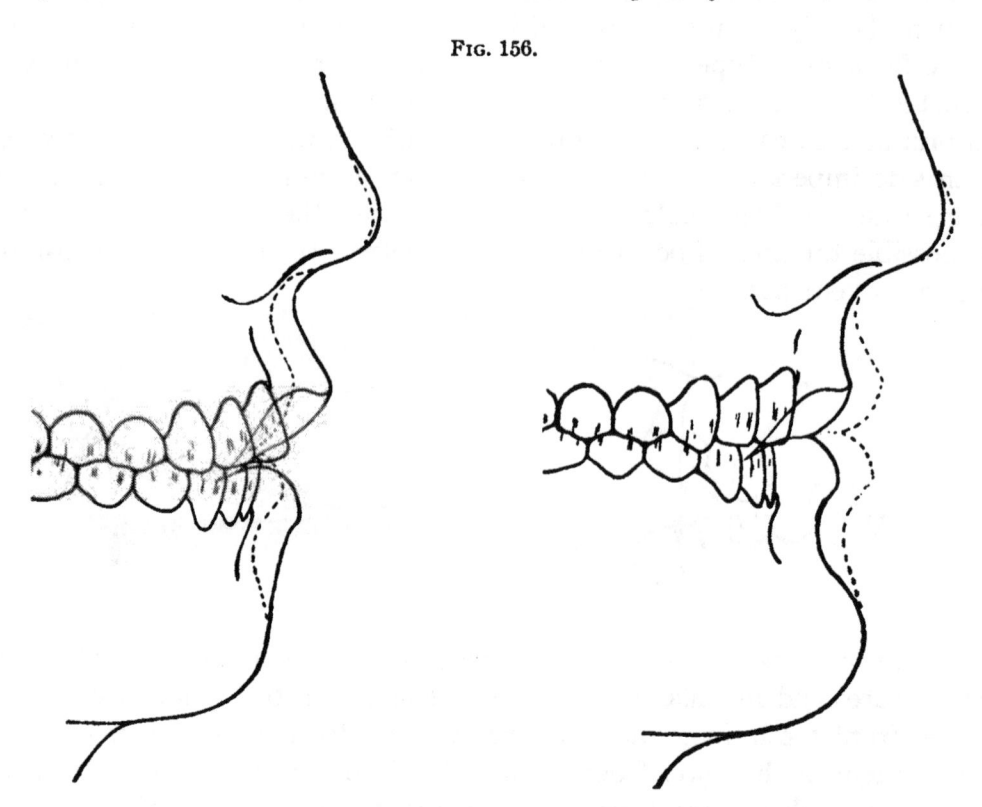

FIG. 156.

the perfect human face as some gradation of these two characters, particularly that of the protrusions. Of the many people we meet whose faces are denominated as plain or homely, if their facial outlines were analyzed from an artistic standpoint, a very large proportion would be found due to a partial or full protrusion or retrusion of both upper and lower lips in relation to the rest of the features, and caused by some degree of protrusion or retrusion of the dentures. As the largest majority of these are stamped with the lesser degrees of these characters, and as the most of them have a typically normal occlusion, no one—or at least very few—ever thinks of correction by orthodontic methods, even though the faces of many could be made beautiful by a very slight movement of the teeth.

Though much has been published by the author within the past fifteen years in regard to bimaxillary protrusion, the great majority of the Angle school orthodontists are very reluctant in recognizing it as belonging to the orthodontic department of practice, because its correction *demands* the extraction of teeth and the consequent breaking down of their ideal *normal* occlusion. They seem to fear that if they let down the bars in one place in their teaching they will have to in other places where extraction is equally imperative. There are many well meaning skillful orthodontists who feel perfectly justified in not acknowledging publicly their belief in and practice of rational extraction, not wishing to set an example to the younger members of this specialty, fearing they might too freely employ it in practice, while others secretly and extensively practice extraction where they believe it is demanded for the best dento-facial results. And yet many of these orthodontists will not acknowledge it at their meetings or even to each other, seeming to fear they will be ostracized or something, not realizing that nine out of ten of the others are doing the same thing.

Some of the older members of the dental profession can remember that amalgam for filling teeth was at one time subjected to the same kind of unreasonable opposition, and wholly due to a few leading spirits who persistently and vehemently denounced its use, being justly actuated, no doubt, by the inexcusable abuse of amalgam, the same as many orthodontists have been and are actuated by the abuse of the principles of rational extraction. The time is now fast approaching when a clearer understanding will show the ultimate futility of all attempts to retard the true question of extraction as in all truths which tend toward true progress.

Bimaxillary Protrusion in its pronounced form is one of the most facially deforming characters of malocclusion which comes into the range of dento-facial orthopedia. It, moreover, is the only character in that large diversified Class I which does not arise in other Classes. As it has been erroneously considered by many to be of very rare occurrence, and its correction not within the province of orthodontia, considerable space is given to this division with the hope that it will become more fully recognized and regarded according to its true importance and possibilities of correction. In Chapter VII, "Etiologic Influences of Heredity," will be found an interesting consideration of a number of variations of heredity which probably have been and are productive of this character of dento-facial malocclusion in its different degrees of prominence. The possibility that Mendel's Law may be an important factor by which this and other types of dento-facial malocclusion arise spontaneously, as it were, from forebears in whom no such condition has ever before occurred, will solve many heretofore mysterious problems of etiology.

The fifteen pronounced cases of bimaxillary protrusion shown in Figs. 157 and 158, arose in the author's practice between the years 1900 and 1912. This personal record of the marked cases of this character, however, hardly begins to represent the comparative number of these cases found among the mixed types of the white race. An observing expert at quick diagnosis of facial outlines will see them everywhere, in the cars and crowded thoroughfares of cities, with physiognomies characterized by protruding mouths and receding chins. The reason why persons of this type do not seek more often for correction, though they may be perhaps embarrassingly conscious of their facial imperfection, is that most of them

FIG. 157.

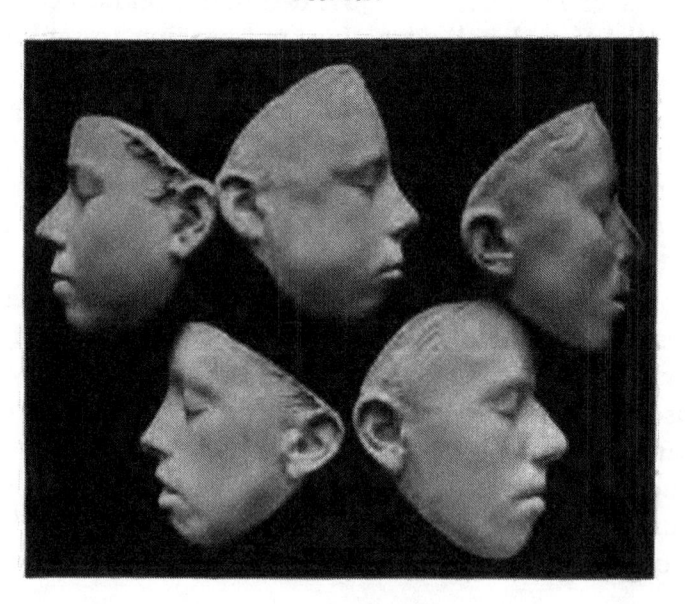

do not imagine that any operation is possible. Moreover, their dentures are so frequently in normal occlusion that even dentists, whose thoughts are engaged in saving teeth, upon seeing these seemingly perfect relations, give little thought to the facial aspect which the dentures produce; or, if they think of it at all, they regard these patients as more or less exceedingly homely, as God or inheritance made them. The same is true of many modern orthodontists who would not consider for a moment the extraction of teeth from mouths in which the dentures are already so nearly or quite in normal occlusion, and who will doubtless tell you that all that is necessary in these cases is to widen the arches and retrude the front teeth. While this might result in a partial improvement in the facial outlines, the teeth would always remain in unpleasant evidence, with an awkward, strained management of the lips, and in a very large proportion of cases, little or no correction is possible in that way. It is a pity to think these patients should be allowed to go through life in that way when perfect correction of the facial outlines is a comparatively easy and sure operation by extracting the first pre-

CHAPTER XXIX. DIVISION 2. CLASS I. 235

molars and placing the remaining buccal teeth in normal occlusion, and retruding all the labial teeth.

Unfortunately, this type is not at present fully recognized by the strict adherents of the Angle system, as belonging to marked malocclusions which demand correction, because in its typical form, the dentures are in normal occlusion. Yet if there is any type in dental orthopedia which demands extensive correction when it occurs in the white race, it is this.

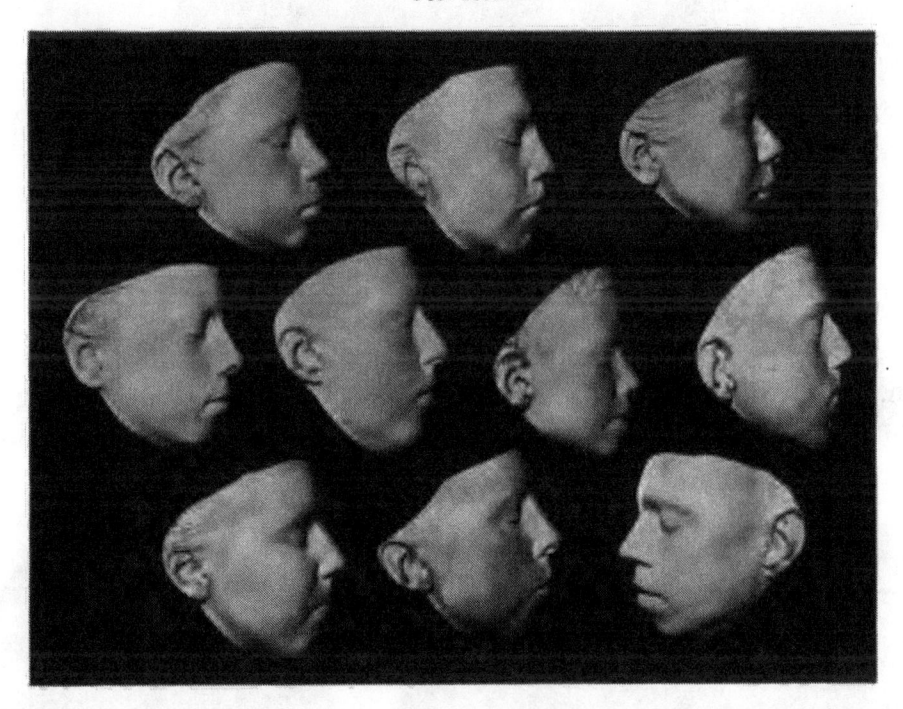

FIG. 158.

When these cases present for treatment, especially as they frequently do after the eruption of the second molars, with the teeth crowded closely together in arches of nearly or quite normal width, with receding chins, and decidedly protruding lips which are closed with difficulty over the protruding dentures, every competent orthodontist must see that there is no way to correct the facial outlines of these patients by an orthopedic movement of the teeth without extraction.

Special attention is called to the two lower cases illustrated in Fig. 157 and fully illustrated in Figs. 159 and 160. In the case shown in Fig. 159, the dentures, with the exception of a slight malposition of the upper right lateral, were in absolute normal occlusion and normal arch width and alignment, and notwithstanding the fact that four premolars were extracted, as shown, followed by the application of the most scientific methods of correction, the dento-facial protrusion is still not wholly reduced. Think what misfortune marred this patient's girlhood because she did not receive proper treatment until after twenty years of age, and wholly because the occlusion of her buccal teeth was normal.

236   *PART VI. DENTO-FACIAL MALOCCLUSIONS*

FIG. 159.

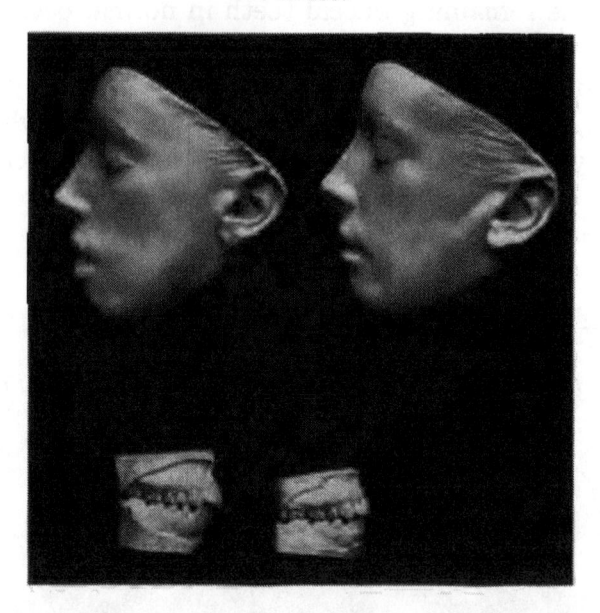

The one case in this group which exhibited a marked irregularity from a normal occlusion, is shown in Fig. 160. It will be seen by carefully examining the first facial cast, that the upper lip is but slightly protruded, which is explained by a

FIG. 160.

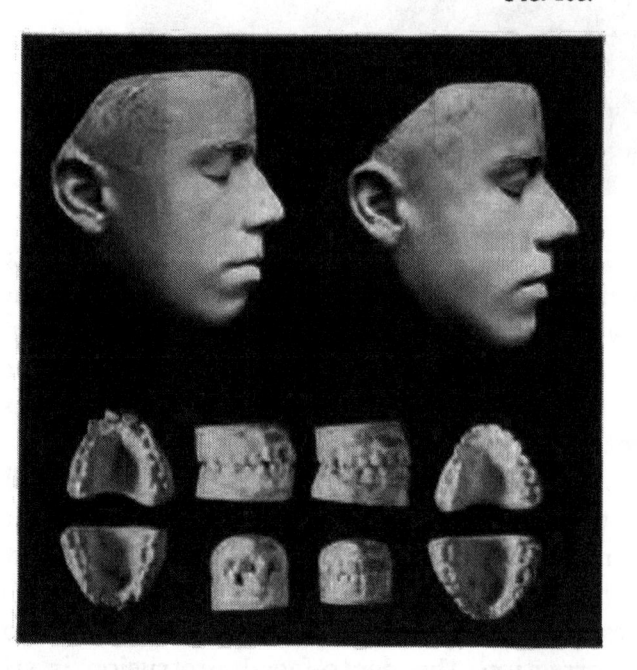

glance at the overlapping malpositions of the upper front teeth, contracting the arch. If the front teeth had been placed in arch alignment with a preservation of all the teeth—the buccal teeth being already in normal occlusion—the result

CHAPTER XXIX. DIVISION 2. CLASS I. 237

could not have been other than a further protrusion of the already protruding lips, with an increase of the receding chin effect. Upon examining the finished faces as they appeared after treatment—one of which is reproduced from a photograph—it appears as if there had been a forward growth of the mandible, because of the greater prominence of the chin and the almost perfect dento-facial outlines, but this is wholly due to the retrusive movement of the labial teeth and the harmonizing effect upon the facial outlines, made possible by the extraction of the four first premolars. Soon after the operation was completed, the young man graduated from Princeton, and because of his phenomenal academic ability and brilliancy, he received from the United States Government an important diplomatic appoint-

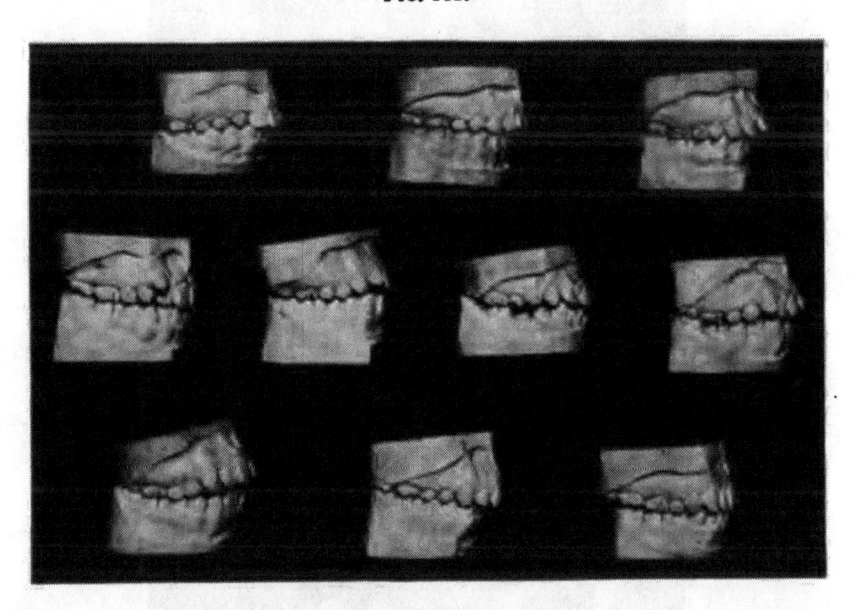

FIG. 161.

ment abroad. As this appointment necessarily entails exacting social functions and relations, one can understand his appreciation of the method of treatment he was finally persuaded to adopt, requiring the extraction of four good premolars, since treatment without extraction would have left a protruding mouth, prominent teeth, and a receding chin, while the result of the other treatment is characterized by comeliness, self-poise, and intellectuality.

In the group of ten bimaxillary protrusions shown in Fig. 158, it will be seen that they present the same marked character of facial outlines as the former group. Fig. 161 is a side view of their dentures in occlusion, showing the same disto-mesially normal relations of the buccal teeth. Only the right side is shown, as the left is practically the same.

Please observe the face on the lower right of Fig. 158, and then turn to Fig. 162, which shows every view of the casts of the dentures of this patient. It will be seen that they are quite as normal in occlusion and arch widths as most dentures

238   PART VI. DENTO-FACIAL MALOCCLUSIONS

which we regard as normal. But when we compare this occlusion with the physiognomy, we can then fully appreciate the fallacy of the teaching that "the full complement of teeth in normal occlusion is necessary to establish the most pleasing harmony to the facial outlines."

Figs. 163 and 164 are the beginning and finished faces of the first two cases shown on the left at the top of Fig. 158. They will serve to illustrate the common results in the correction of this character of bimaxillary malocclusion, performed after the preliminary extraction of the four first premolars. The photographs on the right were taken several years after these cases were finished.

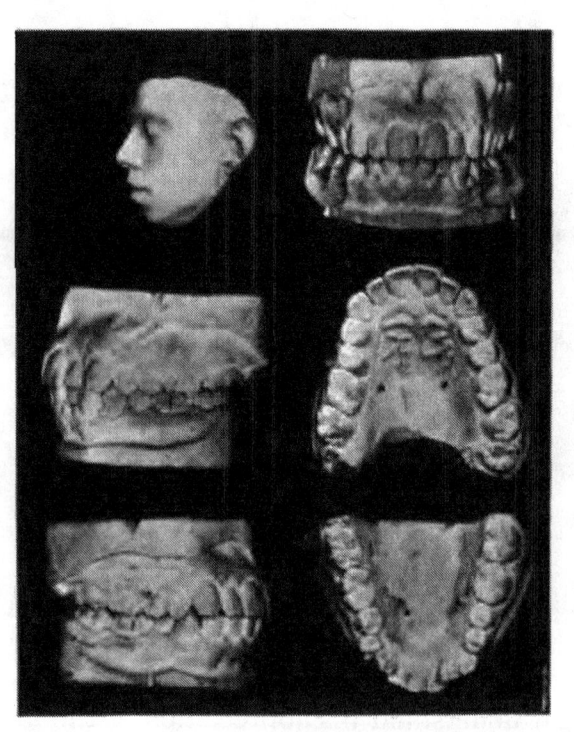

FIG. 162.

The history of the case shown in Fig. 164 is an interesting one from a practical standpoint. When the patient presented at fourteen years of age, it seemed possible to correct the condition without extraction. The teeth were, therefore, placed in normal occlusion, as shown in the intermediate dental cast. While the protrusion over the entire dento-facial outlines, after this operation, was considerably increased by the necessary movement, it was still hoped that the developing growth would harmonize the relations. But after waiting about one year, and still finding no improvement, and wishing to have time to properly correct it before the patient started a course in an Eastern seminary, her parents were consulted, and were also found to be dissatisfied with the result. They had no objection to the extraction of the four premolars if it promised to perfect her features.

CHAPTER XXIX. DIVISION 2. CLASS I.

It was at this time, when the patient was between sixteen and seventeen years of age, that the first facial impression was taken from which the facial cast that is shown on the left was made. The pictures of the facial and dental plaster casts on the right, which show the finished case immediately upon its completion, do scant justice to the beauty of the face or the occlusion of the teeth which obtained later.

FIG. 163.

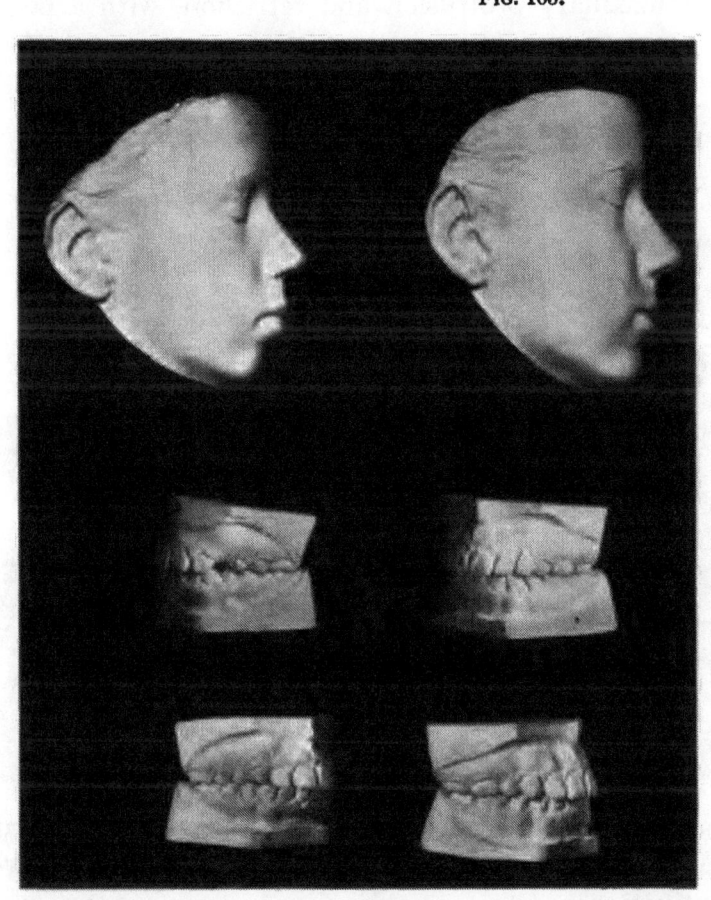

In an extensive practice, one will be called upon to treat every gradation of bimaxillary protrusion and retrusion from the most pronounced types to those of lesser degree; and one will understand also, how this type gradually merges with unbroken gradation into the absolutely normal, with beautiful faces. It has been observed that the imperfections in the facial outlines in a large proportion of these cases, pertain almost wholly to the dento-facial area or that part of the face only, which is supported and characterized by the relative position of the dentures and alveolar processes. In other words, the general labial and buccal surface outline of the dentures constitute the framework of the overlying facial contours. It is hoped, therefore, that it will not be understood that dento-facial harmony, which is the composite type between the extremes of bimaxillary protrusions and retru-

240   PART VI. DENTO-FACIAL MALOCCLUSIONS

sions, is a sure indication of normal occlusion, as has been asserted by a few prominent writers, any more than normal occlusion is a sure indication of dentofacial harmony. It simply means that the framework upon which the soft tissues of the face rest and are dependent for their form and contour, is such as to produce beauty in the facial outlines, though it may be produced by quite irregular teeth.

These principles are well illustrated in Fig. 165, which shows on the left and right, types of pronounced bimaxillary protrusion and retrusion, with a perfect

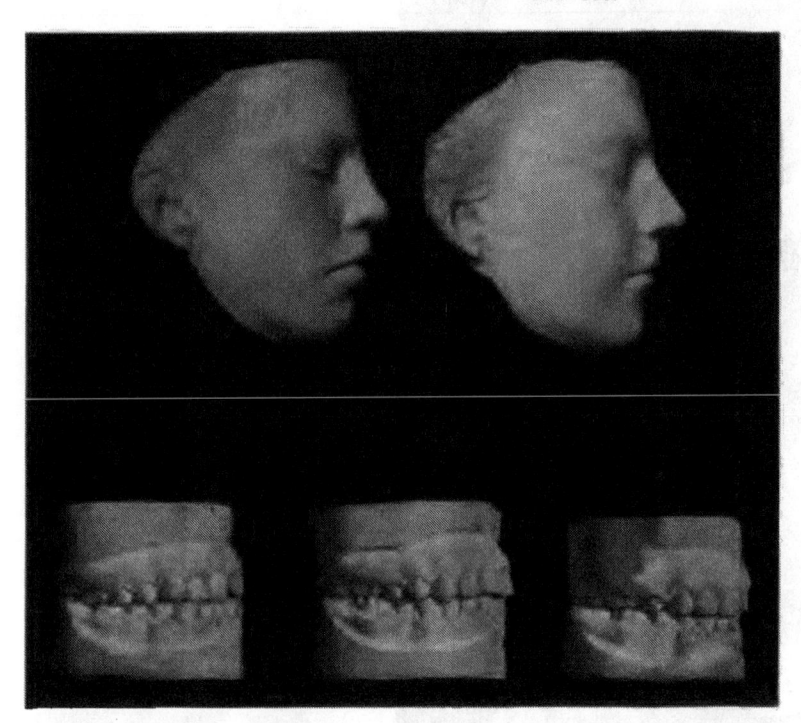

FIG. 164.

dento-facial type above; and yet the dentures of these cases are far from normal in occlusion, and in the central case, with its beautiful face, a number of teeth were missing, because of germ extinction.

In the diagnosis of bimaxillary protrusions, the same rules apply as in the diagnosis of all dento-facial malocclusions. The occlusal relations of the dentures show that they belong in Class I. The true relation of the chin is determined by excluding from the vision the immediate protruded area in order to compare it with the main features of the physiognomy. The relation of the lower lip to the chin, denotes that the lower denture is protruded in relation to the mandible, and with the dentures in normal occlusion and in alignment, the upper must also be equally protruded in relation to the mandible. Therefore, if the chin is in normal relation to the features outside of the dento-facial area, it must be a bimaxillary protrusion. These same diagnostic rules are applicable in the reverse to bimaxillary retrusions.

CHAPTER XXIX. DIVISION 2. CLASS I.

TREATMENT

Bimaxillary Protrusion.—There is no way to correct the facial outlines in extreme cases of bimaxillary protrusion, except by the extraction of four teeth, two upper and two lower, preferably the four first premolars, unless other teeth are considerably broken down from decay and cannot be permanently saved. After the extraction of the premolars, the front teeth are retruded, principally from root-wise stationary anchorages, in the same manner as described for the cor-

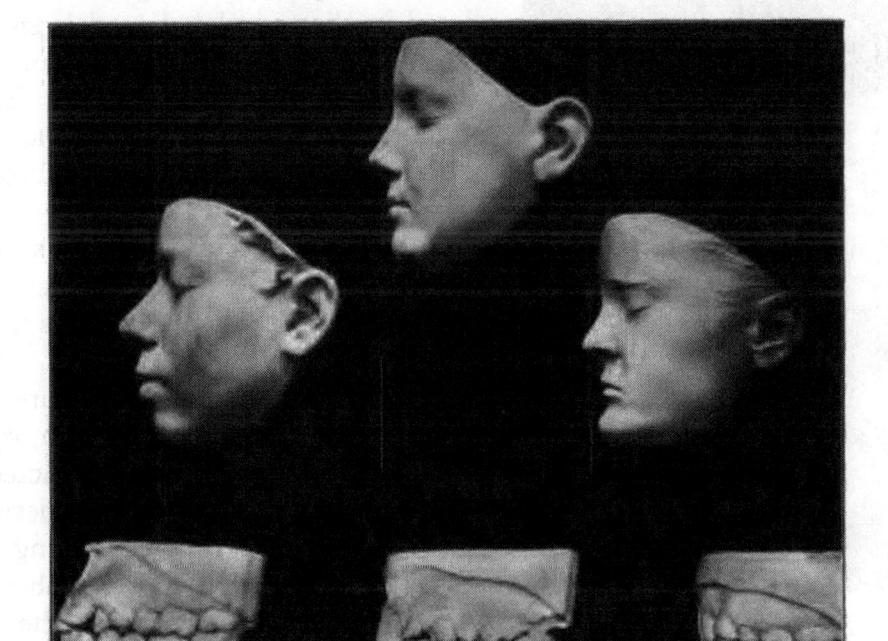

FIG. 165.

rection of upper protrusions. The great object for firm stability of anchorages is to avoid, as far as possible, a mesial movement of the back teeth in order to enable the greatest possible retrusive movement of the front teeth to correct the facial outlines.

In nearly all cases which the author has observed, the protrusion pertains mostly to the coronal zone, and therefore does not often require a bodily retrusive movement. The retruding force, however, should always be applied at the gingival margins, as directed in Practical Treatment of Full Coronal Upper Protrusions.

In the disto-mesial movement of buccal teeth to close spaces of extracted teeth by reciprocal action, or from a stationary anchorage, the employment of root-wise attachments should be considered indispensable in order to avoid an inclination movement by placing the action of the force at a point nearer to the center of alveolar resistance, as has been fully explained in previous chapters. This is especially important in closing spaces after the extraction of molars.

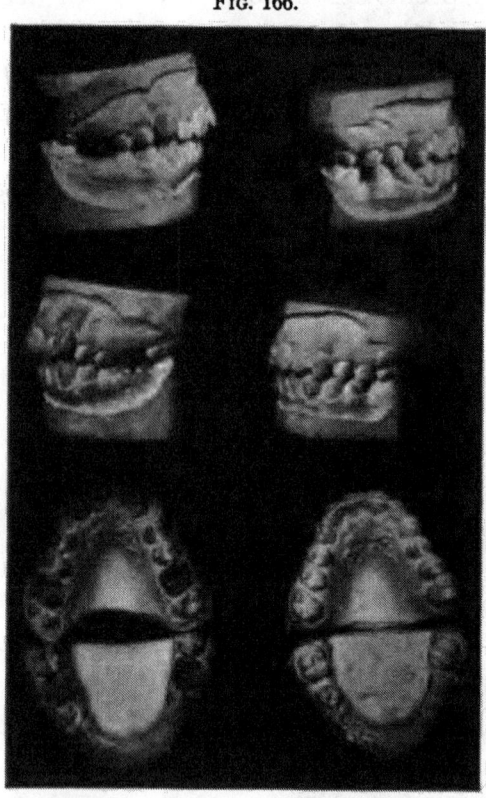

FIG. 166.

Fig. 166 illustrates a case of bimaxillary protrusion which was corrected by extracting the four first molars that were broken down, probably through the action of some eruptive disease. It will be seen that the spaces, except on the right lower, were all closed in the completed models shown by a bodily disto-mesial movement and with no tipping of the adjoining teeth. The cause of the space between the right lower molar and premolar was due to the breakage of the appliance on that side during a summer's outing in a boy's camp. This was soon corrected with a special appliance. The impressions for these illustrations were taken upon his return.

In all cases requiring closure of wide spaces, where teeth have been extracted, the appliances should be constructed with a view to produce a bodily disto-mesial movement and prevent those annoying inverted V-shaped spaces that always otherwise obtain. Fig. 167 shows one of the common methods employed for this purpose. The most important feature is: The power is applied from root-wise extensions. The power bar should be very rigid (No. 18 spring nickel silver) and fitted into long-bearing tube attachments. The upper tube, soldered to the molar band, is No. 19-28, and telescopes into a thin-walled tube, soldered to the premolar band. The upper and lower tubes must move exactly parallel with each other. The arch-bow (No. 19 spring wire), besides acting as a retruding force upon the front teeth, aids in sustaining the rigidity of relations between the molar and the premolar — which is the main principle of this apparatus.

FIG. 167.

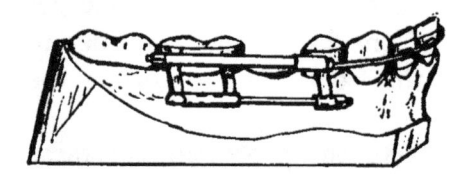

Bimaxillary Retrusions are far more rare in practice than bimaxillary protrusions, and though this type of physiognomy may be quite frequently observed among people we meet, there is no reason why such conditions do not arise from heredity, the same as decided retrusions of a single denture in relation to the

CHAPTER XXIX. DIVISION 2. CLASS I. 243

remaining features, as in retrusion of the lower denture in Division 1, Class II—and retrusion of the upper in Division 1, Class III.

The main reason why these cases do not present for treatment is the same as that which prevents the presentation of bimaxillary protrusions, i. e., because the dentures in these two characters are in normal occlusion, or nearly so, and consequently these patients are rarely, if ever, told that the facial outlines can be easily and greatly beautified by a labio-lingual movement of the front teeth, which can be as easily retained as retrusions and protrusions of single dentures.

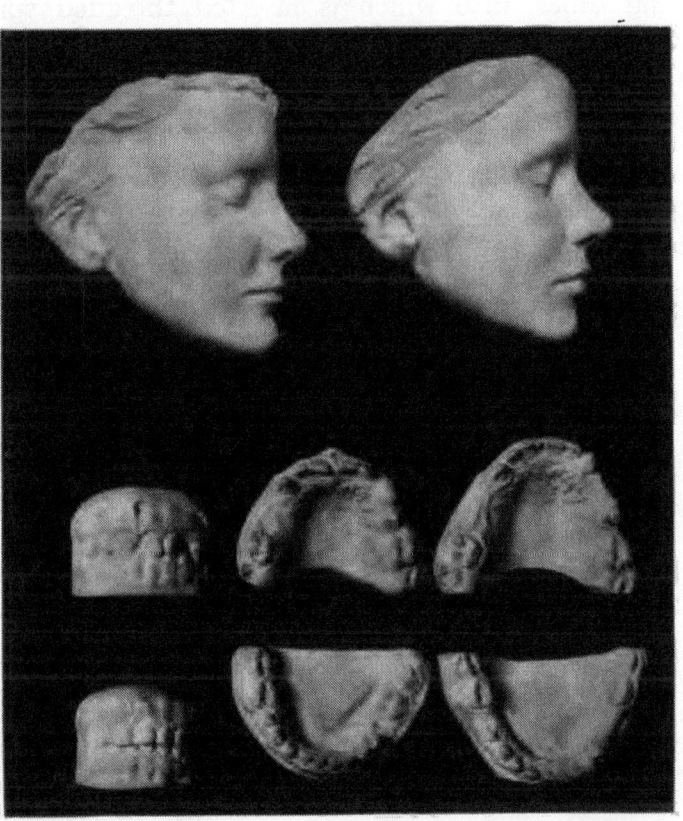

FIG. 168.

There have been only two well defined cases presented for treatment in the author's practice. One of these is shown on the right of Fig. 165. After the case was started some years ago, the family moved away, and the treatment of the case was dropped.

Fig. 168 shows on the left the beginning facial and dental casts of a case which has been recently finished in the author's practice, as shown on the right. It will be seen that the first and second upper and lower premolars on the right side, and second premolars on the left side are missing, the germs being extinct.

The main thing to be accomplished in this case, as in many others where several permanent teeth are missing, is the correction of the facial outlines, leaving the teeth ultimately in a position to permanently support bridge dentures for occlusion and retention. The treatment, after the alignment of the front teeth, consisted in a bodily labial movement of the upper and lower incisors, utilizing the force of the reaction of the fulcrum bow for a labial movement of the cuspids.

One of the most important parts of all operations where considerable bodily labial movements have been accomplished for the correction of decided retrusions, is that retaining appliances must be made so as to keep up the bodily tension on the roots of the front teeth for at least two years after the case is corrected. This is accomplished with the usual six-band retainer (see Fig. 309, Chapter LV), which carries long-bearing tubes, into which is inserted threaded spring bars which extend to open-tube attachments upon molar anchorages. By this arrangement the bodily tension is kept up, and the labial movement can be continued if required.

CLASS II
DISTAL MALOCCLUSION OF LOWER BUCCAL TEETH

Table of Divisions and Types

DIVISION 1: RETRUSION OF THE LOWER DENTURE
- **Type A:** PRONOUNCED RETRUSION OF LOWER DENTURE WITH UPPER NORMAL
- **Type B:** MODERATE RETRUSION OF LOWER DENTURE WITH PROTRUSION OF UPPER

DIVISION 2: PROTRUSION OF THE UPPER WITH LOWER NORMAL
- **Type A:** UPPER CORONAL PROTRUSION
- **Type B:** UPPER BODILY PROTRUSION
- **Type C:** UPPER CORONAL PROTRUSION WITH APICAL RETRUSION
- **Type D:** UPPER APICAL PROTRUSION WITH LINGUAL INCLINATION

Concomitant Characters of Class II

RETRUSION OF MANDIBLE AND LOWER DENTURE
CLOSE-BITE MALOCCLUSION
MALERUPTION OF CUSPIDS   (See Class I, Chapter XXIV)

CLASS II

CHAPTER XXX

INTRODUCTION TO CLASS II

In distal malocclusion of the lower buccal teeth, there arise several Divisions and Types which distinctly differ from each other in their dento-facial characters and demands of treatment. This is fully outlined in the chapter upon Dento-facial Diagnosis, where rules for determining the several characters of dento-facial malocclusion and their general demands of treatment should be carefully studied.

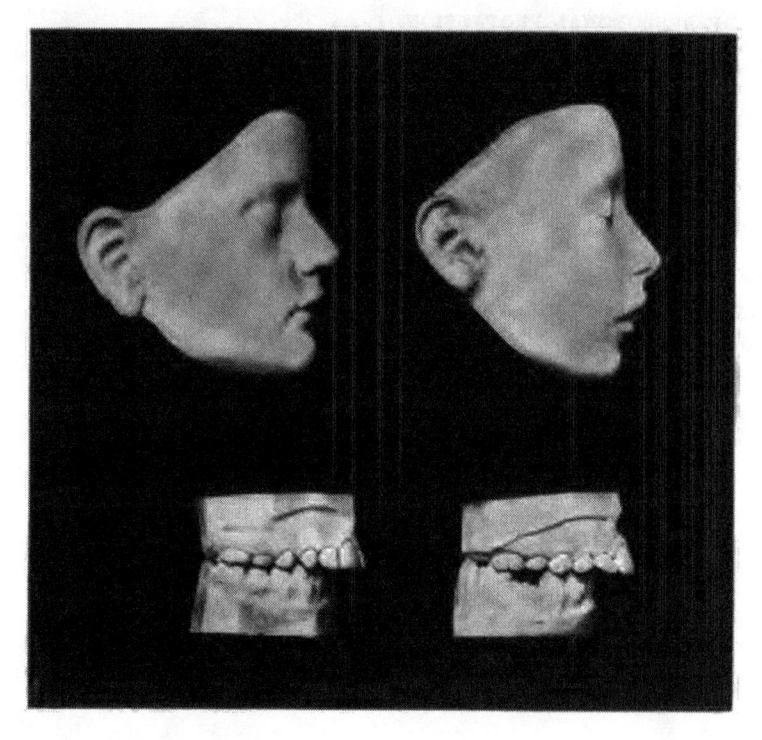

FIG. 169.

The fact that in all of this Class of malocclusions the upper denture is far in front of a normal occlusion with the lower, has led many to the impression that they should be treated all alike, whereas, the facial outlines—which are the only true medium of diagnosis—tell a far different story.

In comparing the facial outlines of the main characters of Divisions 1 and 2 of this Class, the chin in all the Types is in normal dento-facial relation, or nearly

CHAPTER XXX. INTRODUCTION TO CLASS II 247

so. In Type A of Division 1, illustrated on the left of Fig. 169, the lower lip—particularly the labio-mental area—is decidedly retruded in relation to the chin; while in Division 2, illustrated on the right, it is in esthetic outline. In Type A of Division 1, the upper lip is not materially protruded, if at all, in relation to the adjoining facial outlines; while in Types A and B of Division 2, the upper lip is decidedly protruded.

A not uncommon Type of Class II is a retruded position of the chin in relation to dento-facial harmony. This always emphasizes the facial disharmony and increases the difficulties of diagnosis and treatment of all of the dominant characters

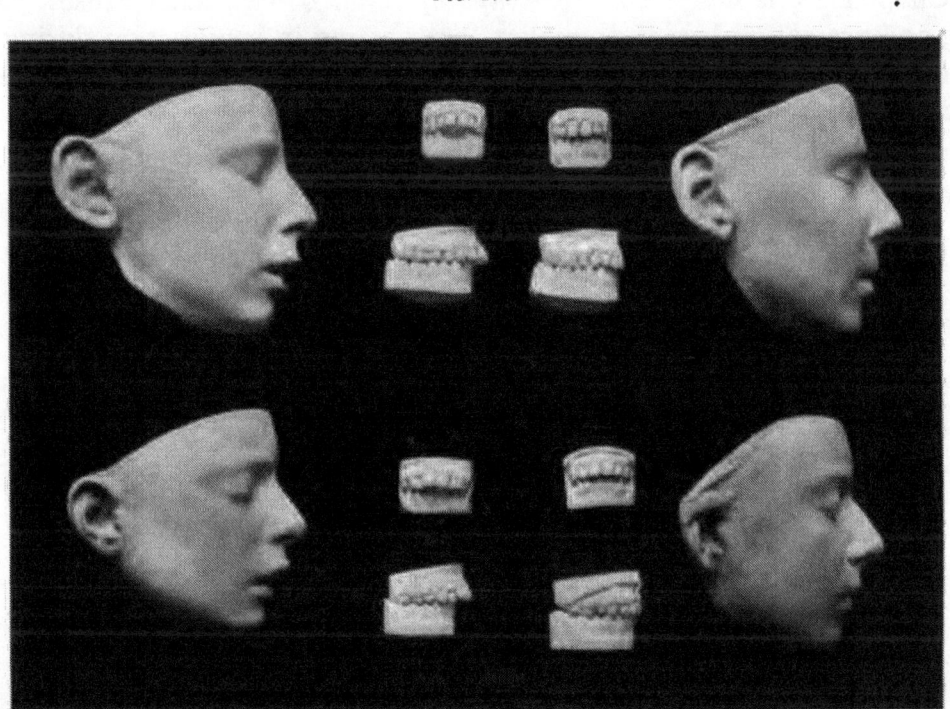

FIG. 170.

with which it occurs. See Fig. 170. As this occurs in both Divisions 1 and 2, it is placed with Concomitant Characters of Class II where the general principles of treatment will be found.

As one advances in the study and practice of orthodontia, he realizes more and more fully the unreliability of depending upon the disto-mesial relations of buccal occlusion as a basis in determining the character and treatment of malocclusions. This is most perfectly and repeatedly exemplified in Class II Malocclusions, which are characterized dentally by a pronounced distal malocclusion of the lower denture in relation to the upper. But in a dento-facial diagnosis, the different characters are found to contain every gradation in character which lies between the extremes of a pronounced retrusion of the lower with the upper normal, and a pronounced protrusion of the upper with the lower normal, all of which demand variations in treatment to obtain the most perfect dento-facial result.

There is no doubt that a large majority of malocclusions of Class II arise through the various forces of some form of heredity; and while it is true that in a large proportion of cases no authentic data of prenatal causes can be obtained that would give rise to the particular character in question, it very commonly is of a Type which no local cause could have produced. On the other hand, there are a number of quite pronounced dento-facial malocclusions of Classes II and III which arise wholly from tonsillar and adenoid influences, and again from other more directly acting local causes.

In Chapter IV is described the *modus operandi* of two local causes, thumb-sucking and premature loss of premolars, both acting in conjunction during early childhood years upon an inherited normal occlusion, may result in one of the most pronounced dento-facial malocclusions of this Class.

CHAPTER XXXI

TYPE A, DIVISION 1, CLASS II

PRONOUNCED RETRUSION OF THE LOWER DENTURE WITH UPPER NORMAL

FIG. 171.

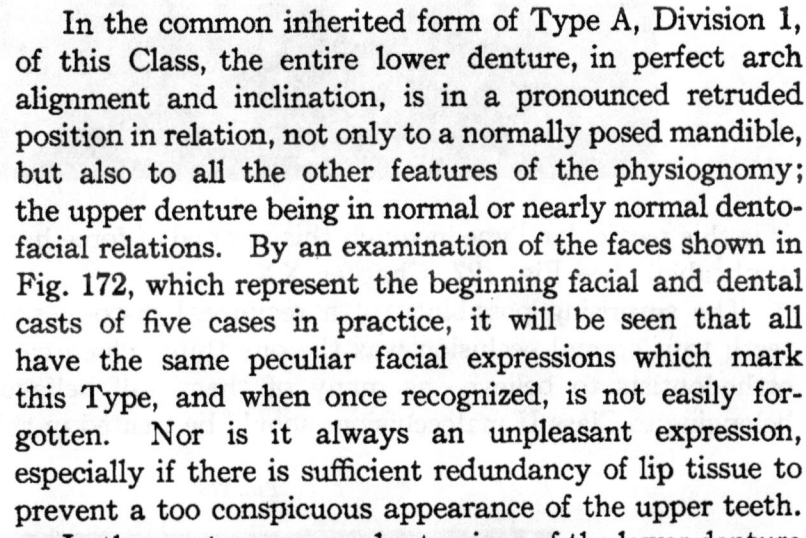

In the common inherited form of Type A, Division 1, of this Class, the entire lower denture, in perfect arch alignment and inclination, is in a pronounced retruded position in relation, not only to a normally posed mandible, but also to all the other features of the physiognomy; the upper denture being in normal or nearly normal dento-facial relations. By an examination of the faces shown in Fig. 172, which represent the beginning facial and dental casts of five cases in practice, it will be seen that all have the same peculiar facial expressions which mark this Type, and when once recognized, is not easily forgotten. Nor is it always an unpleasant expression, especially if there is sufficient redundancy of lip tissue to prevent a too conspicuous appearance of the upper teeth.

In the most pronounced retrusions of the lower denture where the mandible is not also retruded, the chin will appear to be too prominent, and the upper more protruded than it is, because of the immediate retruded relation of the lower lip. The lower lip, in its habit of repose against the incisal edges of the upper front teeth, will usually be curved forward, and produce a defined lateral crease in the deepened labio-mental depression marked by a darkened line of stagnated sebaceous ducts, commonly known as "blackheads."

On the right of Figs. 173 and 174, are fair illustrations of the common results immediately after treatment of all the many cases of this character in the author's practice. But it is a regrettable fact that the disto-mesial shifting of the dentures to a normal occlusion in these cases, as shown, can very rarely be retained permanently even after having been retained artificially in that position for two years or more. In fact, when this particular Type is treated in this way, there are no cases in the author's practice that are as difficult to permanently retain, or more unreliable in the long run in the production of that perfect satisfaction which the immediate results promise.

The principal demand of treatment to correct the facial outlines is a bodily labial movement of the lower front teeth, and a slight lingual inclination movement

249

250 PART VI. DENTO-FACIAL MALOCCLUSIONS

of the upper. As a considerable forward movement of the entire lower denture and a slight retruding movement of the upper can be easily accomplished with young patients, with the intermaxillary force, placing the dentures in normal occlusion,

FIG. 172.

it is this particular Type in which this method of force has seemed to be especially applicable. See Fig. 127, Chapter XXI.

The surprising possibility of a reciprocal disto-mesial shifting of the buccal teeth to a normal occlusion was the one thing which caused the Angle school of orthodontists to believe—as many of them still believe today—that all cases belonging to Class II malocclusions should be treated in this manner.

FIG. 173.

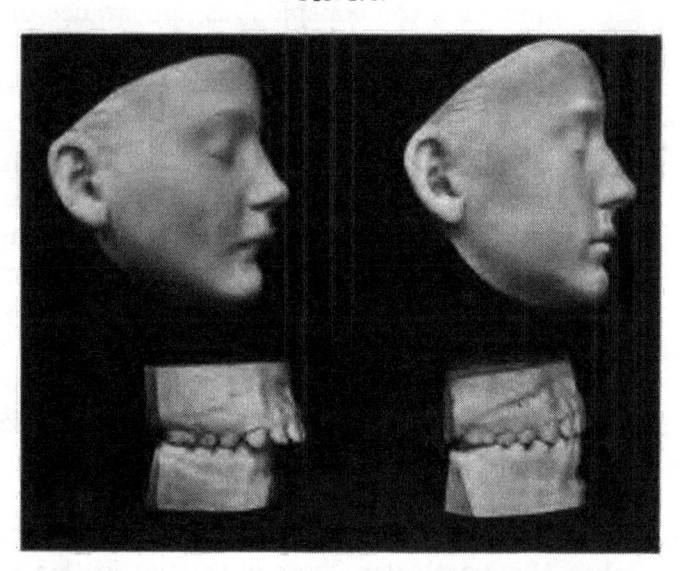

When the dentures have been shifted to a normal occlusion in this way with the intermaxillary force, notwithstanding the so-called "locking force" of normal occlusion, they are usually very difficult if not impossible to retain. First, because this character of malocclusion no doubt arises from a strongly marked hereditary type, or the admixture of inharmonious types, and second, because retention can

CHAPTER XXXI. TYPE A. DIVISION 1. CLASS II.

only be accomplished by the employment of the same intermaxillary forces that were employed in correction. The difficulty of moderating this force to the exact degree required for retention, and the need of having the patient attend to the adjustments presents difficulties that at times are insurmountable.

This is true, moreover, in this method of correcting all disto-mesial malocclusions of the buccal teeth which arise from heredity. If the buccal teeth, through the strong forces of heredity, have assumed that position in relation to the bones in which they are placed—whether or not the bones themselves partake of the malrelation—permanent retention of any extensive movement which is not bodily and interstitially accomplished, is very liable to result in failure.

FIG. 174.

These principles are particularly true of the attempts which are, and have been made, to correct **upper protrusions** in this way; and it no doubt is largely due to this that so many orthodontists have discontinued this method of practice, and adopted the more rational principles of extraction in these cases.

In Division 1, however, if the forward movement of the lower denture can be fully accomplished before the eruption of the second molars, there will be a far greater chance for permanency of retention. The lower denture being quite decidedly retruded in relation to the mandible, it is reasonable to suppose that many instances arise in which the second and third molars do not have room to freely erupt. Therefore, if the first molars and other teeth are moved mesially and bodily in time for the natural development and eruption of the second molars to the required mesial position, the chances of permanency of retention are **very greatly** increased.

After twelve years of age, and at times before, the opening of interproximate spaces for the insertion of artificial lower premolars has become the common treatment in the author's practice for the correction of nearly all Type A cases in this Division of malocclusions, and it is believed that it will prove far more satisfactory than the extensive disto-mesial shifting of the dentures to a normal occlusion. Nor is this an experimental theory, as the same principle has been thoroughly tried out and its value tested in the correction and retention of another character of malocclusion, i. e.—For many years one of the most indispensable methods in the author's practice in the correction of inherited upper retrusions in Class III malocclusions, has been the opening of interproximate spaces for the insertion of buccal teeth. By no other method would it have been possible to retain the teeth, as many of these have been retained for years with no apparent tendency to return to their former malpositions. One of these cases, which was first presented before the First District Dental Society of New York City in 1907, is illustrated in Fig. 229, Chapter XLV.

There is another thing which has appealed to many orthodontists of late in the correction of pronounced Type A malocclusions. It is the demand, from an artistic standpoint, of the bodily labial movement of the lower front teeth to produce a more perfect contour to the retruded labio-mental area.

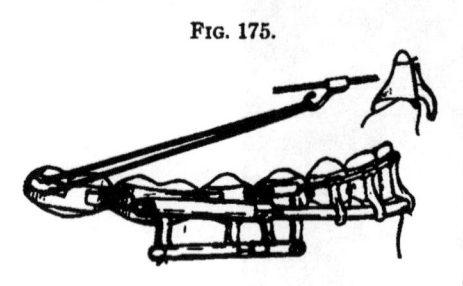

FIG. 175.

The apparatus that is commonly employed for the bodily labial movement of the lower front teeth and for opening interproximate spaces between the premolars, is shown in Fig. 175. The anchorages in this case are on the first and second molars and second premolars. In most instances they are on the second premolars and first molars, and in complications of close-bite malocclusions, they are on the single first molar crowns which are employed to open the bite. In nearly all recent cases, moreover, the anchorage power tube is soldered to rootwise extensions.

In cases of full malinterdigitation, the forces of mastication at twelve years of age and later, will have established an occlusion that is sufficiently needful for all physiologic demands, or one at least which may be easily adjusted with slight disto-mesial and bucco-lingual movements. If in these cases there is a moderate protrusion of the upper denture and a moderate retrusion of the lower in relation to the mandible, the correct treatment of course, would be to shift the dentures to a normal occlusion. But in those very common cases in which the dento-facial malrelation is due wholly or nearly to a retruded position of the lower denture, the method of correction which gives the most lasting satisfaction in the author's practice, consists in a bodily labial movement of the lower incisors with the regular contouring apparatus, with the fulcrum arch-bow anchored to the first lower premolars instead of the molars. This arrangement of the fulcrum force serves two purposes, i. e., it steadies the forward movement of the incisors, keeping them in an upright position, thus aiding the power arch-bow in moving them bodily forward. At the same time, the reaction of the fulcrum force produces a mesial movement of the cuspids and first premolars, opening spaces between the premolars for artificial retaining teeth. If the reaction of the power force upon the stationary anchorages is found to change the original interdigitating occlusion of the buccal teeth, they should be supported with the intermaxillary force. And when greater stability is demanded—as frequently occurs—the tubes should be soldered to root-wise extensions, as shown by numerous illustrations. This method results in an artistic correction of the facial outlines, and insures permanency of retention without materially changing the inherited occlusion of the buccal teeth. See Fig. 210, Chapter XLII.

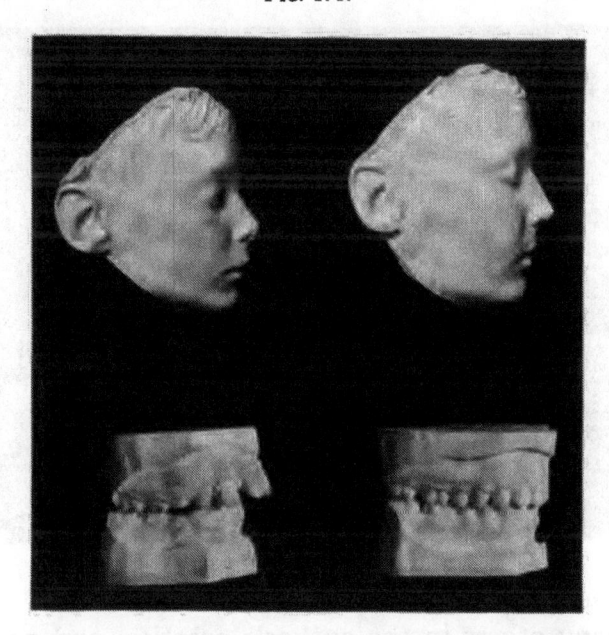

FIG. 176.

Two cases of twin brothers, commenced at twelve years of age, are shown in Figs. 176 and 177. These cases were practically alike, even to the various malalignments of the front teeth; therefore, they presented a most favorable opportunity to test the comparative value of the two methods of correction. That shown in Fig. 176 was corrected by shifting the dentures to a normal occlusion with the intermaxillary force, being careful to produce a much greater mesial movement of the lower than a distal movement of the upper. That shown in Fig. 177, was corrected, as shown, by a bodily labial movement of the six lower front teeth, the first premolars being carried forward by the force of the fulcrum arch-bow of the apparatus, and through the advantage of root-wise attachments on the premolars. When this movement has been properly retained with the working-retainer on the lower, and the spaces are finally locked with the extra premolars, as shown, there can be no doubt of permanency of retention. Whereas, in the other case, like many others corrected in the same manner, *permanency of retention cannot be assured.*

It is not usually a difficult operation to shift disto-mesial malocclusions of Class II to a normal occlusion with the intermaxillary force for youthful patients, providing there are no pronounced complications, and particularly in those cases where an evenly disposed reciprocal force may be employed, as often arises in malocclusions of Type A, Division 1. Nor is it beyond the reach of most orthodontists to obtain beautiful results at the close of operations in this Type by this method, even where considerable complications arise, as may be seen in the illustrations here and elsewhere presented in this work, many of which were complicated with close-bite malocclusions. But that is not the whole question which should be

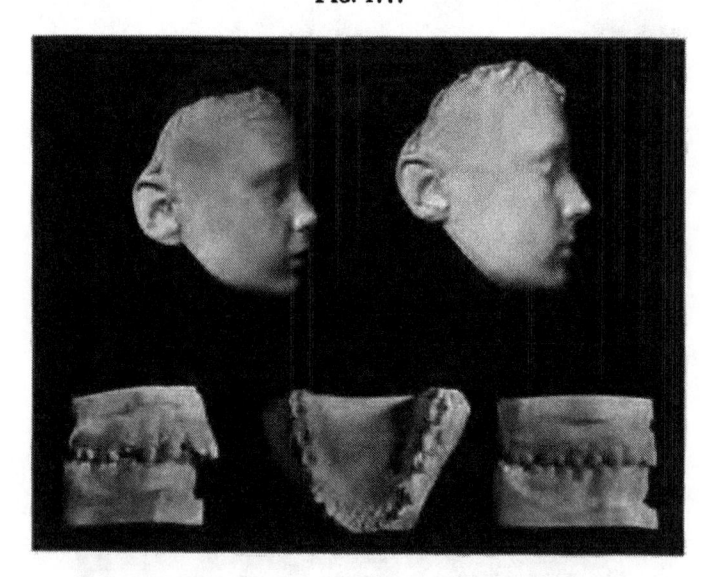

FIG. 177.

considered in the advance practice of orthodontia of today. A number of these same cases and many others in the author's practice, and no doubt hundreds in the practice of other orthodontists, have not retained the perfect positions shown by the finished results, even after being artificially retained for two years or more with the most approved retaining appliances. Why? Because the entire upper and the entire lower dentures have been moved backward and forward of their inherited positions in the jaws, and particularly because there are no stationary means of anchorage by which they can be reliably held in the corrected position until nature can establish their permanency of retention. When the forces of retention are confined to the denture in which the movement has been produced, the degree, direction, and continued stability of these forces can be assured; and this is quite different from being obliged to depend upon the shifting forces of intermaxillary elastics in the employment of which no continuous stability of position can be relied upon.

CHAPTER XXXII

Type B, Division 1, Class II

MODERATE RETRUSION OF THE LOWER DENTURE, AND PARTIAL PROTRUSION OF THE UPPER

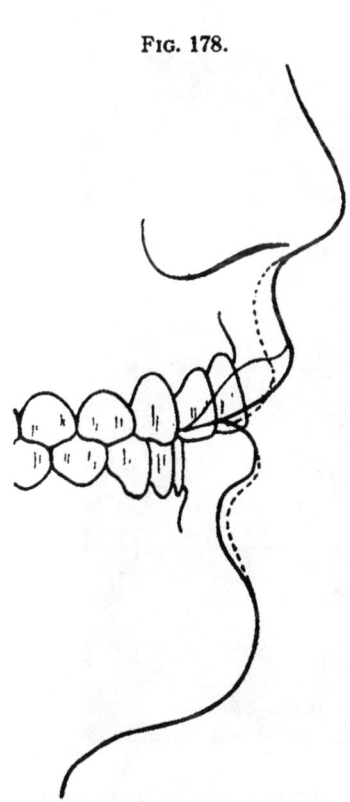

Fig. 178.

In following the rules of diagnosis and treatment in Class II malocclusions, if the chin is found to be in normal pose in relation to the principal features of the physiognomy, and the lower teeth are but slightly retruded, with a concomitant deepening of the **labiomental** depression, and consequently with a more or less pronounced protrusion of the upper teeth and lip, as shown in Fig. 179, it will usually be advisable to extract the first or second upper premolars, with the expectation that the forces required to retrude the upper labial teeth to a position of dento-facial harmony will so react upon the **upper buccal teeth** and all the **lower denture** as to move them slightly forward to the desired degree, and completely close the premolar spaces, and preserve the original disto-mesial interdigitating occlusion of all the buccal teeth.

It will be seen that this Type differs from the ordinary upper protrusion of Division 2, Type A, in the one particular that the lower teeth are retruded. This can only be recognized by a careful study of the facial outlines.

The apparatus indicated for the upper in a purely Type B character, is the same as that illustrated and described in Division 2, and chosen according to the particular Type of the upper protrusion, always being careful to arrange for the application of the several forces, as has been fully described—the appliances always being constructed to retard or accelerate the forward movement of the denture in proportion to its degree of needs. The complete apparatus which the author has found most commonly applicable in these cases is similar to Fig. 185, Chapter XXXIV.

Intermaxillary Force

The intermaxillary force is especially applicable in all reciprocating disto-mesial movements of the buccal teeth. In its application, great care should be exercised to prevent the **extrusion** of the molars—unless this movement be particularly demanded, as in close-bite malocclusions.

256   PART VI. DENTO-FACIAL MALOCCLUSIONS

When the second molars have fully erupted, they should always carry the hooks for the intermaxillary elastics instead of the first molars, unless an extensive movement of the buccal teeth is demanded. The important purpose of placing the attachments for the elastics at the most distal points in the mouth is to keep the force in a horizontal or mesio-distal direction as much as possible. If it is necessary to prevent the extruding tendency of the intermaxillary force, the molar attachments should be anchored down, so to speak, and in such a way so they will not

FIG. 179.

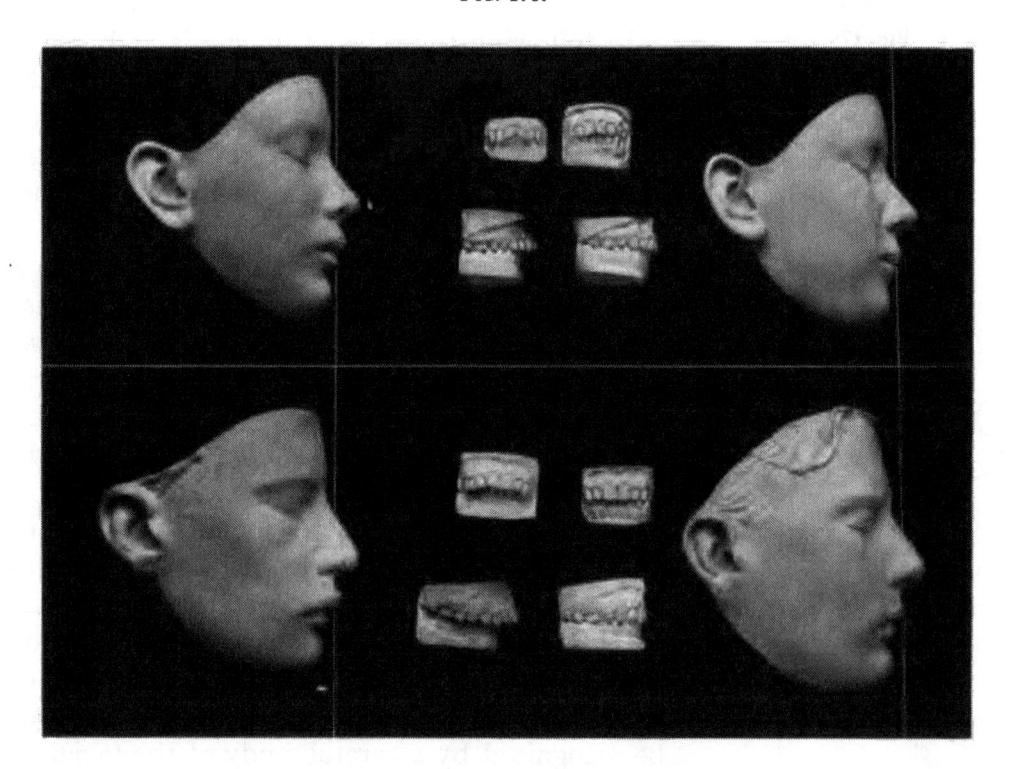

materially interfere with the mesial movement in view. This is accomplished by passing the lower arch-bow under premolar buccal hooks.

If the mesial movement of the lower buccal teeth demanded for normal occlusion is not more than one-half the width of a cusp, it usually may be accomplished for youthful patients with the ultimate preservation of occlusal contact of the molar planes. That is, the inclination which the extent of the movement at first gives to the molars, will ultimately right itself if properly retained.

In the chapter upon **Principles and Technics of Retention** will be found described methods for continuing the application of the intermaxillary force long after the main work of correction is accomplished. This appliance is frequently placed even before the normal relation of the buccal occlusion is attained.

Cases occasionally arise in crowded premolar malalignments for which it seems desirable to utilize all of the intermaxillary force toward a labial movement of the upper or the lower front teeth, with little or no reciprocating movement of the molars. Besides the act of uniting the teeth of one denture so as to retard or prevent a disto-mesial movement, the movement of the other denture from the same force may be increased through the mechanical advantage of applying the force to a few teeth at a time, as mentioned elsewhere.

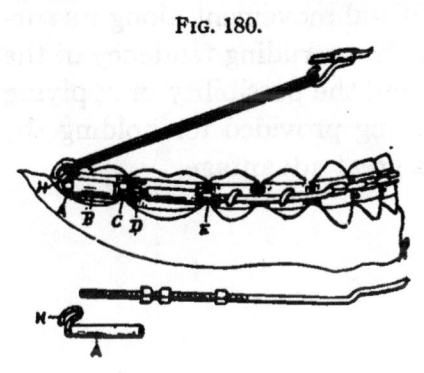

FIG. 180.

In Fig. 180 the **dental arch-bow** (No. 18, or 19, extra hard) engages with the labial teeth by means of the **open-tube attachments,** and passes under the **buccal hooks** of the premolars, and then through No. 18 tubes on the first molars; the threaded ends finally resting in telescope or **sliding tubes A,** within the **anchor tubes B** on the second molars. These tubes have thin walls (No. 32). To one end of tube A (shown disassembled), which is about one-tenth of an inch longer than the attachment tube B, is soldered a hook H, as shown, for the attachment of the elastics. The ends of the bow are threaded to carry nuts C, D, and E, placed as shown. When the apparatus is in position, the nuts C and D are turned back against the sliding tube A, forcing it back until the hook H stands free from the distal end of the anchorage tube B, so that no forward pull is exerted upon the molars when the intermaxillary elastics are attached. The force being directed wholly upon the arch-bow through the medium of the tube A, which engages directly with the nut C, the labial teeth alone to which the bow is attached are forced forward; the hooks H are prevented from coming in contact with the tubes B by means of the nuts C, which are turned back from time to time as the movement progresses.

When the labial teeth have been sufficiently protruded, the premolars are brought forward with either rubber bands, wire, or silk ligatures attached to their buccal hooks and extended from one side to the other around in front of the labial teeth. During this movement, it is well to keep the nuts C and E pressing against the tubes in order to add the anchorage force to that of the intermaxillary. In fact, at any time, the two forces can be used in conjunction.

When the premolar position is corrected, the intermaxillary force is directed to the mesial movement of the first molars by turning the nut D forward against the distal end of the first molar tube, and the nut C, as before. Finally, the second molars are brought forward with the intermaxillary force by turning the nut C forward until the hook H attached to the sliding tube A engages with the distal end of the anchorage tube B.

From this lengthy description, many will doubtless think that this is quite a complicated operation. Yet the construction of the apparatus requires no more skill—if one be supplied with the proper material—than others that appear far more simple. When the apparatus is accurately fitted and in position, the fact that it contains in itself all the elements of complete and successful movements, the subsequent adjusting treatments are reduced to the minimum of time and difficulties.

The combination possesses many important qualities: the horizontal direction of the force, together with the rigid quality of the bow, held down by its engagements to all the buccal teeth, and yet permitting a distal movement along its surface, increases the stability of the anchorage against the extruding tendency of the intermaxillary force when the mouth is opened. Again, the possibility of applying all the force to a few teeth at a time, and means being provided for holding the positions gained, while others are forced forward, is a great advantage.

CHAPTER XXXIII

DIVISION 2, CLASS II

INTRODUCTION

In typical upper protrusions, as in lower retrusions. the upper buccal teeth are always in mesial malocclusion with the lowers, and commonly through the forces of mastication the cusps are in malinterdigitation, or fully the width of a cusp in front of a normal occlusion.

While it is true with this character of malocclusion that the lower teeth are frequently in a more or less retruded position, the present Division will be confined to the description and treatment of the several Types of upper protrusions with the lower normal, and determined solely by the rules of dento-facial diagnosis.

The author is fully aware of the close relationship which this Division bears to certain Types of Division 1, which deal with the same character of malocclusion of the teeth, but which relates mainly to lower retrusions. As the two Divisions, however, represent the extremes of mesio-distal malocclusion, and produce distinctively different facial outlines in character and treatment, they can hardly be considered as belonging to the same Division, notwithstanding the almost indistinguishable blending of intermediate stages.

DIAGNOSIS AND GENERAL RULES OF TREATMENT OF DIVISION 2.

In **Diagnosis,** it should not be forgotten that with upper protrusions the chin will appear to be retruded even when it is in esthetic relation to the unchangeable features of the physiognomy, because of the instinctive tendency to compare it with the immediate malrelation of the upper.

If the upper buccal teeth are in mesial malinterdigitation, as shown in Fig. 181, and the lower teeth, lower lip, and the chin are in esthetic facial relations, the character of the irregularity will be purely that of an upper protrusion. And even when the lower jaw is actually retruded (as in Concomitant Characters of Class II, described in Chapter XXXVIII), if the lower teeth and lip are not retruded *in their relations to the chin*, the act of forcing the lower teeth forward, to aid in the production of normal occlusion, cannot help but make the chin appear more retruded, tending to produce a receding chin effect, which is always to be avoided if possible. There is really no way to properly correct malocclusions of Division 2 in this Class other than by extracting upper teeth—preferably the first premolars. This statement pertains not only to the correction of the facial outlines, but also to that most important of all objectives—permanency of retention.

Like nearly all cases which possess this decided disto-mesial malocclusion, they arise through some form of heredity, and consequently they early establish their malinterdigitation of buccal cusps. In those cases which are truly diagnosed as upper protrusions, why disturb a buccal occlusion (except to make slight necessary adjustments laterally and disto-mesially) which answers all the purposes of mastication? Frequently, the only treatment required is a lingual inclination movement of the six front teeth, and the case is ready for the retainer.

By the other method, which premises that no teeth should be extracted, the case is supposed to be corrected by shifting both dentures disto-mesially to a normal occlusion with the intermaxillary force. Think of this for a moment. If the facial deformity is due solely to a protrusion of the upper denture, as it is likely to be,

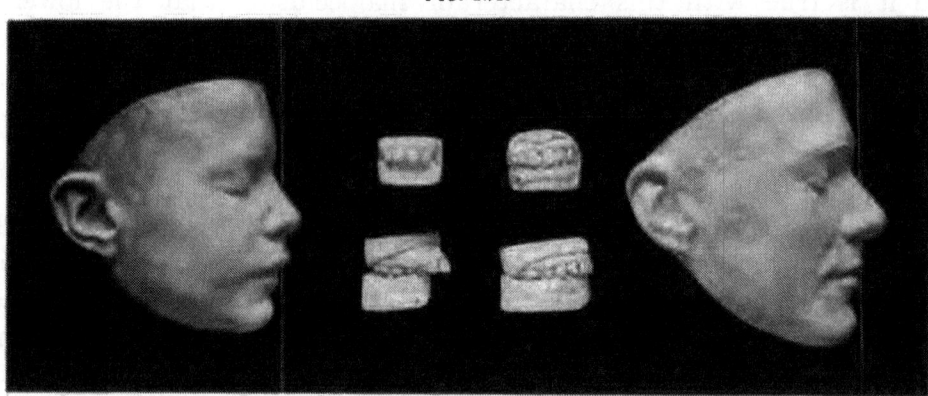

FIG. 181.

the perfect correction of the facial outlines can be accomplished only by a *proportionate retrusive movement of the entire upper denture*. Even if such an extensive movement were possible, as it may be for young children,—provided a sufficient stationary anchorage can be established to prevent the lower denture from moving forward—that position would not be retained, because the oncoming second and third molars would in all probability force the upper denture forward again to its true inherited malposition.

Such an extensive distal movement, however, is probably never accomplished or even expected in the usual operation of shifting the dentures to normal. What *is* accomplished, and what Dr. Angle advocated as his method, is "to move the lower mesially one-half the width of a cusp, and the upper distally the same distance, so that the cusps will occlude normally." Nor could this be accomplished without special stationary anchorages on the lower—of which there has never been a record in that system of practice—because the lower would otherwise move about twice as far forward as the upper would move backward, through a reciprocal action of the intermaxillary force. Right here is the point upon which the whole question of this method of treatment hinges.

CHAPTER XXXIII. DIVISION 2. INTRODUCTORY

With any forward movement of the lower denture, and especially with an extensive movement which that system of treatment portends, *with the lower lip and chin already in normal dento-facial relation, could it do otherwise than abnormally protrude the lower lip?* Therefore, when the dentures are brought to a normal occlusion in this method of treatment, the upper protrusion may be less than one-half corrected, while the lower is reciprocally protruded to an equal abnormal degree, with the result that instead of correcting the facial outlines, *a bimaxillary protrusion is produced* with probably a receding chin effect. This is what Dr. Cryer meant when he said he had seen a number of these cases with protruding mouths right from the hands of orthodontists who claimed they were fully corrected, and that statement—outside of the author's opinion—has been made by many others.

Moreover, the frantic efforts to reduce decided upper protrusions without extraction, have led many to expand upper arches to such an abnormal width that the buccal teeth were in unnatural and unpleasant evidence. It is true that many orthodontists proudly assert that *they* correct these cases dentally and dento-facially without extraction, but if these cases to which they referred had been correctly diagnosed at the start from an artistic standpoint, they would have been classified as lower retrusions of Division 1, Type A or B.

These principles here enumerated are true at any age for all inherited pronounced upper protrusions. And as mentioned elsewhere, they have reference also to the early disto-mesial adjustment of the first permanent molars to normal occlusion—a practice that has been heretofore extensively advocated for all disto-mesial malocclusions of the first molars of children, regardless of inherited types.

CHAPTER XXXIV

Type A, Division 2, Class II

UPPER CORONAL PROTRUSION

A common form of upper protrusion is that which is characterized by a protrusion of the crowns of the labial teeth, with the apical zone normal, or nearly so. This is well illustrated in Fig. 182. By an examination of cases of this Type at the beginning of the operation, it will be seen, first, that the upper buccal teeth are in decided mesial malocclusion, and that the lower lip in relation to the chin is not retruded abnormally, which excludes the case from Division 1 of this Class, and which means that all of the antero-posterior movements of the front teeth for the correction of the labial malposition must be performed on the upper teeth. Second, it will be seen also, that the upper part of the upper lip, or apical zone, is not abnormally protruded. In fact there will often appear to be a deepening of the naso-labial lines at the wings of the nose, as in retrusions of the apical zone due to inhibited development. While the diagnosis of this type is commonly confirmed by an abnormal labial inclination of the front teeth, this must not be taken as a sure indication of coronal protrusion or apical retrusion, because even bodily protrusions—in which the front teeth are supposed to stand in a normally upright position—will at times have decided labial inclinations of the incisors, showing that surface contours of the face do not necessarily follow the exact lines of the framework, but are largely regulated by the immediate thickness of the overlying soft tissues.

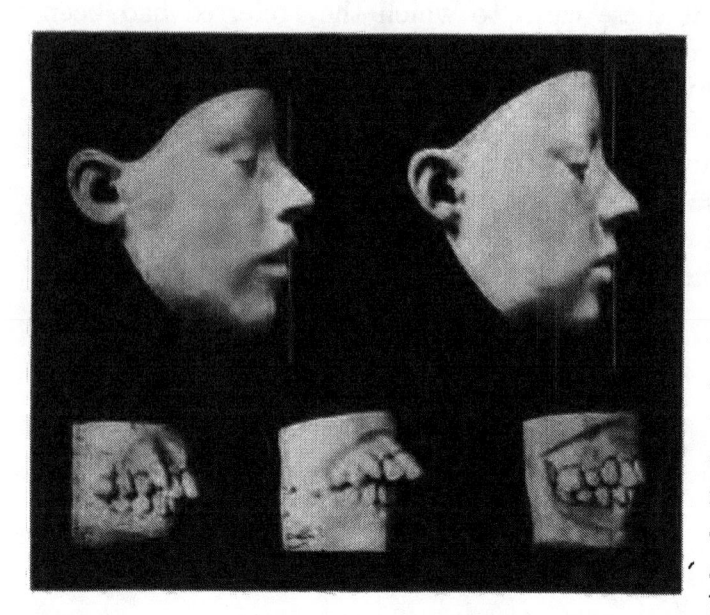

FIG. 182.

If the crowns of the upper front teeth are protruded to the extent of a full width of a premolar, the first premolars should be extracted, unless the second premolars are extensively decayed. Care should be exercised in the construction of the anchorages and the application of forces, so as not to move the back teeth forward and thus use up a part of the space.

CHAPTER XXXIV. TYPE A. DIVISION 2. CLASS II

The dento-facial correction of the disto-mesial malinterdigitation of the back teeth in this Type, which will often be found in perfect masticating occlusion, should appeal to the common sense of all orthodontists, as opposed to a reciprocal movement of all the teeth to a normal occlusion, to say nothing about the correction of facial outlines and the greater possibilities of permanency of retention.

FIG. 183.

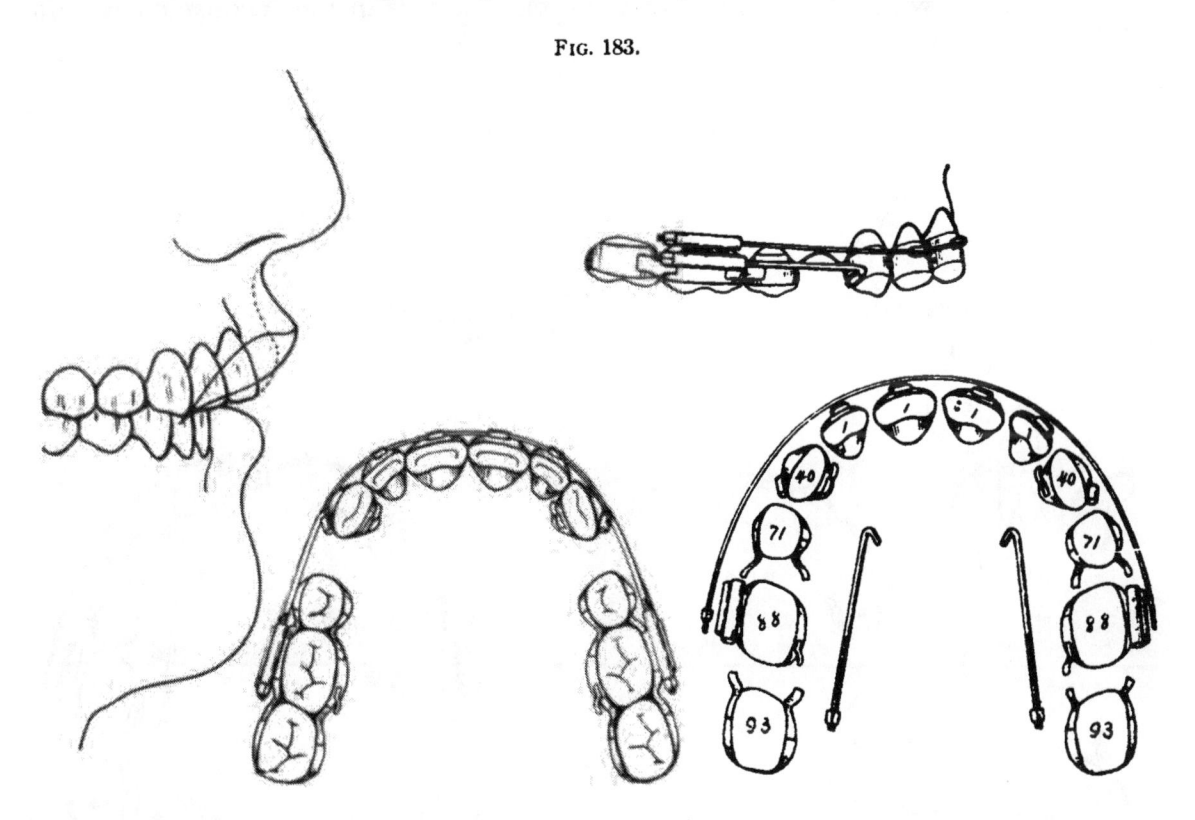

Full Upper Coronal Protrusion.—In Fig. 183, the three-band stationary anchorages carry two buccal tubes. The lower tubes are for No. 19 traction bars for retruding the cuspids, and as shown in the drawing, they are soldered at the gingival border of the bands, but preference is given to the root-wise extensions previously described. The upper tube is for a No. 22 arch traction bow for retruding the incisors. The root-wise position of both tubes aids in the stability of the anchorage. The upper anchorage tube attached to the modern root-wise attachments is commonly the one chosen to move the cuspids, as shown in Fig. 184. See Stationary Anchorages, Chapter XV.

FIG. 184.

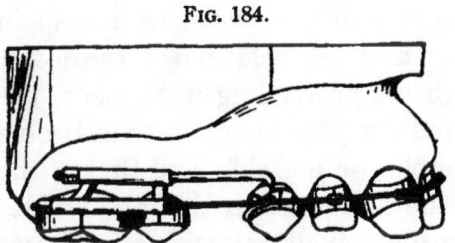

An important feature of the apparatus that should never be omitted, is the lingual hooks for the attachment of elastics to prevent the rotation of the cuspids and aid in their retrusive movement. The open-tube attachments on the incisor bands are of very thin material (20-30), and when these are properly locked around the small wire arch-bow (No. 22), with all sharp edges removed and finished, they present no unpleasant and irritating prominence to the lips. The labial surfaces of the incisor bands should be considerably narrowed, and if they are of nickel silver, they should be covered with 18k gold solder, and this with the small size of the arch-bow aids in the inconspicuousness of the apparatus.

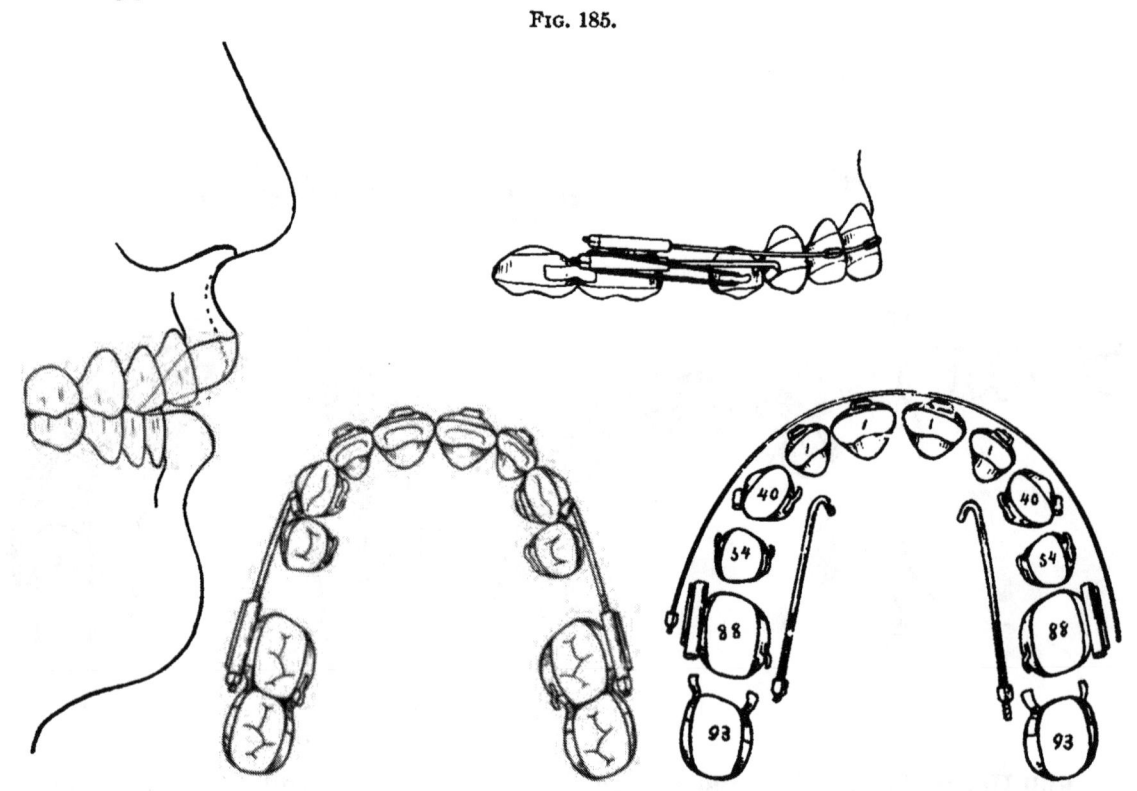

FIG. 185.

When any doubt arises in regard to the stability of the anchorages, the occipital and intermaxillary forces should be employed. In nearly all cases of this Type, the occipital force with post-rest bow A is indicated.

Moderate Upper Coronal Protrusion.—When the upper buccal teeth are in moderate mesial malrelation, or not more than one-half the width of a cusp in front of a normal occlusion, occluding "end on," and the relation of the lower lip to the chin is one that will not bear the slightest protruding movement, the extraction of the second premolars is often indicated for patients older than twelve years. Frequently, the extraction of the first premolar on one side, and that of the second upon the other, is demanded, because of the difference in the mesio-distal occlusion of the buccal teeth. When the malocclusion is bilateral, with a moderate upper protrusion, *be careful that it is not partially a lower retrusion, or sufficiently so as to warrant correction with the intermaxillary force without extraction.*

CHAPTER XXXIV. TYPE A. DIVISION 2. CLASS II.

Fig. 185 is designed for a moderate upper protrusion where the second premolars have been extracted, and is so similar in its construction and application of force to the apparatus shown in Fig. 183, it will be unnecessary to further describe it here.

In moderate upper protrusions with partial mesio-distal malrelations of the buccal teeth of children, for whom there is no positive evidence in the family of inherited upper protrusion, and there are reasons for believing that the malocclusion has arisen from a local cause, extraction should never be considered, but the correction should be accompanied by a distal movement of the upper molars to a normal occlusion, to be followed or accompanied with a retrusive movement of the upper front teeth, wholly through the employment of the intermaxillary and occipital forces.

CHAPTER XXXV

TYPE B, DIVISION 2, CLASS II

UPPER BODILY PROTRUSION

In all upper bodily protrusions the entire maxilla with its upper denture is protruded or prognathic in its relation to the other bones of the physiognomy. This shows conclusively that it is caused from some form of heredity.

In **diagnosis,** the protrusion of the upper apical dento-facial zone is not always at first recognized, nor can this be determined by the inclination of the front teeth, though in upper bodily protrusions the front teeth are more likely to be less labially inclined than in pronounced coronal protrusions of Type A. In nearly all typical bodily protrusions of Type B, however, there will be a general protrusion of the upper lip with a complete obliteration of the naso-labial lines. The lower lip and chin will commonly be in normal pose, the whole producing an expression that is quite as characteristic of this malocclusion as the peculiar facial expressions of all pronounced protrusions and retrusions are characteristic of the Types and Classes to which they belong.

For patients of this Type, as it is not always possible to determine at the beginning of the operation how much may be accomplished by applying the force at the gingival margins of the teeth, the regular Contour Apparatus is not placed at first unless a decided protrusion of the roots is evident.

Fig. 186 represents one of the most common and effective methods in the author's practice for retruding the labial teeth after the extraction of the first premolars.

Its construction admits of the application, separately or in combination, of three characters of retruding force, i. e., Stationary Dental Anchorage, Occipital, and Intermaxillary. The arch-bow No. 19, if employed with the hexagonal lug-nuts at the mesial ends of the cuspid open-tube attachments, as shown in the disassembled apparatus, may be made to exert all of the force from the molar anchorages upon the cuspids alone, or it can be equally distributed to all of the labial teeth according to the degree to which the cuspid nuts are turned in proportion to that of the anchorage nuts.

The force is applied to the incisors at the gingival borders by means of extensions soldered to the labial surfaces of the bands so that the arch-bow will span the interproximate gingivæ. If it is desired to increase the force upon the incisors, or to relieve the anchorage force, and especially if an intruding force is demanded, the **occipital force** may be employed as an auxiliary with the post-rest bow A (See Fig. 78, Chapter XVI), the distal nut being turned only to take up the slack of the

CHAPTER XXXV. TYPE B. DIVISION 2. CLASS II. 267

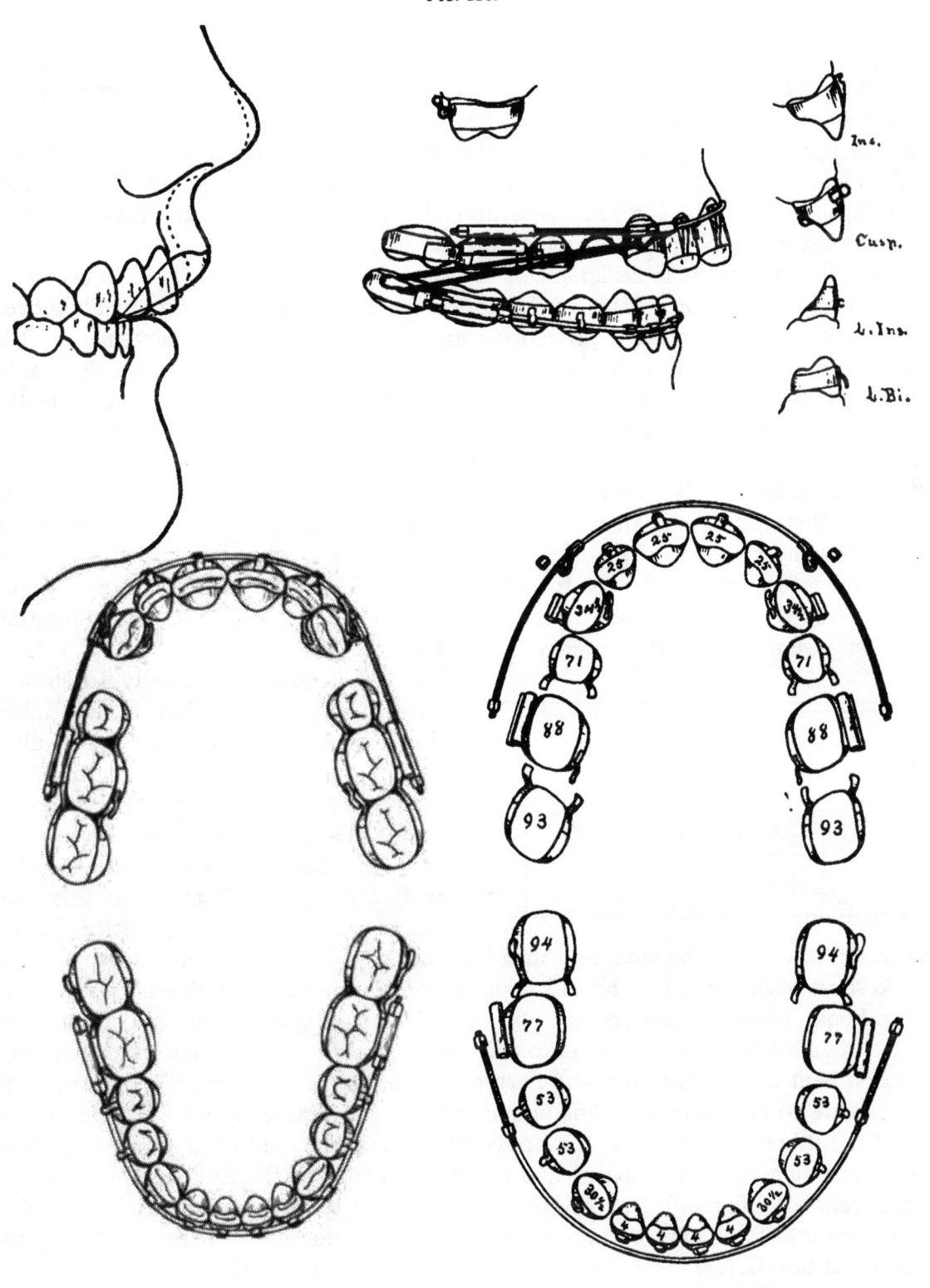

FIG. 186.

arch-bow. The **intermaxillary force,** with sliding hooks engaging directly with the retruding arch-bow through the medium of the nuts, is invaluable as an aid in retruding the labial teeth.

Without the cuspid nuts, the cuspids may be retruded with the intermaxillary force as shown, and supplemented, if desired, with the occipital force. The lingual hooks upon the cuspids are for elastics to the lingual molar hooks, which will often be found useful to control or increase the action. It will be seen that with an intelligent turning of the four nuts upon the arch-bow, the intermaxillary force can be directed only upon the molars, the cuspids, or the incisors.

As the apparatus is designed for Division 2 cases, in which the malocclusion is entirely due to a protrusion of the upper, the lower teeth are quite firmly locked together for the purpose of preventing any mesial or extruding movement. The lower molars carry the regular two-band stationary anchorages, which can be extended to the premolars, if desired, and supplemented with root-wise attachments. The distal intermaxillary hooks on the molar anchorages are wide, buccally convex, and are attached to the disto-occlusal points. The premolars and labial teeth are firmly attached to a No. 19 or 20 arch-bow by means of hooks and open-tube attachments; the arch-bow is then firmly locked to the molar anchorages with mesial and distal nuts.

The intermaxillary hooks for the attachment of the elastics to the upper are soldered to short open tubes, which slide back along the retruding bow and engage with the attachments on the cuspids.

FIG. 187.

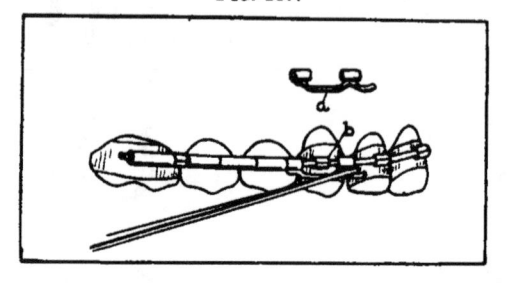

Fig. 187 is presented purely to show a variation in the application of the intermaxillary force and is not intended to illustrate a practical apparatus for this Type of malocclusion. It is frequently desirable to exert a distal intermaxillary force upon the buccal teeth or upon a single molar, without exerting any distal force upon the cuspids or any of the front teeth. This is accomplished with **the span intermaxillary hook,** which is easily made by soldering two short open tubes to a No. 19 wire, the projecting end of which is bent to form the hook, while the central portion "a" is bent to span the cuspid attachment "b" when the tubes are clasped around the arch-bow. In the construction, the wire is first bent the desired form and flattened with a file at the points where the open tubes are to be soldered. This is one of the most practical and effective devices in the author's practice for the application of the intermaxillary force. Instead of the sliding tubes, the span bar may be lengthened to the desired distal point of engagement. Through the medium of the sliding tubes upon the arch-bow, also, the occipital force may be applied directly to the buccal teeth by employing the **occipital bow C.**

CHAPTER XXXV. TYPE B. DIVISION 2. CLASS II.

In all cases of Type B of this Division of Class II, where the facial outlines positively indicate a protrusion of the apical zone of the front teeth, the **regular bodily retruding apparatus** is demanded. This is illustrated in Fig. 193, Chapter XXXVII, where will be found the technic description of the most modern method of construction. A bodily retrusive movement of the front teeth usually requires more force and greater time than a bodily protrusive movement, because it is accomplished wholly by resorption of the walls of the alveoli, acted upon by the force.

FIG. 188.

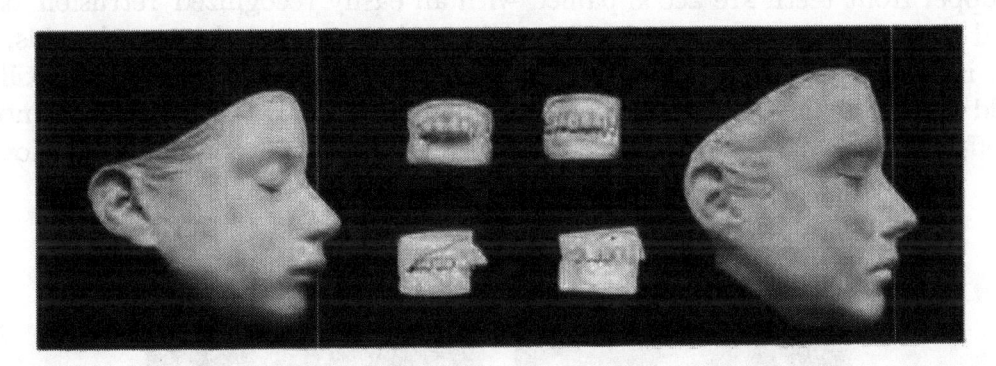

Fig. 188 was made from the plaster casts of a girl thirteen years of age. The beginning facial cast is distinctively characteristic of an upper bodily protrusion; but on account of the decided labial inclination of the front teeth, it was hoped that the retruding force applied at the gingival margin would properly retrude the teeth and correct the facial outlines. It was found, however, after a partial movement by this method, that the protruded apical zone was brought into stronger evidence than at first, and this demanded a bodily retrusive movement, which was accomplished, as shown on the right, with an apparatus similar to that shown in Fig. 193, Chapter XXXVII. The three stages of this very interesting case are fully described and illustrated in Chapter XXI.

CHAPTER XXXVI

Type C, Division 2, Class II

UPPER CORONAL PROTRUSION WITH APICAL RETRUSION

From causes not always possible to discover, protrusions of the crowns of the upper front teeth are accompanied with an easily recognized retrusion of the apical zone. As diseases of the naso-maxillary sinuses, caused from adenoids, may arise in every physical character, inhibiting the development of the maxilla, it would seem that this somewhat rare type illustrated in Fig. 189, is a fair sample of the effect of this local cause upon a case of inherited upper coronal protrusion.

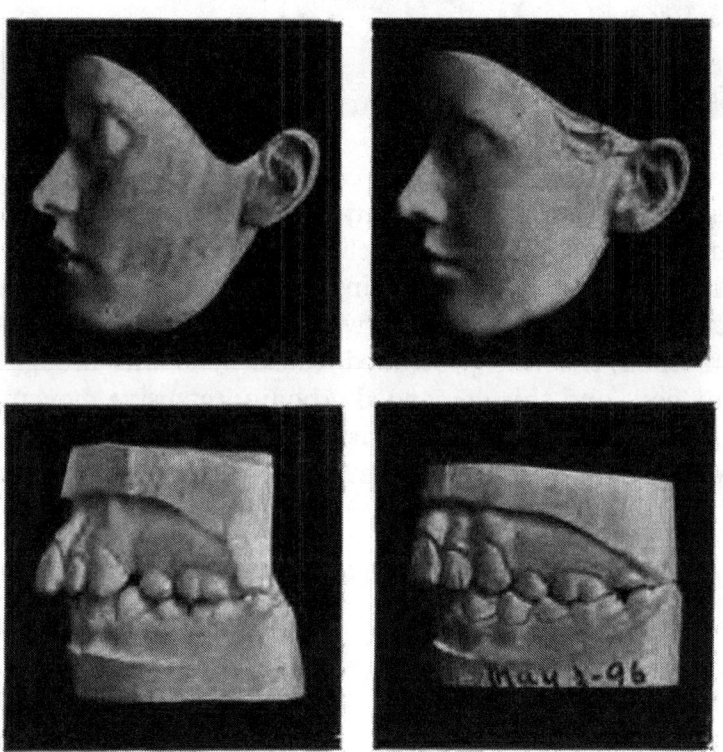

FIG. 189.

The labial inclination of the upper front teeth, with retruded incisive fossæ, will tend to protrude the coronal zone and retrude the apical zone, thus deepening the naso-labial depressions, and often retruding the entire lower portion of the nose in relation to esthetic facial outlines. Of course there is every degree of dentofacial disharmony with the labial teeth in this same inclination, from decided

CHAPTER XXXVI. TYPE C. DIVISION 2. CLASS II. 271

protrusions of the coronal zone with the apical normal, to decided retrusions of the apical zone with coronal normal.

It will be seen that the upper buccal teeth are in full mesial malinterdigitation. In other words, they bite fully the width of a cusp in front of a normal occlusion. When this case presented, the first premolars had been extracted, and an attempt had been made to correct the protrusion. Before this, it was said that the teeth were much more protruded with more decided labial inclination, and this must have enhanced the retruded effect at the upper part of the lip. This retruded

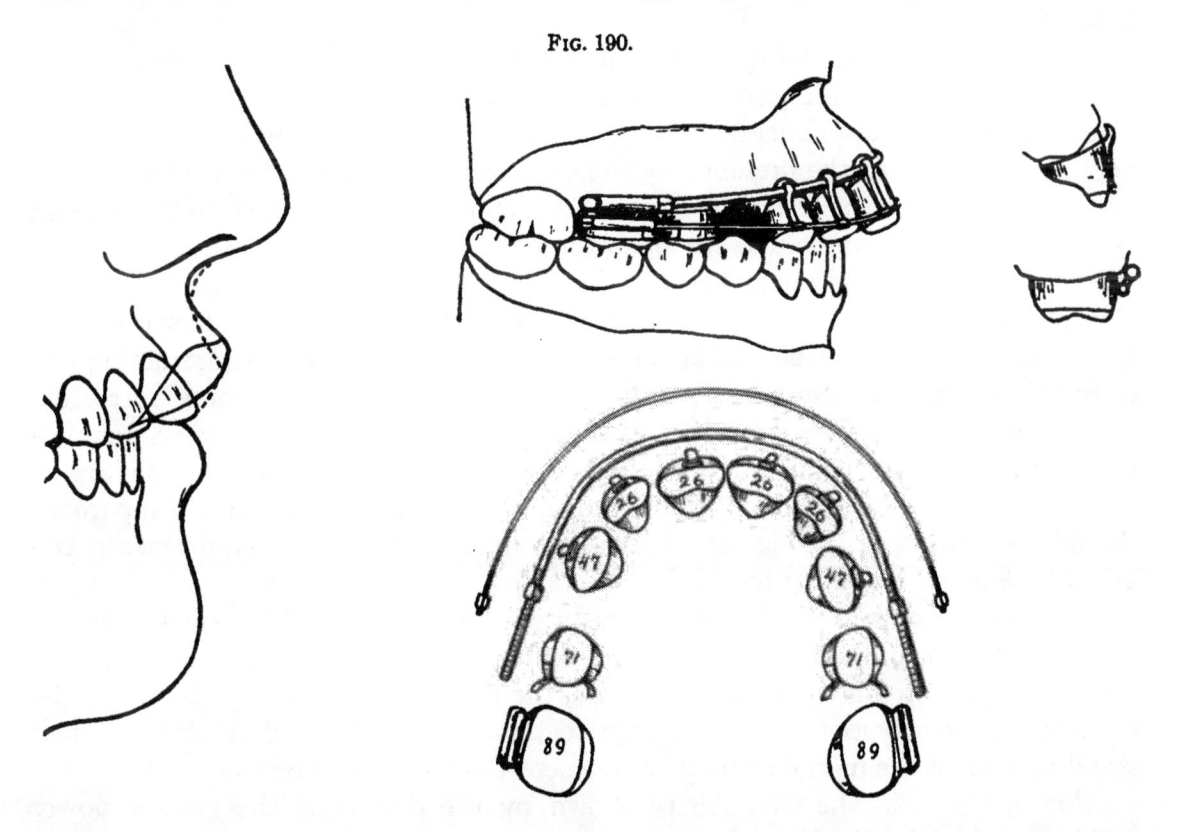

FIG. 190.

effect was quite apparent, as can be seen by the profile model on the left. Even the end of the nose, compared to the finished case, is seen to have been improved in its outlines in the labial movement of the roots and incisive process.

The deepening of the naso-labial lines at the points where they join the wings of the nose, which is apparently caused by the retruded framework supporting the lower end of the nose, is enhanced by the protrusion of the coronal zone, and this produces a peculiar facial expression that at once indicates the character of the dental malposition. It is an expression that is common in protrusions of the labial teeth which arise from thumb-sucking.

Fig. 190 represents one of the regular forms of contour apparatus used for the bodily labial movement of the upper front teeth, and is especially designed for all cases which demand a protrusive movement of the upper apical zone and a retrusive movement of the coronal zone. In fact, the two forces can always be so adjusted that the relative degree of either movement is completely under the control of the operator.

The mechanical principles which underlie the method of applying force for the movement of the roots of teeth are fully explained under "Bodily Movement," Chapter XIV. When this method was first published in 1893, the author named it the "Contour Apparatus" merely for convenience and because it was the first method ever invented that made it really possible to practically contour the dento-facial area.

This method of applying force will never be understood or appreciated by any one who is not willing, or is incapable of skillfully constructing, fitting, and placing the proper appliances for the correct application of this peculiar form of applied force. When the preliminary work is accomplished as it should be, there is no extensive apparatus that will give so little trouble or annoyance to the patient or operator, or one over which the operator has more perfect control of the movements of the teeth, and none that will give so much satisfaction in the final result. This applies particularly to the labial movements of the upper front teeth in Class III, where a full description will be found relative to the details of constructing and fitting the **protruding contour apparatus** for pronounced cases of upper retrusion.

This apparatus differs from that in Class III only in the degree of its possibilities of movement. In all cases where a maximum power is not demanded, as in extensive movements of the roots for the older class of patients, the entire apparatus should be reduced in the size and heft of its parts to meet the requirements and avoid bulkiness. See Chapter XX.

The reciprocal action of the two required forces will nullify each other at the anchorage in proportion to the weaker power, and this is true of all reciprocal forces acting upon a given point; therefore, the resultant should be noted as to the influence it exerts upon the anchorage teeth, and the need of reinforcing their stability against the mesial or distal movement that may be produced.

For instance, in the irregularity shown by the drawings, the greater power will be required for the lingual movement of the crowns; consequently, the excess will tend to move the anchorage teeth mesially. It will be noticed that the buccal teeth of the drawing demand this mesial movement about one-quarter the width of a premolar to correct their interdigitating occlusion; therefore, no more than a two-band stationary anchorage is indicated. But if the cusps of the upper buccal teeth were in full mesial interdigitation, a three-band stationary anchorage would be demanded if possible, and if not, the occipital or intermaxillary auxiliary would be indicated to prevent a mesial movement of the anchor teeth.

In cases where the apical zone of the front teeth is but slightly retruded, the force of a single retruding arch-bow, applied at the incisal zone, will usually be sufficient to tip the roots forward the required distance in the retrusive movement of the crowns, the gingivo-lingual borders of the alveolar process acting as a fulcrum.

In the apparatus shown in Fig. 190, the upper or **"power arch-bow"** No. 16, will act more as a fulcrum, and the lower, or **"fulcrum arch-bow"** No. 20 or 22, will be the moving power, though considerable force will be exerted upon the power arch-bow.

Fitting the Protruding Contour Apparatus

In the fitting and assembling of this apparatus, the power arch-bow, being very rigid, should be perfectly bent so as to lie evenly in its respective attachments without the slightest spring when in position. In the final placing of the apparatus shown in Fig. 190, first cement the anchorage upon one side, and place the end of the power arch-bow in the buccal tube. When the cement is placed in the bands of the other anchorage, slip its tube on to the free end of the arch-bow before carrying the anchorage to place upon the teeth. Then the labial bands are placed one at a time, the gingival hooks lapping on to the arch-bow. The placing of the fulcrum arch-bow needs no direction. In the more modern stationary anchorages for bodily movements, the power tube upon one anchorage is an open-tube, which greatly facilitates assembling and disassembling the power arch-bow, that at times is of the greatest importance.

In the progress of the operation, if it is found that the roots are being protruded more than they should be in proportion to the position of the crowns, the power bow nuts at the mesial ends of the anchorage tubes should be unscrewed, and this will allow the roots to move back. It will be seen with this combination, that the operator has full control over the individual movements of the roots and the crowns of the incisors.

CHAPTER XXXVII

Type D, Division 2, Class II
UPPER APICAL PROTRUSION

Irregularities of this Type are far more rare than their opposites, Type C, probably because they seem to be unassociated with any condition that may have resulted from a local cause. In their pronounced forms, they are characterized by a decided prominence or bulginess along the upper part of the upper lip and base of the nose, completely obliterating the naso-labial lines, while the lower part of the lip is not protruded. In all of these cases, the inherited protruded and en-

FIG. 191.

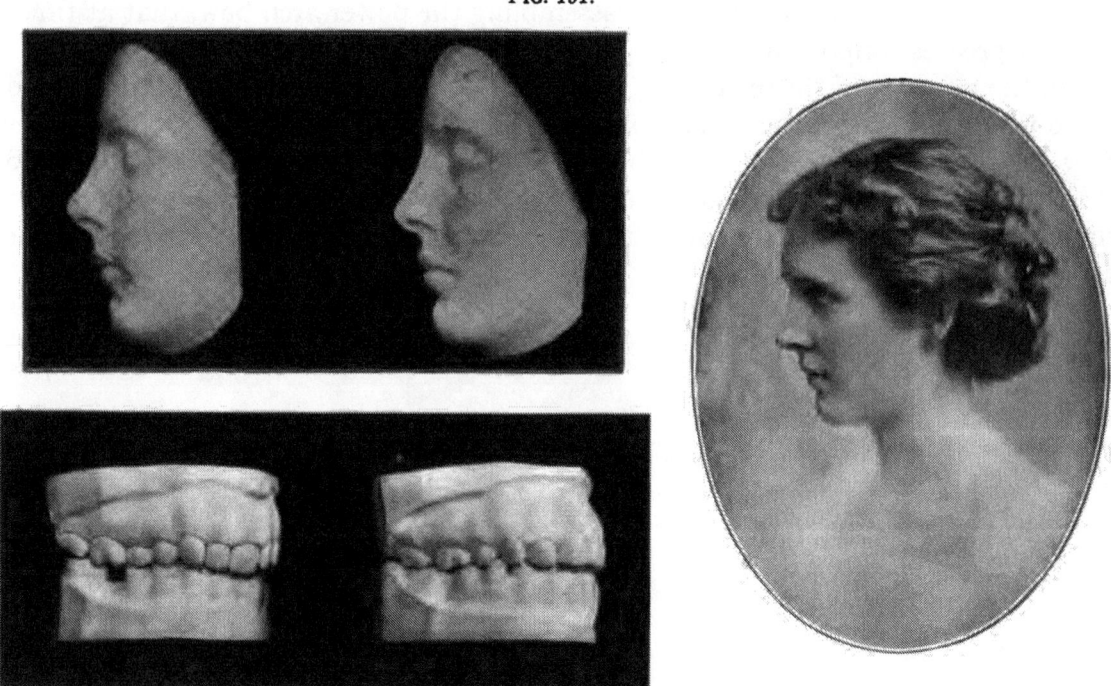

larged maxilla is often quite apparent. If the sizes of the upper teeth are out of proportion to the large maxilla, as Dr. Cryer has proven possible, they would undoubtedly assume a lingual inclination.

In these cases the lips close with difficulty, and rarely with repose, and when the patient is talking or laughing, they often rise to an unpleasant exposure of, not only the entire crowns, but also the gums above; this produces at times an exceedingly displeasing expression.

CHAPTER XXXVII. TYPE D. DIVISION 2. CLASS II. 275

The beginning facial and dental casts shown in Figs. 191 and 192 will serve to illustrate this Type. They were both eighteen years of age at the commencement of the operations. It will be seen that the apical zones were greatly protruded, as shown by the facial casts before treatment. The incisal edges of the centrals in these cases, as is common with this malposition, hugged the lower incisors near their gingival margins. As in all cases of this Type, the occipital force is an important auxiliary, particularly because of its intruding direction.

The photograph on the right of Fig. 191 was taken about ten years after the operation was completed. Note the perfect pose of the upper lip in the finished

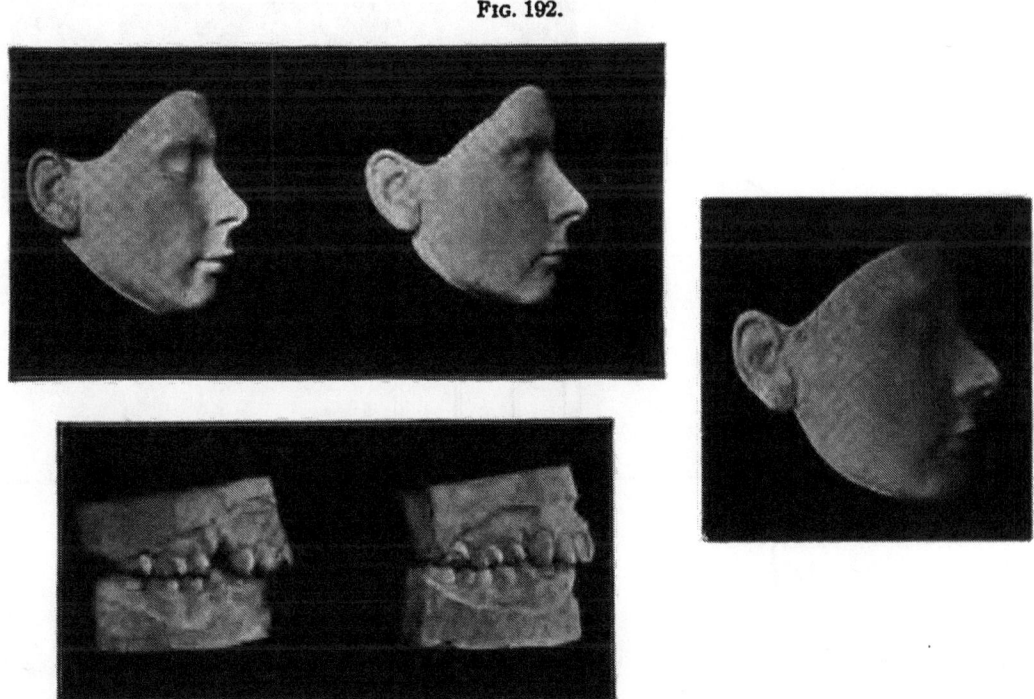

FIG. 192.

illustrations, with the decided protrusion of the upper apical zone and flare of the nostrils entirely removed. This was accomplished by the extraction of the first upper premolars, followed with a bodily lingual movement of the roots of the front teeth, and a slight labial movement of the occlusal zone of the incisors.

Fig. 193 illustrates the common **contour retruding apparatus**. In marked cases of Types B and D of this class the first premolars should be extracted, because every opportunity should be given for the retrusive movement of the roots and alveolar ridge.

The anchorages for all apparatus requiring considerable force are now of the two or three-band stationary type with power applied from root-wise attachments, the construction of which is fully described in Chapter XV. The power arch-bow is No. 16 extra hard nickel silver. The lower, or fulcrum arch-bow is No. 17.

276   PART VI. DENTO-FACIAL MALOCCLUSIONS

The latter, which now acts as a static fulcrum, necessarily exerts a push force, consequently it should be nearly or quite as rigid as the power arch-bow in order to prevent the retrusive force from tipping the crowns lingually. As the retrusive movement progresses, the nuts at the mesial ends of the fulcrum tubes should be turned according to the demands for keeping the front teeth in a normal inclination. For instance, in Type B of this Division, where a general retrusive movement of the front teeth is demanded, the fulcrum nuts are occasionally unscrewed to allow the crowns to move back with the roots. Again, if the protrusion pertains

FIG. 193.

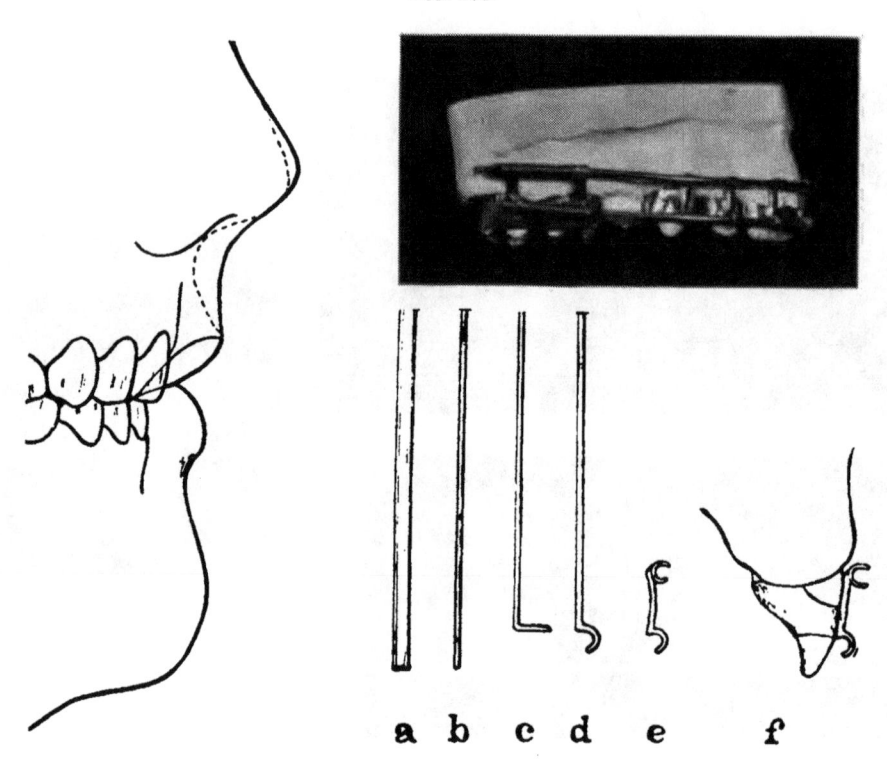

a   b   c   d   e   f

to the apical zone alone, with the crowns lingually inclined, as in the present Type, the fulcrum bow may need to act as a protrusive force to place the incisal ends in proper relation to the lower teeth, while at the same time, the power bow is retruding the roots. In all cases of bodily movements, the power nuts should be given two-quarter turns three times a week.

The labial bands are made of wide No. .0038″ banding material, and when soldered they are placed on the teeth to outline and trim the fronts to a width of about 1/10 of an inch. Upon removal of the bands, flow over their labial surfaces No. 16 gold solder to strengthen and give artistic effect, as fully described in Chapter XX in the construction of the "Midget Apparatus." All the bands are now fitted perfectly to the teeth in the exact position they will occupy in the finished apparatus. Note that the occlusal borders of the incisor bands are even with the

CHAPTER XXXVII. TYPE D. DIVISION 2. CLASS II.

upper border of the fulcrum bow, and that the lower border of this bow is about 1/10 of an inch above the cutting edges. This will indicate the position the occlusal borders of the bands should take upon the lateral incisors, which are usually shorter than the centrals. The occlusal and gingival borders of the central bands should be in line with the bands of the laterals. When the bands are properly fitted to the teeth, a plaster impression is taken; the bands are then carefully removed from the teeth and fitted into their respective positions in the impression, which is filled with strong investment plaster.

The root-wise attachments should be shaped so as to withstand the force, protect the gums, and still not be bulky. In the earlier construction of this apparatus, the power was applied above the gingival margins to obtain the greatest possible mechanical advantage. It has been found in recent years that this is rarely necessary with a proper management of the two forces. In the present apparatus, the power is applied just below the gingival borders directly upon the surface of the crowns and along a line that is even with the highest gingival points upon the lateral incisors. This method has the very great advantage of reducing bulkiness and prominence of the bow and attachments, and particularly the ease of construction.

The root-wise attachments for the front teeth are now made of **No. 16 hook wire.** This is about equal in weight to No. 17 (.045″) rolled to a ribbon thickness of .013″.

In Fig. 193 is shown at "a" and "b" a front and edge view of the hook wire, which after annealing is bent sharply at right angles "c" and curved to form the fulcrum bow attachment "d." This is thinned at the end to form a smooth finish where it partly laps around the bow. In determining the point at which the wire should be cut off for the power attachment, remember that the fulcrum attachments start from the occlusal borders of the bands, therefore, place it upon the model and measure to the gingival border of one of the lateral incisors. The root-wise pieces are cut the same length, and the gingival ends are grooved slightly for the power attachments. These are short sections of thin wall No. 16 open-tubing, which are soldered in place with No. 16 gold solder by holding them in the solder plier ("e"). The pieces are now ready to be fitted and soldered to the bands on the model ("f"). The gold solder that was previously flowed over the front of the bands is usually sufficient for this purpose. In this act, the attachment is held firmly in place with a steel poker dipped in plumbago; or the band may be removed from the model and the parts held in place in the solder plier.

For young patients with less pronounced bodily protrusions, the arch-bows, bands, and attachments may be considerably reduced in size. This is especially true if the appliances are made of platinum-gold.

In assembling the apparatus preparatory to cementing it, the arch-bows should be bent so that when in place they will lie evenly in their attachments without the spring of the material. One of the most important and convenient moves in the construction of all apparatus which require heavy arch-bows, is the employment of **open anchorage tubes** on the right or the left anchorage, fully described and illustrated in other chapters. This is particularly desirable with the present apparatus, as it is quite difficult to force the power and fulcrum bows into closed anchorage tubes after the bands are cemented on the teeth. With the open anchorage tubes, the arch-bows are easily assembled by first placing one end of the power bow in its closed tube and carrying the other end over and fitting it along into the front attachments, and finally into its open-tube on the other anchorage; the fulcrum bow is fitted in the same manner. Furthermore, it is frequently necessary to give final slight bends to the bows here and there so they will lie evenly without tension in the several attachments. This can be easily accomplished if the bows can be readily removed and replaced in the final necessary fitting.

This lengthy description with its necessary detail may lead many to imagine that the construction of this apparatus is fraught with unusual difficulty, whereas, it is no more difficult than other appliances after one gets into the run of the several requirements, and is skilled in the technic, as all orthodontists should be who hope to successfully accomplish the important operations in this specialty of dentistry.

CONCOMITANT CHARACTERS OF CLASS II

CHAPTER XXXVIII

RETRUSION OF THE MANDIBLE AND LOWER DENTURE

Fig. 194.

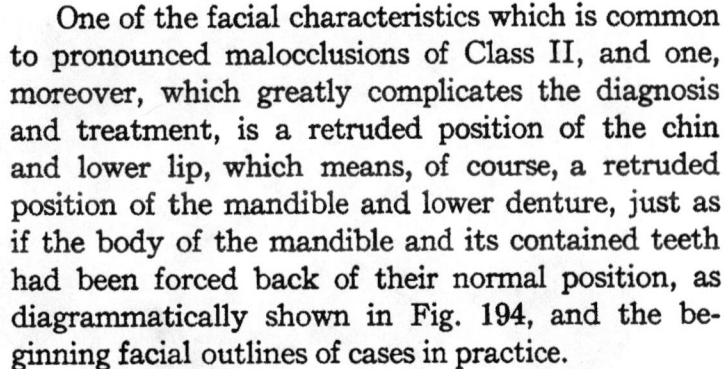

One of the facial characteristics which is common to pronounced malocclusions of Class II, and one, moreover, which greatly complicates the diagnosis and treatment, is a retruded position of the chin and lower lip, which means, of course, a retruded position of the mandible and lower denture, just as if the body of the mandible and its contained teeth had been forced back of their normal position, as diagrammatically shown in Fig. 194, and the beginning facial outlines of cases in practice.

Cases of this character differ quite decidedly in profile outlines and treatment from the other Types of Division 1, in which the lower teeth alone are retruded, while the chin and the body of the lower jaw are in normal relations—though in both characters the same occlusion of the teeth may be exactly alike. Moreover, retrusions of the mandible, in the author's practice, have been found quite as frequent in connection with upper protrusions; and consequently this Type may be considered as belonging properly to Divisions 1 and 2.

Inasmuch as the relative position of the chin varies in different individuals from decided prognathisms to decided retrusions, and as some form of this malrelation may obtain in connection with any other character of irregularity, we therefore find every gradation of this bodily retrusion of the lower jaw and teeth in connection with every gradation of protrusion of the upper teeth.

DIAGNOSIS AND GENERAL TREATMENT

In all cases of marked antero-posterior malrelations of the dentures, one should always strive to prevent being deceived by a facial effect. Where the mandible and contained teeth are decidedly retruded in their esthetic relations, the

280   *PART VI. DENTO-FACIAL MALOCCLUSIONS*

effect is usually that of an upper protrusion, even when the upper lip is nearly or quite in normal relation to the remaining features.

For the perfect correction of occlusion and facial outlines, cases of this Type really demand—if it were possible—the operation known as **"jumping the bite,"** which was introduced by Dr. Norman Kingsley in 1882. This consists in attaching an apparatus to the teeth, which is intended to force the mandible forward the desired distance, and to hold it there until nature has so changed the tempero-maxillary articulation as to render it impossible for the jaw to ever go back to its original position.

FIG. 195.

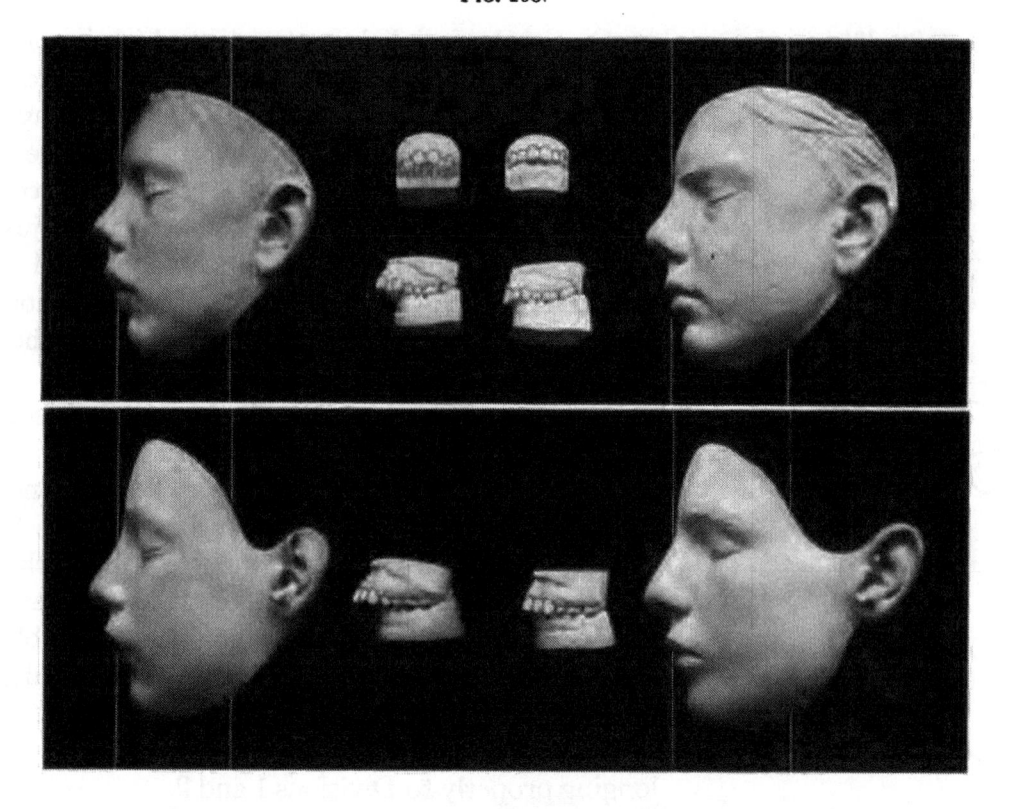

In the Dental Review of May and July 1894, will be found a complete résumé of the literature of "jumping the bite," with the author's description of the difficulties which would need to be overcome in a successful operation of this character; the whole is intended to show the improbability of permanent success. After many long continued trials to "jump the bite" for patients younger than twelve, *all of which ultimately were failures*, and as the author has never seen from the hands of others a single well authenticated case of permanent correction by this method, *he cannot advise anyone to undertake it.*

On the other hand, while it may be possible with this character of malocclusion to bring the teeth to a normal occlusion by an interstitial movement, with the intermaxillary force, this operation in all marked cases should not be attempted, because the lower lip would be forced abnormally forward by the required extreme labial movement of the lower teeth, with the production of a receding chin effect. And in those cases where the upper teeth are considerably protruded, this operation would in all probability result in that most unhappy deformity characterized by a **bimaxillary protrusion.**

In all cases, therefore, of retruded lower teeth and mandible, accompanied with protrusion of the upper, the extraction of upper teeth is always indicated to produce as in all pronounced upper protrusions, the extensive lingual movement of the upper labial teeth to harmonize the facial outlines.

While a lingual movement of the upper labial teeth, even to the full width of a premolar, will not produce the same perfection of facial outlines obtainable in other cases of this Class on account of the retruded position of the lower teeth and chin, still the improvement is always an exceedingly pleasing one, and one, moreover, which is far more liable to retain its position than the operation which requires a movement of all the teeth. In Fig. 195, is shown the results of this method of correction in two cases of this Type. Two cases of this Type are also illustrated under Fig. 170, Chapter XXX.

It is important in the diagnosis of these cases to determine whether an inclination lingual movement of the front is demanded, or a bodily lingual movement. The diagnosis and treatment of these two distinct Types are the same as Types A and B of Division 2 of this Class.

It should never be forgotten that one of the indispensable conditions of permanent retention is an accurate interdigitation of buccal cusps. In nearly all cases of this Type with a full complement of teeth, the upper buccal cusps will be found in mesial malinterdigitation, a condition which is very important to retain. If however, after producing normal width relations of the arches, it is found that the general mesio-distal and bucco-lingual relations are imperfect in this particular they should be intelligently shifted with the intermaxillary elastics. The depth of the labio-mental depression will at once indicate whether a forward movement of the teeth is admissible. Usually, in this Type, such a movement is not advisable, in which case the lower buccal teeth should be firmly united in stationary anchorages and so joined to the front teeth as to prevent a mesial movement from the intermaxillary force. On the other hand, the force should be applied to the upper teeth at points which produce the easiest movement with the least display of power.

In this connection, it may be stated again that a lingual movement of the upper labial teeth, even slightly beyond the normal relation, will produce a far more pleasing facial effect by placing the upper lip in closer harmony with the lower, than will result from a protrusion of the lower lip at the expense of obliterating the labio-mental curve, to say nothing of the possibilities of producing a receding chin effect. It would be well to remember this in cases where the upper is but slightly protruded, or normal, in connection with a decided bodily retruded position of the mandible and teeth.

It will have been observed that in connection with this Type, the rule for extraction is the same as in Division 2. It is needless to say, also, that every device should be taken advantage of to avoid moving the upper anchorage teeth forward; and consequently, the principal movement may demand the intermaxillary and occipital force alone, with an employment of the stationary anchorages mainly for the purpose of taking up the slack of the retruding bow and to retain the positions gained.

In this operation, the intermaxillary force will be a valuable and effective adjunct, if the tendencies of its movement are properly controlled, and especially in cases that are complicated with a close-bite malocclusion, because of the extrusive force which the elastics will exert upon the lower buccal teeth whenever the mouth is opened.

CHAPTER XXXIX

CLOSE-BITE MALOCCLUSION

One of the most common complications of Class II is a **Close-bite Malocclusion,** the lower incisors, upon closure of the jaws, frequently striking into the gums far back of the uppers along the linguo-incisal alveolar ridge. This renders a lingual movement of the upper incisors impossible until provision is first made for permanently opening the bite by methods which are here fully explained.

In the early days of regulating teeth, this character of malocclusion was considered one of the most difficult, if not impossible, to correct, because every attempt to retrude the protruding front teeth would cause the lower incisors to strike deeper into the gums.

The first method which obviated this difficulty, and enabled the author to perform what was considered at that time quite a wonderful correction of a pronounced upper protrusion, was by obliging the unhappy patient, during the time of the operation, to masticate food with the lower incisors striking an extension of a rubber plate which was worn in the roof of the mouth. This method was later presented with a full illustration of a case in practice before the Illinois State Dental Society in 1892. It was believed to be at that time such an advance step in orthodontia, its publication in the Dental Review was copied by a number of textbooks, which unfortunately continued to publish it long after this very crude method had become obsolete.

This incident is mentioned here to show how very few years have elapsed since rubber plates were considered one of the principal means in the regulation of teeth.

FIG. 196.

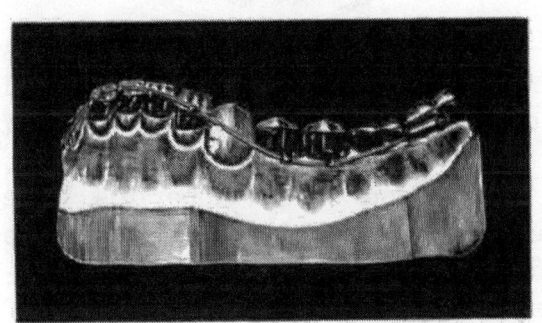

A number of years later, the author introduced another far more efficient and less troublesome method which is illustrated in Fig. 196. To this was added the now indispensable shell crowns instead of bands on the first molars, which at once opens the bite to the desired extent and permits a rapid extrusive movement of the premolars to the new occlusal plane, through the action of the spring arch-bow. The second molar being the youngest tooth and often not fully erupted, will continue its growth to the new functional occlusal plane. Furthermore, the reaction of the spring bow in front exerts an intrusive force upon the incisors, which aids in correcting their supra-occlusal position, and provides room for the

PART VI. DENTO-FACIAL MALOCCLUSIONS

desired retruding movement of the upper front teeth and for the dento-facial and occlusal correction of the entire denture; the whole operation being carried on at the same time and with very little suffering to the patient.

The first molars, being the oldest and strongest, and consequently the most stable teeth in the mouth, are admirably adapted for the crowns to sustain the forces of mastication for the very few months which are required to establish the full masticating position of the other teeth. It would seem that the sudden necessity of commencing and continuing the entire mastication upon these crowns alone

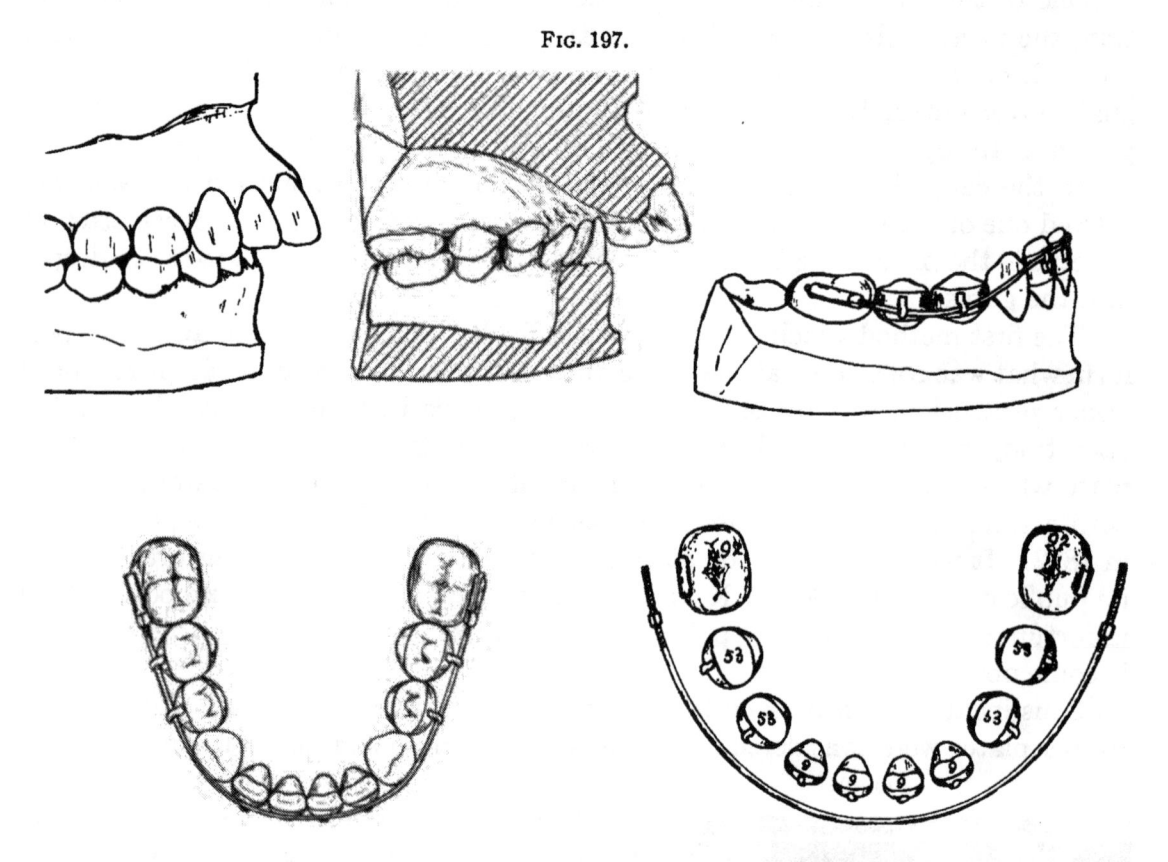

FIG. 197.

would give considerable annoyance and perhaps pain to patients, but one is surprised to hear so little complaint, and to see how quickly they cease to pay any attention to this part of the operation.

Fig. 197 illustrates the most modern construction of this apparatus. The hook and tube attachments on the bands and crowns should be placed so that the resilient force of the bow No. 22 or 23 (.025″ or .0225″) will exert a strong extrusive force upon the premolars and an intrusive force upon the incisors. Instead of seamless round tubes on the molar crowns, U-tubes, open at the top, will enable an easy assembling and removal of the bow.

The shell crowns for the purposes of this work are easily made as follows: Take measurements using wide No. .005″ banding material. After soldering, contour and fit as for ordinary bands, except that the occlusal edges should stand slightly above the occluding surfaces when fitted to place. Now remove the bands and slit their edges so that they can be bent over on the occluding borders with the wood-plugger. When this is accomplished, take bite impressions with modeling-compound or wax, using only sufficient material to partly cover the crowns and the occluding tooth or teeth. Remove the bands and place accurately in the impressions and fill with investing plaster, then set them up in an articulator.

Swage the occluding caps of very thin nickel silver plate No. 35 (.006″) and fit them to the bands so that their edges overlap the occlusal zone. Accuracy of occlusion is not essential at this stage. When these caps are lightly soldered along their borders to the bands, and again placed on the teeth, the patient will be able to indent them with the occluding teeth and thus produce a perfect occluding surface.

Another advantage of thin caps is: when both crowns are placed for *trial fitting*, slight imperfections in the occluding surfaces may be easily corrected by the patient in closing the jaws.

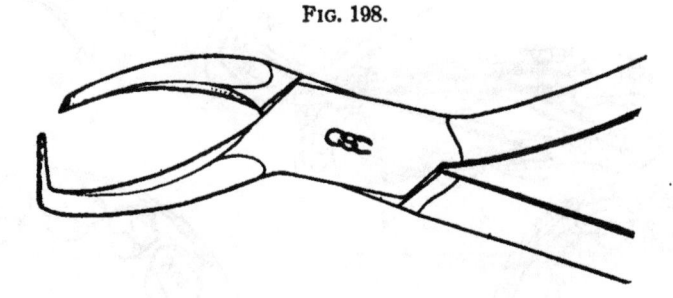

FIG. 198.

Before the crowns are placed on the teeth, bore holes through the mesio-buccal occluding sulci for an exit of excess cement, and particularly for the insertion of the occluding beak of the crown-removing plier, Fig. 198. In finishing the bands, an additional amount of solder may be flowed along the borders of the caps to even the surfaces.

Later, it occasionally becomes necessary to thicken the occluding surfaces by soldering on another cap to each crown so as to open the bite still wider. In removing the crowns for this purpose, and in finally removing them, the cement is burred out of the holes through to the surface of the enamel. The point of the occluding beak of the plier is placed in the hole resting upon the crown of the tooth. This forms a solid fulcrum to the power of the other beak placed under the gingival edge of the crown, enabling one to easily lift it from its attachment, with no wrenching force upon the roots.

When the teeth have become permanently established in their new occlusal positions, the crowns can then be removed and replaced with bands bearing hooks for direct intermaxillary elastics leading to the opposing stationary anchorages for an extrusive movement of these first molars to the new occlusal position. Any linguo-buccal malpositions of occlusion are readily corrected through a proper adjustment of the elastics. For instance, if the lower molars are in buccal malposition in relation to the upper, the elastics are attached to a buccal hook on the lower molar and to a lingual hook on the upper. See Fig. 199. These are readily adjusted and removed by the patient at mealtime. The ordinary "election rings" are usually too large for direct intermaxillary force; therefore, in adjustments, they should be carried forth and back, which doubles their force.

The crowns may at times be dispensed with for young patients, with the expectation of commencing the extruding movement of the lower molars with the intermaxillary elastics at the beginning of the operation, as shown in Fig. 200.

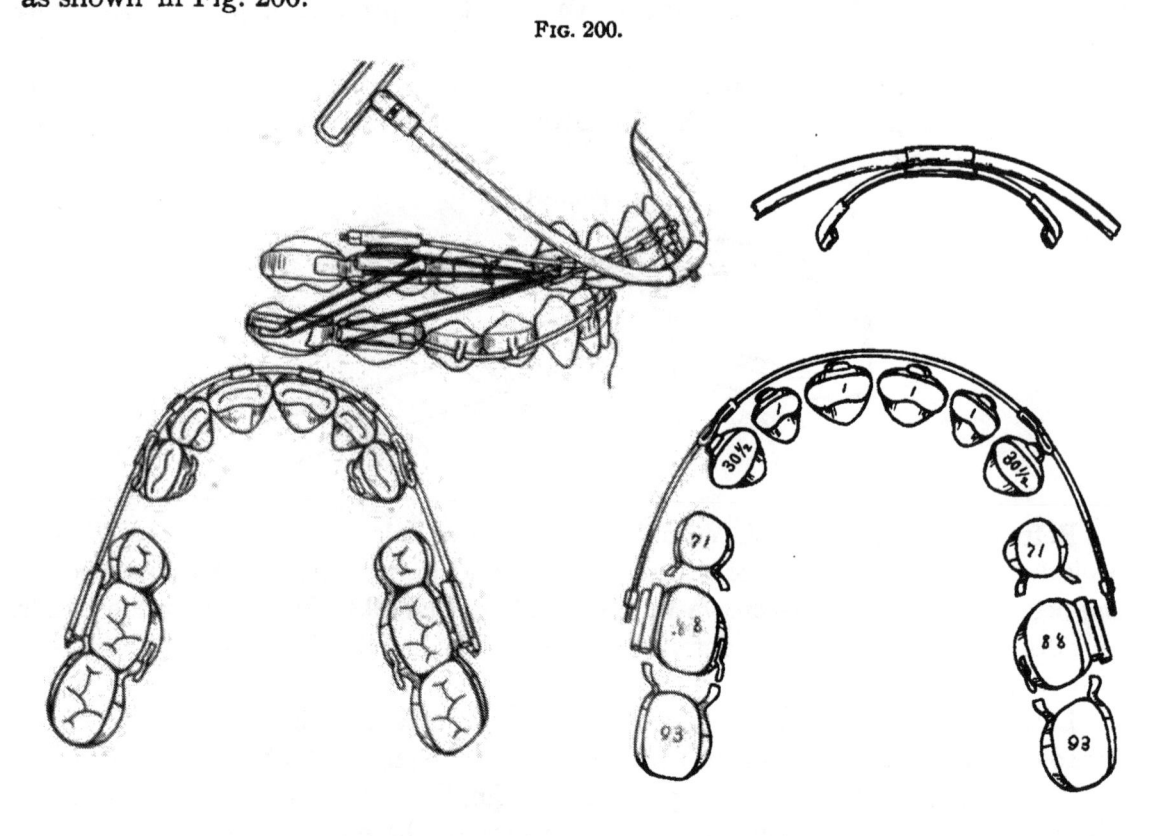

FIG. 199.

FIG. 200.

A two-band stationary anchorage is attached to the molars, with provisions for the attachment of elastics and for the bow to extrude the premolars, etc. This arrangement is particularly applicable for the correction of close-bite malocclusions in Division 2, where little or no mesial movement of the buccal teeth is desired. For cases in Division 1, single bands upon the first and second molars, with short buccal tubes for the bow, would permit a mesial and extruding movement. The intermaxillary elastics passing more directly from one jaw to the other are calculated to exert a direct extruding force upon both the lower and upper buccal teeth.

CHAPTER XXXIX. CONCOMITANT CHARACTERS. CLASS II.

The occipital bow A, in Fig. 78, shown in position, may be exchanged for occipital bow C, shown on the right, if a more direct retruding force upon the cuspids is demanded.

GENERAL BIMAXILLARY INFRA-OCCLUSION

A more rare character of close-bite malocclusion, which may be properly termed **bimaxillary infra-occlusion,** has occasionally fallen under the author's observation for treatment. Though it differs quite decidedly from the typical close-bite malocclusion, it is placed in this Class, because it requires similar methods of treatment.

It refers to cases in which both the front and back teeth are in an infra-occlusal position in relation to a typical dento-facial occlusal plane, shown by the fact that the occlusal edges of the front teeth are in a marked intrusive position in relation

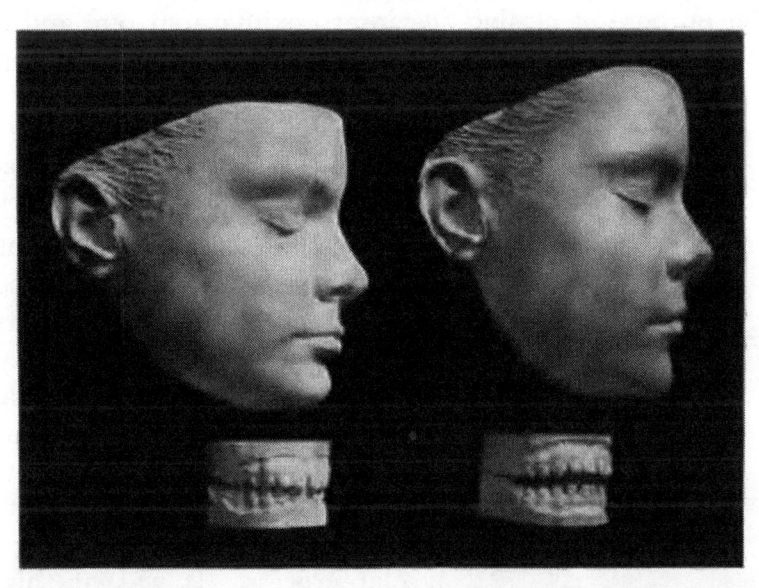

FIG. 201.

to a reposeful parting of the lips, and also by the fact that when the jaws are closed in mastication the lips in contact are forced forward with a marked redundancy of lip tissue. See Fig. 201.

In this case, the difficulty of occluding the teeth, with the production of a painful disturbance at the temporo-maxillary articulation, led to imperfect mastication of food, which was accomplished principally with the incisors alone. On the left is shown the profile cast with the teeth in masticating occlusion. It is unfortunate that it does not fully express the facial disfigurement which was far more pronounced than is here indicated.

The impression for the facial cast on the right was also taken at the same time, but with the dentures held apart with modeling-compound for the purpose of showing the amount of extruding movement that would be necessary to produce a proper facial effect. For this purpose, the modeling-compound was placed between the teeth and the jaws carefully closed to the desired position, at which point the facial impression was taken. Then the modeling-compound bite was removed from the mouth and the dental casts were placed in it and fixed in that position as shown on the right, from which the illustration above was made. The proportionate excess of lip tissue would have permitted the jaws to have opened still wider, without disturbing the ease of a perfect closure of the lips.

The apparatus which was first attached consisted of four crowns placed upon the first molars. This opened the jaws to about one-half the desired extent, to start with. The premolars and labial teeth were all banded with attachments to support **alignment arch-bows** with spurs for the attachment of the **direct intermaxillary elastics,** so as to extrude all of these teeth with a uniform movement, treating the case in this particular as though it were an open-bite malocclusion. Provision was also made for the attachment of the disto-mesial intermaxillary elastics for the purpose of closing the interproximate spaces, and correcting the occlusion by a retruding movement of the upper labial teeth, and a mesial movement of the lower buccal teeth.

Within a few months, all of the intruded buccal teeth, except the crowned molars, were observed to be in perfect occlusion, whereupon, the lower crowns were removed and an added layer soldered to their occlusal surfaces. These being replaced, the several forces were continued as before for a few months, with the second complete closure of occlusal planes; then the upper crowns were treated in the same manner, etc., etc.

FIG. 202.

In this way the teeth were gradually moved to the desired new occlusal plane, which was not in the sense of pulling them *out* of their sockets, but with an apparent concomitant movement of the surrounding gum and alveolar process. It was at this point in the operation that the casts shown in Fig. 202 were made.

The regulating apparatus was now changed for the more delicately constructed and less unsightly retaining appliance. (See Fig. 306, Chapter LIV.) When assured that the positions of the extruded buccal teeth were permanent, the crowns were removed from the first molars and replaced with bands bearing hooks for the direct application of intermaxillary elastics, which finally extruded these teeth to the new plane of occlusion as in the regular cases of close-bite malocclusion.

CHAPTER XXXIX. CONCOMITANT CHARACTERS. CLASS II.

Another case which came for treatment was far more pronounced than any case of bimaxillary infra-occlusion that has fallen under the author's observation. The relative position of the models shown in Fig. 203 were photographed while articulated on the wax bite which produced the proper facial outlines. In other words, the jaws required to be opened that much to produce the best facial effect. An appointment was then made with the patient for the facial cast, but very much to the author's regret, she did not return for it. It is hoped that she fell into the hands of some orthodontist who will fully appreciate the condition, and pursue the proper treatment.

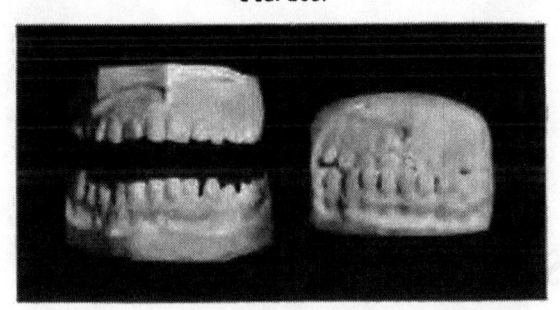

When the jaws were closed in this case, the mandible carried the lower labial teeth in front of the upper, on the same principle that the closure of the jaws of an edentulous mouth will carry the mandible far in front of the maxilla, because of the relative position of the condyles.

CLASS III
MESIAL MALOCCLUSION OF LOWER BUCCAL TEETH

TABLE OF DIVISIONS

DIVISION 1: BODILY RETRUSION OF UPPER DENTURE AND MAXILLA

DIVISION 2: CONTRACTED RETRUSION OF UPPER DENTURE

DIVISION 3: RETRUSION OF THE UPPER WITH PROTRUSION OF LOWER DENTURE

DIVISION 4: RETRUSION OF THE UPPER WITH PROGNATHIC MANDIBLE, COMMONLY ACCOMPANIED WITH OPEN-BITE MALOCCLUSION

CLASS III

CHAPTER XL

PRINCIPLES OF DIAGNOSIS, CAUSES, AND TREATMENT

Upon entering the field of dento-facial malocclusion which is characterized by upper retrusions, we have come to a class of irregularities whose very frequent cause, though often that of heredity, is of local origin, because of the quite prevalent adenoids, rhinological stenosis, and mouth-breathing, which follow each other in sequence, inhibiting the development of the maxilla, and causing conditions which emphasize the abnormality. Certain cases seem to be wholly due to the above local causes, while others are due wholly to heredity, and others again, are due partly to one and partly to the other.

The correction of **upper retrusions** is quite as important and as frequently demanded as upper protrusions. While there will be found quite a similarity in the facial expressions of nearly all the types belonging to this Class, it is nevertheless true that they present a vast variety of dental malrelations, arising as they do from both local causes and heredity—separately and in combination—and frequently demand the highest order of mechanical skill, ingenuity, and artistic ability to correct.

This Class is facially characterized by a retruded position of the entire upper lip in relation to the rest of the features, with an abnormal deepening of the naso-labial lines, and occasionally a retruded position of the end of the nose, as will be seen in many of the illustrations presented.

It will be seen that this Class, therefore, differs from the other two Classes of malocclusion in that all its Divisions and types are stamped with the one characteristic and peculiar facial expression, however much they may differ in other particulars. This means that they all demand bodily labial movement of the upper front teeth, though the apparatus for this movement may have a number of auxiliaries for the correction of other malpositions belonging to the case.

In pronounced cases of upper retrusion—as pointed out in the chapter on Diagnosis—the first mental impression upon the observer is that it is due to a prognathic mandible. This unfortunately has often led to a wrong diagnosis, followed with attempts to correct with occipital force applied to the chin.

Fig. 204 shows the plaster casts before and after treatment of a young man about eighteen years of age. The retruded upper was caused by the extraction of badly decayed and broken-down upper first molars during childhood. It was

292 PART VI. DENTO-FACIAL MALOCCLUSIONS

diagnosed as a prognathic mandible at the International Congress of 1900 at Paris, and the patient was then fitted with a head-cap and chin-piece which he studiously wore at all permissible hours for over a year in a fruitless endeavor to retrude the mandible and lower denture. In the meantime he had entered an Eastern college

FIG. 204.

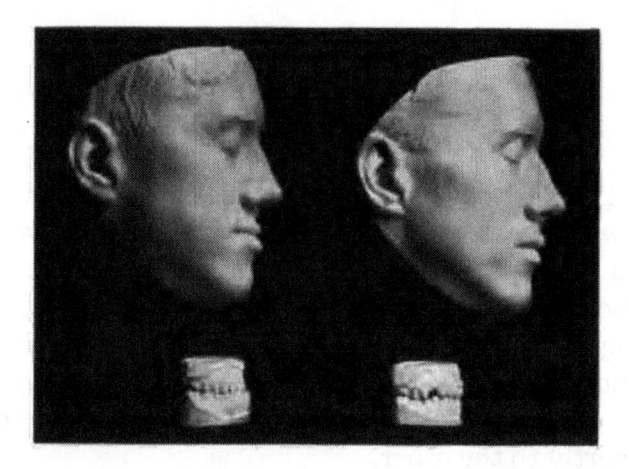

in this country, and was referred to the author by a New York dentist. The facial and dental casts on the left show the condition at that time. The casts on the right, made about a year later, show the effect of a bodily labial movement of the six upper

FIG. 205.

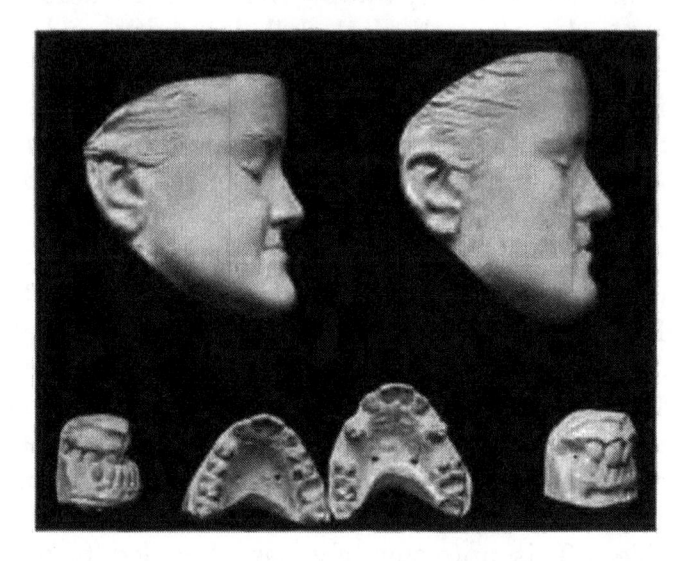

front teeth, and a complete restoration of the facial outlines and normal pose of the chin, though no appliance was placed on the lower teeth, except to act as an auxiliary to the upper for the attachment of the intermaxillary force. To show the remarkable simplicity in the working possibilities of the regular bodily movement appli-

CHAPTER XL. DIAGNOSIS, CAUSES, AND TREATMENT. CLASS III. 293

ances, and the ease and non-irritability of subsequent treatments, the author wishes to state that this case was never seen by him, except at the time required in preparing and stabilizing the appliances, until the patient came for the retainers. The work of adjustment treatments—which consisted in the simple turning of the nuts at regular periods and intermaxillary adjustments—were wholly performed by the young man himself while pursuing his college course.

Even in those cases in which the mandible is really prognathic in connection with retruded uppers, if the lower lip is retruded in relation to the chin—showing

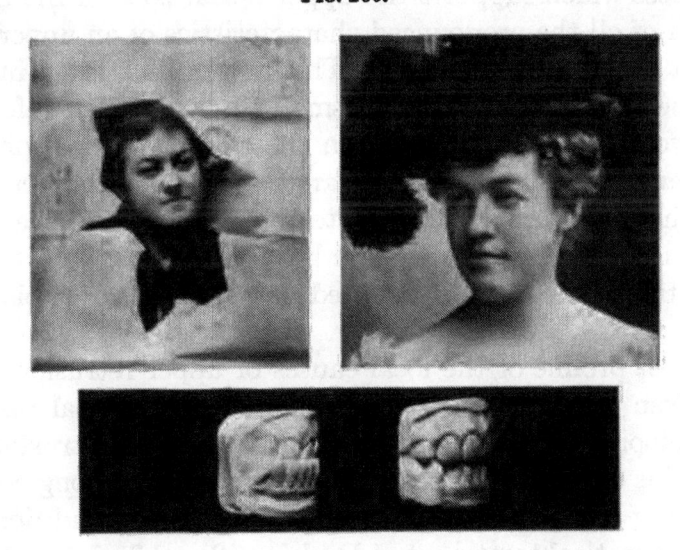

FIG. 206.

that the lower denture is not also protruded with the mandible—the proper bodily correction of the upper, which places the upper and lower front teeth and the lips in harmony, will invariably result in such an improvement to the facial outlines that the former displeasing prognathism of the mandible is lost sight of, and at times it is changed to the beautifying effect of a "Gibson chin."

This principle is perfectly illustrated in Fig. 205, which was made from the facial and dental casts of a miss about eighteen years of age. In connection with the inherited prognathism of the mandible, the upper laterals were missing through extinction of the tooth germs, which no doubt was the main cause of the more extensive upper retrusion. The main object in the correction of this case, as in that of many others of a similar character whose pronounced facial imperfections must inevitably mar the social life and attractiveness of young ladies, was to beautify the facial outlines, though as always, with the view of leaving a good masticating occlusion of the teeth, even if partially artificial.

It can be seen by comparing the palatal views of the casts of the upper denture before and after treatment, something of the degree of bodily labial movement that was necessary to place the upper central incisors and adjoining cuspids in their proper relations to the lower, and thus harmonize the dento-facial area. This necessitated opening spaces for the insertion of four artificial teeth.

Far too many cases of upper retrusion are caused wholly by the injudicious extraction or unnecessary loss of upper permanent teeth. This is fully outlined and illustrated in Chapter XII, under the head of "The Question of Extraction." In addition to this, also, many of these cases are caused by extinction of the germs of upper front teeth, especially the lateral incisors, which permits the upper lip to contrude the underlying front teeth in the early years of their development, so that they bite back of the lowers, causing also a lack of normal anterior development of the alveolar process which supports the upper apical zone of the lip, with the frequent production of all the pronounced characteristics of an upper retrusion, even to the effect of a prognathic mandible. This is well illustrated in Fig. 206. The illustration on the left was made from a small tin-type taken before treatment, at about eighteen years of age. The one on the right is from a photograph taken several years after correction. What appears to be the lateral incisors, are the cuspids, turned slightly and cut off to imitate the laterals in appearance. The first premolars, as is usual in these cases, were brought forward and turned to imitate the cuspids. Artificial teeth were inserted between the premolars for retention and appearance.

One of the most prolific of the local causes of upper retrusions in the author's practice, has arisen wholly or in part from pharyngeo-nasal diseases, resulting in inhibited development of the maxilla, and contracted retrusions of the upper denture. From this cause may arise also the early habit of long continued mouth-breathing, resulting in **open-bite malocclusion.** These conditions are fully described under the practical treatment of Divisions 2 and 3 of this Class.

CHAPTER XLI

Division 1, Class III

BODILY RETRUSION OF THE UPPER DENTURE AND MAXILLA

Fig. 207.

Division 1 of this Class arises from heredity, and is characterized by a retruded malposition of the entire maxilla and upper denture, and produces a retrusion of the entire upper lip, and frequently the end of the nose. In this Division is placed all of that common type of cases of Class III malocclusions in which the entire upper denture is bodily retruded in its dento-facial relations, and the chin and lower lip (mandible and lower denture) are in normal relations to each other and with the main features of the physiognomy, though frequently wrongly diagnosed as prognathic.

The dentures are commonly in fair alignment, the upper front teeth biting back of the lowers, and the premolars and molars in linguo-distal malocclusion.

Fig. 208.

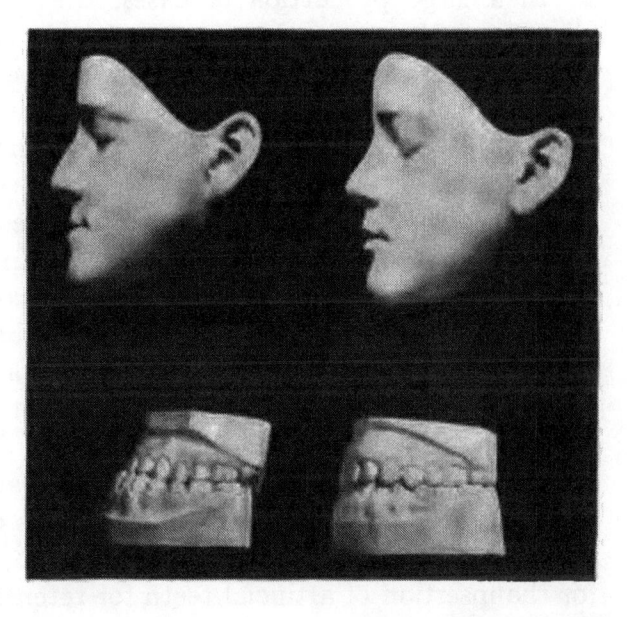

The facial and dental casts on the left of Fig. 208 show a perfect type of this Division. Please note the perfect facial outlines in the finished face on the right, even to the straightening of the nose. The dental models of this case, shown on the right in this illustration, represent the true relations of the dentures in occlusion immediately upon removal of the apparatus which was employed for the bodily labial movement of the upper front teeth and the expansion of the upper arch, also for the retruding movement of the lower with the intermaxillary force. The premature removal of the appliance, before the final adjustment of the buccal occlusion, was made so that impressions could be taken for the casts as shown, to be exhibited as a part of the illustrations of a paper which the author read before the International Dental Congress in 1893.

This was one of the three cases which the author presented at that meeting to show the possibility and practicability of an extensive bodily labial movement with the "contouring apparatus," and an extensive disto-mesial movement of the dentures with the intermaxillary elastic force. The author has never seen this case since its correction, but he learned from friends of the family that "the teeth all went back," which is not at all surprising considering the extensive disto-mesial movement of the entire dentures, and the crude methods of retention then employed.

The main reason why many cases of inherited upper retrusion in the author's early practice seemed impossible to permanently retain, was because in the process of correction, *all* the teeth of the upper denture were moved forward so as to place them in normal occlusion. In other words, the entire upper denture was forced forward of its natural inherited position, accomplished mainly with the intermaxillary force as an auxiliary to the bodily labial movement of the front teeth. When admissible, the lower denture was made to aid in this occlusal correction by a reciprocal retruding movement enabled through the reaction of the elastics, with the result that all the teeth of both dentures were moved considerably from their inherited locations with the sole object of producing a normal occlusion, and with the hope and foolish expectation that a normal interdigitation of buccal cusps would be sufficient to retain them after a reasonable retention with a continuation of the intermaxillary force.

In a large proportion of cases, the intermaxillary principle of retention is all right, and sufficiently effective, but in all strongly marked types of retrusion or protrusion which arise from heredity, the correction of a mesio-distal malocclusion with the intermaxillary force—which is always possible to effect—will almost invariably return to its former malrelations after the intermaxillary retention is stopped. Besides, when dependent upon this kind of artificial retention, it is a most unsatisfactory dernier resort, because patients will not attend to its proper application through the many months required for retention.

The modern reliable method for the correction and permanent retention of all cases of pronounced disto-mesial malocclusion of the dentures which are characterized principally by a pronounced dento-facial protrusion or retrusion of only one denture, with all the teeth in fair alignment and caused by heredity, is not following the arbitrary teaching of shifting the dentures to a normal occlusion, *but it is to move only the front teeth*, which are causing the facial disharmony. This is accomplished in cases of decided retrusions of the upper or the lower dentures by a bodily labial movement of the front teeth, leaving spaces between the premolars for the insertion of artificial teeth for retention and mastication.

Fig. 209 is presented to emphasize the characteristic facial type of Division 1 in this Class, and to show the mature expression which may be caused in the physiog-

CHAPTER XLI. DIVISION 1. CLASS III. 297

nomy of a child twelve years of age by a retrusion of the entire upper lip and lower portion of the nose, with a concomitant deepening of the naso-labial lines. It also illustrates why it is at times necessary in cases of upper retrusion to first force the crowns partly forward of the lowers so they can be grasped by the power and fulcrum arch-bows of the contouring apparatus.

This case was presented in connection with a decided upper protrusion in the chapter on Dento-Facial Diagnosis, to show by intermedial facial casts the progres-

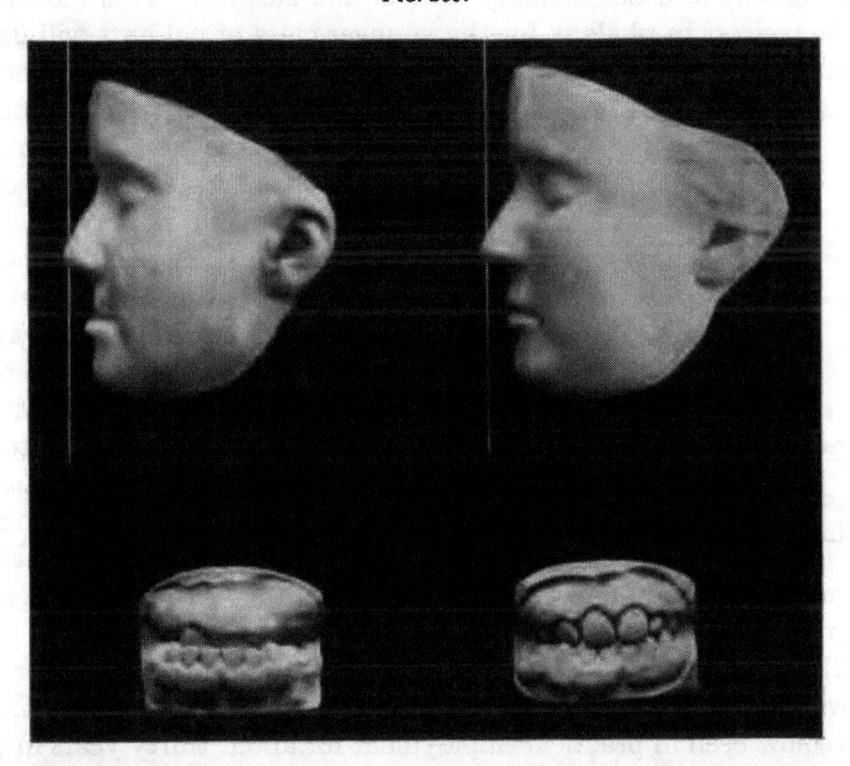

FIG. 209.

sive effect on the facial outlines, first, by an inclination movement of the crowns of the front teeth, and second, by a bodily movement. The intermediate facial casts, Fig. 124, Chapter XXI, to which the reader is referred, plainly show that when the crowns alone are moved, there is no appreciable movement of the apical dento-facial zone. Cases of pronounced upper retrusions, which markedly show a retrusion of the end of the nose, must be due to an abnormally retruded position of the true bone of the intermaxillary process with the nasal spine and cartilaginous septum which supports the end of the nose in its relation to the nasal and malar bones. Therefore, when the end of the nose is brought forward and its lines straightened, it follows that the entire intermaxillary bone with its alveolar process is moved forward with the bodily labial movement of its contained teeth.

CHAPTER XLII

THE PROTRUDING CONTOUR APPARATUS

Nearly all malocclusions of Class III demand a labial bodily movement of the upper incisors and occasionally that of the cuspids. This movement of the roots of the incisors in phalanx for the younger class of patients will usually cause the surrounding alveolar process to move bodily forward with the teeth. For the older class of patients, say from fifteen to sixteen years of age, and later, the movement is more of an interstitial nature—the roots often becoming quite prominent in relation to the surface of the gum. If this becomes especially perceptible, it indicates that the amount of force that is regularly applied each week should be reduced so that the development of the new alveolar process will have a chance to keep pace with the movement of the roots. It is the full normal development of the process that is of the greatest importance in completing and perfecting the framework to give proper form and support to the corrected facial contours.

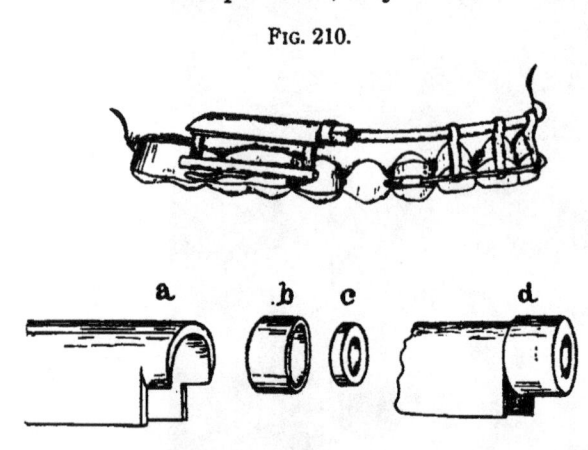

Fig. 210 illustrates the most modern "Contour Apparatus" for the bodily labial movement of the upper incisors, the mechanical principles of which in various forms have now been in practical employment for about thirty years in the successful correction of hundreds of cases of Class III malocclusion.

In recent years, in addition to the two and three-band stationary anchorages which have aways characterized this apparatus, the anchorage tubes for the power arch-bow have been attached to root-wise extensions as shown. This greatly increases the mechanical advantages and offers greater stability to the anchorages, as fully explained in Chapter XX. The scientific principles of bodily movement, particularly those which relate to the labio-lingual bodily movement of the front teeth, outlined in Chapter XIV, are worthy of the deepest study by all who contemplate this operaton.

In descriptions and illustrations of this apparatus in previous chapters, the U-power tubes are open at the top and the threaded ends of the power arch-bows are held in place with counter-sunk lock nuts. A recently improved device for this purpose is shown in working detail in Fig. 210, which is less liable to irritate the tissues and presents greater facilities for assembling and locking the power arch-bow. The mesial end of the U-tube "a" is shaped to telescope into a thin seamless tube "b" into which a short section of tube "c" is soldered to form a shoulder-rest to receive the thrust of the nut. In assembling, the completed thimble "d" is slipped on to the threaded end of the power arch-bow which when placed in its U-tube is then locked with the thimble as shown.

Usually in placing this apparatus, the fulcrum arch-bow is attached to the stationary anchorages, having in mind only the labial movement of the incisors. In all extensive cases, however, when considerable movement is demanded, it is often necessary for the correction of the facial outlines and permanency of retention to open spaces between the anterior buccal teeth for the insertion of artificial retaining dentures. The present apparatus shows how this fulcrum force may be utilized, first, toward a mesial movement of the cuspids, and then the first premolars, so that the artificial retaining teeth will be as inconspicuous as possible. This method particularly applies to the extensive movements demanded in Division 1 of this Class and in Division 1 of Class II where the teeth of the retruded dentures at the beginning of the operation are in fair alignment.

In the construction of this apparatus, the teeth should be properly separated and each finished band and anchorage so perfectly fitted that it can be easily forced on and off with the aid of a wood plugger and band removing plier—shown in Figs. 98 and 99, Chapter XIX—in making slight but necessary changes in the shape or position of the attachments or power arch-bow. The size of the power arch-bow for extensive movements should rarely be larger than No.16 (.050") spring nickel silver. It should be bent first upon the model, and finally at the chair, to conform to the shape of the arch, its ends lying evenly in the **power tubes** without the slightest tension. In the final moves of this important requirement, place the **anchorages** in position and the power arch-bow with the threaded ends lying along the outside of the tubes. Then place the right end in its tube, and see that the other end lies exactly parallel with the left tube and in proper shape and position in front. Then place the left end in its tube with the other end free, and go through the same movements. This may require repeating several times with the greatest nicety of judgment and patience in detail, before you are able to assemble the power arch-bow and anchorages properly together. The heavy **bending pliers**, Fig. 211, are indispensable for this operation.

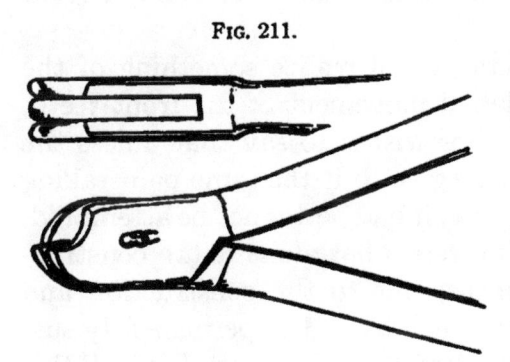

Fig. 211.

After the preliminary fitting of the anchorages, they may be cemented and the power arch-bow placed in position. In assembling the bow, place the left end in its closed tube and carry the other end around beneath the chin and up into the right corner of the mouth back to its position in the U-tube, locking it in place. It is at this time that its final adjustments should be made in its relation to the line of the labial gum and gingival line of the incisor attachments. If the dental arch requires lateral expansion or contraction, the power bow when fitted may be sprung so as to exert a slight force in a buccal or lingual direction.

When this is accomplished, the final preliminary fitting of the incisor bands should be made. Each band should be carried fully to place with its root-wise extension lapping on to the power bow. It will now be seen whether the bow resting in its anchorage tubes is too high or too low to take its place without tension in relation to the root-wise extensions. It will also be found that these extensions will need to be bent lingually or labially, and the upper ends cut off and finished slightly above an even line with the upper border of the power bow. They should perfectly fit against the labial surface of the bow, but in no sense to lap above it, as this would prevent their easy removal in case it became necessary. The fitting, bending, filing, and polishing of this special attachment without distortion or injury to the band is difficult without the use of the **root-wise plier,** Fig. 112, Chapter XX.

Treatment Adjustments.—In applying the force which is to follow the first conscious tension of the nuts, the large nuts of the power bow should be given about two-quarter turns three times a week. As the movement advances it will become necessary to unscrew the fulcrum nut occasionally to allow the incisal zone to move forward with the roots. If the roots are found to be moving dangerously fast for the safety of their vitality, the application of force should be stopped in the power bow, and if necessary, the nuts may be slightly unscrewed. Unscrewing the nut upon the fulcrum arch-bow is also equivalent to reducing the force upon the roots. It may be advisable to remove the fulcrum arch-bow entirely, to be replaced with a new one when the danger is past. The danger line will be indicated by unusual sensitiveness to heat and cold over the root or roots of the affected tooth or teeth; this should not be allowed to arrive to a continual pain. Perfect rest should be afforded to the teeth, and the gum painted with strong tincture of iodine two or three times a week until all irritation subsides.

Those who have followed closely the directions will realize something of the difficulties and skill necessary for the bodily labial movement of the front teeth, and the correction of facial contours. The author wishes to say that unless the operation is considered of sufficient importance to give to it the same painstaking skill that is demanded in other branches of dentistry, it had better not be attempted, as in all probability it will prove a failure. This refers not alone to the construction and application of the regulating apparatus, but to the construction and attachment of the proper retaining appliance that is intended to permanently sustain the position gained. On the other hand, the truly wonderful work which this single apparatus has accomplished in the author's hands, proved now by hundreds of successful cases, convinces him that its work in other hands will cause this principle to grow into great possibilities.

CHAPTER XLIII

DIVISION 2, CLASS III

CONTRACTED RETRUSION OF THE UPPER DENTURE

Division 2 presents quite a variety of dental malpositions which arise mostly from local causes, all of which present the same peculiar facial expression that is characteristic of Class III. Contracted retrusions of the upper denture are due to two main causes: First, from adenoids, etc., inhibiting the growth development of the maxilla, which thus does not give sufficient room for the proper eruption of the permanent teeth in the contracted maxillary arch. In consequence of this, the teeth, and particularly the cuspids, are forced out of alignment, or impacted, with

FIG. 212.

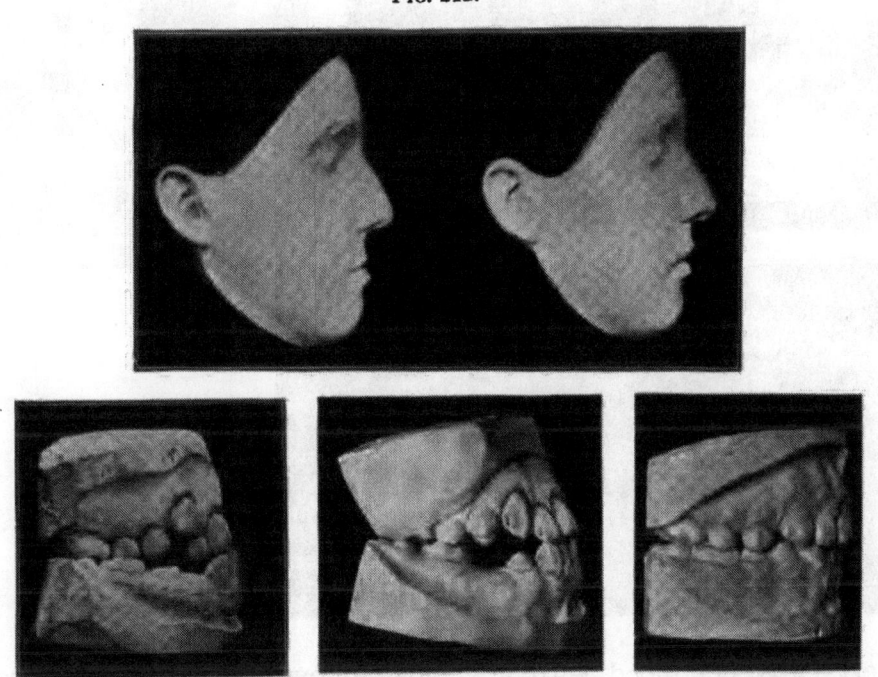

the producton of a dental and alveolar arch that is contracted in its dimensions in relation to the normal. The second form is caused by injudicious extraction, or the premature loss of the deciduous teeth through extensive decay, or the lack of permanent teeth from extinction of the tooth germs.

When any of these local causes are ingrafted upon an inherited upper retrusion, they proportionately increase the dental malposition and facial deformity. Combinations of local causes and inherited retrusions result in many of the most

302   PART VI. DENTO-FACIAL MALOCCLUSIONS

pronounced dento-facial malocclusions of this Class, some of which are illustrated in Division 3.

In Chapter XL, the case illustrated by Fig. 204 was caused by the very early loss of the upper first permanent molars, and those cases illustrated in Figs. 205 and 206 in the same chapter were partly caused through an extinction of the germs of the upper lateral incisors. The most prolific of the local causes, however, start

FIG. 213.

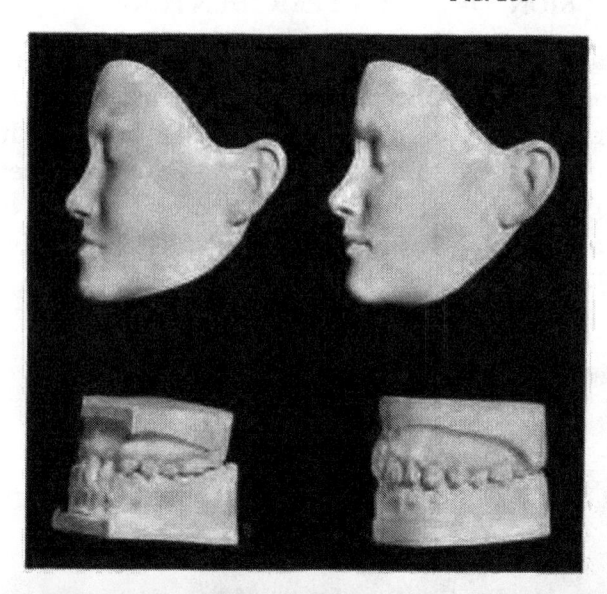

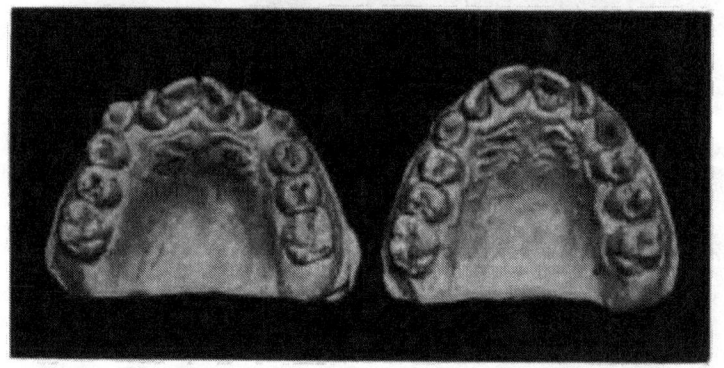

during very early childhood with adenoids, followed by pathogenic conditions of the naso-maxillary sinuses. In these cases, the maxilla and its entire upper dental and alveolar arch is contracted, with high and narrow palatal dome, and usually with a bodily retrusion of the incisor teeth and intermaxillary bone.

This common character of malocclusion is well shown in the beginning dental and facial casts of Fig. 212. The intermediate dental casts show the front teeth in position for the attachment of the apparatus for the bodily labial movement of the incisors. The final dental and facial casts were made upon the removal of

CHAPTER XLIII. DIVISION 2. CLASS III.

this apparatus, and show the teeth in position for the retaining appliance on the front teeth, and the final adjustment of the buccal occlusion. Cases of this character at a youthful age rarely take over one year to correct.

In many cases, the effect of adenoids will result in inhibited maxillary development of the intermaxillary portion of the bone only. When this causes the early erupting incisors to close back of the lowers, inlocking them in that malposition and preventing the development of all the incisive portion of the bone, it produces all the characteristics of an upper retrusion, notwithstanding the normal occlusion of the buccal teeth.

This is fully shown in Fig. 213 which illustrates a case that belongs to Class I, as may be seen by the normal disto-mesal relations of the buccal occlusion at the begin-

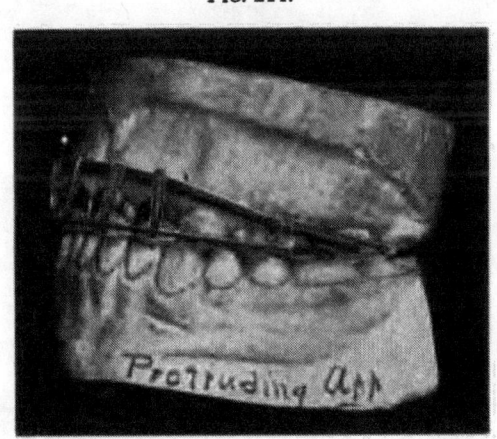

FIG. 214.

ning of the operation. It is presented in this Class, because of its similarity in facial characteristics and demands of treatment. It can be seen by the dental cast made before treatment that the cuspids are crowded out of alignment. But the bodily retruded position of the incisors (shown by their normal inclination) and lingual alveolar ridge plainly indicates that the inhibiting causes operated only in that locality.

The final facial and dental casts show most perfectly the action, effect, and possibilities of a bodily labial movement of the upper incisors, which in this case carried the entire incisive alveolar ridge forward with the movement of the roots, as shown in the enlarged occlusal aspects of the dentures. This case was begun in 1892, and when finished, the casts were mounted and exhibited at the August, 1893 meeting of the International Dental Congress. The profile photograph was taken two or three years afterwards.

Fig. 214 was made from a photo-print of the original apparatus mounted on a set of the finished dental casts. It will be noticed that the power arch-bow was flattened or "ribboned" over the incisive area.

One of the objects in the exhibition of this and other cases from the early practice of the author, is: It will fully disprove the somewhat prevalent assumption

PART VI. DENTO-FACIAL MALOCCLUSIONS

that the bodily movement of teeth arose with the introduction of the Angle "pin and tube" appliances of comparatively recent date. It will also show the practical application and common employment of the disto-mesial intermaxillary force, which was first published in connection with the publication of the birth of bodily movement.

Fig. 215 illustrates a case which no doubt started with the premature extraction or natural loss of the deciduous front teeth, followed with the retrusive malposition of the erupting incisors to such an extent that the mandible was forced to bite the

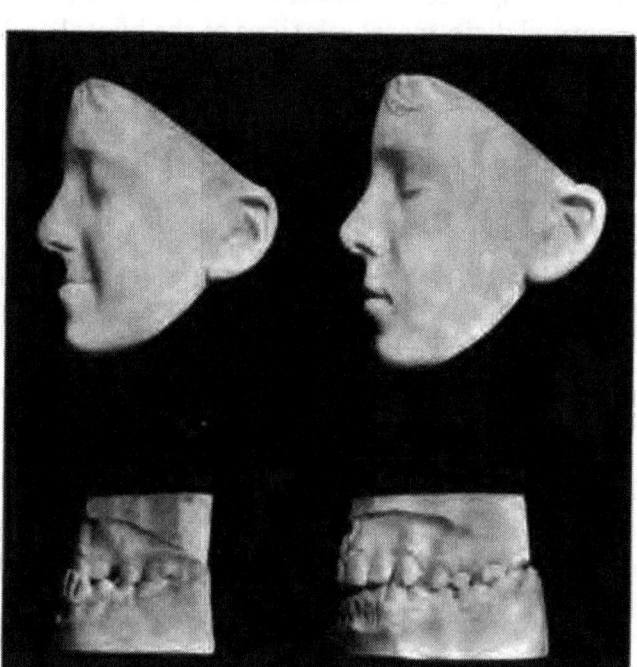

FIG. 215.

lower incisors in front of the uppers to obtain a masticating occlusion of the back teeth. This, in its developing stage caused a lack of development of the incisive or "intermaxillary" process, impacting the cuspids, and a protrusive malposition of the lower front teeth, resulting in a retrusion of the entire upper dento-facial area, and a slight prominence of the lower lip, as seen by the beginning facial cast.

Up to the time of the publication of the first edition of this work in 1908, it was the common teaching in certain schools of orthodontia that "the theory" of bodily movement of teeth was of no practical value. This was emphasized with the fantastic claim that when the crowns of the teeth were moved to place, the roots would soon follow, and the facial outlines would develop to their most harmonious possibilities. Notwithstanding the persistent efforts of the author to counteract this claim, it prevailed among a majority of orthodontists for over twenty years after the first introduction and repeated publication of the present accepted true principles. Through this influence, and the influence of that equally erroneous teaching that no teeth should ever be extracted, the advancement toward the higher principles and practice of orthodontia has been greatly retarded. But fortunately for the world, the brighter rifts of truth are now fast dissipating the clouds which so long prevented many people from enjoying the privileges of the most advanced principles of dento-facial orthopedia.

In every instance where an ordinary expansion arch-bow is employed for correcting the position of incisors that are much retruded, the apical ends of the roots and the incisive process are never moved forward, with the result that when the case is discharged, the crowns of the teeth are in decided labial inclination, and the facial depression is far from corrected. Where such an inclination movement of the incisor teeth in these cases has been accomplished for patients not older than twelve, and the incisal edges retained in that position, the developing influences of growth will perhaps in *some* cases *improve* the retruded position of the roots and alveolar process, but even that is always problematical; whereas, a bodily protruding movement of the roots of the upper incisors and the entire incisive process, with a perfect correction of facial contours *can be accomplished with ease and with perfect certainty* at any time between ten and eighteen years of age. At later ages, the roots of the upper incisors can always be moved bodily forward, and if retained in that position, the alveolar process will fill in around them, though the movement of the bone above, which supports the base and end of the nose, may not always respond to this protruding movement, in consequence of which the facial retrusion is not wholly corrected.

The reactive distal force upon the anchorages in the bodily labial movement of the front teeth demands the most stationary two or three-band anchorages. From this need arose the invaluable root-wise attachments which in recent years have characterized nearly all the bodily movement anchorages in the author's practice. It seems strange, therefore, that in a recent paper read by a prominent orthodontist before the American Society of Orthodontists, that these great principles are still ignored and the single clamp-band anchorages are advocated for all purposes.

It will be noticed in all of these cases that the incisors have been brought forward to a perfectly normal inclination, while in the final facial casts the upper lips and entire upper apical zones have been restored to normal contour, showing that something more than the alveolar process alone has been moved.

Figs. 216 and 217 are quite typical of this Division of malocclusion, both having been caused by inhibited development of the maxillæ from adenoids. It is a great pleasure to again present these two cases, because of the privilege it permits of quoting the words of that most highly respected and beloved brother dentist, the late Dr. Geo. H. Cushing, who referred these cases to the author and opened the discussion on the paper read before the Tri-State Dental meeting at Detroit in 1895. Coming from "Uncle George," who will always be revered for his ability and outspoken honesty of convictions, it reflects great honor upon this work to be able to republish his words founded upon intimate clinical observation of the progress and treatment in these two cases of dento-facial deformity.

"I am not aware that there can be much discussion upon a paper of this character. I do not know that there are any technical objections to the position that the paper assumes as to the possibility of moving the teeth **in phalanx bodily,** the sockets as well as the teeth. If there are any such objections, they must fall before the positive evidence of clinical observation. I think the paper shows conclusively that as Dr. Farrar remarked, 'this demonstrates an era of advance in orthopedic

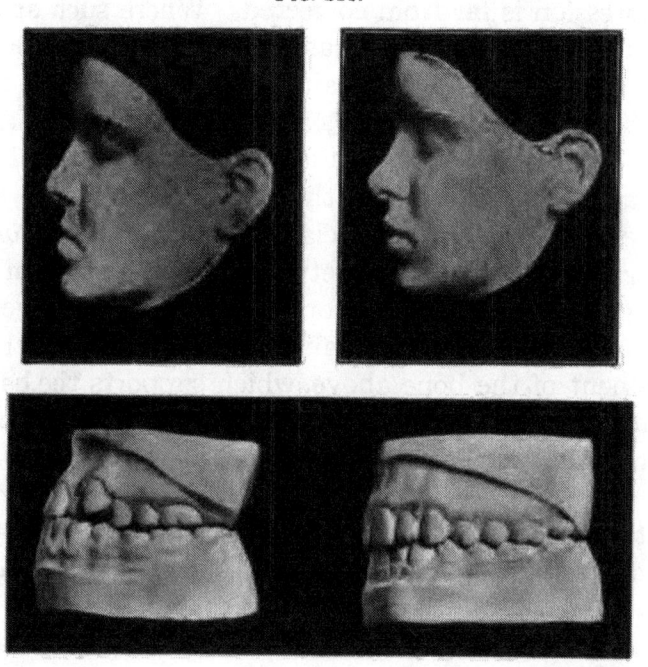

Fig. 216.

surgery.' I think we are most indebted to Dr. Case for an intelligent study of the mechanical principles which govern the movements of the teeth by applied force, in connection with the fact which he has demonstrated, of the possibility of moving the teeth and the processes together. You have seen what he has accomplished, and these models and drawings speak more eloquently than any language can express.

"Two of these cases I have seen under treatment from the first. I cannot begin to tell you the extent of the improvement in the facial expression of the young lady illustrated with the plaster casts (Fig. 216).* The maxillary bone and the process were so receded that there were depressions each side of the median line so deep that you could lay your finger in them. These are now very nearly two-

---

*The case which Dr. Cushing first called attention to is that of a girl about sixteen years of age. The illustration shows the case only partially completed.

thirds obliterated, I should think, and though this mask shows a wonderful improvement, it does not show fully the great change which has been effected, though he has told you that this was one of the cases so difficult to manage because of the rapid absorption of the process from the pressure of the roots. I think he hopes in time to entirely obliterate the deep depression under the alæ of the nose. From my observation, so far as the case has progressed, I have no doubt that he will succeed.

"Of the other case (Fig. 217), I may say that these casts do not begin to show the improvement that has taken place in the short time in which the patient has been under treatment. The boy presented a very disagreeable aspect, as you see

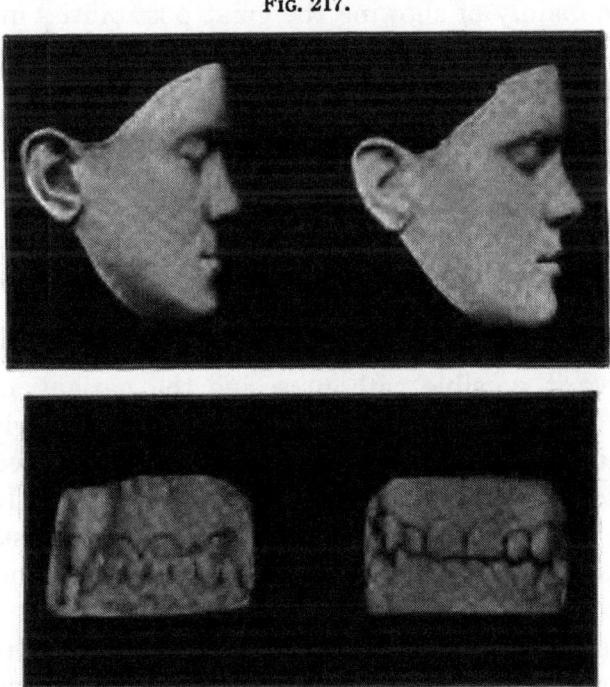

FIG. 217.

here. There is one feature of the case which the author of the paper did not refer to. I do not know whether it passed his mind or not, but it is a feature which is very striking. The boy had a habit of dropping his mouth open continually. He does not do this at all now. I do not know why the movement of these teeth and the contouring of the face by this application of force should have produced that change, but it is a fact that it has. The boy now keeps his mouth closed as other people do. With his chin apparently protruding, owing to the lack of development of the superior maxillary, and the mouth open all the while, you may imagine how very unpleasantly he must have presented himself to his friends. He is now a pretty respectable looking boy, and he was very far from that when he first went into Dr. Case's hands."

Notwithstanding the perfect result shown in this case and the permanency of its retention, which was perfectly sustained with a bridge denture constructed by Dr. Cushing, when the patient was sixteen years of age, the mandible commenced to develop unusual proportions, which at nineteen, had carried the occlusion of the lower labial teeth again far in front of the uppers. When this unexpected movement commenced, the upper contouring apparatus was again attached, with its auxiliary the intermaxillary force, with the hope that an additional forward movement of the upper teeth with a retruding movement of the lowers would correct the condition, but this was soon found impossible, because of the pronounced prognathism which the mandible was assuming. This peculiarity of the forces of heredity assuming sway in the later years of adolescence, is mentioned at greater length in other chapters.

For the purpose mainly of showing the great possibilities in bodily movements of teeth under favorable conditions of health, with the application and control of the various forces, the author has decided at the last moment to publish in this work a brief history of a case in which the movement has been so great and yet free from all unhealthful disturbances of the teeth, that one can hardly believe it possible. This case was commenced about seven years ago at the age of ten years, and has since been treated in interrupted stages according to the demands of physiologic movement, and with the view of stimulating to the greatest extent a revivification of inhibited growth development.

As the extent of bodily movement in this case has been so great that few would be willing to believe it possible without seeing the patient and without having an opportunity to examine the plaster models from the beginning of the work through the different stages of development, the author invited all the orthodontists of Chicago and surroundings to a clinic on February 3, 1921, at which time this case was fully presented. Besides the fourteen orthodontists who were present on that occasion, a number of prominent Chicago dentists have been in touch, more or less, with this case during its treatment.

In Fig. 217½ is shown the illustrations of the facial and dental plaster casts made at the beginning of the operation, and again shortly before the above clinic. One cannot appreciate the perfection of this case without meeting the patient, now a beautiful young lady about eighteen years of age, whose natural facial endowments and perfect form and color of teeth, gave a most favorable foundation upon which to build the present successful result.

In viewing the three stages of the movement shown in the palatal views, please note in the beginning model of the upper denture (a) at the left, the distances from the lateral incisors to the first premolars; then to the second premolars; and finally, to the first molars; and then compare this to the final model of the upper at the right (c) which contains the same teeth, and in addition, the cuspids.

At the beginning of the operation, the actual distance, according to the models, between the upper left lateral and first permanent molar in May, 1914, was ⅝ of an inch, and in December, 1920, it was 1½ inches, showing the remarkable distance of bodily separating movement of ⅞ of an inch between these teeth and

CHAPTER XLIII. DIVISION 2. CLASS III.

without the slightest inclination or tipping movement. On the right side, the movement was about the same, but not completed at that time. And through the whole operation the teeth and gums have remained in a perfectly healthy normal condition.

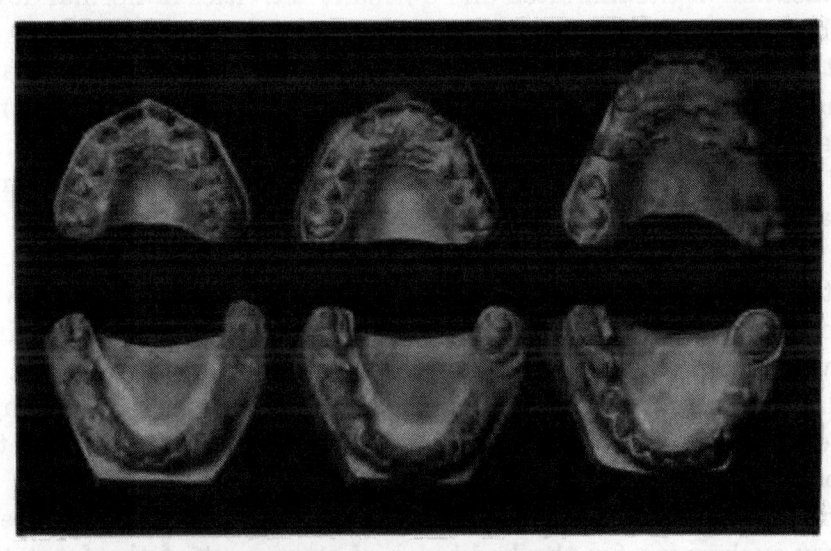

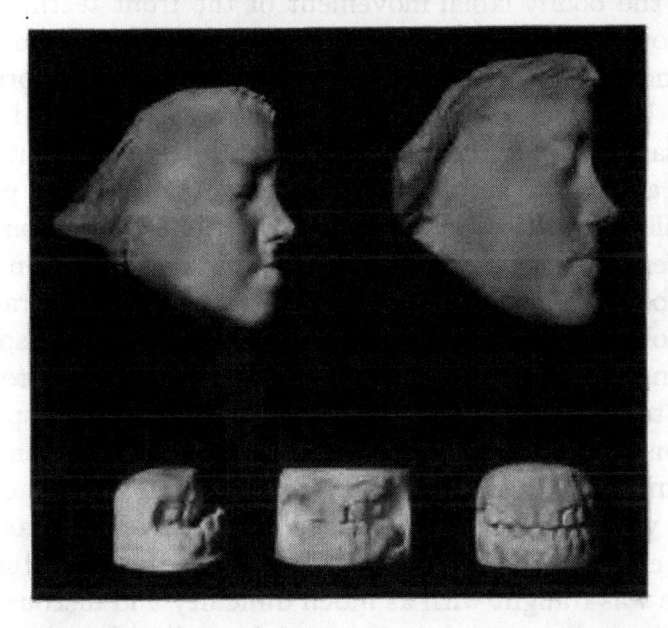

FIG. 217½.

a   b   c

d

The above illustration was made by pressing modeling compound against the labio-buccal surfaces of the teeth while the jaws were closed, and shows the appearance of the left side with the retaining bridge denture in place at the time of the clinic. The upper teeth back of the cuspid are: (1) the artificial premolar, (2) the first premolar, (3) the artificial molar, (4) the second premolar, and (5) the first molar.

The facial casts were made at ten and seventeen years of age. The front occlusal models were made from modeling compound impressions pressed against the front teeth with the dentures in masticating occlusion.

It is not assumed that this extraordinary movement consisted wholly in a bodily labial movement of the upper front teeth, although every effort was employed to prevent a distal movement of the back teeth by locking the three buccal teeth on each side in stationary anchorages carrying power root-wise attachments, in connection with the constant application of intermaxillary force. Nor is it claimed that the extent of this movement was wholly mechanical, but rather one which was greatly aided by the extensively restored growth of the maxilla through the stimulated revivification of the inhibited and dormant activities of normal development. It is possible that a slight distal movement of the anchorage teeth may have caused a retardation in the eruption of the second molars, which only now are about to come through the gums—shown by radiographs. This sluggish eruptive movement, however, has been characteristic of the entire case from the beginning, and no doubt was caused by the same forces that inhibited the development of the maxilla and the germination of six teeth.

At the time of the clinic, the patient was wearing the usual six-band labial retainer with lingual spring bars locked in molar anchorages that are always placed to retain bodily movements of the front teeth. On the left side, the spring bar was connected with the permanent retaining-bridge denture which supplied the spaces with porcelain teeth (d). On the right side, the patient was still wearing an appliance for the bodily mesial movement of the first premolar, the same as that which was worn on the left side in spacing for the artificial teeth.

As previously mentioned, all the upper buccal teeth on each side were employed for stationary anchorages for the bodily labial movement of the front teeth. But toward the latter part of the operation, the first premolars were cut loose from the anchorages, to place them in more proper positions for the ultimate retaining-bridge dentures. In this, as in other bodily movements, in order to keep the teeth in an upright position, it was necessary to apply the force upon root-wise attachments.

This case at ten years of age was a very peculiar one and presented a prospect of almost insurmountable difficulties in the decided inhibited development of the maxilla; the retarded eruption of the permanent teeth; no molars on the lower except what seemed to be the second permanent molars, which recent radiographs show to be the only molars on the lower; no masticating occlusion to speak of; and the lower incisors closing nearly a half-inch in front of the uppers. Note the beginning stage of the lower teeth and the wide abnormal interproximate spaces which had arisen without cause and with no possible occlusion except upon the prematurely erupted second molars. Even after the premolars and cuspids commenced to erupt, their growth was so slow and apparently inhibited with unnatural spacing of the teeth, that the extrusive force to correct the decided infra-occlusion of the buccal teeth in this case was fraught with as much difficulty and discouragement as any part of the operation. Because of these unusual peculiarities, the main object has been to correct the facial deformity by placing the front teeth and their alveolar processes in perfect position so as to present a fine appearance, and to do the best that could be done with the back teeth to place them in position for bridge dentures, to secure proper masticating occlusion.

In all cases of this Class, the intermaxillary force is invariably employed as an indispensable adjunct to support the stability of the upper anchorages. A regular six-band labial retaining appliance with intermaxillary hook attachments forms an admirably stable anchorage for this force, the application of which no doubt prevented the lower teeth from being carried forward in the growth of the mandible, so that now they are in esthetic relation to the chin with the production of that very desirable labio-mental curve. Other than this, no attempt has been made to fully regulate the lower denture, because the spacing of the teeth could be easily accomplished at any time when it seemed desirable to make a lower artificial denture. The main object in this case has been to adjust the upper and lower molar and premolar occlusion to the best advantage for subsequent dentures.

CHAPTER XLIV

DIVISION 3, CLASS III

UPPER RETRUSION WITH PROTRUSION OF LOWER DENTURE

FIG. 218.

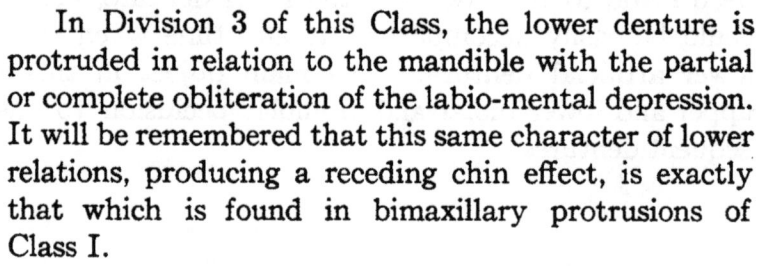

In Division 3 of this Class, the lower denture is protruded in relation to the mandible with the partial or complete obliteration of the labio-mental depression. It will be remembered that this same character of lower relations, producing a receding chin effect, is exactly that which is found in bimaxillary protrusions of Class I.

There is really no local cause that can produce a protrusion of the lower denture in relation to the mandible, which commonly occurs with the upper denture in relation to the maxilla—frequently from local causes explained elsewhere; therefore, this particular character of the lower must always arise from heredity, though the retruded upper—if it *is* retruded—may arise from other causes.

When the cause of "heredity" is mentioned, it is hoped that the student from the previous teaching will understand that it does not necessarily mean a direct inheritance of that particular condition from a parent, which of course is possible; nor does it necessarily mean the direct inheritance of types which are inharmonious when combined in the offspring, because the term heredity applies to a law of generation which is expressed in a variety of ways, as has been fully outlined in chapters relative to the etiology of malocclusion.

TREATMENT

If the malocclusion is slight in this Division, and caused partly by the retruded upper, for patients younger than twelve or fourteen years of age, the dentures should be placed in normal occlusion with the reciprocal action of the intermaxillary force, the student bearing in mind that the natural growth development of the mandible and other bones of the physiognomy is constantly diminishing childhood's protruding disharmonies of the teeth.

In a pronounced protrusion of the lower denture in relation to the mandible and dento-facial harmony, as in pronounced upper protrusions, if it can be seen

CHAPTER XLIV. DIVISION 3. CLASS III

that it has arisen from a marked hereditary strain, the extraction of the first lower premolars is advisable, to be followed with the same rules of treatment as for protruded uppers. The regulation of the upper should be guided by the character and degree of retrusion, while a perfect disto-mesial and bucco-lingual interdigitation of buccal cusps goes without saying.

The quite remarkable improvement to the facial outlines in these cases by the protrusive movement of the upper and the retrusive movement of the lower, is shown by the profile casts of the finished cases. This is no more than any orthodontist may easily obtain in all cases by a scientific application of mechanical force, accompanied with a rational acceptance of necessities, and an appreciation of the highest attainments in facial as well as dental art.

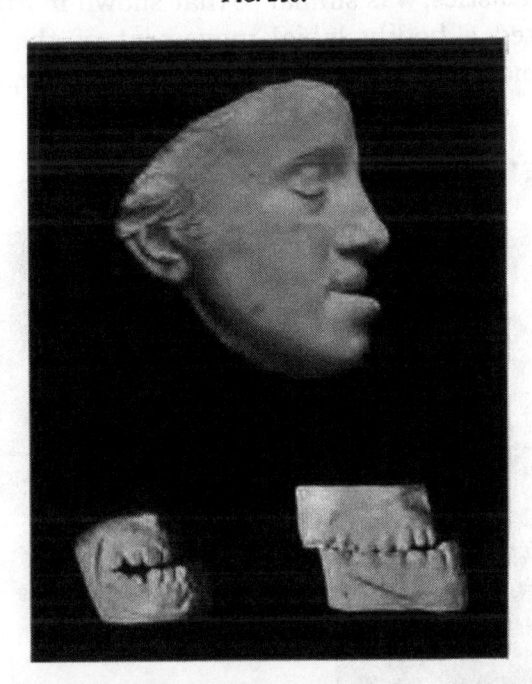

FIG. 219.

Fig. 219 represents a case which has been especially chosen from many of this Division of malocclusion in the author's practice, to illustrate the practical applicability of the foregoing statement. It was made from the facial and dental casts of a woman twenty-four years of age, and represents one of the most pronounced and difficult cases of this type which the author has ever been called upon to treat. Every feature of the physiognomy outside the dento-facial area was perfect, which in connection with the dark brown hair, beautiful eyes, and smooth olive complexion, gave one the greatest desire to correct the deformed area caused by the malocclusion. The occlusion of the teeth was so imperfect that a healthful mastication of food was impossible. The main object of treatment, however, was to get rid of the facial deformity (which she had borne for so many years, not knowing that any correction was possible).

In order to accomplish this, the case was started by extracting the first lower premolar on the right, and a decayed lower molar on the left. The lower apparatus for the right side is shown in Fig. 220, that on the left side being similar. The three molar-band stationary anchorage with buccal and lingual root-wise attachments for the traction bars to the cuspid, was constructed to offer the greatest possible stationary stability so that all the space of the extracted premolar could be utilized in the bodily distal movement of the cuspid. But even with that, it was found necessary later to extract the second premolar. The contour apparatus on the upper, reinforced with the disto-mesial intermaxillary elastics, was similar to that shown in Fig. 210, Chapter XLII. This apparatus effected a bodily labial movement of the incisors and a mesial movement of the cuspids and first premolars sufficient to open spaces between the

FIG. 220.

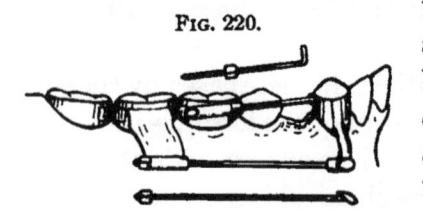

FIG. 221.

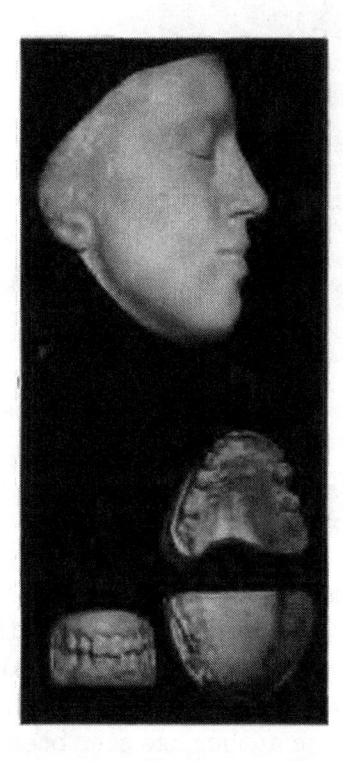

premolars on each side for the insertion of artificial teeth, the advantages of which have been described. The upper anchorages also aided in retruding the lower front teeth. The final result is shown in Fig. 221.

Fig. 222 was made from the facial and dental casts of a miss at eleven and thirteen years of age, which illustrates on the left the effect of a combination of the local cause of adenoids, producing a retruded upper; with that of heredity, producing a protruded lower denture in relation to a normal mandible. The decided

CHAPTER XLIV. DIVISION 3. CLASS III 315

protruded position of the lower front teeth in relation to the upper gave one the impression that the mandible was held forward of the normal masticating position. The late Dr. Chas. Butler, who saw this case in its early stages, believed this to be a fact, until in his effort to make her close her lower jaw further back, she suddenly forced it in the usual functional distance forward of this.

FIG. 222.

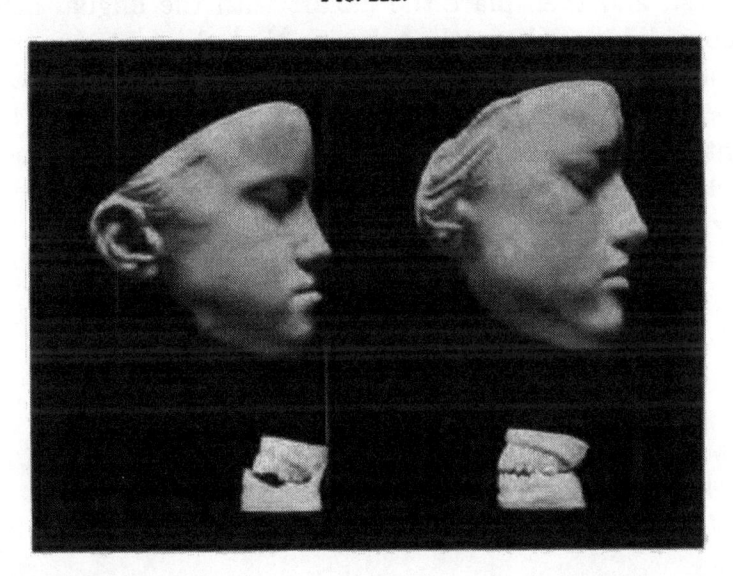

When this case presented for treatment, the deciduous lower cuspids and molars had been removed, leaving on the lower jaw only the fully erupted incisors and first permanent molars with the permanent cuspids just commencing to prick through the gums. Fig. 223 partially illustrates the lower apparatus that was employed in this case, in addition to the apparatus on the upper for bodily labial movement of the incisors. It illustrates the principle of "sustained anchorages" which is fully defined and illustrated in Chapter XV. This was demanded because of the necessity of reinforcing the stability of single molar anchorages on each side. The lingual arch-bow resting in the incisor hooks easily glides into the long-bearing tubes with firmly sustained attachments to heavy molar bands. The labial arch-bow No. 22 or 23 is sustained on the incisors by open tube attachments (not shown by the engraver). It can be seen that the lingual force exerted by this bow upon the incisors cannot possibly tip the molars forward or rotate them on account of the long-bearing lingual tubes, so long as the bands remain firmly cemented to the teeth; consequently, if the molars move at all it must be a bodily movement, which means that their stationary anchorage stability is greatly increased. The more modern root-wise buccal an-

FIG. 223.

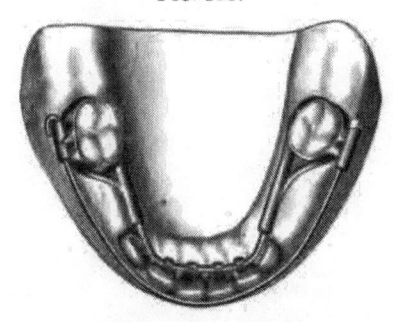

chorage tubes for the retruding arch-bow increases the mechanical advantage by reducing the strain of the band attachments to the molars, as the force would then be exerted nearer the center of resistance to root movements.

It will be seen that the reaction of the sustaining power of the lingual arch-bow on the molars is exerted as an intrusive force upon the incisors, which in this case is very desirable. In the preliminary assembling of this apparatus, place the incisor bands first, and then place the molars with the lingual bow in the tubes. See that the bow glides easily in the tubes so that the retrusive movement of the incisors with the intermaxillary force and labial traction bow is not obstructed.

In connection with the retrusive force of the arch-bow upon the incisors, the disto-mesial intermaxillary force is an important auxiliary. The intermaxillary hooks for the elastics—not shown in the engraving—can always be easily attached to an arch-bow, as explained in the chapter on "technics."

CHAPTER XLV

DIVISION 4, CLASS III

RETRUSION OF THE UPPER DENTURE WITH PROGNATHIC MANDIBLE, COMMONLY ACCOMPANIED WITH OPEN-BITE MALOCCLUSION

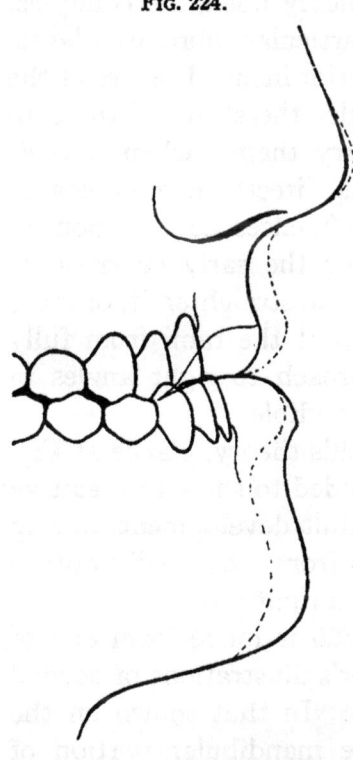

FIG. 224.

In a large proportion of cases which are denominated prognathic mandibles, the chin is in perfect esthetic relation to the main features of the physiognomy, the visual error being due to the immediate relations of a pronounced retruded upper. Real prognathic mandibles, however, arising purely from heredity and rarely from local causes are not uncommon. Prognathic mandibles in connection with normal uppers, and with retruded uppers, may arise from heredity, and be further emphasized by local causes. The latter is well illustrated in Fig. 205, Chapter XL.

The local cause which produces prognathism of the mandible is the same as that which produces open-bite malocclusion, and which can be definitely traced to the early long continued habit of mouth-breathing, which may arise from any abnormal interference with the natural freedom of the nasal air passages, originating mostly from adenoids and continued through the period in which these abnormal growths exert their peculiar local and systemic action.

As the kind of open-bite malocclusion which arises from this cause is almost invariably associated with prognathism of the mandible, it has been deemed advisable, for teaching purposes, to describe this malformation in detail as one of the important characteristics of this Division. The practical treatment of other forms of open-bite malocclusion is fully described under Type G, Division 1, Class I.

In papers read before the Odontological Society of Chicago, in 1894, the American Institute of Dental Pedagogics in 1905, and the National Dental Association in 1917, the author expressed in substance the following summary in regard to the *modus operandi* of this cause: The production of open-bite malocclusion from early mouth-breathing is due to long continued mechanical forces of the ligaments and muscles, mostly during sleep, applied to the developing mandible of childhood at a time when the quality of the bone renders it peculiarly susceptible of being easily deflected from the form of its natural growth.

When the jaws are widely apart during the long sleeping hours of childhood, the mandible under the strain of the various forces is similar to a lever of the second kind. The condyles resting in their sockets are the fulcrum, the power which forces and holds the jaws open is the hyoid muscles attached to the mandible beneath the chin, and the weight acting in the other direction is the masseter and internal pterygoids attached at the angles of the rami. Again, when the jaws are widely open, the condyles, with the intervening interarticular fibro cartilages, are pressed against the posterior inclined planes of the articular eminences and, under the strain of the capsular ligaments, tend to carry them back into their sockets with a force that is directly communicated to the rami. Both these influences acting upon an undeveloped mandible during the early years of its immaturity in form, will tend to straighten it, or more correctly speaking, will prevent the rami from fully assuming their natural approach to right angles in relation to the body of the mandible.

Fig. 225.

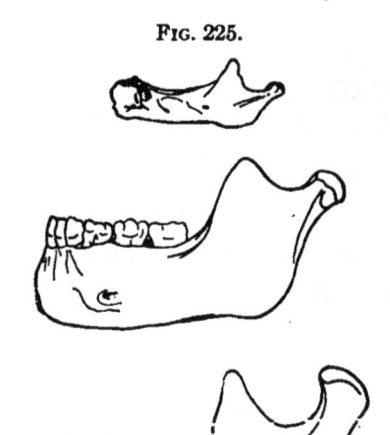

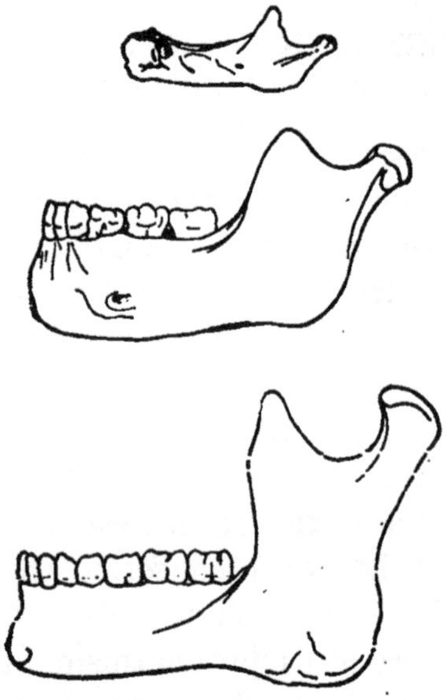

To more fully illustrate this theory, glance at Fig. 225, which was taken from Gray's Anatomy, and is intended to show the relative size and shape of the mandible at birth, puberty, and adult development, during which time the relation of the rami to the body changes from a decidedly obtuse to nearly a right angle.

Fig. 226.

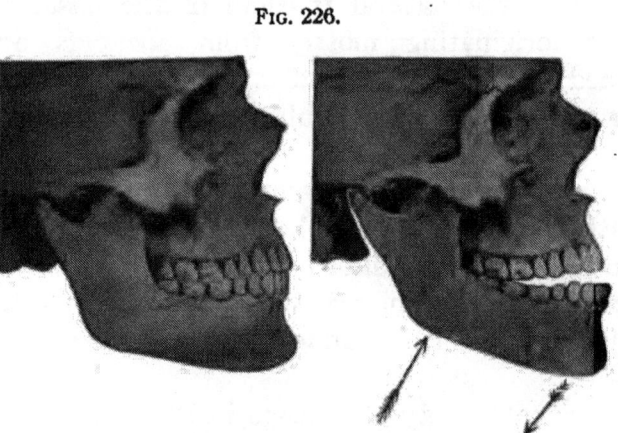

Fig. 226 is made from one of Dr. Cryer's illustrations of normal occlusion. In that shown on the right, the mandibular portion of the picture was removed, cut at the angle, and replaced in the position it might assume during childhood under slight continued force exerted in the direction of the arrows by the muscles while holding the jaws wide apart.

In many cases of open-bite malocclusion caused by early continued mouth-breathing, the relations of the rami and body may be seen, from a profile view of the face, to stand at a more obtuse angle than is normal, and with the frequent production of prognathism; both of which are well shown in Fig. 227, which illustrates four cases in practice before

CHAPTER XLV. DIVISION 4. CLASS III

Fig. 227.

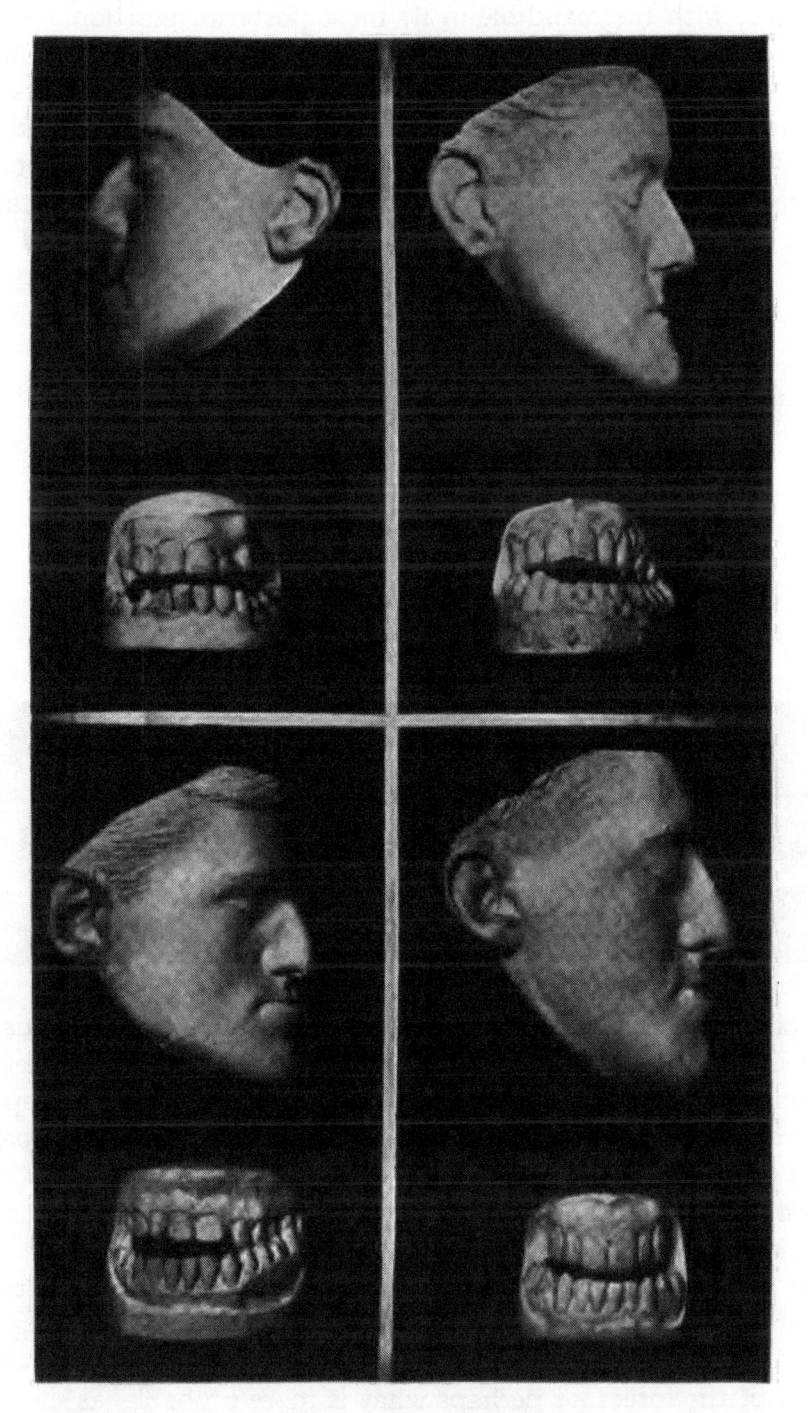

treatment. The dental models shown below the facial casts were made from impressions taken in the usual manner by pressing modeling-compound against the front teeth, with the mandible in its most posterior position. When one considers the mechanism of the cause, it will be seen that this straightening of the mandible, while not inhibiting its growth in other dimensions, increases the distance from the point of the chin to the condyle, with a protruding movement of the body of the mandible and its contained lower denture. Again, when one remembers that the prime cause of obstructed nasal breathing and its resultant open-bite malocclusion is adenoids, which in themselves are the prime cause of inhibited de-

FIG. 228.

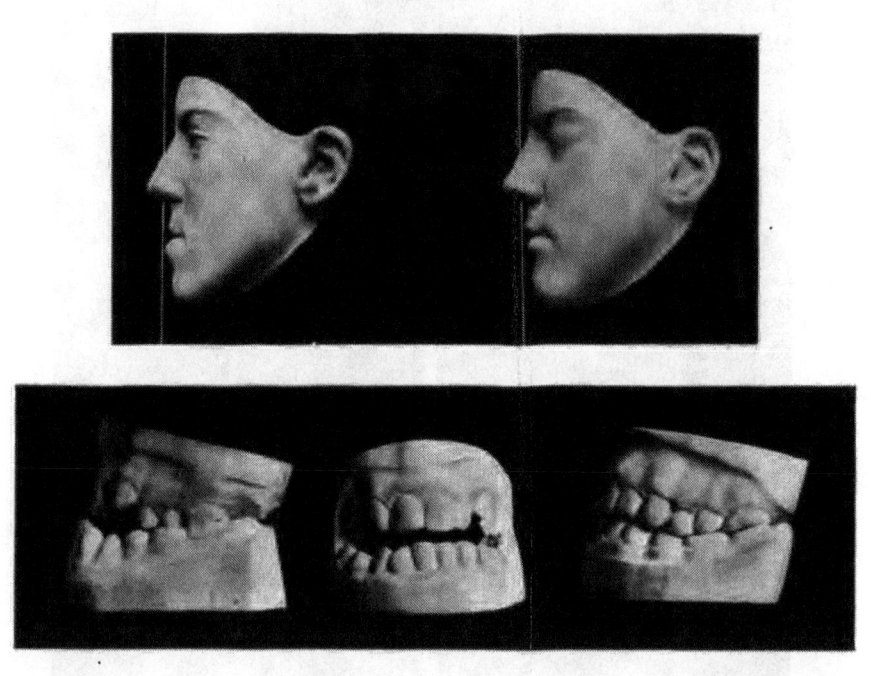

velopment of the maxilla, and which result in the common upper retrusions, one can then appreciate why it is that open-bite malocclusions are so frequently found in Class III, and also why, in so many of these cases, the mandible appears to be so decidedly prognathic in relation to the upper, but which no doubt is partly due to a visual effect in comparing the immediate relations of even a moderately protruded lower with a decidedly retruded upper—the one enhancing in appearance the disharmony of the other.

In three of these cases, as in many others of the same pronounced character, the mandible is bent appreciably to one side, as shown by comparing the relations of the upper and lower front teeth. This condition may be due to an unevenness in the action of the forces, or perhaps what is more probable, as mentioned in the chapter on Lateral Malocclusion, it arises when the mother, either from thoughtlessness or possible necessity, causes the babe to lie upon one side far more than upon the other, which in itself results at times in a permanent bending of the mandible to the opposite side. See Lateral Malocclusion, Chapter XXVII.

For general treatment of open-bite malocclusion, see Chapter XXVIII, Division 1, Class I.

Fig. 228 illustrates a pronounced typical case of this Division, of a girl thirteen years of age, which the author is pleased to present, because it was the very first case in orthodontia in which a bodily protrusive movement of the front teeth was ever attempted. It was the first case also which combined as an auxiliary the disto-mesial intermaxillary force. It was first published in a paper read before the Chicago Dental Society, February 2, 1893, and illustrated with plaster facial and dental casts, as shown, and the original apparatus mounted on the models of the case and set up on an articulator to show the reciprocal action of the intermaxillary elastics in reinforcing the upper anchorages and retruding the lower front teeth. It was later presented with other cases at the International Dental Congress, August, 1893, in which the same character of forces had been employed.

The retruded upper was caused principally through the inhibited development of the maxilla which contracted the entire upper arch with the production of a high and narrow dome, so contracted indeed, that the patient was often obliged to dislodge food from it with her finger. The injudicious extraction of a lateral incisor, by her home dentist, to permit the right upper cuspid to erupt, increased the difficulties of correcting the upper retrusion.

The open-bite malocclusion due to long continued early mouth-breathing, which straightened the form of the mandible, was caused by the same adenoid growths whose influence contracted and retruded the upper.

The fact that the chin in the finished facial cast is not protruded, while in the beginning facial cast the lower lip is quite decidedly protruded in relation to the chin, indicates that the case in this particular was similar to those in Division 3 of this Class. Again, the contracted and retruded upper resulting from local causes, is similar in this particular to Division 2 of this Class.

Attention is called to these fine points of dento-facial relations for the purpose of training the minds of students in the principles of diagnosis.

Fig. 229 illustrates an extreme type of this Division, and the different stages of correction. It will be seen that the required bodily movement of the upper front teeth to correct the facial outlines, opened spaces for the insertion of one artificial tooth on the right side and two on the left. The prosthodontia work completing the case, as shown by the dental casts on the right, was performed by Dr. Hart J. Goslee.

One of the surprising conditions of this case when it presented for treatment, was an artificial extra right lower lateral attached to a slipper crown on the cuspid, which is not distinctly shown by the picture. This peculiarity is worthy of mention at this time, because it is one of the many instances which proves what has been mentioned elsewhere, i. e., that the mandible and other bones which characterize

322   PART VI. DENTO-FACIAL MALOCCLUSIONS

the human physiognomy do not always show inherited disharmonies of size and form in relation to adjoining bones, until sometime after the beginning of adolescence. Nor are pronounced inherited peculiarities and characteristics which pertain to the entire body, indicated at times in a slight degree, until after thirteen or fourteen years of age.

The rapid growth of the mandible, in this case, in response to the forces of heredity after the eruption of nearly all the teeth, opened spaces between the front teeth, notwithstanding their decided lingual inclination. The family dentist who had the case in charge, knowing of no other way to close these spaces, inserted

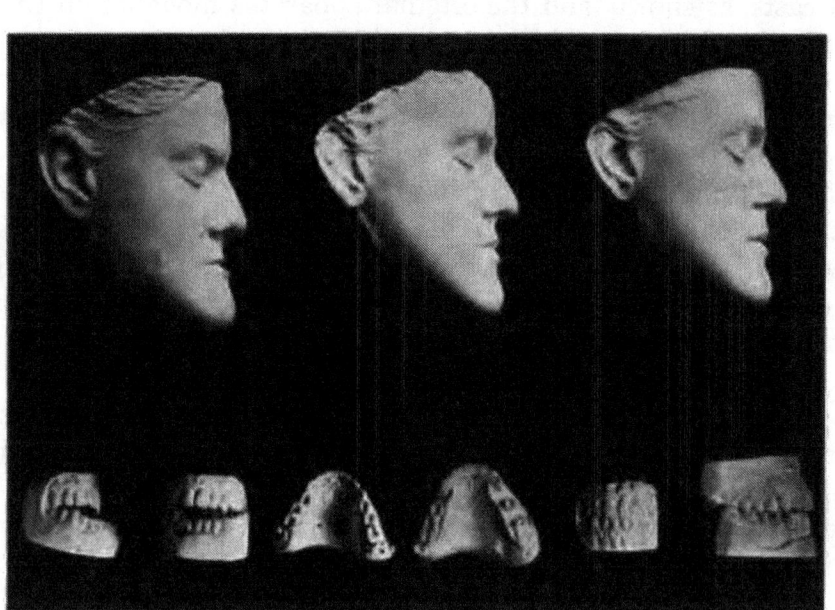

FIG. 229.

the artificial tooth. The removal of this tooth permitted a lingual movement of the roots of the incisor teeth, placing them in a more upright position. At the same time, the extruding movement, with the occipital force, corrected the open-bite malocclusion.

The two following cases, which are quite typical of this Division, were presented with a paper read before the National Dental Association in 1917, mainly to show the possible rapidity of an extrusive bodily movement, with the correction of open-bite malocclusion for patients beyond the age of adolescence. The following is from the published proceedings of that meeting:

"Fig. 230 shows the casts of a young man twenty-one years of age for whom the operation for correction was commenced, May, 1910, and ended, as shown, May, 1911. The mandible in this case was bent to the right carrying its left body and buccal teeth far forward of their normal position, which in connection with the retruded upper, placed the lower left buccal teeth, in a closure of the jaws, fully the width of two premolars in mesial malrelation to the uppers; while on the right side, the disto-mesial malrelation was hardly the width of a single premolar. The early loss of the first lower molar on the right side, however, had permitted the second and third molars to drift forward and thus diminish to that extent the original occlusal malrelations of these teeth. On the upper left side, the loss of the

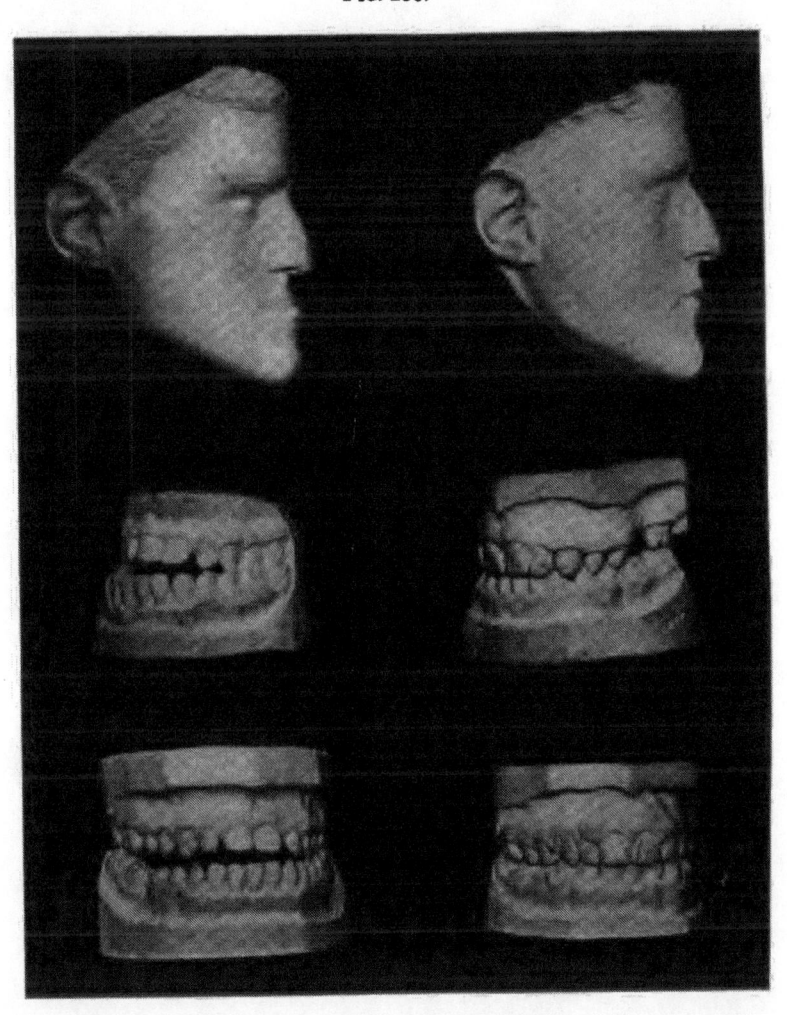

FIG. 230.

crown of the first molar allowed the third molar to close into this space, and thus decrease to that extent the original open-bite.

"The treatment consisted first in the extraction of the first left lower molar, the latter being chosen in this case because it contained a large amalgam filling, and probably a devitalized pulp. This was followed with a bodily retruding movement of the lower premolar and labial teeth, more upon the left side than on the right, and with the usual care, with special apparatus, to close the buccal spaces by a bodily disto-mesial movement. Nothing is so conducive to irritation as in-

324 PART VI. DENTO-FACIAL MALOCCLUSIONS

verted V-shaped spaces between buccal teeth, following the extraction of molars or premolars, or attempts at extensive regulation with single molar anchorages permitting inclination movement, and destruction of perfect masticating occlusion. This movement of the lower, in connection with the upper bodily labial movement, and the artificial closure of the upper first molar space, resulted in quite a perfect

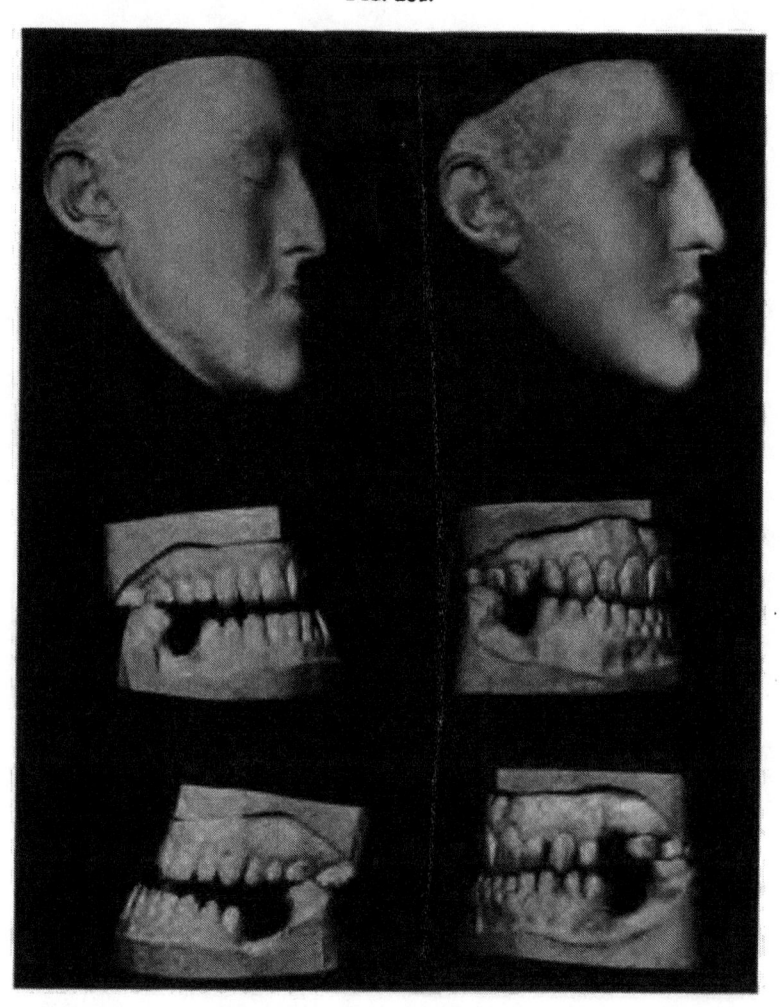

FIG. 231.

masticating occlusion, and a remarkable improvement in the physiognomy, which the final plaster cast inadequately portrays.

"In Fig. 231 is shown the plaster casts of a man twenty-four years of age, a graduate of the University of Michigan, who has recently finished a special postgraduate course at the University of Chicago, and has now entered the law department of that school. He is six feet tall, of robust figure and apparent rugged health. This perfect mental and physical condition is mentioned, because it is remarkable in view of the fact that early untreated adenoids and long continued mouth-breathing inhibited the development of the maxilla and caused a malformation of the mandible and an open-bite malocclusion, which permitted a very imperfect masticating closure upon only the disto-occlusal borders of the second lower molars, so that during all his life from early childhood he had hardly been able to approach the mastication of food.

"The treatment in this case was commenced October 4, 1916—the casts of which are shown on the left. Those on the right were made about one year later when the correction was about two-thirds completed. They were made at that time to aid in the illustration of a paper read before the October, 1917, meeting of the National Dental Society. The principal treatment consisted in a bodily labial movement of the upper front teeth, and a retrusive and extrusive movement of the lower labial teeth and premolars.

"The difficulties on the lower were increased by the loss of the first permanent molars which were extracted at about twelve years of age. This permitted the second molars to tip forward to a decided mesial inclination. The treatment here consisted in shifting the back teeth to proper occlusal relations, and then, by grinding their occluding surfaces, to partially close the open-bite. The occluding position of the original dentures, shown on the left, was placed by Dr. Hart J. Goslee in exact duplication of the beginning labial bite model.

"The entire distal, lingual, and extrusive movement of the lower was accomplished with the intermaxillary and occipital forces. The case was finished with a perfect interdigitating occlusion of the premolars, and with the first molar spaces supplied with artificial teeth, enabling him for the first time in his life to perfectly masticate his food.

"About two weeks before the meeting, the apparatus was removed and the impressions taken for the dental and facial casts shown on the right. He is now wearing a six-band retainer on the lower front teeth which carries the intermaxillary hooks for retaining elastics to the upper, as is usual in such cases."

It is a great pleasure to publish in this connection the following words of Dr. Goslee, who discussed this paper, and who was intimately in touch with the treatment of these and other almost unbelievable corrections in the author's practice.

Dr. Hart J. Goslee, Chicago: "I have no desire to take up your time at this late hour, but I would be very remiss if I did not take occasion to say to the members of this Section that I have seen all these cases. I do not say this to imply in any way that Dr. Case's word is not sufficient, but I have been very closely associated with Dr. Case in much of his work, and wish to add my testimony as to his success in treating these difficult cases of malocclusion. I have been watching his work for twenty years and the results that he has produced in one year in some of these cases are wonderful, indeed they are nothing less than marvelous. And particularly is this true of the case of the young man to which he has referred so extensively, and which case I have observed closely since the beginning."

PART VII

Practical Treatment of Unclassified Malocclusions

UNCLASSIFIED MALOCCLUSIONS

TABLE OF CHARACTERS

INFRA AND SUPRA-OCCLUSIONS
CROWDED MALALIGNMENTS
MALTURNED TEETH
NARROW AND WIDE ARCHES
ABNORMAL INTERPROXIMATE SPACES
IMPACTED TEETH AND THEIR TREATMENT

UNCLASSIFIED MALOCCLUSIONS

FOREWORD

There are certain distinctive characters of irregularity of the teeth all of which arise from local causes, and therefore will be found in each one of the three classes of buccal occlusion, often dominating the character with which they are found. For this reason they cannot be regarded as divisions or types peculiar to any one class.

For purposes of teaching, however, certain dento-facial characters which belong to this group of locally caused malpositions are placed and described under Division 1 of Class I, where they may be intelligently compared with other dento-facial malocclusions with which they frequently become identified.

By referring to the "Table of Characters" on the opposite page, it will be seen that each one of the characters which compose the group now under consideration, is susceptible of assuming a variety of malpositions which may decidedly differ in degree and demands of treatment.

In order to give the student a clear understanding of the most effective methods which are employed for their correction, the most common malpositions of each character are grouped and treated under their respective heads. And though illustrated and described as applicable to only this irregularity, the same methods and principles of force may be employed wherever these malpositions arise in connection with other characters, or in different classes of malocclusion.

The drawings are designed to conspicuously show: first, the malposition of the character under consideration, and every necessary view of the apparatus in position on the teeth, and with special parts in detail; second, the apparatus disassembled from the teeth and shown in its various parts, the whole calculated to render every aid for its correct construction. With this mainly in view, there has been no attempt at anatomic or artistic effect, the principal object being to distinctly show the character of the irregularity and the appliances, or the complete apparatus which the author has successfully used in his practice for its correction.

Accompanying the illustrations will be found a concise description of the character of the irregularity treated, the movement demanded for its correction, the apparatus in detail, with the gauge sizes of its several parts, the special force it is calculated to exert, methods of construction, assembling, adjustment, etc.

CHAPTER XLVI

INFRA AND SUPRA-OCCLUSION

When one or more teeth are above or below the normal occlusal plane, they are in the malposition of **Infra** or **Supra-occlusion**. If, however, one or the other of these conditions involves all the front teeth, they are then in the malposition of **open-bite,** or **close-bite malocclusion.**

For all the ordinary cases of infra or supra-occlusion of one or more teeth, for patients under twelve or fourteen years of age, as in all cases of simple malalignments and malturned teeth, the "Midget Apparatus," described in Chapter XX, is now almost solely employed by the author.

INFRA-OCCLUSION OF CUSPIDS

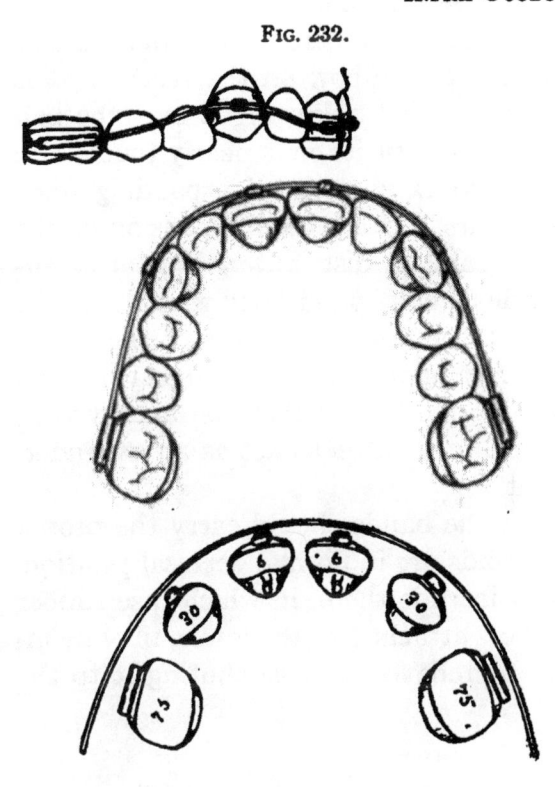

FIG. 232.

The apparatus shown in Fig. 232 is intended for the correction of a very common form of irregularity which may be considered the simplest of that most common malposition which is characterized by **maleruption of the cuspids.** It is placed in this group because a simple resilient alignment bow No. 23, as shown, will commonly correct it with little attention. The effort of nature to erupt crowded cuspids, will at times extrude the centrals. Should all of the incisors demand a slight labial movement to enlarge the arch and give more room for the cuspids, the laterals can also be banded with open-tube, or small hook attachments. If this condition is somewhat marked, it may be necessary to use an expansion arch-bow threaded for nuts at the mesial ends of the molar tubes. Again, if the premolars have been forced into lingual malalignment, or if the premolar area demands a slight expansion, additional appliances will be indicated.

This apparatus is applicable only to those cases in which the cuspids demand slight movement and little artificial aid. For the application of greater force, see

Class I. In this connection, it should always be remembered that in the common course of secondary dentition, the cuspids are often naturally crowded out of their normal alignment, and when the direct cause of this amounts to no more than a slight constriction of the space required, nature will usually correct the malposition for young patients by the natural growth of the jaw.

Infra-Occlusion of Upper Incisors

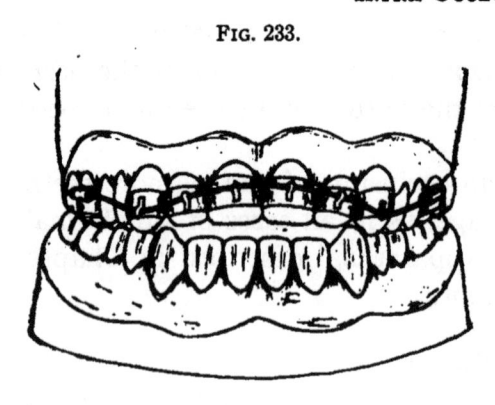

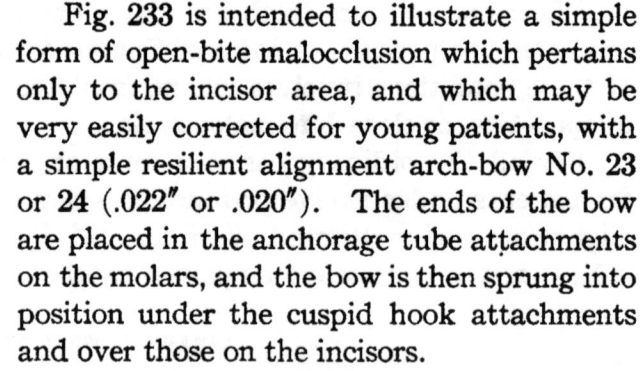

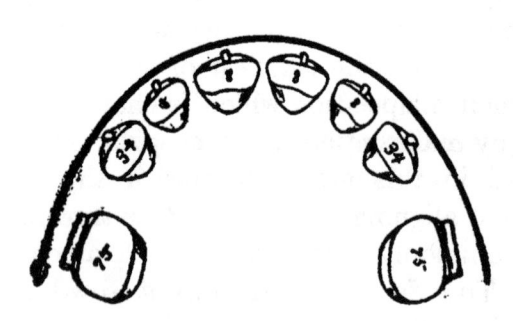

FIG. 233.

Fig. 233 is intended to illustrate a simple form of open-bite malocclusion which pertains only to the incisor area, and which may be very easily corrected for young patients, with a simple resilient alignment arch-bow No. 23 or 24 (.022" or .020"). The ends of the bow are placed in the anchorage tube attachments on the molars, and the bow is then sprung into position under the cuspid hook attachments and over those on the incisors.

It must be remembered before placing any small resilient arch-bow on the teeth, that it should be curved by drawing it over the ball of the thumb until its ends nearly touch, else it is liable to exert a buccal expanding force on the molars. If a lateral expansion of the arch is demanded, distributing lingual extensions made of half-round hook wire should be soldered to the lingual surfaces of the molar bands to rest upon and fit the lingual surfaces of adjoining teeth, and then the uncurved or straight arch-bow may be sprung into its anchorage tubes to act as an expander, according to the potential force that is given it.

If one or more of the teeth are malturned, the bands should carry the proper attachments for rotating them. When the cuspids are in normal occlusal position, if used as fulcrums, this force will abnormally intrude them, in which case rubber bands, extending from the upper teeth to a bow attached to the lower, may be indicated, or the force upon the cuspids may be relieved by distributing it to the premolars.

CHAPTER XLVII

CROWDED MALALIGNMENTS

When one or more teeth occlude lingually, labially, or buccally to the normal line of the arch, they are in malposition or **malalignment**.

Commonly, the teeth are so crowded in the arch that the malaligned teeth cannot regain their normal pose without the aid of artificial force. When a dental arch—especially the upper—is deprived of its natural arch support through the loss or maleruption or malalignment of one or more labial teeth, the influences of muscular action alone will tend to contract its natural boundaries. The contraction of a dental arch in this manner will often cause the opposing arch to also become contracted, and the incisors malposed through the forceful influences of occlusion and muscular action.

The origin of a large proportion of all complex irregularities, be they simple or complicated, may be traced to the premature loss—usually from extraction—of the temporary teeth, followed by a maleruption of the succeeding teeth.

It would seem hardly possible, though true, that the contracting action of the muscles of lips and cheeks could increase a complicated irregularity which may have started from the maleruption, injudicious extraction, or careless loss of a single tooth.

In the contemplation of correction, with a view to permanent retention, the teeth of the opposing jaw, therefore, will frequently require regulating to readjust the occlusion. In the preliminary examination and diagnosis of the more complicated cases, the character of **occlusion** of the **first permanent molars** is of the greatest importance. And in all cases where there is no decided protrusion of one denture or the other, demanding the extraction of premolars, *the teeth should be invariably placed in normal occlusion*. The apparatus should therefore be constructed for the application of forces which will not only laterally expand the arch or arches to normal bucco-lingual relations, but also to normal disto-mesial relations.

In malalignments of the upper, the mesio-buccal cusps of the first upper molars will commonly be found riding too much upon the mesio-buccal cusps of the first lower molars, instead of closing evenly in the sulci between the two lower cusps and overlapping them bucally, as they should. It will be observed that this forward shifting of the upper molars, which is commonly started by the premature loss of deciduous teeth, will tend through occlusal forces, to drive the lower molars forward, and produce either a malalignment of the lower teeth, or a proportionate protrusion of the entire denture. Too much stress, therefore, cannot be laid upon the advisability of intelligently determining the effect which the teeth are destined

334 PART VII. UNCLASSIFIED MALOCCLUSIONS

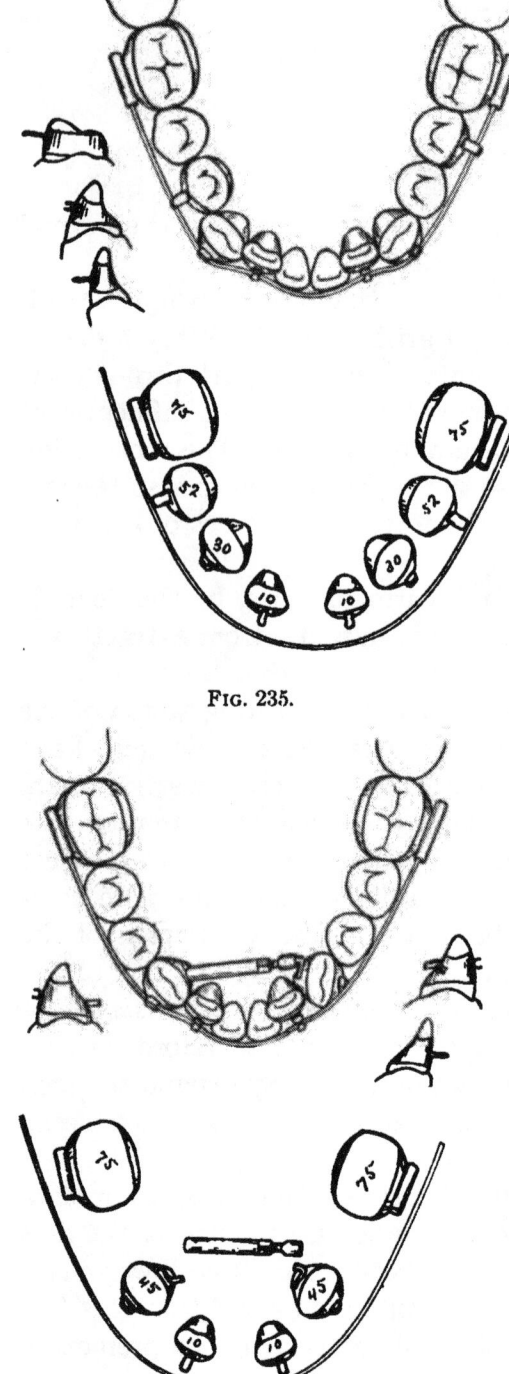

FIG. 234.

FIG. 235.

to have upon the facial outlines, and in deciding whether the occipital or the intermaxillary force is the more applicable for correcting the occlusal malrelations.

If the mesial malocclusion of the upper molars is greater than will be possible to correct by a slight distal movement, which may be brought about by a reaction of the alignment forces of the upper apparatus, provision should be made for the application of the **intermaxillary force,** bearing in mind that the reciprocal action of this force will tend toward a mesial movement of the lower. If this is not advisable, it should be prevented. (See chapter on the application of the intermaxillary force.) It may be that only the occipital force should be employed as an auxiliary.

For nearly all the ordinary crowded malalignments for children, including supra and infra-occlusions, the midget sizes of arch-bows Nos. 24, 25, and 26, will be found effective. For youths and even older patients, when the **malalignment** is **slight** and somewhat similar to the position shown in Fig. 234, a resilient alignment arch-bow No. 22 will usually correct the irregularity with the requirement of few, if any, subsequent adjustments. After the bands are cemented, curve the bow over the ball of the thumb to the form of the arch, and place it in the molar tubes and cuspid rests and then spring it into its attachments on the contruded teeth, bending the hooks closely against the teeth.

When there is a greater lingual malalignment of one or more teeth, it may not be possible or advisable to force the arch-bow to immediate contact with the tooth in the clasp of an open tube or ordinary hook attachment, in which case it may at first be attached to the bow with a wire ligature, or the midget finger spurs, which are fully described in Chapter XIX.

CHAPTER XLVII. CROWDED MALALIGNMENTS

The space for the lower incisors is frequently crowded in upon by the **contrusion of the cuspids,** caused usually by occlusion, and requiring the concurrent regulation of the opposing teeth. Fig. 235 shows the application of a small pinrest jack No. 19 attached to cuspid **bands** for expanding the labial arch. It also shows how to place the jack in case one or both teeth are malturned and require rotating.

FIG. 236.

The lingual jack as shown, is advisable only when the cuspids are in decided lingual malalignment. Ordinarily, the case may be easily corrected for young patients with a No. 20 or 22 expanding arch-bow with the nuts at the mesial ends of the molar anchorage tubes, communicating with strong labial open-tube attachments on the front teeth, and with pin-head lingual attachments on malturned teeth for rotating with wire ligatures.

When all the incisors are in lingual malalignment, they can frequently be easily corrected by lacing them to the arch-bow with a single election ring, as diagrammatically shown in Fig. 236.

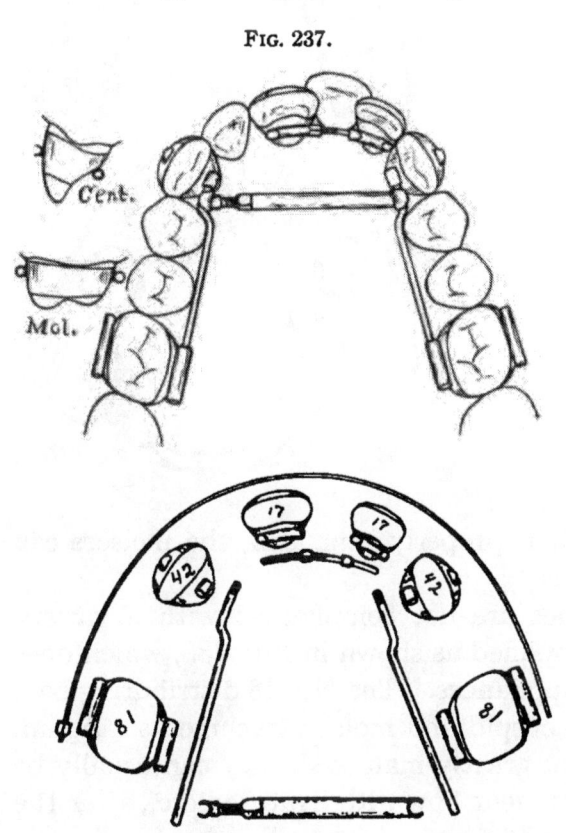

FIG. 237.

In all cases over twelve years of age where the **arch is contracted,** accompanied with malposition of the incisors, it will demand a lateral expansion in order to place the teeth in alignment; moreover, this movement of one denture will often demand the concomitant expansion of the other, else the uncorrected arch will force the other back to its former fixed occlusion.

Fig. 237 shows a common method of expanding the anterior arch as an auxiliary to the labial or lingual curved push bars. The lingual bars No. 18 for distributing the expanding force are threaded at their extreme mesial ends to screw into short threaded lingual tube attachments on the cuspids, or they may be soft-soldered. The principal object of this method of attachment is to preserve the rigidity of the bars, which would not be possible if hard-soldered directly to the bands. The distributing bars are bent to pass the premolars and to afford means of attachment to the bar-rest expanding jack. Their distal ends rest in seamless or open-tube attachments on the molars, or they may be threaded to act as pull or push bars with nuts respectively distal or mesial to the molar tubes. The buccal molar tubes and cuspid open-tube attachments provide means for an alignment arch-bow if needed. If the lingual cuspid attachments are placed at the extreme gingival borders, the straight jack will lie close to the lingual incisal ridge, and will thus not materially interfere with the tongue. When necessary to place the jack further back, the arc jack will be found preferable. The lingual appliance for opening space for the

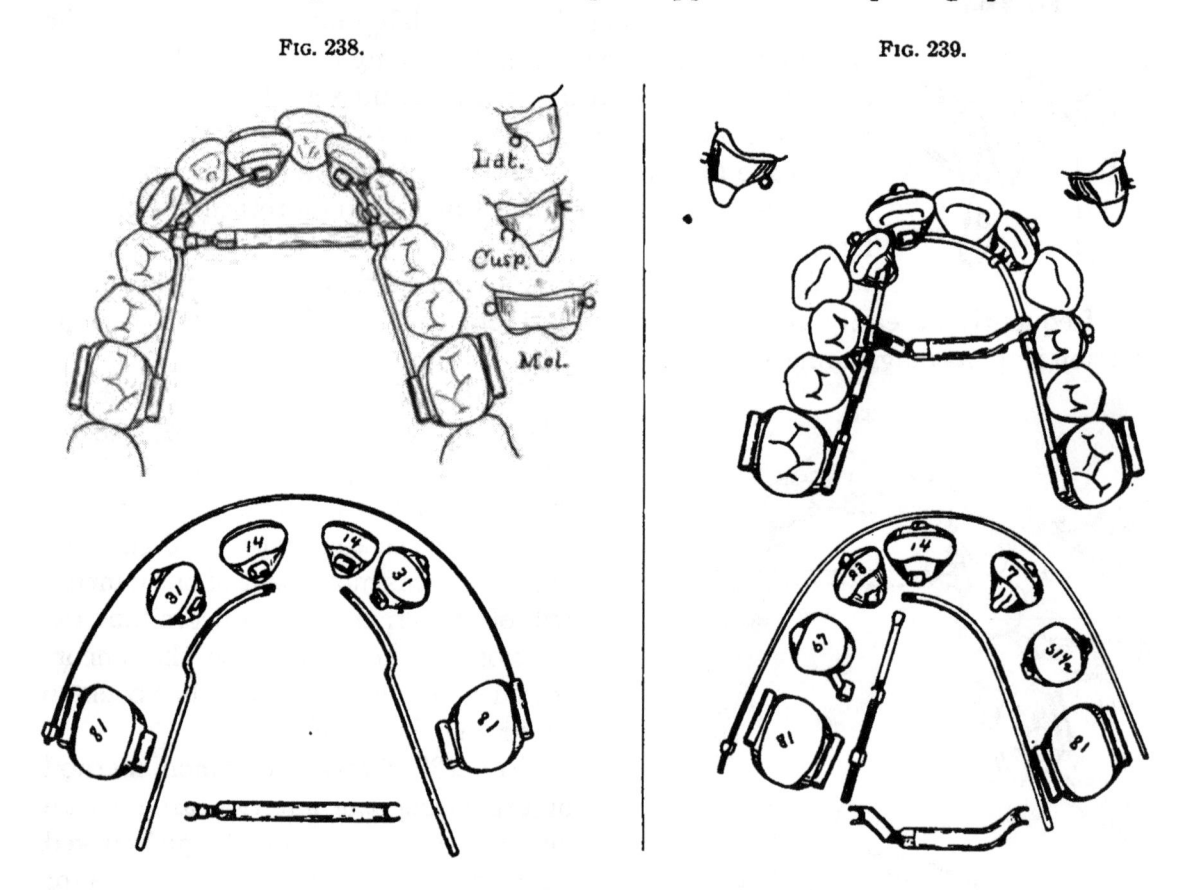

FIG. 238.

FIG. 239.

incisor is obsolete. When the labial arch is properly expanded, the incisors can be usually aligned by very simple methods.

In those cases where the dental arches are not complicated with a variety of malpositions, the apparatus may be simplified as shown in Fig. 238, which does away with the need of the special labial appliances. The No. 18 distributing bars attached to the incisors rest in open-tube cuspid and molar attachments. Again, in those cases where the front teeth are not greatly malposed, they can usually be brought to alignment by the aid of an alignment bow with ligatures, etc., after the arches have been sufficiently expanded with the expanding appliance. In all cases of malalignments with crowded arches, the **foundation principle** of correction lies in first making room for the malposed teeth in the arch, after which the rest of the operation is comparatively easy.

CHAPTER XLVII. CROWDED MALALIGNMENTS

Drop Jack.—In the irregularity shown in Fig. 239, the right premolars and lateral incisor are in decided lingual malalignment, in consequence of which the entire arch on the right side is contracted. The left lingual distributing bar No. 18 is attached to the right central for the purpose of carrying all of the teeth within its grasp to the left. In the combination with the right bar No. 18, the distally reacting force from the lateral incisor can be received either upon the premolar or the molar, it being desired to retrude these teeth to open the space for the cuspid in the general enlargement of the arch, and correct the occlusion. The premolar attachment is peculiarly adapted for producing the greatest amount of inclination movement in proportion to the force exerted. It will be seen also in this combination, that the distal force may be transferred at any time from the premolar to the molar. With this apparatus is introduced the **drop expanding jack,** which is especially valuable in the lateral expansion of the upper arch, where interference with the tongue should be relieved as much as possible.

Occasionally one or two front upper teeth are inlocked in occlusion back of the lowers, demanding considerable force to move them to alignment for patients older than twelve years. In many cases, nothing short of the positive force of a screw jack or lingual push-bow will accomplish the work.

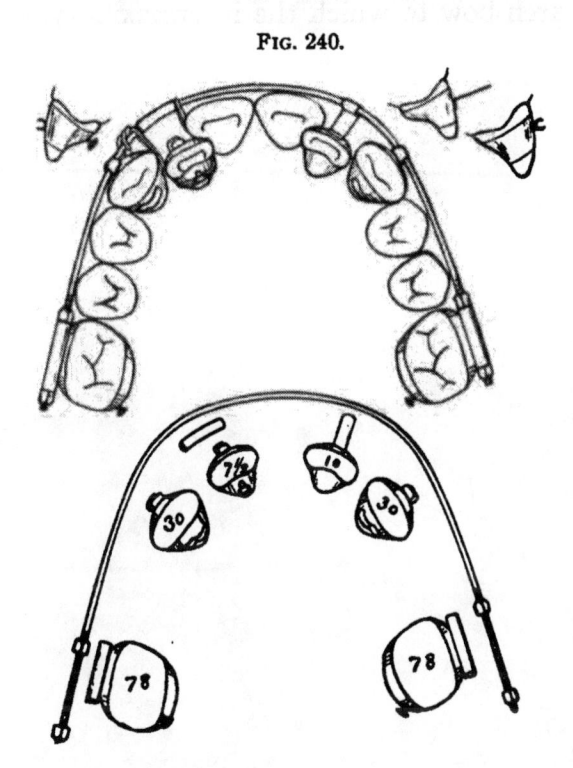

Fig. 240.

For the younger class of patients, the methods shown in Fig. 240 will be found effective. On the right lateral, the ligature wire is passed around the tooth in the form of a double loop and fastened to the bow at the ends of a thin curved tube which is slipped on the bow before it is placed. The curved tube, shown in the illustration, lies between the points of attachment of the wire. The length of the tube can be gauged so that the wire will exert an expanding force upon the adjoining teeth to make room for the lateral.

The Matteson attachment on the left lateral consists of a strip of No. 28 or 30 plate, cut as shown, and soldered to the labial face of the band. The end is lapped over the bow and rolled in under with the pliers. The force is increased from time to time by rolling it up on the bow.

Both of these methods, however, give far more pain in their treatment adjustments than the positive force of a screw, which is always sure, comparatively painless, and therefore to be preferred in the alignment of all *extensive* contrusions, and especially for inlocked upper incisors. The size of the arch-bow may be from Nos. 22 to 19, according to the age of the patient and need of arch expanding force. In the employment of the small sizes of spring arch-bows, the resilient force of the bow is always an advantage, and preferable for young patients where no particular expansion of the arch is required.

The double mesial and distal nuts at the molars are frequently of advantage for expansion arch-bows. They lock the bow firmly in position, and permit a movement of it in either direction by unscrewing one nut and screwing up the other. It should be remembered, however, that this locking of a tooth to a heavy arch-bow increases its immovability, and establishes to that extent a stationary anchorage quality. Therefore, in all instances when a distal movement of the buccal teeth is desired for the correction of the occlusion, a small sized arch-bow instead of a large one is chosen for the bow to hold the teeth in alignment, because it answers every purpose, and yields readily to an inclination movement of the molars. This principle should always be taken advantage of in the application of the disto-mesial action of the intermaxillary force. Moreover, this is one of the principal reasons why it is more scientific and effective to apply this force distally to the molars through the medium of sliding tubes and intermaxillary hooks which glide upon a small resilient archbow, than through the medium of a heavy arch-bow to which the intermaxillary hooks are immovably attached.

CHAPTER XLVIII

MALTURNED TEETH

One of the most common malpositions is that of malturned teeth. During the process of eruption, the front teeth are commonly obliged to crowd their way into the arch between deciduous or permanent teeth, unless deflected completely out of alignment. In so doing, they are naturally malturned by the deflecting influence of their broad and somewhat thin incisal borders coming in contact with adjoining teeth. Later, through the influence of natural growth of the jaws, and muscular action favored by the anatomic shapes of the roots, they commonly assume a normal pose. Where the alveolar arches do not sufficiently enlarge by growth, and where teeth are otherwise prevented from assuming their normal pose through the forces of malocclusion, they become permanently fixed, and so remain malturned and often overlapping until corrected by artificial means.

In the **correction** of malturned teeth, the most important principle to be remembered is that **mechanical advantage** is increased in proportion to the distance from the central axis of the tooth at which the force is applied. Therefore, for the rotation of the labial teeth, the force should be applied at or near the gingival border. See Rotating Movement in Principles of Mechanics, Chapter XIII.

As stated in other parts of this work, the author does not attempt to give every variety of irregularity and complication that may arise in practice, but only some of the common forms of malposition for the purpose alone of showing practical methods of correction, and principally the application of implements and appliances which any ingenious mind will be able to modify to suit the case in hand. The special force exerted by different methods will be briefly described with the appliance.

For the rotation of children's teeth, nothing can be employed that is more effective and that requires less treatment adjustments than that which obtains its motive force from the resiliency of very light arch-bows Nos. 25 and 26. The two most favorable methods for exerting this force for the rotation of front teeth are through the medium of **finger-spurs** and **wire ligatures,** both of which are fully described in detail, with enlarged drawings, in Chapter XIX.

Spring Lever Rotators.—The rotation of teeth with piano-wire bars was first introduced by Dr. E. H. Angle. In a paper presented at the Illinois State Dental Society, in 1894, the author presented the present modification of this principle, which he is pleased to say has rendered this method of rotating teeth one of the most valuable in his practice.

For incisor teeth that are moderately turned, and for cuspids that are slightly turned, the method is quite effective if the principles of the force are understood, mechanically applied, and properly controlled. (See "Rotating Movements," Chapter XIII.)

Where the incisors are malturned and in slight lingual malalignment, resilient bars or levers may be effectively attached in the manner shown in Fig. 241. But it should be remembered that a combination of this character should never be placed upon the teeth without the controlling force of an alignment arch-bow. As explained in Chapter XIII, when a straight spring bar or wire is firmly attached to a tooth and then bent in the form of a bow, and the far end hooked to an easily gliding attachment, it will tend to rotate the tooth on its long axis, providing the tooth is prevented from moving laterally. These two necessary requirements are obtained with an alignment arch-bow. It prevents the tooth from moving into labial malalignment, and also serves as a gliding medium for the hook.

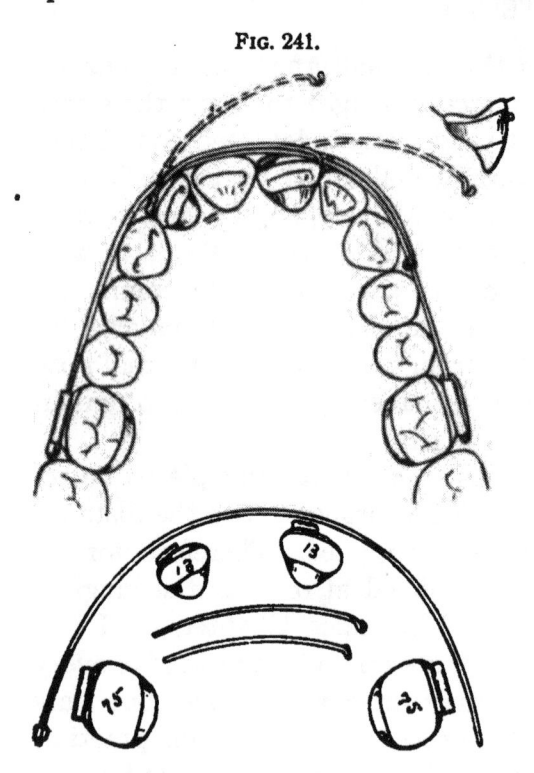

FIG. 241.

The **rotating lever** which the author has found most effective is No. 20 or 22, drawn without annealing from No. 9 extra hard 18 per cent nickel-silver wire. This gives to the wire a resiliency nearly equal to the piano wire, and is quite as effective for all practical purposes without the oxidizing tendency possessed by steel. Cut the wire into 1½-inch lengths, anneal one end and bend it to a hook having the double curve shown in the drawing.

The rotating tube attachments—preferably seamless—should have very thin walls, No. 32 or 34, and should be drawn to fit the bars exactly, so as to hug the band and present no prominent or irritating edges, and to take such position on the tooth, when placed, as will be most effective for its rotation. In placing the lever, see that its length is such as to allow it to hook to the arch-bow at an interproximate position in relation to the teeth, and bend the hook so that when the lever is placed it will lie smoothly along the bow. It will be noticed that the rotating tubes are placed at the most favorable position to obtain the greatest rotating leverage.

Positive Reciprocating Force.—For the rotation of teeth which are extensively turned, especially the cuspids, premolars, and central incisors, the application of positive reciprocating force (a principle which the author introduced in the early 90's) is certainly the ideal method for rotating a tooth upon its long axis, where considerable force and movement is demanded.

CHAPTER XLVIII. MALTURNED TEETH

In nearly all cases which require extensive rotation, and which do not require inclination movement, it will be found by a little study that reciprocating forces can in some form be applied. A not uncommon malposition is that of a central incisor turned one-quarter around and locked in that position by adjoining teeth, as shown in Fig. 242. A No. 19 **fork-end jack,** resting on a lingual spur hook on the malturned incisor, exerts a rotating force, the reaction of which being received upon the lingual bar attached to the right central, cuspid, and molar, sustains the integrity of the arch, and exerts a uniform expanding force to open the space; while

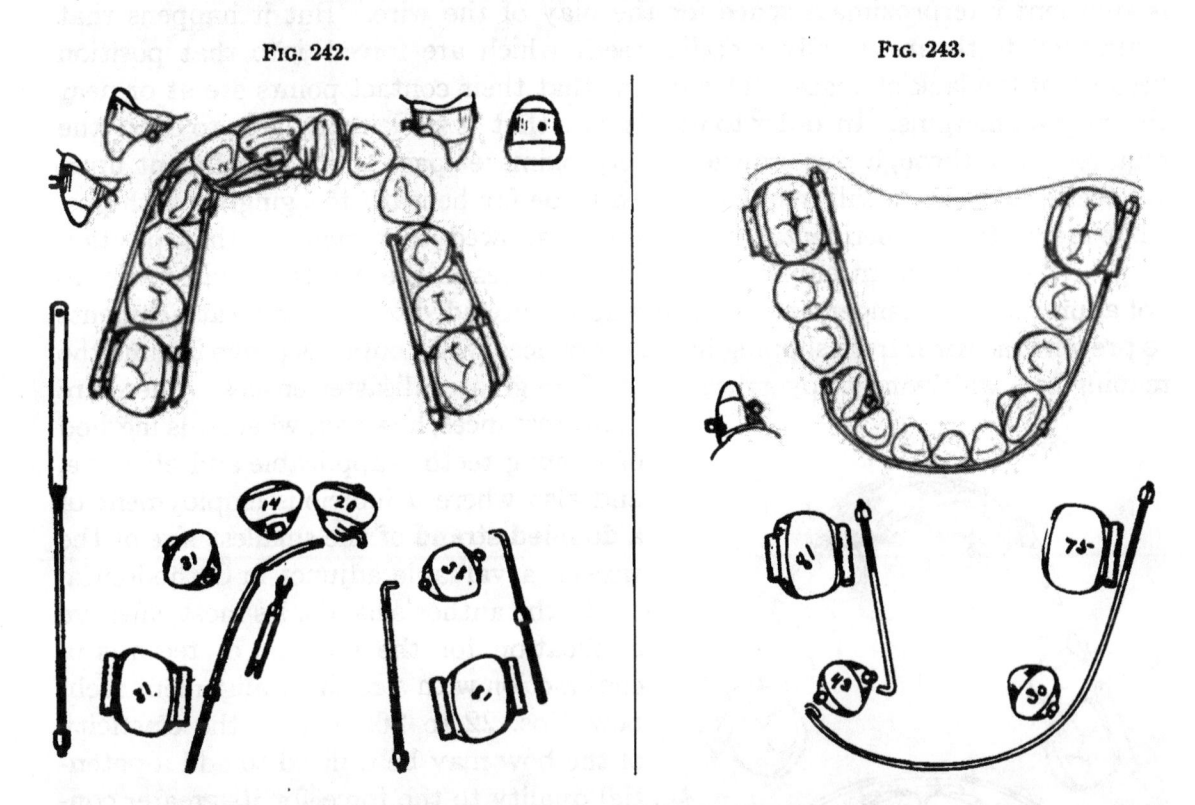

Fig. 242.

Fig. 243.

the **ribbon end-traction bar,** buttoned to the labial face of the malturned incisor from a molar anchorage, completes the reciprocating rotating combination.

In the drawing will be seen a malturned upper first premolar which frequently offers great resistance to rotation on account of its bifurcated roots. A simple and very effective method is here shown for the application of the reciprocating forces of pull and push bars connected to the premolar band with hinge attachments from a molar anchorage.

When one cuspid is decidedly malturned, for patients older than twelve or fourteen, and seems to offer considerable resistance to rotation, a very effective appliance, offering the application of direct positive force, is shown in Fig. 243. A No. 22 (.025″) traction arch-bow is cut in two, giving the proper length for each piece. Short pieces of No. 22-30 tubing are soldered to the buccal and lingual surfaces of the cuspid band, and form the attachments as in the former appliance for rotating the first premolar. The cut ends of the bow are slightly annealed to form hooks which, when passed through the tube attachments, are bent back on themselves. The rest of the apparatus is plainly shown. The labio-buccal portion of the bow may be employed as a basis for correcting malpositions of other front teeth the same as if it were a complete arch-bow.

Wire Ligatures for Rotating.—As before mentioned, the employment of **wire ligatures** is an effective method of rotating and aligning teeth, especially when there is sufficient interproximate space for the play of the wire. But it happens that malturned teeth are usually *crowded* teeth which are forced into that position because of the lack of space. This means that their contact points are at or near the gingival margins. In order to pass a wire that is sufficiently large to exert the required force through this crowded interproximate space to its attachment upon the teeth, its passage will frequently need to be far beneath the gingivæ with possible injury to the peridental membrane if allowed to remain in that position long. The too frequent employment of these wires in the hands of many who do not appreciate this danger, and especially upon unbanded teeth with no attachments to prevent the wires from slipping into the crevices, will doubtless prove in time the reaping of a whirlwind of pyorrhea cases, if no greater disaster ensues. There are many instances, however, where this method of moving teeth is applicable and effective, and also where a judicious employment of a **doubled strand** of the smallest size of the wires is a valuable adjunct in Orthodontia.

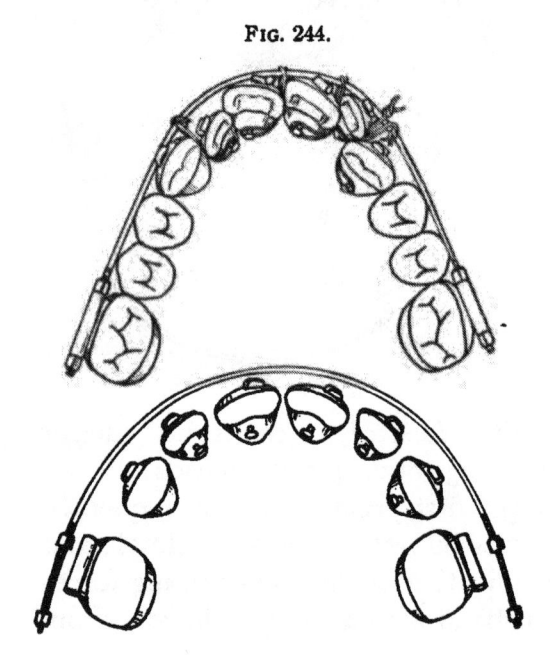

FIG. 244.

In the author's hands, its most effective application for the rotation of teeth is in conjunction with a resilient alignment arch-bow Nos. 22 to 26, so that the elasticity of the bow may be utilized to add a potential quality to the force for its greater continued action.

In Fig. 244, the ends of the wires are shown more twisted than they would be at first, especially upon a heavier bow, the purpose being to show how they may be twisted upon the lighter spring arch-bows whose potential resiliency would exert a more gradual force and not require the repeated painful renewals of the ligatures which commonly break with a subsequent twist. The projecting ends of the wires are intended to be tucked back out of irritating prominence.

The most perfect method of applying the wire ligatures is described by Dr. Angle as follows: "When applying a wire ligature, a piece long enough to be firmly grasped by both hands should be used so that strong tension may be exerted when making the twist. This should never be more than three-fourths of a turn at first. The surplus ends are then clipped off, leaving projections one-eighth of an inch long. These ends are then curled under the arch, thus providing a smooth surface to the lips."

Elastic Rings for Rotating.—One of the most convenient, effective, and easily adjusted methods of rotating contruded lower incisors and other teeth which are not extensively malturned, is with the employment of elastic rings. Those who have witnessed the wonderful results accomplished by the intermaxillary elastics will not question the adequacy of the continuous force when properly applied for the rotation of teeth.

There are many ways in which the elastic rings may be applied that will suggest themselves to ingenious minds according to the conditions and requirements.

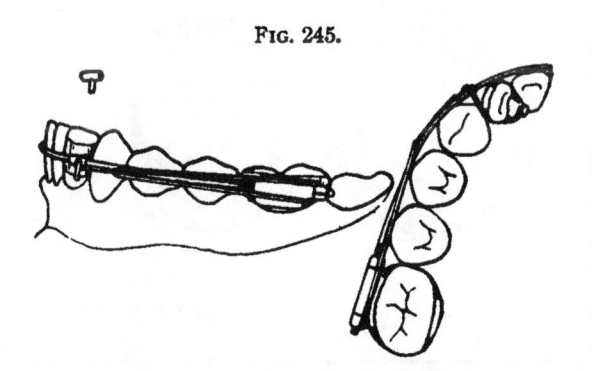

FIG. 245.

When only one tooth requires rotating, a loop of "Corticelli A" silk ligature may be passed over a lingual pin-head attachment, and the ends carried under a "T" attachment on the arch-bow and tied to an election ring which is looped over the anchorage attachment, as shown in Fig. 245. In this way you can increase the elastic force to any desired degree by doubling the ring back on itself. The "T" attachment is made by soldering a spur to a short thin-walled tube of a size to exactly fit the arch-bow to which it is soft-soldered at the required position. Were it not for this attachment on the bow, the force of the elastic upon the cuspid over which it would pass would contrude it, unless it was secured to the bow with a band attachment.

Silk Ligatures for Rotating, Etc.

Silk and linen thread have been used for all time in the regulation of teeth; but the honor is due to Dr. W. J. Younger for first practically demonstrating the remarkable effectiveness of very small silk ligatures, and for special methods of securing them to teeth to obtain the greatest possible advantage of their qualities.

For malturned teeth that require a slight rotating force for their correction, and for the prevention of rotation movement from the action or misapplication of other forces, "Corticelli A" silk ligatures, if properly applied, will be found invaluable. The retention of a rotating ligature when tied to a tooth, and its subsequent potential action, is due quite as much to the elastic resilient quality—found only in the smallest of silk threads—as to the method of its application. An important advantage of the smaller sizes is they are not so liable to become foul, which is one of the unpleasant conditions common with the larger ligatures.

344 PART VII. UNCLASSIFIED MALOCCLUSIONS

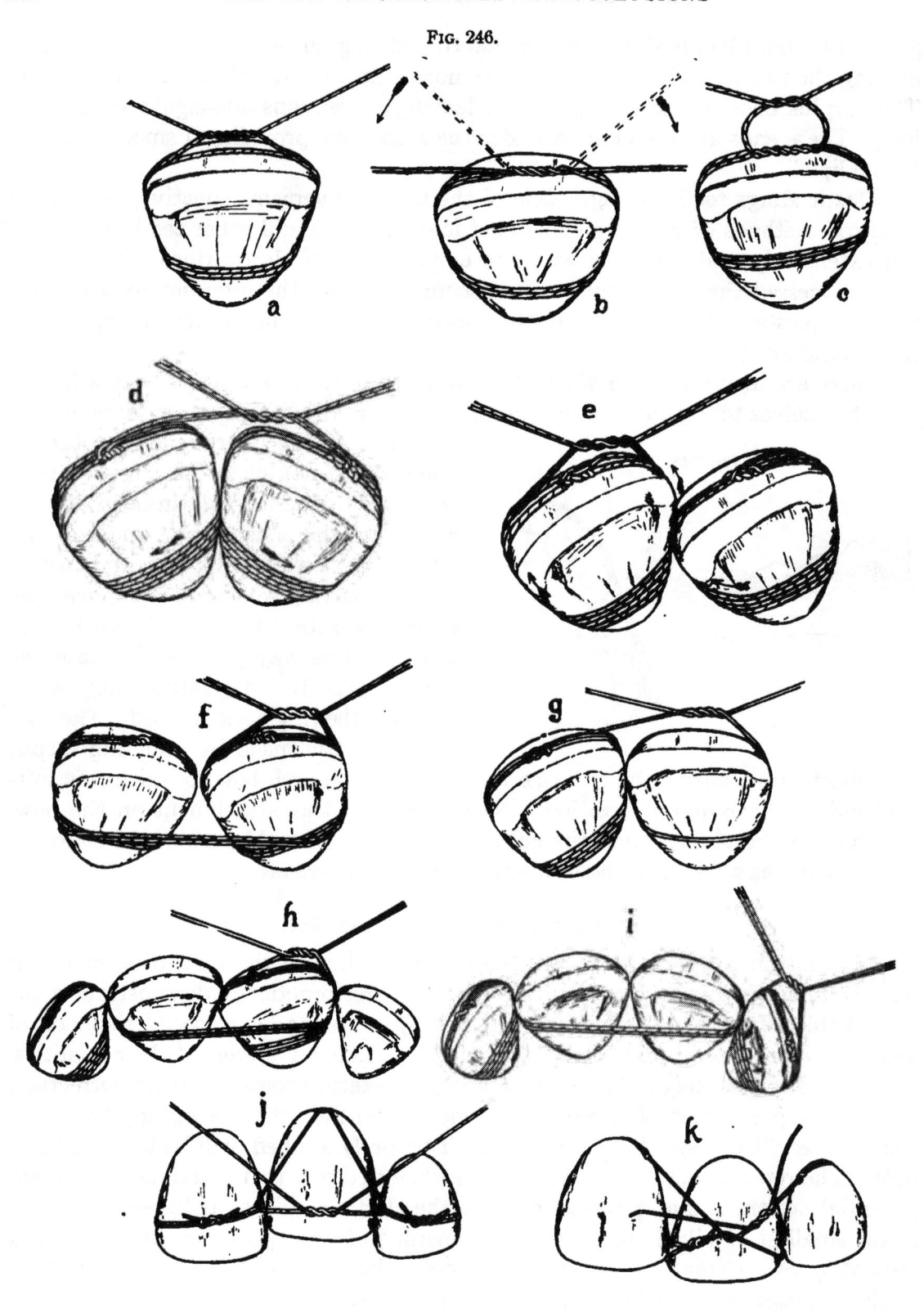

Fig. 246.

CHAPTER XLVIII. MALTURNED TEETH

To tie a silk ligature to a tooth that will not slip while exerting a rotating force, requires special methods of procedure. First: the ligature should be thoroughly waxed, except at that portion of the middle which is sufficient to pass *twice* around the tooth to be rotated. Second: after passing the unwaxed portion *twice* around the tooth, the first half of the knot should be made by passing one end through the loop *twice*, as in the sailor's tie to prevent it from slipping after drawing it tightly to place. Third: while grasping the ends of the ligature firmly, lift the tie from the tooth with all the force which the ligature will bear (see "a," Fig. 246) then suddenly drop the hands while keeping up the tension, to take up all the slack ("b"). By repeating this movement once or twice, it insures drawing the double loop around the tooth to its fullest tension. Fourth: the rest of the knot is finished by passing the end through the loop *once*, either way, and drawing it firmly to place with a slight right and left movement ("c"). Fifth: the double strand is grasped and carried in the direction of the desired force.

The methods of rotating the central incisors labio-mesially are shown by "d." After tying the ligatures to both teeth as described, the double strands are again passed around the teeth in the direction of the desired force, and tied with a sailor's knot at the most prominent point on the face of one of the teeth. The same movements in tying the first half of this knot should be made as in the first knot, "a" and "b," as much of the effectiveness of the method lies in storing up all the potential force which the resiliency of the silk fibers will permit without breaking. To prevent the first half of this tie from slipping back while the rest of the knot is made, it is usually necessary for the assistant to hold it with a piece of orangewood. The ends are then cut off close to the knot.

"e" shows method of rotating adjoining incisors that are malturned in the same direction.

"f" shows method of rotating central incisors labio-distally.

"g" shows method of rotating a single incisor. After carrying the double strand around the tooth, it is separated and tied to an adjoining tooth so as to produce no rotating force upon the latter. Whenever possible, the double strand should be tied to a double strand from another tooth which requires rotating, though it may be quite distantly located. The potential resiliency of the ligature is increased in proportion to its length. With this in view, the author frequently ties the double strand from a single malturned incisor to that of another double strand from a molar anchorage.

"h" shows method of rotating a central and lateral in the same direction.

"i" shows method of rotating the laterals in opposite directions, or labio-mesially.

"j" and "k" show methods of extruding and intruding a single incisor with silk ligatures.

CHAPTER XLIX

NARROW AND WIDE ARCHES

Laterally Contracted Arches of various forms and from various causes constitute one of the common characters of irregularities of the teeth.

In the early history of the correction of irregularities by means of dental plates, the lateral expansion of the arch was considered the all important and necessary preliminary step in nearly all cases that required room for placing the teeth in alignment. Indeed, so prevalent did this idea become, with the frequent expansion of arches to unnatural and disfiguring widths by the use of the "Coffin" and other expanding plates, that even today it is difficult to eradicate that impression and substitute in its place the far more important **distal movement** of the premolars and molars when demanded, to restore them to their inherited positions of normal occlusion, from which they may have drifted forward through the premature loss of deciduous teeth, or malalignments of the permanent teeth. The lateral expansion of dental arches, however, will always remain one of the important movements in correction.

The two principal means employed by the author for the lateral expansion or contraction of the dental arch are those afforded, first, by the resilient force of a **spring arch-bow,** and second, by the positive force of a screw. The former is especially applicable for expanding or contracting the buccal area, particularly in the molar region, because its greatest action is at the ends of the bow with a diminishing movement as it approaches the center of the bow; while the latter, through the aid of several forms of jacks, can be made to locate the force at any lateral area upon either side of the arch, or distribute it evenly to the two sides for a general expansion.

For extensive expansions of the arch for youths and adults, especially at the cuspid and premolar areas, nothing will ever equal in efficiency the positive force of a screw applied on the lingual area. The methods which are here presented for applying the positive forces have been brought to a high degree of perfection toward the elimination of irritating influences, through the medium of the "arc," "drop," and "turn-buckle" jacks. Occasionally it is desired to apply an independent lingual expanding force through the medium of sigmoid shaped wire springs which are bent to conform to the lingual surfaces of the gum and dome of the arch. The regular expansion arch-bow, however, which is placed on the outside of the dental arch, is far more frequently demanded, and it is certainly more valuable for the general expansion of dental arches in all directions, because it enables the application of a variety of auxiliary forces for the correction of malalignments, protrusions, and retrusions, and bodily movements of the front teeth.

CHAPTER XLIX. NARROW AND WIDE ARCHES

EXPANSION OF ARCHES FOR CHILDREN AND YOUTHS

For the general expansion of dental arches to correct crowded malalignments for children and youths, extra spring nickel silver or platinized gold expansion arch-bows No. 19 will be found sufficiently effective. In fact, for children under ten years of age, Nos. 23, 22, and 20, are commonly employed. These bows are threaded at the ends for nuts at the mesial ends of the molar tubes. The remarkable effectiveness of the smaller sizes of spring arch-bows in the general expansion of dental arches is due to their resiliency when sprung into attachments from one tooth to the other. This forces the malaligned teeth, in their movements toward correction, to act as expanding wedges toward enlarging the arch—an advantage that is only possible with the smaller bows. This is the secret also of the wonderful effectiveness of the midget sizes, Nos. 24, 25, and 26, which the author now commonly employs for the correction of malalignments of children's teeth, and which can accomplish the object only through a general expansion of the dental arch.

For the lateral expansion of narrow arches for older patients as an auxiliary to other forces to correct protrusions, etc., the larger sizes of arch-bows are commonly demanded, and are frequently placed to act independently of the other correcting forces of the apparatus. Often, this independent expanding force is placed on the lingual aspect of the arch, and composed of different forms of wire springs and expanding jacks.

BODILY EXPANSION

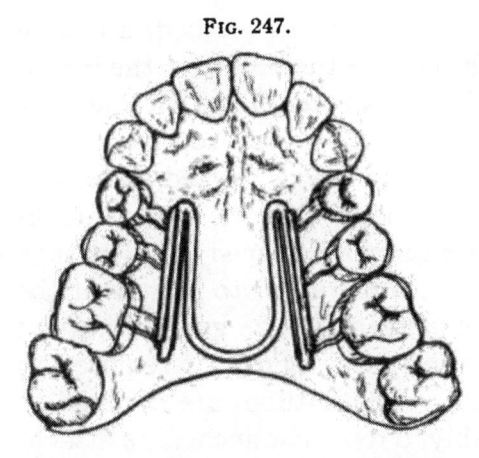

FIG. 247.

When bodily expansion movement is desired—which is frequently of the greatest importance on the upper arch—the expanding force, whether from the lingual or buccal aspect, should be applied to the teeth through the medium of **root-wise attachments,** in order to place the line of its directed force nearer to the center of alveolar resistance. This may be accomplished by soldering root-wise extensions to the bands of the teeth which are chosen to transmit this force. See Fig. 247; also see Anchorages, Chapter XV.

In the employment of any labio-buccal expansion arch-bow, it will be found of great advantage to have an open anchorage tube on one side, instead of both being closed, or seamless. By placing one end of the spring bow in the closed tube, and then by springing the other end into its seating in the open-tube, the full spring force of the bow is obtained. If necessary for greater security, it may be locked in place. One of the greatest advantages is: it enables an easy unlocking of the arch-bow for renewing its force, or changing it in any way. The open mouth of the tube should stand slightly inclined toward the gum, in order that the expanding force of the bow when sprung into it will firmly retain its seating without otherwise locking it. This is especially important when plain bows—without nuts—are employed.

When the expansion arch-bow is attached to single molar anchorages, the molar bands should always carry lingual yoke extensions, made of round or half-round wire fitted to the gingival margins of the adjoining teeth, to distribute the expanding force.

The *bodily* expanding property of an arch-bow can be further increased by taking advantage of torsional force which may be imparted to the bow by giving to its ends a twisted spring force before locking them into their anchorage tubes. The method is fully described in the chapter on Bodily Movement, and illustrated in Fig. 63, Chapter XIV. It was presented in a paper read before the American Society of Orthodontists in 1917.

In a desired bodily lateral expansion of a dental arch, if it were possible, hypothetically speaking, to attach an elastic buccal pull or push force to the apical ends of the roots to act in conjunction with a direct lateral expansion arch-bow, it would certainly express the ideal principles of bodily buccal expanding force.

In the process of assembling the torsional bow, the ends are twisted and locked firmly in the anchorage tubes in such a manner as to retain their potential torsional force, in addition to the direct expanding force of the bow. This will have a great tendency toward accomplishing a bodily buccal movement of buccal teeth and alveolar process.

For all the ordinary expansion of arches for children by this method, a No. 20 (.032″) spring arch-bow is sufficiently heavy. The ends of the bow over the buccal area are flattened to a ribbon form about ⅔ or ½ the diameter of the wire, leaving the labial portion of the bow round. The object of this is, first, to give a more resilient spring to that portion of the bow that is forced into a twisted state, and second, to afford a means for holding it firmly in that position at the molar attachments. To fulfill the requirements, the anchorages carry a flattened seamless tube on one side, and an open U-tube on the other, both constructed to loosely fit the ribboned ends of the bow. The U-tube should be made of No. 28 gauge platinum gold, or nickel silver, well reinforced with solder, as great rigidity is required to prevent the torsional force from opening the tube. The U-tubes are soldered to the buccal surfaces of the molar bands, or preferably to root-wise anchorage attachments, so they will stand slightly inclined toward the median line. When one of the flattened ends of the arch-bow is placed in the lock-tube, as shown on the left of Fig. 63, Chapter XIV, the mere lifting of the other end to position twists the end that is locked. In order to twist the other end of the bow before seating it in the lock-tube, it must be firmly grasped with suitable pliers and forcibly twisted to its locked position; this gives one something of an idea of the force of reaction exerted upon the roots of the teeth. The bow in the illustration has the appearance of being flattened only at one end; this was the engraver's error.

LINGUAL SPRING EXPANDERS

Laterally contracted arches are not uncommon with no other irregularity except that the front teeth are forced into a more or less protruded state, demanding an expansion of the buccal area to correct the front teeth and the occlusion of the back teeth.

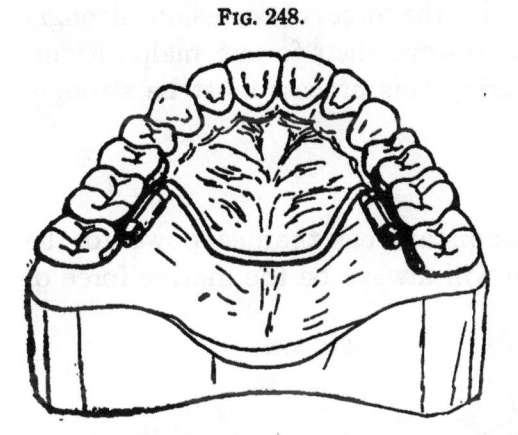

FIG. 248.

If the teeth do not require a bodily expanding movement, Fig. 248 illustrates one of the most simple appliances in technic construction and future management. The sizes of the lingual expanding bows range from Nos. 18 to 16 spring nickel-silver wire. The object of employing a bow of a large size is to obtain a more positive force to lower the range of its spring potentiality, and thus avoid the possibility of too much movement. The bow is fitted to lie evenly along the surfaces of the teeth and conform to the dome of the arch. It is then sprung outward to a point of equilibrium that is slightly beyond the desired movement. The lingual open-tubes are soldered to single molar bands in connection with yoke distributing attachments made of half-round wire fitted to the lingual surfaces of adjoining teeth, by which means the expanding force of the bow is communicated to all the buccal teeth. The sizes of the spring expanding bows range from No. 18 to 16, determined by the age of the patient, etc. These molar bands usually carry buccal tubes for the regular arch-bows. In assembling, one end is placed in its tube attachment, and the other end sprung into place. The distal nuts shown in the drawing are not usually necessary.

There are other ways in which a lingual expanding bow may be bent so as to conform to other demands. To produce a greater resilient capacity, instead of crossing the dome of the arch immediately upon emerging from the mesial ends of the tubes, the bow may be bent sharply back to pass root-wise of the tubes and then turned to cross the arch further back, or the two ends may be bent in the form of the letter S.

Instances arise during or after considerable lateral expansion of arches, even with the employment of correct methods for bodily expansion, and especially when both arches have expanded, in which the crowns are tipped sufficiently to greatly disturb their occlusion. When the broad occlusal surfaces of molar teeth have established a perfect masticating occlusion by use, whether or not it be a normal interdigitation of the cusps, any inclination movement, especially in a buccal direction, as in expanding movements, will tilt the surfaces so that only the lingual cusps strike, and when this expanding movement has occurred with the teeth of both jaws, it often leaves a wide buccal inter-occlusal space. If they are firmly retained in that position, the forces of occlusion will slowly move the roots bodily to

350   PART VII. UNCLASSIFIED MALOCCLUSIONS

a perfect masticating closure of the crowns; and this is true of every inclination of molars, unless opposed by stronger forces. It is remarkable, however, how much more quickly the correction can be effected by direct intermaxillary elastics attached to hooks on the gingivo-buccal surfaces of the upper and lower molar teeth. See Direct Intermaxillary Force, Chapter XVI. It must be remembered, however, that the forces of these elastics in combination with the forces of occlusion, strongly tend toward a lingual movement of the crowns toward their former malpositions, and consequently, their expanded positions during this process must be strongly retained by lingual or labio-buccal arch-bows.

Drop Jack

While spring bow expanders are applicable for distal areas, the ideal power for the enlargement of dental arches in every direction will always be the motive force of a screw.

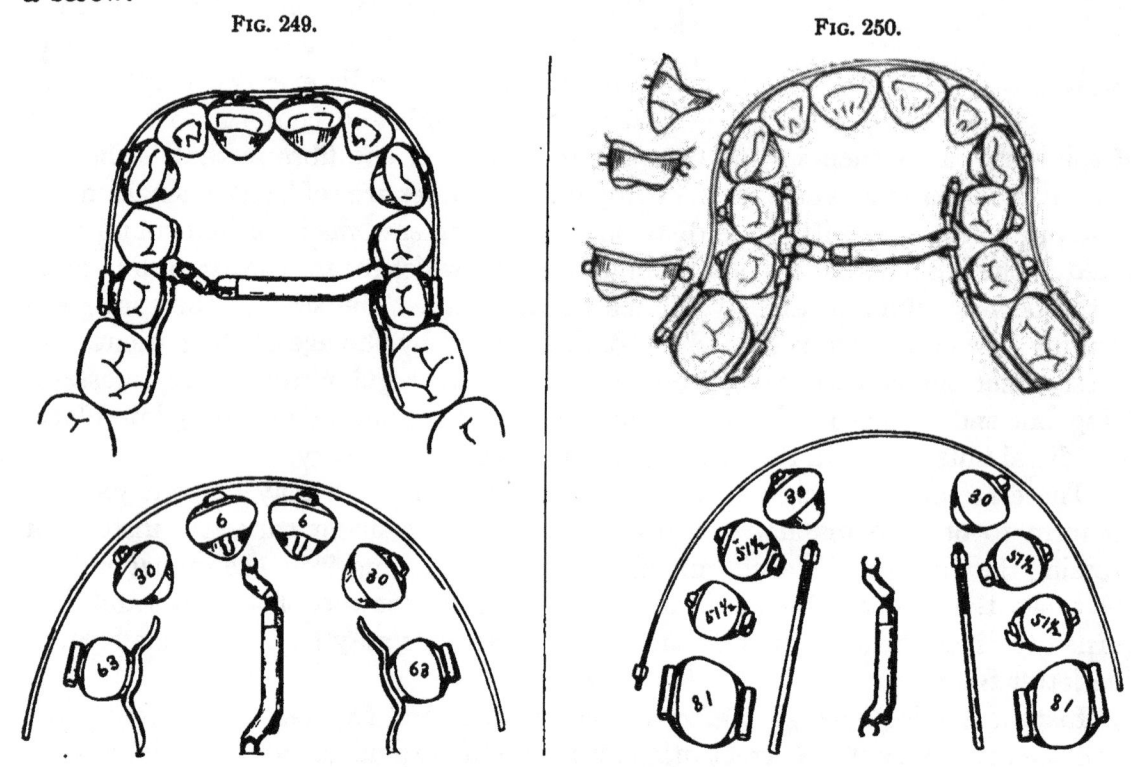

Fig. 249.   Fig. 250.

In Figs. 249 and 250 is shown the application of the **Drop Jack** used here for the ateral expansion of the arch. The **Drop** and **Arc Jacks** are far superior to the straight jacks for crossing the upper arch back of the anterior ridge, as they do not present the same unpleasant obstruction to the action of the tongue. Patients who are greatly annoyed and irritated with the one, will wear the other without complaint.

In the irregularities shown, the "club-shaped" arches are flattened across the front, and narrowed at the premolar and first molar areas. In addition to the

CHAPTER XLIX. NARROW AND WIDE ARCHES

action of the expanding jack, a resilient arch-bow No. 20 or 22, shaped the same as that shown in the disassembled appliance, is sprung into the attachments as illustrated. These forces will tend to bring the arches to a position preparatory to the final truing with the regular arch-bow.

When bodily expansion is demanded, and it is desired to employ the lingual jack-screw force, root-wise extensions may be soldered to stationary anchorages

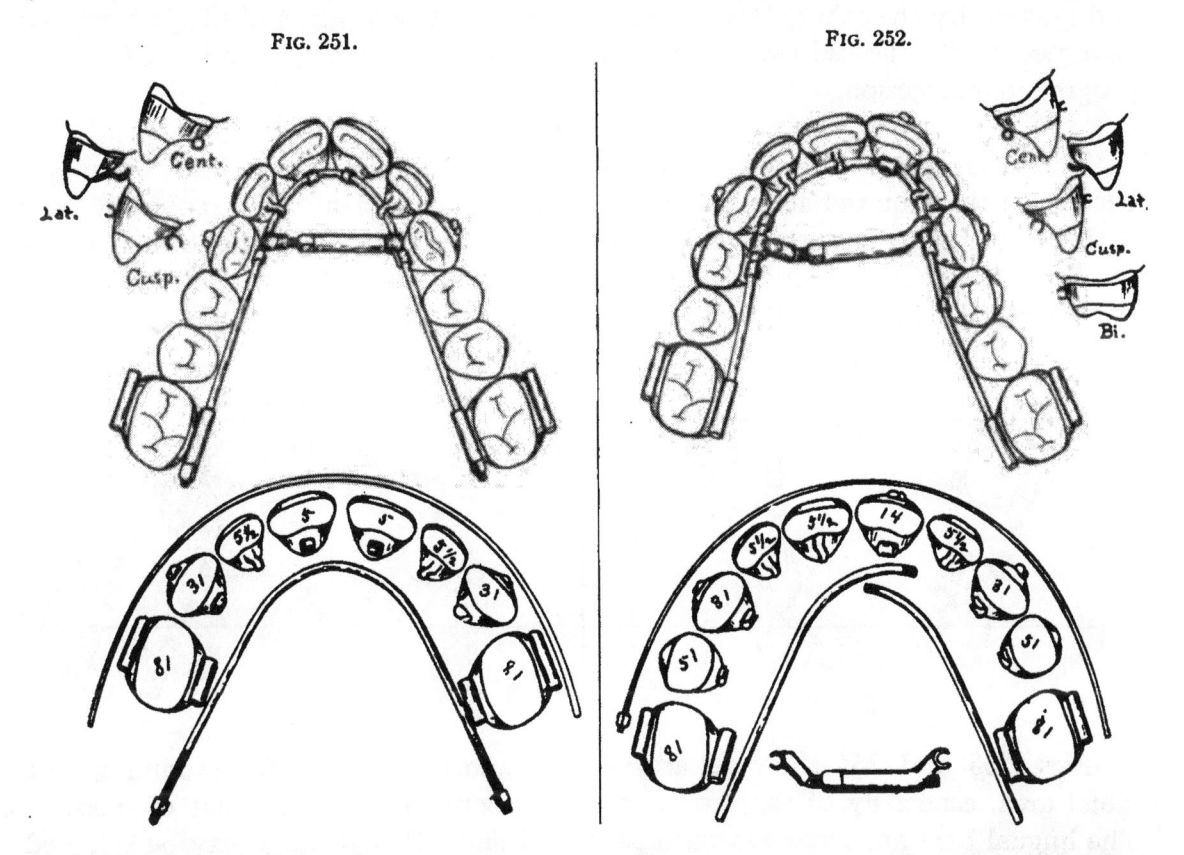

FIG. 251.

FIG. 252.

involving two or three teeth on each side, and a drop jack, or even a straight jack may be made to rest firmly in position upon the lingual bars that are soldered to the root-wise extensions. Or the extensions may be bent and fitted before soldering to form the bars upon which the jack rests.

V-shaped arches, similar to that shown in Fig. 251, may be expanded, and the incisors brought to normal arch alignment with an expanding jack No. 14, resting upon an **annealed, or semi-hard lingual bow,** No. 18, attached as shown by the drawing. It will be seen that the lateral expansion of the bow in a line with the cuspids, will retract and enlarge its anterior curve, and—if the anchorages are stationary—will retrude the front teeth to the full extent of this movement. If the contraction of the arch is not symmetrical—one side being contruded slightly more than the other—the bow may be annealed at the point of greatest contrusion, and this will enable it to more readily bend outward under the strain of the jack.

If **one side** of the dental arch is **contruded,** the normal side should be united to receive and distribute the force of reaction so as to permit no movement of the united phalanx. In Fig. 252, the right lingual distributing bow is extra-hard No. 18 wire screw attached to the left central band, and bent so as to rest evenly upon the lingual surfaces, and grasped by the attachments of the other teeth, as shown. The left lingual bow is **semi-hard** No. 18 wire, screw-attached also to the left central, and grasped by the other attachments, as shown. The location of the jack will be governed by the desired movement, and its position changed, as indicated, in the progress of correction.

Arc Jacks

The **expansion** of the **lower arch** is somewhat more difficult than the upper, because of the required action of the tongue, though patients will frequently bear without complaint or special irritation a straight jack crossing the lower arch as far back as the first premolar. But an extensive distal location is now made unnecessary by the use of the **Arc** and **Turn-buckle Jacks.**

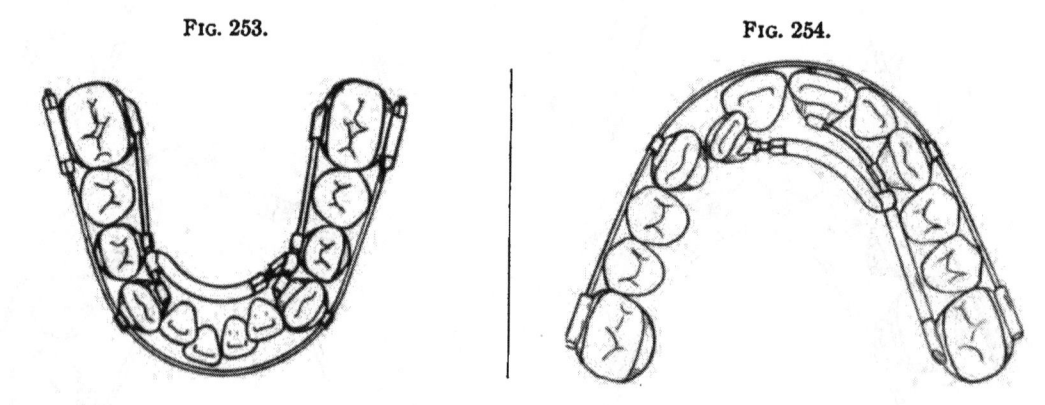

Fig. 253.

Fig. 254.

Figs. 253 and 254 show apparatus particularly designed for expanding the labial area, especially of the lower, to make room for the alignment of incisors. The lingual bars are screw-attached at mesial ends, though they may be soldered directly to the bands. The malposed incisors are usually brought to place and rotated, if necessary, through the medium of a resilient arch-bow, with various kinds of attachments on the incisor bands. Fig. 255 exhibits one of its advantages over the straight jack, and shows its relation to the dome in expanding the arch at the premolar area. The action of this jack differs from the drop jack in that the height of its curve increases, taking it farther out of the way of the tongue as the arch expands.

Fig. 255.

The **Arc Jack** is one of the most important implements designed for expanding the dental arch, and for other purposes in orthodontia. It has come in response to the same need which created the Drop and Turn-buckle jacks, and for many conditions it is far superior. It is made with different kinds of attachments. Through

CHAPTER XLIX. NARROW AND WIDE ARCHES

its end attachments it can be placed so that the arc is toward the dome or toward the labial arch. The latter is especially useful in expanding the lower labial arch, and for the correction of many malpositions where a straight jack would interfere with the tongue.

TURN-BUCKLE JACK

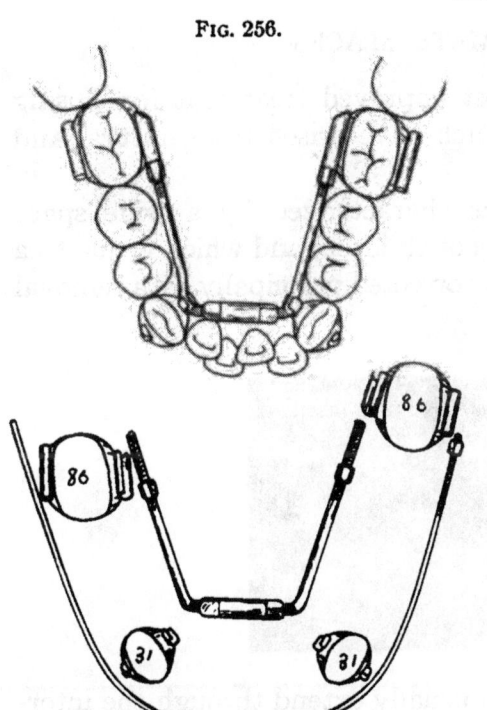

FIG. 256.

The **lateral expansion** of the **lower buccal teeth, including the cuspids,** is most successfully accomplished with the **Turn-buckle Expanding Jack,** shown in Fig. 256. The distal ends of the arms may be threaded, as shown, for hexagonal nuts to be placed mesially to the open-tube rests on the molars.

In assembling the Turn-buckle Expanding Jacks, the arms should first be bent and shaped to lie evenly in the buccal attachments, and then finally sprung outward so as to exert a more forcible pressure upon the posterior teeth, to act somewhat similar to the spring bows at the distal areas. The advantage of the turn-buckle over the spring bow expanders and contractors is that the screw movement permits locating the force at the anterior portion of the arch.

Care should be observed in springing the arms in either direction with the hands, with the view of causing the appliance to exert a greater force at the distal area, as it will be seen in such a movement that its greatest strain is brought upon the points where the arms enter the turn-buckle, and consequently upon the weakest parts of the arms, where they are deeply threaded, which may break them, or bend them, so as to obstruct a free action of the screw. Furthermore, as the bends should usually be made at the angles near the threaded and weakest parts, the **heavy wire benders** (see Fig. 211, Chapter XLII) are indispensable for this purpose, unless the arms are unscrewed and otherwise grasped.

FIG. 257.

The "bending pliers" will also be found convenient for shaping the arms to conform to the teeth, and for all purposes within and without the mouth where heavy bars require to be given short bends.

The cuspid attachment shown in Fig. 257, is usually more applicable than that shown in Fig. 256, as it permits locating the turn-buckle at a more distal position.

CHAPTER L

ABNORMAL INTERPROXIMATE SPACES

This chapter will describe in detail the most approved treatment for closing all kinds of abnormal interproximate spaces which have arisen from natural and artificial causes.

First Character.—The malposition which is characterized by a wide space between the upper central incisors in the mouths of children, and which is due to a low attachment of the frenum of the upper lip, is corrected principally by a removal

FIG. 258.

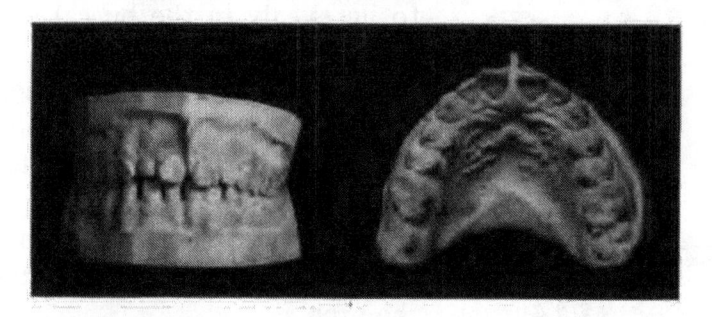

of the cause. The muscular fibers of the frenum usually extend through the interproximate space between the centrals to an attachment on the lingual aspect, with the result that every movement of the lip causing a contraction of these muscular fibers tends to keep this space open. In fact, the action of the fibers will frequently produce quite a deep groove in the interproximate alveolar process. To verify its lingual attachment, grasp the frenum between the thumb and finger with a slight pulling movement which will cause the linguo-mesial gingivæ to turn white, and will show that this is the true aponeurosis of the muscle.

Besides the abnormal appearance which this malposition produces, it frequently interferes with the perfect enunciation of the linguo-dental aspirates.

THE OPERATION

Under the effect of a local anesthetic, the frenum is grasped in locking artery forceps (see Fig. 259), and its connection with the lip is first completely severed with narrow short-beak scissors. Then with a heavy round-end gum lance, and while pulling slightly on the forceps, completely sever the attachments on each side clear to the bone, and continue its extirpation through between the teeth including its lingual attachment. To completely detach the fibers between the teeth, it may be necessary to use a narrow hoe excavator or pointed scaler. All these

CHAPTER L. ABNORMAL INTERPROXIMATE SPACES

FIG. 259.

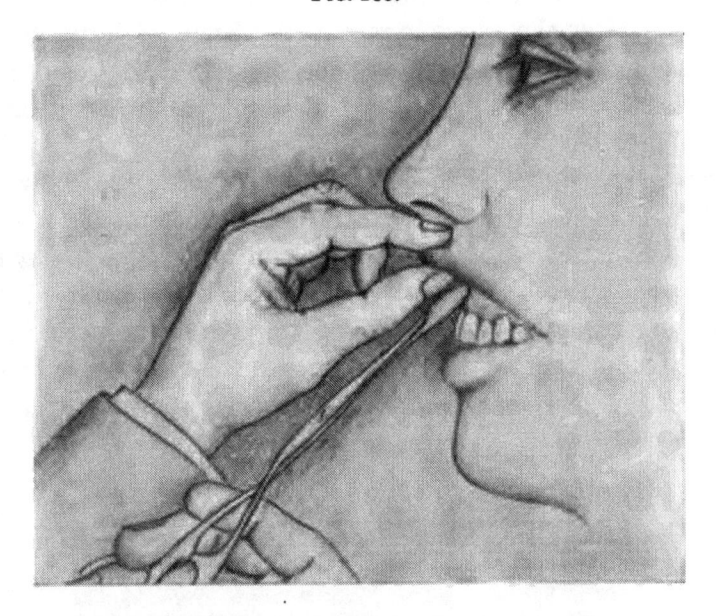

instruments should be very sharp and perfectly sterilized. It is not sufficient as a rule to cut out a V-shaped piece of the frenum, because the deeper located

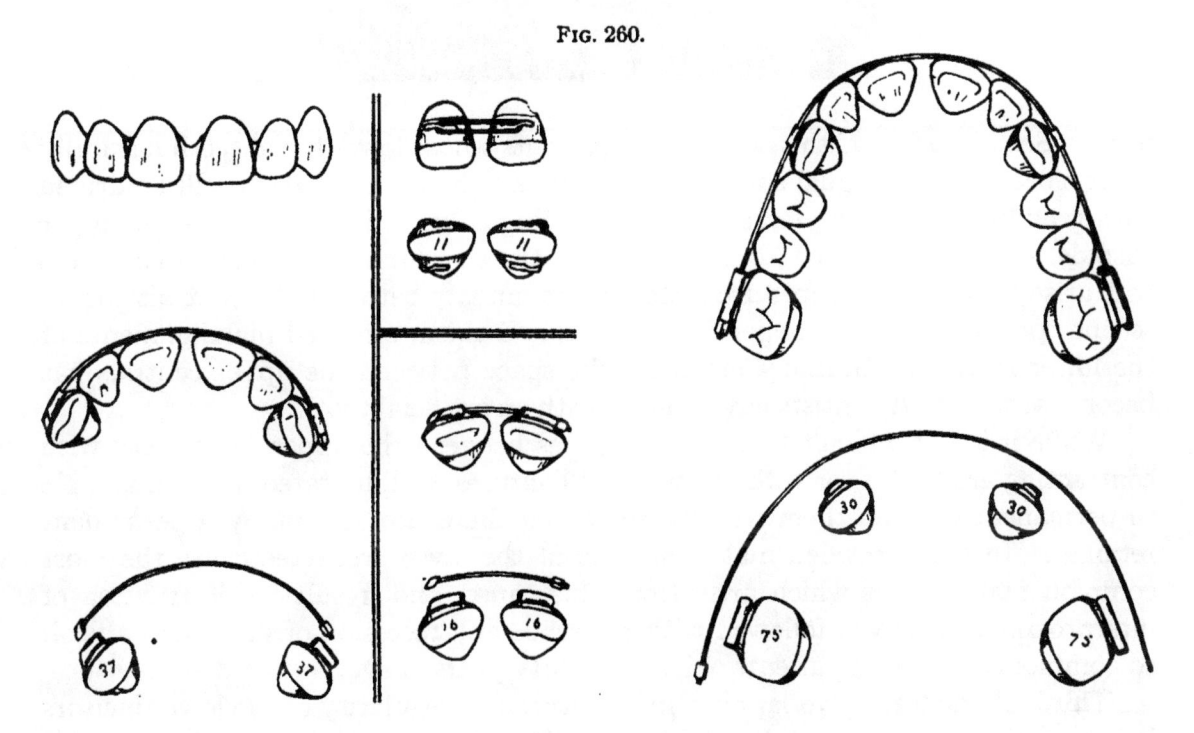

FIG. 260.

fibers in the groove will soon develop into another frenum, and thus continue the cause. When this operation is performed skillfully and thoroughly, it causes the patient no pain and should require no more time than it takes to describe it.

For quite young patients, the teeth will usually assume their normal position with little or no aid after the cause is removed. Even with much older patients, if this is the sole cause, and it has been thoroughly removed, very simple appliances, shown under Fig. 260, will readily close the space; also retention can be assured with a very moderate effort.

Second Character.—When abnormally wide spaces arise between the centrals, and occasionally between all the front teeth, for patients older than twenty-five or thirty years of age, and they aver that this condition is of somewhat recent date, and that the spaces seem to be gradually increasing, it is usually due to the wearing away of masticating surfaces, which allows the jaws to come closer together with a forward movement of the entire lower denture, the latter movement being due to the position of the tempero-maxillary articulation in relation to the occlusal

FIG. 261.

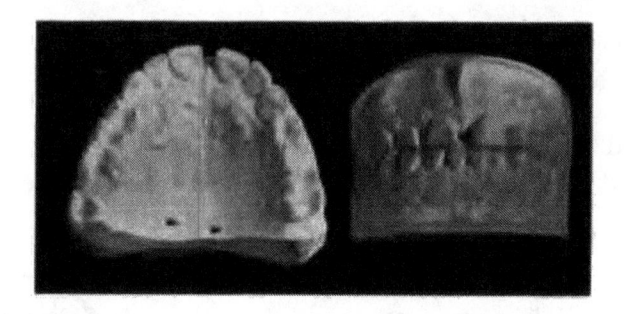

plane. See Fig. 261. If this occurs with patients whose lower labial teeth naturally shear closely to the lingual surfaces of the upper, the lower phalanx will be driven with gradually increasing force between the lingually inclined planes of the upper cuspids, and against the incisors, with one of three results: First, abnormal spaces will arise between the upper front teeth—commonly between the centrals alone; second, protrusion of the upper front teeth; and third, crowded malalignments of the lower incisors. In many instances the space between the upper centrals has become so wide that dentists have filled it with an artificial tooth.

While it is not difficult to close the spaces between the upper front teeth with contracting arch-bows, or with elastics and ligatures, as illustrated, it is impossible to permanently retain them without removing the cause, except by a permanent retainer. In fact, crowded malalignments of the lower front teeth are the most common malpositions which arise from this cause, and result in destruction of interproximate gingivæ, followed with pyorrhea and recession of gums and alveoli so commonly seen with patients older than forty years of age.

Third Character.—Overlapping and malturned irregularity of the lower incisors is one of the forms of dental malposition. This is commonly caused by a lateral contraction of the arch, which demands the expansion of both arches. At times this irregularity will occur with the arches in normal width, the upper teeth regular,

CHAPTER L. ABNORMAL INTERPROXIMATE SPACES

and the buccal teeth in normal occlusion. This seems to be due to the fact that the lower teeth are inharmonious in size in relation to the upper. If it is due to the fact that the lower buccal teeth are in slight mesial malocclusion, and the patient is young, and the occlusion has not assumed a fixed position, the correction should consist in retruding the lower buccal teeth with the intermaxillary elastic force.

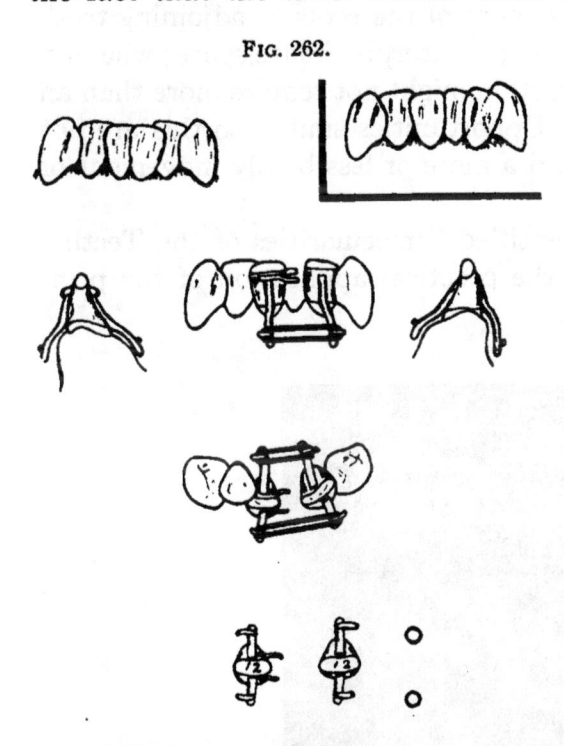

Fig. 262.

Crowded malalignments of the lower incisors are not uncommon with patients older than thirty-five years of age. This frequently arises from the same cause that produces the wide spaces between the upper centrals, i. e., the wearing down of the occlusal surfaces of the buccal teeth. This causes the jaws to come closer together and forces the lower forward with a contraction of the arch.

As the incisors are thus forced into malturned positions, the gingivo-interproximate spaces become gradually closed, severing the normal union of gum tissue between the teeth, causing exposure and death to the peridental membranes, and resulting in absorption and pyorrhea, as shown in Figs. 262 and 264.

In these cases the demand for the extraction of a lower incisor is *imperative*, and if this is followed with a proper closure of the space and regulation, it will frequently be the means of saving all of the lower labial teeth, and restore the surrounding tissue to a healthy condition; otherwise they would succumb to the abnormal conditions with ultimate loss.

In closing the space caused by the extraction of an incisor preparatory to aligning the teeth in the correction of an irregularity where this operation is demanded, the principal object is to avoid leaving an inverted V interproximate space which will usually occur with the ordinary inclination movement of the crowns.

A choice of the particular tooth to be extracted should be guided by the apparent relative distances of the apical ends of the roots from each other—everything else being equal—choosing that one if possible which is between adjoining teeth whose roots are nearest together. A novice will commonly choose the tooth which is farthest out of alignment. More often than otherwise this is wrong, because in the natural inclination movement of the crowded crowns, the root of the malposed tooth acts as a fulcrum, and forces the apical ends of the adjoining teeth farther apart; and as the difficulties of correction lie mainly in the necessity of bodily moving the roots toward each other, the extent of the root movement is of the greatest importance.

This is well shown in the upper drawings of Fig. 262. If the left lateral which is far out of alignment is extracted, the movement of the roots of adjoining teeth would need to be considerable to properly close the interproximate space; whereas, by the extraction of the left central, the correction might not require more than an inclination movement of the crowns alone. Opportunities similar to this are not rare. The usual conditions, however, demand a more or less bodily movement of the adjoining teeth.

The late Dr. J. N. Farrar, in his work entitled "Irregularities of the Teeth," published in 1888, was the first to publish the practical application of the prin-

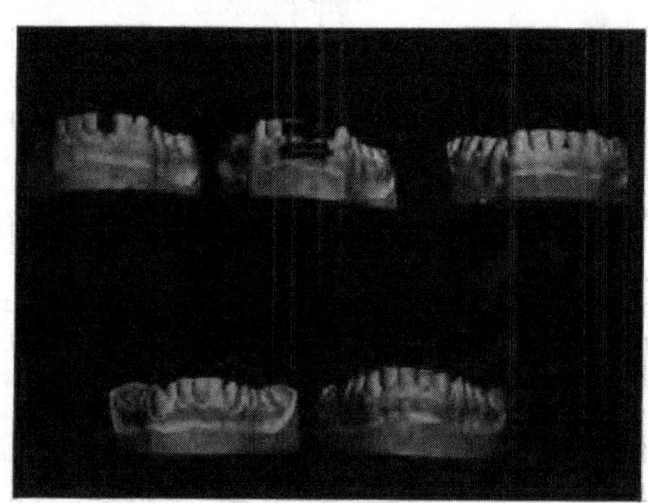

FIG. 263.

ciples of a lever of the third kind for the bodily lateral movement of the lower incisors to close wide interproximate spaces. The principles of his apparatus may be briefly explained as follows:

By attaching a traction bar at the gingival margins of the incisors having an open space between, an inclination movement will occur until the contact points of the crowns touch, and then if they are prevented from sliding by, this point will become a static fulcrum, the teeth becoming levers of the third kind with force and movement transferred to the roots. The mechanical advantage of this force will be increased in proportion to the nearness to the apical ends of the roots to which the power is applied, this being the object of the root-wise extensions.

An effective method for closing spaces between lower front teeth after extraction is shown in Fig. 262. To wide long-bearing bands fitted to the desired teeth, No. 18 root-wise bars are soldered and shaped to conform to the gum, as shown. To the ends of these are soldered short T's for the attachment of elastics. To prevent rotation, which would naturally occur with force applied at so great a distance from the central axis of the tooth, the root-wise bars are attached to both the labial and lingual surfaces of the bands. This enables one to govern the amount of movement. If irritation to the tissues is caused by the unnecessary length of the bars, they are easily bent in a distal direction which is equivalent to shortening them. The fork attached to the occluso-proximal border of one of the bands will prevent the teeth from overlapping when they come into contact.

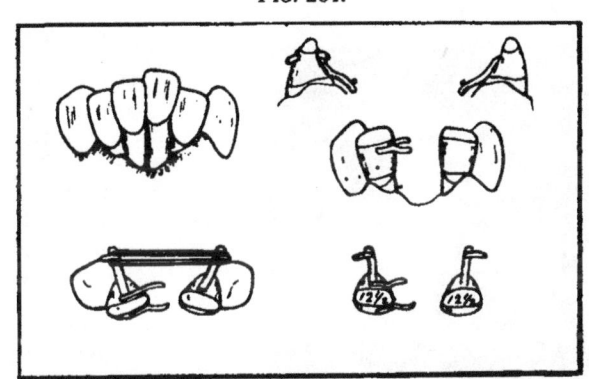

Fig. 263 shows the common results of a bodily movement of the incisors to close the space of an extracted tooth.

Fig. 264.

Fig. 264, illustrated by the drawing, is that of a case in practice, shown in Fig. 265 which was made from the dental casts of a patient thirty-five years of age, whose lower incisors were affected with pyorrhea and with decided gingival and alveolar absorption, and resulted in the necessary loss of the two centrals. The space was closed with the apparatus, as shown, and the disease was completely eradicated, and terminated in a most satisfactory restoration of the surrounding tissues.

Fig. 265.

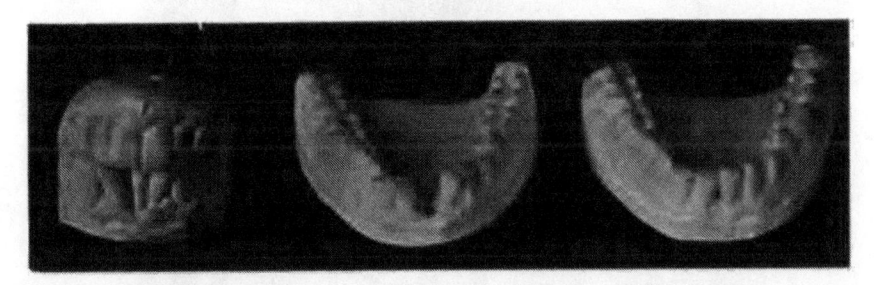

This case is a fair illustration of many similar cases older than forty years which were corrected with equal success in the author's practice.

Fourth Character. The Closure of Molar Spaces after Extraction

An interruption in the development of the crowns of the first permanent molars during dentition is not so very rare. Nor is it rare to find the crowns of these teeth at ten, eleven, and twelve years of age, so broken down with the ravages of decay that their permanent preservation is questionable. When this occurs in a denture which shows by every indication that it is decidedly protruded in its dento-facial relations, the defective molars, instead of the premolars, should be unhesitatingly

360   *PART VII. UNCLASSIFIED MALOCCLUSIONS*

extracted, and appliances placed that will close the wide molar spaces by a bodily movement of the adjoining teeth. See improved appliances for the bodily disto-mesial movement of buccal teeth to close interproximate spaces, described and illustrated in various chapters.

Fig. 266 was made from the casts of a patient eleven and twelve years of age. The first four molars were of the character mentioned above. As it was a protruded upper, the lower first molars were temporarily filled, and the upper were

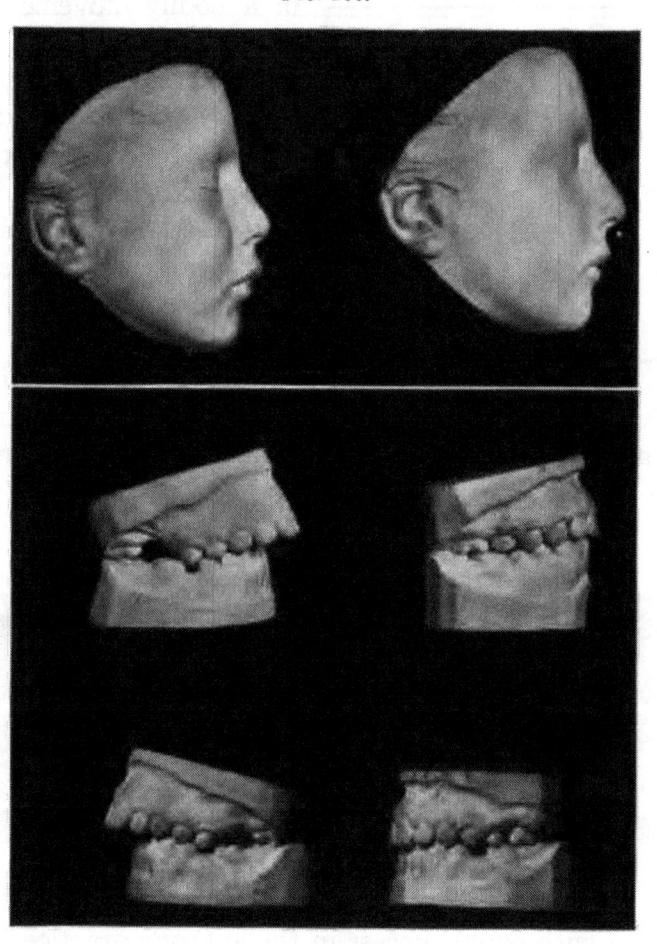

FIG. 266.

extracted. The closure of the wide spaces by a bodily distal movement of the premolars and lingual movement of the front teeth was accomplished through a root-wise application of traction intermaxillary and occipital force. On the left is shown the beginning facial cast and dental models after the extraction of the first upper molars. On the right is illustrated the finished work. It will be seen by the casts that the molar spaces are now completely closed without the slightest inclination of the adjoining teeth, and that the dento-facial protrusion has been wholly reduced.

CHAPTER L. ABNORMAL INTERPROXIMATE SPACES

When nature is left to close wide spaces after the extraction of first molars, the second molars usually tip forward, destroying perfect occlusion, with the production of a sulci into which food is crowded into inverted V interproximate spaces. This is exceedingly annoying, and often results in injury to the teeth and surrounding membranes. This is true, moreover, with any mechanical movement that is not especially constructed to apply the proper forces for a bodily movement.

FIG. 267.

FIG. 268.

When the above mentioned brokendown condition of the first molars arises in a case of bimaxillary protrusion, they are the teeth to be extracted instead of the first premolars, which otherwise is the rule. Fig. 267 illustrates a case of a young man seventeen years of age. This case is fully described under Bimaxillary Protrusions in Class I, and illustrated by Figs. 166 and 167. Fig. 268 shows the buccal appliances which were employed in this case for bodily closing the spaces between the second molars and second premolars.

The student is referred to the more modern methods in root-wise attachments for the bodily closing of buccal spaces in Chapter XV on Stationary Anchorages.

CHAPTER LI

IMPACTED TEETH AND THEIR TREATMENT

The failure of certain permanent teeth to erupt long after their normal periods of dentition has long been the cause of unhappy conditions which demand the highest order of skill to remedy. This is particularly true of deep alveolar impactions, especially before the days of modern facilities, when surgeons and dentists were groping in the dark in search of a problematical cause of some profound condition, which they could not see or absolutely know existed. And even when they were quite certain that the condition was caused by an impacted tooth, it was impossible for them to locate its position, which now is regarded practically as an indispensable preliminary to the operation.

ADVANTAGES OF THE X-RAY

Since the discovery of the Roentgen ray, many of the difficulties which formerly confronted the operator have been removed. The development and perfection of dental radiography makes it now possible to determine with certainty the presence or absence of a missing tooth which is suspected of being impacted, and which gives no outward indication of its presence. The ordinary radiogram will also give a very fair idea of the relative position and location of wholly imbedded teeth to any one who understands the peculiar shadow distortion which the ray is liable to throw upon the plate. This is a feature of considerable importance to one who desires to know the exact posture and the location of an impacted tooth, as will be seen later.

The X-ray will expose certain causes for the impaction, that would otherwise be unknown, which if removed will permit the tooth or teeth to erupt sufficiently at least to allow the attachment of force devices for its final adjustment in the arch. This refers particularly to supernumerary teeth and odontomata, which are wholly imbedded in the process with the normal teeth, and in such a manner as to obstruct their eruption, and which frequently give no outward appearance to the overlying gum that would indicate their presence.

ORDER OF IMPACTIONS

In the author's practice, the teeth most liable to be impacted are: (1) the upper cuspids; (2) the lower second premolars; and (3) the upper central incisors. The third lower molars, however, are perhaps far more liable to become impacted than any of the other teeth; and the third upper molars, upper second premolars, and lower cuspids, are occasionally in this condition. Dr. Cryer, in a paper published

CHAPTER LI. IMPACTIONS

in the Dental Cosmos, January, 1904, places the order of frequency of impacted teeth as follows: (1) the lower third molars; (2) the upper cuspids; (3) the upper third molars; (4) the upper central incisors; (5) the lower second premolars; (6) the upper second premolars; and (7) the lower cuspids. His opinion should receive respect, based as it is largely upon an examination of numberless clinical cases and dried skulls.

CAUSES

The common cause of dental impactions is the absence of room in the arch for their free and normal eruption. The spaces for the third molars, which are at present rarely more than sufficient in Caucasian races for the normal eruption and occlusion of these teeth, seem to be gradually diminishing through a foreshortening of the jaws under the forces of evolution. These spaces, moreover, which normally arise for the third molars in the final development and growth of the jaw, are doubtless frequently encroached upon by slight retruding movements of the buccal teeth, through the forces of mastication seeking occlusal interdigitation of the cusps. This may be one of the principal causes for the retarded eruption and impaction, especially of lower third molars, which are frequently crowded back under the angles of the ascending rami.

In Chapter X it will be seen that Dr. Cryer has pointed out the dangers of a *considerable* distal movement of the buccal teeth to correct occlusion, which has been recently advocated as an advanced step in Orthodontia, but one which could only be practiced in a thoughtless disregard of physiologic demands in the normal eruption of third molars.

A frequent secondary, or concomitant cause for the impaction of lower third molars and other teeth is doubtless the deflecting influence of impinging roots of adjoining teeth, which the crowns of the erupting teeth come in contact with, at a time when their roots being uncalcified, the crowns are easily deflected from their true perpendicular positions and growth movements. This turning of the crown from its true course, which with upper cuspids seems to be caused by the roots of the deciduous cuspids, cannot help but divert and misdirect the forces of resorption which are necessary for the growth movement of the tooth, and which tends always to project it along the line of its central axis. Moreover, the malposition which may commence at first with a slight deflection is probably further enhanced by the forces of eruption and development of the root. This would seem to be true in those frequent cases of impacted upper cuspids which lie imbedded nearly or quite parallel to the occlusal plane and with their crowns just back of the incisor roots; this would indicate that the malinclination had principally if not wholly occurred before the roots were developed, and that the resorptive, eruptive, and developing forces had all tended to carry the tooth forward along the misdirected line of its growth. See Fig. 269.

In a very large proportion of the impactions of lower third molars, they lie in a decided mesial inclination, frequently parallel with the occlusal plane, and with their

364   PART VII. UNCLASSIFIED MALOCCLUSIONS

occlusal surfaces resting against the distal surfaces of the roots of the second molars, and frequently with the points of the cusps locked in the disto-cervical depressions, as shown in Fig. 270.

FIG. 269.

FIG. 270.

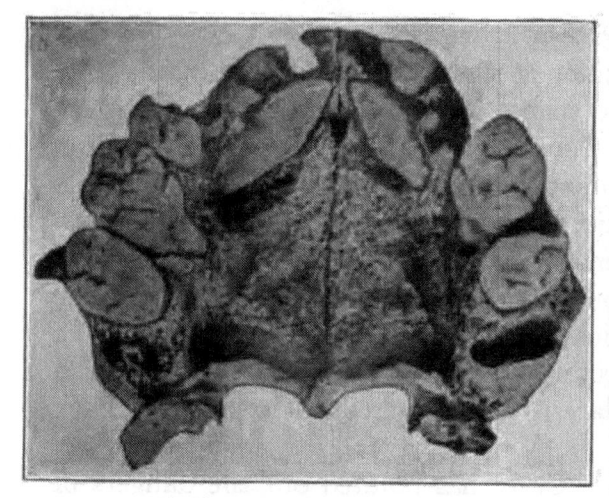

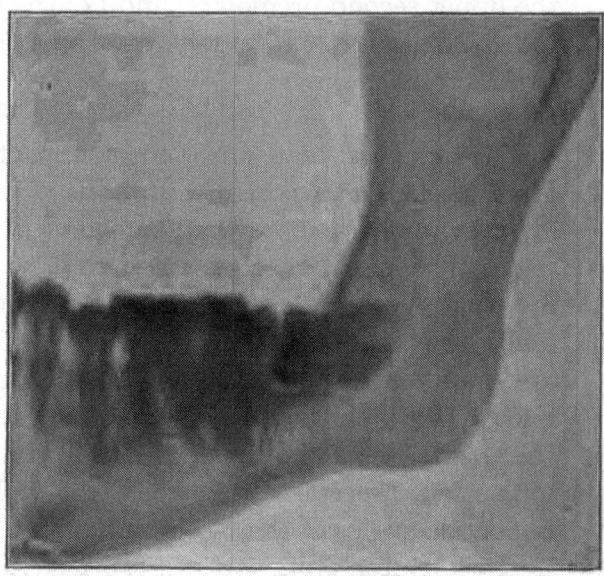

Two impacted canine teeth. (Cryer)

An impacted second premolar and a third molar. (Cryer)

In Fig. 271 is most perfectly illustrated one of the possibilities which may arise with impacted third molars.

When **first lower molars** are moved distally at an early age, the crowns of the second molars, whose roots may not be wholly calcified, are pressed back with an

FIG. 271.

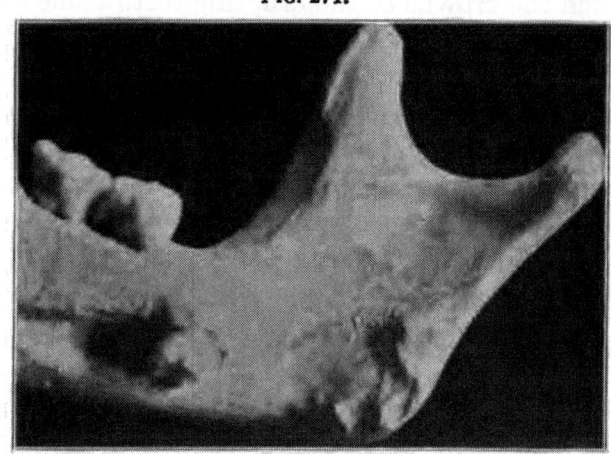

Inverted third molar. (Cryer)

inclination movement. It would seem, in this distal movement and inclination of the second molar, that the overhanging distal surface of its crown, impinging and pressing down upon the mesio-occlusal angle of the third molar crown, which at twelve years of age usually lies imbedded in the apical zone without roots, mesially inclined, would tend to hold it down at that point, while the eruptive forces would tend to lift the distal portion of the crown and turn its occlusal surface forward against the second molar. The ultimate calcification of its roots in that position causes them to extend back beneath the angles of the rami, with an impaction of the tooth which often demands a severe surgical operation for its removal. If at eight or nine years of age the first lower molars are forced back half the width of a cusp, as has been recommended for the purpose of attaining a typically normal occlusion, the unerupted second molars whose roots at that age are uncalcified, are doubtless moved distally to an unnatural position in the jaws. If held in that unnaturally retruded position, it is not strange that the mesio-occlusal portion of the partially developed crown of the third molar should be projected forward beneath the growing roots of the second molar, and thus prevented from following the natural course of its eruption to an upright position, with the production of an impaction that would not otherwise have occurred.

The late Dr. C. N. Pierce, on page 646, Vol. III, American System of Dentistry, truly says: "An impacted third molar at the base of the coronoid process is capable of giving as much excruciating and persistent suffering as is possible for human nature to endure. Indeed, there is no abnormality or mission coming in the province of the oral surgeon which demands more prompt action, or for the time more thoroughly taxes to the utmost his best judgment and skill. The removal of the anterior molar is often indicated for the purpose of giving relief; indeed, when the third molar is imbedded so that it cannot be reached, it is the only remedy." This, in the practice of Orthodontia, should be well considered before blind and thoughtless attempts are made to apply the intermaxillary force to the teeth of youths of tender ages, in a frantic endeavor to produce a typically normal occlusion in cases of inherited disto-mesial malocclusions.

In a paper read before the Chicago Dental Society, January, 1905, entitled "Impacted Teeth, Their Liberation and Correction," the author exhibited twenty-nine cases comprising thirty-seven impactions. Of these a few of the most interesting have been selected to illustrate this chapter. Of the impactions, **eleven** were upper cuspids; **six** were upper central incisors; **ten** were lower second premolars, and **one** was an upper second premolar.

Of the **cuspids,** eight were accompanied, up to the date of presentation, with the deciduous cuspids, nearly all of the roots of which were not decalcified. It may be that the roots of deciduous cuspids, which from some cause the resorptive forces do not attack, are the principal causes of the impaction of cuspid teeth. Again, the deflection of the crowns may originally arise from some other cause which enables the projecting forces of growth to carry them so far to one side that the decalcifiation of the deciduous roots does not occur. Thus the deciduous cuspids not being shed because of the unabsorbed roots, and remaining firmly seated in their alveoli, are probably allowed to remain because of the doubt which arises as to the presence of the permanent cuspids, which only the X-ray is able to definitely determine.

Two of the **cuspid** impactions were caused by the presence of supernumerary lateral incisors, and one by the premature loss of the deciduous cuspid which permitted the adjoining teeth to close the space.

Of the impacted **central incisors,** four were caused by the presence of supernumerary teeth, and two by odontomata.

Of the impacted **second premolars,** ten were caused by the premature loss of the second deciduous molars, and one by the delayed extraction of the second deciduous molar. The last character is quite commonly observed by dentists. In the many years of the author's private and clinical practice, no less than fifteen cases of impacted lower second premolars from this cause alone have presented. When a second deciduous molar is not thrown off by the eruptive forces of the second premolar, the growth and crowding nature of the adjoining buccal teeth will cause their crowns to overhang and entrap it in their dovetailing inclinations until it is forcibly extracted. If, as in all cases of this character which the author has observed, the roots of the deciduous molars are completely decalcified, it is not difficult to force the crowns out through the buccal or lingual interproximate spaces—the impacted premolars being found immediately beneath. In this connection it is interesting to note the difference in the growth altitudes of the deciduous and advanced permanent occlusal planes.

Treatment

In all cases where the impacted teeth are necessary for the perfection and preservation of the dental arch, every means should be employed to restore them to their normal positions. The treatment should consist, first, in a removal of the causes, and all obstructions to their free eruption. Where adjoining teeth partially or completely close the space, the proper appliances should be attached for widening the space and retaining it until the position of the impacted tooth is corrected. **Deciduous, and supernumerary teeth, and odontomata,** should be removed, and the overlying gum and process freely cut away so as to expose at least the occlusal portion of the crown. If the tooth is imbedded deeply in the process, it may require several operations to keep the wound open. The inflammation that ensues is advantageous toward a stimulation of the eruptive forces, which having lain dormant for years are slow to be aroused to renewed activities of tooth growth. During adolescence, after the obstructions to the growth of impacted teeth are removed and the channels of eruption kept open, without other aid they will usually erupt to a sufficient degree at least to enable the placing of lightly attached bands or caps arranged for the attachment of rubber ligatures to co-operating appliances. If the tooth is found to be much out of position or decidedly malturned or inclined, a more firmly attached band can be placed later to permit the application of positive forces.

CHAPTER LI. IMPACTIONS

With older patients it may be found impossible to arouse natural growth movement; or the position and inclination of the impacted tooth may be such that the propelling direction of its growth movement is of little use, even if possible. In either event, means for the application of artificial force will be found necessary; and as its position precludes the possibility of a band attachment, a small pit may be bored into the crown to attach a hook for a rubber ligature. But this should never be attempted until the crown is sufficiently uncovered to determine the relative position of the tooth and the exact anatomic area of the exposed surface, in order that the hole may be bored at some point on its lingual surface that will not ultimately deface the tooth when filled, and particularly to avoid endangering the vitality of the pulp.

With impactions of the labial teeth, to which these precautions apply only, the position of the pit should be chosen on the lingual surface of the crown at a point so that the drill may be directed safely as regards the pulp, and if possible, at right angles to the direction of the required force in order that only a moderate depth will be necessary to insure the stability of the post hook. The choice of position may also be influenced by the possibility of the force producing an unnecessary or necessary rotation of the tooth in its movement to place.

With teeth that are so deeply imbedded that a visual examination is not possible, these requirements often demand a most careful and intelligent indirect digital diagnosis, with an instrument calculated to sensitively impart the character and anatomic conformation of the freed area.

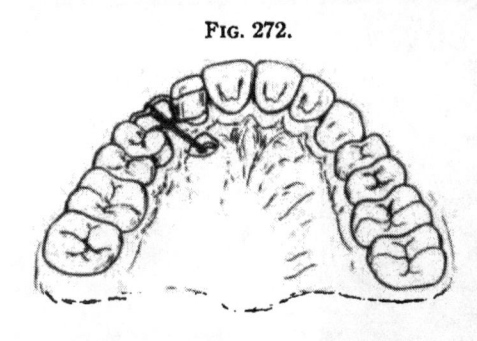

FIG. 272.

Fig. 272 illustrates the common appliance employed for hastening the eruption of completely imbedded teeth. The adjoining teeth are banded, and a bar is soldered from one band to the other so as to take a position at the extreme occlusal zone. This acts as a retainer where the space has been widened and as a means for attaching elastic bands to the impacted tooth. The hole that is bored into the tooth for this purpose need not be deep if it takes the proper direction.

The drill for boring the hole, and the wire which should exactly fit it—with no attempt to screw it in—should be about No. 19 or 20. In placing and forming the hook, use a straight piece of wire about five inches long, well annealed at the attachment end. After cementing in place, cut the wire off, leaving sufficient length to bend it close to the surface of the gum and opposite the direction of force. This will cause the rubber ligatures to hug the tooth and thus exert little force upon the wire attachment to dislodge it. When the impacted tooth has been forced out of its imbedment sufficiently to enable the attachment of a band, it will commonly require another appliance to place it in normal position.

368 PART VII. UNCLASSIFIED MALOCCLUSIONS

A more forcible action of the elastics may be obtained by attaching them to the teeth of the opposing jaw. Figs. 273 and 274 illustrate an ingenious and effective method which was proposed by Dr. E. H. Angle in 1891. As early as 1868

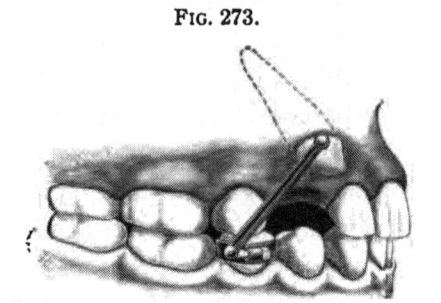

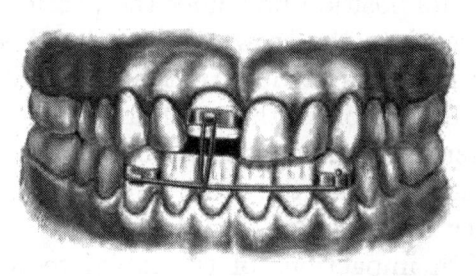

FIG. 273.

FIG. 274.

Dr. Jerry A. Robinson of Jackson, Michigan, employed this same principle, using silk ligatures instead of rubber, by tying them to the necks of the teeth in a case quite similar to Fig. 274, for a young man living in his family. The traction ligature was removed at meal times. The correction was accomplished in a short time, and retained by tying the ligatures to adjoining teeth.*

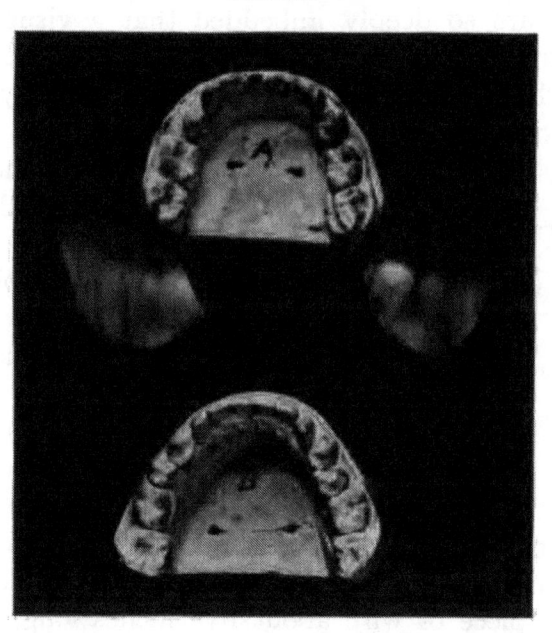

FIG. 275.

Dr. Angle would probably not advocate today the boring of a hole in the face of a cuspid, as shown in Fig. 273. When a band or lightly attached cap with a hook attachment cannot be secured to a tooth, a hole can usually be bored for

---

*The author, who was a student of Dr. Robinson's during the time of the above operation, was told that this was the common method of correcting the position of "short teeth." From this it may be seen that direct intermaxillary force was employed in dentistry much earlier than has been supposed.

CHAPTER LI. IMPACTIONS

a pin at a point where it will not ultimately be a defacement. In Chapter XVIII under "Construction of Regulating Bands," is described the method of banding partially erupted cuspids.

The Impaction of Second Bicuspids

Fig. 275 shows casts and radiograms of a boy fourteen years of age. The premature loss of the lower second deciduous molars had permitted the adjoining teeth to completely close the space for the second premolars, as shown by model "A." The accompanying radiogram shows the impacted premolars. The proper appliances for opening and retaining the spaces and correcting the malocclusion

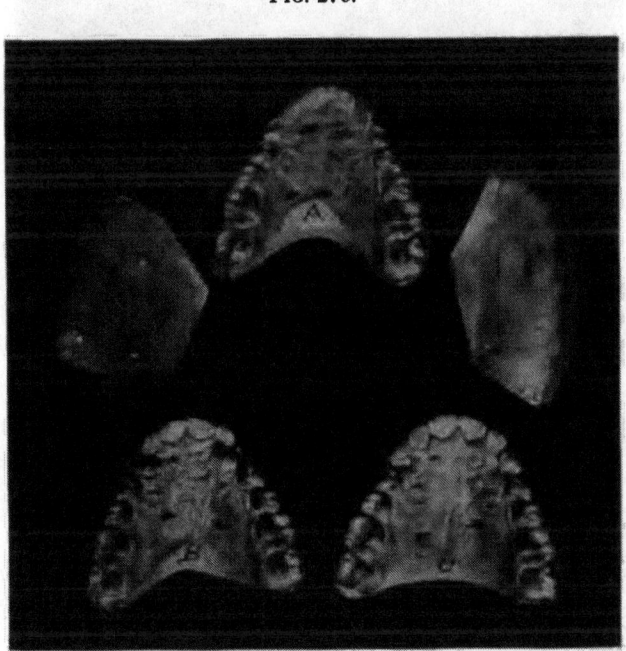

FIG. 276.

were attached, and this caused the impacted teeth to erupt as seen in Model "B." This case practically illustrates the common cause and results of impaction of this character.

Impaction of Upper Cuspids

Fig. 276 is from casts and radiograms of a girl fourteen years of age. In an examination of cast "A" which represents the case when presented, there will be found no abnormal prominences of the gum surface to indicate the presence of the permanent cuspids.

It is important to note in this and other cases to be shown, the shadow distortion of the position of the impacted teeth which the ordinary radiogram is liable to produce. Here they have the appearance of lying imbedded in the process at an inclination of 45° as compared to the normal, and with the apical ends of the roots quite distally located.

370   PART VII. UNCLASSIFIED MALOCCLUSIONS

In cast "B," which shows the cuspids as they naturally erupted after the removal of obstructions, and cast "C," after their malpositions are corrected, they are seen to be in perfect inclination in relation to the normal, a position which they could not have attained had their roots been located as indicated by the radiogram. This is far better shown by the cast of this case.

Fig. 277 is from casts of a young man about twenty-five years of age. Slight prominences of the gum surface indicated the presence of the impacted cuspids.

FIG. 277.

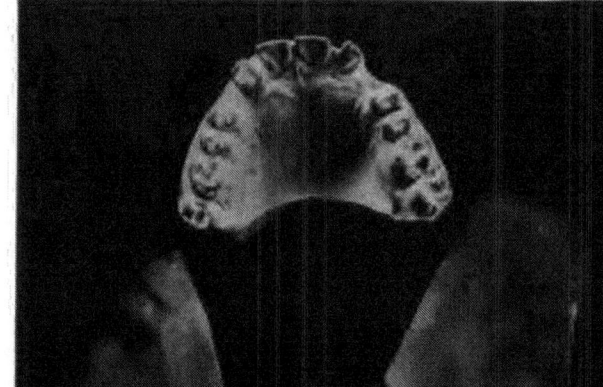

The radiograms also give to them the appearance of quite a mesial malinclination, which their erupted positions, shown by cast "C," by no means confirm. It would have been impossible to have turned these teeth to the nearly or quite normal inclinations, shown by the cast, had they been imbedded in the process in the position which the shadow distortion of the X-ray shows them. In this case, the projecting force of eruption has carried the points of the crowns well forward toward the lingual aspect of the central incisors, demanding quite a decided distal movement in lifting and forcing them into alignment. One of the hooks for the attachment of the elastic force is shown on the right cuspid of cast "B," just as the tooth is emerging from the gum. Cast "C" shows the cuspid sufficiently erupted to place

CHAPTER LI. IMPACTIONS

bands for the attachment of the lingual reciprocating jack for the final rotation and lateral movement of the crowns into alignment.

Fig. 278 illustrates the case of a girl sixteen years of age. The beginning casts "A" and "B" show two fairly well formed upper laterals on the right side and that no cuspid has erupted on that side. No prominence of the gum indicated the presence of the missing cuspid. The supernumerary lateral is plainly located as the one next to the central, by its larger size and slight difference in shape as compared to the other

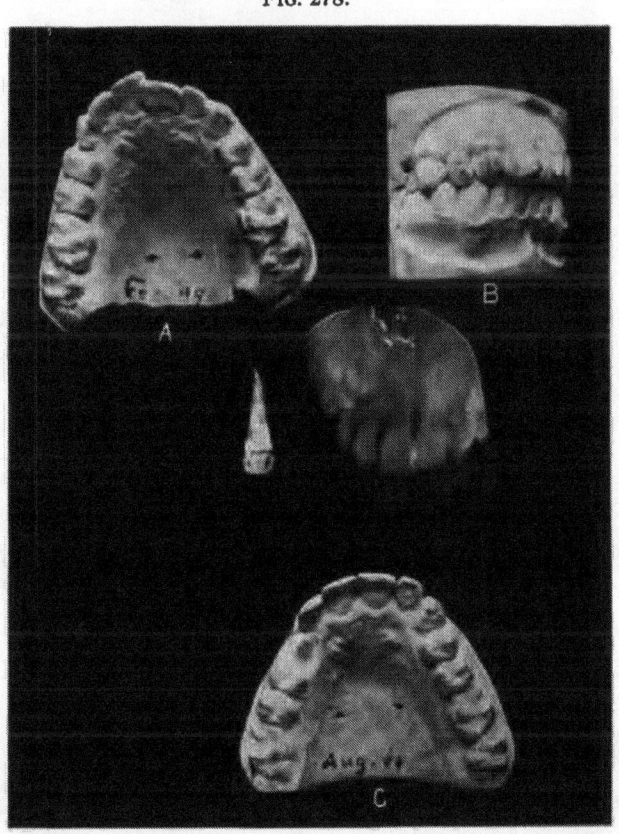

FIG. 278.

two laterals. Notwithstanding the fact that the supernumerary lateral was badly disfigured by a yellowish channel across its labial face, shown by the preserved tooth and cast, not one of the good dentists who cared for her teeth thought to look for an impacted cuspid by the aid of the X-ray now shown by the radiogram. As shown by cast "C," the supernumerary was removed, the distally located lateral was forced forward to place, and the impacted cuspid, now in a partial state of eruption, is ready for the final adjustment.

IMPACTION OF UPPER CENTRAL INCISORS

Fig. 279 illustrates the case of a girl fourteen years of age. Cast "A" made from an impression taken at beginning of operation shows no prominence of the gum surface to indicate the presence of the missing incisors. The radiogram shows the

372   PART VII. UNCLASSIFIED MALOCCLUSIONS

two central incisors above two impacted supernumerary teeth, all imbedded in the process. Below these in the radiogram is seen the right lateral, which marks the occlusal plane. The radiogram plate, unfortunately, was cut too narrow to show the left lateral. The extracted supernumeraries are seen on each side of the radiogram. Cast "B" shows left incisor in partial state of natural eruption, and the right incisor ready to burst through the gum.

Fig. 280 shows casts, etc., of a boy thirteen years of age. Casts "A" and "B" represent the appearance of the case when presented. The linguo-incisive alveolar

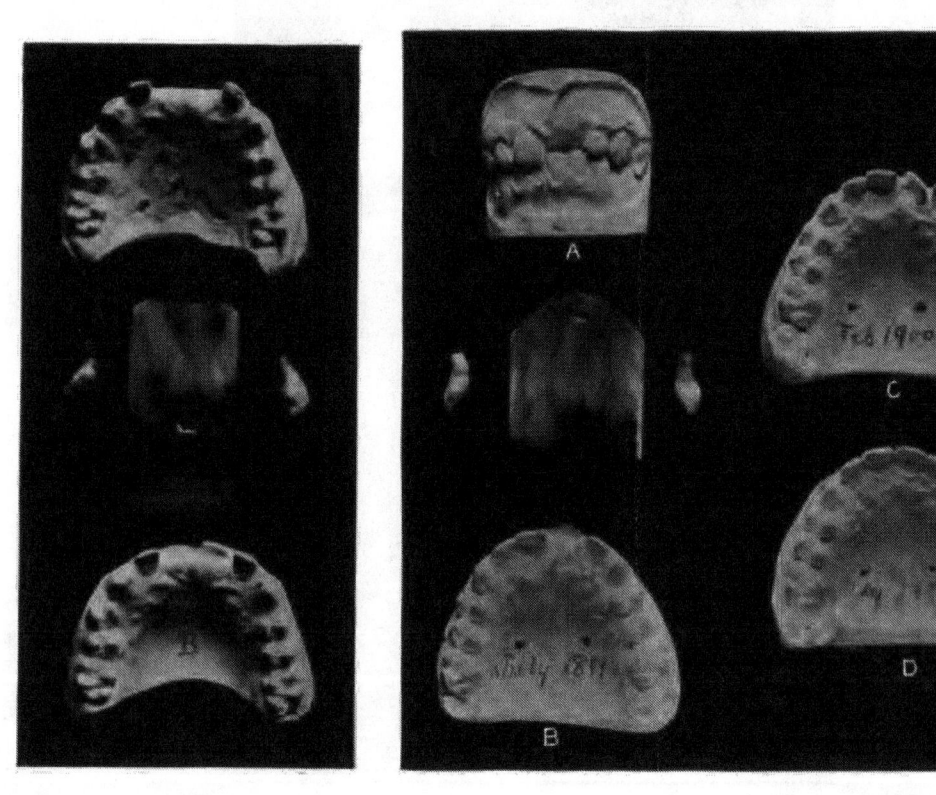

FIG. 279.   FIG. 280.

ridge is somewhat prominent but hardly sufficient to assure the presence of the missing incisor, which is seen in the radiogram wedged between two impacted supernumerary teeth. The latter were extracted and are now shown on each side of the radiogram. Cast "C" shows the incisor in a partial state of natural eruption after the obstructions were removed. At this time band appliances were attached for the regulation, with the final result shown by cast "D."

Fig. 281 shows casts, etc., of a boy of seventeen years. Cast "A" and radiogram on the left show dental arch and location of the impacted incisor. By carefully observing the radiogram, the shadow of a small dense body is seen to lie at the incisal edge of the impacted tooth in the pathway of its natural eruption. This proved to be an **odontomata** about half the size of an incisor crown which was

CHAPTER LI. IMPACTIONS

loosely imbedded in a partially absorbed area of the process. Having no power of its own to erupt, and composed of a structure that resisted the resorptive elements it remained as a permanent obstruction in the pathway of the natural growth of the impacted incisor. Upon examining it after its removal, its irregular surfaces,

FIG. 281.

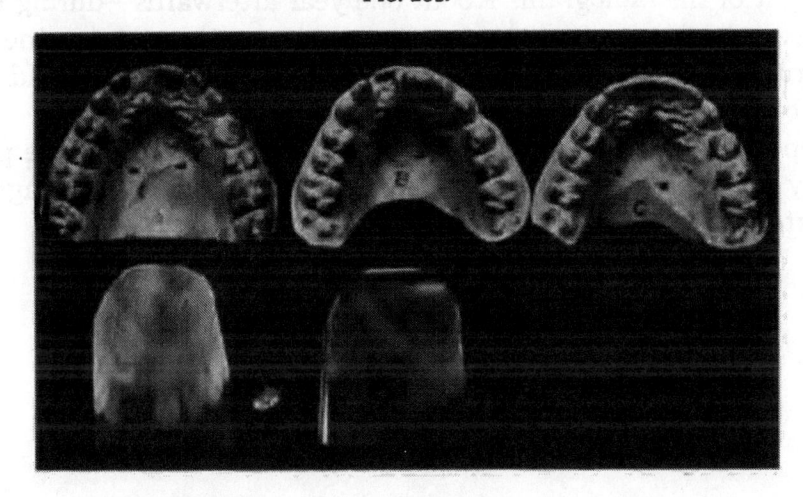

studded here and there with enamel prominences, demonstrated at once its odontomatous character. As the tooth one year after this time presented no signs of erupting, the second radiogram on the right was made, which shows the incisor

FIG. 282.

at a somewhat advanced stage, but evidently retarded in its growth by dormant physiologic processes or obstructed by the overlying secondary dense tissues which closed the original wound. This was freely removed as before. In another year the case again presented with the incisor sufficiently erupted, as shown by cast "B," to attach a band appliance for its final correction, which resulted as shown in cast "C."

Fig. 282 was made from the radiogram and casts of a girl sixteen years of age at presentment. The surface of the surrounding gum, as shown by cast "A," gave no indication of the impacted incisor, which in the radiogram is seen to be interrupted in its physiologic eruption by an odontomata located at its mesio-incisal area. This was removed—with the overlying process—and can now be seen at the right of the radiogram. About one year afterwards—during which time there were several minor operations to remove obstructing tissue—the tooth was sufficiently erupted for the attachment of a band, which enabled a rapid correction, as shown by cast "B."

Let us hope that familiarity with the advantages presented by the possibilities of the X-ray will lessen the number of cases of unnecessarily lengthy dental impactions after the usual ages of normal eruption.

PART VIII

Principles and Technics of Retention

RETENTION IN DENTAL ORTHOPEDIA

CHAPTER LII

PRINCIPLES OF RETENTION

The art of moving teeth in the correction of irregularities has always been regarded in the past as so nearly the whole of Orthodontia that the **retention** of corrected teeth has been largely considered a matter of course, and its importance, difficulties, and uncertainty of permanency have been lost sight of, or regarded thoughtlessly as a very minor branch of the art of regulating. It is possible and even probable that the art of retention will never approach so nearly to an exact science as that of regulating, because of certain natural influences over which one can have little or no control. Yet it is nevertheless a fact that the principal failures along this line have been and are largely due: first, to a lack of recognition and appreciation of the forceful influences of heredity; second, to a wrong system of regulation, which has led to placing too much dependence upon the normal locking interdigitation of masticating cusps, after extensive disto-mesial movements of the dentures to a normal occlusion; and third, it has been due to inadequate retaining methods and appliances, and the unfortunate tendency among a large class of orthodontists to avoid everything which demands personal technical skill.

Nearly all writers of note upon this subject, from Dr. Norman Kingsley to the present time, have emphasized the importance of moving the teeth to positions of normal occlusion, except when inadvisable for the correction of facial deformities, and always advising **proper occlusal relations** with the interdigitation of buccal cusps. In fact, that has always been the prime object of every one of even ordinary ability who has undertaken the correction of malposed teeth. It would seem that anyone of ordinary ability must know that when teeth are moved and left in a position where the masticating forces will drive them along the inclined planes of opposing cusps, that there can be only one result so far as that influence individually is concerned. But on the other hand, even when the cusps perfectly interdigitate, and even though a state of *normal* occlusion is established, if the teeth have been artificially moved to that position it is no positive evidence that the occlusion *per se* will retain even the buccal teeth; nor that this occlusion and retention will insure the retention of the regulated front teeth.

Failures of seemingly perfect operations have so frequently and persistently arisen because of the impermanency of retention, that it is not strange many dentists have abandoned attempts at regulating through lack of confidence in the utility of an operation which is fraught with so many difficulties and probabilities of ultimate failure. Nor is it strange that orthodontic operations are so commonly discredited among the laity.

In the earlier years of his practice, the author seeing the failure of retaining some of his most successful cases and realizing the inadequacy of the retaining plates and devices which were then employed, would have returned to the general practice of dentistry had it not been for the discovery or invention of the present system of retention, which in its developed stage is outlined in this work.

Those who practice advanced principles of dental and dento-facial orthopedia and fully grasp the underlying principles of retention, and appreciate its difficulties and advantages, and who are able and willing to devote to it that high order of mechanical skill which adequate retaining appliances demand, will find few things in dentistry that will bring quite the satisfaction and permanent pleasure as the branch they have chosen to practice. And even these men must be prepared to meet cases in which the forces of heredity will move the teeth back toward their former malpositions soon after the artificial restraint is removed, though perfectly retained a seemingly sufficient time.

Influences of Heredity

The inheritance of any family type of irregularity, from that of a single malturned incisor to extensive protrusions and retrusions, will be found the most difficult to correct, especially if a wrong method of regulating is employed. In cases of decided disto-mesial malocclusal relations of the dentures—the upper or the lower being protruded or retruded—which are so frequently due to heredity through the admixture of inharmonious types, one of the great principles of correction with a view to permanency of retention in these cases is **that fixed inherited occlusions of the buccal teeth must not be changed,** except to slightly adjust them to a more perfect interdigitation. In order, therefore, to correct the dento-facial outlines and relations of these cases in protrusions they frequently demand the extraction of teeth, and in retrusions they demand opening spaces between the premolars for the insertion of retaining artificial teeth.

The longer orthodontia is practiced, the more respect the author has for the general teachings enunciated forty years ago and published in that inestimable work entitled "Oral Deformities," by that most ingenious of all men of his day, Dr. Norman W. Kingsley. While the implements and appliances used for retention in those days were very crude as compared to those of the present time, the difficulties arising in certain conditions and the influences of natural laws remain the same and continue to engage our most earnest endeavors, often in futile attempts to permanence of retention, even with the most perfectly constructed modern appliances. Dr. Kingsley expressed thousands of ideas that are as true and applicable today as when first written. Indeed, we continually see in print these and many time-worn important thoughts reclothed and represented in a new and forceful light, and too often introduced and claimed as discoveries of modern origin. He sums up in the following words all that need be said relative to the influences of inheritance: "In hereditary cases of extensive character which have been delayed until at or near maturity, we can never feel certain that the original tendency to malposition so long unbroken will not reassert itself at any time that we abandon retaining fixtures."

Local Influences

The physical reacting forces which tend to impair or destroy permanency of retention of regulated teeth, are by far the most prolific.

When teeth are moved from a natural or acquired position, the strong elastic and resilient fibers of the peridental membrane and surrounding alveolar process are strained, stretched, and bent, and unless these are held a sufficient time for nature to rearrange the molecules to a new state of equilibrium, or supply the necessary elements for their fixation, they are sure to assert their power in forcing the teeth back toward the former malpositions.

Occlusal Influences

In regard to the influences of occlusion before and after regulation, the author cannot do better than quote Dr. Kingsley at some length:

"The occlusion of the teeth is a most potent factor in determining the stability in a new position. If occlusion of the teeth will be such as to favor the retention of moved teeth in their new position, then considerable movement may be attempted at almost any age at which it might be desired, and with an expectation of success; but if, on the other hand, the occlusion would be bad, with a tendency to drive them to their former malpositions, then all efforts at regulating would be folly at any age.

"Teeth could only be retained in changed positions under such circumstances by constantly wearing fixtures which would jeopardize their durability and permanence. The wearing of retaining plates as well as all other fixtures upon the teeth is undesirable and objectionable; they are an evil, necessary in some cases, but to be avoided as much as possible. Nevertheless, the fruits of a skillful and successful effort in regulating teeth must not be lost by neglecting to retain them in place until they not only become firm, but the tendency to return to their former malpositions has been seemingly overcome."

Dr. Edward H. Angle in his work entitled "Malocclusion of the Teeth and Fractures of the Maxillæ," has also expressed many valuable thoughts relative to the principles of retention, which are worthy of the careful consideration of all who essay the regulation of teeth. A small part of this teaching is as follows:

"It should ever be borne in mind that unless the conditions which have been operative in producing or maintaining malocclusion be removed or modified, the establishing of permanent normal occlusion can rarely be hoped for. For example, if the arches have been narrowed and the teeth forced to take malpositions as a result of mouth-breathing due to pathological conditions of the nasal passages, it will be very improbable that the teeth remain in correct occlusion after the removal of the retaining device, regardless of the time it may have been worn, unless normal breathing be established, so that the mouth may be closed, and the teeth not deprived of occlusion and the normal restraint and support of the lips the requisite amount of time.

"Again, if irregularities of the upper teeth have followed as a result of the diminished size of the lower arch, from an overlapped or irregular condition of the lower teeth, it would be folly to expect the teeth of the upper arch to be permanently maintained in their new positions unless occlusion be established by harmonizing the proportionate sizes of the arches by correction of the positions of the lower teeth."

Importance of Interdigitation of Buccal Cusps

In the text matter of this work, and especially throughout specific methods of regulating, in Parts VI and VII, the careful reader has observed that one of the indispensable principles of regulation is to place the teeth in positions where ultimate self-fixation will not be obstructed by malocclusion. In the opening paragraphs of Chapter XI, this feature of the subject is particularly dwelt upon.

While a normal occlusion of the teeth is eminently to be desired and striven for in regulation, if for no other reason than the aid it affords to retention, we should not forget that it is somewhat rare to find an anatomically normal occlusion even among dentures which we would never think of regulating. But that which we do almost invariably find in all cases that are not open-bite malocclusion, is that the masticating forces have caused the teeth to adjust themselves, so that the cusps of one set are fitted into the depressions and sulci of the other with considerable accuracy, showing that this relation, whether or not in a normal occlusion, must be attained, else nature will attain it before she rests; nor can permanence of retention of the masticating teeth be assured before. In other words, a malocclusion with interdigitation of cusps is nearly, if not quite, as capable of fixing and retaining the relative positions of teeth as a normal occlusion. It is only in rare cases that we can hope to actually improve the masticating function of an acquired and fixed occlusion of even quite irregular teeth. For this reason an acquired or inherited mesio-distal malinterdigitation of buccal cusps with arches in normal width should never be disturbed except in those cases where one denture is protruded and the other is retruded; and even then there are many exceptions to this rule, as pointed out in Class II and elsewhere.

Importance of Extraction

There are many instances of irregularity for which esthetic relations cannot be perfectly attained without extraction; nor can those cases which have been possible to regulate without extraction always be retained with the same assurance of permanency, because of the forceful influences of heredity and tendencies of crowded buccal teeth to assume their former malpositions. The author refers to excessive protrusion of the upper or lower teeth, with the teeth of the opposing jaw in normal dento-facial relation, also to full bimaxillary protrusions.

In the above cases, correction without extraction would mean that all of the teeth of the protruded arch or arches would require to be moved back fully the width of a premolar. While the author admits that it would be possible to move the buccal teeth of the upper jaw distally that distance, with a long continued and heroic application of the occipital and intermaxillary forces for some patients not older than twelve years, the same amount of movement would not be possible with the lowers, because of the impossibility of applying the occipital force; nor in bimaxillary protrusions would it be possible to apply to the lower a sufficient power from the combination of the occipital and intermaxillary forces. And in any event, with molars which had naturally erupted in that position—or in other words, which had not drifted mesially because of the premature loss of deciduous teeth —such an extensive movement would in all probability produce a decided distal inclination of the crowns, with no perfect occlusion thus robbing the operation of its principal if not the only element of retention; while the tipped occlusal planes would constantly tend to force the teeth back to their former malpositions. Moreover, permanence of retention would still not be assured without the ultimate extraction of the third molars. And so after all, to satisfy a sentiment, this prolonged and questionable operation resolves itself into the question whether it is not better to extract a premolar on each side, followed by ease of correction and assurance of retention, than subject the patient and operator to far greater difficulties, with questionable possibilities of retention and the final extraction of the third molars.

Removal of Causes.—Narrow upper arches with high domes, protruded V-shaped labial curves with the buccal cusps occluding in the sulci of the lowers instead of on the buccal aspect, and the upper buccal teeth not lingually inclined, are not uncommon, and usually are caused by a lack of proper development of the maxillary bones due to early diseases of the maxillary and nasal sinuses, adenoid vegetations, degeneracy, etc. As has been pointed out, correction would be futile without a removal of the cause. There is another equally important requirement which pertains directly to retention, i. e., the bodily lateral expansion of arches. See Chapter XLIX.

Importance of Bodily Movement

If the molar teeth have been tipped mesially or distally in regulation, or if linguo-buccal inclination of the crowns is produced, as would probably occur from an expanding jack as it is ordinarily applied, or through the action of an expansion arch-bow, to which the crowns of the teeth are attached with wire ligatures, the occlusal planes, especially of the molars, will subsequently be forced back to a more normal occlusal attitude. This has frequently been the main cause of a general failure of retention, and shows the importance of a bodily movement of buccal teeth.

To this might also be added the teachings of those eminent writers and authors of textbooks, Drs. Farrar, Guilford, Bogue, Goddard, Jackson, and others on this side and across the water, to further show that all men of large experience in orthodontia recognize and lay special stress upon the importance of the influences of inheritance and occlusion, in considering the permanent retention of regulated teeth. Beyond this, the author will not attempt an outline of the various causes which operate to destroy the retention of moved teeth, nor describe in detail the imperfections and inadequacies of retaining plates and fixtures that have been and are still being employed.

SUMMARY OF PRINCIPLES

The most important underlying principles which should be borne in mind are:

First: Teeth that are moved by orthodontic processes from one relative position to another are for a considerable time—often for years—subjected to the physical forces of surrounding tissues which tend to move them back toward the irregular positions they formerly occupied.

Second: That these forces continue to operate until the stretched and bent fibrous structures are brought to equilibrium in their changed positions by the physiologic processes of nature. To most successfully aid nature in the upbuilding of sustaining elements and structures, the moved and loosened teeth should be held *relatively* still during the entire period that is required for their permanent retention.

Third: A somewhat proportionate relation will be found to exist between the degree of the forces required for movement and the reactive forces opposed to retention. In other words, if the movement will have required considerable force, the retaining fixtures will need to be of proportionate strength and stability, unless the teeth are brought to positions of positive self-fixation by occlusion. Again, the reaction will always be along the lines in the opposite direction to that of the movements—either rotation, inclination, bodily, or a compound of these three elementary movements—consequently the fixture should be so constructed and applied to completely overcome these reactive tendencies, the directions of which may be determined by comparing the beginning and final casts.

Fourth: As a rule, teeth that have been moved slightly are far more difficult to retain than those of extensive movements, because—as in ethical relations—ties of attachment that are slightly strained are far more liable to regain their former relations than if completely broken up. Adult patients frequently apply for treatment with no more than slight malturned lateral incisors, under the impression that successful correction can be easily and inexpensively accomplished; but these corrections more often than otherwise will demand a permanent fixture to retain them. In these cases the movement should be carried considerably beyond the required position in order to sever as much as possible the original attachments, and then be allowed to slowly return to nearly the required position when the retainer is attached.

Fifth: Teeth that have been moved slowly will not require the same strength of artificial retention, or the same length of time as those that are moved rapidly, because nature has had time to partially complete the upbuilding elements of retaining bone structure.

Sixth: While it is a fact that teeth regulated during youth are more easily retained than if regulated at maturity, or later in life, no rule can be laid down as to the time retaining appliances should be worn proportionate to age, so varied are the conditions and influences that obtain with different patients. In nearly all cases where the teeth do not receive the positive self-retaining support of occlusion, the fixture should be worn at least two years. During this time *it should be removed as often as there is any doubt of the slightest imperfection in its cement attachments to the teeth*. At these times the teeth should be thoroughly cleaned, and slight malpositions, which the loosened appliance has permitted, should be corrected with silk ligatures before recementing the appliance, which in the meantime has been cleaned and properly prepared for re-attaching. Though a retainer may at times be worn from one to two years without removal and without injury to the teeth, six months should be the limit, though seemingly perfect in its cement attachments.

IMPERATIVE DEMANDS IN RETAINING FIXTURES

To render the most aid in the upbuilding of tissues for the permanent retention of regulated teeth, the retaining fixture should be one that so firmly grasps the teeth that the several opposing forces are completely held at bay, except for the slight normal movements occasioned by mastication, etc.

Anything in the form of a retaining plate which requires frequent removals for cleansing is objectionable and far inferior to a cement-attached appliance for holding the teeth firmly in the desired positions.

The fixture should be as perfectly fitted and cemented to the teeth as a bridge denture, and so constructed that the teeth and gums can be kept in a healthy condition while it is worn, with the same comfort and unconsciousness that a filling or artificial crown produces.

To fulfill these demands, its appearance in the mouth is of the utmost importance. Patients will submit to long, tedious, and painful operations, often with cumbersome and unsightly apparatus, stimulated by the hope of ultimate success, but when the teeth are finally brought to a satisfactory position, they naturally object to a long and continued use of any form of appliance objectionably conspicuous or annoying.

One of the greatest objections to an attached fixture is the danger from decaying detritus lodged in the pockets of imperfectly cemented bands and uncemented extensions, which if allowed to remain will wreck the underlying enamel. To avoid this, the best of retaining appliances should be carefully examined every two or three months, and patients also should be warned in regard to the danger of leaving the appliance upon the teeth after they discover that any one of the bands has become loosened and is in any way pocketing decaying foods or unhealthful secretions.

CHAPTER LIII

LABIAL RETAINING FIXTURES

It will be observed in the following description of **retaining appliances** for front teeth, that the author avoids as far as possible the employment of uncemented extensions or bars lying upon unbanded teeth. Though they may at times be used with safety, he prefers that retaining fixtures shall be composed of **united bands,** which are perfectly fitted and cemented at all parts in contact with enamel. Another important object in firmly cemented bands is to secure relative immovability against the strong tendencies of the forces of reaction, thus preventing anything more than the slight normal movements of mastication. Moreover, it is a somewhat rare occurrence even with minor irregularities, that all of the front teeth are not moved more or less, and therefore demand a proportionate retaining fixture.

As a rule, all fixtures—even those for the retention of a single tooth—demand at least two carefully fitted and cemented bands. When more than two teeth are involved in a labial fixture, the **pier bands** are the only ones which need to completely encircle the teeth; and these may be quite narrow in front to be less conspicuous. The bands for the intervening teeth are cut away in front, leaving only a small portion to lap on either side, and joined with a solid clip to insure a stable grasp, as will be described.

QUALITY AND THICKNESS OF BANDS

The pier bands of the appliance are narrowed in front and usually cut to conform to the gingival border. These are now made of platinum-gold. The cuspid bands in a six-band appliance, as in Fig. 290, are .0045" in thickness. In a four-band appliance attached to the incisors alone, the pier bands are .004". For intervening bands, the fronts of which are nearly cut away, **nickel-silver** is preferable, because of its greater strength and sufficiently high fusibility. These bands rarely need to be thicker than .003".

Bands for retainers should always be as thin as the required strength will permit in order to leave the smallest possible spaces at contact points while the appliance is in position. Also all portions of the fronts that are not absolutely required for stability of retention should be narrowed or cut completely away.

All exposed surfaces of the intervening nickel-silver bands should be completely covered with platinum-gold in the reinforcing and soldering process. In an appliance involving four or more teeth, a **clasp-metal plate,** No. 28 gauge, is swaged and soldered to the lingual surfaces of the bands, as will be described, to reinforce the stability of the fixture.

CHAPTER LIII. LABIAL RETAINING FIXTURES

Technics of Construction

To illustrate the principles which have been outlined, we will first consider a simple irregularity. See Fig. 283.

Fig. 284 is a common but very questionable retaining fixture which consists of a bar passed through a rotating tube attachment, or soldered directly to the band. This fixture can be made less irritating to the lips and more inconspicuous and permanent by bending a D clasp-metal wire to conform to the labial surfaces and

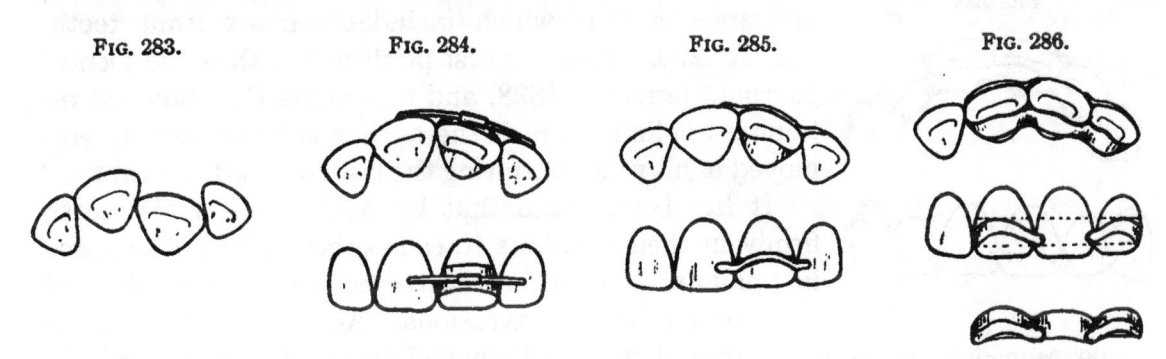

FIG. 283. FIG. 284. FIG. 285. FIG. 286.

soldering it to a perfectly fitted platinum-gold band. The labial borders of the bands are then trimmed nearly to the wire, and the whole perfectly finished and gold-plated. See Fig. 285. The uncemented extensions, which lie upon the adjoining teeth, should be slightly convex on the under surface and perfectly finished, and the patient required to frequently clean them with floss silk.

As **uncemented extensions** are at best often dangerous to the enamel upon which they rest, for young and somewhat careless patients the author prefers the appliance shown in Fig. 286. The outer pier bands of all retainers are platinum-gold, with joints on the lingual aspect, and the intervening bands are nickel-silver with joints on the labial. The joints of all retaining bands are soldered with 22k gold solder.

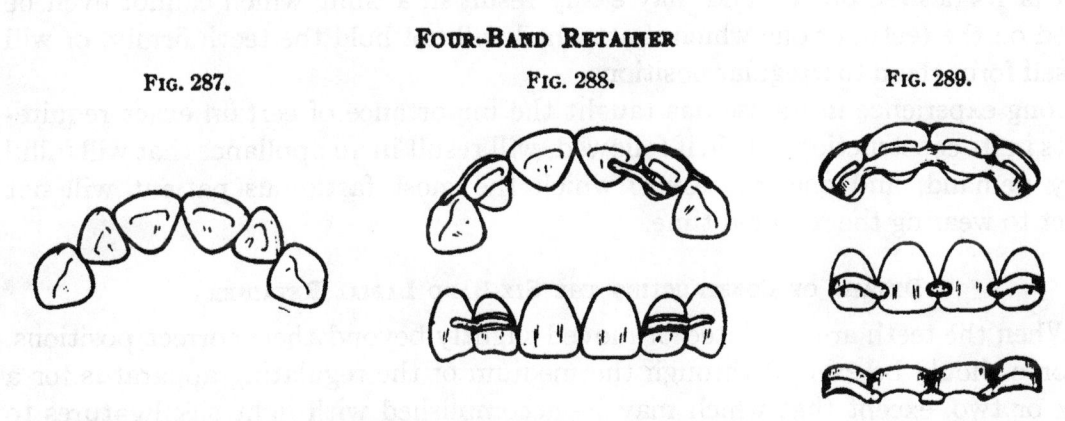

Four-Band Retainer

FIG. 287. FIG. 288. FIG. 289.

In Fig. 287, both laterals are malturned.

Fig. 288 shows an improvement over the bar attachment that is commonly recommended. In construction it is similar to Fig. 285.

Fig. 289 shows the appliance which is far preferable. Its technic construction is similar to the "six-band retainer." It will be found equally applicable where all of the incisors are malturned but in alignment with cuspids that are properly posed.

Six-Band Labial Retainer

In a large proportion of irregularities, all of the labial teeth are more or less malposed, or require to be moved to bring about a proper arch alignment and occlusal relation; therefore, the most common retaining appliance is that which includes the **six front teeth.** See Fig. 290. This was first published in the Ohio Dental Journal, January, 1898, and represents the standard retaining appliance which the author has successfully employed in his practice during the last twenty-five years.

Fig. 290.

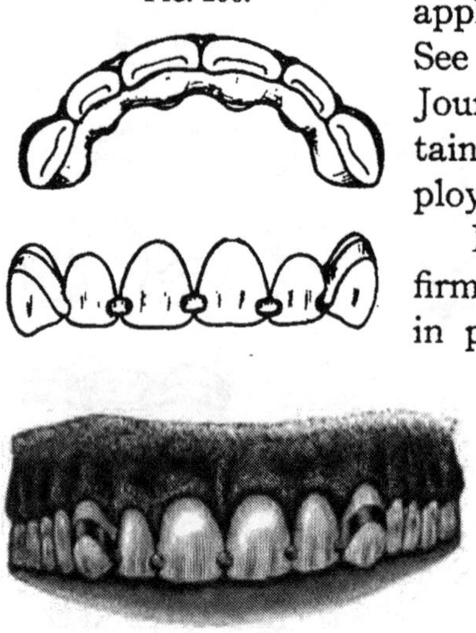

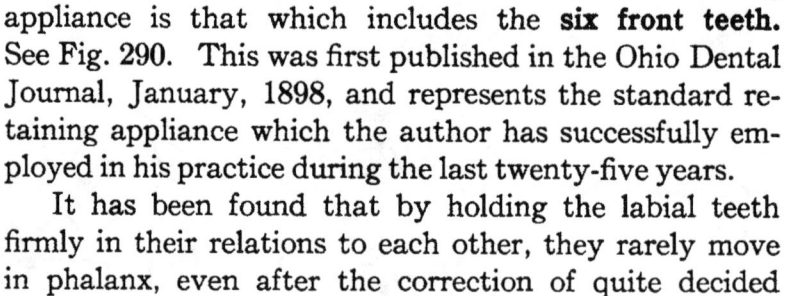

It has been found that by holding the labial teeth firmly in their relations to each other, they rarely move in phalanx, even after the correction of quite decided protrusions or retrusions. Again, after the correction of narrow V-shaped arches, by preventing the labial teeth from reacting, the premolars and even the molars rarely move, though not otherwise sustained. In cases of decided protrusions and retrusions, however, and particularly when the incisors have been moved bodily in phalanx, provision is always made for lingual bars to the molars to overcome the tendency toward reaction. Supplementary attachments to the labial retainers will be found fully described in Chapter LIV.

Unless the labial retainer can be constructed with the same skill required for crown or bridge dentures, it had better not be attempted, because it will fall short of its desired object, and may easily result in a thing which cannot even be placed on the teeth, or one which if attached will not hold the teeth firmly, or will in itself force them to irregular positions.

Long experience in its use has taught the importance of certain exact requirements in its construction which, if followed, will result in an appliance that will fulfill every demand, and one, moreover, which the most fastidious patient will not object to wearing the required time.

Details of Constructing the Six-Band Labial Retainer

When the teeth are regulated or moved slightly beyond their correct positions, no force should be exerted through the medium of the regulating apparatus for a week or two, except that which may be accomplished with light silk ligatures to hold the teeth or true them up. As it is always desirable to place the retainer the same day that the apparatus is removed, an early appointment is made in order

CHAPTER LIII. LABIAL RETAINING FIXTURES

to have plenty of time; though in an expert handling of the work, two and sometimes three of these appliances can be made and placed in one day.

When the regulating apparatus is removed, the teeth are cleaned preparatory to taking the measurements and fitting the bands, as described. At this time it will frequently be found that the teeth are not quite in the exact positions they appeared before the apparatus was removed, or they may have sprung slightly out of place after its removal. This is especially true of malturned teeth which have not been carried **beyond** their normal positions—as they should be. In this event a skillful tying and management of "Corticelli A" silk ligatures will usually correct the positions during the time the bands for the retainer are being soldered preparatory to fitting. Occasionally, they will require a second tying, and at times it will be well to postpone fitting the bands until the next day to obtain the required positions.

FIG. 291

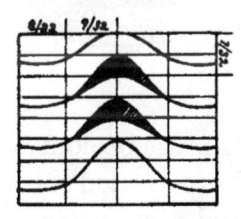

In order that cuspid bands—which are the only ones in the six-band retainer which encircle the teeth when finished—be as inconspicuous as possible, they are cut after a pattern (Fig. 291), which provides for a wide lingual portion with joint, and a narrow labial portion, which conforms to the gingival line. When properly soldered, fitted, and contoured, this pattern will be found to fit perfectly every cuspid.

In preparing to construct the cuspid pier bands, a piece of platinum-gold, .0045" in thickness and 1⅛" wide, is annealed and marked as shown by the straight lines in Fig. 291. A little

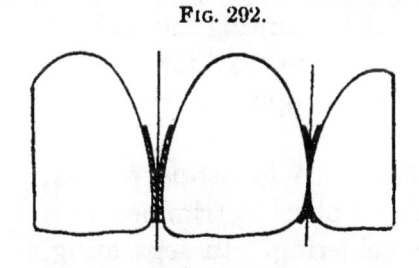

FIG. 292.

practice will enable one with a delicate pair of curved manicure scissors to cut the band according to the pattern shown below. The thickness of this band with that of the adjoining one will produce about as much space between the cuspid and lateral as would be caused by two layers of common writing paper; and this can be reduced at the contact point, if desired, with a paper disk. See Fig. 292.

The incisor bands should never be thicker than .003", preferably of nickel silver. Alternate bands—as for instance the right lateral and left central—may be sufficiently wide to extend beneath the interproximate gingivæ. The extra width insures the interproximate portions of alternate bands to serve as **entering wedges** in the first placing of the appliance after it is soldered. This will be more fully appreciated in the later description, and especially in practice.

Preparatory to fitting the bands on the teeth, the labio-gingival borders of the incisor bands may be trimmed, as shown in Fig. 293, though this is not important. The occlusal borders should be trimmed free from the incisal edges, being sure that the **contact points** of the teeth are well covered. It is next to impossible to fit a thin wide band that requires forcing on and off the teeth several times without proper tools. The hardwood plugger and band-removing plier will be found invaluable in this operation.

The bands are perfectly fitted and burnished to the inequalities of the lingual surfaces of the teeth, and a partial impression is taken in **investing plaster,** using only sufficient material to submerge the bands. The bands are then carefully removed from the teeth with the removing-plier, and accurately placed in their respective positions in the impression, Fig. 294, and the approximating surfaces are filled with Taggart's wax, using the point of a hot spatula to drive it between

FIG. 293.   FIG. 294. 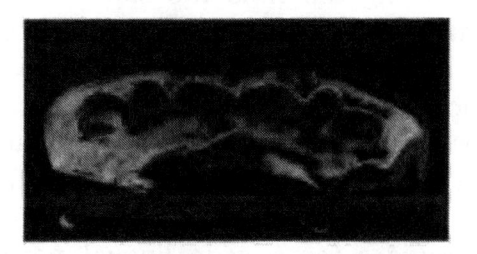   FIG. 295.

the bands. Any slight portion of the wax which runs into the bands must be completely removed, and the surface scraped. A thin solution of plumbago is used for separation. This should thoroughly cover the plaster surfaces and the *insides of the bands*. If it were not for the wax between the bands, the plumbago would flow between their interproximate surfaces and prevent the flow and perfect union with the gold solder. Again, if wax is allowed to remain on the inner surfaces of the bands, it will cause the solder to flow there. The object in painting the surfaces with plumbago is to prevent the slightest portion of solder from reaching and adhering to these surfaces, as this might easily prevent the entire appliance from going to place.

FIG. 296.

FIG. 297.

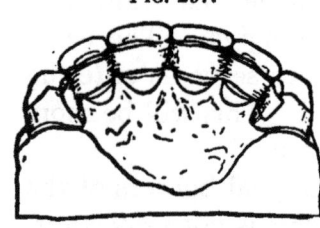

The impression is now filled with **investing plaster,** and the model with the bands in place is trimmed to a minimum size of stability for soldering. In separating, the **lingual portion** of the impression is saved, as shown in Fig. 295, from which is obtained the **die** for swaging the lingual reinforcement-plate, which is made of No. 28 gauge clasp-metal. This is well shown in Figs. 296 and 297, swaged, trimmed, and placed in position to solder. It should be cut a little narrower than the bands to facilitate placing and drawing the gold solder beneath, which should finally be flowed over its entire surface. It is of the utmost importance to stiffen in this way the six-band labial retainer to prevent the reacting forces from changing the corrected curve of the arch, especially in all cases where the arch has been laterally expanded.

CHAPTER LIII. LABIAL RETAINING FIXTURES

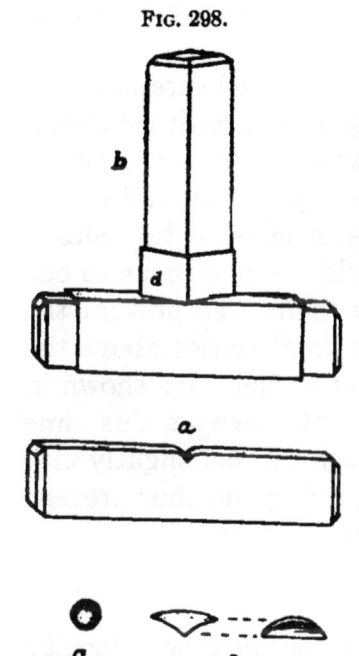

Fig. 298.

To avoid an excess of solder with its contracting possibilities, an important device is now employed for filling and finishing the labial portion of the interproximate extensions which lap on to the labio-proximate angles of the incisors—the intervening portions of the bands being cut away. This consists in striking up small gold clips which exactly fit the sulci and leave slightly convex labial surfaces for artistic finish.

The dies for this device are easily made as follows: From a ⅜-inch square steel rod (or any scrap piece of steel) cut two pieces, "a" and "b," Fig. 298. Across the center of "a," cut a groove with a sharp-edged file in the form of the labial interproximate sulci. The other piece is for the plunger die "b." First fit one end perfectly to the groove, and then cut out a place with a round file and slightly concave it with a round corundum stone to form the space in which to strike the clip.

The clips are made of scrap clasp-metal pieces weighing about two grains, and are fused on the solder-block to form tiny balls, "c," which being placed at the center of the groove "a" with the die evenly in position are quickly struck to the desired forms. Two views of the clips and the original ball of metal are shown enlarged at "c" and "e." A convenient guide "d" to the plunger is easily made of 28-gauge plate. A square is made and fitted to the counter-piece, with an opening cut for the groove. To this is soldered a box which fits and guides the plunger die directly into the groove.

The investment containing the bands should be trimmed to stand on a firm base with the labial surfaces uppermost. When it is thoroughly dried with a blow-pipe, and the interproximate spaces luted with fused borax, place on edge in each one of the sulci a small piece of No. 18k gold solder and flare the soft blaze back and forth over the entire piece from a direction that will cause a part of the heat to reach the lingual surfaces. With this movement, the solder when fused will be drawn through between the teeth and will thoroughly penetrate and fill the entire interproximate spaces. The three central clips can now be placed, being careful to place them exactly over the contact points of the teeth, and with the same character of blaze draw them to position using a steel-pointed instrument dipped in plumbago for a teaser. It is usually necessary to add small pieces of solder to their edges to complete the work.

The investment piece is then partly tilted upon its ends to facilitate placing and soldering the other two clips. Now turn the investment over, resting it firmly in a concaved block. The entire lingual surfaces of the bands being luted with fused borax, adjust and fit the clasp-metal reinforcement piece, and hold it firmly in place at the center with a teaser, while tacking it at this point, and then at the ends. Place fairly large pieces of solder at one edge of the reinforcement, and draw them first beneath it by directing the heat mostly at the other edge. Finally, smooth and finish with a minimum amount of solder.

After the borax is removed in the sulphuric acid bath, the lingual surface is first finished at the lathe. In finishing the front, use a thin-edged stone with the dental engine, and grind around the clips until the inter-portions of the bands to be cut away are nearly or quite severed. Finally, finish with sandpaper disks, and polish.

In the entire process of finishing, the piece should be handled with delicacy and with special care to avoid bending the frail interproximate extensions to one side or the other, as this will tend to fracture or weaken them. To prevent the solder from producing thickened portions in the interproximal spaces above the contact point, the bands should be pressed closely together at the stage shown in Fig. 294, before filling the impression. Another **important move** at this time is to burnish the gingivo-lingual edge of the band firmly against and slightly into the plaster impression, as it is liable to contract in the soldering and thus prevent the appliance from going fully to place over the linguo-gingival ridges.

PLACING THE APPLIANCE

The general flare of the labial teeth often occasions considerable difficulty and pain in placing the appliance when finished. This has been one of the greatest drawbacks to its general adoption, though much has been due to the lack of perfect accuracy and care in its construction, and partly due to the natural contraction of the solder. Therefore, the smallest amount of solder permissible in obtaining a smooth finish should be used.

As an extra precaution toward aiding in the easy placing of the appliance, narrow thin separating tape is placed between the banded teeth (Fig. 293) and cut off close *just before taking the impression.* At this time also, light adjustment ligatures for the final truing up of the teeth may be placed if required.

The difficulty in forcing a six-band appliance to place for the first time makes it usually necessary to place it **temporarily,** to remain about a week to allow the teeth to become adjusted to it, so that the final placing can be made with the rapidity required by the setting cement.

Moreover, this first placing of the appliance will rarely be possible if started at the cuspids. It should be started between the centrals, then the laterals, and finally the cuspids. When it is forced to a starting position upon all of the teeth, it can then be easily malleted to place with a **wood-plugger,** and finally with a thin unserrated foot plugger, to drive home the interproximate portions. The interproximo-gingival extensions of alternate bands, previously mentioned, will act as **entering wedges,** and often facilitate the first placing, especially with beginners. In the author's practice, however, where two of these appliances are made and placed in one day, this feature of the operation is rarely found necessary.

Though it may seem to be impossible at times to place or even start a six-band appliance of this character on the teeth on account of the disto-mesial flare at the occlusal zone, yet in the hands of an expert that same appliance could be readily placed, and in fact it could be placed by anyone after a little experience. However, when it is or seems to be absolutely impossible to place the appliance, as sometimes occurs, there is no objection to sawing it in two through the lingual section of one of the centrals. This will enable a temporary placing of the separate pieces for a few days, then an impression is taken, etc., as described for the bands, and the sawed surfaces are soldered.

After the appliance has been worn for about a week, to aid the final placing, it should be removed and finished for the permanent placing. All interproximal extensions and labial lappings of the incisor bands are cut down around the contact points to the minimum requirements for strength. The labial clips should be allowed to lap upon the teeth sufficiently to hold them firmly in grasp; especially upon teeth that have been rotated, and at points where the greatest reactive force will be exerted. After the appliance has been worn for a few months, or has become loosened at any point demanding its removal, the extent of the laps may often be safely reduced, so that no more appears than is often seen with proximal gold fillings. See Fig. 290.

Removal of the Appliance

It is *imperative* that a retaining appliance be removed *immediately* upon the discovery that any portion of it has become loosened from its cement attachments to the teeth, because these loosened places serve as pockets for the retention of decaying detritus which soon attacks and destroys the integrity of the enamel.

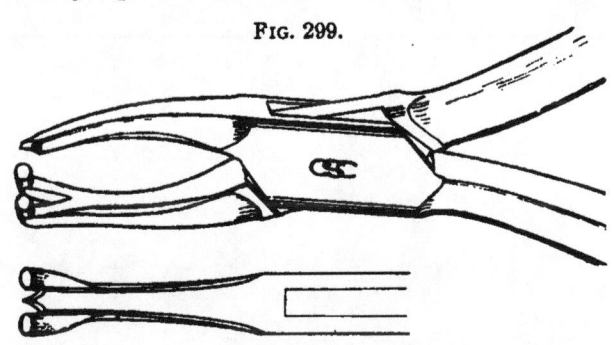

Fig. 299.

The need of removing a retaining appliance intact for the purpose of reattaching it, which is necessarily very frail at its interproximal extensions, and which is usually firmly cemented and attached at nearly all points, cannot well be accomplished without proper pliers, to say nothing of the pain that would be produced by a free-hand attempt to lift or pull it from its attachments to the teeth. This is especially true of the six-band labial retainer. In many instances, the plier shown in Fig. 99, Chapter XIX will answer the purpose, but the one which is especially adapted for this part of the operation is that shown in Fig. 299.

Restoring Broken Interproximate Extensions

It occasionally happens with the most careful handling that one or more of the proximal extensions will be torn off. Any attempt to repair it by soldering the broken edges together would be futile, because of its exceeding thinness at this point, which should not be thickened with a reinforcing piece or overflow of solder. It can, however, be very easily and perfectly restored in the following manner: Cut the appliance nearly or quite in two with a thin saw, by commencing at the occlusal border and following the proximal line marked by the broken edge. Now place the appliance in position on the teeth, and form a new T-extension by fitting and burnishing to the place a piece of narrow thin banding material, which has been doubled to the form of a T, as shown in Fig. 300. An impression is then taken in plaster and the appliance removed with the T, and carefully placed in the impression. When this is filled with investing plaster, the cast when removed holds the T in place ready for soldering. The solder should be flowed between all surfaces of the T which lie in contact. Finally, fit and solder the finishing clip to form the labial face of the new proximal extension. This when finished will be quite as strong and perfect as the original piece.

Fig. 300.

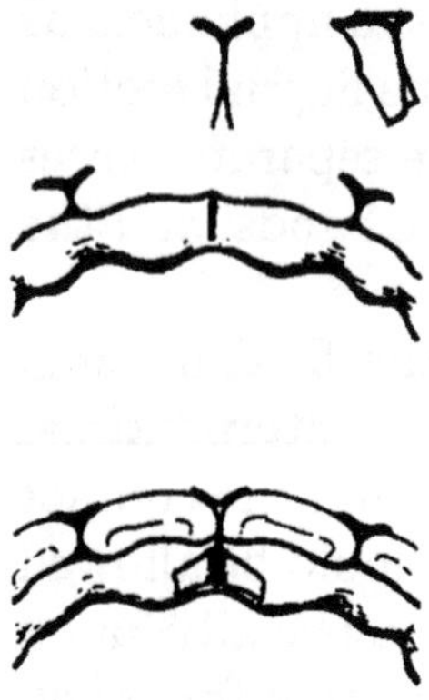

CHAPTER LIV

SUPPLEMENTARY RETAINING ATTACHMENTS AND APPLIANCES

In a very large proportion of all malocclusions, if the **six-band labial retainer**, described in Chapter LIII is properly constructed and attached, it will be commonly found sufficient in itself to perfectly retain the teeth, even though the buccal teeth which have been considerably moved are not involved in the grasp of the fixture. This of course presupposes that the upper and lower teeth have been brought to the desired relative positions, and that the cusps of the buccal teeth perfectly interdigitate, though perhaps not in a typically normal occlusion.

There are, however, a number of important supplements to this appliance which will be demanded for the retention of extensive movements.

Retention of Lateral Expansions

If one arch has been laterally expanded to the desired occlusion with a normal opposing arch which has not been moved, the simple **six-band labial fixture** will usually retain the expansion and any changed curve or malalignment of the labial arch. But if the operation has been performed without due regard to the forces of occlusion and the opposing arch has been allowed to remain laterally contracted, the stability of these unmoved teeth will surely drive the expanded teeth back to their former malpositions. This force of occlusion will frequently be sufficient to bend or displace any labial retainer that is not of unusual proportions, and will finally complete the failure of the operation after the retainer is removed.

Fig. 301.

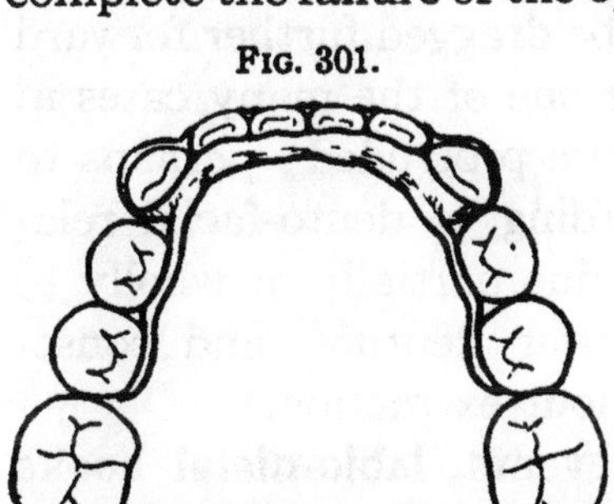

When both arches have been laterally expanded, as they should be in the last-named condition, if the lower six-band retainer is reinforced with a **clasp metal bow**, No. 17, soldered to the lingual face of the six-band labial retainer, as shown in Fig. 301, the forces of occlusion in connection with the regular upper labial retainer, shown in Fig. 290, will usually be sufficient to hold both arches in position.

With certain occlusions it may be found expedient to attach the **lingual bow** to the upper instead of the lower, and in some instances to both arches. The length of the arms and size of the wire for the lingual bow will be governed by the demands of the case. If the distal area has been much expanded, with a demand that the arms extend to the molars, they should be supported by thin lingual tubes soldered to No. 36 gold molar bands, and with every precaution in finish for cleanliness and non-irritability.

RETENTION OF RETRUDED MOVEMENTS

Fig. 302.

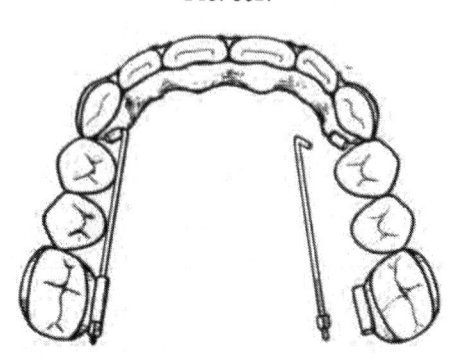

When all of the upper or the lower labial teeth have been retruded to reduce decided protrusions and close spaces occasioned by the extraction of premolars, the **labial retainer** should carry No. 19 thin wall tubes soldered to the linguo-distal borders of the cuspid bands, as shown in Fig. 302, for the purpose of attaching the appliance to the molars, either at the start or upon the first indication of a return movement. The **traction bars** are No. 19 or 20 nickel-silver, and usually should be provided with mesial and distal nuts to firmly lock them in the lingual tubes attached to gold molar bands. This will enable one to keep all interproximate spaces closed, and if at this time the occlusion is perfected it will be found sufficient.

In many cases in which the age of the patient and position of the teeth, etc., favor permanency of retention, the **lingual bars** and **molar bands** are not at first attached, though the lingual cuspid tubes in these cases should always be placed on the retainer, to be employed if found necessary. The tubes being small, lying close to the gum and properly finished, give no irritation or annoyance.

INTERMAXILLARY RETENTION

In cases which are purely protrusions of the upper to the extent that the buccal cusps interdigitate fully the width of a premolar in front of a normal occlusion (such cases being usually corrected by the extraction of the first or second premolars), the buccal teeth may be forced slightly forward of an interdigitating occlusion if employed as the sole anchorage force for retruding the labial teeth, and if employed as the sole means of retention, will tend to be dragged further forward by the reacting force of the front teeth. Or it may be one of the many cases in which the upper teeth in relation to the lower teeth were protruded—perhaps to the extent of the full width of a premolar—but according to dento-facial relations was found to be due partially or wholly to a retrusion of the lower denture, and consequently corrected without extraction.

Fig. 303.

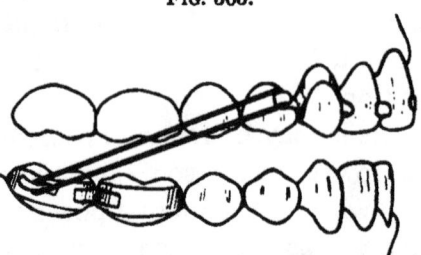

In both of these events, **labio-distal hooks** should be soldered to the labial retaining appliance as shown in Fig. 303 for the purpose of continuing the **intermaxillary force.**

The hooks are made of No. 28 clasp-metal or round platinum-gold wire soldered to the labio-distal surface of the cuspid bands, and formed to protect the premolars from the action of the elastics.

CHAPTER LIV. SUPPLEMENTARY RETAINING ATTACHMENTS

In all cases where the intermaxillary force has been extensively employed for the disto-mesial correction of malocclusion, nothing but a continuation of this character of force, in a milder degree, seems capable of retaining the position gained, notwithstanding the fact that the teeth at times have been brought to perfect or normal interdigitating occlusion. Moreover, where the final movements for the disto-mesial correction of malocclusion can be accomplished with the intermaxillary force alone, the labial retainer may be attached for this purpose as soon as the six front teeth are corrected in relation to each other. This is a most important proposition, and one which all orthodontists will take advantage of in those cases where it is indicated, as soon as they understand and appreciate the value of a properly constructed **labial retainer,** because it permits the early removal of unsightly regulating apparatus. It is of special importance where one or the other arch is decidedly retruded, and the opposing arch but slightly—if at all—protruded, as the locking of the labial teeth together in phalanx in this way increases their stability opposed to movement, as in stationary anchorages.

Intermaxillary Anchorage Methods for Retention

In determining the character of the opposing anchorage appliances for applying the intermaxillary force for disto-mesial movements, warning cannot be too often repeated in regard to the care that should be exercised in the application of a mesial force through this medium, as the same rules here obtain as in major movements. These are in the main:

First: When no mesial or extruding movement of the buccal teeth is desired, the anchorage hooks for the elastics should be placed at the most distal points possible, and attached to a two or three-band stationary anchorage. See Fig. 303.

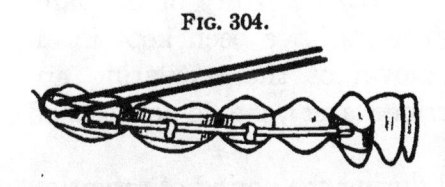

Fig. 304.

Second: If a mesial force or movement is desired, and the extruding tendency of the elastics is feared, the intermaxillary hooks should be attached to the most distal points of single molar bands—preferably to the second molars—which are anchored down with No. 19 or 18 bars, the distal ends of which rest in short tubes upon the anchor molars and pass forward under hooks or through short open-tube attachments on the first molars and the premolars to **rests** upon the cuspids. See Fig. 304. All of these bands should be as thin as the desired strength will permit. With this combination, the extruding force will be distributed to all the buccal teeth, while a mesial tipping of the crowns will be induced through the possibility of the contact points sliding upon each other. If an arch-bow is employed instead of the bars, the incisors may also be attached to it if desired.

Third: If an extruding force or movement is desired, following the correction of a close-bite malocclusion with apparatus shown in Fig. 197, the elastics should be attached to single **first molar bands,** or to the **crowns** which were employed to open the bite, and the rest of the apparatus arranged to distribute the force to the premolars.

Co-operating with a Lower Labial Retainer.—In a large proportion of cases, the lower dental arch and malaligned or malturned incisors which have been corrected demand the employment of a six-band labial retainer. In these instances it is frequently desirable to directly connect the retainer to the intermaxillary anchorages which are employed as a retrusive force to the upper teeth. This will afford a complete relief upon the premolar area, so that these teeth will not be crowded out of line. It is one of the common methods employed by the author in the mesial action of the **intermaxillary force** upon the lower or upper arch when the front teeth are in alignment. See Fig. 305. To the labio-dental surfaces of the cuspid bands of the retainer are soldered **flattened tubes,** which are bent to receive the mesial ends of No. 18 or 19 bars, the distal ends of which are locked with mesial and distal nuts in buccal tubes upon the first molar bands or regulating crowns. When the intermaxillary elastics are looped over the distal nuts or attached to special hooks, the force may be distributed directly to the labial teeth in phalanx. The bars may also be employed to correct or retain the premolars.

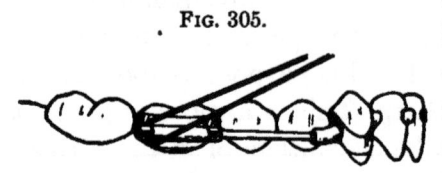

RECIPROCAL RETAINING ACTION OF INTERMAXILLARY FORCE

The most common malocclusion for which the **intermaxillary retainer** is especially applicable is that of Class II in which the upper buccal teeth are the width of a cusp in front of a normal occlusion.

Where the lower or upper front teeth have been moved labially or lingually to a considerable extent, it is presumed that the incisors have been kept in an upright position by a bodily movement. Upon removal of the regulating appliances, the **bodily retaining apparatus** (Fig. 310, described later), should be attached in connection with the **intermaxillary force.**

The amount of intermaxillary force to be applied during the period of retention should be governed by the needs of the case. It should not be at any time in excess of a force sufficient to retain the position gained—that is providing the teeth are fully corrected when the retainer is placed—as this would necessitate stopping the force every once in a while and allowing the teeth to go back, and it is this swinging back and forth in the sockets that is especially opposed to the formation and solid fixation of a permanent retaining alveolus. It is far more advisable that the heft of the elastics be gauged to the required degree of force, to hold the teeth perfectly so that the elastics can be worn continuously.

Faber No. 5 (Ticket Rings) are the same size in circumference but only about one-half the heft of No. 6 (Election Rings). The latter, single and double, are commonly used for regulating. No. 7 (Thread Bands) are the same heft as No. 6, but being about twice the size, will exert less intermaxillary force than No. 5.

After correcting the labial malrelations of the arches and placing the front teeth in proper arch alignment, the author frequently places the retaining apparatus shown in Fig. 305, before the disto-mesial malocclusion is wholly corrected, knowing that the intermaxillary force can be gauged to any degree, and will if properly applied, act quite as perfectly in retaining or moving the teeth as with the regulating apparatus. The teeth are not so liable to be forced out of alignment, and the appliance is far less conspicuous than the usual regulating appliance; moreover, the rigidity of the retainer, holding the labial curve of the arch in its corrected position, is of the greatest aid in preventing the reactive forces from laterally contracting the entire arch.

Direct Intermaxillary Retention

The correction of extensive **open-bite malocclusions** has always been more difficult to retain than any other character of irregularity, because of the impossibility in most cases of obtaining a stable hold upon which to anchor a retainer that would successfully combat the force of reaction. If a lingual or labio-buccal bow is anchored to the molar teeth for this purpose, the reactive forces of the originally open-bite labial teeth will usually force the distal extremities of the bow and anchorages in the opposite direction, extruding the molars, which in itself will open the bite still further, as any movement at this point will be magnified in its action upon the front teeth. The intermediate teeth which are also employed in this method as fulcrums to the elastic force of the bow are frequently intruded.

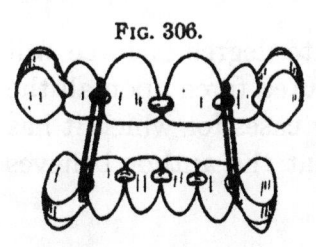

FIG. 306.

These difficulties are now overcome by soldering small **spurs** to the upper and lower labial retainers, as shown in Fig. 306. To these the patient attaches direct intermaxillary elastics, which are worn continuously at all times that do not interfere with required functions. This force should be continued until the forces of reaction are completely overcome.

As a large proportion of these cases are mouth-breathers at the time of the operation—the habit having continued long after the causes are removed—the elastics also subserve the purpose of aiding the patient in overcoming this unhealthful habit. Fig. 307 illustrates a common open-bite malocclusion which was principally corrected with the retaining apparatus as shown.

Occipital Retention

In the correction of many cases of decided **upper protrusions**, especially those in which the incisors are in an extruded position and thus in unpleasant evidence in relation to short upper lips, and particularly when complicated with close-bite malocclusions, the **occipital force** with its upward and backward direction of movement has proven an indispensable auxiliary in the author's practice. Again, in the correction of open-bite malocclusions complicated with lower protrusions (Division 4, Class III), the **occipital force,** through the medium of the lower occipital bow is

FIG. 307.

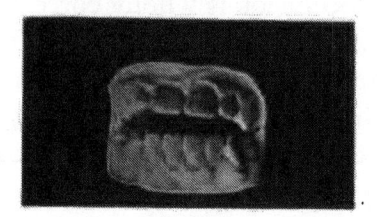

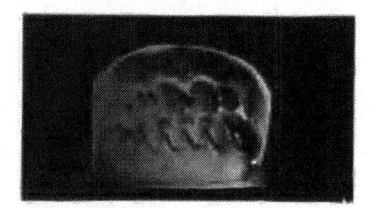

one of the most valuable and effective forces for closing the bite and aiding the retrusive movement of the lower labial teeth after the extraction of premolars. (See Occipital Force, Chapter XVI.)

FIG. 308.

In both of these characters, the tendency of the reactive forces are often difficult to overcome for a time with dental retainers alone. Nor does one always obtain the full desired results of these movements at the time when the case is otherwise corrected and ready for the usual retaining appliances. In these cases, therefore, a **platinum-gold wire,** size .040″, is soldered to the interproximal extensions of the **six-band labial retainer,** and in such a position as to span the central incisors, as shown in Fig. 308. The bar which crosses well above the median T-extension of the appliance forms a perfect **rest** for the **occipital bow A** on the upper, and **bow B** on the lower. Small rings soldered to the bar on each side of the lips of the **rest** prevent lateral motion.

The occipital apparatus, worn at night, with a moderate degree of force will give little or no annoyance, and will exert an evenly distributed force upon all the labial teeth to which the retainer is attached. In the many cases for which it has been employed in this way, it has accomplished results that the author believes would have been otherwise impossible.

Retention of Bodily Movements

In the contemplation of retaining teeth which have been moved bodily, the magnitude and peculiarity of the force of a lever of the third kind, which is the active mechanical principle in the bodily movement, is equally important to consider when we come to the retention of this movement.

The retaining appliance capable of fully sustaining this movement must be one that will forcibly combat the great reacting tendency of the elastic bone and tissue fibers to return to equilibrium. As this force is exerted along the entire length of the root, it must be seen that the stress upon the comparatively narrow zone of the crown which is grasped by the retaining appliance increases as the force approaches the apical end of the root, on the same principle that the advantage of a

CHAPTER LIV. SUPPLEMENTARY RETAINING ATTACHMENTS

lever of the first kind is increased by lengthening the power arm. Therefore, the necessity is apparent in this character of retention of employing distally extended arms with stable attachments to the retainer. This is especially true of **bodily labial movement** of the front teeth which so commonly carries the entire alveolar ridge forward in a manner that could not be accomplished other than by bending and stretching the cancellous structure of the alveolar process at the apical zone of its attachments. With **bodily retruding movements** of the labial teeth, the obstructing alveolar process in the pathway of the moving roots is to a very large extent resorbed, and consequently they are far more easily retained.

FIG. 309.

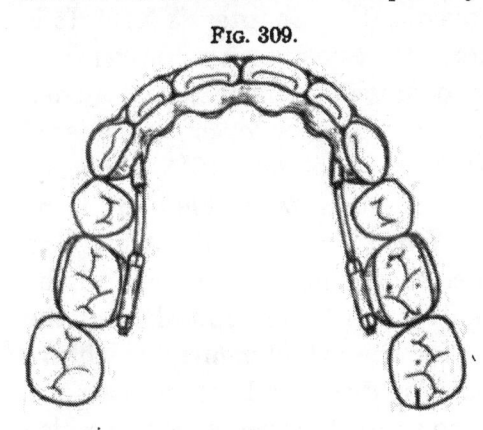

When a bodily protruding or retruding movement of the incisors has been produced and has not been accompanied by a movement of the roots of the **cuspids,** the six-band labial retainer, attached firmly as it is to the cuspid teeth, will greatly aid in retaining the root movement of the incisors, though it should always be supplemented with **lingual bars** to the molars. Fig. 309 represents the common retainer employed in these cases. Resilient clasp-metal or platinum-gold (.032″) bars are closely fitted into long-bearing elliptical clasp-metal tubes which are soldered to the lingual surfaces of the regular **six-band retainer.** The bars rest in lingual molar **open-tube attachments,** with lock-nuts to insure stability. In the final assembling and placing of the appliance, the bars are bent up or down so that when sprung into the tubes they will exert a slight extra force upon the roots in the direction of their movement. Then the anchorage tubes are closed around the bars and the projecting edges and corners are smoothed to prevent irritation of tissues. In addition to retaining the teeth, the forces of movement may be increased by bending the bars and turning the nuts.

FIG. 310.

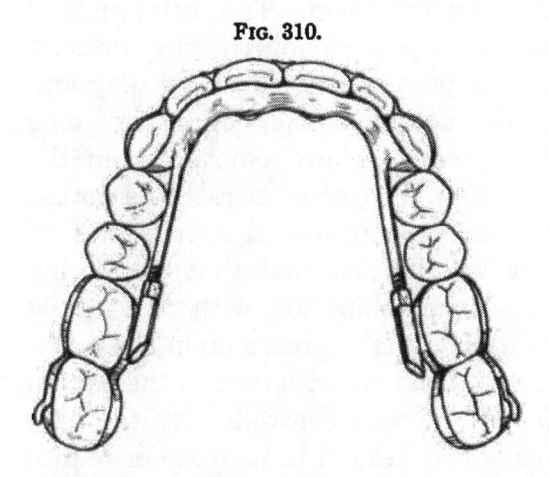

Where extensive **bodily labial movements** have been accomplished, the bands of the labial retainer should be sufficiently wide to cover the entire lingual surfaces to which they are perfectly fitted, in order to produce a wide and perfect grasp upon the crowns. When resilient bars are firmly attached to these long-bearing bands, and the ends sprung into **open-tube attachments** on the molars, they exert a push force at the gingival zone which is transmitted to the entire root. In connection with this, if the ends of the bars are threaded for mesially acting nuts, the appliance can be made to exert a similar—though less powerful—force to that of the regular contour apparatus. See Fig. 310. Because of its inconspicuousness, it may be preferably employed as a working retainer from the start in minor bodily protruding movements of the incisors. In all cases where it seems desirable to remove the regular apparatus before the full completion of its work, it will be found invaluable for holding the position gained, and for continuing the movement. This apparatus is described as follows:

The Working Bodily Movement Retainer, shown in Fig. 310, is designed to retain extensive bodily labial movements for the older class of patients; the lingual bars being much larger than those usually employed. (See Chapter XX.) It is constructed with a view to combat the reaction of extensive root movement; also to continue this force, and if necessary the bodily movement to a lessened degree. To the lingual surfaces of the labial retainer (upper or lower) is soldered a nickel-silver, or preferably **platinum-gold wire bow** (.045″ or .040″), threaded at the ends for mesial nuts. The contact surfaces of the bow are filed to fit the lingual surfaces of the appliance before soldering. When smaller resilient bars are employed, it is important that their spring temper should not be removed in the soldering process, especially if they are of nickel-silver. A favorite method of the author's is to use elliptical gold-platinum tubing for the attachments, which are soldered to the usual lingual reinforcement plate. The distal ends of the bars are threaded to lie in **open lingual tubes** upon the molar anchorages which are also provided with buccal **intermaxillary hooks.** The same care should be exercised in fitting the bow or bars to lie along the lingual surfaces of the teeth, and the ends to lie evenly in the tubes, as was described in fitting the power bow in the regular contour apparatus. Finally, with this apparatus the ends of the bow or bars are bent at the points where they join the labial retainer toward the occlusal plane, so that in the final assembling, after the cement has hardened, the ends are sprung toward and into the open tubes which are then closed around them. The distal ends of the tubes and bow should be beveled and finished to present no irritating surfaces.

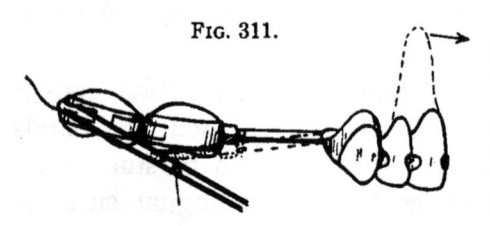

FIG. 311.

Fig. 311 is presented to illustrate diagrammatically the action of the lingual retaining bars. The premolars are removed from the drawing to show the lingual bars. The dotted lines and arrows indicate the principles of action. It will be observed that the spring of the bars in combination with the rigidly attached labial retainer is calculated to exert a bodily labial force upon the roots. This force will be in proportion to the amount of bend that is given to the bars in the final placing, while the labial force will be otherwise controlled by the nuts at the mesial ends of the tubes. If at any time it is desired to increase or reduce the force upon the roots of the labial teeth, the bars can be easily bent with the **curved wire benders** shown elsewhere. The intermaxillary force is an important auxiliary in sustaining the stability of the anchorages and as an aid toward a general protrusive movement of the upper teeth and retrusive movement of the lower.

When this apparatus is employed principally for bodily labial movement of the incisor teeth—as it may be in all minor cases—with the view of forcing the cuspids and first premolars forward by inclination movement with push bars from the anchorages, or with the production of a mesial movement of all of the buccal teeth with the intermaxillary force—the incisors should first be placed in relative alignment and the **four-band labial retainer** should be constructed with the lingual bow attached, etc., as described above. If the cuspids and first premolars are to be moved forward with the view of inserting artificial premolars to sustain the arch, buccal tubes should be soldered to the anchorages for No. .040" push bars to be employed for this purpose later in the operation.

The author was pleased to have Dr. Angle take advantage of this invention in the presentation of his pin and tube "working retainer" in 1910, the mechanical principles of which are exactly the same as that which was published and illustrated as above in the first edition of this work. The difference being that he obtained bodily force action through the torsional spring of a very small labial arch-bow instead of the direct spring of lingual bars. His employment of this principle in his practice no doubt led to his appreciation and sudden enthusiastic acceptance of the possibilities and value of bodily movement, which resulted in his applying this pin and tube method to regulating appliances, etc., and now to the general acceptance of the great value of the bodily movement of teeth.

Permanent Retaining Fixtures

In most cases where the teeth have been properly corrected, and a perfect retaining appliance has been subsequently worn for two years, with the attention that should be given to it, the positions of the teeth will not materially change. It unfortunately is a fact that occasionally after a perfect and seemingly adequate retention, there are instances in which the teeth when unrestrained will move more or less back toward their former malpositions.

As it is impossible to determine in each case the absolute time that a fixture should be worn to insure permanency of retention, it has been the author's custom to insist upon keeping the appliance on the teeth much longer than would ordinarily seem necessary. As a result of experience in this department, the time limit for wearing retaining fixtures has gradually lengthened in the last twelve years, from about six months to two years; and in some instances of marked inherited irregularities, they are now worn three years.

As the need of lengthening the retaining period has developed, it has called for a gradually increasing perfection of retaining appliances to avoid injuring the teeth, and to present an acceptable appearance. The need of such an appliance produced the retaining fixtures and methods described in the two previous chapters. It now remains to describe a final method of retention for the treatment of those comparatively few cases which demand a **permanent fixture,** or at least one that will need to be worn many years, indeed too long to ask a patient to keep in the mouth an appliance that in any way mars the natural appearance of the teeth, to say nothing of the increased danger to the teeth that is caused by cemented bands worn during long periods.

The most conspicuous of the irregularities which demand a permanently attached fixture is that which is characterized by **abnormal interproximate spaces** between the upper incisors, most frequently found between the central incisors, and which are commonly impossible to retain without a permanent fixture. This character of irregularity is fully described and illustrated in Chapter L, where the causes and treatment will be found with specific methods of correction.

The teeth which assume this special irregularity present the most continued opposition to retention after correction of any of the malpositions, even though the apparent local cause be wholly removed. In a number of instances of this character, which were perfectly retained for two years, upon removal of the retainer, the teeth soon showed signs of returning to their former malposition and with no apparent cause for it other than the unaccountable forces of nature. Therefore, if we hope to correct this irregularity which frequently mars perfect enunciation, and is conspicuously unpleasant in appearance, the proposition of permanent retention must be considered. Any form of band retainer is objectionable, because of its appearance and possible injury to the teeth.

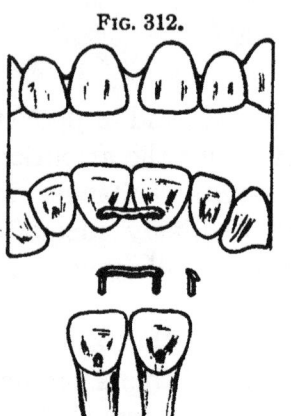

FIG. 312.

The retainer which the author has employed with the greatest satisfaction, where the space is between the centrals, is in the form of a **staple,** which doubtless has been used for years in various forms and positions.* When constructed according to the methods here proposed, and properly placed in position, it is seen only upon the lingual aspect as a flattened gold bar which extends from the lingual fossa of one tooth to the other, formed and finished to present the least possible obstruction and irritation to the tongue. See Fig. 312.

This may be made of gold wire No. 16. The ends are bent at right angles at the proper distance apart, and **filed** down to enter No. 19 holes bored in the teeth, as will be described. The No. 16 wire is of sufficient size to permit beveling the bar to fit the beveled borders of the holes, marginal ridges of the teeth, and conform to the interproximal gingivæ. The exposed or lingual surface of the bar is also beveled in a line with the plane of the enamel surfaces and finished to present no greater prominences than demanded for strength.

A staple retainer of this character was constructed for one of Dr. Thos. L. Gilmer's patients in 1894, since which time it has been worn **without removal,**

*Presented at the meeting of the Odontological Society, April, 1903, and published in the Dental Review, February, 1904.

CHAPTER LIV. SUPPLEMENTARY RETAINING ATTACHMENTS 403

and with no perceptible change or injury to the teeth. This is shown in Fig. 313. The two casts on the left are before and after correction. That on the right is from an impression taken over ten years afterward with the appliance on the teeth.

FIG. 313.

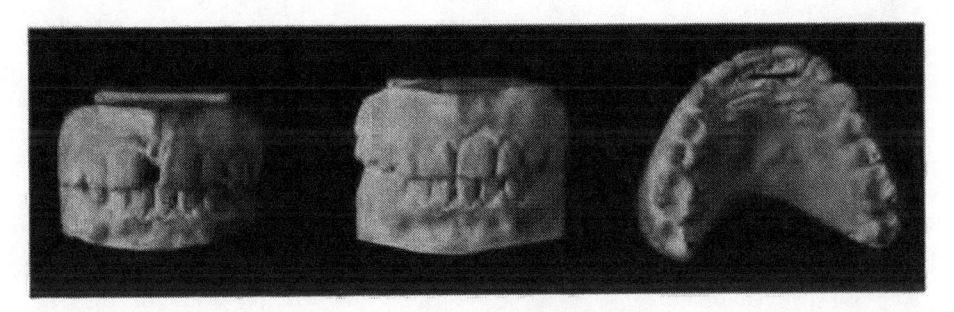

The late Dr. Joseph Wassall suggested a very practical modification in the technic construction of this retainer, especially applicable when employed to retain more than two teeth. When the pits in the teeth are prepared, by boring all the holes exactly parallel, place in them straight short posts of No. 19 gold wire and take a plaster impression. To insure pulling the **posts** out of the **pits** with the impression, they may be roughened, or the projecting ends bent. When the impression is filled with investing material, and carefully separated so as to avoid dislodging the **posts** from the model, it will enable one to solder to them the **spanning bar.** After this the surplus projecting ends are cut away, and the appliance finished and placed as before. Fig. 314 shows an appliance of this kind placed in a position to be forced to its final seating for uniting the centrals and cuspids.

FIG. 314.

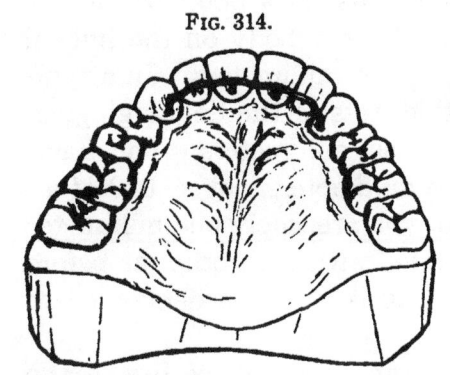

The spanning bar should be shaped to conform to the line of lingual ridges of the teeth and gingivæ over which it rests, being careful that it freely spans the median interproximate gingivæ, as any pressure upon the tissue at this point will cause inflammation and swelling. Moreover, there should be no attempt to make it fit accurately to the teeth, as might be accomplished by grinding grooves in the marginal ridges. In fact, it would be better to leave the under surface of the bar rounded and sufficiently free from the enamel to allow the removal of accumulations, with dental floss, etc. In fitting the bar on the model, place it at one side of the projecting posts, either occlusally or gingivally as seems best to meet the requirements and avoid occlusal contact, or separate bars may be fitted between the posts.

By making a labio-lingual section of a central incisor, as shown in Fig. 315, it will be found that the thickness and shape of the linguo-cervical wall will safely permit the boring of a hole of sufficient size and depth, if started in a line with the **middle** of the wall and carried **parallel to the central axis** of the tooth.

The location and direction of the proposed hole can easily be determined by the eye. In gazing root-wise at a labial tooth, take such a position as will bring

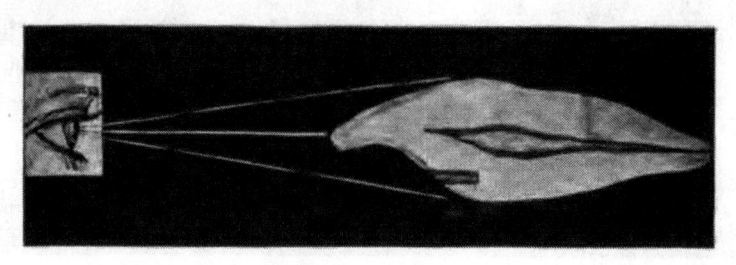

FIG. 351.

the cutting edge exactly in the center between the gingivo-labial and gingivo-lingual borders of the crown, and you will be looking directly along the line of the central axis of the tooth.

Use a No. 19 drill and start the hole in the lingual fossa at a point whose line of direction, parallel to the central axis, will leave sufficient body on the lingual side of the pit, and then bore to the depth of about three millimeters. In a typically formed central incisor of ordinary size, the thickness of the linguo-gingival wall is about three millimeters to the depth of at least six millimeters. The diameter of a No. 19 drill is about .035 of an inch. One millimeter is over .039 of an inch. Consequently, if the proper course is pursued, you are safely one millimeter from either wall. The holes should be perfectly parallel with each other as before stated, with margins very slightly countersunk, and no larger than demanded to closely fit the posts.

The safety and continued permanency of this form of appliance lies in the fact that the holes can be bored without injury to the adjoining enamel. But no attempt should be made to cover in the surrounding enamel surfaces with small pieces of plate or washers, however accurately they may be fitted, because the intervening cement will soon wash out and leave pockets for decaying detritus which will ultimately cause decay of the teeth. On the contrary, the bar where it leaves the pins and passes over the marginal ridges should lie upon the natural enamel surfaces with free rounded contact so as to permit perfect cleansing.

One is occasionally called upon to treat patients older than twenty-five years of age with protruding upper incisors, having wide interproximate spaces between the centrals and at times between all of the labial teeth which are not caused or held in that position by the occlusion of the lower teeth.

There should be no hesitation in regard to correction in these cases, even though the apparent cause is pyorrhea. In fact, with proper preliminary treatment, nothing will tend more favorably to throw off the dormant conditions of pyorrhea and restore health than the required movement of the teeth. In many instances, the irregularity may have arisen from inherent tendencies, or from the thumb-sucking habit, which forced the deciduous and permanent labial arch forward. In any event there seems to be no accounting for that continued wide-spaced malposition of the incisors opposed constantly and perhaps from the time of their eruption, by the contruding force of the lips.

If the cuspids are not involved in the protruded condition, and if after the lingual movement of incisors they will not retain their position, even after having been held perfectly with the labial retainer for two years—they can be surely and safely retained with the **permanent retaining fixture.** This may at times be attached only to the cuspids and central incisors. The fact that it is completely out of sight and can be easily removed at any time, and the small holes filled with gold, makes this form of retainer superior to the six-band appliance in all cases of this character which require very long or permanent retention. In those cases in which it is applicable, and which seem to demand a permanent fixture, and also those which indicate the need of retention an unusual length of time, this method is the only one employed by the author.

In recommending this appliance, which doubtless will appeal to many because of its apparent simplicity and ease of construction, it is hoped that a careful and skillful application of the rules laid down for boring and preparing the holes will be closely observed. This is by far the most important part of the operation. The next is in the accuracy of fittings at the margins of the holes. The bars should conform somewhat to the shape of the surfaces over which they lie, and take the position best calculated for freedom from the tongue and lower teeth. This can be accomplished on the model preparatory to soldering to the pins; the final adjustments to correct slight imperfections being made at the chair preparatory to cementing the completed fixture.

PART IX

The Prosthetic Correction of Cleft Palate

THE PROSTHETIC CORRECTION OF CLEFT PALATE

CHAPTER I

GENERAL PRINCIPLES IN THE MECHANISM OF SPEECH, AND THE TRAINING OF CLEFT PALATE PATIENTS AFTER OPERATION

In taking up the study of correction of Cleft Palate, the student is referred to any one of the main works upon Oral Surgery for the history, the etiology, and the peculiar physical and anatomic characteristics of this unfortunate deformity.

For the purposes of our present work which pertains purely to the practical correction of speech by prosthesis, for cleft palate patients, the student should fully

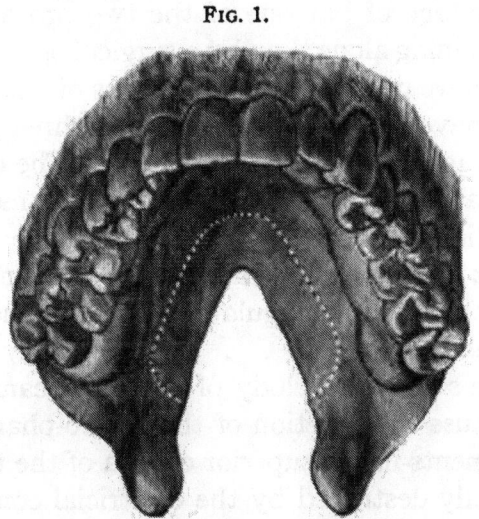

FIG. 1.

A typical single cleft of the palate. The dotted line shows the border should not extend back of the most anterior attachment of the velum-palati.

realize at the outset that the real object of a cleft palate operation, whether by surgery or prosthesis, is to fully restore the deficient parts in a manner that will enable the muscles, in connection with the restoration, to perform all the functions of normal speech, so that the patient will be able, with proper training, to speak with perfect articulation and normal voice tone quality.

One cannot appreciate the many requirements that are demanded of an artificially or a surgically restored palate until he fully understands the normal mechanism of speech and the main principles of phonology, and particularly the part which is played by the velum-palati, whose function is destroyed by the cleft. This knowledge is quite as important in our college teaching in pointing the way to the successful treatment of cleft palate, as it is to teach that occluso-proximate fillings in dentistry are for something more than closing the cavity in the tooth, and why the really successful operation demands the restoration of anatomic form and contact contours which nature has found imperative for the preservation of masticating occlusion and the future healthfulness of interproximate tissue. If these imperative foundation principles were not taught in the operative departments of our dental colleges, what hope would there be for the future success of our graduates in practice?

After operations, proper **intelligent instruction** in the art of speaking correctly is quite as important to cleft palate patients as the operation itself. In regard to this it is a pleasure to quote from the late Dr. G. Hudson-Makuen,* whose extensive experience in the teaching of cleft palate pupils to speak, renders his opinion of the greatest value. In speaking of the comparative value of training pupils to speak before and after *surgical* operations, he says:

"In the adolescent or adult cleft palate patient, *training will do more for the improvement of speech than will the surgical operation.* In other words, a patient who can have the advantage of but one of the two procedures can probably be given better speech by training alone than by a surgical operation alone. The reason for this is apparent when we consider the limitations of the operation. In the first place, the speech as I have shown, is defective in three important particulars, namely, in resonance, in melody, and in articulation. The extent to which we can improve the resonance and melody of the voice by the mere closure of the cleft [with a surgical operation] is very slight, because however well the operation may be done, the patient will have but limited control of a more or less tense velum, and he will be unable, therefore, to regulate the size of the opening between the oro-pharynx and the naso-pharynx. . . . Moreover, the rapid changes in pitch which result in the so-called melody of the voice cannot be made with any degree of accuracy, because the function of the palato-pharyngeal muscles, which have their lower attachments in the superior cornua of the thyroid cartilage of the larynx, is at least partially destroyed by the cicatricial contractions which follow the operation, and by the atrophy which has taken place from the disuse of these muscles before the operation was performed."

This concisely expresses the truth in regard to the value of nearly all surgical operations for the correction of cleft palate when operated upon after early infancy, and it also applies to a very large proportion of the infantile operations.

There is one very important thing which he does not mention: It is only in very rare cases of cleft palate at three years of age that there is a sufficient length of soft palatal tissue—when the borders of the cleft are brought together and per-

* "Oral Surgery," Dr. T. W. Brophy, Chap. XXX.

CHAPTER I. GENERAL PRINCIPLES

fectly united—to close the oro-nasal passage, and after that age, with or without an operation, this lack of palatal tissue increases until adult life, because of a lack of functional growth development.

A recognition of the necessity for a more complete closure of this passage in fulfillment of the demands of perfect speech has led many skillful surgeons to the performance of quite wonderful plastic operations in lengthening the velum with the view of enabling it to properly functionate as an organ of speech. In regard to these more extensive operations it is unfortunate but true that the greater the extent of the operation, the greater is the functional destruction of important muscular tissue for the necessary surgical building, with a proportional amount of

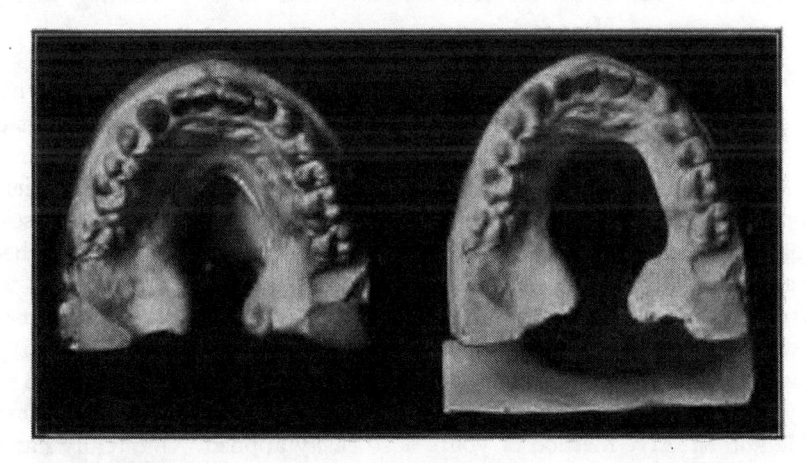

FIG. 2.

The above illustration was made from the models of a case which originally was a typical cleft with plenty of normal palatal tissue, but now is a wide cleft with cicatricial remnants of the soft bifurcated palate, after several frantic attempts had been made to close the cleft surgically. On the right, is seen the present obturator in position.

tense cicatricial rigidity in the resultant palate, which consequently is lacking in every requirement of functional activity demanded by this indispensable organ of speech.

When one becomes thoroughly acquainted with the physical character and functions of the normal velum which enables it to make the almost lightning-like movements demanded in the rapid utterance of the oral elements of words, and then compare this to the rigid cicatricial structure of the surgically formed velum with no possibility of anything like functional movement, *or even possible closure of the passage of air and voice sounds to the nose* beyond its tensely drawn posterior border, one then can realize how futile are these efforts toward a surgical production of this organ of speech.

In view of the voluminous amount of evidence which proves that the surgical operation when performed after infancy rarely enables patients to speak without the characteristic cleft palate imperfections—to say nothing of the thousands of utter failures to even unite the borders of the cleft—and in view also of the many evidences which have been exhibited at clinics and before important societies and extensively published, which prove that the modern velum obturator when properly constructed and followed with proper training enables cleft palate patients to speak with absolute perfection in tone and articulation, it would seem that the common instincts of humanity would lead all honest surgeons to hesitate before taking the chance of wrecking the lives of so many patients by an operation which at best is purely experimental, with results which so frequently deprive them of all future possibilities of perfect speech.

It was the natural and effective action of the Velum-Obturator which led the late Dr. John B. Murphy, whose name is known throughout the world, to write one of his characteristic generous letters to the author in regard to a cleft palate patient who came under his observation after wearing the obturator a little more than a year. He says in part:

> "I am more than happy to say that I was pleased and surprised to observe that such perfect correction of speech could be accomplished for a cleft palate with an obturator. I feel that the result obtained by the obturator cannot be excelled, even if equalled, by the most successful operation. Your patient not only spoke well with perfect enunciation and tone, but seemed to be unconscious of the palate in her mouth in any position of the head. And though not attached to a dental plate which I had supposed was always necessary, it seemed to rest securely in position, responding in every detail to movements of the muscles of speech, deglutition and inhalation, just as though it were the natural palate and velum. *Its motion really seems uncanny, it is so natural.* It is really sad that so many patients are permitted to go through life with defective palates, when this simple and effective method of yours is so easily applied. One really has to see the result to appreciate the great benefit that is derived from it."

Importance of Proper Instruction

Those who perform cleft palate operations—surgical or prosthetic—should fully understand the imperative mechanical requirements of perfect speech, and should also be able to give to their patients after operations at least proper foundation instruction, with appropriate notes and illustrative matter for practice exercises and for future systematic training. Nor should the responsibility of the operator stop here: He should require his patients to return to him after a few months that he may correct errors they have failed to suppress, etc. If patients are left to parents or friends for occasional correction, with no intelligent or guiding rules for instruction or continued admonition along the line of correct practice, they may never learn to speak with perfect enunciation and tone even when they are supplied with the most perfect surgical or artificial palate, because of the difficulty of overcoming long continued habits of false muscular movements which may have been acquired through years of frantic efforts to be understood. Moreover, parents and members of the family cannot as a rule be relied upon to give adequate instruction, because they have learned to understand everything the cleft palate member says, however imperfectly articulated, and therefore will not stop him as they should, at the very first oral element of speech which he fails to utter perfectly. Even the best teachers of elocution rarely employ the methods which are of the greatest importance in the teaching of cleft palate pupils.

Therefore, the surgical or prosthetic operation should be regarded as the preliminary work in giving to the patient the proper foundation to become a competent pupil in the acquirement of perfect speech. The success in the training branch of the operation will depend, first, upon the character and effectiveness of the operation, and second, upon the ability and persevering determination of the pupil. If the restoration is one which does not promise to give him full control of the speaking functions of the breath blasts, or on the other hand, if he does not appreciate the importance of perfect speech, the results are very likely to be unsatisfactory.

Practical Teaching

The teaching of cleft palate patients to speak perfectly commences in the author's practice, usually at the first or second sitting, because it takes about two weeks, in connection with other duties of practice, to make and fit the velum-obturator. This time may be very advantageously employed by the patient in practicing "tongue and lip gymnastics" or the *voluntary* placing of the tongue and lips in every possible position, which will often be of great help later when he is supplied with means for fully directing and controlling the breath blasts. Moreover, as cleft palate patients are often from distant localities, and though required to remain at least two weeks after the completion of the obturator, the time is barely sufficient to start them properly in the course of training, which really should be continued afterward under efficient tutelage.

At the first sitting the case is diagnosed with a view to determine the character of the cleft, and particularly the form of the nasal floor and adjoining sinuses to decide the method that should be employed in taking the impression. At this sitting or the next, a thorough diagnosis of the speaking qualifications is made by having the patient pronounce as distinctly as possible short words containing collectively all the consonant oral elements of speech according to the illustrated chart. Reference notes of the pupil's failures, with directions for correction, should be marked under each of the oral elements on the chart, to be later given to the pupil for reference in the absence of the teacher; or the chart may be supplemented with notes and small pencil drawings showing the relative positions of the oral organs of speech illustrated by the chart and verified by the teacher.

The vowel oral elements will be found to be quite perfectly articulated by all cleft palate patients, though lacking in proper resonance and tone quality, which will come through special training after the muscles have learned to completely close the oro-nasal passage with the aid of the obturator.

In these first lessons, the operator will be able to determine which of the consonant oral elements are imperfectly made, and those which will require the most practice. At this time, the patient should be shown the positions of the tongue in the enunciation of one or two of the simple sounds which require the least amount of air pressure, with instruction to practice these elementary sounds alone until quite perfect before attempting to join them to the vowels or short syllables. This later may require patiently repeated showings with every aid that will enable the pupil to place the tongue properly, whose control and direction will likely be as awkward and difficult as a child learning to walk, as he has never before had these same muscles directed by the nerves into the speaking movements or positions. The most arduous but necessary part of the teacher's work is the repetition, over and over again, of the required sounds, not only to show the requisite position and action of the oral organs, but to instill into the mind of the pupil a true conception of the required sounds, and the fixation of the sound-images.

Sound-Images

The "sound-image" of an oral element of speech is the individual cognition of the exact sound of that element, so that one is able to detect the slightest imperfection in or variation from it when it is made by others or himself, in the same way that a teacher of singing is able to detect the slightest flat or sharp of a musical note. All cleft palate patients, who have been obliged to speak perhaps for years in their imperfect way, have acquired false sound-images of all the utterances which have been impossible for them to articulate perfectly—with the result that they are absolutely unconscious of their own imperfections and wonder why they are not understood, often becoming quite indignant when people who are not accustomed to hearing them speak do not understand them. This is true also of some singers who will persist in flatting or sharping certain notes because they have acquired false sound-images of those notes.

Albert Salisbury in his work on "Phonology and Orthoëpy" makes the following statement: "The exact quality and character of each oral element is determined by the requisite position and relation of the several organs of speech. Correct enunciation depends primarily on correct position of these organs; it is therefore of vital importance that the teacher should, in the first place, know *what the correct sounds are*, to the ear, and, in the second place, what the correct positions are, in the mouth, for producing the exact sound required. When the teacher finds in the pupil a wrong habit of sound-production, the first point of attack should be the securing of a correct sound-image; the next should be the securing of the proper position of the organs for producing that sound."

This applies to pupils whose organs are physically normal, or at least capable of development to normal activities. With cleft palate pupils, after competent operations, it is usually necessary to reverse this order and teach them, first, the positions of the tongue, etc., which enable them to make the proper sounds.

One of the greatest difficulties encountered by teachers in the correction of defective speech, and particularly with cleft palate pupils, is the fixed acquirement of false sound-images of certain oral elements when uttered by the pupils themselves, though they may have the keenest sense of the proper sounds of these elements when made by others. One of the most effective methods of instilling the cognition of the correct sound which they fail to recognize when uttered by themselves, is for the teacher to repeat distinctly the sound over and over again while very close to the pupil, and *accompanied in each utterance by the pupil* in an effort to make the same sound. By dropping the utterance occasionally, leaving the pupil to make it alone, the progress may be noted; but most important, the pupil will be led to recognize the difference between the false sound he makes and the true one, which will stimulate an involuntary effort toward a closer imitation. In other words, when the sound-images become fixed in the mind of the pupil as regards his own utterances, he is not satisfied until they are correctly articulated.

When a word or syllable is found to be imperfectly articulated, it should be at once divided into its oral elements and the pupil required to practice upon the isolated elementary sounds in which he fails, until he becomes proficient in that part, before he attempts to pronounce the whole word.

It can be seen by this, that the psychologic development of the mental concepts of correct articulate sounds of the oral elements of spoken words is quite as important as the restorative operation and the physical development of the inhibited activities of the muscles. Nor will true development in either case arise until the cleft palate patient is first supplied with adequate physical means that will ultimately enable an exact duplication of the indispensable functions of the velum-palati.

Practical Application of Methods of Instruction

When the obturator is finished and the patient becomes an accredited pupil in phonology and orthoëpy, the real instruction commences toward giving him the proper foundation for speaking—not only in perfect articulation, but in normal voice tone and resonance.

It is the custom of the author to give lessons to the pupil in a closed room free from the embarrassment of listeners, and to pursue the teaching for fifteen or twenty minutes, and then leave him alone for an hour's practice. As a supplement and variation from the breath sounds of the consonant oral elements, the pupil should practice on the phonetic sounds of the vowels—especially that of **a**, as **ā** in **ale**, **ă** in **at**, **â** in **all** and **ä** in **ah**, made with a strong forcible gutteral expression not once or twice, but at least fifty times, one after the other. This may then be joined to the acquired sounds of all the explosives and continued with the same forcible utterance. The object of this exercise is to strengthen and develop the pharyngeal and palatal muscles so that they will firmly and involuntarily close around the artificial velum completely preventing the vocalized air from escaping into the nose. Tongue gymnastics are of the greatest importance in revivifying the inhibited activities of the tongue by voluntary movements in direction, position, and rapidity. Along this line the rapid utterance of all the explosive oral elements joined to each one of the vowels, as **bā, bē, bī, bō, bū,** taking up each one of the explosives shown by the chart in succession, commencing with the labials **bă** and **pă,** followed with the labio-dentals **fă,** the linguo-dentals **thă,** and the linguals **dă, tă, chă, ka, gă.** When all these are distinctly uttered, follow this practice by joining the explosives to all the phonetic sounds of the vowels. Again, the rapid utterance of single elementary sounds in musical rhythm as, **la—-lalala—la,—la,** etc., will be found very difficult for most cleft palate pupils to utter rapidly at the start.

The pupil may quietly practice all the voiceless breath sounds of the consonants when not otherwise engaged. Even the sibilants of **c** and **s** may be practiced quietly at almost all times, at home or on the street, when there are no interferences.

The patient should be kept in training under immediate supervision and instruction until there is every reason to believe he will follow up the instruction, aided by the drawings, or that he will be placed in the hands of competent teachers.

With patients too young to understand and appreciate the requirements and the necessity of continued practice until they have fully acquired the correct utterances and "sound-images" of the oral elements they fail to articulate, the instruction sheets should be given to the parents for their own instruction as teachers, or for the information of teachers who are employed for this purpose.

If a **surgical operation** has been performed during infancy, or before the child has commenced to talk (and this in the opinion of the author is the only time when a surgical operation for cleft palate should ever be performed), the rule in regard to the instruction sheets should be considered quite as imperative, and should include all the consonant oral elements of speech which cleft palate patients in general fail to articulate distinctly. Instruction should then begin *at the very first word* the child attempts to articulate. In that way he will very soon acquire the sound-image, and his efforts to reach it *will act as a mechanical stimulation* toward natural growth development of the velum and co-operating muscles. It is the lack of velum tissue growth in proper proportion to the growth and development of surrounding parts, due to the disuse of the speaking muscles, which causes most of the failures that result from infantile surgical operations. If the cleft is closed skillfully at that time, and the surgically corrected velum is *sufficiently adequate* to close the oro-nasal passage when the child *commences to speak,* and if from that time on there is intelligent *insistence* that he shall speak distinctly, the results without doubt would be all that could be desired.

IMPORTANCE OF SYSTEMATIC INSTRUCTION IN THE MANAGEMENT OF THE LIPS, TONGUE, VOICE, ETC.

The operator or teacher will frequently be surprised to find how much improvement can be made by proper instruction in the speech of nearly all patients, even before they are supplied with any other aid. This is easily accounted for by the fact that they rarely have received from their parents or school teachers the slightest systematic instruction in regard to the management of the lips, tongue, or voice, because it is an exceedingly sensitive subject at home and abroad, evoking only pity for this terrible deformity, of which the immediate friends are inclined to believe that nothing except an operation will enable them to speak more perfectly. Besides this, the fact that the family soon learn to fully understand everything the patient says, causes him to believe that he speaks quite perfectly. For instance, nearly all cleft palate patients before receiving aid will make fairly close imitations with the throat muscles, of the sibilant and many other aspirate and explosive sounds to whose defects they are wholly blind, though quite noticeable and to strangers not always intelligible. As the sibilant is such an important element of correct speech when made properly at the tip end of the tongue with a high thin whistle, and as it requires but a slight pressure of air, it is usually their first lesson. Occasionally they succeed in distinctly sounding **s** in **yes,** even before the artificial palate is inserted, though never having properly made it before.

Again, one will meet patients with large open clefts who will distinctly pronounce words containing certain oral elements which the majority of patients cannot intelligibly approach before the operation. And perhaps this same patient may have the greatest difficulty in acquiring the perfect enunciation of other articulate sounds that are usually quite easy to acquire. One patient twenty-five years of age rapidly learned to speak with remarkable distinctness except in joining the elements of **t** and **o** in **toe,** which took months of persevering practice to acquire. Another patient, about sixteen years of age, who otherwise spoke perfectly, was unable for months to unite the sound of **b** with **gȧ,** in the word **began.**

One of the patients who was exhibited by the author at a clinic of the National Dental Association in 1918, distinctly articulated—and mostly with strong oral resonance—even the most tongue-twisting words that were given to her by the members, except the plural of words ending in **g.** In pronouncing **dogs,** she gave the clear sibilant as in **cats,** instead of the vocalized sibilant **z.** As this patient had been wearing the obturator only a short time, it is needless to say that this important element of speech was soon acquired.

Another patient eleven years of age was also presented, for whom the construction of the obturator had just been started. The impression and the method of taking it was described; also there was shown in the mouth the modeling-compound trial model of the obturator, which though much heavier than the final hard-rubber one, perfectly retained its position without being sustained artificially. This exhibition was quite an advantage, because it enabled the author to show clearly the action of the pharyngeal muscles in relation to the veil of the obturator in the act of closing the passage to the nose. This little patient had been operated upon seven times surgically for the closure of the cleft, with the result that all the soft palatal tissue and a portion of the pharyngeal tissue were destroyed. The object in mentioning this case here is to say that even before the insertion of the obturator, and notwithstanding the loss of so much tissue, she could distinctly enunciate—after a very little preliminary training—a large number of the explosive and aspirate oral elements of speech, and seemingly with a normal action of the tongue and lips, although not sharply or fully without the nasal tone. This in itself is very unusual before receiving thorough instruction.

To continue the history of this interesting case: One week after the finished obturator was placed in the mouth, many of the most prominent surgeons and dentists of Chicago came by invitation, to see the obturator in action, and all were surprised by her very rapid acquirements in so short a time.

One of the most important peculiarities of the present velum obturator, and the one which places it on a scientific basis in its relation to all the requirements of articulation and resonance, is the feature that—in its typical state—*it does not require any attachment to a plate or other dental device to hold it in position;* it being sustained through its perfectly fitted nasal and palatal extensions, and mostly because of the peculiar form and position of the veil and its relation to the walls of the pharynx and the action of the pharyngeal and palatal muscles.

The importance of doing without a supporting plate for the obturator is not merely one of convenience to the patient, but it is the one principle which permits all the requirements of normal speech.

The most potent factors of the remarkable success of this form of obturator in the restoration of speech are its extremely light weight and its free mobility and quick response to the slightest movement of the muscles; and when it is surrounded and within their grasp in its act of completely closing the passage to the nose, it takes the same favorable position in relation to the vibratory voice blasts as the normal velum-palati, whose function and activities it seems to imitate closely, and as Dr. Murphy said: "Its motion really seems uncanny, it is so natural." This will be appreciated when we come to study all the requirements in the mechanism of speech.

In works upon general phonology and orthoëpy, it has not been regarded as especially important to understand the anatomy and physiology of the palatal and pharyngeal muscles, or the exact details, with illustrations, of the relative positions and action of the tongue and other oral organs of speech; nor is there any particular stress laid upon the importance of a complete closure of the oro-nasal passage, because general instruction in the art of speaking perfectly pertains to that class of pupils whose muscles and controlling nerves are sufficiently unimpaired to require no more than the developing stimulation of right teaching and practice toward the psychologic acquirement and attainment of the exact sounds of the oral elements not properly articulated.

In the training toward this object, the specialized organs of speech intuitively take the right positions without being told, so to speak, whereas, the requirements of teaching are quite different with cleft palate pupils, who up to the time of the operation have been debarred the power to control the force and direction of the speaking breath blasts for the utterance of nearly all the consonant oral elements, and who therefore have been driven, in their efforts to be understood, to a wrong and inadequate employment of those muscles which were not intended for speech, and a complete disuse of the muscles which should control the main organs of normal speech, with the result that the function and action of the principal speaking muscles and guiding nerves are wholly untrained, and in addition to this the palatal and pharyngeal muscles are more or less atrophied. Consesequently, the functional position and action of the voluntary oral organs of speech must be carefully and specifically taught before they can be expected to make the proper utterances.

Moreover, one of the greatest difficulties to overcome arises from the fact that the muscles have acquired false habits of action in their efforts to produce intelligible speech, which is mainly due to the acquirement of false conceptions of the articulate sounds the pupil utters. But when the proper sound-image is stamped indelibly upon his mind, it will then be surely followed by the involuntary movement of the right muscles for its production, providing the physical machinery is sufficiently adequate. In the same manner that the pupil at the piano must at first be taught how and where to place the fingers on the keys to get the required sounds, while later this is followed with hardly a thought of the fingers, which are now almost wholly directed by the efferent motor impulses from ganglia under the subconscious control of the brain, that is thinking only of the musical staff or the tone-images which it indicates.

The training of cleft palate pupils, therefore, should be that which will most successfully utilize the impaired palatal and pharyngeal muscles with the view of stimulating their development toward a revivification of their inhibited activities, for no really successful prosthetic or surgical operation can be accomplished without their functional co-operation. Furthermore, in order that patients receive the full benefit of the operation, a character of teaching and training that is especially adapted to this class of pupils is of the utmost importance. The responsibility of this must lie with the operator, or a teacher who has full knowledge of the special needs and methods which should be employed. This can only be accomplished, as stated before, with a perfect understanding of the phonologic mechanism of normal speech and those principles of teaching which should be employed with pupils who have been wholly deprived of the use of the principal organs of speech.

CHAPTER II

PHYSIOLOGIC AND PHONETIC PRINCIPLES IN THE ART OF SPEAKING

It will be impossible in the short space of this chapter to give more than a glance at the general principles of phonology, omitting much that should be regarded as of great importance, found in works upon general phonology and orthoëpy, to which the student is earnestly referred.

Those principles, however, which pertain especially to this particular work are given here in the fullest detail, arranged by the author for the teaching of cleft palate pupils to speak; and designed especially to emphasize the importance of methods whose employment—though not so material in the general teaching of phonology—is of the greatest importance in this department of dentistry. Therefore, much stress has been laid upon the functions of the palate—particularly the velum-palati—and to the peculiar defects in the mechanism which arise from its impairment. In order to arrive at the most successful correction of those special imperfections, the author has found it necessary to divide or classify the consonant oral elements upon a basis which it is hoped will more sharply illustrate slight but important differences in enunciation which might otherwise be easily overlooked.

As all the **vowel elements** are distinctly enunciated by persons with open cleft palates—*though with imperfect tone*—the need of teaching the required position of the tongue, etc., in these utterances, may be considered, in this work for the instruction of cleft palate patients, of lesser importance. Consequently, there has been given to the vowel branch no more than a cursory explanation, with no illustrations; the principal teaching being devoted to the more exhaustive and systematic explanation and illustration of the consonant utterances which cleft palate patients have been unable to enunciate properly.

It would be well to state, however, in this connection, that the vowel or vocal utterances are the most important elements of speech, as they are the only elements which are purely composed of the vibratory voice blasts; consequently, they are the only parts of speech which present the vocally vibratory audible sounds, except when certain consonant utterances are intoned at the vocal cords, as in pronouncing **z,** whereas, the true voiceless consonant sounds are made by a forcible expelling of the unvocalized air through constricted openings and regulated passages in their function of giving the beginning and finishing touches to the vocals. Notwithstanding the fact that nearly all vowel utterances with open cleft palates are distinctly articulated, they are completely lacking in the important elements of tone and resonance, because the vocalized air passes freely into the nasal chambers, imparting to the sound the nasal quality. One can see by this how a complete closure of every passage to the nasal chambers is necessary for the perfect utterance of the vowels as well as of the consonant oral elements.

The Physiologic Mechanism of Speech

The framework of the speaking machine is the thorax, the trachea, the pharynx, the oral and nasal cavities, the jaws, the dentures, and the roof of the mouth. The active or mobile parts of this machine are the diaphragm, intercostal muscles, vocal cords, pharyngeal, palatal, lingual, labial, and buccinator muscles. To these may be added the hyoid and masseter muscles, which aid in regulating the different required sizes of the oral cavity by opening and closing the jaws. The action of this co-ordinated machinery, which is fed with expirations of air from the lungs, and whose product is spoken language, is worthy of the deepest study by dentists and oral surgeons, whose every department of applied science is concerned in perfecting or in marring its mechanism.

The sensations which we cognize as sounds of every character, reach the brain through the auditory apparatus, which is thrown into functional activity usually by vibratory wave movements of air striking the drum or diaphragm of the ear. A somewhat prolonged and forcible expiration of breath from the lungs throws into vibrations the vocal cords of the larynx, which in turn impart their vibrations to the air, and give rise to the sound we call voice. Its quality, pitch, and loudness are regulated by the character of the tissues which compose the cords, their tension, and the force of the air blasts.

As these speaking air blasts are forced upward through the trachea, the volume of air upon leaving the glottis is divided by the action and inaction of the vocal cords into a rapid succession of vibrating and unvibrating zones. The vibrating portions are the voice sounds, which are employed in enunciating the vowel oral elements of speech, and in giving to them their peculiar individual timbre and normal voice tone quality and resonance. The voiceless or unvibratory air blasts, when forced into the oral cavity, are converted into the explosives and fricative sounds which compose the oral elements of the consonants.

As the column of speaking breath travels through the mouth, it comes under the influence of certain definite muscular movements and restrictions, which stop or interrupt its free passage or force it into certain chambers or channels of different forms by which it is molded into speech or vocal language. Therefore, to speak distinctly, there are certain physical requirements which must be fulfilled. Among the foremost of these is the necessity of completely closing the oro-nasal passage so that in all parts of speech, except the sounds of **m, n,** and **ng,** not a particle of the expired breath used in talking can escape into the nose; otherwise, as will be shown, it is impossible to enunciate properly and distinctly all vowel and nearly all consonant utterances, except in phenomenal cases.

In the involuntary intermitting function of closing and opening the passage to the nose, the velum-palati acts with almost lightning-like rapidity in the perfect enunciation of rapidly spoken words, and especially those words in which certain oral elements which demand that this passage be open, are joined to, or lie between, other oral elements which demand that it be closed. For instance, in the word **and,** the beginning vowel **a** requires this passage closed for resonating quality, the **n** requires with equal importance that it be open for its peculiar nasal tone quality, and the **d** that it be again fully closed for its distinct explosive articulation.

One can understand by this example alone something of the difficulties which confront the surgical operator in an endeavor to not only close extensive clefts of the hard and soft palate for patients older than five years, but to construct a plastic velum, necessarily composed largely of cicatricial tissue, which will act with that light sensitive mobility that is demanded of the normal palate in its activities of perfect speech; and also how impossible it would be to accomplish these indispensable requisites of speech with any form of artificial palate or obturator that is attached to a dental fixture, or one that will not quickly and rapidly move, as does the normal velum, with the very lightest touch of the muscles which control it.

The Velum-Palati

In order to obtain an intelligent comprehension of the scientific principles and practical activities of a modern obturator in the correction of speech, it may be well to first briefly call attention to the indispensable functions of the velum-palati, because it is solely through the loss or impairment of this important organ that renders perfect speech impossible. Therefore, anything which is capable of restoring the possibilities of perfect speech to cleft palate patients—whether by surgical or prosthetic methods— must also be capable of imitating the action and function of the normal velum.

The first and most indispensable part of the involuntary function of the normal velum is its act of completely closing the oro-nasal passage, in order that the air blasts of speech may be wholly directed and forcibly thrown into and through the oral cavity, to be formed into the articulate sounds of speech. This is absolutely necessary for the perfect enunciation of all the oral elements of speech, except those of **m, n,** and **ng,** which will be explained later.

The second important part of its function is its light sensitive rapidity of movement, which will be appreciated when we remember that the oro-nasal passage must be closed and opened at the very beginning and ending of nearly every oral element in a large proportion of spoken words which we distinctly enunciate, and that the words of the English language contain from one to eight oral elements, which when spoken rapidly, require an almost inconceivable rapidity of muscular movement.

The third important part of its function pertains to normal voice tone quality and resonance. When we consider that the main resonating chambers of our wonderful speaking instrument lie above the hard and soft palate, we can fully understand how necessary it is that the voice vibrations must be freely and uninterruptedly imparted to these chambers in order to produce the required tone and melody of perfect speech.

The complete closure of the oro-nasal passage, principally by the velum-palati, enables the performance of two indispensable functions of speech. First, it enables the forcing of the unvocalized air into and through the speaking tube of the mouth with that forcible pressure which is necessary for the distinct and perfect enunciation of the consonant explosive and aspirate oral elements, and which would not be possible with this passage open, any more than it would be possible for a syringe or a chip-blower to functionate with a hole through its side. Second, in this act of closure, it enables the production of natural voice tone quality and melody of resonance, in both speaking and singing, which also would not be possible with this passage open. It would seem that the vibratory voice blasts of the vocals, when confined to the oro-pharyngeal speaking tube, are thrown into more intensified vibrations, whose wave impacts are thus more effectually communicated and transmitted through the medium of the velum-palati and surrounding tissues to the resonating chambers of the head.

The student will appreciate this if he will forcibly utter the vowel oral element **ah,** and note the strong natural oral tone and resonating voice quality, which in the less rapid vibrations of low tone registers, produces a perceptible quivering of the throat tissues, easily felt by the fingers on the outside of the throat. Now make the same effort with the palate dropped so that the vibrating air can pass freely into the nose, and note the nasal tone and lack of forceful resonating voice quality. In this process, the thin sensitive velum-palati, stretched backward in drum-like tenseness toward the walls of the pharynx to co-operate with the pharyngeal muscles in closing the passage to the upper pharynx and nose, is an admirable transmitter of the voice waves to the real sounding-board of the head. An important feature in this act is the position of the velum lying almost at right angles to the voice blasts directly from the glottis. It is this position of the veil of the obturator, also, that enables it to so closely imitate the action and function of the normal velum.

It will be observed that the attainment of natural voice quality, with its resonance and melody in both speaking and singing, is not accomplished by allowing the original vibratory air of the voice to enter the nasal chambers, otherwise there would result an unpleasant nasal tone, devoid of true resonating richness. The vocalized air is therefore completely and wholly stopped at the velum-palati, which in consequence is thrown to greater vibratory and transmitting activity, imparting its intensified sound waves to the upper resonating chambers, where it is properly molded and sent forth to the outer air as natural speaking and singing voice tones.

Resonance

The quality of voice known as resonance and melody, which is quite as important to perfect speech and vocal music as distinct articulation, no doubt starts to be imparted to the voice in the trachea and continues to characterize its tone by different forms of the pharyngeal and oral channels through which it passes in the mechanism of speech.

The principal portion of normal speech resonance, however, is imparted to the voice in the nasal chambers where resides the real "sounding-board" of the speech mechanism. The vibratory air itself, from the vocal cords, does not enter these chambers except when uttering the nasals—**m, n,** and **ng**—it being prevented principally by the velum-palati through which the voice vibrations readily pass. This complete closure of the passage to the nose is important in the production of normal tone resonance. The failure to close this passage completely in the utterance of all the vocals, characterizes the sounds as more or less nasal, and to that extent destroys the true resonating and resounding quality of perfect vocal speech; whereas, its complete closure intensifies the vibrations of air, and consequently the sound above the velum.

A person outside of a thin hermetically sealed door can be distinctly understood by one on the inside if he speaks loudly enough, and yet not a particle of the vibratory air of voice, *per se*, penetrates the door. The substance of which the door is composed is a transmitter of the voice vibrations.

It will be seen, therefore, that the velum-palati in the normal state is not only the chief organ in distinct articulation by completely closing the oro-nasal passage, but it is also a perfect transmitter of voice vibrations which gives to speech its main resonating quality. In fact, pure resonance and clear vocal tone quality in all vowel utterances of the English language seem to require this closure—a thing which cannot be said of the French and possibly many other languages. In speaking any of our vowels with a forcible gutteral prolongation, we notice the distinctly marked difference in the character and quality of the tone with this passage closed and with it open; this plainly indicates the functional mechanism by which the voice in nearly all requirements of speech readily passes through a closed palate to the upper resonating chambers, and not back of an open or partially open palate.

It is only through an understanding of the functions of the velum-palati that we gain a true conception of its indispensable action in the mechanism of speech and are able to realize fully the object and difficulties of an operation for the restoration of a cleft palate by surgical or artificial means. It forms also an important foundation for an intelligent comprehension of the art of speaking correctly.

The Oral Elements of Vowels and Consonants

The alphabetical symbols which stand for the oral elements of speech in the English language are divided into vowels and consonants. An **oral element,** or elementary sound, is one which is uttered with a single impulse, always with the same mechanism, and which cannot be divided into separate sounds. Words are composed of oral elements the same as chemical compounds are composed of chemical elements. Like chemical elements also, they are represented to the eye by symbols composed of one or more letters of the alphabet. For instance, in the word **cat,** there are three oral elements, whose phonism may be represented to the eye as **kă-ă-tŭ,** whereas, in **ought,** a word of five letters, there are only two oral elements, **au-tŭ.**

In practicing separate utterances of the oral elements which are represented in written language by the alphabet, or symbols of speech, they should be enunciated with a short quick utterance so as to avoid mixing the voiceless breath consonant sounds with the adjoining voice sounds of the vowels. In representing to the eye of the student or the pupil the detached phonetic sounds of the explosive oral elements, for teaching purposes in this work, the symbol **u** or **a** (i. e., short) is added to the consonant letter. Thus in representing the explosive oral element of **b** in the word **but,** it is **bŭ,** uttered with a quick breath emission by the sudden parting of the lips, and by not permitting the sound to run into the vocal sound of the vowel **u.** The oral element of **u** in **but** is sounded like **uh,** and the **t** is represented as **tă** or **tŭ,** and is made with a sudden explosive breath emission, etc.

While it is a fact that in the perfect pronunciation of a word the explosive elements are indistinguishably joined to the vowel elements, the sounds are there nevertheless, and their distinct and separate utterance should be considered as the first requirement in teaching cleft palate pupils to enunciate any of the words in which the explosives occur, as these are the utterances in which they most often fail, because of the impossibility of accumulating a sufficient pressure of potential air back of the stop before it is suddenly let loose.

When a syllable or a word is pronounced properly, it is characterized by a succession of all the **oral elementary sounds** of which it is composed. *Each one of these sounds requires a different muscular movement, and however quickly the word is spoken, if uttered distinctly, all the movements and positions necessary for the utterance of each separate element must always occur in the succession of their position in the word.*

In papers which have recently been read before medical and dental societies in regard to the function of speech, there seems to be no recognition of distinguishing differences between the sounds of the letters of the alphabet and the sounds of the oral elements of speech of which the letters are nothing more than the visual symbols. While all the vowel elementary sounds are similar to the phonetic sounds of the vowel letters, the names of the consonant letters when written or spoken are composed of two or more oral elements, which when pronounced may have very little semblance in sound to the oral element in speech which this letter or symbol stands for.

In other words, in pronouncing the names of the letters which stand for the vowel elements—**a, e, i,** etc.—we find that the different sounds compare favorably with the elementary sounds of these letters in speaking the words in which they occur—except in diphthongs and silent letters—because the naming of any of the vowels is in itself an utterance similar to their phonetic elemental sounds in spoken words. In this particular they differ quite decidedly from the *names* of the consonants, each one of which requires a vowel in its pronunciation, and in the spelling of its name, as **be, de, te,** etc. Therefore, in speaking the names of the consonants, we are not uttering the oral elements which they stand for in words, but two or more oral elements—thus **b** is a sudden short explosive breath sound, **bŭ**, added to a vowel element, **e**—otherwise they would have no character if uttered alone as do the vowels.

Furthermore, the spoken name of several of the consonants shows little or no resemblance to the oral element which the consonant symbol stands for in speech. For instance, in pronouncing the name of the letter **h,** we find that it is composed phonetically of two oral elements, **ā** and the breath emission **ch**, but its *oral element* in the words **horse, house,** etc., is an open aspirate which is simply a forced breath sound made at the back of the mouth or in the throat, and quite different in sound from the word **aich,** which is made principally at the front of the mouth. Again, in the phonetic pronunciation of the name of the letter **w,** it is found to be composed of four oral elements, **dŭ-bŭ-l-u,** which in combination is quite unlike the open aspirate oral element made at the lips which the symbol stands for in **wood, wet,** etc. Note the sound that is emitted before it starts the vowels **o** and **e.**

There is another distinguishing difference between vowels and consonants. Each vowel has a number of oral elements which are quite distinctly different phonetically in sound, and are made with a slightly different mechanism, as, **ā (ale), ă (at), â (all), ä (ah),** etc.; whereas, the consonant oral elements are characterized by a single sound and mechanism. While this is true in regard to the mechanism of the consonants, there is an apparent difference in the initial and final sound of a number of them, **l, r, n, m, f,** because in the initial they always join the vowel with an explosive-like sound, and in the final, the organs and mechanism remain in the set position until the sound of the element stops.

Broadly speaking, the vowels are the body or framework of speech, and the consonants are the finishing touches which give to speech its sharply defined characteristics. The vowels are the open voice sounds, and the consonants are the forced breath sounds, and while the latter are frequently vocalized, their main function is to give distinct enunciatory quality. In order to understand the composition and mechanism of the oral elements of speech, a clear conception of the distinctive parts of speech which enter into their formation, together with the distinctive characters of physiologic movements and positions they require, is of imperative importance.

The Vowels

The Vocals, or **Vowel Oral Elements,** whose symbols in the English language are **a, e, i, o, u,** and final **y,** are those utterances which impart to speech its main voice tones; and whether uttered with voice or whispers, they are the open or the least interrupted of all the elementary sounds of spoken language. They are characterized by the different forms of the pharyngeal and oral cavities through which they pass more or less freely. They demand for their perfection of tone and resonance a complete closure of the oro-nasal passage, though they may be uttered quite distinctly in a nasal tone by all cleft palate persons.

While the vowel sounds seem to be the most hopeful parts of speech to correct in the preliminary examination of a cleft palate patient, they are almost invariably the last in which perfection of tone is acquired. The reason for this is evident. The vowel utterances of cleft palate pupils are at first so much more perfect than the consonant utterances, that they are given little thought in the primary efforts to articulate distinctly, until finally when quite perfect articulation is acquired, we have lingering that unpleasant nasal resonance which is so common with those wearing vela or obturators attached to plates, or those with surgically corrected palates. This shows (1) the demand in vowel utterance of an absolute closure of the oro-nasal passage, and (2) the need of a palate which will have the voice-transmitting properties of the natural palate.

The Consonants

The Consonant Oral Elements are the forcible breath sounds of speech produced by forcing the unvocalized air blasts through more or less constricted openings, or against full stops to be suddenly opened. While many of them are uttered without voice, others are intoned by vibrations of the vocal cords from the very start, which finally blend into the true sounds of the vowel tones. They give to spoken language its real enunciatory quality. Under normal conditions they demand for distinct and perfect articulation the full functional involuntary activity of the velum-palati to completely close and open the nasal passage; consequently they are the most difficult for persons with an open cleft of the palate to utter intelligibly. They may be properly classified upon the basis of the peculiar character of sound which is made in their perfect utterance by an open and by a complete closure of the nasal passage.

Intrinsic Value of Illustrations

It may be well to state that phonologic illustrations showing positions of the tongue, lips, etc., in different movements of correct articulation, as in the **Classified Charts** herewith, are really not necessary to a competent teacher who speaks distinctly, except that it may aid him in making the drawings for his pupils, showing the proper positions for the utterance in which they fail. Every person who speaks with accurate articulation and tone, utters each oral element in exactly the same manner and with the same action and position of the muscles and oral organs of speech. The sounds may differ in their timbre, their melody, and their resonating quality, but each of the elementary utterances of perfect speech is always made with the same mechanism; and this is true of all languages, the oral elements differing as the languages differ. If the teacher or anyone is capable of dividing the words of his language into their **oral elements,** he would then only need to note the positions and form of the tongue and lips, and the relation they bear to the teeth and roof of the mouth in uttering, first, all the phonetic sounds of vocals or vowels, and second, in uttering all the unvocalized air sounds, unmixed with the vocals, which constitute the consonants.

The teacher, therefore, may easily make the required drawings, as did the author when making the accompanying charts, without reference to or a thought of other published illustrations, commencing at the front of the mouth and going back, i. e., the labials, the labio-dentals, the linguo-dentals, and the linguo-palatals. The author has adopted this same order in placing the consonant oral elements in the classification illustrated by the Charts.

Classification of Consonant Oral Elements

In a classification of the consonant oral elements for the purpose of instructing those who may be called upon to teach cleft palate patients to speak perfectly after operations, and to confine the work to purely practical methods adapted to our purpose, the author has not attempted a full outline of all the elementary sounds important in general phonology and orthoëpy, the main object being to base the classification upon the sounds requiring the perfect functions of the velum-palati, of which these pupils have hitherto been deprived—hoping in this way to enforce the acquirement of the higher possibilities and full activities of the velum-obturator, or of the surgical palate. A more extensive and erudite endeavor would only serve to complicate and cloud the efforts of these unfortunates, whose only object is to learn to speak distinctly, and who therefore are not supposed to acquire the advanced educational principles of the science of speaking which are mainly intended in this work for teachers, or those who it is hoped will undertake the teaching of their cleft palate patients, and who therefore should fully understand the basic principles of phonology, which strictly pertain to this department.

Slight differences between the sounds and mechanism of the same consonant oral elements uttered by different persons, which may be acquired by association with different provincial sounds of the vocals, and possibly with different provincial pronunciations, have always rendered it impossible for authors to determine whether certain oral elements should be placed in one class or the other. The principal object of a classification to a pupil whose mechanism has always been deficient is: that different sound utterances should be systematically grouped solely on the basis of their phonation and mechanism, so that they will aid him in acquiring not only correct sound-images, but the manner of their construction.

The special classification which is here adopted and shown by the charts divides the consonant oral elements into four classes: **Nasals, Explosives, Open Aspirates** and **Explosive Aspirates**. This is a system which has gradually developed in the author's practice through many years of prosthetic correction of cleft palate and the subsequent teaching of these patients to speak. It is made mainly with the view of presenting important distinctions between the sound-images of elements whose mechanism is quite similar and consequently difficult for the patient to acquire without special drilling.

This has particular reference to certain elements in "open" and "explosive" aspirates, which will be appreciated when one distinctly enunciates the initial oral

CHAPTER II. PHYSIOLOGIC AND PHONETIC PRINCIPLES

elements of **p** and **b** in **pay** and **bay**, and **w** and **wh** in the words **watt** and **what**, each pair being made at the lips with exactly the same positions but with different breath or fricative force. Cleft palate pupils who may easily acquire a perfect articulation of the initial sounds of **pŭ, tŭ,** and **wă**, etc., will often work for weeks on the initial sounds of **bŭ, dă,** and **wh**, not that they lack in physical means, but they fail to acquire a fixed and retentive conception of the difference in the sound-images, when uttered by themselves.

In this connection, note the explosive and open aspirate difference in the initial and final **l** and **r** in the words, **late** and **still**, and **run** and **bur**, showing the necessity of dividing the Aspirates into two Classes. This is fully explained in the explanatory notes following the Charts.

THE NASALS

FIG. 3.

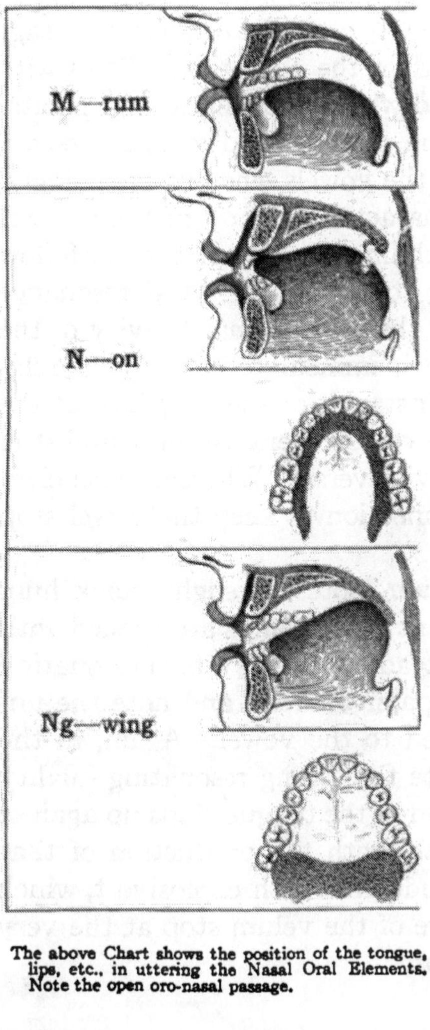

The above Chart shows the position of the tongue, lips, etc., in uttering the Nasal Oral Elements. Note the open oro-nasal passage.

The **Nasals** are the only elements of speech in which the oro-nasal passage is required to be open for the free passage of the air blasts. Nasals are composed of the intoned consonant sounds, **m, n,** and **ng,** which it will be found, demand closed stops to drive the column of vocalized breath directly into the nasal chambers for the production of that peculiar nasal resonance characteristic of these utterances. Therefore, they are the only sounds which most patients with open clefts will perfectly utter with proper tone and resonance. The resonance and enunciatory characters of each of the nasal elements are regulated by the points at which the stops occur, and which determine the size of the oral cavity back of the stop as a part of the resonating area.

The **Nasal Oral Elements** are made with a sound similar to musical humming tones, but of course with short quick action, like nearly all oral elements; the vocalized breath being driven by the aid of the full stops directly into the nasal chambers.

For the oral element which the symbol **m** stands for, the stop is formed by a complete closure of the lips. In the word **mother** it is the sound which comes before **other,** and like all the nasals it ends with a slight explosive as it merges into the vocal.

For **n,** the stop is formed by a complete closure at the end and sides of the tongue against the anterior part of the hard palate and along the gingival borders.

For **ng,** the stop is formed by a closure of the dorsum of the tongue against the anterior portion and sides of the soft palate.

As previously stated, in the advanced stage of training cleft palate pupils to speak a nasal resonance running into and destroying the true resonance of connecting vowels, is commonly found to be the most difficult to eradicate of all the imperfections of their speech. This is largely because it is so difficult for them to overcome the habit of years in hearing their own voice utter the vowel sounds with the passage to the nose open, so that they do not readily cognize the difference between the true resonating tones of the vowels and the nasal tones which they have so long imparted to these important elements; though they may be very quick to recognize the false sounds when uttered by someone else. This is one of the most marked defects which almost invariably characterizes the speech of cleft palate patients whose clefts have been closed surgically, and too, for the very good reason that it is impossible for them to completely close the oro-nasal passage with a surgically constructed velum, however perfect the operation. Even with patients who possess perfect velum-obturators, and whose pharyngeal and palatal muscles are fully capable of completely closing the passage, and who, moreover, will perfectly enunciate all the phonetic sounds of the vowels when uttered singly, will still unconsciously allow the nasal tone to characterize many of their vowel utterances. This is particularly true of vowels which immediately precede or follow **m** and **n,** and which demand for true resonating tone that the nasal resonance must not run into the vowel resonance; indicating that the normal activity of the two stops which regulate these two sounds and their immediate harmonious relation must work with lightning-like rapidity. For instance, at the very instant the nasal stop at the lips and tongue is opened for the vowel utterance the vowel stop at the oro-nasal passage is completely closed, and vice versa. Whereas, with cleft palate pupils there is a great tendency in this connection to keep the vowel stop open.

In the proper pronunciation of the word **mother,** note the slight quick hum of the **m** with its nasal quality up to the very instant that the lips are opened with an explosive-like sound in starting the **o.** Now instead of making a firm resonating utterance of the **o,** allow the velum to drop with passive effort, and note the unnatural nasal quality that is immediately imparted to the vowel. Again, in the proper forcible articulation of the word **won't,** note the strong resonating quality of the vocal element **o,** up to the instant that the end of the tongue claps up against the roof of the mouth just back of the front teeth, with the production of that slight nasal hum immediately followed by the sudden breath explosive **t,** which would be impossible without the immediate closure of the velum stop at the very instant the tongue is released from the nasal element.

In this short description applied to the nasals, may be found examples of training which in principle apply to the articulation of every word in our language, and the utterance of every oral element in the four classes shown by the Classified Charts.

The competent teacher should be fully capable of intelligently analyzing his own speaking activities, not only as regards the position and action of the organs of speech in correct articulation, but in the psychologic cognition of true sound-images. This will enable him to intelligently impart the requisite kind of knowledge to his pupils as an indispensable part of the teaching curriculum of the operation.

THE EXPLOSIVES

FIG. 4.

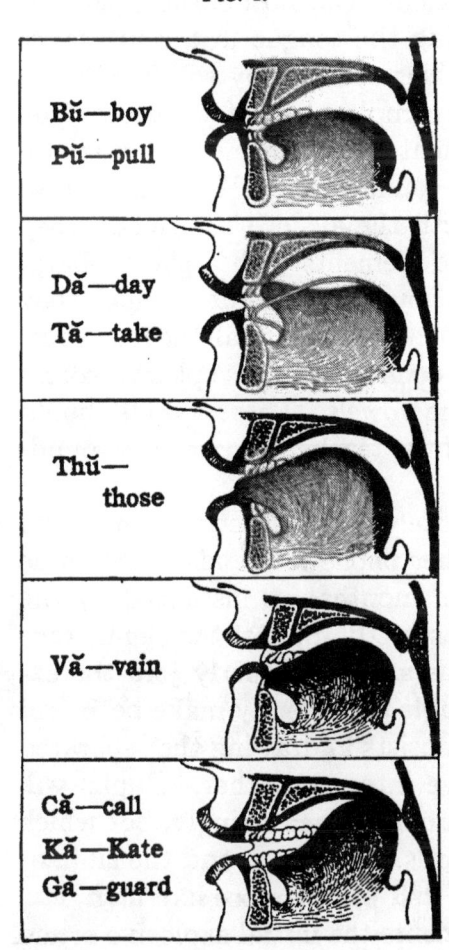

Bŭ—boy
Pŭ—pull

Dă—day
Tă—take

Thŭ—those

Vă—vain

Că—call
Kă—Kate
Gă—guard

The above Chart shows the position of the tongue, lips, etc., in uttering the Explosive Oral Elements. Note the closed oro-nasal passage.

Explosives are the elements of speech which demand quite a pressure of breath back of a full stop, to be followed immediately with a sudden opening of the stop for the emission of the completed utterance or explosive, which may occur at the beginning or ending of a syllable or word.

The English symbols which represent the **Explosive Oral Elements** are b, d, c (hard), g (hard), k, p, t, th, and initial y.

For the purpose of definitely symbolizing the sounds of the explosive oral elements which these letters stand for in words, the author, as before mentioned, has chosen the short sound of **a** and **u**—pronounced **uh** with a short, quick utterance —to complete the symbol, because its utterance comes nearer than any other one sound in representing the completed explosive when uttered alone. When the explosive oral elements are thus phonetically symbolized and arranged respectively as regards positions and mechanism of utterance from the front to the back of the mouth, they are as follows:

For **bŭ** as in **boy, pŭ** as in **pull,** the stop occurs between the lips.

For **vă** as in **vain,** between the lower lip and upper front teeth.

For **thŭ** as in **the, those,** etc., between the flattened end of the tongue and upper front teeth.

For **dŭ** as in **do, tŭ** as in **take, kŭ** or **cŭ** (hard) as in **Kate, call,** etc., and **gŭ** (hard) as in **go,** the stops occur between the tongue in various positions and points on the roof of the mouth from the front teeth to the middle of the soft palate. These positions and points will be somewhat varied with different individuals.

The illustrations under **Explosives** show the position of the oral organs and stops at the start of the utterance. Where two positions of the tongue are shown, the one indicates its position at the tip end when the stop occurs to *start* the explosive element, and the other shows the position which immediately follows, to complete its full utterance.

The Explosive and Aspirate Oral Elements are among the most difficult for cleft palate pupils to enunciate distinctly. This is not surprising when one remembers that the proper placing and utterance of all breath sounds requiring full stops and small constricted channels made at the front of the mouth, have—with rare exceptions—never been fully accomplished by them. The most of these patients know absolutely nothing about placing and shaping the tongue in the utterance of the greater proportion of these sounds; and in their efforts they will handle the tongue with a degree of awkwardness indicative of a complete lack of mental control. Often they will never arrive at the correct movement except through an involuntary action of the muscles in efforts to imitate the sound-image. When they have acquired the proper sounds by repeated efforts with the aid of the teacher, they should be required to practice these isolated sound elements with a short, sharp, distinct, forcible utterance before attempting to pronounce the words in which they occur. When this is perfectly acquired, they may then be joined to all the long vocal sounds of the vowels, as **bā, bē, bī, bō, bū**, etc.—connecting the explosive sound elements with all the phonetic sounds of each of the vowels. These sounds should never be practiced at first, except in the presence of the teacher, or until the sound-image is acquired. .

Often it will be found that pupils will immediately and correctly connect the explosive with one sound of a vocal, while with other phonetic sounds of the same vowel they will require practice for days and even months—as instanced by the patient who rapidly acquired the ability to utter distinctly most of the elementary sounds, but who practiced for weeks before he was able to properly join the explosive **tŭ** to **o** in **toe,** or **oo** in **too,** though he was able to perfectly make both oral elements separately. In these cases, the practice consists in drawing the separated sounds closer and closer together until they merge into each other. Pupils will frequently soon learn to enunciate perfectly certain oral elements singly, but which require days of practice to smoothly unite into words. Thus, **yă,** and the sibilant **s** in **yes,** will sound like **yets.** Again, **fe** and **sh** in **fish** will be more like **fitch,** etc.

It will be observed that in some of the oral elements the initial explosive sound is started with the voice or vocalized breath, as **dŭ** in **day;** while with other explosive-like sounds, as initial **f,** it starts with the expelling of unvocalized breath but ends with a distinct explosive as it joins the vocal in **fŭ, fall.** This is an example of many fine distinctions in the enunciation of the explosives, the teaching of which possibly has not been found necessary in the general teaching of pupils with ordinary defects.

CHAPTER II. PHYSIOLOGIC AND PHONETIC PRINCIPLES

But its recognition and application is nevertheless of very great importance in teaching those who have never made a correct approach to distinctness in explosive and aspirate utterances. It is partly this which led the author to divide Aspirates into the "Open" and "Explosive" Classes.

With all initial explosive sounds, uttered with perfect distinctness, there invariably occurs a more or less sudden liberation of the utterance before it joins the vocal. This plainly indicates preliminary accumulation of compressed breath back of a full stop, which could only be possible with the palatal passage completely closed. With certain explosive oral elements, however, the explosive sound is almost imperceptible, because it is drowned by the aspirate part of its utterance, as in initial **f, l, ch,** in **fate, late, choose,** etc. This has led authors to classify these utterances solely under "Aspirates," and also because when used as finals they are clearly open aspirates. But inasmuch as it is found that the distinctive part of the utterance which cleft palate pupils fail to make is the explosive part, or the part which demands a sudden liberation of compressed breath, however inaudibly it is sounded, they are placed in our classification under "Explosive Aspirates," because it is so important in our teaching that phonetic differences should be sharply defined, and that we should not be obliged to cling to a classification that is inadequate in *our* field of orthoëpy, however well established it may be phonologically.

While it is possible in seemingly well spoken language that certain oral elements, which should have distinct explosive utterance, are slurred into sounds more like aspirates without special notice, nevertheless in teaching pupils who have never intelligibly, or at least distinctly, uttered these sounds or employed the proper methods, the author believes it to be imperative that the sharp and distinct utterance of these elements, especially those with stops, should be insisted upon. One of the main reasons for this particular kind of training is that it is the *only* way in which the undeveloped muscles in conjunction with the obturator can be taught to involuntarily close the oro-nasal passage. In the continued efforts toward this accomplishment the inhibited growth and dormant activities of the palatal and pharyngeal muscles, through lack of use, will become revivified and no doubt stimulated toward assuming their normal inherited properties and proportions.

Again in correct speech in pluralized words having final explosives, the explosive termination of the element is not sounded but is lost in the sibilant, as in **cats,** etc.

THE ASPIRATES

The **Aspirates** are the parts of speech uttered with a forcible expulsive or fricative emission of the breath through a constricted opening. They are characterized by the form of the opening and oral channel through which the breath is forced, and a variety of muscular actions which render them quite distinctive in the quality and character of their utterance. The sounds of the aspirate oral elements may be divided into "Open" Aspirates and "Explosive" Aspirates.

Open Aspirates

The **Open Aspirate** elements are continuous sounds, mostly voiceless breath sounds, with no abrupt or explosive beginning or ending, and blend evenly into the **vowel tones** to which they are joined. The English symbols which represent the open aspirate elements are **c** (soft), **f, h, l** (final), **r, s, sh, wh, z,** and **x** (final). When phonetically symbolized and arranged respectively as regards position and mechanism of utterance they are as follows:

In the utterance of **wh** as in **when, what,** etc., the breath blast emission is at the lips.

In **f** (final) as in **half, stiff,** etc., between the lower lip and upper teeth.

In **c** (soft), **s** and **z**, as in **cell, so, zeal,** etc., at the tip end of the tongue and anterior palatal surface.

In **sh** as in **shame, show,** etc., between the broadened blade of the tongue and anterior hard palate.

In **l** (final) as in **still,** etc., see fuller explanation under "Notes relative to the Chart."

In **r** (final) as in **for, fur,** etc., between the soft palate and dorsum of the tongue with depressed blade.

In **h** as in **her, horse,** etc., between the dorsum of the tongue and contracted throat muscles.

The pure sibilants s, c, and **x** (final), consist of a fine sharp whistle, made as shown, through a tiny opening at the tip end of the tongue. The lower figure shows the contact linguo-palatal area. While in ordinarily correct speech, the sibilant is a fricative or hissing sound, the author considers it quite important that cleft palate pupils should learn to make the phonetic **high clear thin whistle at the tip of the tongue** which is laid down in all phonologies as the *perfect sibilant sound*. Nothing adds so much to the perfection of speech and its distinctive characterization as this sound when properly and distinctly made and which forms such an important part of our spoken language.

Z, the cognate of **s,** is the same with the addition of vocalization, the vibrations of which can be felt in the throat.

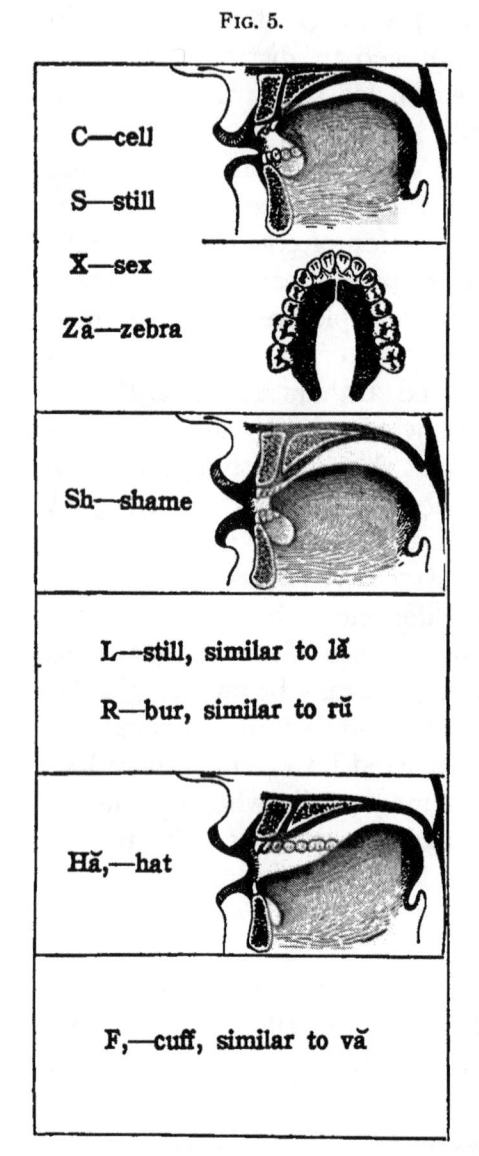

Fig. 5.

C—cell
S—still
X—sex
Ză—zebra
Sh—shame
L—still, similar to lă
R—bur, similar to rŭ
Hă,—hat
F,—cuff, similar to vă

The above Chart shows the position of the tongue, lips, etc., in uttering the Open Aspirate Elements. Note the closed or o-nasal passage.

CHAPTER II. PHYSIOLOGIC AND PHONETIC PRINCIPLES

Sh is made by forcibly expelling the breath through a broad thin opening between the retracted end of the tongue and anterior alveolar ridge, with the lips pushed forward as a part of the characterization of the sound.

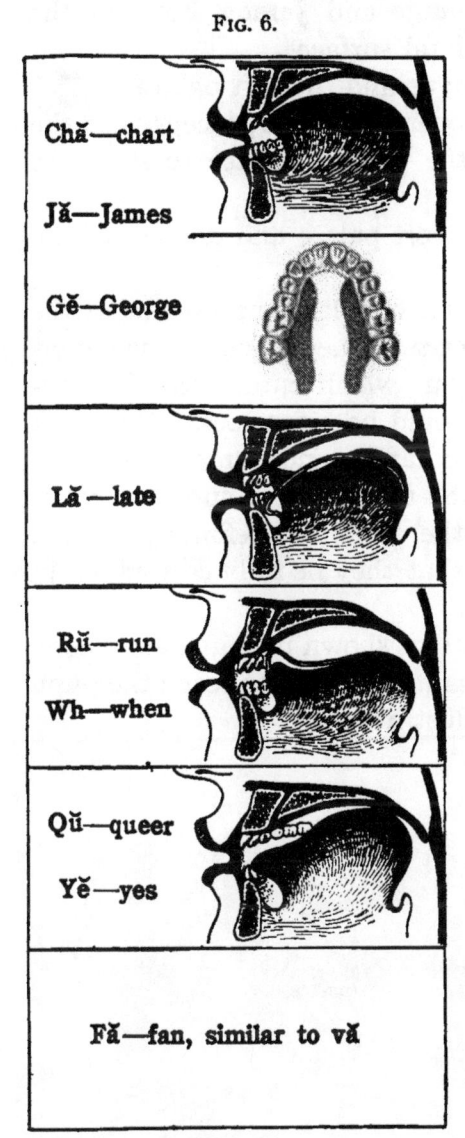

Ch, J, G. With the explosive aspirate elements, **ch, j,** and soft **g,** the second and main position of the tongue following that of the partial explosive is similar to that of **sh,** but with no special action of the lips.

L. Note the difference in the mechanism of l final and l initial. With the former, or open aspirate sound **ŭl,** as in **full,** the element is *completely* ended while the end of the tongue rests against the upper alveolar ridge, the vocalized breath escaping at both sides of the tongue; whereas, in the explosive aspirate **lŭ** as in **lot,** the aspirate part of the element is made in the same way, but is interrupted by a sudden dropping of the end of the tongue to emit the explosive to join the vowel element. (See **La,** under explosive aspirates.)

R. The open or aspirate part of the sound of **r** as in **bur** is made by forcing the vocalized breath through a somewhat constricted opening at the dorsum of the tongue and on over its concaved surface, the sides and tip being slightly raised. In the explosive aspirate **rŭ** as in **run,** the r sound is interrupted by the end of the tongue momentarily approaching the roof to produce a more forcible and sudden emission.

The mechanism of the other oral elements is well shown.

THE EXPLOSIVE ASPIRATES

The **Explosive Aspirate** elements are those which are uttered with a somewhat sudden expelling of the breath, not unlike explosives, as it joins the vocal, though the principal part of the sound is aspirate. The difference between open and explosive aspirates will be recognized in pronouncing **when** and **went.**

The English symbols which represent the "explosive aspirate" elements are **ch, f, g j, 1 (hard), q, r, w,** and initial **y.** Arranged respectively as regards position and mechanism of utterance they are as follows:

In **w,** as in **watt, was,** etc., the emission occurs at the lips.

FIG. 6.

Chă—chart
Jă—James
Gĕ—George
Lă—late
Rŭ—run
Wh—when
Qŭ—queer
Yĕ—yes
Fă—fan, similar to vă

The above Chart shows the position of the tongue, lips, etc., in uttering the Explosive Aspirate Elements.
Note the closed oro-nasal passage.

In **f** (initial), as in **few, fur,** etc., between lower lip and teeth.

In **l** (initial), as in **late, lot,** etc., at the sides of the tongue with the end touching the anterior alveolar ridge.

In **ch,** as in **church, g** (soft), and **j,** as in **George** and **James,** between the flattened blade of the tongue and the anterior palatal surface.

In **q,** as in **quick,** between the dorsum of the tongue and the soft palate.

In **r** (initial), as in **run, rat,** etc., same as the open aspirate **r,** except that the end of the tongue is brought into contact with the palatal surface to start the sound.

In (initial) **y,** as in **yet, yoke,** etc., between the soft palate and dorsum of the tongue with end depressed.

The position and form of the lips in the utterance of a large proportion of the oral elements are quite as important in characterizing the articulate sound as the form, position, and relation of the other organs which enter into the construction of the elements. In this connection it should be remembered that cleft palate patients or pupils, before operations, have rarely and sometimes never used the lips, the teeth and lips, or the end of the tongue, in a speaking functional sense; therefore, special instruction with the positions definitely defined should be given by the teacher with an insistence that they be fully carried out in their practice, even to a pronounced degree at first.

The teacher should verify all the muscular positions shown here and elsewhere, in uttering the different oral elements of the consonants, in order to teach the pupil the correct positions by practical instruction and illustrations.

CHAPTER III

THE TECHNIC CONSTRUCTION OF THE VELUM-OBTURATOR

The Impression and Model of the Cleft

With an understanding of the physiologic functions of the normal organs of speech, one cannot fail to recognize the requirements that are necessary in an instrument which is calculated to restore vocal articulation and resonance to congenital cleft palate patients. The most important technic requirements of this accomplishment lie (1), in obtaining an accurate adequate **impression,** and (2), in forming the veil of the obturator.

The impression is not taken by placing plaster in a prepared tray and forcing the mass into place, as in prosthodontia, but most of the impression is made by carrying the plaster into place a little at a time on the tip end of a spatula. This necessitates a jelly-like consistency of the plaster, a condition which is obtained with some of the best slow-setting plasters by thoroughly stirring the proper mix, and not by mixing it thin and waiting for it to partially set. A perfect impression of the required portion of the floor of the nares is impossible in any other way. It is also necessary that the nasal portion of the impression should easily separate at the cleft from the lingual portion, otherwise it could not be removed; all of this will be fully explained.

A perfect plaster impression of an ordinary typical cleft for the velum-obturator requires no more skill than ordinary impressions for partial and full dentures, which skillful dentists obtain daily. It is necessary that the **working-model** (Figs. 19 and 20) from the impression should duplicate only the **hard parts** on the lingual and nasal surfaces of the palatal process where the body of the obturator should exactly fit (Fig. 7). The lingual **lateral wings** of the obturator should extend no farther laterally and anteriorly upon the roof of the mouth than is required to correct the curve of the dome of the arch for speaking purposes, and give security to the obturator without impairing its mobility.

The nasal extensions, shown on the right in Fig. 7, should fit the floor of the nares over a sufficient area to prevent not only the body of the obturator from dropping directly down when in position, but to prevent the possibility of its dropping at all *until it has passed directly back along the floor from ¼ to ⅜ of an inch.* In connection with this, if the **velum** of the obturator has the proper form and relative position, as will be described, the involuntary action of the palatal and pharyngeal muscles will not only prevent it from falling, but will *at once force it back to place,* if it starts to become dislodged.

438   PART IX. THE PROSTHETIC CORRECTION OF CLEFT PALATE

Before taking the impression, the mental and physical sensitiveness of the tissues should be dulled. If the throat muscles are exceedingly sensitive, with tendencies to contract or gag upon the slightest touch, as they commonly are, they should be freely manipulated with the finger, a brush, or an instrument, until this is reduced and the patient's fears wholly allayed. This may require more than

FIG. 7.

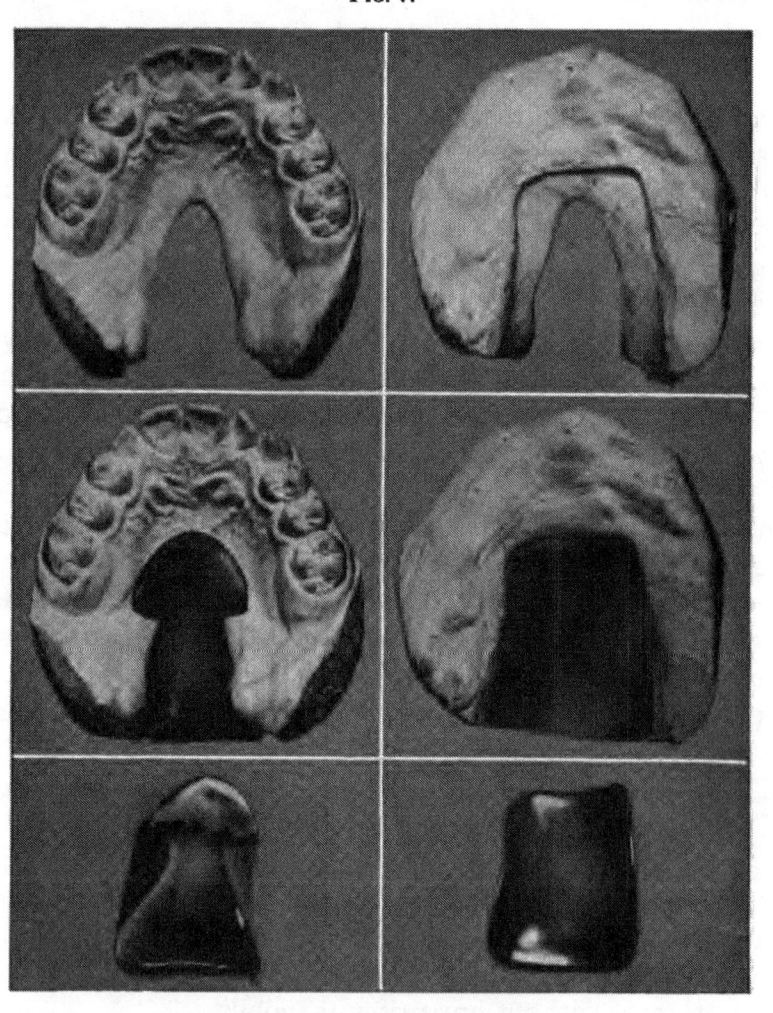

On the left is an oral view, 1st, of a typical cleft; 2d, the velum-obturator in position; 3d, the velum-obturator. On the right are the nasal aspects.

one sitting. The author has never found it necessary to anesthetize the tissues, though there is no special objection to it.

As a part of this preliminary diagnosis, the operator, with electrical mouth lamp and light rubber or celluloid probes bent at different angles—which can be easily made from knitting needles—should become thoroughly acquainted with all the physical conditions: the cleft, the floor of the nares and its lateral recesses, if any, and all irregularities arising from unusual adhesions. The examination

CHAPTER III. TECHNIC CONSTRUCTION OF VELUM-OBTURATOR

should particularly pertain to the form and surfaces of the inferior meatus over which the nasal portion of the obturator is to extend, in order to determine if this portion of the impression is to be taken in one or two sections, to prevent the possibility of getting it dovetailed in this cavity. In the normal state, the lateral walls at the points of entrance to the nares from the naso-pharynx, are often more or less constricted or drawn in toward the median line, which would prevent this portion of the impression, if taken in one piece, from being forced back sufficiently to drop out of the cleft. Occasionally, the vomer is united to one border of the cleft, presenting complications that will be described later.

This would also be a favorable time to commence the study of the positions and action of the palatal and pharyngeal muscles, and also the walls of the pharynx with the muscles relaxed and contracted along the zone to be selected for the position and extent of the rim of the veil of the obturator.

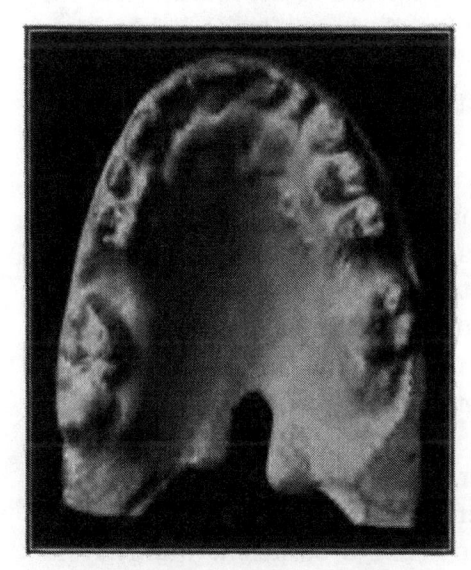

SMALL CLEFTS

FIG. 8.

A cleft of the soft palate or velum-palati.

Impressions of **small clefts** (Fig. 8) which extend only through the soft palate, or those which extend no more than a half-inch into the hard palate, are usually far more difficult to obtain than those of larger clefts, because it is difficult to prevent starting involuntary muscular contractions, by the required movements of the spatula when introducing the plaster. These should always be allowed to subside before further steps are taken.

It should be remembered that the object of the impression in every case is principally to obtain an exact reverse duplication of the **hard nasal floor,** sufficiently far forward and laterally, to sustain the body of the obturator; in the same manner as will be described for larger clefts; and that no attempt should be made to obtain an exact impression of any part of the bifurcated velum.

If a sufficiently extensive impression can be taken of the floor of the nares, whether for small or large clefts, there is no reason why an obturator for one should not be worn quite as successfully as for the other, without a sustaining device, and consequently with perfect restoration of speech capabilities; providing of course that the most scientific part of the work on the veil of the palate is properly performed. This statement is well attested in the author's practice with congenital clefts of almost every character and size.

The case shown in Fig. 8 arose in practice before the days of the present obturator, and is the smallest congenital cleft that the author has ever attempted to correct. The operation for its correction consisted of a soft rubber artificial velum buttoned to a thin narrow very flexible platinum-gold ribbon which extended from a narrow plate across the roof of the mouth sustained with clasps around the first molars. The nasal portion of the obturator was limited and yet sufficient to sustain it in place when held forward by the plate. Its veil was similar to the Kingsley vela. This of course required frequent renewals, because of the rapid deterioration of the soft rubber. One of the objectionable features in the employment of soft rubber vela is: patients will not have them renewed as they should.

In the construction of the present form of obturators for very small clefts, where there is a possibility of its falling into the grasp of the swallowing muscles, it is always advisable to start the patient with a sustaining device similar to that described, though the author is confident this will be found unnecessary, when the muscles become educated in sustaining its position. One of the greatest advantages in this particular with the hard rubber obturators is its extremely light weight.

The sustaining device should not be firmly buttoned to the obturator with the view of carrying both into place together, but the posterior end of the retainer should be bent in the form of a hook that will drop into its fitted place after the obturator has been inserted.

In taking the impression of a very small cleft for an obturator, it may be possible to extend the plaster further forward on the floor of the nares than it may be found practical or advisable to extend the nasal portion of the obturator. This extension on the model, however, should be preserved and duplicated in the *metal* casts, as it may be found useful later. Besides the nasal portion, the working model must also duplicate the required hard palatal surface, and, moreover, the two surfaces—the nasal and the palatal, for both small and large clefts—must bear exact impressional relations to each other. This is not possible if the nasal section has been ever so slightly raised from its seating, or if the sections have not been exactly readjusted outside of the mouth.

This is not a very difficult feature with larger clefts, as will be shown; nor would it be difficult with small clefts if the plaster could be properly introduced with a spatula and permitted to retain its position while a sufficient quantity is added and brought down through the cleft to make a reliable broad bearing joint with the palatal section.

Where this is not possible, the impression may be taken by the use of a special tray. If a tray is employed—the form of which in certain essential particulars must of necessity be left to the ingenuity of the operator—as no two cases are alike—it should be of that character to enable passing it back far enough to then quickly carry it upward and forward into place, and of a form to hold sufficient plaster to be forced over the floor of the nares.

The cup of the tray (Fig. 9) may be made of block tin that can be easily bent to curve forward over the bifurcated velum-palati and palatal process. To this, firmly soft-solder a No. 9 nickel-silver wire handle, as shown. The cup portion may

CHAPTER III. TECHNIC CONSTRUCTION OF VELUM-OBTURATOR 441

be further extended with a thin sheet of wax and carried into place while it is soft; this should leave plenty of room for the plaster, and avoid forcing the yielding tissues too far out of place. Though this is of little importance, as the duplicated uvula and softer portion of the velum-palati, whatever their positions, are cut

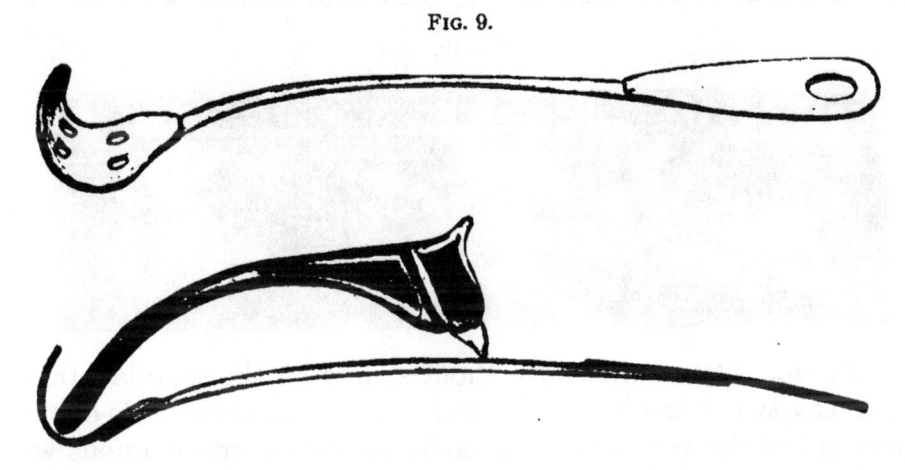

FIG. 9.

away on the model. The illustration shows a cross-section of the tray in position. It will be noticed that the wire handle leaves sufficient space for placing the lingual portion with a spatula.

When the tray and plaster are carried to place, allow the handle to rest upon the incisor teeth to firmly steady it, and maintain this position while the second or lingual section is introduced and hardened.

In those cases of non-irritability of the soft palate, or when cocainized, the introduction of the tray containing the plaster may be immediately preceded by first introducing considerable plaster above the cleft with the spatula, as in larger clefts. This will insure obtaining a more extensive impression of the nasal floor. A large mouth-mirror should be held back of the plaster so as to prevent it after it leaves the spatula, from falling from its lodgment into the throat. If a sufficient mass of the plaster can be forced in this way forward of the attachment of the velum-palati, it will retain its position and thus eliminate the need of introducing so much on the tray, which may therefore be reduced in size. After the plaster has set, there should be no special difficulty in carrying it backward, downward, and out of the mouth.

Two-Section Impression

For the ordinary typical cleft, or those similar to Figs. 1 and 7, which extend well into the hard palate, but not forward of the commencement of the alveolar process, the nasal section can usually be taken in one piece, providing it is found upon examination there is no obstruction which will prevent the impression from being easily forced back and out upon its removal. The head of the patient, for all cleft palate impressions, should not be thrown back any farther than is absolutely necessary to obtain ease of manipulation. The plaster being well stirred, but nothing added to hasten its setting, may be rapidly and deftly introduced from the point of a spatula—being careful to not arouse the sensitive activity of the soft palate.

The **spatula** should be about a half-inch wide and squared at the end with corners and edges rounded so as to avoid injuring the mucous membranes, and formed to carry as much plaster as possible at the very end past the border of the cleft. The **plaster** should be of that slow-setting gelatinous consistency that will enable

FIG. 10.

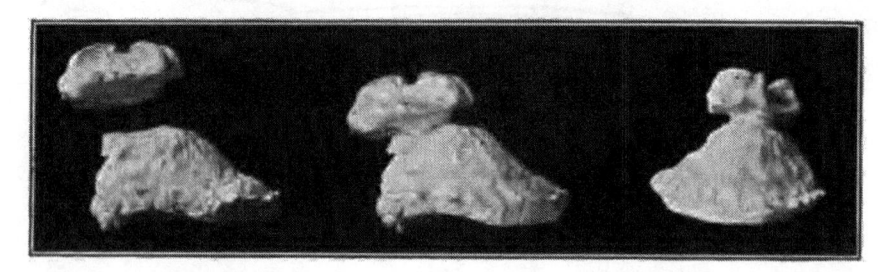

lifting a goodly quantity on the end without sliding off the spatula. Introduce it into the nasal cavity one side at a time, and scrape if off the spatula on the edge of the cleft forward of the velum and, by rapid additional introductions which will act as **followers,** the plaster can be forced back along the floor of the nares to the fullest extent.

Complete one side before going to the other. Then fill the central portion and level it between the cleft along a line which represents its nearest approaching borders; finally, remove all superfluous plaster adhering to the lingual surface. In this first part of the operation, great care should be exercised so as not to start the contracting activities of the muscles. There is always plenty of time with one batch of slow-setting plaster, if moderately rapid movements are made. If a particle is allowed to drop into the throat, or on to the tongue, it should *at once* be removed. Or if the plaster is carried or is allowed to float back on the upper lateral borders of the velum, as may arise in an endeavor to obtain an impression of the posterior lateral surfaces, it is very liable to cause gagging and destroy the impression.

The exposed portion of the nasal section between the borders of the cleft is now thoroughly lubricated with a soft camel's hair brush, and another batch of plaster is brought and carefully spread over it and on to the roof of the mouth with a spatula, and continued out even with the linguo-occlusal surfaces of the teeth. See Fig. 10. Or the first lingual portion when partially hard may be followed with very soft plaster in a rimless tray, with no attempt to carry the plaster beyond the occlusal surfaces of the teeth. In either method, great care should be employed not to raise the nasal section, as a slight pressure from below might easily raise it from its seating upon the floor of the nares without detection, and thus destroy the grasping fit of the obturator. In the removal of the lingual portion, it should separate freely and cleanly from the nasal portion, and then the nasal piece is slow-

CHAPTER III. TECHNIC CONSTRUCTION OF VELUM-OBTURATOR

ly and carefully teased back with a pointed instrument and protected from dropping into the throat with a mouth-mirror. It is quite important that the exposed surface of the nasal section between the cleft be *thoroughly lubricated* to facilitate its separating easily from the lingual portion.

FIG. 11.

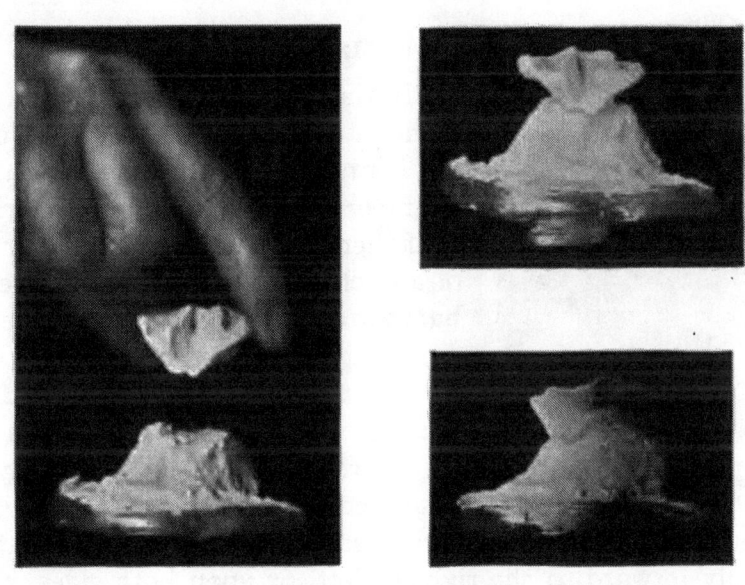

A simple two-section impression.

With quite an extensive experience with clefts of the character described above, which have been found "favorable" in diagnosis, the author has yet to experience a single instance where the nasal section with the usual precautions could not be taken in one piece and easily removed without severe pain or injury. This

FIG. 12.

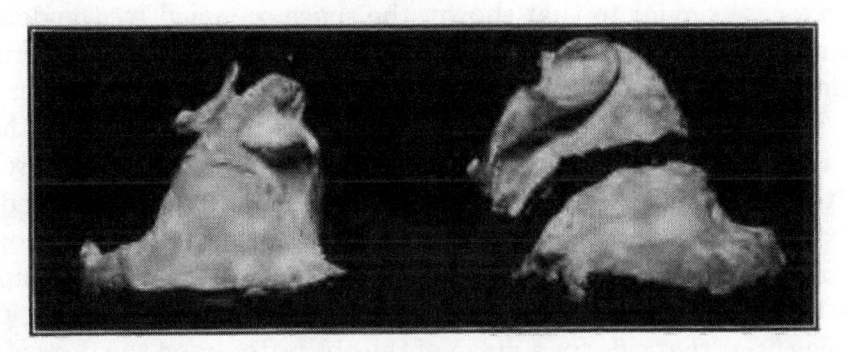

A complicated two-section impression.

no doubt is due to the yielding nasal tissues. Fig. 11 shows different views of a two-section impression of a symmetrical cleft, taken as described.

Fig. 12 shows a two-section impression where the thin ear-like extension on the right side of the nasal section shows how the plaster had been forced into the middle meatus. The impression illustrates the possibility of removing an extensive and apparently impossible nasal section in one piece. The impression was removed without a break, notwithstanding the fact that one of the extensions was only a little thicker than a blotter. This nicely illustrates the yielding and releasing possibilities of the nasal organs, on the same principle that an impression of an ear can be easily removed, which would be impossible if its framework was composed of unyielding bone.

Three-Section Impressions

Fig. 13.

A three-section impression.

If the lateral borders at the posterior entrance to the nares from the naso-pharynx are contracted so that the width of the nasal chamber is wider than its posterior entrance, or if there are deep lateral sulci or attachments of any character that would prevent the **direct backward movement** of the one piece nasal section, the impression of the nares should be taken in two sections, making a three-section impression. Fig. 13 is made from an impression taken in this way, as will be described later.

With more **extensive clefts** entirely separating the hard palate, or which extend diagonally forward to the right or left, or upon both sides, along the line which would have been the intermaxillary suture, or as in Fig. 14 where the whole intermaxillary process has been removed leaving a wide cleft in front, the obturator should not extend forward of a point that is about even with the lingual border of the alveolar ridge. Therefore, this part of the cleft which is not needed for the working-model, should be filled with **dough** (made by mixing flour, powdered soapstone, and water) so that the plaster cannot dovetail into this section. See Fig. 15. In a case similar to that shown, the space occupied by the dough should be filled finally with a hard-rubber piece attached to a removable restoring bridge. The restoring piece is made from an impression taken after the obturator is finished and in the mouth. The object of the denture is to completely close the anterior portion of the cleft, restore the normal lines of the lingual speaking arch and the contour of the upper lip, and permit free nasal breathing. See Figs. 40 and 41.

Occasionally, the vomer will be attached to the hard palate on one side or the other of the cleft, presenting a hard smooth wall which extends upward and toward the median line. At times this will involve the whole of one side, preventing the advantage upon that side for a grasp of the obturator upon the floor of the nares. At other times only a portion will be closed, leaving a roundish opening at its anterior border extending on to the floor of the nares. It is usually desirable to take advantage of this opening to a moderate degree, to aid in sustaining the obturator upon that side, but never to the extent of preventing its easy removal. If

CHAPTER III. TECHNIC CONSTRUCTION OF VELUM-OBTURATOR

the impression-plaster is allowed to freely enter this opening, it might cause trouble. It should, therefore, be prepared by stuffing it with **dough,** leaving a free border, but with a depression of sufficient depth for a slight rim of the plaster and the final obturator to fit into.

It should be understood by this that it is not absolutely necessary to obtain a clinging nasal seating for the obturator on *both* sides of the cleft, and especially not, if *one* side has a broad seating, as the veil of the obturator which rests upon the velum-palati on the other side where it merges into the hard palate, will prevent

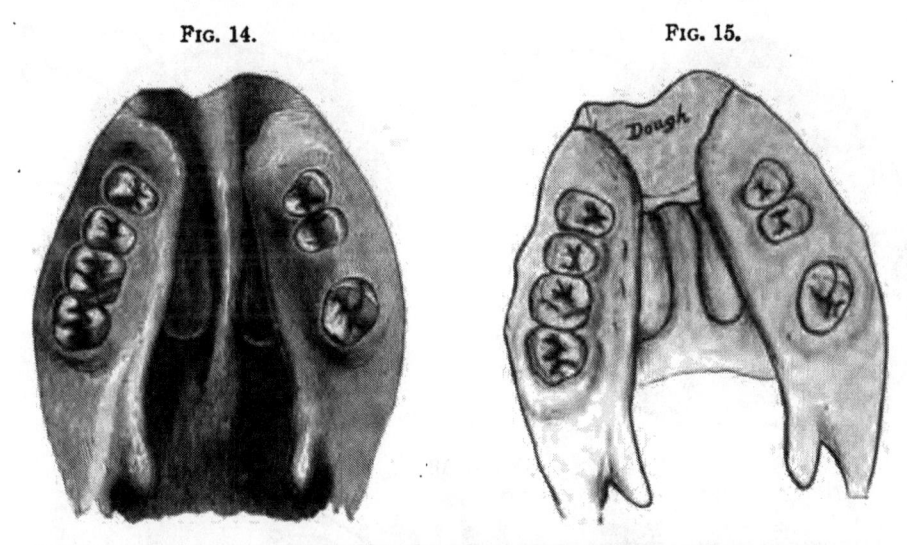

FIG. 14.   FIG. 15.

The above is a representation of a large double cleft. On the right is shown the position of dough to prevent the nasal portion of the impression from dovetailing.

it from tipping or falling. An obturator of this character, shown on the left of the upper group in Fig. 39, is worn with perfect unconsciousness of its presence, though it is not sustained by a supporting plate. Notwithstanding the fact that this patient was over thirty-five years of age when the obturator was first inserted, she has been one of our best patients at clinics, where she has kindly appeared to show how a cleft palate patient can be made to speak perfectly at quite an advanced age, if he has ambition and perseverance.

TECHNICS OF THREE-SECTION IMPRESSIONS

With all impressions of clefts which demand that the nasal portion should be taken in two sections the plaster is managed and introduced the same as for the first half of a single section, pressing it back along the floor of the nares upon one side as before, but stopping it at the border of the cleft by slightly slanting the exposed surface "a," Fig. 16, upward toward the median line. Finish this first half-section by removing all portions of plaster adhering to the palatal surface and also the thin friable edges which have lapped on to the palatal border "b," leaving a narrow flange "c" to fit the palatal section when introduced. The mesio-nasal end

446 PART IX. THE PROSTHETIC CORRECTION OF CLEFT PALATE

"d" of this section is then covered with a perfect separator, and the **second section** "e," Fig. 17, for the opposite side is introduced and finished much in the same manner. This will leave a wide space "f" between the two sections, which touch only at their mesio-nasal ends "d," where they are intended to unite to complete the impression of the floor of the nares. Any lateral branching of the cleft that would be liable to dovetail the plaster, should first be corrected with **dough** "g." It is very important that all of the sections should easily separate from each other at the

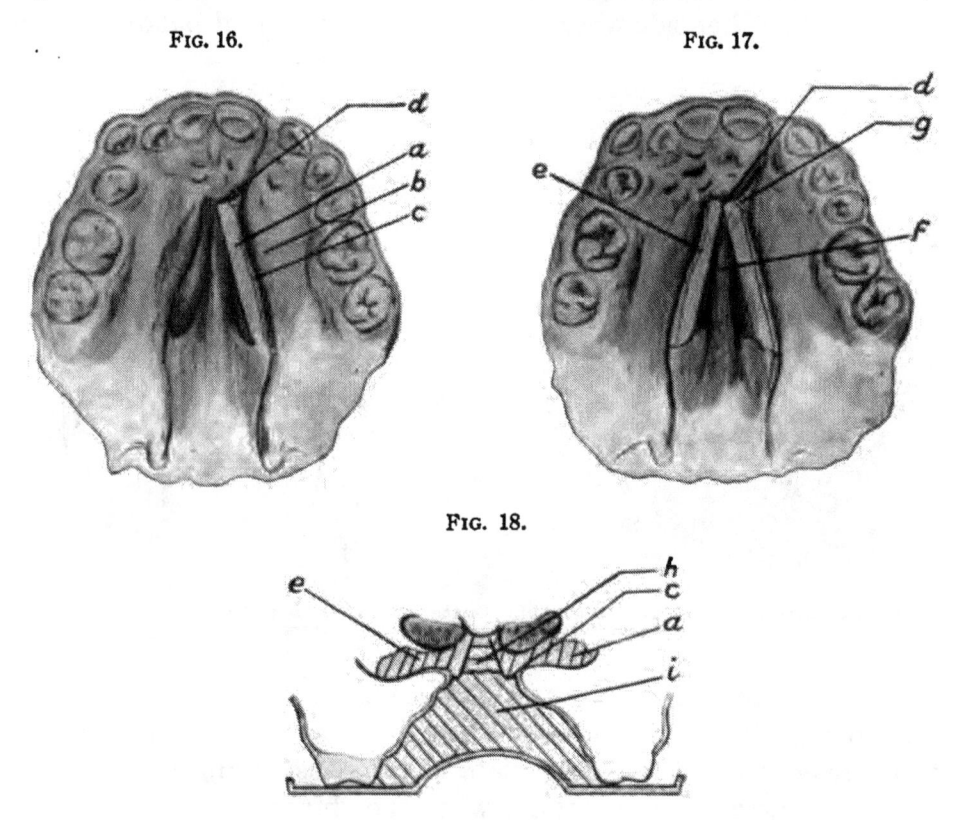

FIG. 16.   FIG. 17.

FIG. 18.

The above on the left, shows the first plaster nasal section in place, in a three-section impression. On the right, both sections in place, and below a transverse of the three sections: a, e, i, and the dough, h.

time of removal, because so little force can be exerted without causing considerable pain to the patient. There is always the chance that they will cling together so firmly that the objects and advantages of sectional parts will be lost. For this reason, when the first and second sections join at "d," the joint should be no larger than necessary to complete the impression at this point upon the nasal floor. Again, the surfaces of the plaster that are to join the section to follow, should be smoothed with the spatula in its final finishing. The author has found no lubricant more perfect at this time than Brophy's Separatine, followed with a solution of soap, carefully painted over the surface with a soft brush.

The inverted V-shaped space "f" between these sections is then partially filled with dough "h," shown in the transverse section, Fig. 18, leaving a well de-

CHAPTER III. TECHNIC CONSTRUCTION OF VELUM-OBTURATOR

fined edge "c" along the border which is intended to join the **third section** "i" with a clean cut fitting when the sections are finally removed and joined outside of the mouth.

The object of the dough here is to prevent the plaster of the third section "i" from extending too high upon the diagonal walls of "a" and "e" or over their tops and debar its easy removal. Still, this part of the impression should be perfectly marked with well defined edges at "c" so there will be no doubt of perfect readjustment of the pieces. Therefore, before starting to take the third section, the exposed surfaces of the first two should be quite perfectly smoothed, while soft, and thoroughly lubricated. The time required for these lengthy necessary instructions should not lead one to imagine that he has time to throw away at this particular stage of the operation, because at any moment an irresistible contraction of the palatal or pharyngeal muscles will be very liable to draw the posterior ends of the sections together, dislodging them from their seating before the palatal section can be placed to secure them. This has often led the author to omit the dough for very sensitive patients, using special care in placing the plaster with the spatula for the palatal section so as to span the space. After the removal of section "i" and the dough "h," Fig. 18, the posterior part of the nasal sections is slightly drawn back and forth toward the center with a teasing movement to loosen it from its seating. It is then teased backward and out, allowing it to take its easiest path. The opposite section is removed in the same manner. When the three sections are united, they should give a perfect impression of all that is required, and without great difficulty in removal.

The one thing of the greatest importance, and the one which demands the greatest care and delicacy of movement in taking these sectional impressions, is to avoid changing in the slightest degree the seating of the nasal sections during the processes of the successive work, and thus disturb their true final relations to each other. If the soft plaster in its introduction is allowed to float back upon a sensitive soft palate, or a particle drops on the back of the tongue or in the throat, it is very liable to start contractions of the muscles which will lift one or both of the nasal sections from their attachment to the mucous membrane. If this occurs before the final lingual section is placed, one might as well stop and begin again—but without discouragement, because of the advantage that is always derived from the experience, to both patient and operator.

Again, in clearing off the plaster that has overlapped the borders of the cleft, and in smoothing and shaping the exposed surfaces preparatory to introducing the last section, or in placing the **dough** between the sections, and even in lubricating the surfaces, and finally the introduction of the section with the spatula until the dome of the arch is filled to the occluding surfaces of the teeth, all of this should be performed deftly and rapidly with the one idea in view that the nasal sections *must not be lifted from their seating, or their positions disturbed in the slightest degree;* otherwise, the exact relations of the lingual and nasal surfaces of the working-model will be destroyed, and to an extent that will destroy the true working possibilities of the obturator.

The greatest danger to this special distortion of the model lies in the fact that it is not detected at the time, or perhaps not until the obturator is found to be too loose, because its upper and lower wings do not have that close grasp upon the hard palate that they should. There should never be any hesitation in taking another impression to correct an imperfection, or when there is a possibility of improving a desired extent of the impression of the nasal floor, or even to correct it if there is any doubt as to its perfection. It is rare for the author to be satisfied with less than three impressions, even when the first one seems to be quite perfect. This gives an opportunity to compare results and choose the best one. Operators of less experience, therefore, should never hesitate to try many times if not fully satisfied; though it may be well to postpone the operation to another day to prevent undue irritation or tetanic contraction of the throat muscles.

The Plaster Working-Model of the Cleft

Great care should be exercised in adjusting the several sections of the impression together, preparatory to filling for the **plaster working-model** (Figs. 19 and 20), as the slightest particle of plaster or debris between the joints at this time will detract from the fit of the obturator. When the sections are fastened firmly together with wax at points which do not encroach upon the impression, cover with a *thin* coat of brown shellac for demarcation. When *dry*, follow with a coat of sandarac varnish, and when this is *dry*, soak the impression *thoroughly* in water just before filling. As soon as the plaster is hard, commence separating, which will be facilitated by occasional dippings in water. Another way is to thoroughly coat with Brophy's Separatine following the sandarac, and follow this by soaking in soapy water.

Preparatory to **filling the impression,** it will be well to remember what has been said of the lingual and nasal extensions of the obturator, and it will then be seen that the only duplicate surfaces of the **model** desired from the impression are: the cleft, and all that portion of the nasal floor obtainable, and the required lingual surfaces. Therefore, unnecessary excess of plaster in filling, and consequently a deal of work in separating and trimming may be avoided.

While the plaster model should be at first of sufficient body in front to avoid breaking its lateral halves apart in the process of constructing and fitting the **modeling-compound model** of the obturator, it should be remembered also that it must be trimmed down ultimately so as to occupy only about one-quarter the surface contents of the **cleft palate flask** in which the obturator should take a central position. These details are given because dentists who are in the habit of filling impressions for "models" for dentures, etc., may feel it necessary to cover the entire surface of the impression, and build it over the top.

In the selection of plaster, employ the kind that will give a hard, smooth, strong model. To avoid air bubbles, pour off the surplus water from the bowl at the

CHAPTER III. TECHNIC CONSTRUCTION OF VELUM-OBTURATOR

moment the last particles of plaster are sinking beneath the surface. After quickly mixing, the remaining air bubbles are removed by a rotary movement of the bowl, causing plaster to float upon the sides of the bowl, and by occasionally jogging it upon the bench. This procedure should be followed in pouring all the plaster and investment models in the flask. Hold the impression in one hand and pour the plaster from the bowl held in the other, commencing in front, and causing it to flow back on each side of the cleft, shaking it into another bowl. Repeat this several times, until the required surfaces are covered. Then with the spatula, build it to the desired thickness, height, and width. This should leave the upper part of the nasal and posterior portions uncovered.

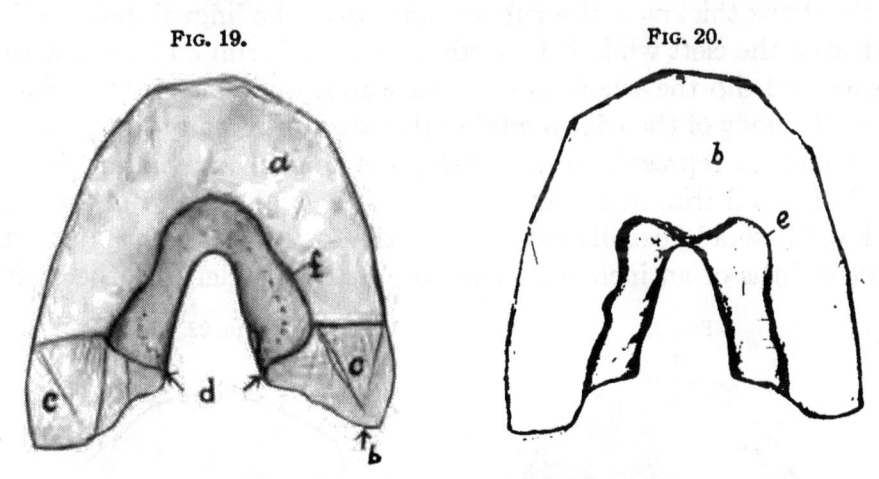

FIG. 19. FIG. 20.

The lingual and nasal aspect of plaster working-model A.

Figs. 19 and 20 represent respectively, **lingual** and **nasal** views of a plaster model of a typical cleft similar to that shown in Fig. 1. In trimming the model, the surfaces "a" and "b"—lingual and nasal aspects—should be trimmed parallel to the occlusal plane. The distance between these two surfaces will make the body of the model about one-half to three-fourths of an inch thick; though when fitted to the flask, it will be much thinner. Preserve the model of the nasal floor to its outer borders "e" and the lingual surface "f" to about one-quarter of an inch beyond that required for the palatal or lingual extensions of the obturator, shown by the dotted lines. Trim the posterior ends "c" "c" of the model diagonally, as shown, for the final drawing surfaces of the casts. If the posterior borders of the model of the cleft at "d" are drawn toward each other, as they usually are, making the cleft narrower at that point, trim them parallel so that the **trial-model** will readily slip back and out of the model of the cleft during its forming and fitting. It will be shown later how these are restored on the model so that the obturator will allow full play of the velum-palati in swallowing, etc.

CHAPTER IV

THE TRIAL-MODEL OF THE OBTURATOR

The surface of the plaster model being rubbed with fine soapstone, select a piece of tough modeling-compound and form it into a solid ball about the size of a hickory nut, and press it into the cleft of the model and spread it out above and below to about the thickness of a rubber plate over the lingual and nasal surfaces. Remove it from the cleft while it is partially soft and trim off excess with scissors. Then replace and dip the whole into warm water, and continue the forming and trimming of the **body** of the **trial-model** in this way until ready to try in the mouth.

Figs. 21 and 22 represent respectively, the lingual and nasal views showing the partially formed trial-model in position. The oral portion of the trial-model, shown in Fig. 21, should usually extend over the roof of the mouth no further than about three-eighths of an inch from the borders of the cleft, be the cleft large or

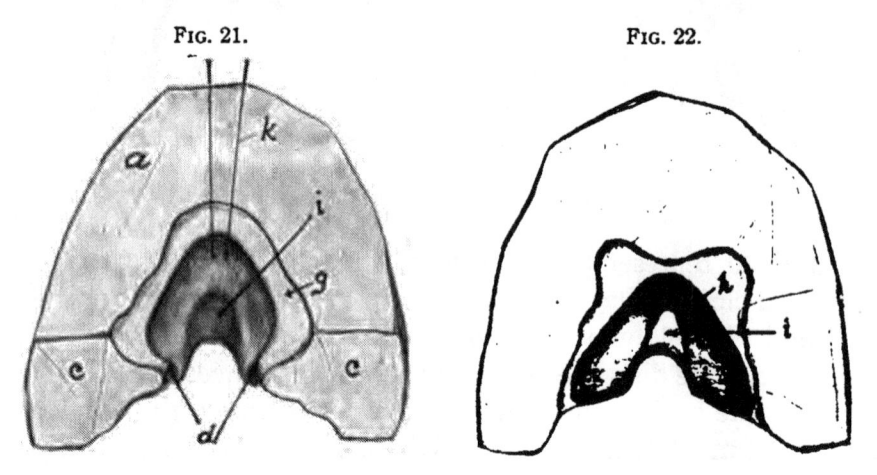

FIG. 21.   FIG. 22.

small, its posterior borders should stop well in front of the attachments of the velum-palati. This will leave a narrow space "g" on the plaster-model, to be finally concaved for the seating of the central or palatal plaster and metal casts. The anterior and lateral nasal extensions "h," Fig. 22, may be very much abridged as shown, for the early trials. This will enable a much easier adjustment in the fitting process to carry the trial-model back into the throat before lifting it, to bring it forward to its seating in the cleft. This is especially important in the trial fitting of the veil. The central portion "i" between the cleft, which in the final preparation is mainly cut away, should be left for strength during the trial movements, it being curved forward, as shown, to obtain a clear view of the pharyngeal wall and muscles during the fitting of the veil.

CHAPTER IV. THE TRIAL-MODEL OF THE OBTURATOR

A strong silk ligature "k," Fig. 21, is usually attached to facilitate the introduction and removals of the trial-model, and to recover it from the grasp of the throat muscles, in case of its accidental falling. With one or more fingers resting on the under surface of the trial-model, and with the ligature held tautly with the other fingers, a sufficiently firm hold may be obtained to carry it back in the mouth until the lateral nasal extensions "h," Fig. 22, will allow it to be carried far back, up and forward to place. Another very important object of the ligature is that the trial-model can be held safely forward in position by passing the ligature between two of the teeth with a knot in front. This will allow the patient to close the mouth and take time to become somewhat accustomed to it, and he will be able to note if there are any points of irritation in swallowing, etc. These rests with the trial-model in place are of the greatest advantage later in the forming and fitting of the veil. This is the time to observe if the fit is perfect and if it will securely retain its position when the nasal wings are extended.

To the posterior borders of the trial or obturator model, where the lateral wings of the lingual portions curve over the borders of the cleft "d," Fig. 21, to join the nasal portions, the surfaces must permit the free action of the muscles in swallowing, etc. This can be determined with the trial-model in the mouth. Occasionally, the attachment of the palatal muscles is so far forward along the edges of the osseous cleft, it will be found necessary to scrape the inner surfaces of the model which will leave a space shown at "d" between the borders of the plaster and trial-model at this point, especially if the plaster-model has been trimmed off to parallel the edges. Later, upon completion of the final model of the obturator, these spaces must be closed. This procedure is described in Chapter V.

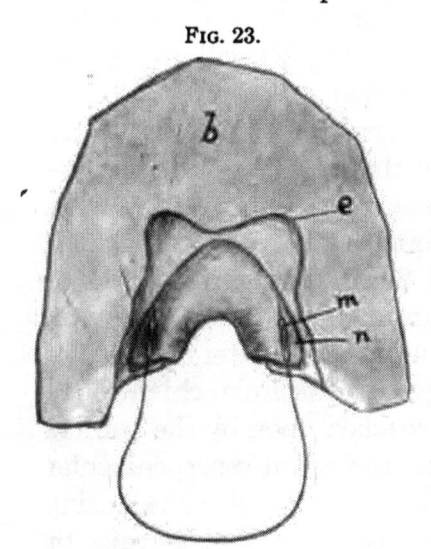

FIG. 23.

The Veil of the Obturator.—When satisfied with the form and fit of the body of the trial-model, showing that another impression will not be necessary to secure perfect coaptation to the hard surfaces for this portion of the obturator—the next move is to arrange for a wire loop guide for forming and fitting the veil of the obturator.

CONSTRUCTING THE VEIL OF THE OBTURATOR

Fig. 23 is a nasal view of the plaster-model with the partially formed trial-model in place, showing short pieces of tubing "m" (No. 23 nickel-silver rotating tube) imbedded in the compound, with a **copper wire** "n" in position, the loop being bent to conform somewhat to the size and form of the **pharyngeal walls.** This is for the purpose of exactly gauging the extent and position of the veil of the obturator by a visual observation of the pharyngeal walls above and below the loop, during a physiologic action of the muscles. This enables one to form and place the wire and ultimate border of the veil exactly along the lines of physiologic demands, thus freeing this most important part of the whole operation from the "guesswork" of former methods which have always debarred the scientific advancement of the prosthetic correction of this deformity.

In the first trials, force the loop well into the tubes to insure against having it too large, and to accustom the patient to its introduction. It can then be enlarged and shaped to conform to the **pharyngeal walls** during the contraction of the zone which is to determine the outline of the borders of the final veil.

In the preliminary and present study of the pharynx, one should note first, the position of the greatest **forward extension** of the **superior pharyngeal muscle.** This can easily be ascertained by titillating the throat tissues to the point that starts the act of gagging. By watching at that moment the otherwise smooth posterior pharyngeal wall, a transverse fold will be seen to stand forward along the zone where the velum-palati rests in closing the oro-nasal passage. This is the superior pharyngeal muscle in its somewhat abortive effort to imitate its more normal action. Its position is usually below the line of direction of the hard palate, and usually below the orifices of the Eustachian tubes. With cleft palate patients it is rarely developed as in normal conditions, or as it will be later (if the patient is not too old) under the stimulation induced in co-operating with the artificial veil, in performing the important function of closing the oro-nasal passage, which is its main function under normal conditions in the activities of speech.

The position of this muscle will be a guide to the **height** and **line** of the loop at that point, as the lower edge of the border of the veil should be an eighth of an inch or more above the line of the **greatest extension** of this muscle and it should no more than **barely touch** the veil. The subsequent development of this and other pharyngeal muscles will complete the necessary occlusion. Fig. 24 will give something of an idea of the relation of the veil to the superior pharyngeal muscle, but it should not be regarded as an invariable guide to modern treatment, as it will frequently be advisable to raise the posterior border of the veil above the relative position shown in this picture. It will be found necessary to frequently **induce** a **contraction** of the throat muscles by titillating the soft palate, or by asking the patient to partially swallow with the mouth open. If the loop of wire touches or presses upon the contracted pharyngeal muscles at any point, it should be bent away, or perhaps forced farther into the tubes. At the posterior lateral angles of the pharynx, and **above** the line of the veil, the entrances to the **Eustachian tubes** should be seen. These should **never be covered,** or encroached upon by the borders of the veil. Below these openings the walls are frequently thrown into perpendicular folds, which if prominent, as they occasionally are, and the desired zone during contraction of the muscles is not smooth, it may be necessary to slightly raise or lower the angle of the veil at that point to a smoother zone, or to more closely fit it to the irregularities to assure the probability of a complete closure of the oro-nasal passage.

CHAPTER IV. THE TRIAL-MODEL OF THE OBTURATOR 453

However, there can be no cut and dried rules in regard to the exact position of the veil in relation to the superior pharyngeal muscle, except that it should rest in such a position in the relaxed state of the muscles, that the palatal muscles in swallowing, will **raise** it **above** the greatest contractility of all the pharyngeal muscles, so that they cannot get it within their grasp to cause its downward move-

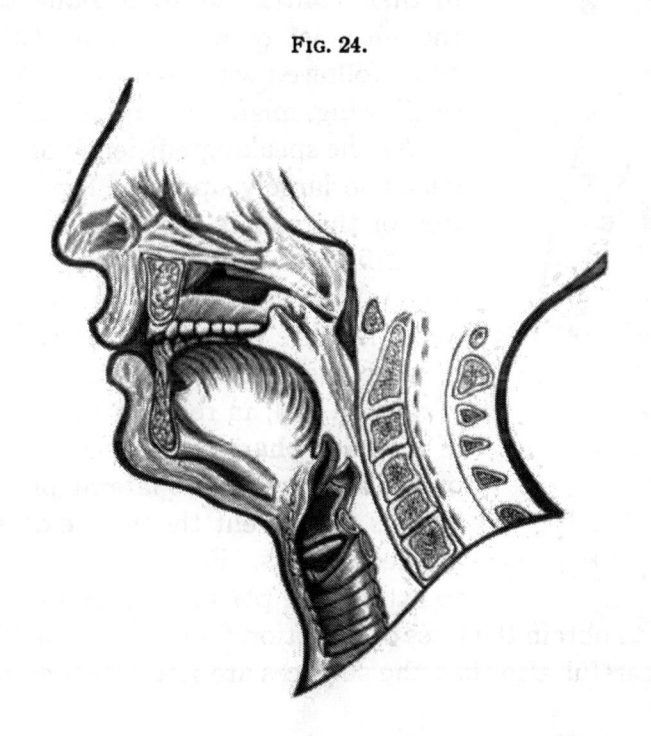

FIG. 24.

ment. In one instance it was necessary to place the posterior border three-eighths of an inch above the superior pharyngeal to obtain the most practical use of the obturator.

A **roll** of **modeling-compound** a trifle larger than one-half the diameter of a pencil, and of sufficient length to more than reach around the loop, is now warmed at one end over a small jet of a Bunsen Burner, with sufficient heat to enable its firm cohesion to the trial-model at the point "n," Figs. 23 and 25, where the loop emerges from the tube. Then with slight warmings, carry it around the loop imbedding it in its substance to the other end; finally, cut off the surplus and attach the end as before. This is shaped by the fingers, so as to leave the outer border rounded and the inner ("o") pinched to a V-edge to evenly join the line of the final thin central portion of the veil.

A proper degree of judgment based upon the position and action of the muscles and their requirements in speaking, will enable this preliminary shaping of the loop and border of the veil to its relations with the pharyngeal walls. When in place, it can easily be seen where the contracted muscles press too hard upon it, even though the patient may not complain of irritation in swallowing; these places should be trimmed, or warmed and pressed back, and their positions confirmed by repeated trials.

Great care must always be exercised in the repeated necessary introduction and removal of the model, to prevent changing its form. This danger debars softening the border of the model sufficiently to obtain an exact impression of the muscles in their contracted state along the desired zone, though a jet of warm air or water upon limited areas followed with repeated acts of the patient's swallowing, might accomplish this.

Fig. 25.

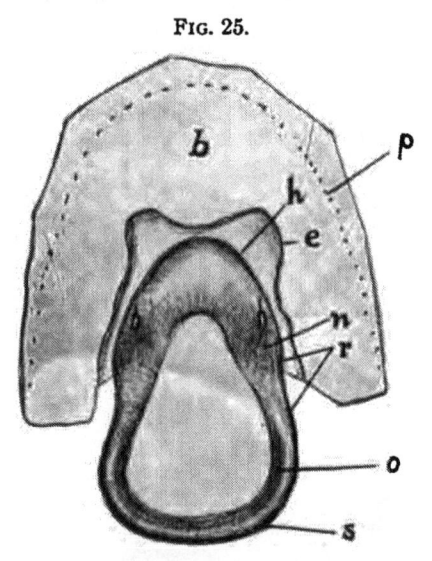

Nasal view of the completed model of the obturator placed on the plaster working-model.

As the speaking efficiency of the obturator depends so largely upon the form and relative position of the veil, it should be regarded as the most scientific part of the whole operation, and proportionate care and skill given to forming the model.

It is quite necessary to obtain a close coaptation of the anterior lateral borders of the veil ("r," Fig. 25), in relation to the contracted walls of the **naso-pharynx**, especially when there is little or no activity of the lateral pharyngeal muscles. This is to prevent the escape of air into the nose at these points. For this reason one should strive to extend the plaster impression to these surfaces far enough at least to obtain the lines of direction for correctly molding this portion of the veil, being careful also that the surfaces are not extended so far as to produce irritation.

Remember that the line of the posterior peripheral surface "s," Fig. 25, of the entire border of the veil should follow the contour lines of the muscles along the pathway of the chosen zone at the moment of their greatest contraction, and should never be allowed to more than barely touch at any point. Later, after the first obturator is vulcanized and worn for a few days, if it is found needful to extend the border at any place to aid the patient to more completely close the oro-nasal passage, it can easily be accomplished by scraping the metal casts, and if too long, the obturator can be reduced. These movements should be done cautiously, however, if the obturator-model has been properly formed, because the subsequent functional efforts of the muscles to completely close an almost closed opening in uttering all of the oral elements, except **m, n,** and **ng,** will cause these muscles which have never been used under speech impulses, to develop surprisingly. *To leave the largest possible space at the posterior border of the veil when the muscles are relaxed*, is of the greatest importance to speech and healthful breathing (Fig. 26).

This part of the work should not be done hastily, or with lengthened sittings, as an irritated condition of the sensitive pharyngeal mucous membrane will start a tetanic contraction of the muscles that will lead to a very deceiving estimation

CHAPTER IV. THE TRIAL-MODEL OF THE OBTURATOR

of the size of the pharynx in its apparently relaxed state. One will often be surprised after a supposedly perfect fitting of the veil, to find on a later day that it should be considerably extended.

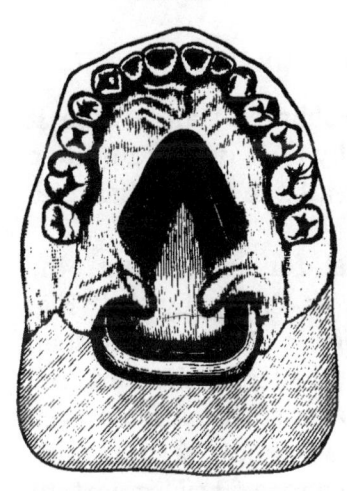

FIG. 26.

Designed to show the trial-model of the obturator in position with the central portion open, and the usual distance between the posterior borders of the veil and the pharyngeal walls when the muscles are completely relaxed.

It would be well to state at this time that one is likely to meet with an unusual variation in the form of the pharynx and the position and action or inaction of the pharyngeal muscles. This is not easily discernible, and may allow the obturator to unexpectedly fall from its safe position, even when a perfect impression has been secured, shown by the difficulty in removals of the trial-model and final obturator. It seems to occur during a relaxation of the muscles in a sudden forcible intake of the breath, and is usually remedied by tipping the veil of the obturator up to a higher position in the pharynx. Only in one instance, in the author's practice, has this resulted in danger of swallowing the obturator. It occurred with a woman about forty years of age, whose obturator was seemingly perfect and worn at all hours during several weeks of speech training. About two weeks after she returned to her somewhat distant home, while talking and laughing with her friends, the obturator dropped into her throat and apparently was swallowed. Fortunately it produced an almost immediate nausea and vomiting, with its recovery. It was found upon her return to the office several weeks later that the attachment and action of the posterior lateral muscles were very much higher in the throat than is common, and in a forcible drawing in of the breath with her head thrown back, the obturator slipped backward—which is a common movement with all obturators—and instead of the muscles forcing it back to place as they should, it dropped sufficiently to be partly swallowed. By bending the posterior portion of the veil upward so that its rim when in the most posterior position rested above the Eustachian tubes—which in this case were quite low—it was found impossible to dislodge it as before.

In order to have her feel perfectly safe with it, however, a very light retaining-plate was made as described, but with the belief that it will be abandoned as soon as confidence is restored.

If the rules here given are followed and a proper choice of the palato-pharyngeal zone is made, together with a perfect and sufficiently extensive fitting upon the nasal floor, the velum-obturator should be worn with comfort, safety, and unconsciousness of its presence in the mouth during all waking and sleeping hours, and without a supporting plate in most instances *from the very start*. Patients under twenty years of age soon learn to speak with the velum-obturator with such perfect articulation and tone, that strangers do not suspect their deformity.

CHAPTER V

THE LABORATORY TECHNIC CONSTRUCTION OF THE OBTURATOR-MODEL

The remaining portion of the operation is **purely mechanical;** and while it may seem to be somewhat complicated to a novice, and really does demand quite a high degree of exactness in mechanical technic, it is after all the same character of procedure which is familiar to skilled dentists.

In preparing the modeling-compound **obturator-model** for investment, the nasal wings "h," Figs. 22 and 25, should now be extended as shown by "r," Fig. 30, and then the entire model should be finished to no thicker at any point than a thin rubber plate. The part which represents the inner border of the **veil** "o," Fig. 25, Chapter IV, should be concaved on its upper and lower surfaces to an even knife-blade edge, leaving the rounded peripheral border "s" about ⅛ of an inch thick. Great care must be exercised that the position and shape of this important peripheral rim of the velum is not changed from its original formation in the mouth. All the **central portion** of the **obturator-model** within the loop, as shown in Fig. 25, is cut away to more accurately determine the thickness of the nasal and lingual walls of the body, and the line "o." When this is finished, cut a pattern from a thin business card by first outlining it with a pencil along the inner borders of the open loop. This when bent to the proper curve to form the dome of the arch, should be waxed evenly in place along its outer edge to form the central portion of the obturator-model. There is, however, no objection to spanning this space with a *very thin* sheet of wax. The **tubes** at the ends of the **wire loop** which extend into the body of the trial-model, if exposed, may be cut off and removed. The rest of the loop imbedded in the modeling-compound border of the veil, should be allowed to remain, if possible, to strengthen this frail portion of the model which has cost so much labor and skill to form.

If the impression of the **nasal floor,** shown by the plaster-model, is more extensive than seems to be necessary to support the obturator, the added **nasal-wings** of the **obturator-model** need not extend to its outer borders ("r," Fig. 30). Later, if desired, the **nasal metal cast** which fills this space may be cut back to allow a greater extension.

It is of the greatest importance that the finished **obturator-model** be reduced to the minimum of thickness and heft to meet the demands of strength and durability of the obturator, being careful to leave a sufficiently wide and firm peripheral rim at the border of the veil, to aid the pharyngeal muscles in closing the oro-nasal passage, not only to aid in the safe support and retention of the obturator, but also to increase its possibilities in the activities of speech. The finishing and

CHAPTER V. LABORATORY TECHNIC CONSTRUCTION

smoothing the surfaces of the **obturator-model** are best accomplished with light sharp scrapers, being always careful to avoid changing the relative position of the veil. It will be remembered that its dimensions at any point may at any time be increased by scraping the metal casts, and decreased by scraping the obturator.

With the finished **obturator-model** in position on the **plaster working-model,** restore with plaster as mentioned under Fig. 19 the posterior borders of the cleft by filling the V-shaped spaces "d," Fig. 21, which represent the natural contracted position of the border of the cleft at the point where the natural velum joins the hard palate. These restorations can be further finished on the plaster-model, if edges are presented after the final removal of the **obturator-model** from its investment, as will be described. Before filling these V-shaped spaces, however, the **obturator-model** must be removed to permit deepening and roughening the surfaces so that the added plaster will perfectly adhere. The above restoration, however, is not always necessary with every cleft. One should fully appreciate that this original model of the cleft (Figs. 19 and 20) represents the only surfaces which the obturator is supposed to exactly fit the hard parts of the mouth and nasal cavity. It should, therefore, be carefully protected from injury through the many technic trials to which it is subjected.

In preparing the **plaster working-model** for investment in the flask, the posterior ends "c," Fig. 21, should extend no farther than the requirements of the lingual portion of the obturator, with surfaces slanting slightly upward and forward. Space should be allowed at the lingual borders of the obturator for a concave seating "g," as will be described later.

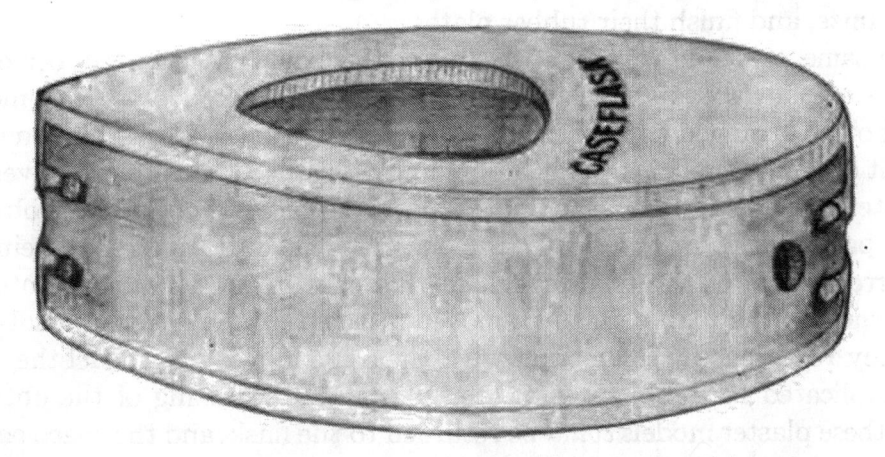

FIG. 27.

THE FLASK

Fig. 27 illustrates the cleft palate flask closed with its lingual and nasal covers (named according to their relations to the cleft), and provided with fittings to hold the parts firmly in position during vulcanizing, etc. The body of the flask is beveled and finished on the inside, as shown by Fig. 28, which gives an interior view of a vertical antero-posterior section through the body. The beveled planes divide the contents of the flask into lingual and nasal halves, which permit the separation and removal of the casts from the flask, and from each other. The round

FIG. 28.

holes in the sides of the flask are for the insertion of a screw-driver to separate the upper and lower metal casts after they have been poured, and also after vulcanizing. These should be filled with investment to present a smooth surface on the inside of the flask, until needed.

PRELIMINARY PRINCIPLES

With the **model** of the obturator finished and on the working-model of the cleft, the object now is to completely invest the **obturator-model** in parts in plaster which may be easily removed from the flask, and cleanly separated from each other and the obturator-model intact. It therefore must be apparent that when these plaster parts are duplicated in **metal** and the space of the **obturator-model** is packed with rubber and vulcanized, the hard rubber obturators can be easily removed from the metal casts ready for finishing, in the same way that dentists pack, vulcanize, and finish their rubber plates.

On the same principle that dentists invest the trial plate of a rubber denture in plaster—one surface of which is represented by the model of the mouth—and the whole so arranged that when the flask is opened and the trial plate removed, the space it occupied is packed with rubber and vulcanized, so also, the investment of the plaster-model made from the impression, and the trial-model of the obturator in a cleft palate flask is practically the same. The only difference being: the plaster surroundings of the trial-model, in this case, must be divided into parts that are formed so they can be easily removed intact from the flask and trial-model, because they represent in connection with the original working-model the models that are duplicated in Babbitt's metal for the final vulcanizing of the obturator. Of course, these plaster models *could* be returned to the flask, and the space occupied by the trial-model could be packed with rubber and vulcanized to form an unfinished obturator, the same as dentists pack their rubber plates, but the models for future obturators, which have cost so much time and skill to prepare would be destroyed, and what is of great importance, you would be deprived of the opportunity to skillfully correct slight imperfections in the obturators by making required changes in the casts. This is one of the principal features of this system, which pertains to the entire life of the patient.

The somewhat intricate processes that are necessary in the duplication of this first set of plaster models in metal which surround the obturator in the flask have always been a great stumbling block to students, largely because they do not think out for themselves the absolute need of these movements, which have been freed as far as possible from every complication during many years of practice. If they should take one of these plaster parts as a pattern to a foundry to be duplicated in metal, they would easily understand that the molder would first surround it with sand in such a way as to remove the pattern and fill the space it occupied with the metal. In that case the walls of the chamber after the pattern is removed are composed wholly of sand and are the exact impression of the peripheral surfaces of the pattern. In our duplication of these models or patterns in metal, the walls or chambers of each one are made up of the flask upon one side, and the investment plaster models on the other sides; and then as each cast is poured, it becomes one of these parts, so that when all of them are poured they fit perfectly together in the flask; and being duplicates of the first set of plaster models, they form a chamber for vulcanizing the obturator—as will be fully explained.

To many practitioners of dentistry who contemplate undertaking this work, the detailed descriptions and repetition of words and ideas will doubtless seem to be quite unnecessary and verbose, but possibly excusable when they remember that it is written mainly for the education and guidance of college students by an author who has been engaged in teaching for many years and fully realizes this necessity.

The **metal casts** and the **flask** for each individual case should be regarded as the valuable life property of the patient, and if not given into his hands at the close of the operation, they should be kept in a fire-proof safe to be turned over to him upon demand, so that if necessary, other dentists can renew the obturators.

The First Set of Plaster Models

In preparing the **first set of plaster models** which are to surround the obturator-model and are ultimately to be duplicated in **metal,** the important feature is the carrying into the combination, as one of its parts, the **original plaster working-model A** (Figs. 19 and 20), made from the impression of the cleft. The plaster models should be of the strongest possible quality of plaster, because from these are made the investment models for making the final **metal casts,** and are consequently subjected to conditions that tend to injure or break them. The easy removal of plaster casts from the flask is possible only *by keeping the inside surfaces of the flask polished and oiled.*

As before outlined, in fitting the **plaster-model A** (Figs. 29 and 30) to the flask, it is placed in such a position that the **obturator-model** will occupy a central position in the flask, leaving sufficient room "g" between the top of the flask and the

460 PART IX. THE PROSTHETIC CORRECTION OF CLEFT PALATE

outer edges of the lingual wings of the obturator-model for the seating of that portion of the "palatal" or lingual cast C, Fig. 31. Preliminary to fitting it into the flask, therefore, the lingual surface A, Fig. 29, should be evenly trimmed parallel to the line of the lingual wings and general plane of the obturator-model. Then by outlining with a pencil the inner edge of the flask upon the model, as shown by the dotted line in Fig. 25, it can be roughly trimmed, and the space between it and the flask filled with plaster. The nasal surface of this plaster-model should be beveled even with the dividing line of the flask "b," Fig. 30.

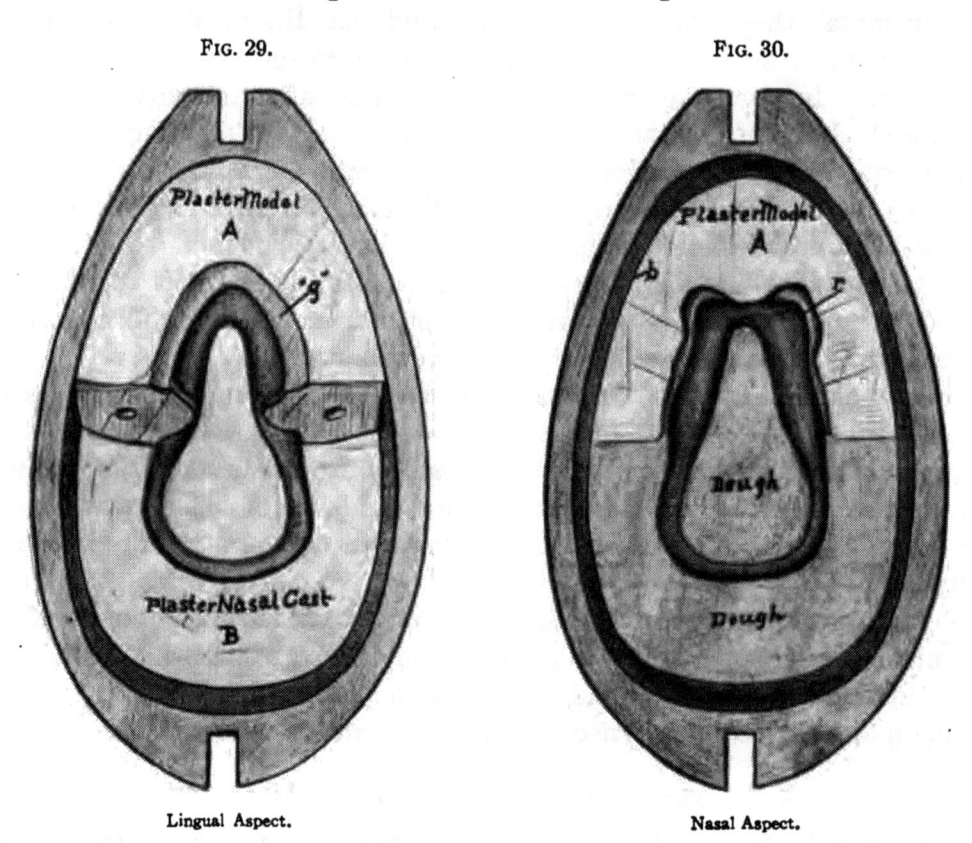

FIG. 29. FIG. 30.

Lingual Aspect. Nasal Aspect.

After fitting and securing with plaster the **model A** in position, it should be removed from the flask and finally trimmed as above, and then returned to the flask for making the rest of the surrounding models. The **plaster nasal model B**, Fig. 31, may be made first as follows: With the model A and the obturator-model in position, fill the rest of the upper half of the flask with **dough** to produce a matrix to pour against. See Fig. 30. **Dough** is easily and quickly prepared, it yields at the slightest touch, and will not, therefore, force the delicate rim of the **veil** out of position in placing it, and yet it possesses sufficient stability to retain its integrity against the introduction of the plaster. The **dough,** where it joins the other parts, should be smoothed with a wax spatula even with the line of the plaster-model and along the proper dividing and separating lines around the obturator-model of the **veil**, and the parting line of the beveled planes of the flask. Along the surfaces of the **veil rim**, "s" and "o," Fig. 25, the dough should be placed so that the plaster cast, about to be poured, will **draw**, else this delicate structure will be broken in the removal of the cast from the flask. Remember, that you are now preparing the natural parting lines of the future metal casts from which the hard vulcanized rubber obturator is to be removed.

Fig. 30 is the **nasal aspect** showing the lingual half of the flask filled with the **plaster-model A,** and the **dough,** with the **obturator-model** in position ready for pouring the **plaster nasal model B** (see Figs. 29 and 31). In Fig. 30, the central part of the veil is shown filled with dough. A later and more preferable method is to span this loop with a pattern cut from a thin card as before described. The exposed surfaces of the plaster-model A should receive a thorough coat of Brophy's Separatine, and when dry, cover all the surfaces with thin soapy water before pouring the plaster. If sandarac varnish is used it must not touch the modeling-compound, as it will dissolve its surface and stick it to the model. In other places, sandarac followed with thin oil is a good separator.

One can readily understand that it is necessary, in separating irregular surfaces and frail forms of plaster casts from each other and from the flask without breaking, that all surfaces must be arranged to *draw*, and then covered with a good separating material. In separating the most difficult facial casts from plaster impressions, a thick coating of sandarac varnish is used, followed by soaking in water. But soaking in water weakens cleft palate plaster casts and renders frail portions liable to break. In the construction and necessary duplication of the many plaster casts for each cleft palate case, do not forget that the **flask** should be **thoroughly cleaned,** and its beveled surfaces oiled after the removal of *every plaster casting*, which should never be left in the flask long, as rust will soon make its removal difficult. The success of the entire operation demands the highest order of cleanliness and accuracy at every step of the undertaking.

The Plaster and Investment Models

In the process of pouring the **plaster models** the plaster should be of just the right consistency which is best obtained in the manner described in filling the impression. With the flask held in one hand, pour the plaster from the bowl into the mold, commencing at an extreme border causing it to flow rapidly over the surfaces, and then with a quick movement throw it back into the bowl, repeating the movements until it is filled. This should drive the air out of all the pockets. Scrape the surplus plaster off even with the edge of the flask.

Fig. 29 represents the lingual aspect, after the **dough** has been removed, showing the original **plaster-model A** with the **obturator-model** in position in the lingual half of the flask and resting now upon the **plaster nasal model B,** which has just been poured into the flask, and finished ready for pouring the **plaster palatal model C,** Fig. 31. Remember after each plaster and investment model is poured, all

462   PART IX. THE PROSTHETIC CORRECTION OF CLEFT PALATE

the parts should be removed from the flask for finishing the newly poured model and preparing the flask for the next pouring. In removing the plaster models from the flask after pouring, the flask is held loosely in the hand with the fingers and thumb doubled under and lightly touching the edges of the model to prevent it from suddenly falling out and breaking, the flask is then tapped sharply with a light hammer on the under side of one of its ends, the fingers being able to detect and guide the slightest movement of the model as it falls from the flask. If the

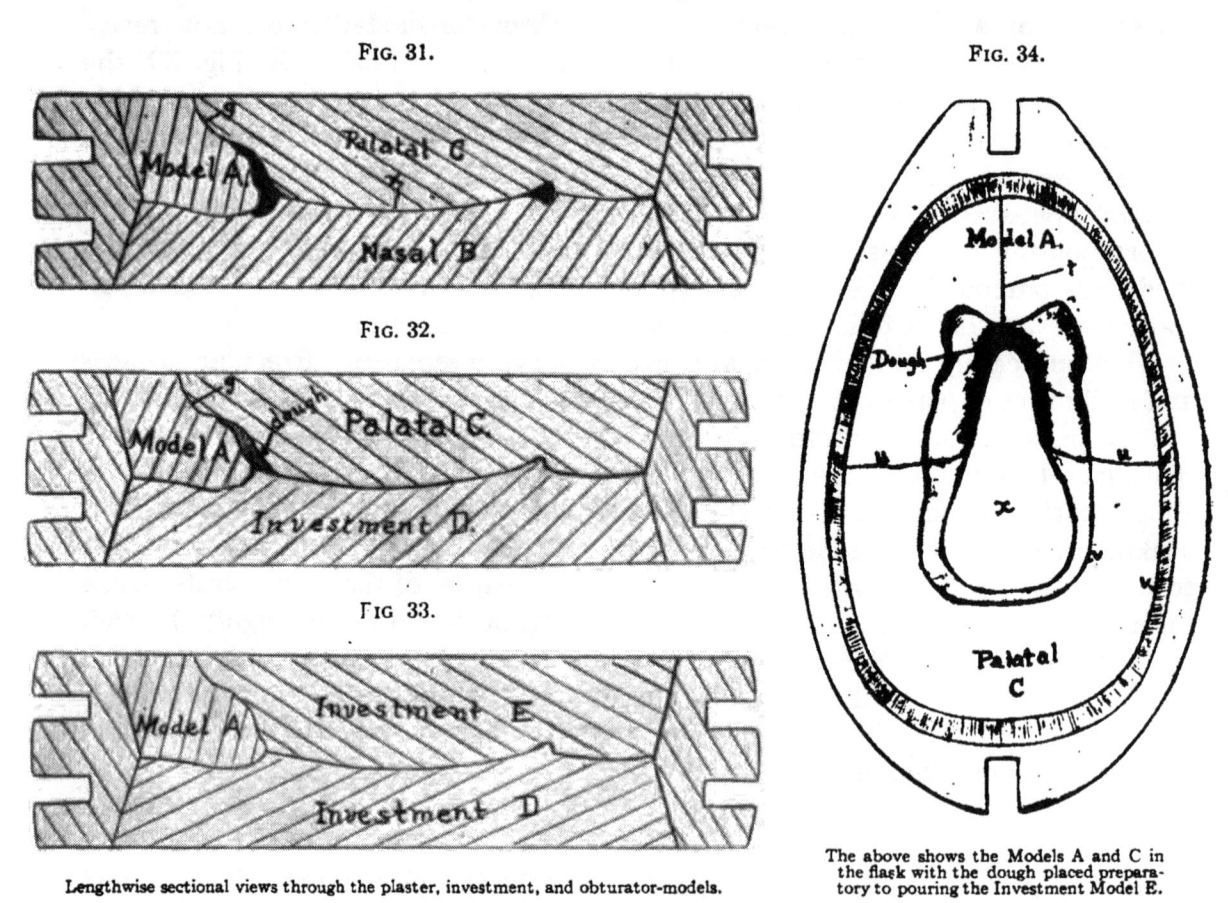

FIG. 31.

FIG. 32.

FIG 33.

Lengthwise sectional views through the plaster, investment, and obturator-models.

FIG. 34.

The above shows the Models A and C in the flask with the dough placed preparatory to pouring the Investment Model E.

plaster model clings to the **model of the veil,** showing that it has lapped beyond its true drawing line, loosen it carefully with a spatula. After its removal, its finishing consists in correcting all drawing and overlapping lines at "v" "v" and parting edges at "u" "u," Fig. 34.

Before returning the casts to the flask, varnish only the surfaces that are to come in contact with the next model to be poured. Finally, if oil is used over the surfaces of the mold before pouring, stand the flask on edge that the excess oil in pockets may drain off.

One of the most important movements in the whole process is to secure *absolute coaptation* of the models at "g" and "x," Fig. 31, in **replacing** them in the flask

CHAPTER V. LABORATORY TECHNIC CONSTRUCTION

preparatory to pouring subsequent plaster or metal casts. This is especially imperative preparatory to pouring the models B and C around the model A, Fig. 31, or in fitting together the subsequent investment models (E and D, Fig. 33) to form a mold for duplicating this important model A in plaster, or metal; it being a duplicate of the cleft and the hard surfaces which the obturator must exactly fit. If an excess of separating fluid or a slight particle of plaster or dirt is allowed to come between the contact surfaces of the models, or between them and the beveled surfaces of the flask, which might arise with a slovenly procedure, so that the models A and B, or B and C, do not come absolutely together, the same misfit will be produced that would arise if the nasal and palatal sections of the impression are not exactly replaced. Again, the expansion of the plaster models will at times make it impossible to properly replace them in the flask. This should be corrected by scraping their outer surfaces where they come in contact with the flask. Furthermore, the models should be grasped in such a manner during the process of pouring, that they can be held firmly together until the first stage of hardening has taken place.

All of these lengthy preliminary directions, which need not be repeated, are of especial importance preparatory to the final duplications in metal, which may frequently require a number of recastings before a perfect cast is secured, and which means also the reduplication of the investment models, if they are broken.

Fig. 31 illustrates a side view of a vertical-median section after pouring the **plaster palatal model C.** The model of the obturator is now completely surrounded with parts in plaster, which when **duplicated in metal** and properly prepared, will form the final castings in which the rubber obturators are vulcanized. This completes the first set of models, all of which should be carefully preserved; first, to enable making the investment sets for pouring the casts, and second, as original patterns, by the aid of which—in case of an accident—a new set of metal casts or parts thereof can be made.

Trim the top and bottom surfaces even with the flask, and then with the nasal model B downward, tap the flask gently on the underside with precautions as described, and when B is removed, trim off any surplus plaster from the inside of the flask which may have run down between it and the nasal model, etc.

In like manner, the models A and C, containing the obturator-model, are removed from the flask, the model C should be carefully separated from the model A and the obturator-model. As it would be impossible to remove the obturator-model from the plaster-model A, because of the added portion at "d," Fig. 21—and also for other reasons—it is necessary to saw the plaster-model A in two, along the line "t," Fig. 34, using a very thin "jeweler's saw," and cut nearly to the obturator-model, and then *break* the two halves apart by inserting a thin pry, and carefully separate them from the obturator-model. See that the edges of the added portions of plaster "d," Fig. 21, are smoothed even with the lines of the model A, and remove all portions of plaster which may have been extended out upon the surfaces. The object in breaking the rest of the sawed cut instead of sawing it all the way through, is to prevent the right and left models A, in subsequent movements, from closing the cut and thus changing their true relative positions. Separating the model A into two pieces is necessary also for the castings to enable an easy removal of the hard obturators after vulcanizing.

THE INVESTMENTS TO FORM THE MOLD FOR THE METAL CASTS A

It is evident that if these plaster models which surround and invest the **obturator-model** are to be duplicated in metal, each part must be regarded as a **molder's pattern,** or model, to be invested or surrounded with other parts composed of some material against which metal can be poured, and so arranged that the parts can be opened, the pattern or model cleanly removed without dragging, and the parts accurately readjusted to form an exact mold or impression into which the metal is poured for the casts. It is evident also, that there is no further need of the **obturator-model,** since we have the impression of all its surfaces in the form of a mold, still it is well to preserve it intact in case some unforeseen accident occurs.

It is advisable to make the metal casts of the **model A** first, because it is usually the most difficult to obtain, with the absolute accuracy required of the nasal and palatal surfaces. It is also necessary to make the subsequent investments and metal duplicates of this model in two pieces, as explained.

INVESTMENT MODELS

Fig. 34 is a nasal view of the **model A,** and the **palatal model C** in position in the lingual part of the flask with the **obturator-model removed,** preparatory to pouring the **investment nasal model D** (Fig. 32), which is to form part of the **mold** for casting the right and left duplicates of the **model A.** It will be noticed that the space which was filled by the lingual portion of the **obturator-model** is now filled with *dough* up to the line which represents the nearest approaching borders of the cleft (Fig. 34), for the purpose of stopping the plaster at that point. The lingual cover of the flask is now placed and fastened with the pins to prevent the models from moving. The exposed surfaces of the models are covered with two coats of Brophy's, or any good separating fluid, carefully oiled and drained, and then the flask is filled with any good investment.

In describing the method of obtaining metal casts for the Kingsley Velum (Cosmos, June, 1885), the author employed sand for the molds; but for many years some of the market mixtures of investments have been far preferable. Choose an **investing-compound** that will pour easily, leave a smooth surface, become very hard, and that will sustain considerable heat without shrinking or cracking, and will not break in separating it from the casting. This is important in the effort to produce exact duplication and to avoid the possible necessity of making a whole new set of investment models in case a metal cast is imperfect.

Fig. 32 illustrates a transverse section, showing the **investment D** in place after being poured. When this is hard, all the models are removed from the flask and the surfaces prepared for the next investment model. With the **plaster palatal model C,** and the dough removed, and the plaster model A, and investment model D in position, the **investment model E** is poured. Fig. 33.

It will be seen that the space which was occupied by the **obturator-model** is now entirely **closed,** and that any one of the component parts can be readily duplicated by removing it and filling the space which it occupied. As it is necessary to duplicate in metal the casts of the **model A** in two parts, one-half of this model is removed (Fig. 35, Chapter VI), and the space is then filled with investing-compound forming one-half of **investment model A.** Before and during the pouring of this model with investment or metal, the parts in the flask should be exactly fitted and held firmly together, as any variation in this will detract from the fit of the obturator. After pouring this **investment model A,** remove the entire model A and smooth the surface of the investment where it joins the sawed surface of its fellow. It will then be seen if the parts were exactly together, and if not, another should be poured.

Fig. 36 shows the space after the removal of the other half of the **plaster-model A.** The case is now composed entirely of investment-compound, and ready for pouring the first **metal cast A.** Before drying the investment-models for this purpose, it is always advisable at this stage to make new exact duplicates of the original **plaster model A,** in case the original is broken. This is easily done by pouring new plaster halves of the model A in the spaces which they occupied, commencing as arranged for the metal cast in Figs. 35 and 36.

CHAPTER VI

TECHNICS OF THE METAL CASTS AND OBTURATOR

The **metal casts** of the right and left **plaster models A** are obtained as follows: With the **investments** in place in the flask, as shown in Fig. 36, and the nasal cover secured in position with the pins, thoroughly dry the case until not a particle of moisture appears on a cool dry piece of glass. Haskell's Babbitt metal has been found to produce the most satisfactory castings. This is especially mentioned, as there is such a vast difference in the general commercial product of this metal.

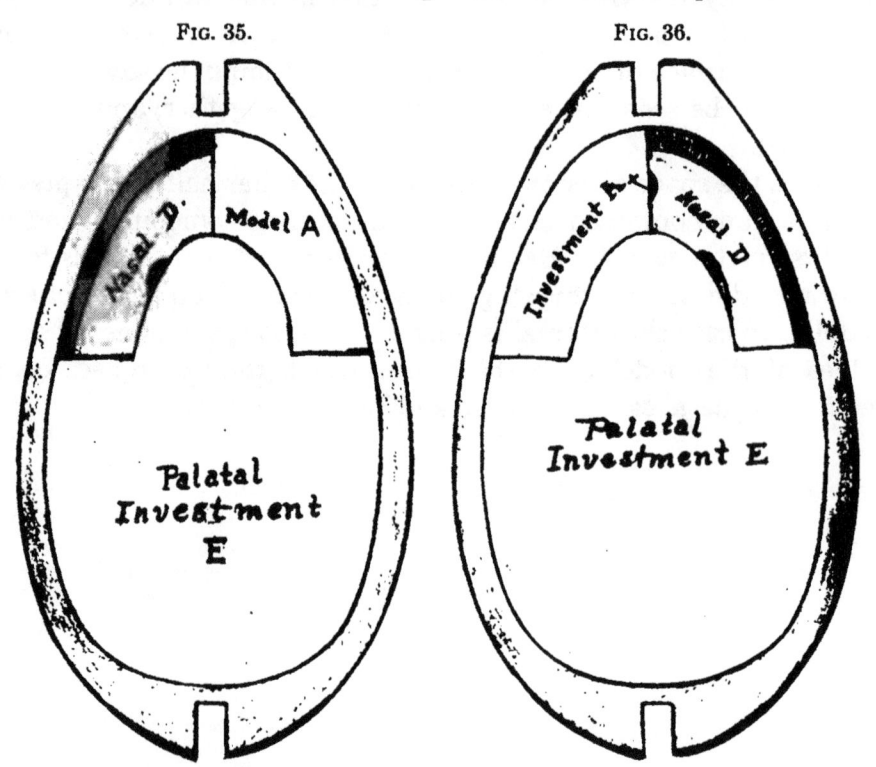

FIG. 35.   FIG. 36.

It possesses a favorable degree of fusibility and should make a sharp casting without shrinkage. During the pouring, hold the case in one hand with a padded holder, with the thumb pressing firmly the palatal investment E, and jog the case by striking the back of the hand upon the bench. This will cause the metal to flow sharply and the air bubbles to rise to the top in case of air pockets. Before the metal has congealed, the excess should be quickly scraped off even with the top of the flask. One should never get discouraged if he has to pour several casts before one is secured that is perfect, though this may rarely happen.

CHAPTER VI. TECHNICS OF THE METAL CASTS AND OBTURATOR

After pouring, as soon as the casting has cooled sufficiently, remove the investments and **metal cast A,** from the lingual half of the flask by gently tapping the flask on the side so that they will all fall out together. Then carefully part them from the metal cast A, with the view to prevent fracturing the now more or less fragile **palatal investment,** and thus avoid the necessity of making new ones with the lengthy drying process for the casting of the other half of the model A, or for the recasting of the first one in case it is found imperfect.

Each metal casting as it is obtained is henceforth used as a part of the combination in the flask for subsequent castings; the exposed surfaces to be poured against being covered with a thin coating of plumbago. If the first pouring of the **metal cast A** is found to be perfect, it can be immediately replaced in the flask with the **Investment E** (if not broken) and without further drying (if it is still hot) the second half of the **cast A** can be poured.

When the two pieces which form the metal duplicates of the **model A** are secured, the next castings to be obtained are the duplicates of the original **nasal** and **palatal models B** and **C,** which surround the model of the obturator. Fig. 31.

The Metal Casts of the Original Plaster Models B and C

It makes no difference which of the two remaining models of the original set is cast first, though it is usually easier to duplicate the **nasal cast B** last. In this description, however, the nasal cast B is made first, i. e.: Place the right and left metal castings A in the flask with the original **plaster nasal model B,** Fig. 37.

Fig. 37.

Before doing this secure a perfect coaptation of the contact surfaces of the metal casts and plaster model, especially along the border "y" which may be understood as representing the entire border of the nasal portion. The interferences to the perfect coaptation of the plaster and metal pieces are commonly due to imperfections of the metal castings at their outer borders next to the flask where they have followed slight fractures of the investment model. The fitting is usually done outside of the flask, either by cutting away the metal or the plaster at interfering points. Finally, see that the surface of the **plaster model B** is well coated with lubricants, and the nasal cover of the flask secured in place to prevent the slightest displacements. Then pour **investment G** jogging it so that it will flow and completely fill to their very outer borders the deep interspaces, which represent the nasal extensions of the obturator. It helps to shorten the time of the drying out, in casting duplicates of models B and C, by using no more investment material than is necessary to represent the desired impression surfaces of the model to be duplicated.

When the investment is hard, the nasal cover of the flask is removed, and the **plaster nasal model B** *alone* is carefully removed from the flask by lightly tapping the flask as before described. If the adjustments have been perfect, little or no investment will have flowed out upon the castings beyond the designated borders of the obturator. If this has occurred, however, to a slight extent, remove it and define the borders. Again, if the investment has not wholly filled the space, or air-holes have arisen, they should be filled. When it is remembered that in this impressional surface is represented the entire upper nasal surface of the obturator, with one-half the border of the veil, it will be seen that it should be regarded as a model of that part of the obturator and finished to represent the proper thickness and extensions of the nasal wings, and evenly defined borders throughout. Slight changes which seem advisable toward *reducing* the size or thickness of the original obturator-model, may be made at this time without harm, in as much as it is possible to make corrections by *enlarging* the final castings. The surfaces of the investment at the posterior edges of the castings at "u," Fig. 34, should be made to join evenly, and the excess of plaster removed from the sides of the flask above its dividing beveled line "v."

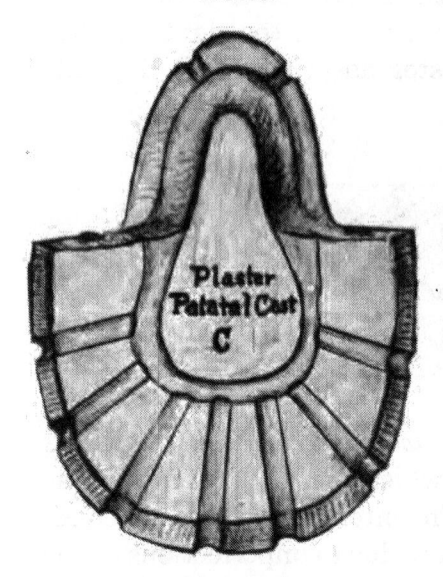

FIG. 38.

When properly prepared, the metal surfaces are coated with plumbago; the case is then thoroughly dried, and the **metal cast of B** is poured in the same manner as described for the castings of **A.** Great care should be exercised to prevent melting the metal casts which are in the flask while drying the investments for pouring subsequent castings. The danger point of heat may be determined by placing a small fragment of the metal on the heater beside the flask. This, when it starts to melt will be a warning to reduce the heat.

When the **metal cast B** is secured, the original **plaster model C** (Figs. 31 and 38), next to be duplicated, is fitted to the metal casts in the same manner as described for **B.** As it is necessary to press this **plaster model C** firmly to place—after sufficient investment material has been placed in position to fill the interspaces occupied by the obturator-model—numerous gates should be cut extending to the top edge of the cast for the free overflow of investment. See Fig. 38. In the fitting of the **plaster model C,** the seating "g," Figs. 29 and 37, of the **metal cast A,** should be corrected and polished, though not to change the sharply outlined edge of the obturator, where there should be perfect coaptation of the casts. After thoroughly

CHAPTER VI. TECHNICS OF THE METAL CASTS AND OBTURATOR

preparing the surfaces of the **model C** for separating, as described with **B,** and with the **metal casts A** and **B** in the flask secured with the nasal cover, place only the required amount of investment in the mold to fully fill the interspaces; then press the **plaster model C** firmly to place, holding it in position until the investment is partially hard. It will be seen that if this cast does not go fully to place, the only harm it does is to thicken the palatal and veil portion of the obturator beyond that which was designed to be the proper dimensions when the **obturator-model** was prepared. If this thickened condition is more than a slight scraping of the plaster surfaces will correct, all the casts should be removed from the flask, and cleaned and freed from every possible obstruction that may have prevented them from being forced fully to place. It may be that the plaster model C has slightly expanded, indicating that the surfaces which join the flask should be scraped. More than likely the investment-compound was mixed too thick, etc.

In the removal of the **plaster model C,** great care should be used so as to not dislodge or cause the slightest movement of the **metal casts A,** lest the thin investment extensions which represent the palatal wings are thrown from their seating on the casts. This may be accomplished by holding the casts firmly in place with the fingers while the model is tapped lightly, without turning the flask over. It then may be carefully lifted with a screw-driver thrust into the posterior hole or if one dislikes to disturb the stopping of this hole, which would necessitate filling it again, the **model C** can be lifted from its seating by prying it up from the back with a sharp pointed knife. One can see by this the need of perfect lubrication of **model C,** before pressing it to place. After the removal of **model C,** all excess investment which covers the **metal casts A** and **B,** beyond the defined borders of the obturator, should be removed. It will be seen that the investment-impression at this stage is a duplicate—or should be—of the entire lingual surfaces of the **obturator-model.** Before pouring the **metal cast C,** all the metal surfaces of the mold should be covered with plumbago, the lingual cover of the flask is fastened in place, and the case is thoroughly dried, etc., as before described.

Note: As before stated, if it is found after pouring each of the metal casts A, B, or C, that they are imperfect, due mostly to not sufficiently drying the investments, and if it is found also, that the investments are not broken, as should obtain with good material, another cast should be poured at once, as the heat of the first casting may have completed the drying of the investment. In fact, several pourings are often made with the same investment.

PREPARATORY TO PACKING AND FINISHING THE OBTURATOR

The casts are now finished and polished on all the obturator surfaces, except those which represents the nasal and lingual surfaces of the castings A, which are simply brushed and burnished. The entire inside surfaces of the casts are then covered with a coating of common bar washing soap to prevent the rubber from clinging to the casts upon removal. Heavy tin-foil may also be used for this purpose, which is especially desirable when the velum-obturator is to be made of flexible rubber, because of the impossibility of further finishing the soft rubber after vulcanizing.

The case is warmed and packed similar to that of dental rubber plates. Remember that the fusibility of Babbitt's metal is much lower than lead and that an excess of heat through forgetfulness, etc., may spoil all the work. In packing, do not use an excess of rubber. The amount may be roughly estimated by the weight or by the water displacement of the **obturator-model.** Force the casts to place in a press after packing, and continue by placing the whole in boiling water until the lingual and nasal covers of the flask can be fully fastened with the pins. After vulcanizing, warm in hot water and insert a screw-driver into one of the holes in the sides of the flask, and carefully pry the casts apart, etc. The finishing is similar to that of rubber dental plates.

Notwithstanding the very great difference in the sizes of congenital clefts of the palate, the principles involved in the technic are the same, with slight variations to meet differences in form. Moreover, the forms of obturators are all quite similar in their general characteristics as shown in Fig. 39, from open double-clefts to the one on the right of the lower row for a cleft extending into the hard palate about three-eighths of an inch only.

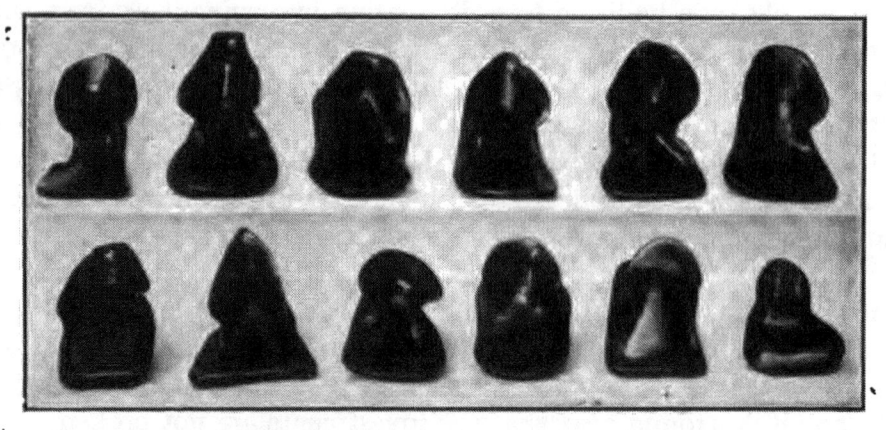

FIG. 39.

There is no reason in the world why the general practitioner of dentistry should not consider the whole operation of the prosthetic correction of cleft palate as a part of his profession, because it is so similar in its mechanical requirements to that in which he is necessarily skilled. It certainly would result in bringing incalculable relief and happiness to the lives of thousands of sufferers, because it would restore to them the fair opportunities of humanity for intellectual, social, and commercial advancement. It, moreover, would prevent many harmful surgical operations.

CHAPTER VII

COMPLICATIONS WITH IRREGULARITIES AND SURGICAL FAILURES

With all extensive congenital clefts, especially among those which extend entirely through the maxillary bone at one side of the incisive process or both, and also through the lip, there commonly arise, through a lack of normal development, abnormalities of the upper jaw and denture. These conditions are frequently of such a serious character that they demand correction preliminary to the insertion of the obturator if one hopes to obtain a condition that will enable the patient to acquire perfect articulation, to say nothing of the desirability and advantage of correcting decided facial deformities.

Malpositions and lack of development of upper front teeth, loss of the entire intermaxillary process and incisor teeth in double clefts, lack of development of bone with decided malpositions and impactions of anterior teeth in complete single clefts, with consequent retractions and retrusions of the teeth and anterior supporting processes, have quite as much influence in preventing the distinct enunciation of certain oral elements of speech as has the cleft of the palate itself. Imperfect surgical operations on the upper lip leaving the patient with V-shaped fissures and an excess of cicatricial tissue, will frequently mar the correct articulation of labials and labial explosives which demand distinct utterance. One occasionally meets with the surgical results of an operation on a double-fissured lip, with and without the intervening incisor teeth and process, which in the contracted, retruded, and tightly drawn cicatricial condition of the upper lip destroys its natural contour and functional activities. Skillful plastic surgery will accomplish wonders in the restoration of these cases.

Labial explosives as in **bŭ, boy,** etc., demand for a perfect acquirement of distinct enunciation a perfect closure of the lips, which is impossible if there is the slightest opening through which the compressed breath can escape. **Labio** and **linguo-dentals,** as in **vŭ, vain, fŭ, fall,** and **thŭ, those,** etc., require an even line of occlusal edges of the upper front teeth. The anterior **linguo-palatals,** both **explosives** and **aspirates,** in words containing the oral elements, **tŭ, dŭ, chŭ, s, z,** and **sh,** cannot be perfectly uttered without an occluding surface for the tongue, which resembles in its form the anterior linguo-palatal ridge.

In extensive cases it is rare to find the full complement of teeth, impacted or otherwise, the germs being extinct or having been destroyed. In two instances in the author's practice, the intermaxillary or incisive process and the incisors were missing, which was doubtless caused by the surgeon who operated on the lip in early infancy not understanding that the nodular fleshy process, hanging at the tip end of the nose at birth with infants having double clefts and hare-lips, contains the germs of an important part of dental and facial anatomy. Believing it to be a useless abnormal appendage, these "would be surgeons" heedlessly snip it off, oblivious of the fact that they are depriving the patient's future of the main portion of the upper lip, all the upper incisor teeth and the entire intermaxillary process with its nasal spine and cartilaginous septum supporting the upper lip and the end of the nose.

Even with extensive single complete clefts through the maxillæ, some of the front teeth are commonly missing, others are frequently deformed, decidedly malposed, or deeply impacted, so that orthodontic and prosthodontic operations are demanded, if one aspires to accomplish a perfect correction. If in these cases it seems necessary to sustain the obturator with a plate denture—which is now rare in this stage of our advancement—a gold plate denture may be constructed with a pink rubber attachment to restore the facial contour and fill the anterior portion of the cleft. But a removable bridge denture with porcelain restorations is preferable by far. It is nearly always advisable in these cases to first correct the positions of the remaining teeth, and widen the arches. In wide-open clefts at birth, the space in front will usually be found closed at ten years of age, however much the jaw may be deprived of front teeth and intermaxillary processes. This extensive settling together of the two lateral sections of the maxilla is partly due to the contracting force of the surgically closed upper lip, which also causes the decided upper retrusion so often found in these cases.

Besides correcting the alignment of the remaining teeth, the restoration of impacted teeth and the extraction of deformed teeth, the cleft maxillæ should be widened to restore the parts to their normal positions in order to place the buccal teeth in masticating occlusion with the lowers and to round out the arch for the proper placing of the artificial denture and restoration auxiliaries. The extensive lateral expansion of the arch will of course widen the cleft, but that is a matter of no moment so far as the fitting and action of the obturator is concerned, while the cleft forward of it can be quite as easily and properly closed.

The strong tendency of the widened arch and cleft to go back to its former position demands a firmly attached fixed retaining bridge. If a removable bridge is employed, it must be of that construction which will effectually prevent this possibility. There is such a variety of conditions that will arise no rules can be laid down, as much will depend upon the ingenuity and skill of the operator.

Fig. 40 made from the dental casts of a girl 15 years of age, illustrates a case on the left in which a wide anterior cleft bereft of the entire intermaxillary portion had become closed in front, so that the right cuspid nearly touched the second premolar on the opposite side—the loss of the intervening teeth and tissues doubtless occurred from the cause referred to. In observing the decidedly abnormal retruded position of the remaining front teeth in relation to the lower denture, one can imagine something of the facial deformity which this produced, as shown on the left

CHAPTER VII. IRREGULARITIES AND SURGICAL FAILURES 473

of Fig. 41. On the right of Fig. 40 will be seen the expanded arch and corrected position of the teeth, resulting in a good masticating occlusion of the buccal teeth,

FIG. 40.

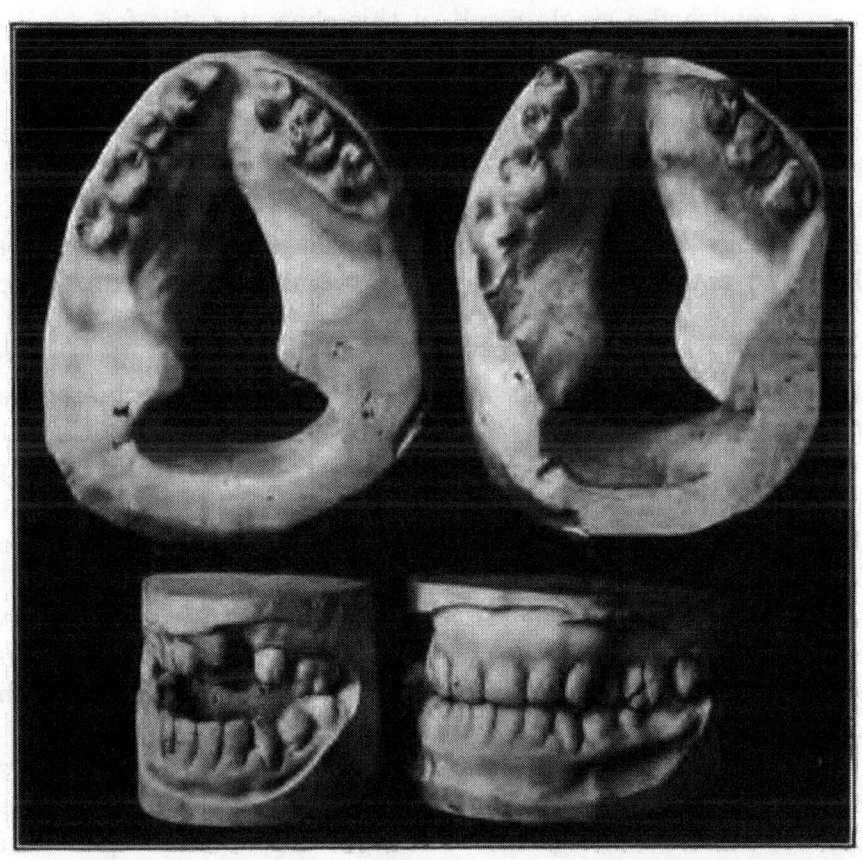

FIG. 41.

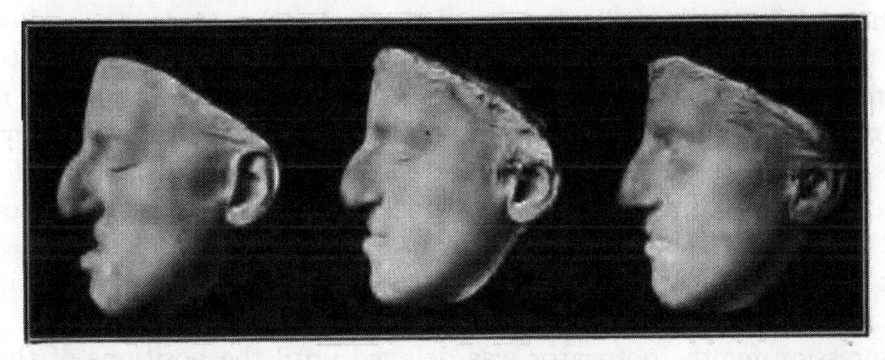

The above dental and facial casts show (1) the results following the deprivation of intermaxillary process and front teeth, with the abridged and cicatricially contracted upper lip, (2) the expanded arch and widened cleft in preparation for the restoration denture and obturator, and (3) the final completed conditions.

preparatory to the construction of the removable bridge restoring denture. The central facial cast below was made after the dental restoration, and the one on the right, after the plastic operation by Dr. L. L. McArthur of Chicago.

With the restoration of the facial outlines and functions of mastication, and with a velum-obturator which enables her to speak with perfect articulation and tone, this now quite attractive looking young woman is a useful and happy member of society, endowed with all the possibilities which make life worth the living. To one who has accomplished a single result of this character, the fee, be it little or much, is nothing compared to the great satisfaction of knowing that he has been instrumental in restoring to physical, social, and intellectual manhood or womanhood a deformed human being whose life otherwise would have been a constant embarrassment, a humiliation, and a burden.

One patient wearing a velum-obturator delivered the valedictory of his class, another the salutatory, and a third—a girl—the class poem. Two others are now practicing law, and another is a member of a prominent glee club. One young man gave quite a remarkable exhibition in an extemporaneous speech at the meeting of the International Dental Congress in 1904 at St. Louis, and spoke so perfectly that Dr. Platschick, a prominent Paris dentist, made the following remark in the discussion: "While Dr. Case speaks well, his patient speaks more distinctly. At least it is easier for me to understand him." Many other patients might be mentioned who are now filling prominent positions in social and business life which would have been otherwise impossible without the aid of these obturators.

The author does not wish to infer that success has always been the invariable result, except with those who commenced wearing the velum-obturators under twenty-five years of age; though a number learned to speak perfectly with its aid at thirty-five years of age, and one after forty years of age.

Fig. 42, at the top, illustrates the dental casts of a boy at fourteen years of age. His upper central incisors besides being decidedly retruded and malturned, were almost wholly buried under the gums. The right cuspid was impacted, and the left cuspid just pricking through the gum was in decided mesial inclination. The width of the arch in the buccal area placed the molars in extreme buccal occlusal relation to the lowers. In fact, there were only two points where his teeth touched in occlusion. The cleft was unusually large and wide, partly due to loss of natural tissue in frantic and futile surgical operations to close it during infancy. His speech was so imperfect, because of his extensive palatal and dental deformity, that it greatly hindered him at school and whenever he attempted to talk to strangers. And yet, he was a boy of more than usual intelligence and brightness, just arriving at the age when he was beginning to feel intensely the humiliating and depressing forces of his misfortune.

The impression for the obturator was delayed until the positions of the teeth were partially corrected as shown by the models in the lower half of Fig. 42, which also shows his obturator in position. It was necessary to take the impression in three sections in this case, as described and illustrated in Chapter III. This impression shown in Fig. 13 was photographed before filling for the working-model.

The first, or test obturator was of flexible rubber, but before the close of the day this was substituted for a hard polished rubber obturator, which remained in his mouth during that first night, and every night since, without a retaining plate. This patient was presented at the November, 1914, meeting of the Odontological Society of Chicago about two weeks after the first insertion of his obturator, and even at that early stage he could perfectly articulate nearly all the oral elements of speech when pronounced for him separately, and most of the single syllable words which are difficult for cleft palate patients to utter.

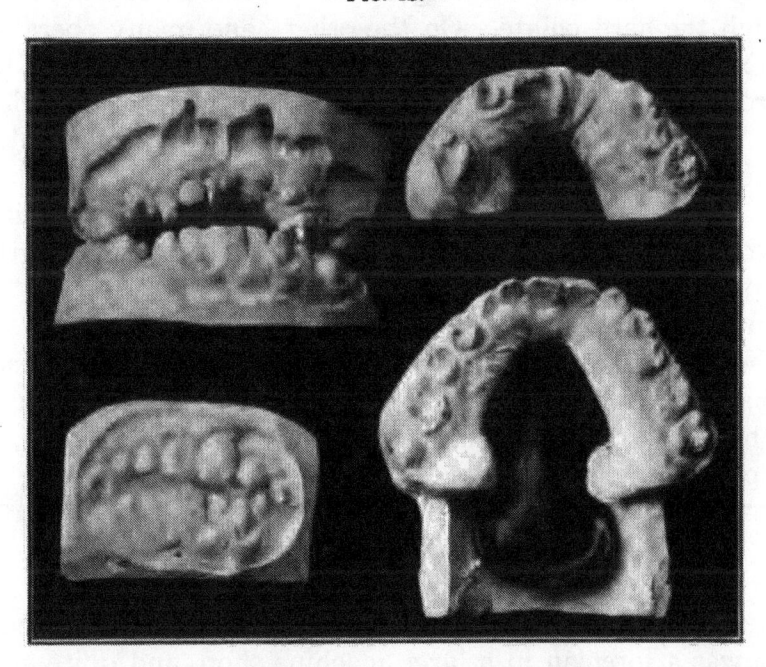

FIG. 42.

The above shows (1) a not uncommon lack of development and malocclusion. (2) Below, the partial correction of the upper front teeth, preparatory to the construction of an obturator which is seen in place

His mother wrote the author about a year afterwards: "He is now taking his place in his school classes with the greatest satisfaction to his teachers and friends, speaking nearly all his words with quite distinct articulation, except when he forgets himself and speaks rapidly. We feel it will not be many months before he completely corrects these former habits of speech." With this change and its possibilities in his speech and voice, there will come into his countenance the happy animated expression of boyhood which will take the place of the former dull look of despair.

One of the most difficult and at times discouraging conditions which confronts the specialist in the mechanical treatment of cleft palate, is the appeal for help from those whose clefts have been partially or completely closed by imperfect or inadequate surgical operations, which leave them without the possibility of ever perfecting their speech unless something else can be accomplished.

It is a mistaken idea among surgeons that an equally successful artificial palate can always be constructed after surgical operations prove to be failures. For even in those cases where they have not succeeded in uniting any portion of the cleft, much will depend upon the amount of scar tissue that is left, which will proportionately inhibit the free functional mobility of the palatal muscles upon which the obturator almost wholly depends for its perfect action.

A common form of surgical failure that frequently comes before the author, and one which is more unfortunate than no surgical union, is where the patient is left with a partial closure of the cleft—generally through the velum—the history of which usually indicates that the surgeon was unable by repeated trials to close the cleft through the hard palate. On the other hand, many operations are performed upon extensive clefts with the view of closing *only* the soft palatal cleft, in the very wrongful belief that when the remainder of the cleft is closed with an artificial plate, which any dentist can construct, the patient will speak intelligibly. At any rate the assurance is given that all has been accomplished that is possible for the patient. The statement will apply here that was mentioned in reference to all surgically corrected palates that are decidedly inadequate in length for closing the oro-nasal passage.

The most unfortunate feature in regard to all cases in which the original cleft extends into the hard palate, and which is united surgically only at the soft palate is: the fact that few patients are willing to have these partially united palates disunited for the insertion of an obturator, even though there may be, through this means, a fair promise of all the possibilities of perfect speech. One patient over twenty-five years of age with a large cleft, and with only a small part of the cleft through the soft palate surgically united, after hesitating for more than a year before permitting its disunion for the obturator, finally consented to the operation; and then because of a favorable decree of an Oracle which he said he had consulted. This man who was a foreman in a large machine shop, and quite well educated, learned to speak so perfectly with an artificial palate that he had evening classes for teaching the foreigners of the shop to speak English correctly.

Fig. 43 shows the models and obturator of a boy twelve years of age whose soft palate when presented was surgically united, and though the opening through the hard palate was closed with a plate, his speech was quite as imperfect as any patient with an open cleft. The correction of this case would not have been so successful with the obturator alone or without the preliminary correction of his teeth, the expansion of the arch, and the insertion of the bridge denture which also corrected a decided facial deformity.

A finale far more to be regretted is where the patient is left with a complete surgically closed cleft, but with the velum-palati so inadequate in its length and possibilities of functional action that it leaves a wide opening at the oro-nasal passage, and consequently the speech rarely if ever is improved. Many of the surgical operations on cleft palate, though complete crass failures in the restoration of speech, when considered from a surgical standpoint, are worthy of being classed among operations of the very highest order, demanding a degree of consummate skill and ingenuity in not only closing extensive clefts, but in lengthening the soft palatal tissues in a manner that is truly wonderful. In the more skillful and extensive operations of this character, when performed during infancy, vocal articulation is frequently quite perfect, though almost invariably lacking in normal tone and resonance; the speech being characterized by the peculiar nasal or "cleft palate quality." It is a deplorable fact, however, that the larger number of surgical operations of today are of a lower order, and that there are so many cleft

FIG. 43.

The above illustration shows (1) a partial surgical union; (2) Expansion of the arch; (3) Restoration denture, and (4) The obturator in position.

palate operations attempted at all ages and upon all sizes of clefts, often with no apparent effort or expectation of doing more than to barely unite the borders of the cleft. These supposedly successful cases especially, and in fact all cases where the clefts have been completely united with results which debar the patient from acquiring perfect speech, are particularly to be deplored, because it is rare that persons so afflicted or their friends will consent to the destruction of an operation which has been attained through such incalculable hardships. Nor can they be assured, under the circumstances, that the usual perfect result of prosthetic treatment will be attained.

Fig. 44 was made from the models of a man over twenty-five years of age. It will serve to illustrate the not uncommon appearance of a surgical closure of a cleft. The distance from the posterior border of the velum-palati to the nearest extended position of the posterior pharyngeal wall was fully three-fourths of an inch, and consequently his speech had all the imperfect characteristics of open cleft palates. The surgically closed cleft was opened for the insertion of a flexible velum; and while the result was far from perfect, his speech and voice-tone were considerably improved. This was before the days of the velum-obturator which doubtless would have been far more successful.

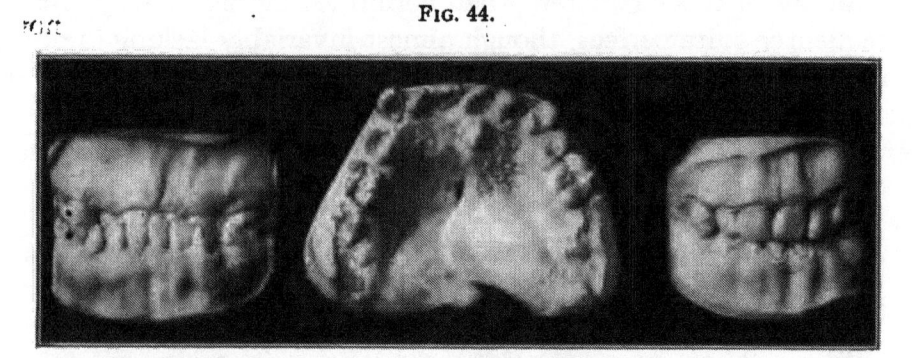

FIG. 44.

The above dental casts show (1) the original occlusion of the front teeth; (2) the common result of an imperfect surgical operation. and (3) after the correction of the teeth preliminary to opening the cleft for the insertion of an obturator.

The case is presented here principally to show the common malocclusion of the teeth in connection with extensive clefts and what may be accomplished in their correction at quite an advanced age.

While it is true that a very large porportion of cleft palate patients who have received unsatisfactory surgical treatment are unwilling to try what they believe to be "another experiment," especially those who have obtained a complete and even partial closure of the cleft, it happens to be true also that nearly one-half of the many patients for whom the author has inserted artificial palates, have at some time during earlier life—mostly during infancy—received surgical treatment for the correction of their cleft palates.

Let us hope that the proportion of surgical failures will be greatly lessened in the future by the general resolve that must come to all well informed honest surgeons, to confine their future operations to infants, and even then to accept only the most favorable cases, with the determination to follow them up with proper instruction for the acquirement of speech. Among the poorer classes, where this deformity seems to most frequently arise, the most favorable physically disposed tissues and perfect surgical closure of the clefts of infants are not very likley to be followed at the proper stage of development by the parents or the surgeon with the necessary persistent endeavor toward the kind of training that will teach the child to commence and continue the articulation of the oral elements in proportion to the development of his speech. The general history of these cases is that the child grows up speaking about the same as he would have done without an operation. The only advantage, therefore, in operations for the closure of congenital clefts under these circumstances resolves itself into a temporary display of surgical skill for a few, or to show one of the great accomplishments in oral surgery before an

CHAPTER VII. IRREGULARITIES AND SURGICAL FAILURES

admiring class. This is particularly true if the patient is older than five years, and the inexcusability of the operation increases in proportion to the time after that age.

While it no doubt is true that the surgical treatment of cleft palate for children born of wealthy parents could meet with the highest degree of success, because of the care and teaching that could be given, still, up to the present time, because parents and even surgeons are not informed in regard to the value and necessity of early speech training, the results in these cases are quite as likely to be as unsatisfactory as others.

This failure to speak perfectly is seen on every hand among cleft palate children and adults in all social degrees of life, who have been operated upon during infancy. Even among the wealthy and most refined people, where no expense has been spared in the procurement of the most prominent surgeons who have been given a free hand to choose the time and character of the operation, many of these children go through life greatly handicapped with embarrassingly imperfect speech.

It is hoped that the time is not far distant when there will be an appreciation of the value of the velum-obturator, and what may be accomplished in proper speech training.

INDEX

ABNORMALLY enlarged mandible, 317, 319, 322
    Abnormal Interproximate Spaces, 354
Advanced Principles of Technics, 155
Alignment, definition of, 10
    arch-bows, 263, 332, 334, 355
Alveolar process and alveoli, 66
Anchorages, technics and principles of, 118
    reciprocating or movable, 125, see "Intermaxillary"
    rootwise, 122, 242, 252, 298, 314, 361
    stability of, 120, 124
    stationary, 121, 286
    sustained, 123, 124, 315
Anæsthetics, local, 354
Angle's bodily movement, 114
    direct intermaxillary force, 368
    teaching, 80, 379
    wire ligatures, 342
Anterior, definition of, 12
Apparatus, important requisites of, 95
    alignment, 168, 331, 334
    assembling and fitting, 172, 211, 273, see Part VII
    bodily movement, 170, 173, 252, 271, 276, 298
    contracting and expanding, see "Expansion"
    extruding and intruding, 283, 284
    midget, 159, 166, 168
    rotating, 340, 341, 342, 343
Application of force, see "Force" 95, 109
Arch-bows, definition of, 11
    alignment, 211, 263, 332, 334, 355
    arch push bow, see protruding and expanding
    contraction, 263, 267, 355
    expansion, 116, 337, 346, 347, 348
    labio-buccal, 267
    lingual, 349, 351
    lingual yoke, 211
    lug, 206, 207, 208
    protruding and expanding, 206, 207, 209, 271
    protruding contour power, 170, 172, 271, 298
    midget, 168, 169, 170, 172
    resilient, 161, 166, 168, 169, 283, 331, 332, 334
    retruding, 263, 267, 355
    spring, 116, 349, 350
    torsional, 116
Arch, dental, definition of, 11
    club or saddle shaped, 350
    contracted and expanded, 335, 346, 350, 351
    expansion of lower, 334, 352, 353
    narrow, 116, 347, 349

Arch, normal, 61
    unilateral contraction of, 351
    V-shaped, 351
Arrangement of teeth, 61
Art, 5

BANDS, fitting of, 155, 385, 387, 388
    band material, 148, 150
    construction of, 147, 171, see "Incisor bands"
    finishing and plating, 162
    measurements of partially erupted cuspids, 151
    midget, 159
    soldering of, 151
    plugger, 157
Bars,
    lug pull, 242, 314, 355, 361
    lug push, 206, 207, 208, 252, 335
    pull or traction, 263, 264, 341, 394
    push, 208, 212, 314, 336, 341
    resilient, 107
    ribbon, 341
Basic Principles of Practice, 61
Batteries, 163
Bicuspid, see "Premolar"
Bilateral, definition of, 14
    maleruption of cuspids, 200, 209, 215
Bimaxillary supra and infra-occlusion, definition of, 10
Bimaxillary Protrusion and Retrusion, 232, 233, 241
Biology, laws of, 37
    heredity, 38
    natural selection, 40
    natural variation, 39
    environment, 40
Black, 14, 61
Blowpipe, 152, 159
Bodily expansion, 116, 347, 349, see "Expansion"
Bodily movement, principles of, 109
    buccal, 347, 349
    disto-mesial or lateral, 242, 252, 314, 361
    labial or protruding, 170, 173, 252, 271, 298, 303
    lingual or retruding, 276
Bodily protrusion of upper denture, 266
Bodily retrusion of upper denture, 295
Bodily working retainer, 175, 176, 399
Bows, see "Arch-bows"
Bracket and hook, 162
Buccal, definition of, 13, see "Bodily movements"
Broomell, 69

CANINE and cuspid, definition of, 14
    Casts, dental and facial, 139, 141, 142, 146
Causes, see "Etiology"
Chin retractors or caps, see "Occipital Force" 133, 135
Chin, importance of in diagnosis, 54, 76, 183, 192, 234
    retruded, 279
Class I Normal disto-mesial occlusion of the buccal teeth, 199
Class II Distal malocclusion of lower buccal teeth, 245
Class III Mesial malocclusion of lower buccal teeth, 290
Classes, dento-facial malocclusions, 180
Classes, table of, 19
Cleft palate, prosthetic correction of, 409
    impressions, 437, 439, 441, 444
    trial-model, 450
    working-model, 448
    flask, 457
    plaster models, 459
    investment models, 461, 464
    metal casts, 467
    packing, vulcanizing, and finishing obturator, 469
    complications with irregularities and surgical failures, 471, see "Speech"
Close-bite malocclusion, definition of, 10
Close-bite malocclusion, 283, 287
Closing of abnormal spaces, 242, 354, 356, 357, 358, see "Bodily disto-mesial movements"
    molar spaces, 359, 361
Concomitant characters of Class II, 279
Construction of Bands, see "Bands"
    midget appliances, 159
Contour apparatus, see "Bodily Movement Apparatus"
Contrude, definition of, 13
Coronal zones, 156, 186
Coronal protrusions, upper, 262, 270
Crowded malalignments, 333, 357
Crowns for opening bite, 284, 285
Counter-sunk nuts, 175
Cryer, 68, 81, 261, 318, 362, 365
Cushing, 305
Cuspid bands for retaining appliances, 387
Cuspids, bodily movement of, 242, 314
    bilateral maleruption of, 209, 215
    impaction of, 364, 367, 369, 371
    maleruption of, 200, 205, 208
    rotation of, 341, 342
    unilateral maleruption of, 205

DARWIN, 40, 51
    Deciduous teeth,
    importance of preserving, 30
    premature loss of, 30
Dental Orthopedia, definition of, 3
Dento-facial malocclusions, Part VI
    dento-facial area, definition of, 9, 183, 185, 186
    observation training, 192
    practical diagnosis, 193
    principles of diagnosis, 181, 190
    zones of movement, 186

Diagnosis, principles according to Classes, 195
Direct and disto-mesial intermaxillary force, see "Intermaxillary Force"
Distal and mesial, definition of, 11
Dome, definition of, 11

ELASTIC bands, see "Occipital and Intermaxilliary Force"
Elliptical tubing, 212, 336, 352, 399
Environment, 40
Etiology, 23
    biological laws, influences of, 37
    causes in relation to treatment, 26
    comparison of childhood and adult physiognomies, 35
    compound causes, 24
    influences of deciduous dentures, 30, 33
    influences of heredity, see "Heredity"
    maleruption of labial teeth, 32
    thumbsucking, 33
    unknowable causes, 23
Expansion and contraction of dental arches, see "Arches"
Expansion and contraction
    bodily, 116, 347, 349
    disto-mesial, 207
    jacks, 350, 351
    lateral, 346, 353
    lingual arch, 351
    of premolar area, 347, 349, 352
    spring, 347, 349
    torsional, 116, see "Force"
Extraction,
    considered by Dr. Cryer, 73
    importance of, 79, 380
    in bimaxillary protrusion, 88, 89, 236, 239, 240
    injudicious, of permanent teeth, 83, 84, 294
    in maleruption of cuspids, 84, 85, 90
    in mesial malocclusion of upper, 127, 128
    in protrusion of upper with lower normal, 188, 269
    in protrusion of upper with retrusion of lower, 197, 260
    in protrusion of upper apical zone, 274
    judicious, of permanent teeth, 83, 87
    of deciduous teeth, 30
    rules of, 83
Extruding and intruding apparatus, 283, 284
Extrusive and intrusive, definition of, 13
    apparatus, 283, 284
    force, 108

FACIAL impressions and casts, 141, 142, 146
    Facial outlines in diagnosis, 190
Farrar, 80, 95, 306, 358
Finger spurs, 160, 161
Fitting and assembling apparatus, 172, see "Primary Principles" in Parts IV and V.
Flask, cleft palate, 457
Force, principles of, 95, 109

Force, elastic, 126, 225, 343
    expanding, 347, 351, see "Expansion"
    intermaxillary, see "Intermaxillary Force"
    laws of, 112, 118
    linguo-buccal, 132, 225, 286
    misapplication of, 104
    occipital, 126, 132
    reciprocating, 340, see "Intermaxillary Force"
    rootwise, 347, see "Anchorages"
    screw, 95, 96
    spring, 107
    torsional, 116, 166, 170, 348
Frenum, treatment of abnormal, 354, 355

GENERAL Bimaxillary Supra- and Infra-occlusion, definition of, 10
German silver, see "Nickel Silver"
Gingival, definition of, 13
Gold and platinum bands for appliances, 384, 385, 387
    plating solution, 163
    soldering, 151, 160
    wires and arch-bows, 169, 171, 398, 400
Goslee, 321, 325
Gray, 177, 185, 318
Grinding teeth in the correction of open-bite malocclusion, 231

HABIT of mouth-breathing, 227, 229, 230
    Harmony, dento-facial, 182
Headgear, see "Occipital apparatus," 133
Heredity, 38, 43, 378
    ethnologically considered, 43
    influences of, upon deciduous dentures, 33
    law of, 38
    Mendel's Law, 39, 44
    principles of, 53
Hook and bracket, 162
Huxley, 51
Hygienic requirements, 165
Hypertrophied gums, 76

IMPACTED teeth, 362
    Angle's method of treatment, 368
    general treatment, 366
    lower third molars, 363, 364
    second premolars, 369
    upper central incisors, 371, 372, 373
    upper cuspids, 364, 367, 369, 371
Impressions and casts,
    dental and facial, 139, 141
    of cleft palate, 437
Impression trays, 140
    anchorage, 121
    occlusal, 141
Incisors,
    bands for, 148, 155
    bodily movement of, 103, 109, 111, 170
    inclination movement of, 97

Incisors, inlocked, 337, 338
    impacted, 371, 372, 373
    intrusive and extrusive movement of, 230, 231, 283, 284, 286
    protruding movement of, 111, 170, 252, 257, 298
    retruding movement of, 103, 263, 264, 267, 276
    rotation of, 340, 341
Incisive or intermaxillary bone (Gray), 185
Inclination, of teeth, Black's definition of, 64
    movement, 96, 97
Inferior, definition of, 13
Influences of heredity upon deciduous dentures, 33
Infra-occlusion, definition of, 10
    bimaxillary, 287
    of cuspids, 331, 367, 368
    of incisors, 230, 231, 332
Injudicious extraction, 84, 86, 294
Instruction in speech, 409, 420, see "Speech"
Interdigitate, definition of, 10
Intermaxillary force, principles of, 126
    apparatus, 213, 252, 257, 267, 268, 286, 394
    bucco-lingual, 132, 286
    direct or extrusive, 132, 209, 211, 230, 286, 368
    disto-mesial, 213, 231
    for extensive movements, 257
    lateral, 225
    linguo-buccal, 132, 225, 286
    span hooks, 129, 268
    tube hooks, 129, 257, 267
    tube Ts, 230, 343, 358, 397
Interproximate spaces, 354, 356
    between lower front teeth, 354, 356
    between buccal teeth, 359, 361
Introduction of band material, 148, 150
    impression trays, 140
    waxed tape, 147
Intrusive and extrusive, definition of, 13
    apparatus, 283, 284,
    force, 108
Irregularities, definition of, 8
    caused by injudicious extraction of permanent teeth, 84, 86, 294
    resulting from loss of deciduous teeth, 30

JACKSCREWS,
    arc, 352
    bar rest, 208, 335, 336, 351, 352
    drop, 336, 350
    elliptical spur rest, 334
    expanding, 207, 334, 351, 352, 353
    fork end, 208, 336, 341
    pin rest, 334
Jackscrews, reciprocating, 340, 341
    turnbuckle expansion and contraction, 353
Judicious, or rational extraction, principles of, 87
Jumping the bite, 280

KINGSLEY, 80, 378, 379

LABIAL, definition of, 13
    Labio-mental curve, definition of, 9
Lateral expansion and contraction, 346, 353
Lateral incisors inlocked, 335, 336, 337
Lateral malocclusion, 220
Lateral movement of cuspids, 353
Laws of Biology, 37
Law of Force, 112, 118
Law of Levers, 97
Law of Heredity, 38
Levers, 97
Lever rotator, 107, 339, 340
Ligatures, rubber, 335, 343
    silk, 343, 344
    wire, 337, 342
Lingual, definition of, 13
Lock-nuts, 172, 298, 399
Lug nut attachment, 207, 335
Lower protrusions, 312
    prognathism, 317
    retrusions, 249, 252, 255, 279, 283

MAKUEN, 410
    Malalignment, definition of, 10
Malalignments and crowded complications, 333
Maleruption of cuspids, see "Cuspids"
    of labial teeth, 32
Mallet, lead, 158
Malocclusion, definition of, 10
    bimaxillary short-bite, 287
    close-bite, 283
    dento-facial, 181
    etiology of, 23
    mesial, of lower buccal teeth, 291
    open-bite, 227, 317
    unclassified, 327, see Part VII
Malposed, definition of, 10
Malturned, definition of, 12
Malturned teeth, 339
Mandible, abnormally enlarged, 317, 319, 322
Matteson, 337
Measurements, partially erupted cuspids, 151
    taking of, 148, 156
Mechanics, principles of, 6, 95
Mechanism of speech, 409
Mendel's Law, 39, 44
Mesial and distal, definition of, 11
Mesial malocclusion of lower buccal teeth, 291
Methods of, closing abnormal buccal spaces, 242, 361
    closing labial spaces, 354, 357
    cutting cuspid retainer bands, 387
    drilling holes for staple retainer, 402, 403
    introducing tape, 147
    opening space, 335
    restoring broken interproximate extensions, 391
Midget apparatus, 159, 166, 168
Modeling compound, 140
Molar, anchorage, 120, 124
    bands, 150

Molar, bodily movement of, 361, see "Rootwise Anchorages"
    crowns, 284, 285
    impactions, 363, 364
    measurements, 150
Mouth-breathing habit, 227, 229, 230
Movements, primary, 96
    bodily, 96, 103, 109, 359
    extrusive or intrusive, 96, 108
    inclination, 96
    lateral, 98
    protrusive or retrusive, 111, 127
    rotating, 96, 106
Murphy, Dr. J. B., 412

NARROW and wide arches, 334, 346
    Naso-labial folds, definition of, 9
Natural selection, 40
Natural variation, 39
Negro and Caucasian skulls, 74
Newton, 118
Nickel silver, 164
Nomenclature, 8
Normal and anatomic, definition of, 9
Normal occlusion, 61, see "Arrangement of Teeth"
Nut, counter-sunk, 175
    lock, 172, 298, 399

OBSERVATION training, 192
    Obturator, 411, 438, 455, 470, 475, 477
Occipital apparatus, 133, 213, 236
    dental movement of buccal teeth, 213
    extruding lower, 231
    force, principles of, 126
Occlusion, definition of, 9
    influences which characterize, see "Etiology of Malocclusion"
    principles of, 78
    relations of, 78
    typical and atypical, 68
Occlusal plane, definition of, 10, 12
Odontomata, 24, 362, 366, 372
Open-bite malocclusion, 173, 227, 317
    causes of, 229
    definition of, 10
    grinding of teeth in correction of, 231
    treatment, 230
Oral element, 14, 424
Origin, use and misuse of intermaxillary force, 126
Oro-nasal, definition of, 14
Orthodontia, definition of, 3, 8
Orthodontic principles of diagnosis, 181
Orthopedia, definition of, 3, 9
Osborn, 47

PACKING and finishing the obturator, 469
    Part I Preliminary Principles of Practice, 3
Part II Etiology of Malocclusion, 23
Part III Basic Principles of Practice, 61

Part IV Technic Principles of Practice, 95
Part V Primary Principles of Practice, 139
Part VI Practical Treatment of Dento-Facial Mal-
    occlusions, 181
Part VII Practical Treatment of Unclassified Mal-
    occlusions, 327
Part VIII Principles and Technics of Retention, 377
Part IX The Prosthetic Correction of Cleft Palate,
    409
Pericementitis caused by movements, 300
Pericemental membrane, injury from wire ligatures, 342
Physiognomies, 35
Pierce, 365
Placing bands, 157, see "Bands"
Plaster casts and impressions, 139, 141, 146
Plates, 346
    Coffin, 346
Plating apparatus, 163
    of bands, 162
    solution, 163
Platinum-gold, 163, 164, 172, 384, 385
    wires, 169, 171, 398, 400
Pliers, band, 149, 150
    band removing, 158
    band slitting, 158
    bending, 299, 353
    burnishing, 151
    contouring, 156
    crown removing, 285
    retainer, removing, 391
    rootwise, 172, 300
    solder, 151
    step, 162
    tape, 148
Plugger, band, 157, 388, 390
Plumbago, as luting, 151, 388
Posed, definition of, 10
Premolar, definition of, 14
    extraction of, 83, 202, 215, 216, 263
    impaction of, 369
    movable attachment, 209, 211
    rotation of, 341
Primary principles and technics, 147
Primary principles of practice, 139
Principles of dental anchorages, 118
    diagnosis and treatment, 181, 193, 195
    force, 96
    intermaxillary and occipital force, 126
    mechanics, 95
    occlusion, 78
    practice, 3, 61, 93, 139
Principles of retention, 375, 377
Prognathic appearance (Cryer), 76, 317
    jaws, 312, 317, 318, 319
Prosthetic correction of cleft palate, 409
Protrude, definition of, 12
Protruding contour apparatus, 170, 252, 271, 298, 303
    fitting of, 172, 273, 298, 300
Protrusions, bimaxillary, 232, 233, 241

Protrusions, inherited, 197, 280
    locally caused, 35, 190, 218
    of lower denture, 313, 315
    of upper, 197, 247, see Div. 2, Class II
    of upper apical, 274, 275
    of upper bodily, 266, 269
    of upper coronal, 262, 270
    of mandible 292, 322
Pyorrhea, cause of irregularities, 356, 357

QUESTION of extraction, 83
    injudicious, of permanent teeth, 83, 84, 294
    judicious, or rational, of permanent teeth, 87
    rules of, 83

RADIOGRAMS, 24, 310, 362
    Reactive force, 118
Receding chin, 232, 234, 235, 236, 239, 240
Reciprocating or movable anchorage, 125
Reinforcements, 116, 348, 350
Relation of coronal zones, 156, 186
Removal of bands, 158
    of crowns, 285
    of retainers, 391
Resilient arch-bows, 161, 166, 331, 346
Retaining fixtures, 384, 399
    attachments, 393
    bodily movements, 398, 399, 400
    construction technics, 385, 386
    die for swaging clips, 389
    direct and occipital, 397, 398
    four band, 385
    intermaxillary, 394
    intermaxillary anchorage methods, 395
    lateral expansions, 393
    permanent, 401, 402
    placing the appliance, 390
    removal, 391
    restoring broken extensions, 391
    retruded movements, 394
    six band, 386
Retention, principles of, 377
    imperative demands of, 383
    importance of bodily, 381
    importance of extraction, 380
    importance of interdigitating cusps, 380
    influences of heredity, 378
    local influences, 379
    occlusal influences, 379
Retractors, chin, 133
Retrude, definition of, 12
Retruding contour apparatus, 276
Retrusion,
    bimaxillary, 232, 242
    inherited, 249 Division 1, Class II
    lower denture, 249, 250, 251, 253
    mandible, 236, 238
    mandible and lower denture, 279, 280
    upper apical, 270, 271

INDEX

Retrusion, upper bodily, 295, 297, see Class III
    upper coronal, 274
Ribbon bars and jacks, 341
Rise and development of intermaxillary force, 126
Robinson, 131, 368
Rootwise, definition of, 13
    anchorages, 122, 242, 252, 276, 298, 314, 347, 361
    bars and extensions, 122, 347, 357
Rotate, definition of, 12
Rotating movement, 96, 106, 344
    of cuspids, 341, 342
    of incisors, 340, 341
    of premolars, 341
    with finger spurs, 161
    with levers, 107, 339, 340
    with elastics, 343
    with silk, 343, 344
    with wire, 339, 342

SALISBURY, 414
    Science, 5
Scissors, curved, 155
    tape, 148
Scope of dento-facial field, 184
Scope of Dental Orthopedia, 3
Screw force, 95, 96
Separating tape, 147
Short-bite malocclusion, 287
Silk elastics, 134
    ligatures for rotating, 343, 344
Silver, nickel, 164
Skiagraphs, see "Radiograms"
Sliding tubes, 131, 213, 257, 268
Slitting of bands, 158
Solder, gold, 149, 153, 155, 160, 164
    silver, 154
    soft, 211
Solder pliers, 151
Soldering of attachments, 152, 159
    bands, 151, 152
Spaces, abnormal interproximate, 354
    closing of buccal, see "Rootwise Anchorages"
    closing of incisor, 355, 357, 359
Span, intermaxillary, 129, 268
Speech, mechanism of, 409, 421
    aspirates, 433, 434
    classification consonant oral elements, 428
    explosives, 431, 435
    methods of instruction, 415
Speech, nasals, 429
    oral elements, 424
    sound images, 414
    vowels and consonants, 426, 427
Spring arch contractor and expander, see "Expansion"
    lever rotator, 107, 339, 340
Stability of anchorage, 120
Stackpole, 56
Staple retainer, 402
Stationary anchorages, 121, 123, 175, 286

Superior, definition of, 13
Supplementary retainers, 393
Supernumerary teeth, 362, 366
Supra-occlusion, definition of, 10
Surgical failures, 471
Sustained anchorages, 123, 315

TATTACHMENTS for elastics, 176, 230, 343, 358, 397
    premolar attachments, 206
Table of classes, 19
    of characters, 328
Taggart, 388
Tape, waxed, 147
    method of introducing, 147
    scissors, 148
    sizes of, 147
Teaching, principles of, 3, 410
Technics of dental anchorage, 118
    of attachments, 170
    of band fitting, 155, 156
Thumbsucking protrusions, 33, 218
Torsional force, 116, 166, 170, 348
Tooth levers, 101
Traction bars, see "Bars"
Training, observation, 192
Trays, impression, 121, 140, 141
Trimming of casts, 141
Trudo, definition of, 12
Tubing, elliptical, 212, 336, 352, 399
    open, 129, 211, 278, 298, 399
    U, 160, 170, 174, 176, 298
Tying of ligatures, 344
Types, table of in Class I, 199
    in Class II, 245
Typical and atypical occlusion of the teeth, 68

UNCLASSIFIED malocclusions, 329
    Unilateral, definition of, 14
    maleruption of cuspids, 205
Unimaxillary, definition of, 14

VELUM-OBTURATOR, 411, 438, 455, 470, 475, 477
    palati, 422
V-shaped arches, 351

WALLACE, 51
    Working retainer, 175, 176, 400

X RAY, 24, 310, 362

YOKE bow, lingual, 211
    Younger, 343

ZONES, definition of, 11
    dento-facial, see "Diagnosis" Chapter XXI
    of movement, 186
    relation of coronal, 156, 186